THOMAS MERTON

Selected Essays

THOMAS MERTON
Selected Essays

Edited with an Introduction by
PATRICK F. O'CONNELL

ORBIS BOOKS

Maryknoll, New York 10545

Founded in 1970, Orbis Books endeavors to publish works that enlighten the mind, nourish the spirit, and challenge the conscience. The publishing arm of the Maryknoll Fathers and Brothers, Orbis seeks to explore the global dimensions of the Christian faith and mission, to invite dialogue with diverse cultures and religious traditions, and to serve the cause of reconciliation and peace. The books published reflect the views of their authors and do not represent the official position of the Maryknoll Society. To learn more about Maryknoll and Orbis Books, please visit our website at www.maryknollsociety.org.

Library of Congress Cataloging-in-Publication Data

Merton, Thomas, 1915-1968.
  [Essays. Selections]
  Selected essays / Thomas Merton ; edited with an introduction by Patrick F. O'Connell.
      pages cm
  Includes bibliographical references (pages   ).
  ISBN 978-1-62698-023-5 (cloth); 978-1-62698-092-1
  I. O'Connell, Patrick F. II. Merton, Thomas, 1915-1968. White pebble. III. Title.
BX4705.M542A25 2013
230—dc23
                                                        2012048170

Contents

Foreword, by Patrick Hart, OCSO   vii

Introduction: Merton the Essayist   ix

SELECTED ESSAYS

1. The White Pebble   3
2. St. John of the Cross   15
3. Poetry and Contemplation: A Reappraisal   23
4. Boris Pasternak and the People with Watch Chains   39
5. The Recovery of Paradise   52
6. Notes for a Philosophy of Solitude   65
7. Theology of Creativity   86
8. Christian Culture Needs Oriental Wisdom   102
9. A Letter to Pablo Antonio Cuadra concerning Giants   113
10. Peace: A Religious Responsibility   126
11. The Humanity of Christ in Monastic Prayer   150
12. Message to Poets   172
13. A Tribute to Gandhi   177
14. From Pilgrimage to Crusade   185
15. Religion and Race in the United States   205
16. Rain and the Rhinoceros   216
17. The Contemplative Life in the Modern World   225
18. Day of a Stranger   232

19. Symbolism: Communication or Communion?   240

20. The Other Side of Despair: Notes on Christian Existentialism   258

21. The Time of the End Is the Time of No Room   277

22. Blessed Are the Meek   284

23. Events and Pseudo-Events: Letter to a Southern Churchman   296

24. The Spiritual Father in the Desert Tradition   310

25. Is the World a Problem?   331

26. A Christian Looks at Zen   342

27. Terror and the Absurd: Violence and Nonviolence
    in Albert Camus   361

28. The Monastic Renewal: Problems and Prospects   382

29. "Baptism in the Forest": Wisdom and Initiation
    in William Faulkner   401

30. Ishi: A Meditation   426

31. Learning to Live   433

32. The Wild Places   442

33. Final Integration: Toward a "Monastic Therapy"   452

Appendix: Merton's Essays: A Chronology   463

Bibliography   478

Index   481

Foreword

PATRICK HART, OCSO

DURING THE YEARS 1955-1965, when Thomas Merton served as novice master at the Abbey of Gethsemani, he spent much of his limited amount of time for writing engaged in doing shorter essays and poetry on subjects that interested him. The same pattern continued after August 1965 when he entered the hermitage where he would spend the last three years of his life. He would later collect the various essays, with some revisions, for book publication. The range of his topics was enormous, from monastic history to literary criticism, from Native Americans to Zen. Many of these essays addressed social issues, such as racial justice or nuclear warfare.

What I recall vividly, after half a century, about Father Louis, as we called Merton in the monastery, was his reaction to the system of censorship in the Cistercian Order. With regard to his essay on the philosophy of solitude, for example, I remember that Merton commented to a reader who had complimented him on the depth of his insights into the topic, "Well, it should be good because it took several revisions before it finally passed Trappist censorship!" Within the Order there was a suspicion of an exaggerated interest in the subject of the hermit life or solitude in the context of the monastic cenobium. As secretary to Abbot James Fox during the time Merton was novice master, it was my job to deliver to Father Louis the censors' reports, since Dom James preferred not to confront Fr. Louis directly. The latter would mutter such humorous complaints as, "My God, if you quote the Our Father, the censors would demand a footnote."

The greatest trial for him in this regard was a collection of articles on war and peace, which brought a strong negative reaction from the Abbot General, Dom Gabriel Sortais, who wrote Merton that he could write on peace but not on war! His manuscript, *Peace in the Post-Christian Era*, was typed up and ready for publication when the ban arrived from Rome. As I recall, Dom James delayed passing on the negative report to Fr. Louis for several months, which allowed a number of these articles on nuclear warfare and the obligation to work for peace to appear in journals like *Commonweal* and *The Catholic Worker*. In 1963, shortly after Pope John XXIII published his encyclical *Pacem in Terris*, which delighted Merton enormously, he wrote to the Abbot General with tongue in cheek that it was a good thing the pope didn't have to get *Pacem in Terris* passed by Trappist censorship. He commented that the pope had condemned the use of nuclear weapons much better than he himself could have done with his writings. (Ironically, *Peace in the Post-Christian Era* was finally published long after the death of both Merton and the Abbot General and is more relevant today than at the time it was written and banned.)

What a great gift it is to now have this volume of *Selected Essays* of Thomas Merton, a wonderful companion volume to the selected journals, letters, and poetry published previously. Editor Patrick O'Connell has a comprehensive knowledge of Thomas Merton's entire corpus, so we are presented with a wise choice of Merton's work in this genre, ranging across the entire spectrum of his shorter writings. This collection will serve as a useful compendium for those already familiar with the breadth and depth of Merton's vision and as a splendid introduction for those encountering Thomas Merton for the first time.

Introduction

Merton the Essayist

IN A CHARACTERISTICALLY WRY comment early in *Conjectures of a Guilty Bystander*, Thomas Merton notes one consequence of his reputation as a prolific author: "Don R—, prominent in Italian Catholic Action and editor of a rather lavish magazine, writes a pleasant breezy note, asking for an article on 'The Holiness of the Church': just like that! People are now convinced that I secrete articles like perspiration. This is clearly more my fault than theirs, and something has to be done about it."[1] As Merton himself is ruefully aware, this impression of abundant, perhaps overabundant, productivity, particularly of shorter prose pieces, during this period of his life was not inaccurate, but the apparent expectation that he could or would provide comforting, uncontroversial restatements of standard religious sentiments no longer reflected Merton's sense of his vocation as a writer, if it ever did. In the original June 29, 1961, journal entry on which this passage was based (in which we learn that the editor in question was "Don Giovanni Rossi—head of Pro Civitate Christiana"), Merton merely comments that he "shall politely decline" the invitation,[2] but in the considerably expanded version put together some four years later for *Conjectures* Merton goes on to consider how his writing has moved away from conventional reflections on conventional topics, such as Don Rossi seemed to be looking for, to explorations of issues for which "ready-to-serve Catholic answers" are inadequate. "It seems to me," he writes, "that one of the reasons why my writing appeals to many people is precisely that I am not so sure of myself and do not claim to have all the answers. In fact, I often wonder quite openly about these 'answers,' and about the habit of always having them ready. The best I can do is to look for some of the questions" (*Conjectures*, 38). While Merton

---

1. Thomas Merton, *Conjectures of a Guilty Bystander* (Garden City, NY: Doubleday, 1966), 38.

2. Thomas Merton, *Turning Toward the World: The Pivotal Years. Journals, vol. 4: 1960-1963*, ed. Victor A. Kramer (San Francisco: HarperCollins, 1996), 135.

certainly does more than simply raise questions in the profusion of articles on a vast range of issues that make up so considerable a proportion of his writing, particularly in the final decade of his life, his willingness to dispense with pre-fabricated conclusions, to consider all sides of a question, to bring his deeply spiritual, profoundly Catholic sensibility to bear on matters beyond the usual "religious" and "monastic" milieu, to write "essays" in the etymological sense of efforts, attempts to reach greater clarity through the very process of reflection, make many of his works in this genre among the most characteristic, most chal-lenging, most eloquent, and most significant of his writings.

In his 1966 essay "Is the World a Problem?" Merton distinguished between "the author of *The Seven Storey Mountain*, which seemingly a lot of people have read" and "the author of more recent essays and poems which apparently very few people have read."[3] Yet in the more than four decades since his death Mer-ton's sustained reputation and continued influence have been due at least as much to these essays (if not the poems) as to his celebrated autobiography. As in his journals and letters, the astonishing breadth of Merton's interests and con-cerns is evident in his essays, so varied in both voice and subject matter, while the scope of the essay allows for greater depth of consideration than is generally provided by those more spontaneous genres. Very many people have now read them and found them to be an indispensible source of insight on topics rang-ing from interreligious dialogue to racial justice, from the laconic *verba* of the fourth-century desert fathers to the novels of Faulkner and Camus, from the nuclear threat to the "philosophy of solitude," all grounded explicitly or implic-itly in what Merton considered to be the "one root truth" of whatever he had written: "that God calls human persons to union with Himself and with one another in Christ, in the Church which is His Mystical Body."[4]

Merton's "career" as an essayist can be conveniently divided into two approximately equal periods, 1947-58 and 1958-68. The second is by far the more important, but the first reveals that his affinity for the essay form did not suddenly develop in the final decade of his life. It actually emerges[5] during the period between the completion of *The Seven Storey Mountain* in late 1946 and its publication two years later, and continues to develop, if somewhat fitfully and sporadically, until in the late 1950s it breaks through the somewhat nar-

---

3. Thomas Merton, *Contemplation in a World of Action* (Garden City, NY: Doubleday, 1971), 144.

4. Thomas Merton, "Concerning the Collection in the Bellarmine College Library," in Thomas Merton, John Howard Griffin, and Monsignor [Alfred] Horrigan, *The Thomas Merton Studies Center* (Santa Barbara, CA: Unicorn Press, 1971), 14.

5. A few premonastic essays survive; see the appendix.

row channels to which it had hitherto been confined. On November 5, 1947, Merton wrote to his friend and former Columbia professor Mark Van Doren, "I am tremendously busy with writing. Magazines are beginning to be after me, and I have to do a lot of judicious refusing. I can only write for magazines on condition that I keep myself in one field & on one plane—and the nearer it is to mystical theology the better. My superiors have more or less let me go off on my own & make all my own decisions as far as writing is concerned with the one exception—they won't let me give it up."[6] His first substantial article, "Poetry and the Contemplative Life," had appeared that July in *The Commonweal* (as it was then called), where he had been regularly publishing poetry since mid-1946; a second, "The Trappists Go to Utah," came out at the end of August, and "Active and Contemplative Orders" was published exactly a month after his letter to Van Doren.

Over the next two years further articles, all of them focused to one degree or another on aspects of the contemplative life, appeared in *The Commonweal* and in other, generally small Catholic magazines, including *Messenger of the Sacred Heart, Integrity, Marian Literary Studies, Dublin Review,* and *Cross and Crown.*[7] As early as September 1947, when only the first two pieces were in print, Merton was already thinking about gathering them together for a book,[8] an idea he was still considering as late as April 1950,[9] though by that time "Poetry and the Contemplative Life" had been included as an appendix to his third book of verse, *Figures for an Apocalypse,*[10] and "Active and Contemplative Orders" had become part of the epilogue to *The Seven Storey Mountain.*[11] The revival of the plan was perhaps prompted by publication the previous month of what would turn out to be Merton's last original article for *The Commonweal* until late 1958.

In any case, nothing came of the idea, and by that time a combination of

6. Thomas Merton, *The Road to Joy: Letters to New and Old Friends,* ed. Robert E. Daggy (New York: Farrar, Straus, Giroux, 1989), 21.

7. See the appendix for a chronological list of all Merton's essays, with bibliographical details.

8. See Thomas Merton, *Entering the Silence: Becoming a Monk and Writer. Journals, vol. 2: 1941-1952,* ed. Jonathan Montaldo (San Francisco: HarperCollins, 1996), 105.

9. See Thomas Merton, *Witness to Freedom: Letters in Times of Crisis,* ed. William H. Shannon (New York: Farrar, Straus, Giroux, 1994), 127.

10. Thomas Merton, *Figures for an Apocalypse* (New York: New Directions, 1947), 93-111.

11. Thomas Merton, *The Seven Storey Mountain* (New York: Harcourt, Brace, 1948), 414-19; this had been done at the suggestion of Fordham University professor Francis X. Connolly. See Merton's November 12, 1949 letter to Sr. Thérèse Lentfoehr (*Road to Joy,* 197).

factors seems to have shifted Merton's attention away from writing shorter articles—the success of his autobiography, and perhaps even more so of *Seeds of Contemplation*,[12] published the following year, led him to concentrate on book-length projects, while the subsequent difficulties he experienced in trying to bring what would become *The Ascent to Truth*[13] to completion became a major preoccupation around this time. He had also been warned by Cistercian Abbot General Gabriel Sortais not to become too committed to periodical publication. As early as August 20, 1948 he writes in his journal, "Dom Gabriel told me not to let myself get roped into any magazine as a *collaborateur*, i.e., not to get my name on the mast-head as a staff writer, and be slow to accept work. They are all commercial. They ruin you. Told me to refuse book-reviews except in exceptional cases" (*Entering the Silence*, 226). He had written a five-part scholarly essay, very different in tone from the articles for popular magazines, published in the Order's journal *Collectanea Ordinis Cisterciensium Reformatorum* in 1948-50, and an autobiographical essay for a collection entitled *Where I Found Christ* that was also published in abbreviated form in *Sign* magazine in July 1950, but virtually all the rest of his prose in magazines through 1952 were excerpts of material that had been or would be published in books (or, in the case of *The Seven Storey Mountain*, of unpublished portions of the manuscript that Merton's friend and correspondent Sr. Thérèse Lentfoehr had selected). By early 1952, as his godfather Ed Rice began planning his photo-magazine *Jubilee*, Merton wrote to Sr. Thérèse, "I am supposed to have backed out of the magazine field altogether. The Abbot General definitely told me to keep my name off the masthead of any magazine—even as advisor" (*Road to Joy*, 210).

In 1953, the eight-hundredth anniversary of the death of St. Bernard, there was a flurry of Merton articles on his great Cistercian predecessor, including the first of what would eventually be a significant number of contributions to *Jubilee*, but once again there was very little original periodical publication for the next couple of years. Merton even told Sr. Thérèse in November 1956, a year after he had taken on the position of novice master at Gethsemani, "Father Abbot will not allow me to write *anything* whatever" (*Road to Joy*, 226), though this was evidently a typically Mertonian overstatement, even with regard to shorter pieces, since that very month "Notes on Sacred and Profane Art" was published in *Jubilee*, and "Time and the Liturgy" appeared in *Worship* in December. There is also evidence that Merton had been assembling a collection of unpublished essays on aspects of spiritual guidance developed during his

---

12. Thomas Merton, *Seeds of Contemplation* (New York: New Directions, 1949).
13. Thomas Merton, *The Ascent to Truth* (New York: Harcourt, Brace, 1951).

early months as novice master, which was probably abandoned in mid-1956.[14] But in fact articles on art, liturgy, and spiritual direction, many of them published over the next few years in *Sponsa Regis*, a magazine for women religious put out by the Benedictines of Collegeville, MN and edited by Merton's friend Fr. Kilian McDonnell, marked a definitive return to the essay form, but one that was soon to lead in a quite different, much more creative direction.

One clear indication that Merton was entering a new phase is the rewriting of his very first *Commonweal* article as "Poetry and Contemplation: A Reappraisal," published in the same magazine in October 1958, marked by a broadened understanding of contemplation as encompassing all of life and a more expansive recognition of its compatibility with artistic creativity (and implicitly with other types of activity as well). That the transition was a gradual one is suggested by a journal entry from October 1958, where Merton writes, "Took the thought of articles for nuns to direction—Is it better to write fast, easy (useless) articles for nuns or slow, difficult, important articles on Le Douanier Rousseau, Pasternak, etc.? . . . . Meanwhile, I'll write all articles—both kinds."[15] The following April he is still somewhat ambivalent, but the shift is more apparent:

> One thing is certain—it is useless for me to turn out easy essays for extern sisters. For a while I was wondering: there is always a temptation to do what is easy and obvious on the ground that the most obvious is the Will of God. This is too obvious and I am glad. On the other hand it is possible that the things I am interested in (articles on Pasternak, Le Douanier Rousseau, etc.) are not obvious enough. Or not obvious enough to those who get worried about such things. (*Search for Solitude*, 274)

No article on the French primitive painter was ever written,[16] but a pair of articles on the author of *Dr. Zhivago*, which had literary and political as well as spiritual dimensions, mark a breakthrough—while he never completely stops

---

14. For details see the introductory note to Thomas Merton, "Your Will and Your Vocation," *The Merton Seasonal* 34.2 (Summer 2009), 3.

15. Thomas Merton, *A Search for Solitude: Pursuing the Monk's True Life. Journals, vol. 3: 1952-1960*, ed. Lawrence S. Cunningham (San Francisco: HarperCollins, 1996), 222.

16. Some indication of his interest is found in comments related to natural contemplation in conferences given to newly ordained monks in 1961. See Thomas Merton, *An Introduction to Christian Mysticism: Initiation into the Monastic Tradition* 3, ed. Patrick F. O'Connell (Kalamazoo, MI: Cistercian Publications, 2008), 134-35.

writing the equivalent of "easy essays for extern sisters," his move into more adventurous, more controversial, and more satisfying areas was now irreversible.

Soon, in the vivid if somewhat imprecise words of Paul Wilkes' script for *Merton: A Film Biography*, "With the force of a dam bursting, he began to write for dozens of secular publications on an astonishing variety of subjects."[17] In fact, though his essays would appear in such prestigious journals as *Hudson Review* and *Sewanee Review* and in mass-market monthlies such as *Harper's* and *Holiday*, the majority of his articles continued to be published in religiously oriented periodicals, but now they were typically progressive, lay-edited Catholic magazines like *Commonweal, Jubilee, The Catholic Worker, The Critic, Continuum,* and *Ramparts* (soon to become secularized); the circle widened to include Protestant publications like *Motive,* ecumenical ones like *Katallagete,* even non-Christian, non-American ones like *Mountain Path, Gandhi Marg,* and *The Eastern Buddhist.*

Moreover, in at least one of its metaphorical guises, the dam did not in fact burst: for most of his remaining years he had to contend with various forms of censorship operative in the Cistercian Order. He was initially forbidden by the Abbot General himself to publish his first article on Pasternak, as writing about a novelist was considered improper for a cloistered contemplative; another key text of this transitional period, which would eventually become "Notes for a Philosophy of Solitude," was repeatedly rejected by the censors for the apparently opposite reason that Merton's emphasis on the solitary dimension of life both within and beyond the monastery was thought to undermine the communal focus of the Trappist vocation; and of course the official ban on all writing about war handed down by the authorities in April 1962 is one of the best-known episodes in Merton's later life.[18] Not until 1967, in the wake of the Second Vatican Council, did the Order's requirement to submit writings for publication to official censors begin to be dismantled, though there was a way "around the dam" in that material appearing in publications that were "very small and of very limited influence,"[19] which included a fair proportion of those Merton was writing for, did not require censorship.

In any case, with or without censorship, the main point of Wilkes' comment, the truly astonishing output of articles as well as other work continued unabated

---

17. *Merton: A Film Biography,* a film by Paul Wilkes and Audrey L. Glynn (1985).

18. For an overview of the censorship issue, see Christine M. Bochen, "Censorship," in William H. Shannon, Christine M. Bochen, and Patrick F. O'Connell, *The Thomas Merton Encyclopedia* (Maryknoll, NY: Orbis Books, 2002), 47-49.

19. Thomas Merton, *The Hidden Ground of Love: Letters on Religious Experience and Social Concerns,* ed. William H. Shannon (New York: Farrar, Straus, Giroux, 1985), 258.

until and, as far as publication goes, even beyond Merton's death at the end of 1968. In the last ten years of his life Merton published an average of about eighteen articles per year; 1965 saw the appearance of twenty-six, and 1967 of no less than thirty-three! Little wonder that editors such as Don Rossi thought he "secrete[d] articles like perspiration." He periodically bemoaned this fecundity, declaring in his journal as early as December 1959, "More and more I see the necessity of leaving my own ridiculous 'career' as a religious journalist. Stop writing for publication—except poems and creative meditations" (*Search for Solitude*, 350); five months later he pledges "to *write less*, to write what I need to say to myself and to God, not for the public. And to *withhold publication except in special cases*," though he immediately wonders "to what extent I owe a certain amount of writing to the Church" (*Search for Solitude*, 392-93). The pace certainly did not diminish, and after his retirement as novice master and withdrawal to his hermitage in August, 1965, the amount of time available for writing increased substantially, as did his output; in March of 1968 he is still noting, "I have tried to keep up with articles, etc. I am asked to write—or get myself into writing."[20]

From 1960 onward about half the books he published were collections of essays, beginning with the aptly titled *Disputed Questions* (which would describe even more accurately much of his subsequent work in this form), a rather heterogeneous gathering that included both his reflections on Pasternak and his essay on solitude. Subsequently, articles on political and social issues were brought together in *Seeds of Destruction* and *Faith and Violence*, on liturgy in *Seasons of Celebration*, on Eastern religions in *Mystics and Zen Masters* (along with essays on Christianity) and in *Zen and the Birds of Appetite*, with more "creative" pieces appearing in *The Behavior of Titans* and *Raids on the Unspeakable* (which overlapped in content to a considerable extent). The process continued after his death with articles on monastic renewal gathered in *Contemplation in a World of Action*, and more traditional, generally earlier monastic essays in *The Monastic Journey*; articles on Native Americans in the slim *Ishi Means Man*, and a comprehensive collection of writings on literature in the massive *Literary Essays*; both Gordon Zahn and William Shannon edited volumes of social and political articles, many of them previously uncollected; finally, *Love and Living* was a sort of successor to *Disputed Questions* in its inclusion of essays from Merton's last years on a wide variety of topics.[21] In this way the essays have reached a far wider audience than (with very few exceptions) they would have had in their initial periodical publication, and many have taken their place among the most

---

20. Thomas Merton, *The Other Side of the Mountain: The End of the Journey. Journals, vol. 7: 1967-1968*, ed. Patrick Hart (San Francisco: HarperCollins, 1998), 63.

21. See the bibliography for publication details on these volumes.

appreciated and most influential of Merton's writings—readily accessible, yet distributed throughout multiple volumes.

While there have been a number of anthologies that have included a variety of Merton's writings in multiple genres, such as *A Thomas Merton Reader* (for which Merton himself worked very closely with editor Thomas McDonnell in selecting material), and Lawrence Cunningham's very fine *Thomas Merton: Spiritual Master*, and there have been posthumous essay collections bringing together articles on a particular subject—social issues, literature, Native Americans—no previous volume has provided a broad cross-section of Merton's work as an essayist that allows readers to get some sense of the full range of his achievement in this form. It is this perceived need that the present collection is intended to satisfy, thereby complementing the recent one-volume selections of Merton's journals, letters, and poetry.[22]

Of the approximately 250 essays Merton wrote, thirty-three have been chosen for inclusion here. They are arranged chronologically rather than thematically, not only to give some indication of Merton's development as an essayist but to show how his attention could be occupied in rapid succession, or even simultaneously, by widely disparate topics, as when, for example, he was working on the contemporary social analysis of "Events and Pseudo-events" and the historical study "The Spiritual Father in the Desert Tradition" at exactly the same time.

Among the criteria for selection, in addition to the intrinsic merit of each piece, was the desire to include representative essays across the whole spectrum of Merton's interests, concerns, and enthusiasms: solitude and the contemplative life as intrinsic dimensions of contemporary existence; the interaction of Christianity with culture, both historically and currently; monastic history and monastic renewal; key social issues, especially war and peace and racial justice, as well as concern for the environment; the spiritual implications of literature, particularly the work of three modern authors with whom Merton resonated most deeply—Pasternak, Faulkner, and Camus; reflections on his own aesthetic theory and practice; dialogue with other religious traditions; the centrality of the Christian mystery to authentic human identity.

There has also been an effort to make available examples of the diversity of voice and tone found in the essays: the combination of autobiography and scrip-

---

22. Thomas Merton, *The Intimate Merton: His Life from His Journals*, ed. Patrick Hart and Jonathan Montaldo (San Francisco: HarperCollins, 1999); Thomas Merton, *A Life in Letters: The Essential Collection*, ed. William H. Shannon and Christine M. Bochen (San Francisco: Harper One, 2008); Thomas Merton, *In the Dark before Dawn: New Selected Poems*, ed. Lynn R. Szabo (New York: New Directions, 2005).

tural imagery in "The White Pebble"; the informal, conversational voice, similar to that found in the journals, of "Rain and the Rhinoceros," "Day of a Stranger," "Is the World a Problem?"; the passionate anguish of "A Letter to Pablo Antonio Cuadra concerning Giants"; the more measured combination of description and prescription in "Peace: A Religious Responsibility"; the movement from meditation to exhortation in "Blessed Are the Meek"; the broad scope of "From Pilgrimage to Crusade" and "The Other Side of Despair," in contrast to the precise focus of "The Time of the End Is the Time of No Room"; the more objective, even scholarly perspective of "The Humanity of Christ in Monastic Prayer" and "The Spiritual Father in the Desert Tradition"—though even the most deeply researched and heavily annotated essays are never presented as being of merely academic interest to author or audience. The selection intends to highlight both the range of Merton's style and subject matter and the underlying unity of vision that informs the entire collection. Whether primarily personal, critical, or expository, each of these essays is marked by what Merton called a sapiential, or sophianic, perspective—an intuitive, participatory awareness of the "hidden wholeness" of all reality,[23] which he described in the essay on Faulkner included here as "a kind of knowledge by identification, an intersubjective knowledge, a communion in cosmic awareness and in nature . . . . a wisdom based on love."

In the selection process, the definition of "essay" has been interpreted in a fairly strict sense. No transcriptions of Merton's talks or conferences, such as those given to religious women in Alaska before leaving for Asia, or his presentation on "Marxism and Monastic Perspectives" given just hours before his death, have been considered. Introductions written for Merton's own compilations, such as those for *The Wisdom of the Desert* or *The Way of Chuang Tzu*, or even the wonderful "Herakleitos the Obscure," which precedes Merton's reworkings of the fragments of the pre-Socratic philosopher, have been somewhat regretfully excluded, although the Faulkner article that prefaced the collection *Mansions of the Spirit* has been included, along with "The Recovery of Paradise," Merton's main contribution to the exchange with D. T. Suzuki that was originally intended to precede the sayings in *The Wisdom of the Desert*. Book reviews that are simply summary and evaluation were eliminated, but review essays that consist primarily of Merton's own reflections on events and issues raised by a particular book, such as "Ishi—A Meditation" or "The Wild Places" or "Final Integration," form a significant segment of Merton's shorter prose writings and are amply represented here.

---

23. Thomas Merton, *The Collected Poems of Thomas Merton* (New York: New Directions, 1977), 363.

By no means are all of Merton's essays, as he himself repeatedly observed, of the same quality or significance, but there are numerous other very fine pieces that could have been selected. No doubt many readers will regret the absence of a particular favorite or two. But it is hoped that the collection as presently constituted accomplishes its main purpose, to provide a representative and comprehensive anthology that accurately reflects the breadth and depth of Merton's work as an essayist.

The essays are generally presented in their final published form. Occasional misprints are silently corrected, and British forms and spellings in some essays have been regularized to conform to American usage. The format for Merton's notes has been regularized, and all notes have been located at the foot of the page. In a couple of cases original titles have been restored, for reasons that are explained in the headnotes. For two of the essays, the text provided differs substantially from that previously available; again, the rationale for the changes is provided in the headnotes. These introductory comments preceding each selection include information on the process of composition and details of publication, along with brief discussion of the content and context of the essay that gives some indication of why it has been chosen for the collection. Also included in the volume is an appendix providing a complete chronological listing of all Merton's essays, along with a bibliography of works in which Merton's essays are to be found.

In conclusion, I would like to express my deep gratitude for the friendship and encouragement of the wonderful community of Merton scholars, many of whom made helpful suggestions that have resulted in a better book. Particular appreciation is due to Patricia Burton, whose magnificent bibliographical work benefitted this volume in so many ways; to Paul Pearson, Director and Archivist of the Thomas Merton Center at Bellarmine University, the principal archive of Merton's papers, whose expertise and support have been invaluable; and to Brother Patrick Hart, Thomas Merton's last secretary and a wise guide and mentor for generations of Merton readers and scholars alike, not only for providing the lovely foreword to this volume but for his generous assistance and encouragement in this and numerous other projects. Finally, as always, my wife, Suzanne, and our children have been a constant source of sustenance and inspiration; in a special way this collection is dedicated in love to them, and to our grandchildren, with the hope that many years from now they may experience something of the same enjoyment, fascination, and intellectual and spiritual nourishment in these essays that their grandfather has found over the past four decades since he first encountered Thomas Merton.

Selected Essays

1

The White Pebble

This little-known autobiographical essay appeared in a collection of conversion stories entitled *Where I Found Christ*, edited by John A. O'Brien (Garden City, NY: Doubleday, 1950), 235-50. Like a number of the other pieces in the volume, it was also published, in somewhat abbreviated form, in *Sign* magazine just prior to its appearance in the book (29 [July 1950], 26-28, 69); it was also included in the second volume of the British edition, collectively entitled (from a compilation of similar articles published the previous year) *The Road to Damascus* (London: W. H. Allen, 1950), 156-69. It was not subsequently reprinted. It had been completed by October 1, 1949, when Merton wrote to ask Abbot James Fox to pass it on to the censor (*School of Charity*, 17). The essay does not simply summarize Merton's life story as found in *The Seven Storey Mountain*, but, using the image of the white pebble with the hidden name written upon it from Revelations 2:17 as a symbol of one's authentic identity, discusses his ongoing conversion from baptism through entry into monastic life to his recent priestly ordination (which took place on May 26, 1949), thus serving not only as a coda to the autobiography but as a supplement to the journal that he was currently writing, which would appear as *The Sign of Jonas* in 1953, and in complete form as *Entering the Silence*.

I N THE APOCALYPSE, St. John puts these words upon the lips of God. "To him that overcometh, I will give the hidden manna, and will give him a white counter, and in the counter, a new name written, which no man knoweth, but he that receiveth it."[1] The "counter" in this sentence means a pebble, a token that might be given out as a lot in a game of chance. Each one in the game is identified by his lot, or his counter, or his pebble.

So it is with our lives, in the eyes of God. The supernatural destinies of the elect are hidden in the hands of God. Our vocation to the faith, and to the particular, individual part that each one of us must play in the life of the Church, is a secret gift of God. Our supernatural identity is hidden in a little white counter,

---

1. Apocalypse 2:17.

a little white pebble in the hand of God. If we want it, we must reach out and take it from His hand.

If we do not accept it, we shall never know our true name. We shall never find out who we were meant to be. And we shall fall into a hopeless and everlasting void that is peopled by all the missing persons who have never found out that they really had a name and a character and an identity reserved for them in heaven, that they were destined for life instead of death, if only they had known how to reach for their pebble and make the effort to begin to live.

Each one gets his pebble from the hand of Christ. The hands of Christ are pierced by nails. He bought us our supernatural life with His own human life. The white counters that he gives to those who "overcome" are tokens of a share in His divine life. All true life flows into the souls of men from the wounds of Christ on the Cross.

St. Paul says, "We . . . are baptized in His death. We are buried together with him by baptism into death; that as Christ is risen from the dead by the glory of the Father, so we also may walk in newness of life."[2] And this new life is a divine life. "We are dead to sin but living to God in Jesus Christ our Lord."[3] It is no longer we who live, but Christ lives in us.[4]

We too often tend to think of supernatural life as a gift given to individuals for themselves alone, as if the Kingdom of Heaven were a conglomeration of strangers drawn together like a football crowd—men who have little in common except that they are all sitting in the same stadium and are all excited about the same game. It is as if we thought supernatural life were a gift dealt out to each one without any reference to the other elect—like the graded series of prizes in a lottery. Each one takes his prize and goes off by himself to enjoy it as best he can.

According to this view, we tend to think of conversions to the faith as phenomena that are completely understandable when you tell the story of how an individual got to be baptized. When he is baptized, he is "in." He has been initiated. He is a fellow Christian. Of course conversion stories do stand on their own merits. They do express their own significant lessons. Nevertheless, each conversion is only really understandable in the light of the *Parousia*—the second coming of Christ—and of the *Pleroma*—the fullness of the Mystical Christ.

We are all baptized into *one* supernatural life, into one Christ. "In one Spirit we are all baptized into one Body."[5] Our lives are thenceforth so intimately iden-

---

2. Romans 6:3-4.
3. Ibid., 11.
4. Galatians 2:20.
5. I Corinthians 12:13.

tified that "if one member suffer the others suffer with it and if one member glory the others glory with it."[6] We are all like grains of wheat ground into flour and baked into one Host and consecrated as the Body of Christ: "For we, being many, are one bread, one body, all that partake of one bread."[7]

Now this Mystical Christ, the "whole Christ," head and members, is not a static moral organization. It is a living and growing organism which is developing toward a definite end which will be the perfect manifestation of the power and the Kingship of Christ, the full and final expression of His victory over death and sin. The Mystical Body of Christ is not simply a kind of mythical clearinghouse through which individuals pass in order to enter into a reward. It is *the central reality of all creation*. This "one new man"[8] made of the union of the elect with the Incarnate Son of God is the whole reason for the existence of the universe because, as St. Paul tells us, God "chose us in Him [Jesus] before the foundation of the world . . . and predestinated us unto the adoption of children through Jesus Christ unto Himself . . . unto the praise of the glory of His grace in which He hath graced us in His beloved Son."[9] It is this "one Man" who gives God perfect glory. This Mystical Christ gathers into Himself everything in heaven and on earth, because God reveals through His Son "the mystery of His will" which is to "restore all things in Christ"—*instaurare omnia in Christo*.[10] There is no other purpose in the world than this: that God be perfectly glorified by the "whole Christ." The day when that perfect glory will be given has not yet arrived. But it is coming. The "whole Christ" is constantly growing and advancing toward that "day of Christ Jesus," the day of "the perfecting of the saints"[11] when the Body will be complete, when the number of the elect will be filled up, and we will all "meet into the unity of faith and of the knowledge of the Son of God, unto a perfect man, unto the measure of the age of the fullness of Christ."[12]

All the rest of creation, below man, also awaits without realizing it the "day of Christ Jesus," this day of fulfillment. For "every creature groaneth and travaileth even until now . . . waiting for the adoption of the sons of God."[13]

The final end of this development is the perfect union of all the elect with

---

6. I Corinthians 12:36.
7. I Corinthians 10:16.
8. Ephesians 2:15.
9. Ephesians 1:4-6.
10. Ephesians 1:10.
11. Ephesians 4:12.
12. Ephesians 4:13.
13. Romans 8:22-23.

God, in one Spirit. "For by Him we have access both in one Spirit to the Father."[14] This will be the final, perfect, mystical union of the "whole Christ" with the Godhead, revealed by Jesus in the seventeenth chapter of St. John's Gospel, that stupendous unity of love and vision in which all the saints become absorbed, without losing their personal identities, in the depths of the intimate life of the Blessed Trinity. They all become one with God and one with one another as the three divine persons are one. The same divine life flows through the exultant body of the elect. They see God as He sees Himself, for they see Him and all things in His Word. They love God and one another as He loves Himself, for they are all caught up into the uncreated flame of Love which bursts forth from the Father and the Son and unites them in Love—the Holy Spirit.

IT SEEMS TO ME that it is extremely important for a full and normal development of the Christian life and spirit that Christians should acquire this long-range view of their baptism and their individual vocation. Everyone should see his baptism in the light of eschatology. Every Christian should regard his Christian life in relation to the *Parousia* and to the *Pleroma*—the final fulfillment of the life of the whole Christ. Jesus Himself constantly reminded His hearers that the Master who had given various talents to His servants would one day return and ask for an accounting. These parables should not merely be understood in the light of personal justification and sin. It is not merely a question of making certain that one is personally discovered at the hour of death to be in the state of grace. Supernatural life itself is a talent which is given us to be developed. The virtues of faith, hope, and charity, by which we are united to God, are talents given us to be developed. And they are given us that we may develop them not only on our own account but for everybody else in the Mystical Body.

The final perfection of the "whole Christ," the final glory that the resplendent Bride will give to God in the "day of Christ Jesus," depends in some measure upon each one of us, because it depends on the use we make of God's gifts. These gifts are given us, remember, not for ourselves alone, but for others as well.

No man enters heaven all by himself. We either bring others in with us or we are brought in by others. The sublime economy of divine love, the feast of love which is the heart's blood of the body of Christ, demands this sharing in merits and graces, because every gift that is shared with another is sweeter and more meritorious. One of the most fundamental laws of life is the need to multiply itself, and this law applies to the supernatural life as well. Good is diffusive of itself. The grace that is given to *me* must pour out into *your* heart through works

---

14. Ephesians 2:18.

of love, through prayer, through sacrifice. The more fully one enters into the Christian life, the more he feels the necessity of communicating that life to others, if not by word, then by prayer and by the deep, sweet anguish of desire, the craving for souls that burns in the depths of the heart of the priest.

Here, then, are our principles: We are baptized into the whole Christ. Baptism implies a responsibility to *develop* one's supernatural life, to nourish it by love of God, to reproduce and spread it by love for other men. All this is ordered to the final perfection of a plan that extends far beyond our own individual salvation: a plan for God's glory which lies at the very heart of the universe. This mystery we must believe and seek to understand if we would make anything of conversion and vocation.

I might add that every baptism implies a distinct individual vocation, a peculiar function in the building up of the Mystical Body. This follows clearly from St. Paul's teaching on the functions of the different members. Each one has something to do. We are not called merely to vegetate in the Mystical Body, but to act and to grow and to help the growth of other members.

Finally, every circumstance of every individual life, every grace, every trial, every joy, every suffering, every gift, and every loss, must be seen in the light of this same universal plan. It is all part of our vocation. It is all sent to us by God as a means for working out our own salvation and perfecting the Mystical Body. There is nothing on earth which cannot be made to contribute to the good of the elect and of the "whole Christ." "And we know that to them that love God, all things work together unto good."[15]

I know from my own experience that baptism was not the end of my conversion but only the beginning. I was baptized twelve years ago. I came to the font seeking what most people seek—faith, truth, life, peace. I found all that the first day, and yet I have continued to seek and have continued, also, to find. This seeking and finding goes on more and more. The pursuit becomes more ardent and more calm. The experience of discovery is something deeper and more vital every day.

The faith, the love of God, the light of God's presence, the sense of rich and living spiritual union with my brothers in God, all this grows and broadens with the ordinary joys and sufferings of life. You do not always have the sense that you are getting somewhere, and yet, whether you feel it or not, this expansion and deepening is always going on. The life of a Christian who does what he can to develop his Christian life is every day more serene and more profound. I say, by way of parenthesis, the life of the Christian who *does what he can*. Many Chris-

15. Romans 8:28.

tians inhibit the growth of the life within them by their morbid depression at not being able to do what they can't. One of the great secrets of the Christian life is the kind of peaceful humility which trusts in God for results and does not get too disturbed by the constant failures of human weakness.

The story of my own conversion has been told elsewhere in considerable detail.[16] There is no need to go into it all again here, except to say that I had tried most of the typical solutions that men apply to their problems before I became a Catholic. I found that all these other solutions were inadequate. I knew something of the life of the artist and intellectual because my father was an artist and I was brought up, for better or for worse, as an intellectual.

I went through schools and colleges in America and France and England. After a year at Cambridge I came back to Columbia and then went into teaching and writing. That was what I was up to when I finally found my way into the little church of Corpus Christi on 121st Street, just off Broadway, at the edge of the Columbia campus.

Meanwhile I had tried to construct a philosophy of life on four different foundations. I had begun with plain, atheistic hedonism—which is a fancy title for a life of absolute selfishness. Believe in nothing, have a good time, and try to satisfy all your capacities for pleasure without hurting other people too much. It was what my generation believed in, when it was entering into manhood after having considered the society of its elders during the 1920s. In order to give this vague and irrational code an intellectual structure, I rebuilt its foundations with the fragments I was able to gather from a hasty and superficial reading of Freud and Jung.

The reason why one had to lead this life devoted to self-satisfaction was that mental health depended on keeping one's mind from becoming a tangle of repressions. This made me excessively introspective. In order to escape into the world outside myself, and also in order to take revenge for my own disgust with myself by venting it all on a "scapegoat," I became a communist sympathizer and unloaded all my sins on the back of the bourgeoisie. It made me feel good, but not for long. Campus communism at Columbia was untidy and feeble, and I did not take well to the incantation of slogans as a substitute for thought. When it became clear that the unprincipled opportunism of the party line had no other end than to promote the interests of those in power in "the party," I gave up communism in complete disgust.

Then I tried to return to the religion of my childhood—a vague Protestantism. It was too vague. I wanted a solid foundation of doctrinal truth to build on, and I could not find any. Protestantism was so highly subjective that each

---

16. *The Seven Storey Mountain* (New York: Harcourt, Brace, 1948).

individual was isolated with his own personal experience, and faith had become, in practice, almost incommunicable. It was almost impossible to find out exactly what my Protestant friends really *believed*. Nevertheless, the element of personal experience in religion fascinated me, and I explored the literature of oriental mysticism without much profit except that I came away with the conviction that man could, by detachment from created things and by a profound interior transformation, enter into direct experimental contact with God.

The fact that God could exist had meanwhile been impressed upon me by Gilson's *Spirit of Medieval Philosophy*. When I began to find out more about scholastic philosophy and theology by reading Jacques Maritain and parts of St. Thomas, and when I began to understand something of the nature of the soul and its life, my conversion followed quite logically.

The intellectual basis of my conversion was simply this: I found that God existed, and that He was the source of all reality; was, in fact, Reality, Truth, Life itself. He was pure actuality. On the other hand, I found that I had an intellect made to apprehend the highest and most perfect Truth in a supernatural intuition born of love, and that I had a free will that was capable of turning all the powers of my being either toward that Truth or away from it. Finally, since I could not attain this consummation by my own unaided natural powers, I would have to enter into the economy of means and helps called "graces" won for me by Christ. Therefore I was baptized and became a Christian at least in name.

IT IS EVIDENT THAT the story of my life up to the day of my baptism is hardly the adequate story of my "conversion." My conversion is still going on. Conversion is something that is prolonged over a whole lifetime. Its progress leads it over a succession of peaks and valleys, but normally the ascent is continuous in the sense that each new valley is higher than the last one.

I have said that the problem of the Christian life is not solved by baptism alone. Sanctifying grace, which makes us "live in Christ" and nourishes us with the fruits of His Passion and endows us with a share in His risen glory, is a talent that has to be increased and developed. We must enter deeper and deeper into this life of Christ. We must give ourselves over more and more fully to the mighty and transforming power of grace. Why? Because, as I have said, the purpose of our lives is to make us more and more productive members of the Mystical Body of Christ.[17]

We increase and deepen our participation in the life of the Body by the activity of our minds and wills, illuminated and guided by the Holy Ghost. We

17. John 15:1, 2, 6, 8.

must therefore keep growing in our knowledge and love of God and in our love for other men. The power of good operative habits must take ever greater and greater hold upon us. The Truth we believe in must work itself more and more fully into the very substance of our lives until our whole existence is nothing but vision and love.

What this means in practice is summed up by one word that most men are afraid of: *asceticism*. "We are debtors not to the flesh to live according to the flesh. For if you live according to the flesh, you shall die; but if by the spirit you mortify the deeds of the flesh, you shall live."[18] Our divine sonship and our inheritance of the joys of the divine life depend on our union with Christ who died for us on the Cross. We are only "joint-heirs with Him," "if so we suffer with him that we may be glorified with him."[19] "For they that are Christ's have crucified their flesh with its vices and concupiscences."[20]

The reason for this is not purely negative. Penance and mortification are not imposed on us merely as a vindictive punishment. We tend to forget the medicinal value of penance. We must deny our faculties the satisfactions proper to a lower form of life in order to accustom them, little by little, to the higher life of the Spirit in which God is known and loved as He is in Himself and not as He appears reflected in His creatures. Asceticism is essential to the Christian life. Without self-denial we cannot be Christ's disciples. "If any man will come after me, let him deny himself and take up his cross and come, follow me."[21]

It took me almost a year to discover that it was not possible to live a life exactly like that led by non-Christians and remain a Christian, no matter how convinced one might be of the truth of Christianity. I admit that it is possible and necessary for many Christians to live immersed in "the world" and all that it implies, but they are precisely the ones who ought to practice the most difficult asceticism. If they are to live as true members of Christ and radiate the divine influence among the men with whom they are in contact, they will be obliged to develop rich interior lives of union with God, and this union will have to be deep enough to weather the demands of hard work and constant contact with things that would defile a weaker spirit.

My own weakness convinced me that I ought to take upon myself the obligations of a higher state of life, not because I felt strong enough to live up to these obligations, but because I realized that they implied special helps and graces from God. I became a Cistercian novice in the Trappist Abbey of Gethsemani,

18. Romans 8:12-13.
19. Romans 8:17.
20. Galatians 5:24.
21. Matthew 16:24.

Kentucky. God had been exceedingly generous with me. In exchange for a half-articulate acknowledgment of my absolute helplessness, He had called me to one of the most austere orders in the Church. And a few years before, I had been quite convinced that I did not have good enough health to lead the ordinary life of men in the world.

If I began a meditation on this second great step in my conversion, I would go on for pages and fill another book, which would perhaps be tedious to everyone but myself, because the mystery of God's goodness to me is something that dazzles me more and more from day to day and I cannot exhaust its fascination.

The monastic life is nothing but a search for God, a search that has been streamlined and intensified by the rejection of every other concern. A Christian living in the world can temper his pursuit of God's Truth with other secondary interests, as long as these do not conflict with his Christian vocation. But God becomes the monk's whole reason for existing. Nothing that does not lead to God, nothing that does not give him glory, is of any account. The monk, and especially the Trappist Cistercian, is by profession a contemplative. He is immersed and swallowed up in the tide of life and vision that is poured out upon the world through the Passion of Our Divine Savior. The monk's life is a life of ardent love for Christ, who is "the way, the truth and the life."

And yet, however great may be the grace of monastic profession, it still falls far short of the priesthood. There is no greater gift given by Christ to the members of His Church than the grace of the priesthood. Ordination impresses upon the soul an indelible character which identifies a man with Christ as priest and victim. The grace of the priesthood sinks a man into the very depths of the Christ-Life, places him at the heart of all that is real and vital, and arms him with the power which has secretly shaped all history until now and which is fast preparing the final revelation of the glory of the sons of God, in Christ Jesus. The priest holds in his hands the Judge and Savior of men. He speaks five words and the Life of the world is present on the altar before him. He holds between his fingers the Heart that is throbbing in the deepest center of all the hearts of the saints. He holds the life of all the saints; he holds God Himself in his hands!

Is IT POSSIBLE TO imagine a man, endowed with such power from God, not being completely transformed by his daily exercise of it?

I cannot write much here about this third and most tremendous step in my conversion. Its effects are only just beginning dimly to dawn upon me. I am just beginning to see something of the breadth of the new horizons that are opened up before me by the Christ of my daily Mass.

At four o'clock in the morning, after the choir has finished chanting the night office begun at 1:30 or 2 A.M., in the Basilica of the Abbey, the Cistercian priests file through the shadows of the transept into their sacristy. High up in the belfry the little bell tolls for Masses that are about to begin. We take off our white cowls and put on our vestments, and depart severally to our dim altars in the candlelit side chapels. And the great Sacrifice begins, as we bow at the foot of the altar of God. We go up to God with our hearts steeped in the peace of the Psalms, our minds swimming in the calm wonder of revelation. We offer the host and the chalice to God, for His blessing upon the Sacrifice.

We bow down before the thrice Holy God, and begin the Canon, drawing into the heart of our Mass the lives and souls of all those whom Christ's Heart loves in our hearts. We press them to His Heart in our hearts, as more than once during the Canon we cry out to God with a great cry that shakes our depths, the cry of those who are still divided and separated in some measure from the perfect union of the saints in Christ. We bow in silence, holding the thin white host. Everything becomes luminous and calm. With a simplicity and a peace that are more powerful than all thunder, Christ utters Himself through us and is present upon the altar. The might of His Spirit sings within us, and the Spirit cries, "Abba, Father!" and prays for us within us with a pleading too deep and too magnificent for us to understand.

It is a sweet and terrible thing to feel the fire of that wonderful pleading grow up and begin to burn in the secret depths of your being. Yet, by the mercy of God, you are not consumed, and your hand does not tremble when you lift up the body and blood of Christ and offer Him to the Father: all honor and glory! You are sustained by the expectation of the final act, the Communion that completes the Sacrifice. The wonderful calm anguish, generated within your heart by the prayer of the Spirit, is quenched in the chalice of your Communion and you sink into the clear-eyed peace of Christ, the peace which is the peace and simplicity of an Eternal Child!

Then, for an hour, perhaps more, it is this peace that prays within you with an ineffable power. You go off somewhere in the dark recesses of the church and kneel behind something, and half the time you forget where you are.

Day after day it is the same external act: but always with a new inner meaning. Morning after morning you go to the dim altar weaker and more lowly than you have ever been before, and leave it lost in a more incomprehensible greatness than you have ever known before. A few months of the Mass have emptied me more and filled me more than seven years of monastic asceticism.

I used to have what I considered a degree of prayer. It was something I thought I could refer to as "my prayer." I rested in it, and it was silent and sweet. It seemed to me to be something rich and beautiful. Now I have no prayer. I am possessed by the prayer of One who is Almighty. And His prayer in me is something more than prayer because it is an infinite Sacrifice.

Prayer used to rise out of my soul as a desire that raised me up to God. It was my desire, and I could see where it was going, and I could take complacency in it. Now prayer is an earthquake which rends the rocks on which the substance of my being is built, and I do not know where it is going or what it is doing: sometimes it raises the dead, but only to assuage my terror. And sometimes it throws me to the living, the way the early Christians were thrown to the lions.

The Mass has made an end forever of what I used to treasure as an interior solitude. It has shown me the way to a height of solitude I never dreamed of because its paradox was utterly beyond my own imagining. This is the solitude of Christ in the Blessed Sacrament. Jesus in the host is alone, not because He is remote and isolated from everybody, but because He is *given to everybody, given utterly*. And because He is given to everybody, He can belong exclusively to nobody. And yet He is so alone that He belongs entirely to each one who possesses Him.

If you are afraid of love, never become a priest, never say Mass. The Mass will draw down upon your soul a torrent of interior suffering which has only one function—to break you wide open and let everybody in the world into your heart. If you are afraid of people, never say Mass! If you want to guard your heart against invasion, never say Mass! For when you begin to say Mass, the Spirit of God awakes like a giant inside you and bursts the locks of your private sanctuary and calls all the people in the world to come into your heart. If you say Mass, you condemn your soul to the torment of a love that is so vast and so insatiable that you will never be able to bear it alone. That love is the love of the Heart of Jesus, burning within your own miserable heart, and bringing down upon you the huge weight of His pity for all the sins of the world!

Do you know what that love will do to you if you let it work on your soul, if you do not resist it? It will devour you. It will kill you. It will break your heart.

I wish I could speak intelligibly about the absolute imperiousness of Christ's love in the heart of a priest. Without actually doing violence to your heart (for Christ's love always works with a power that is smooth and delicate, even when it smashes you!), the Spirit strikes like lightning as soon as there is the slightest opening in your will, and in a flash He is upon you with His new demand. And almost every time it seems to be a sweeping demand for your whole self, everything, a holocaust.

Where is there a hiding place, where is there a high mountain or a deep forest or an unvisited desert, where a poor priest can go to escape from the voices of men that are brought to the ears of his soul by the Holy Spirit? Where can a creature without courage and without virtue, and almost without faith, hide his head and blot out the image of the faces that look at him and hands that reach out to him? Where can he go to stop his ears against the voices that cry, "Die for me! Die for me!"?

That is not all. It is not only the ones we must die for that terrify us: it is most of all the ones we must live for. They demand not only our strength and our health and our time, but if we listen to the voice of Christ in them, there will be many among them who will claim, as an imperious right, the deepest recesses of your heart and soul: because we are their Christ and we have to love them with the same love with which Christ loves them. "This is my commandment, that you love one another as I have loved you."[22] It is not enough to be a mere agent of God, transacting His business and then retiring within ourselves. We have to do the work of Him that sent us, which is to live consumed in the suffering of love.

"A WOMAN WHEN SHE is in labor hath sorrow because her hour is come; but when she hath brought forth the child she remembereth no more the anguish for joy that a man is born into the world."[23] The great work of Christ would be completed more quickly if we were more willing to bear the anguish of His love. Yet is it any wonder that we flee from a love that destroys us? Alas, we forget that it destroys us only to transform us. The things the Spirit of God demands of us in order to form the Mystical Body of the Whole Christ, in order that "a man may be born into the world," contradict our own ideals of a sanctity in which we ourselves are not sacrificed, consumed, and transformed.

We resist the exigencies of a love that seeks to fulfill us by melting us down in the crucible from which the *Pleroma* is to emerge. But it is only in Christ, in the whole Christ, that each individual personality can be completely perfected and fulfilled. For Christ is our life, and until we live perfectly in Him, and He in us, we still fall short of the man we were intended to be, because something of our life is still lacking to us.

Let us all enter into the great prayer of the Church, which centers upon the Sacrifice of Christ in the Mass, and in that prayer let us remember one another, readers and writer, priest and faithful. Let us ask God through Christ, and in the unity of His Spirit, to give us the courage not to run away from His love, not to run away from His fire, and not to run away from the divine love we find in one another.

---

22. John 15:12.
23. John 16:21.

2

St. John of the Cross

This brief introduction to the life and work of St. John of the Cross was first published as one of twenty essays in the collection entitled *Saints for Now*, edited by Claire Boothe Luce (New York: Sheed & Ward, 1952), 250-60. It was reprinted as part of the "Mentors and Doctrines" section of *A Thomas Merton Reader* (306-14; rev. ed., 285-94). Focusing principally on his geographical and cultural setting in sixteenth-century Spain, his poetry (including a partial translation of the "Spiritual Canticle"), and his sanctity, with its integration of "natural suffering and supernatural joy" in a life of charity at once perfect and obscure, it is a more personal and more "popular" treatment of the saint about whom Merton had recently written extensively in *The Ascent to Truth* and in his five-part article "The Transforming Union in St. Bernard and St. John of the Cross" (*Collectanea OCR*, 1948-1950; reprinted in *Thomas Merton on St. Bernard*, 159-226). Here Merton explains in what sense he can call St. John "the most accessible of the saints" and endeavors to show how the saint also "makes us accessible to ourselves by opening our hearts to God within their own depths."

I F YOU HAVE NEVER seen El Greco's view of Toledo, you might take a look at it. It will tell you something about St. John of the Cross. I say it will tell you something—not very much. St. John of the Cross and El Greco were contemporaries; they lived in the same country; they were mystics, though by no means in the same degree. In other ways they were quite different. Father Bruno, in the best life of St. John of the Cross so far written, reminds his reader several times not to go imagining that St. John of the Cross looked like an El Greco painting. He was more like one of Zurbaran's Carthusians. Even that comparison is not altogether exact. The original and authentic portrait of the saint shows him to have an innocent and rather expressionless face. He does not look in any way ascetic. In fact you would think you were looking at the portrait of a Madrid shopkeeper or of a cook.

El Greco's view of Toledo is very dramatic. It is full of spiritual implications. It looks like a portrait of the heavenly Jerusalem wearing an iron mask. Yet there is nothing inert about these buildings. The dark city built on its mountain seems to be entirely alive. It surges with life, coordinated by some mysterious, providential upheaval which drives all these masses of stone upward toward heaven, in the clouds of a blue disaster that foreshadows the end of the world.

Somewhere in the middle of the picture must be the building where St. John of the Cross was kept in prison. Soon after the beginning of St. Theresa's reform he was kidnapped by opponents of the reform, and disappeared. No one had any idea where he had gone, and, as St. Theresa lamented, nobody seemed to care. He was locked up in a cell without light or air during the stifling heat of a Toledan summer to await trial and punishment for what his persecutors seriously believed to be a canonical crime. The complex canonical and political implications of the Carmelite reform had involved the saints of that reform in the kind of intrigue for which they alone, of all Spain, had no taste. And even St. Theresa, whose dovelike simplicity was supported by an altogether devastating prudence in these adventures, seems to have rather enjoyed them.

John of the Cross found little that was humanly speaking enjoyable in his Toledo jail. His only excursions from his cell came on the days when he was brought down to the refectory to be publicly scourged by his jailers, who were scandalized at his meek silence, believing it to be the sign of a reprobate conscience, hardened in rebellion. Why didn't the man do something to defend himself?

Here in Toledo, in what he called "the belly of the whale," the saint, wisely more silent than the prophet Jonas, dealt not with men but with God alone, waiting patiently for the divine answer that would end this dark night of his soul. No one knows when or how the answer came, but when St. John made his miraculous escape during the octave of the Assumption, in 1578, he carried in his pocket the manuscript of a poem which respectable critics have declared to be superior to any other in the Spanish language. These critics range from Menendez y Pelayo, who may be deemed to be respectable in a rather stuffy sense, to more recent and more advanced writers. Even the London magazine *Horizon* included two very competent articles on St. John of the Cross in a series of "studies of genius." As far as I know, John of the Cross was the only saint in the series.

El Greco was painting in Toledo when St. John of the Cross was in prison there. But the imprisonment of St. John of the Cross and the *Spiritual Canticle* which bloomed miraculously in the closet where he was jailed had little to do with the exiled Greek. The color scheme is quite different. The painter's view of the city must be a winter view, black, purple, green, blue, and gray. And the movement is a blind upheaval in which earth and sky run off the top of the canvas like an ebb-tide in the Arctic Ocean. The color scheme of John's imprisonment is black and ocher and brown and red: the red is his own blood running down his back. The movement is centripetal. There is a tremendous stability, not merely in the soul immobilized, entombed in a burning stone wall, but in the depths of that soul, purified by a purgatory that those alone know who have felt it, emerging into the Center of all centers, the Love which moves the heavens and the stars, the Living God.

The last place in the world where one would imagine the *Spiritual Canticle* to have been written is a dungeon!

I will try to translate a little of it:

My Beloved is like the mountains.
Like the lonely valleys full of woods
The strange islands
The rivers with their sound
The whisper of the lovely air!

The night, appeased and hushed
About the rising of the dawn,
The music stilled
The sounding solitude
The supper that rebuilds my life
And brings me love.

Our bed of flowers
Surrounded by the lions' dens
Makes us a purple tent,
Is built of peace.
Our bed is crowned with a thousand shields of gold!

Fast-flying birds
Lions, harts, and leaping does[1]
Mountains, banks, and vales
Streams, breezes, heats of day
And terrors watching in the night:

By the sweet lyres and by the siren's song
I conjure you: let angers end!

---

1. I lift this line bodily from the translation of Professor E. Allison Peers.

And do not touch the wall
But let the bride be safe: let her sleep on!

Only the saint and God can tell what distant echoes of an utterly alien everyday common life penetrated the darkness of the jail cell and the infinitely deep sleep of the peace in which his soul lay hidden in God. *Touch not the wall* . . . but the religious police could not disturb the ecstasy of one who had been carried so far that he was no longer troubled at the thought of being rejected even by the holy!

NO ONE CAN BECOME a saint without solving the problem of suffering. No one who has ever written anything, outside the pages of Scripture, has given us such a solution to the problem as St. John of the Cross. I will not speculate upon his answers. I will merely mention the fact that they exist and pass on. For those who want to read it, there is the *Dark Night of the Soul.* But this much must be said: Sanctity can never abide a merely speculative solution to the problem of suffering. Sanctity solves the problem not by analyzing but by suffering. It is a living solution, burned in the flesh and spirit of the saint by fire. Scripture itself tells us as much. "As silver is tried by fire and gold in the furnace, so the Lord trieth hearts" (Prov. 17:3). "Son, when thou comest to the service of God, stand in justice and fear and prepare thy soul for temptation. Humble thy heart and endure; incline thy ear and receive the words of understanding and make not haste in the time of clouds. Wait on God with patience; join thyself to God and endure, that thy life may be increased in the latter end. Take all that shall be brought upon thee, and in thy sorrow endure and in thy humiliation keep patience. For gold and silver are tried in the fire and acceptable men in the furnace of humiliation" (Eccles. 2:1-5).

Sanctity does not consist in suffering. It is not even directly produced by suffering, for many have suffered and have become devils rather than saints. What is more, there are some who gloat over the sufferings of the saints and are hideously sentimental about sufferings of their own, and cap it all by a voracious appetite for inflicting suffering on other people, sometimes in the name of sanctity. Of such were those who persecuted St. John of the Cross in his last days, and helped him to enter heaven with greater pain and greater heroism. These were not the "calced" who caught him at the beginning of his career, but the champion ascetics of his own reformed family, the men of the second generation, those who unconsciously did their best to ruin the work of the founders, and who quite consciously did everything they could to remove St. John of the Cross from a position in which he would be able to defend what he knew to be the Teresian ideal.

Sanctity itself is a living solution of the problem of suffering. For the saint, suffering continues to be suffering, but it ceases to be an obstacle to his mission, or to his happiness, both of which are found positively and concretely in the will of God. The will of God is found by the saint less in *manifestations* of the divine good-pleasure than in God Himself.

Suffering, on the natural level, is always opposed to natural joy. There is no opposition between natural suffering and supernatural joy. Joy, in the super-natural order, is simply an aspect of charity. It is inseparable from the love that is poured forth in our hearts by the Holy Ghost. But when sanctity is not yet mature, its joy is not always recognizable. It can too easily be buried under pain. But true charity, far from being diminished by suffering, uses suffering as it uses everything else: for the increase of its own immanent vitality. Charity is the expression of a divine life within us, and this life, if we allow it to have its way, will grow and thrive most in the very presence of all that seems to destroy life and to quench its flame. A life that blazes with a hundredfold brilliance in the face of death is therefore invincible. Its joy cannot fail. It conquers everything. It knows no suffering. Like the Risen Christ, Who is its Author and Principle, it knows no death.

THE LIFE OF CHARITY was perfect in the great Carmelite reformer, St. John of the Cross. It was so perfect that it can hardly be said to shine before men. His soul was too pure to attract any attention. Yet precisely because of his purity, he is one of the few saints who can gain a hearing in the most surprising recesses of an impure world. John of the Cross, who seems at first sight to be a saint for the most pure of the Christian elite, may very well prove to be the last hope of har-lots and publicans. The wisdom of this extraordinary child "reaches from end to end mightily." Lost in the pure wisdom of God, like God, and in God, he attains to all things. This saint, so often caricatured as an extremist, is actually beyond all extremes. Having annihilated all extremes in the center of his own humility, he remains colorless and neutral. His doctrine, which is considered inhumanly hard, is only hard because it is superhumanly simple. Its simplicity seems to pres-ent an obstacle to our nature, which seeks to hide itself from God in a labyrinth of mental complexities, like Adam and Eve amidst the leaves of Paradise.

The hardest thing to accept, in St. John of the Cross, is not the Cross, but the awful neutrality of his interior solitude. After all, as he so reasonably points out, when the soul is detached, by the Cross, from every sensible and spiritual obstacle, its journey to God becomes easy and joyful: "The Cross is the staff whereby one may reach Him, and whereby the road is greatly lightened and made easy. Wherefore Our Lord said through St. Matthew: My yoke is easy and my burden is light, which burden is the Cross. For if a man resolve to submit himself to carrying his cross—that is to say, if he resolve to desire in truth to meet trials and to bear them in all things for God's sake—he will find in them great relief and sweetness wherewith he may travel on this road, detached from all things and desiring nothing."[2]

The two words "desiring nothing" contain all the difficulty and all the simplicity of St. John of the Cross. But no Christian has a right to complain of them. They are simply an echo of two words that sum up the teaching of Jesus Christ in the Gospel: *abneget semetipsum.* "If any man would come after me, let him *deny himself.* ..."

This total self-denial, which St. John of the Cross pursues into the inmost depths of the human spirit, reduces our interior landscape to a wasteland without special features of any kind whatever. We do not even have the consolation of beholding a personal disaster. A cataclysm of the spirit, if terrible, is also interesting. But the soul of the contemplative is happy to be reduced to a state of complete loneliness and dereliction in which the most significant renouncement is that of self-complacency. Many men are attracted to a solitude in which they believe that they will have the leisure and the opportunity to contemplate themselves. Not so St. John of the Cross: "These times of aridity cause the soul to journey in all purity in the love of God, since it is no longer influenced in its actions by the pleasure and sweetness of the actions themselves ... but only by a desire to please God. It becomes neither presumptuous nor self-satisfied, as perchance it was wont to become in the time of its prosperity, but fearful and timid with regard to itself, finding in itself no satisfaction whatsoever; and herein consists that holy fear which preserves and increases the virtues.... Save for the pleasure indeed which at certain times God infuses into it, it is a wonder if it find pleasure and consolation of sense, through its own diligence, in any spiritual exercise or action.... There grows within souls that experience this arid night (of the senses) care for God and yearnings to serve Him, for in proportion as the breasts of sensuality wherewith it sustained and nourished the desires that it pursued are drying up, there remains nothing in that aridity and detachment save the yearning to serve God, which is a thing very pleasing to God."[3]

The joy of this emptiness, this weird neutrality of spirit which leaves the soul detached from the things of the earth and not yet in possession of those of heaven, suddenly blossoms out into a pure paradise of liberty, of which the saint sings in

---

2. *The Ascent of Mount Carmel,* ii, 7. *Complete Works of St. John of the Cross,* translated and edited by E. Allison Peers (Westminster: Newman, 1945), vol. I, p. 91.

3. *The Dark Night of the Soul,* i, 13. Peers, ed., *Complete Works of St. John of the Cross,,* vol. I, p. 393.

his *Spiritual Canticle*: it is a solitude full of wild birds and strange trees, rocks, rivers, and desert islands, lions and leaping does. These creatures are images of the joys of the spirit, aspects of interior solitude, fires that flash in the abyss of the pure heart whose loneliness becomes alive with the deep lightnings of God.

IF I SAY THAT St. John of the Cross seems to me to be the most accessible of the saints, that is only another way of saying that he is my favorite saint—together with three others who also seem to me most approachable: St. Benedict, St. Bernard, and St. Francis of Assisi. After all, the people you make friends with are the ones who welcome you into their company. But besides this, it also seems to me that St. John of the Cross is absolutely and in himself a most accessible saint. This, to those who find him forbidding, will seem an outrageous paradox. Nevertheless it is true, if you consider that few saints, if any, have ever opened up to other men such remote depths in their own soul. St. John of the Cross admits you, in the *Living Flame*, to his soul's "deepest center," to the "deep caverns" in which the lamps of fire, the attributes of God, flash mysteriously in metaphysical shadows; who else has done as much? St. John reveals himself to us not in allegory, as does St. Theresa (in the *Mansions*) but in *symbol*. And symbol is a far more potent and effective medium than allegory. It is truer because it is more direct and more intimate. It does not need to be worked out and applied by the reason. The symbols that spring from the depths of the heart of St. John of the Cross awaken kindred symbols in the depths of the heart that loves him. Their effect, of course, is supported and intensified by grace which, we may believe, the saint himself has begged for the souls of those who have been called to love him in God. Here is a union and a friendship of the soul with God Himself. Earth knows no such intimacies. Those who love St. Peter from the Gospels, and react in vivid sympathy for his all too human experiences, do not come as close to Peter as the one who meets St. John of the Cross in the depths of prayer. We know St. Peter on a more exterior surface of life—the level of passion and emotion. But on that level there is less communion, and less effective communication, than in the depths of the spirit.

And thus St. John of the Cross not only makes himself accessible to us, but does much more: he makes us accessible to ourselves by opening our hearts to God within their own depths.

In the end, however, I may as well have the courtesy to admit one thing: St. John of the Cross is not everybody's food. Even in a contemplative monastery there will be some who will never get along with him—and others who, though they think they know what he is about, would do better to let him alone. He upsets everyone who thinks that his doctrine is supposed to lead one by a way that is exalted. On the contrary, his way is so humble that it ends up by being no way at all, for John of the Cross is unfriendly to systems and a bitter enemy of all exaltation. *Omnis qui se exaltat humiliabitur.* His glory is to do without glory for the love of Christ.

John of the Cross is the patron of those who have a vocation that is thought, by others, to be spectacular, but which, in reality, is lowly, difficult, and obscure. He is the patron and the protector and master of those whom God has led into the uninteresting wilderness of contemplative prayer. His domain is precisely defined. He is the patron of contemplatives in the strict sense, and of their spiritual directors, not of contemplatives in the juridical sense. He is the patron of those who pray in a certain way in which God wants them to pray, whether they happen to be in the cloister, the desert, or the city. Therefore his influence is not limited to one order or to one kind of order. His teaching is not merely a matter of "Carmelite Spirituality," as some seem to think. In fact, I would venture to say that he is the father of all those whose prayer is an undefined isolation outside the boundary of "spirituality." He deals chiefly with those who, in one way or another, have been brought face to face with God in a way that methods cannot account for and books do not explain. He is in Christ the model and the maker of contemplatives wherever they may be found.

When this much has been said, enough has been said. St. John of the Cross was not famous in his own lifetime and will not be famous in our own. There is no need that either he, or contemplation, should be famous. In this world in which all good things are talked about and practically none of them are practiced, it would be unwise to make contemplative prayer a matter for publicity, though perhaps no harm has been done, thus far, by making its name known. God Himself knows well enough how to make the thing known to those who need it, in His designs for them.

Let it suffice to have said that this Spanish saint is one of the greatest and most hidden of the saints, that of all saints he is perhaps the greatest poet as well as the greatest contemplative, and that in his humility he was also most human, although I have not said much to prove it. I know that he will understand that this essay about him was written as a veiled act of homage, as a gesture of love and gratitude, and as a disguised prayer. He knows what the prayer seeks. May he grant it to the writer and to the readers of these words.

3

Poetry and Contemplation: A Reappraisal

As Merton himself points out in the headnote that opens this article, it is a revision of the essay "Poetry and the Contemplative Life," first published in *The Commonweal* 46 (July 4, 1947), 280-86, and reprinted (in slightly revised form) as an appendix to his third book of verse, *Figures for an Apocalypse* (93-111). It is thus the first in a series of revisions of early writings that Merton made during this period that included the transformation of *Seeds of Contemplation* into *New Seeds of Contemplation* and *What Is Contemplation?* into *The Inner Experience*. The new version likewise appeared first in *Commonweal* 69 (October 24, 1958), 87-92, and was reprinted, again with slight revisions, in the first edition of Thomas Merton, *Selected Poems* (107-35; in the 1967 "enlarged edition" of *Selected Poems* the essay was replaced by additional poems drawn from the 1963 volume *Emblems of a Season of Fury*). The essay has been most readily available in *A Thomas Merton Reader* (436-50; rev. ed., 399-415) and in *The Literary Essays of Thomas Merton* (338-54). (For a comparison of the two versions see Patrick F. O'Connell, "Poetry and Contemplation: The Evolution of Thomas Merton's Aesthetic," *The Merton Journal* 8.1 [Easter 2001], 2-11.) Appearing in the year of Merton's "Fourth and Walnut" epiphany, which is usually taken as marking his "turning toward the world" during the final decade of his life, the revised essay emphasizes that contemplation is not "*a separate department of life*" but "*the very fullness of a fully integrated life*," and that therefore the conflict he analyzed in the original version between artistic creativity and contemplative realization is "*largely, an illusion*"—less a problem to be resolved logically than a mystery to be lived out in the particular circumstances of one's own unique life and vocation. It marks not only Merton's return to composing poetry on a more regular basis from the mid-1950s until the end of his life, but his growing awareness that the will of God is to be discovered less in conforming to abstract principles than in recognizing and responding to the signs of the times, which may call one to poetry as well as to prayer, may find both contemplation and action essential to a deepening relationship with both Creator and creation.

Author's Note

Ten years ago I wrote an article called "Poetry and the Contemplative Life" which was published first in Commonweal *and then appeared in a volume of verse,* Figures for an Apocalypse.

In its original form, this article stated a "problem" and tried to apply a rather crude "solution" which, at the time, was rather widely discussed by people interested in religious verse and, at least by implication, in religious experience. Many of them were inclined to accept the "solution" that was proposed. Others wisely rejected it because of its somewhat puritanical implications.

As time passed I have found that the confident pronouncements made in my early writing lay more and more heavily on my conscience as a writer and as a priest, and while it is evidently impossible to correct and amend all my wrong-headed propositions, at least I would like to revise the essay of 1948. The revision is unfortunately not fully satisfactory precisely because it is no more than a revision. But I do not want to write a whole new article, approaching the subject from an entirely different angle. I believe it is necessary to revise the earlier article and to restate the case in the same context, arriving at a different conclusion.

One of the unavoidable defects of this kind of revision is that it retains an altogether misleading insistence on the terms "contemplation" and "contemplative life" as something apart from the rest of man's existence. This involves a rather naïve presupposition that "contemplation" is a kind of objectivized entity which gets "interfered with" by such things as aesthetic reflection. There is a certain amount of truth behind this supposed conflict, but to state it thus crudely is to invite all sorts of misunderstanding. In actual fact, neither religious nor artistic contemplation should be regarded as "things" which happen or "objects" which one can "have." They belong to the much more mysterious realm of what one "is"—or rather "who" one is. Aesthetic intuition is not merely the act of a faculty, it is also a heightening and intensification of our personal identity and being by the perception of our connatural affinity with "Being" in the beauty contemplated.

But also, and at the same time, the implied conflict between "contemplation" as rest and poetic creation as activity is even more misleading. It is all wrong to imagine that in order to "contemplate" divine things, or what you will, it is necessary to abstain from every kind of action and enter into a kind of spiritual stillness where one waits for "something to happen." In actual fact, true contemplation is inseparable from life and from the dynamism of life—which includes work, creation, production, fruitfulness, and above all love. *Contemplation is not to be thought of as a separate department of life, cut off from all man's other interests and superseding them. It is the very fullness of a fully integrated life. It is the crown of life and of all life's activities.*

Therefore the earlier problem was, largely, an illusion, created by this division of life into formally separate compartments of "action" and "contemplation." But because this crude division was stated so forcefully and so frequently in my earlier writings, I feel that it is most necessary now to try to do something to heal this wound and draw together the two sides of this unfortunate fissure.

In this present article, the wound is still evident, and it is meant to be so. I am attempting to patch it up, and probably do not fully succeed. If this is true, I do not care so much, as long as it is clear that I am stitching and drawing the wound together, pouring in the disinfectant, and putting on a bandage.

1

IN AN AGE OF SCIENCE and technology, in which man finds himself bewildered and disoriented by the fabulous versatility of the machines he has created, we live precipitated outside ourselves at every moment, interiorly empty, spiritually lost, seeking at all costs to forget our own emptiness and ready to alienate ourselves completely in the name of any "cause" that comes along. At such a time as this, it seems absurd to talk of contemplation; and indeed a great deal of the talk that has been bandied about timidly enough on this subject is ludicrous and inadequate. Contemplation itself takes on the appearance of a safe and rather bourgeois "cause"—the refuge of a few well-meaning Christians who are willing to acquaint themselves with St. Thomas and St. John of the Cross, and to disport themselves thereafter in such Edens of passivity and fervor as cannot be disapproved by the so-called "Masters of the Spiritual Life." For others, safer still, contemplation means nothing more than a life of leisure and of study: in many cases more a fond hope than an accomplished fact.

The relative timidity of these adventures, and the hare-brained chase after more exotic forms of spirituality, should not make us too prone to laugh at every symptom of man's acute need for an interior life. For one of the most important and most hopeful signs of the times is in the turbulent, anarchic, but fully determined efforts of a small minority of men to recover some kind of contact with their own inner depths, to recapture the freshness and truth of their own subjectivity, and to go on from there not only to God but to the spirit of other men. In the face of our own almost hopeless alienation, we are trying to get back to ourselves before it is too late. One of the most outstanding examples of this struggle is seen in the almost symbolic career of Boris Pasternak, whose more recent poetry and prose can most certainly qualify in a broad and basic sense as *contemplative*.

The contemplative is not just a man who sits under a tree with his legs crossed, or one who edifies himself with the answer to ultimate and spiritual problems. He is one who seeks to know the meaning of life not only with his head but with his whole being, by living it in depth and in purity, and thus uniting himself to the very Source of Life—a Source which is infinitely actual and therefore too real to be contained satisfactorily inside any word or concept or name assigned by man; for the words of man tend to limit the realities which they express, in order to express them. And anything that can be limited cannot be the infinite actuality known to the contemplative without words and without the mediation of precise analytical thought. We can say, then, that contemplation is the intuitive perception of life in its Source: that Source Who revealed Himself as the unnameable "I Am" and then again made Himself known to us as Man in Christ. Contemplation is experience of God in Man, God in the world, God in Christ; it is an obscure intuition of God Himself, and this intuition is a gift of God Who reveals Himself in His very hiddenness as One unknown.

Contemplation is related to art, to worship, to charity; all these reach out by intuition and self-dedication into the realms that transcend the material conduct of everyday life. Or rather, in the midst of ordinary life itself they seek and find a new and transcendent meaning. And by this meaning they transfigure the whole of life. Art, worship, and love penetrate into the spring of living waters that flows from the depths where man's spirit is united to God, and draw from those depths power to create a new world and a new life. Contemplation goes deeper than all three, and unites them, and plunges man's whole soul into the supernal waters, in the baptism of wordless understanding and ecstatic prayer.

There can be various levels of contemplation. There is contemplation in a broad and improper sense—the religious intuition of the artist, the lover, or the worshiper. In these intuitions, art, love, or worship remain in the foreground; they modify the experience of ultimate reality, and present that reality to us as the "object" of aesthetic vision, or adoration, or love. In an even less proper sense, "contemplation" loses sight of ultimates and becomes preoccupied with a beautiful thing, or a meaningful liturgy, or a loved person.

But in its proper meaning, contemplation transcends all "objects," all "things," and goes beyond all "ideas" of beauty or goodness or truth, passes beyond all speculation, all creative fervor, all charitable action, and "rests" in the inexpressible. It lets go of everything and finds All in Nothing—the *todo y nada* of St. John of the Cross.

On a dark night, kindled in love with yearnings—O happy chance—
I went forth without being observed, my house being now at rest.

In darkness and secure, by the secret ladder, disguised,—O happy chance—
In darkness and concealment, my house being now at rest.

In the happy night, in secret when none saw me
Nor I beheld aught, without light or guide save that which burned in my
        heart

This light guided me more surely than the light of noonday
To the place where He (well I knew who!) was awaiting me
A place where none appeared.

Now when we speak of a possible conflict between poetry and contemplation, it is clearly only contemplation in the last, most perfect sense that is intended. For when we speak of contemplation in the more broad and improper sense, we find it uniting itself with art, with worship, and with love. It is not only compatible with poetic creation, but is stimulated by it, and in its turn inspires poetry. And in the realm of worship, contemplation in this broad sense is stimulated by meditation, by prayer, by liturgy, and arises out of these religious activities. Above all, in the sacramental life of the Church, we find contemplation in this broad sense should normally be the fruit of fervent reception of the sacraments, at least sometimes. That is to say that the reception of the sacraments should produce, once in a while, not only interior and unfelt grace but also a certain dim awareness of the presence and the action of God in the soul, though this awareness may be very fleeting, tenuous, and almost impossible to assess. Nor should people trouble their heads about whether or not they feel it, because some are not supposed to feel it: feelings are not important, and what they will experience without realizing it too clearly is the fervor of love and the desire to dedicate themselves more perfectly to God. Such things we can call in a broad and improper sense "contemplative" experiences.

This is *active* contemplation, in which grace indeed is the principle of all the supernatural value and ordination of our acts, but in which much of the initiative belongs to our own powers, prompted and sustained by grace. This form of the contemplative life prepares us for contemplation properly so called: the life of *infused* or *passive* or *mystical* contemplation.

Contemplation is the fullness of the Christian vocation—the full flowering of baptismal grace and of the Christ-life in our souls.

Christian contemplation is not something esoteric and dangerous. It is simply the experience of God that is given to a soul purified by humility and faith. It is the "knowledge" of God in the darkness of infused love. "This is eternal life, that they should know Thee, the One True God, and Jesus Christ Whom Thou hast sent" (John 17:3) or "But we all, beholding the glory of the Lord with open face, are transformed into the same image from glory to glory, as by the Spirit of the Lord" (II Corinthians 3:18). St. Paul, in his Epistle to the Hebrews, rebuked those who clung to the "first elements of the words of God" when they should have been "Masters," and he urged them to relinquish the "milk" of beginners and to desire the "strong meat" of the perfect, which is the contemplation of Christ in the great Mystery in which He renews on earth the redemptive sacrifice of the Cross. "For every one that is a partaker of milk is unskillful in the word of justice: for he is a little child. But strong meat is for the perfect: for them who by custom have their senses exercised to the discerning of good and evil" (Hebrews 5:13-14). *Omnis qui ad Dominum convertitur contemplativam vitam desiderat*, said St. Gregory the Great, and he was using contemplation in our sense: to live on the desire of God alone; to have one's mind divested of all earthly things and united, insofar as human weakness permits, with Christ. And he adds that the contemplative life begins on earth in order to continue, more perfectly, in heaven. St. Thomas echoed him with his famous phrase: *quaedam inchoatio beatitudinis* (contemplation is a beginning of eternal blessedness). St. Bonaventure goes further than any of the other Doctors of the Church in his insistence that all Christians should desire union with God in loving contemplation. And in his second conference on the Hexaemeron, applying Christ's words in Matthew 12:42, he says that the Queen of the South who left her own land and traveled far to hear the wisdom of Solomon will rise up in judgment against our generation, which refuses the treasure of divine wisdom, preferring the far lesser riches of worldly wisdom and philosophy.

Infused contemplation is a quasi-experimental knowledge of God's goodness "tasted" and "possessed" by a vital contact in the depths of the soul. By infused love, we are given an immediate grasp of God's own substance, and rest in the obscure and profound sense of His presence and transcendent actions within our inmost selves, yielding ourselves altogether to the work of His transforming Spirit.

By the light of infused wisdom we enter deeply into the Mystery of Christ Who is Himself the light of men. We participate, as it were, in the glory that is radiated mystically by His risen and transfigured Humanity. Our eyes are opened to understand the Scriptures and the mystery of God's intervention in man's history. We become aware of the way in which the infinite mercy and wisdom of God are revealed to men and angels in the Mystery of the Church, which is the Body of Christ. The contemplative life is the lot of those who have entered most fully into the life and spirit of the Church, so that the contemplatives are at the very heart of the Mystery which they have begun really to understand and to "see" with the eyes of their soul. To desire the contemplative life and its gifts is therefore to desire to become in the highest sense a fruitful and strong member of Christ. But it means also, by that very fact, to desire and accept a share in His sufferings and death, that we may rise with Him in the participation of His glory.

Now whether we speak of contemplation as active or passive, one thing is evident: it brings us into the closest contact with the one subject that is truly worthy of a Christian poet: the great Mystery of God, revealing His mercy to us in Christ. The Christian poet should be one who has been granted a deep understanding of the ways of God and of the Mystery of Christ. Deeply rooted in the spiritual consciousness of the whole Church, steeped in the Liturgy and the Scriptures, fully possessed by the "mind of the Church," he becomes as it were a voice of the Church and of the Holy Spirit, and sings again the *magnalia Dei*, praising God and pointing out the wonder of His ways. The Christian poet is therefore the successor to David and the Prophets, he contemplates what was announced by the poets of the Old Testament: he should be, as they were, a mystic, full of divine fire. He should be one who, like the prophet Isaias, has seen the living God and has lamented the fact that he was a man of impure lips, until God Himself sent Seraph, with a live coal from the altar of the heavenly temple, to burn his lips with prophetic inspiration.

In the true Christian poet—in Dante, St. John of the Cross, St. Francis, Jacopone da Todi, Hopkins, Paul Claudel—we find it hard to distinguish between the inspiration of the prophet and mystic and the purely poetic enthusiasm of great artistic genius.

Consider also what a tremendous mine of literary inspiration is in the liturgical life. The Liturgy itself contains the greatest literature, not only from Scripture but from the genius of the Patristic and Middle Ages. The Liturgy stands at the crossroads of the natural and supernatural lives, and exploits all the possibilities of both in order to bring out every possible meaning and implication that is in them with respect to our salvation and the praise of God. It surrounds those founts of all supernatural vitality, the Sacraments, with a music that is perfect in its integrity and dignity, and with ceremonies that are most meaningful by reason of their tremendous, dramatic simplicity, not to mention all the resources of pictorial and plastic art still unknown in this land which has never yet possessed a Chartres or an Assisi.

THE LITURGY IS, THEN, not only a school of literary taste and a mine of marvelous subjects, but it is infinitely more: it is a sacramental system built around the greatest Sacrament, the Blessed Eucharist, in which Christ Himself is enthroned, in mystery, in the very heart of His wonderful creation.

Christ on the Cross is the fount of all art because He is the Word, the fount of all grace and wisdom. He is the center of everything, of the whole economy of the natural and supernatural orders. Everything that is made subsists in Him and reflects His beauty. Everything points to this anointed King of Creation Who is the splendor of the eternal light and the mirror of the Godhead without stain. He is the "image of the invisible God, the firstborn of every creature . . . in Him were all things created, by Him and in Him . . . He is before all and by Him all things consist . . . in Whom it hath pleased the Father that all things should dwell . . . for in Him dwelleth all the fullness of the Godhead corporeally," that in all things He may hold the primacy (Colossians 1 and 2).

The Christian's vision of the world ought, by its very nature, to have in it something of poetic inspiration. Our faith ought to be capable of filling our hearts with a wonder and a wisdom which see beyond the surface of things and events, and grasp something of the inner and "sacred" meaning of the cosmos which, in all its movements and all its aspects, sings the praises of its Creator and Redeemer.

No Christian poetry worthy of the name has been written by anyone who was not in some degree a contemplative. I say "in some degree" because obviously not all Christian poets are mystics. But the true poet is always akin to the mystic because of the "prophetic" intuition by which he sees the spiritual reality, the inner meaning of the object he contemplates, which makes that concrete reality not only a thing worthy of admiration in itself, but also and above all makes it a *sign of God*. All good Christian poets are then contemplatives in the sense that they see God everywhere in His creation and in His mysteries, and behold the created world as filled with signs and symbols of God. To the true Christian poet, the whole world and all the incidents of life tend to be sacraments—signs of God, signs of His love working in the world.

However, the mere fact of having this contemplative vision of God in the world around us does not necessarily make a man a great poet. One must be not a "seer" but also and especially a "creator"—a "maker." Poetry is an art, a natural skill, a virtue of the practical intellect, and no matter how great a subject we may have in the experience of contemplation, we will not be able to put it into words if we do not have the proper command of our medium. This is true. But let us assume that a man already has this natural gift. If the inspiration is helpless without a correspondingly effective technique, technique is barren without inspiration.

2

CHRIST IS THE INSPIRATION of Christian poetry, and Christ is at the center of the contemplative life. Therefore, it would seem fairly evident that the one thing that will most contribute to the perfection of Catholic literature in general and poetry in particular will be for our writers and poets to live more as "contemplatives" than as citizens of a materialistic world. This means first of all leading the full Christian sacramental and liturgical life insofar as they can in their state. Obviously, the poet does not have to enter a monastery to be a better poet. On the contrary, what we need are "contemplatives" outside the cloister and outside the rigidly fixed patterns of religious life—contemplatives in the world of art, letters, education, and even politics. This means a solid integration of one's work, thought, religion, and family life and recreations in one vital harmonious unity with Christ at its center. The liturgical life is the most obvious example of "active contemplation," but it is hard enough to find a parish where the liturgical life is anything more than a bare skeleton. The eccentricities and obsessions of occasional faddists should not prejudice us against the immense vitality and permanent value of the true liturgical revival. It is quite certain that one of the most valid achievements in the realm of Christian art in our time is to the credit of the monks of Solesmes, with their revival of Gregorian chant.

A sincere and efficacious desire to enter more deeply into the beauty of the Christian mystery implies a willingness to sacrifice the things which are called "beautiful" by the decadent standards of a materialistic world. Yet the Christian contemplative need not confine himself to religious, still less to professionally "pious" models. He will, of course, read Scripture and above all the contemplative saints: John of the Cross, Theresa of Avila, John Ruysbroek, Bonaventure, Bernard. But no one can be a poet without reading the good poets of his own time—T. S. Eliot, Auden, Spender, Rilke, Pasternak, Dylan Thomas, García Lorca. One might add that a fully integrated vision of our time and of its spirit presupposes some contact with the genius of Baudelaire and Rimbaud, who are Christians turned inside out.

Contemplation has much to offer poetry. And poetry, in its turn, has something to offer contemplation. How is this so? In understanding the relation of poetry to contemplation the first thing that needs to be stressed is the essential dignity of aesthetic experience. It is, in itself, a very high gift, though only in the natural order. It is a gift which very many people have never received, and which others, having received, have allowed to spoil or become atrophied within them through neglect and misuse.

To many people, the enjoyment of art is nothing more than a sensible and emotional thrill. They look at a picture, and if it stimulates one or another of their sense-appetites they are pleased. On a hot day they like to look at a picture of mountains or the sea because it makes them feel cool. They like paintings of dogs that you could almost pat. But naturally they soon tire of art, under those circumstances. They turn aside to pat a real dog, or they go down the street to an air-conditioned movie, to give their senses another series of jolts. This is not what one can legitimately call the "enjoyment of Art."

A GENUINE AESTHETIC EXPERIENCE is something which transcends not only the sensible order (in which, however, it has its beginning) but also that of reason itself. It is a suprarational intuition of the latent perfection of things. Its immediacy outruns the speed of reasoning and leaves all analysis far behind. In the natural order, as Jacques Maritain has often insisted, it is an analogue of the mystical experience which it resembles and imitates from afar. Its mode of apprehension is that of "connaturality"—it reaches out to grasp the inner reality, the vital substance of its object, by a kind of affective identification of itself with it. It rests in the perfection of things by a kind of union which sometimes resembles the quiescence of the soul in its immediate affective contact with God in the obscurity of mystical prayer. A true artist can contemplate a picture for hours, and it is a real contemplation, too. So close is the resemblance between these two experiences that a poet like Blake could almost confuse the two and make them merge into one another as if they belonged to the same order of things.

This resemblance between the experiences of the artist and of the mystic has been extensively discussed in the long and important article on "Art and Spirituality," by Fr. M. Leonard, S.J., in the *Dictionnaire de Spiritualité*.

This theologian pushes the dignity of the aesthetic intuition practically to its limit. He gives it everything that it is ontologically able to stand. He insists that the highest experience of the artist penetrates not only beyond the sensible surface of things into their inmost reality, but even beyond that to God Himself. More than that, the analogy with mystical experience is deeper and closer still because, he says, the intuition of the artist sets in motion the very same psychological processes which accompany infused contemplation. This would seem to be too much; but no, it is not. It fits in with the psychology of St. Augustine and St. Bonaventure and the latter's notion of contemplation *per speculum*, passing through the mirror of created things to God, even if that mirror may happen to be our own soul. It also fits in with the ideas of the Greek Fathers about *theoria physica*, or "natural contemplation," which arrives at God through the inner spiritual reality (the *logos*) of the created thing.

The Augustinian psychology, which forms the traditional substratum of Christian mystical theology in the Western Church, distinguishes between an *inferior* and a *superior* soul. Of course, this is only a manner of speaking. There is only one soul, a simple spiritual substance, undivided and indivisible. And yet the soul insofar as it acts through its faculties, making decisions and practical judgments concerning temporal external things, is called "inferior." The "superior" soul is the same soul, but now considered as the principle or *actus primus* of these other diverse and multiple acts of the faculties which, as it were, flow from this inner principle. Only the superior soul is strictly the image of God within us. And if we are to contemplate God at all, this internal image must be re-formed by grace, and then we must enter into this inner sanctuary which is the substance of the soul itself. This passage from the exterior to the interior has nothing to do with concentration or introspection. It is a transit from objectivization to knowledge by intuition and connaturality. The majority of people never enter into this inward self, which is an abode of silence and peace and where the diversified activities of the intellect and will are collected, so to speak, into one intense and smooth and spiritualized activity which far exceeds in its fruitfulness the plodding efforts of reason working on external reality with its analyses and syllogisms.

IT IS HERE THAT mystical contemplation begins. It is into this substance or "center" of the soul, when it has transcended its dependence on sensations and images and concepts, that the obscure light of infused contemplation will be poured by God, giving us experimental contact with Himself without the medium of sense species. And in this contact, we are no longer facing God as an "object" of experience or as a concept which we apprehend. We are united to Him in the mystery of love and its transcendent subjectivity, and see Him in ourselves by losing ourselves in Him.

Yet even in the natural order, without attaining to God in us, and without perceiving this "inner spiritual light," the aesthetic experience introduces us into the interior sanctuary of the soul and to its inexpressible simplicity. For the aesthetic intuition is also beyond objectivity—it "sees" by identifying itself spiritually with what it contemplates.

Obviously, then, when the natural contemplation of the artist or the metaphysician has already given a man a taste of the peaceful intoxication which is experienced in the suprarational intuitions of this interior self, the way is already well prepared for infused contemplation. If God should grant that grace, the person so favored will be much better prepared to recognize it, and to cooperate with God's action within him. This, as a matter of fact, is a tremendous advantage. The artist, the poet, the metaphysician is, then, in some sense already naturally prepared and disposed to remove some of the principal obstacles to the light of infused contemplation. He will be less tempted than the ordinary man to reach out for vulgar satisfactions and imaginable thrills. He will be more "spiritual," if not more "religious." He will be more ready to keep himself detached from the level of crude feeling and emotionalism which so easily corrupt the integrity both of the artist and of the man of prayer. The mere fact of the artist's or poet's good taste, which should belong to him by virtue of his art, will help him to avoid some of the evils that tend to corrupt religious experience before it has a chance to take root and grow in the soul.

3

MYSTICAL CONTEMPLATION IS ABSOLUTELY beyond the reach of man's natural activity. There is nothing he can do to obtain it by himself. It is a pure gift of God. God gives it to whom He wills, and in the way and degree in which He wills. By co-operating with the work of ordinary grace we can—and, if we really mean to love God, we must—seek Him and even find Him obscurely by a love that gropes humbly for truth in the darkness of this life. But no amount of generosity on our part, no amount of effort, no amount of sacrifice will make us into mystics. That is a work that must be done by God acting as the "principal agent" (the term is that of St. John of the Cross). If He is the principal agent, there is another agent: ourselves. But our part is simply to consent, to listen, and to follow without knowing where we are going. All the rest that we can do amounts to the more or less negative task of avoiding obstacles and keeping our own prejudiced judgments and self-will out of His way. St. Bonaventure tells us in many places that prayer and ardent desire can persuade God to give us this gift, and that *industria* on our part can open the way for His action. The term *industria* stands for active purification, and St. Bonaventure means, by that, precisely the same thing that St. John of the Cross talks about all through the "Ascent of Mount Carmel," namely the active emptying of the soul, clearing it of all images, all likenesses of and attachments to created things, so that it may be clean and pure to receive the obscure light of God's own presence. The soul must be stripped of all its selfish desires for natural satisfactions, no matter how high, how noble, or how excellent in themselves. As long as it rests in things for their own sake, seen and possessed as "objects" to gratify our own self-love, it cannot possess God and be possessed by Him, for the love of the soul for objectivized beings is darkness in the sight of God.

It is the common doctrine of Christian mystical theologians that a great obstacle to "unitive" or "connatural" or "affective" knowledge of God by infused contemplation (the terms are those of St. Thomas and his followers) is attachment to objectivized human reasoning and analysis and discourse that proceeds by abstraction from sense images, and by syllogizing, to conclusions. In other words, a man cannot at the same time fly in an airplane and walk along the ground. He must do one or the other. And if he insists on walking along the ground—all right, it is no sin. But it will take him much longer and cost him much more effort to get to his destination, and he will have a much more limited view of things along his way. What the Holy Spirit demands of the mystic is peaceful consent and a blind trust in Him; for all this time, since the soul does not act of itself, it remains blind and in darkness, having no idea where it is going or what is being done, and tasting satisfaction that is, at first, extremely tenuous and ineffable and obscure. The reason is, of course, that the soul is not yet sufficiently spiritualized to be able to grasp and appreciate what is going on within it. It remains with nothing but the vaguest and most general sense that God is really and truly present and working there—a sense which is fraught with a greater certitude than anything it has ever experienced before. And yet if one stops to analyze the experience, or if one makes a move to increase its intensity by a natural act, the whole thing will evade his grasp and he will lose it altogether.

Now it is precisely here that the aesthetic instinct changes its colors and, from being a precious gift, becomes a real danger. If the intuition of the poet naturally leads him into the inner sanctuary of his soul, it is for a special purpose in the natural order: when the poet enters into himself, it is in order to reflect upon his inspiration and to clothe it with a special and splendid form and then return to *display it to those outside.* And here the radical difference between the artist and the mystic begins to be seen. The artist enters into himself in order to *work.* For him, the "superior" soul is a forge where inspiration kindles a fire of white heat, a crucible for the transformation of natural images into new, created forms. But the mystic enters into himself, not in order to work but to pass through the center of his own soul and lose himself in the mystery and secrecy and infinite, transcendent reality of God living and working within him.

Consequently, if the mystic happens to be, at the same time, an artist, when prayer calls him within himself to the secrecy of God's presence, his art will be tempted to start working and producing and studying the "creative" possibilities of this experience. And therefore immediately the whole thing runs the risk of being frustrated and destroyed. The artist will run the risk of losing a gift of tremendous supernatural worth, in order to perform a work of far less value. He will let go of the deep, spiritual grace which has been granted him, in order to return to the reflection of that grace within his own soul. He will withdraw from the mystery of identification with Reality beyond forms and objectivized concepts, and will return to the realm of subject and object. He will objectivize his own experience and seek to exploit and employ it for its own sake. He will leave God and return to himself, and in so doing, though he follows his natural instinct to "create," he will, in fact, be less creative. For the creative work done directly in the soul and on the soul by God Himself, the infinite *Creator Spiritus*, is beyond all comparison with the work which the soul of man itself accomplishes in imitation of the divine Creator.

Unable fully to lose himself in God, doomed by the restlessness of talent to seek himself in the highest natural gift that God has given him, the artist falls from contemplation and returns to himself as artist. Instead of passing through his own soul into the abyss of the infinite actuality of God Himself, he will remain there a moment, only to emerge again into the exterior world of multiple created things whose variety once more dissipates his energies until they are lost in perplexity and dissatisfaction.

There is, therefore, a likelihood that one who has the natural gift of artistic intuition and creation may be unable to pass on to the superior and most spiritual kind of contemplation, in which the soul rests in God without images, without concepts, without any intermediary. The artist may be like the hare in the fable, who far outstrips the tortoise without talent in the beginnings of the contemplative life, but who, in the end, is left behind. In a word, natural gifts and talents may be of great value in the beginning, but contemplation can never depend on them. They may, indeed, prove to be obstacles, unless by some special grace we are completely detached from them. And so the artist may well receive the first taste of infused prayer, for, as St. John of the Cross says, that is granted to relatively many souls, and often quite soon in their spiritual life, especially where conditions are favorable; but, because of this tragic promethean tendency to exploit every experience as material for "creation," the artist may remain there all his life on the threshold, never entering into the banquet, but always running back into the street to tell the passers-by of the wonderful music he has heard coming from inside the palace of the King!

4

WHAT, THEN, IS THE conclusion? That poetry can, indeed, help to bring us rapidly through that early part of the journey to contemplation that is called active; but when we are entering the realm of true contemplation, where eternal happiness is tasted in anticipation, poetic intuition may ruin our rest in God "beyond all images."

In such an event, one might at first be tempted to say that there is only one course for the poet to take, if he wants to be a mystic or a saint: he must consent to the *ruthless and complete sacrifice of his art*. Such a conclusion would seem to be dictated by logic. If there is an infinite distance between the gifts of nature and those of grace, between the natural and the supernatural order, man and God, then should not one always reject the natural for the supernatural, the temporal for the eternal, the human for the divine? It seems to be so simple as to defy contradiction. And yet, when one has experience in the strange vicissitudes of the inner life, and when one has seen something of the ways of God, one remembers that there is a vast difference between the logic of men and the logic of God. There is indeed no human logic in the ways of interior prayer, only Divine paradox. Our God is not a Platonist. Our Christian spirituality is not the intellectualism of Plotinus or the asceticism of the Stoics. We must therefore be very careful of oversimplifications. The Christian is sanctified not merely by always making the choice of "the most perfect thing." Indeed, experience teaches us that the most perfect choice is not always that which is most perfect in itself. The most perfect choice is *the choice of what God has willed for us*, even though it may be, in itself, less perfect, and indeed less "spiritual."

It is quite true that aesthetic experience is only a temporal thing, and like all other temporal things it passes away. It is true that mystical prayer enriches man a hundredfold in time and in eternity. It purifies the soul and loads it with supernatural merits, enlarging man's powers and capacities to absorb the infinite rivers of divine light which will one day be his beatitude. The sacrifice of art would seem to be a small enough price to lay down for this "pearl of great price."

But let us consider for a moment whether the Christian contemplative poet is necessarily confronted with an absolute clean-cut "either/or" choice between "art" and "mystical prayer."

It can of course happen that a contemplative and artist finds himself in a situation in which he is morally certain that God demands of him the sacrifice of his art, in order that he may enter more deeply into the contemplative life. In such a case, the sacrifice must be made, not because this is a general law binding all artist-contemplatives, but because it is the will of God in this particular, concrete case.

But it may equally well happen that an artist who imagines himself to be called to the higher reaches of mystical prayer is not called to them at all. It becomes evident, to him, that the simplest and most obvious thing for him is to be an artist, and that he should sacrifice his aspirations for a deep mystical life and be content with the lesser gifts with which he has been endowed by God. For such a one, to insist on spending long hours in prayer frustrating his creative instinct would, in fact, lead to illusion. His efforts to be a contemplative would be fruitless. Indeed, he would find that by being an artist—and at the same time living fully all the implications of art for a Christian and for a contemplative in the broad sense of the word—he would enjoy a far deeper and more vital interior life, with a much richer appreciation of the mysteries of God, than if he just tried to bury his artistic talent and be a professional "saint." If he is called to be an artist, then his art will lead him to sanctity, if he uses it as a Christian should.

To take yet another case: it might conceivably be the will of God—as it certainly was in the case of the Old Testament Prophets and in that of St. John of the Cross—that a man should remain *at the same time a mystic and a poet* and ascend to the greatest heights of poetic creation and of mystical prayer without any evident contradiction between them. Here again, the problem is solved not by the application of some abstract, *a priori* principle, but purely by a practically practical appeal to the will of God in this particular case. We are dealing with gifts of God, which God can give as He pleases, when He pleases, to whom He pleases. It is futile for us to lay down laws which say when or how God's gifts must be given, to whom they can be given, to whom they must be refused. It remains true that at a certain point in the interior life, the instinct to create and communicate enters into conflict with the call to mystical union with God. But God Himself can resolve the conflict. And He does. Nor does He need any advice from us in order to do so.

The Christian life is the life of Christ in the soul. Christian wisdom is the wisdom of God's only-begotten Son, Who is begotten Wisdom—*sapientia genita*. To be wise with the wisdom of Christ, we must let Christ be born and live within us in His own way. He does not come to all in the same way, because we all have different functions in His Mystical Body. "There are diversities of graces, but the same Spirit, and there are diversities of ministries but the same Lord; and there are diversities of operations, but the same God Who worketh all in all. And the manifestation of the Spirit is given to every man unto profit" (I Corinthians 12:4-7).

We may apply the last words of this text to our present case. If the Christian poet is truly a Christian poet, if he has a vocation to make known to other men the unsearchable mystery of the love of Christ, then he must do so in the Spirit of Christ. And his "manifestation of the Spirit" not only springs from a kind of contemplative intuition of the mystery of Christ, but is "given to him for his profit" and will therefore deepen and perfect his union with Christ. The Christian poet and artist is one who grows not only by his contemplation but also by his open declaration of the mercy of God. If it is clear that he is called to give this witness to God, then he can say with St. Paul: "Woe to me if I preach not the Gospel." At the same time, he should always remember that the hidden and more spiritual gifts are infinitely greater than his art, and if he is called upon to make an exclusive choice of one or the other, he must know how to sacrifice his art.

4

Boris Pasternak and the People with Watch Chains

This essay, the earliest reflections by Merton on the work of the Russian poet and novelist Boris Pasternak (with whom he engaged in a brief but significant correspondence [see *Courage for Truth*, 87-93]), first appeared in *Jubilee* 7 (July 1959), 17-31. Merton indicates an interest in writing about Pasternak on September 9, 1958, while reading *Dr. Zhivago* (*Search for Solitude*, 216-17), and by Thanksgiving (November 29) has completed the article, a process that he calls "enlightening for me" (*Search for Solitude*, 233). Permission to publish was initially denied by the Cistercian Abbot General "on the grounds that novels are worldly things and the dog should not return to his vomit" (*Search for Solitude*, 250), but later granted when it appeared (erroneously, as it turned out) that Pasternak had been taken into custody by Soviet authorities. The article was sent to Pasternak who indicated his own appreciation of it (see *Courage for Truth*, 99). Subsequently Merton published "The Pasternak Affair in Perspective" in *Thought* 34 (Winter 1959-1960), 485-517; he combined the two essays with a new introductory section ("*In memoriam*") in *Disputed Questions* as "The Pasternak Affair" (3-67) in which the initial article became section 2, "*The People with Watch Chains*" (7-24). The complete essay is also found in *Literary Essays* (37-83) as well as in *Merton & Hesychasm* (343-95). Because of the length of the final combined article, only "*The People with Watch Chains*" (under its original title) can be included in the present volume. Merton sees the Pasternak of *Dr. Zhivago* not as a political writer in any narrow sense but as a "sign of contradiction" to both East and West, to "our age of materialism, collectivism, and power politics." He is both a solitary and an authentic revolutionary, testifying to the primacy of life and freedom over any and all closed systems. Immersing himself during this period in the wisdom theology of Orthodox theologians, Merton finds in *Zhivago* "the cosmic liturgy of Genesis," the "sophianic world" of Eden that Yurii and Lara briefly experience despite being subjected to and sharing in the deeply flawed and radically fallen human condition of their disrupted society. "Where precisely does [Pasternak] stand?" Merton asks in his concluding paragraph: "The answer is that like life itself he stands nowhere, but *moves*—and moves 'with the freedom of the sons of God'" that refuses to conform to the stifling prescriptions of "the people with watch chains," whether communist or capitalist, who try, and ultimately fail, to reduce the richness of life to the confines of their own ideology.

My sister-called-life, like a tidal wave breaking
Swamps the bright world in a wall of spring rain:
But people with watch-chains grumble and frown
With poisoned politeness, like snakes in the corn.

From My Sister Life

I T IS PERHAPS not quite fair to start a discussion of Pasternak with lines from an early poem. He repudiated his earlier style, together with much that was written by the Futurists and Symbolists who were his friends forty years ago. (He did not, of course, repudiate his friends. For someone like Pasternak, friends cannot become "nonpersons.") He may or may not have pardoned us for enjoying the freshness of this early verse, but in any case it is clear that Life who was his "sister" in 1917 became his bride and his very self in *Dr. Zhivago* ("Doctor Life"). Life is at once the hero and the heroine (Lara) of this strange, seemingly pessimistic but victorious tragedy: not, however, Life in the abstract, certainly not the illusory, frozen-faced *imago* of Life upon which Communism constructs its spiritless fantasies of the future. Life for Pasternak is the painful, ambivalent, yet inexhaustibly fecund reality that is the very soul of Russia. A reality which, with all its paradoxes, has certainly manifested itself in the Russian revolution and all that followed, but which overflows all the possible limits of recorded history. Hundreds of pages of turbulent and exquisite prose give us some insight into the vastness of that reality as it was experienced, quite providentially, by one of the few sensitive and original spirits that survived the storm. And since Life cannot be confined within the boundaries of one nation, what Pasternak has to say about it overflows symbolism, into every corner of the world. It is the mystery of history as passion and resurrection that we glimpse obscurely in the story of the obscure Doctor who gives his name to the novel. This frustrated, confused, and yet somehow triumphant protagonist is not only Pasternak himself and even Russia, but mankind—not "twentieth-century man" but man who is perhaps too existential and mysterious for any label to convey his meaning and his identity. We, of course, are that man.

That is the mark of a really great book: it is in some way about everybody and everybody is involved in it. Nothing could be done to stop the drab epic of Zhivago, like the downpour in the 1917 poem, from bursting on the heads of all and swamping them whether they liked it or not. For that is exactly what Life cannot refrain from doing.

The appearance of *Dr. Zhivago*, and all the confused and largely absurd reactions which followed upon it, form a very meaningful incident at the close of an apparently meaningless decade. Certainly the surprise publication and instant success of the novel everywhere (including Russia, where it has been avidly read in manuscript by all the young intellectuals who could get hold of it) has more to say in retrospect than all the noise and empty oratory of the Soviet fortieth anniversary. This significance will of course be missed by all those who insist on taking a purely partisan and *simpliste* view of events, and who therefore interpret the book as all black or all white, all good or all bad, all left or all right. The dimensions of Pasternak's worldview are more existential and spiritual and are decidedly beyond left and right.

In bursting upon the heads of all, *Zhivago* inevitably deluged first of all those simple and pontifical souls whose Gospel is passive conformity with the politicians and bigshots, with the high priests of journalism and the doctors of propaganda: upon those who though they no longer decorate their paunches with cheap watch chains, still thrive on conformity with the status quo, on either side of the iron curtain.

Zhivago is one of those immensely "popular" books that has not really been popular. It has been bought by more people than were able to read it with full understanding. No doubt many of those who have had Pasternak's heavy volume in their hands have approved of it only vaguely and for the wrong reasons. And others who have read it have put it down with the unquiet feeling that it was somehow not sufficiently businesslike. For such as these, "life" has ceased to mean what it means to Pasternak. For the people with watch chains, a life that gets along independently of the plans of politicians and economists is nothing but a reactionary illusion. This has been brought home to Pasternak in no uncertain terms by his devoted confrères in the Soviet Writers' Union. But the same judgment has finally worked its way out in the West also, where Isaac Deutscher, the biographer of Stalin, has accused Zhivago of being another Oblomov and scolded him for considering the revolution "an atrocity." Let us face it, the people with watch chains can easily reconcile themselves with any atrocity that serves their own opportunism, whether it be in the form of a revolution or of an atomic bomb. Life (claimed as a sister by escapists and cosmopolitan mad dogs) had better learn to get along in these new circumstances. The atrocities are here to stay.

ALL GREAT WRITING IS in some sense revolutionary. Life itself is revolutionary, because it constantly strives to surpass itself. And if history is to be something more than the record of society's bogging down in meaningless formalities to justify the crimes of men, then a book that is at the same time great in its own right, and moreover lands with a tremendous impact on the world of its time, deserves an important place in history. The reason why *Dr. Zhivago* is significant is precisely that it stands so far above politics. This, among other things, places it in an entirely different category from Dudintsev's *Not by Bread Alone*. Attempts to involve Pasternak in the Cold War have been remarkable above all by their futility. The cloud of misunderstandings and accusations that surrounded the affair did not engulf Pasternak; the confusion served principally to emphasize the distance which separated him from his accusers and his admirers alike.

Both as a writer and as a man, Pasternak stands out as a sign of contradiction in our age of materialism, collectivism, and power politics. His spiritual genius is essentially and powerfully solitary. Yet his significance does not lie precisely in this. Rather it lies in the fact that his very solitude made him capable of extraordinarily intimate and understanding contacts with men all over the face of the earth. The thing that attracted people to Pasternak was not a social or political theory, it was not a formula for the unification of mankind, not a collectivist panacea for all the evils in the world: it was the man himself, the truth that was in him, his simplicity, his direct contact with life, and the fact that he was full of the only revolutionary force that is capable of producing anything new: he is full of love.

Pasternak is then not just a man who refuses to conform (that is to say, a rebel). The fact is, he is not a rebel, for a rebel is one who wants to substitute his own authority for the authority of somebody else. Pasternak is one who *cannot* conform to an artificial and stereotyped pattern because, by the grace of God, he is too much alive to be capable of such treason to himself and to life. He is not a rebel but a revolutionary, in the same way that Gandhi was a revolutionary. And in fact those who have said: "Passive resistance is all right against the English but it would never work against Russia" must stop and consider that in Pasternak it did, to some extent, work even in Russia. Pasternak is certainly a man to be compared with Gandhi. Though different in so many accidental ways, his protest is ultimately the same: the protest of life itself, of humanity itself, of love, speaking not with theories and programs but simply affirming itself and asking to be judged on its own merits.

Like Gandhi, Pasternak stands out as a gigantic paradox in a world of servile and mercenary conformities. His presence in such a world has had an inescapable effect: it has struck fear into the hearts of everyone else, whether in Russia or in America. The reaction to Pasternak, the alternate waves of love, fear, hate, and adulation that have rushed toward him from every part of the world were all set in motion by the *guilt* of a society that has consciously and knowingly betrayed life, and sold itself out to falsity, formalism, and spiritual degradation. In some (for instance, the pundits of Soviet literature) this guilt has produced hatred and rage against Pasternak. The fear he aroused was intolerable. His colleagues in the Soviet Writers' Union began to yell for his blood, and yelled all the more loudly in proportion as they were themselves servile and second rate. There were a few notable exceptions, rare writers of integrity and even talent, like Ilya Ehrenburg.

The politicians of the Kremlin, on the other hand, not being writers, not thoroughly understanding what it was all about anyway, were less moved to guilt, felt less fear, and were slow to do much about the case at first.

In the West the reaction was different. We felt the same guilt, the same fear, but in a different mode and degree. On the whole our reaction was to run to Pasternak with fervent accolades: to admire in him the courage and integrity we lack in ourselves. Perhaps we can taste a little vicarious revolutionary joy without doing anything to change our own lives. To justify our own condition of servility and spiritual prostitution we think it sufficient to admire another man's integrity.

I THINK THAT LATER pages of this study will show that Pasternak's witness is essentially Christian. That is the trouble: the problematical quality of Pasternak's "Christianity" lies in the fact that it is reduced to the barest and most elementary essentials: intense awareness of all cosmic and human reality as "life in Christ," and the consequent plunge into love as the only dynamic and creative force which really honors this "Life" by creating itself anew in Life's—Christ's—image.

As soon as *Dr. Zhivago* appeared everybody began comparing Pasternak with Tolstoy and Dostoevsky. The comparisons were obvious, sometimes trite, but basically legitimate. However, they run the risk of creating misconceptions. Pasternak does not merely work on an enormous canvas, like the classical novelists of the nineteenth century. Sholokhov also has done that, and Pasternak is immensely more important than Sholokhov, competent as the latter may be. But to be a twentieth-century Tolstoy is in fact to disqualify oneself for comparison with one who was an original and unique genius of his own age. The thing that makes Pasternak a new Tolstoy is precisely the fact that he is *not* Tolstoy, he is Pasternak. He is, that is to say, a writer of great power, a man of new and original vision, whose work takes in an enormous area, creates a whole new world. But it is not the world of *War and Peace* and it is not constructed in the same way. In fact, Pasternak has as much in common with Joyce and Proust as he has with Tolstoy. He is a poet and a musician, which Tolstoy was not, and the structure of *Zhivago* is symphonic, thematic, almost liturgical. Both writers are "spiritual" in a very deep way, but the spirituality of Tolstoy is always more ethical and pedestrian.

Like Dostoevsky, Pasternak sees life as a mystic, but without the hieratic kenoticism of the *Brothers Karamazov*. The mysticism of Pasternak is more latent, more cosmic, more pagan, if you like. It is more primitive, less sophisticated, free and untouched by any hieratic forms. There is therefore a "newness" and freshness in his spirituality that contrasts strikingly with the worn and mature sanctity of Staretz Zossima purified of self-consciousness by the weariness of much suffering. Pasternak's simple and moving poem on "Holy Week" illustrates this point. It is the death and resurrection of Christ seen in and through nature. Only discreetly and for a brief moment do ritual forms present themselves, as when we see a procession emerge from a country church. The birch tree "stands aside" to let the worshippers come forth but the procession soon returns into the church.

> And March scoops up the snow on the porch
> And scatters it like alms among the halt and lame—
> As though a man had carried out the Ark
> And opened it and distributed all it held.

All the reality of Holy Week is there, but in a very simple, elementary shape—a shape given to it by Pasternak's humility and contact with the "sacred" earth.

The very scarce and slight expressions of explicit spirituality in *Dr. Zhivago* are uttered by people who might have qualified for a place in the *Brothers Karamazov* (Uncle Nikolai and the seamstress of Yuriatin), but they have about them the ingenuousness of a spirituality that has never yet become quite conscious of itself and has therefore never needed to be purified.

If Pasternak's view of the universe is liturgical, it is the cosmic liturgy of Genesis, not the churchly and hierarchal liturgy of the Apocalypse, of pseudo-Dionysius, and of the Orthodox Church. And yet Pasternak loves that liturgy, and belongs to that Church. It even occurs to him to quote from the liturgy frequently and in strange places: for instance, these words which he declared indicate a basic liturgical inspiration in the poets Blok and Mayakovsky:

> Let all human flesh be silent and let it remain in terror, and in trembling, and let no living being think within itself. For behold, there cometh the King of Kings and the Lord of Lords to offer Himself in immolation and to become the food of the faithful.

Notice, though, in what a subdued and apologetic manner Pasternak himself makes use of this powerful text. In the last stanza of the poem on "Holy Week," we read his lines on the Easter Vigil:

And when midnight comes
All creatures and all flesh will fall silent
On hearing Spring put forth its rumor
That just as soon as there is better weather
Death itself can be overcome
Through the power of the Resurrection.

To say then that Zhivago has a liturgical character is not to accuse it of hieratic ceremoniousness. On the contrary, it is to praise the spontaneity with which cries of joy and reverence spring up on every page to hymn the sanctity of Life and of that Love which is the image of the Creator.

AND SO, THOUGH PASTERNAK is deeply and purely Christian, his simplicity, untainted by ritualistic routine, unstrained by formal or hieratic rigidities of any sort, has a kind of *pre-Christian* character. In him we find the ingenuous Christianity of an *anima naturaliter Christiana* that has discovered Christianity all by itself. It is a Christianity that is not perfectly at home with dogmatic formulas, but gropes after revealed truth in its own clumsy way. And so in his Christianity and in all his spirituality Pasternak is exceedingly primitive. This is one of his most wonderful qualities and we owe it no doubt to the persecution of Christianity by the State in Russia. Where the Church was free we got the complex, tormented Christianity of Dostoevsky. Where the Church is confined and limited we get the rudimentary, "primitive" Christianity of Pasternak.

What *Zhivago* opposes to Communism is therefore not a defense of Western democracy, not a political platform for some kind of liberalism, and still less a tract in favor of formal religion. *Zhivago* confronts Communism with life itself and leaves us in the presence of inevitable conclusions. Communism has proposed to control life with a rigid system and with the tyranny of artificial forms. Those who have believed in this delusion and yielded themselves up to it as to a "superior force" have paid the penalty by ceasing to be complete human beings, by ceasing to live in the full sense of the word, by ceasing to be men. Even the idealistic and devoted Strelnikov becomes the victim of his own ideals, and Lara can say of him:

It was as if something abstract had crept into his face and made it colorless. As if a living human face had become the embodiment of a principle, the image of an idea. . . . I realized that this had happened to him because he had handed himself over to a superior force that is deadening and pitiless and will not spare him in the end. It seemed to me that he was a marked man and that this was the seal of his doom.

The fact that this judgment is so closely akin to Freudianism and is yet explicitly Christian gives one much food for reflection. The Christian note is sounded in a strong and definite way at the very beginning of the book, as one of the themes which will recur most strongly in all its various parts. The "beast in man" is not to be tamed by threats, but must be brought into harmony with life and made to serve creativeness and love by the influence of inner and spiritual music.

> What has for centuries raised man above the beast is not the cudgel but an inward music; the irresistible power of unarmed truth, the powerful attraction of its example. It has always been assumed that the most important things in the Gospels are the ethical maxims and commandments. But for me the most important thing is that Christ speaks in parables taken from life, that He explains the truth in terms of everyday reality. The idea that underlies this is that communion between mortals is immortal, and that the whole of life is symbolic because it is meaningful.

The words about the "irresistible power of unarmed truth" are pure Gandhi. The rest, about the inextricable union of symbolism and communion, in life itself, is what gives Pasternak's vision of the world its liturgical and sacramental character (always remembering that his "liturgy" is entirely nonhieratic and that in him sacrament implies not so much established ritual form as living mystery).

Everyone has been struck, not to mention embarrassed, by the overpowering symbolic richness of *Dr. Zhivago*. In fact, Pasternak, whether he knows it or not, is plunged fully into midstream of the lost tradition of "natural contemplation" which flowed among the Greek Fathers after it had been set in motion by Origen. Of course the tradition has not been altogether lost, and Pasternak has come upon it in the Orthodox Church. The fact is clear in any case: he reads the Scriptures with the avidity and the spiritual imagination of Origen and he looks on the world with the illuminated eyes of the Cappadocian Fathers—but without their dogmatic and ascetic preoccupations.

However, it is not with scriptural images that Pasternak is primarily concerned. The Fathers of the Church declared that the Scriptures are a recreated world, a Paradise restored to man after Adam had disturbed the cosmic liturgy by his fall. Pasternak is not the prophet of this regained Paradise, as were Origen and Gregory of Nyssa. Rather he is a prophet of the original, cosmic revelation: one who sees symbols and figures of the inward, spiritual world, working themselves out in the mystery of the universe around him and above all in the history of men. Not so much in the formal, and illusory, history of states and empires that is written down in books, but in the living, transcendental and mysterious history of individual human beings and in the indescribable interweaving of their destinies.

IT IS AS ARTIST, symbolist, and prophet that Zhivago stands most radically in opposition to Soviet society. He himself is a man of Eden, of Paradise. He is Adam, and therefore also, in some sense, Christ. Lara is Eve and Sophia (the Cosmic Bride of God) and Russia. One should examine, for instance, the description of the Edenlike garden at Duplyanka in the very beginning of the book. The fragrant fields, the heat, the flowerbeds, the lonely coppice where Yurii speaks with his angel or his mother whose presence (again a sophianic presence) seems to surround him here. Here too Lara, as a girl, is shown to us in the beginning of the book (in one of those innumerable coincidences which Pasternak himself regards as of supreme significance in his novel):

> Lara walked along the tracks following a path worn by pilgrims and then turned into the fields. Here she stopped and, closing her eyes, took a deep breath of the flower-scented air of the broad expanse around her. It was dearer to her than her kin, better than a lover, wiser than a book. For a moment she rediscovered the purpose of her life. She was here on earth to grasp the meaning of its wild enchantment, to call each thing by its right name, or, if this were not in her power, to give birth out of love for life to successors who would do it in her place.

The allusion to that primeval, Edenic existence in which Adam gave the animals their names is transparently obvious. And Eve is the "Mother of all the living."

Yurii and Lara will be united in another Eden, at Varykino, but a strange Eden of snow and silence, lost in a vast landscape wasted by armies. There Yurii will give himself, in the night, to his most fruitful work of poetic creation.

In contrast to the Eden image which symbolizes the sophianic world of Yurii and Lara, of Adam, of Christ, stands the House of the Sculptures in Yuriatin. One of the most significant chapters of the book is called "Opposite the House of the Sculptures." It is the one where the seamstress develops the typological figures of the Old Testament, speaking by lamplight in the same enchanted atmosphere of warmth that pervaded the fields of Duplyanka. The opposition is obvious.

> (Lara) Antopova lived at the corner of Merchant Street opposite the dark, blue-grey house with sculptures. . . . It did indeed live up to its name and there was something strange and disturbing about it. Its entire top floor was surrounded by female mythological figures half as big again as human beings. Between two gusts of the dust storm it seemed to him as if all the

women in the house had come out on the balcony and were looking down at him over the balustrade. . . .

At the corner there was a dark grey house with sculptures. The huge square stones of the lower part of its façade were covered with freshly posted sheets of government newspapers and proclamations. Small groups of people stood on the sidewalk, reading in silence. . . .

With uncanny insight, the poet has portrayed the bourgeois world of the nineteenth century, a grey façade covered with "sculptures"—enormous and meaningless figures of nothingness, figures for the sake of figures. Yet a dust storm gives them an illusory life. Decorations with no inner reference: advertisements of a culture that has lost its head and has run soberly raving through its own backyards and factories with a handful of rubles. All that remained was for the house itself behind the façade to be gutted and emptied of its semihuman content: then everything was set for the Posters and Proclamations of the Red state. If the editors of *Novy Mir* read *Dr. Zhivago* with understanding they would have found in this passage a much more profound condemnation of Communism than in the description of the Partisan battle which they picked out for special reproof.

On the one hand we have the revolution: "what they mean by ideas is nothing but words, claptrap in praise of the revolution and the regime. . . ." Against this pseudo-scientific array of propaganda clichés stands the doctor and poet, the diagnostician. One of his greatest sins (the term is chosen advisedly) is his belief in intuition. By his intuition, he is able to get "an immediate grasp of a situation as a whole" which the Marxists vainly hope to achieve by pseudo-science. But what does he seek most of all? What is his real work? As poet, his function is not merely to express his own state of mind, and not merely to exercise his own artistic power. Pasternak's concept of the poet's vocation is at once dynamic and contemplative: two terms which can only be synthesized in the heat of a prophetic ardor.

Language is not merely the material or the instrument which the poet uses. This is the sin of the Soviet ideologist for whom language is simply a mine of terms and formulas which can be pragmatically exploited. When in the moment of inspiration the poet's creative intelligence is married with the inborn wisdom of human language (the Word of God and Human Nature—Divinity and Sophia) then in the very flow of new and individual intuitions, the poet utters the voice of that wonderful and mysterious world of God-manhood—it is the transfigured, spiritualized, and divinized cosmos that speaks through him, and through him utters its praise of the Creator.

Language, the home and receptacle of beauty and meaning, itself begins to think and speak for man and turns wholly into music, not in terms of sonority but in terms of the impetuousness and power of its inward flow. Then, like the current of a mighty river polishing stones and turning wheels by its very movement, the flow of speech creates in passing, by virtue of its own laws, meter and rhythm and countless other relationships, which are even more important, but which are as yet unexplored, insufficiently recognized, and unnamed. At such moments, Yurii Adreievitch felt that the main part of the work was being done not by him but by a superior power that was above him and directed him, namely the movement of universal thought and poetry in its present historical stage and in the one to come. And he felt himself to be only the occasion, the fulcrum, needed to make this movement possible.

This is the very key to Pasternak's "religious philosophy." He is a complete existentialist (in the most favorable and religious sense of the word). One might ask, in the light of this passage, if his Christian images were nothing more than secondary symbols, subordinated to this great, dynamic worldview. The answer is no. What we have here is a Christian existentialism like that of Berdyaev, and of course far less articulate and less developed than that of Berdyaev. The Christian cosmology of Dante, for example, was static and centripetal. But Christianity is not bound up with Ptolemaic astronomy. Pasternak is absorbed in his vision of a fluid, ever-moving, ever-developing cosmos. It is a vision appropriate to a contemporary of Einstein and Bergson; but let us not forget that it is also akin to the vision of St. Gregory of Nyssa.

It is not necessary at this point to investigate further the depth and genuineness of the Christian elements in Pasternak. They are clearly present, but their presence should not delude us into any oversimplifications in his regard. There are many differences between his Christianity and the Protestant, or even the Catholic Christianity of the West. To what extent are these differences fundamental? We may perhaps return to this question elsewhere. Sufficient to remember that if in the first pages of the book Christ becomes a kind of ideological or symbolic center for the whole structure, this does not alter the fact that Uncle Nikolai propounds his belief in the following terms, which cannot help but perplex the average believer:

One must be true to Christ. . . . What you don't understand is that it is possible to be an atheist, it is possible not to know whether God exists or why, and yet believe that man does not live in a state of nature but in history, and that history as we know it now began with Christ, and that Christ's Gospel is its foundation.

Without commenting on this passage, let us simply remark that it is typical of the "religious statements" made here and there in the book which very frequently are much tamer and more simple than they appear to be at first sight. Here the difficulty arises largely from a misuse of the word "atheist." What Pasternak really means, in our terminology, is "agnostic," as is clear from his own explanation. Note that Pasternak does not necessarily make himself personally answerable for the theology of Uncle Nikolai, and that he records with full approval the remarkable discourse of Sima on the miracles of the Old Testament as "types" of the greatest miracle, the Incarnation. It is clear that Christ, for Pasternak, is a transcendent and Personal Being in the sense generally understood by such orthodox theologians as Soloviev or the Russian existentialist Berdyaev. The Christ of Pasternak is the Christ of Soloviev's "God-manhood." His view of the cosmos is, like Berdyaev's, "sophianic" and his "sister Life" has, in fact, all the characteristics of the Sancta Sophia who appeared to Soloviev in Egypt. His protestation that for him "believing in God" or in "the resurrection" is not quite the same thing as it might be to the popular anthropomorphic mind is, after all, quite legitimate self-defense for one who has no pretension of talking like a professional theologian. So much for his terms. But as for his intentions and his spirit, of these there can be no doubt: they are genuinely religious, authentically Christian, and all the more so for their spontaneous unconventionality.

But the important thing to realize is that here, as with all deeply spiritual thinkers, to concentrate on a strict analysis of concepts and formulas is to lose contact with the man's basic intuitions. The great error, the error into which the Communists themselves plunge headlong at the first opportunity, is to try to peg genius down and make it fit into some ready-made classification. Pasternak is not a man for whom there is a plain and definite category. And we must not try to tag him with easy names: Christian, Communist; anti-Christian, anti-Communist; liberal, reactionary; personalist, romanticist, etc.

As Lara says, in one of her most "sophianic" moods: "It's only in mediocre books that people are divided into two camps and have nothing to do with each other. In real life, everything gets mixed up! Don't you think you'd have to be a hopeless nonentity to play only one role all your life, to have only one place in society, always to stand for the same thing?" Both the admirers and the enemies of Pasternak have tried to do him this great dishonor: to write him into one of their own "mediocre books," and to make of him a stereotype to fit and to excuse their own lamentable prejudices. Thus do the "people with watch chains" complain—and not too politely—"like snakes in the corn."

It is true that some names fit Pasternak better than others, and that he is certainly very much of a Christian and not very much of a Communist. Nevertheless his Christianity is first of all quite personal, then quite Russian. His politics are personal first of all and then again Russian, though it might be a lot safer to say that he is antipolitical rather than political. But it would be utterly false to say (as his accusers said) that he had rejected the Russian revolution as a whole.

Where precisely does he stand? The answer is that like life itself he stands nowhere, but *moves*. He moves in a definite direction, however, and this is what must be taken into account if he is to be properly understood. From the very first we must realize that this direction does not lie, simply, west of Russia. Pasternak's tendencies are neither geographical nor political. His movement is into the new dimension of the future which we cannot yet estimate because it is not yet with us. He looks beyond the rigid, frozen monolith of Soviet society; he looks beyond the more confused, shifting, and colliding forms that make up the world of the West. What does he see? Freedom. Not the freedom of Soviet man after the mythical "withering away of the state." Not the chaotic irresponsibility that leaves Western man the captive of economic, social, and psychological forces. Not even that vision which has been irreverently described as "pie in the sky," but really the freedom of the sons of God, on earth, in which "individual life becomes the life story of God and its contents fill the vast expanses of the universe."

5

The Recovery of Paradise

In 1959 Merton began a correspondence with D. T. Suzuki concerning the possibility of the noted Japanese scholar of Zen contributing an introduction to Merton's collection of translations from *Verba Seniorum*, the sayings of the Desert Fathers, published in 1960 as *The Wisdom of the Desert* (see the correspondence in *Hidden Ground of Love*, 560-69). In the event, Cistercian authorities objected to having a non-Christian introduce the monastic material, with the result that Merton provided his own introduction, and the exchange between Suzuki and Merton, which included a headnote by Merton, Suzuki's original introduction, a substantial reflection in response by Merton, and briefer addenda by both writers, appeared in 1961 in *New Directions in Prose and Poetry* 17 as "Wisdom in Emptiness, A Dialogue: D. T. Suzuki and Thomas Merton" (65-101). It was later included as Part II of *Zen and the Birds of Appetite* (99-138). Suzuki's article arrived on October 23, 1959 (see *Hidden Ground of Love*, 566), and Merton's contribution, entitled "The Recovery of Paradise," was finished by November 20 (see *Road to Joy*, 234). While this part of the dialogue responds to Suzuki's reflections, it is able to stand alone as a significant exploration of Merton's understanding of desert spirituality, and was included, in somewhat abridged form, in *A Thomas Merton Reader*, for which Merton was very much involved in assembling materials (509-15; rev. ed., 481-88). While Merton was later critical of the theological language of his "final remarks" in the dialogue, "an example of how *not* to approach Zen" (*Zen and the Birds of Appetite*, 139), "The Recovery of Paradise" itself is not only the earliest extended expression of Merton's fascination with Zen and engagement in interreligious dialogue, but one of his most articulate discussions (along with portions of *The New Man*) of a central element of his spiritual teaching, reaching all the way back to the title of his autobiography with its allusion to Mount Purgatory with the Garden of Eden at its summit: salvation as union with the "New Adam" who restores the primordial unity and harmony of creation that had been shattered by the fall. Drawing on Dostoevsky, St. Augustine, John Cassian, and of course the sayings of the Desert Fathers translated in his anthology, and responding to Suzuki's own sensitive reading of these stories as exemplifying a return to innocence and "emptiness," Merton presents his fundamental understanding of the Paschal Mystery of dying and rising with Christ as a restoration of "the lost innocence, the emptiness and purity of heart which had belonged to Adam and Eve in Eden," and a "recovery of that 'unity'"—both inner integration and social communion—"which had been shattered by the 'knowledge of good and evil.'"

∞

I

ONE OF DOSTOEVSKI'S "saints," the Staretz Zosima, who speaks as a typical witness to the tradition of the Greek and Russian Church, makes an astonishing declaration. He says: "We do not understand that life is paradise, for it suffices only to wish to understand it, and at once paradise will appear in front of us in its beauty." Taken in the context of the *Brothers Karamazov*, against the background of violence, blasphemy, and murder which fill the book, this is indeed an astonishing statement. Was Zosima perfectly serious? Or was he simply a deluded idiot, dreaming the frantic dreams inspired by the "opium of the people"?

Whatever the modern reader may think of this claim, it was certainly something basic to primitive Christianity. Modern studies of the Fathers have revealed beyond question that one of the main motives that impelled men to embrace the "angelic life" (*bios angelikos*) of solitude and poverty in the desert was precisely the hope that by so doing they might return to paradise.

Now this concept must be properly and accurately understood. Paradise is not "heaven." Paradise is a state, or indeed a place, on earth. Paradise belongs more properly to the present than to the future life. In some sense it belongs to both. It is the state in which man was originally created to live on earth. It is also conceived as a kind of antechamber to heaven after death—as for instance at the end of Dante's *Purgatorio*. Christ, dying on the cross, said to the good thief at His side: "This day thou shalt be with me *in Paradise*," and it was clear that this did not mean, and could not have meant, heaven.

We must not imagine Paradise as a place of ease and sensual pleasure. It is a state of peace and rest, by all means. But what the Desert Fathers sought when they believed they could find "paradise" in the desert was the lost innocence, the emptiness and purity of heart which had belonged to Adam and Eve in Eden. Evidently they could not have expected to find beautiful trees and gardens in the waterless desert, burned by the sun. Obviously they did not expect to find a place, among the fiery rocks and caves, where they could recline at ease in shady groves, by cool running water. What they sought was paradise within themselves, or rather above and beyond themselves. They sought paradise in the recovery of that "unity" which had been shattered by the "knowledge of good and evil."

In the beginning, Adam was "one man." The Fall had divided him into "a multitude." Christ had restored man to unity in Himself. The Mystical Christ was the "New Adam," and in Him all men could return to unity, to innocence, to purity, and become "one man." *Omnes in Christo unum.* This meant, of course, living not by one's own will, one's own ego, one's own limited and selfish spirit, but being "one spirit" with Christ. "Those who are united to the Lord," says St. Paul, "are *one spirit.*" Union with Christ means unity in Christ, so that each one who is in Christ can say, with Paul: "It is now not I that live but Christ that lives in me." It is the same Christ who lives in all. The individual has "died" with Christ to his "old man," his exterior, egotistical self, and "risen" in Christ to the new man, a selfless and divine being, who is the one Christ, the same who is "all in all."

The great difference between Christianity and Buddhism arises at this juncture. From the metaphysical point of view, Buddhism seems to take "emptiness" as a complete negation of all personality, whereas Christianity finds in purity of heart and "unity of spirit," a supreme and transcendent fulfillment of personality. This is an extremely complex and difficult question which I am not prepared to discuss. But it seems to me that most discussions on the point, up to now, have been completely equivocal. Very often, on the Christian side, we identify "personality" with the illusory and exterior ego-self, which is certainly not the true Christian "person." On the Buddhist side there seems to be no positive idea of personality at all; it is a value which seems to be completely missing from Buddhist thought. Yet it is certainly not absent from Buddhist practice, as is evident from Dr. Suzuki's remark that at the end of Zen training, when one has become "absolutely naked," one finds himself to be the ordinary "Tom, Dick, or Harry" that he has been all along. This seems to me, in practice, to correspond to the idea that a Christian can lose his "old man" and find his true self "in Christ." The main difference is that the language and practice of Zen are much more radical, austere, and ruthless, and that where the Zen-man says "emptiness" he leaves no room for any image or concept to confuse the real issue. The Christian treatment of the subject makes free use of richly metaphorical expressions and of concrete imagery, but we must take care to penetrate beyond the exterior surface and reach the inner depths. In any case the "death of the old man" is not the destruction of personality but the dissipation of an illusion, and the discovery of the new man is the realization of what was there all along, at least as a radical possibility, by reason of the fact that man is the image of God.

These Christian themes of "life in Christ" and "unity in Christ" are familiar enough, but one feels that today they are not understood in all their spiritual depth. Their mystical implications are seldom explored. We dwell rather, with much greater interest, on their social, economic, and ethical implications. I wonder if what Dr. Suzuki had said about "emptiness" ought not to help us to go deeper than we usually do into this doctrine of our mystical unity and purity in Christ. Anyone who has read St. John of the Cross and his doctrine of "night" will be inclined to ask the same question. If we are to die to ourselves and live "in Christ," does that not mean that we must somehow find ourselves "dead" and "empty" with regard to our old self? If we are to be moved in all things by the grace of Christ should we not in some sense realize this as action out-of-emptiness, springing from the mystery of the pure freedom which is "divine love," rather than as something produced in and with our egotistical, exterior self, springing from our desires and referred to our own spiritual interest?

St. John of the Cross compares man to a window through which the light of God is shining. If the windowpane is clean of every stain, it is completely transparent, we do not see it at all; it is "empty" and nothing is seen but the light. But if a man bears in himself the stains of spiritual egotism and preoccupation with his illusory and exterior self, even in "good things," then the window pane itself is clearly seen by reason of the stains that are on it. Hence if a man can be rid of the stains and dust produced within him by his fixation upon what is good and bad in reference to himself, he will be transformed in God and will be "one with God." In the terms of St. John of the Cross:

> In thus allowing God to work in it, the soul (having rid itself of every mist and stain of creatures, which consists in having its will perfectly united with that of God, for to love is to labor to detach and strip itself for God's sake of all that is not God) is at once illumined and transformed in God, and God communicates to it His supernatural being in such wise that the soul appears to be God Himself, and has all that God Himself has. . . . All the things of God and the soul are one in participant transformation; and the soul seems to be God rather than the soul, and is indeed God by participation. (St. John of the Cross, *Ascent of Mount Carmel*, II, 5. Peers trans., vol. 1, p. 82)

This, as we shall see, is what the Fathers called "purity of heart," and it corresponds to a recovery of the innocence of Adam in Paradise. The many stories of the Desert Fathers in which they are shown to have exercised an extraordinary control over wild animals were originally understood as a manifestation of this recovery of paradisiacal innocence. As one of the early writers, Paul the Hermit, declared: "If anyone acquires purity, everything will submit to him as it did to Adam in paradise before the fall" (quoted in Dom Anselm Stolz, *Théologie de la Mystique*, Chevetogne, 1947, p. 31).

If we admit Staretz Zosima's statement that paradise is something attainable because, after all, it is present within us and we have only to discover it there, we may still pause to question one part of his statement: "one has *only to wish to understand it*, and at once paradise will appear before us in all its beauty." That seems to be a little too easy. Much more is required than a simple velleity. Anyone can make a wish. But the kind of "wishing" that Zosima refers to here is something far beyond daydreaming and wishful thinking. It means, of course, a complete upheaval and transformation of one's whole life. One has to "wish" for this one realization alone and give up wishing for anything else. One has to forget the quest of every other "good." One has to devote himself with his whole heart and soul to the recovery of his "innocence." And yet, as Dr. Suzuki has so well pointed out, and as the Christian doctrine of grace teaches us in other terms, this cannot be the work of our own "self." It is useless for the "self" to try to "purify itself," or for the "self" to "make a place in itself" for God. The innocence and purity of heart which belong to paradise are a complete emptiness of self in which all is the work of God, the free and unpredictable expression of His love, the work of grace. In the purity of original innocence, all is done in us but without us, *in nobis et sine nobis*. But before we reach that level, we must also learn to work on the other level of "knowledge"—*scientia*—where grace works in us but "not without us"—*in nobis sed non sine nobis*.

Dr. Suzuki has, in his own terms, very aptly pointed out that it would be a serious error to think that one could hoist himself back by his own bootstraps into the state of innocence and go on blissfully with no further concern about the present life. Innocence does not cast out or destroy knowledge. The two must go together. That, indeed, was where many apparently spiritual men have failed. Some of them were so innocent that they had lost all contact with everyday reality of life in a struggling and complex world of men. But theirs was not true innocence. It was fictitious, a perversion and frustration of the real spiritual life. It was the emptiness of the quietist, an emptiness that was merely blank and silly: an absence of knowledge without the presence of wisdom. It was the narcissistic ignorance of the baby, not the emptiness of the saint who is moved, without reflection or self-consciousness, by the grace of God.

At this point, however, I would like to question Dr. Suzuki's interpretation of the story of the "great hermit" who had the robbers arrested. I am tempted to wonder if there is not, in this reaction of his, a touch of what might be called "overcompensation." There is, in fact, quite a lot of Zen in this story of the robbers and of the "great hermit." At any rate, it is the kind of story a Western reader might be tempted to spot right away as having affinities with the spirit of Zen. And perhaps Dr. Suzuki is too much on his guard against such an interpretation which would, of course, tend toward the old accusation of antinomianism.

Certainly the "great hermit" does not seem to have much respect for laws, jails, and police.

But if we look at the story a little closer we find that the point is quite a different matter. No one is saying that robbers ought not to go to jail. What is pointed out is that hermits have no business sending them there. The robber should, certainly, respect property rights; but the hermit, consecrated to a life of poverty and "emptiness," has forfeited his right to be concerned with possessions, with property or with material security. On the contrary, if he is what he ought to be, he will do what Dr. Suzuki's farmer did, and help the robbers with a ladder. But no, these monks are spiritually sick. Far from being empty of themselves, they are full of themselves; they rise up in anger when their selfish interests are touched or even menaced. They revenge wrongs that are done to them because they are all bound up with a "self" that can be wronged and feel outraged. In the words of the "Path of Virtue" (*Dhammapada*):

> He verily is not an anchorite who oppresses others;
> He is not an ascetic who causes grief to another.

This is almost identical with one of the sayings of Abbot Pastor:

> He who is quarrelsome is no monk; he who returns evil for evil is no monk; he who gets angry is no monk. (*The Wisdom of the Desert*, XLIX)

So the outraged hermits are in reality much more to blame than the robbers, because precisely it is people like these who cause poor men to become robbers. It is those who acquire inordinate possessions for themselves and defend them against others who make it necessary for the others to steal in order to make a living. That at least is the idea of Abbot Poemen and in telling "great hermit" to let the robbers out of jail he was being neither antisocial nor sentimental; he was just giving his monks a lesson in poverty. They did not wish to know the paradise that was within them through detachment and purity of heart; but rather they wanted to keep themselves in darkness and defilement by their love of their own possessions and their own comfort. They did not want the "wisdom" that "tastes" the presence of God in freedom and emptiness, but the "knowledge" of "mine" and "thine" and of violated rights "vindicated" by recourse to the police and to torture.

II

THE FATHERS OF THE Church have interpreted man's creation in the "image of God" as a proof that he is capable of paradisiacal innocence and of contemplation, and that these are indeed the purpose of his creation. Man was made in order that in his emptiness and purity of heart he might mirror the purity and freedom of the invisible God and thus be perfectly one with Him. But the recovery of this paradise, which is always hidden within us at least as a possibility, is a matter of great practical difficulty. Genesis tells us that the way back to Paradise is barred by an angel with a flaming sword "turning every way." Yet that does not mean that the return is absolutely impossible. As St. Ambrose says: "All who wish to return to paradise must be tested by the fire" (*Oportet omnes per ignem probari quicumque ad paradisum redire desiderant. In Psalmum* 118, xx, 12. Quoted in Stolz, p. 32). The way from knowledge to innocence, or the purification of the heart, is a way of temptation and struggle. It is a matter of wrestling with supreme difficulties and overcoming obstacles that seem, and indeed are, beyond human strength.

Dr. Suzuki has not mentioned one of the main actors in the drama of the Fall: the devil. Buddhism certainly has a very definite concept of this personage (*Mara*—the tempter) and if ever there was a spirituality more concerned with the devil than that of the Egyptian desert, it is the Buddhism of Tibet. In Zen, however, the devil appears relatively little. We see him occasionally in these "Sayings of the Fathers." But his presence is everywhere noted in the desert, which is indeed his refuge. The first and greatest of hermits, St. Anthony, is the classic type of the wrestler with the devil. The Desert Fathers invaded the devil's own exclusive territory in order, by overcoming him in singlehanded combat, to regain paradise.

Without attempting the delicate task of fully identifying this ubiquitous and evil spirit, let us remind ourselves that in the first pages of the Bible he appears as the one who offers man the "knowledge of good and evil" as something "better," superior, and more "godlike" than the state of innocence and emptiness. And in the last pages of the Bible the devil is finally "cast out" when man is restored to unity with God in Christ. The significant point is that in these verses of the Apocalypse (12:10) the devil is called "the accuser of our brethren . . . who accused them before God day and night." In the Book of Job, the devil is not only the one who causes Job's sufferings, but it is understood that he also acts as a "tempter" through the moralizing of Job's friends.

The friends of Job appear on the scene as advisers and "consolers," offering Job the fruits of their moral *scientia*. But when Job insists that his sufferings have *no explanation* and that he cannot discover the reason for them through conventional ethical concepts, his friends turn into accusers, and curse Job as a sinner. Thus, instead of consolers, they become torturers by virtue of their very morality, and in so doing, while claiming to be advocates of God, they act as instruments of the devil.

In other words, the realm of knowledge or *scientia* is a realm where man is subject to the influence of the devil. This does nothing to alter the fact that knowledge is good and necessary. Nevertheless, even when our "science" does not fail us, it still tends to delude us. Its perspectives are not those of our inmost, spiritual nature. And at the same time we are constantly being misled by passion, attachment to self, and by the "deceptions of the devil." The realm of knowledge is then a realm of alienation and peril, in which we are not our true selves and in which we are likely to become completely enslaved to the power of illusion. And this is true not only when we fall into sin but also to some extent even when we avoid it. The Desert Fathers realized that the most dangerous activity of the devil came into play against the monk only when he was morally perfect, that is, apparently "pure" and virtuous enough to be capable of spiritual pride. Then began the struggle with the last and subtlest of the attachments: the attachment to one's own spiritual excellence; the love of one's spiritualized, purified, and "empty" self; the narcissism of the perfect, of the pseudo-saint, and of the false mystic.

The only escape, as St. Anthony said, was humility. And the Desert Fathers' concept of humility corresponds very closely to the spiritual poverty Dr. Suzuki has just described for us. One must possess and retain absolutely nothing, not even a self in which he can receive angelic visitations, not even a selflessness he can be proud of. True sanctity is not the work of man purifying himself; it is God Himself present in His own transcendent light, which to us is emptiness.

III

LET US LOOK MORE closely at two Patristic texts on science (*scientia*) or knowledge, as it occurred in the fall of Adam. St. Augustine says:

> This science is described as the recognition of good and evil because the soul ought to reach out to what is beyond itself, that is to God, and to forget what is beneath itself, that is bodily pleasure. But if the soul, deserting God, turns in upon itself and wishes to enjoy its own spiritual power as though without God, it becomes inflated with pride, which is the beginning of all sin. And when it is thus punished for its sin, it learns by experience what a distance separates the good it has deserted and the evil into which it has fallen. This then is what it means to have tasted the fruit of the tree of the knowledge of good and evil. (*De Genesi contra Manichaeos*, ix. Migne, PL 34:203)

And again in another place:

> When the soul deserts the wisdom (*sapientia*) of love, which is always
> unchanging and one, and desires knowledge (*scientia*) from the experi-
> ence of temporal and changing things, it becomes puffed up rather than
> built up. And weighed down in this manner the soul falls away from bless-
> edness as though by its own heaviness. (*De Trinitate* xii, 11. Migne, PL
> 42:1007)

A few brief words of comment will clarify this concept of "knowledge" and of
its effects. First of all, the state in which man is created is one of un-selfconscious
"reaching out" to what is metaphysically higher than himself, but nevertheless
intimately present within his own being, so that he himself is hidden in God and
united with Him. This is what, for St. Augustine, corresponds to the innocence
of paradise and to "emptiness." The knowledge of good and evil begins with the
fruition of sensible and temporal things for their own sakes, an act which makes
the soul conscious of itself, and centers it on its own pleasure. It becomes aware
of what is good and evil "for itself." As soon as this takes place, there is a complete change of perspective, and from unity or wisdom (identified with emptiness and purity) the soul now enters into a state of dualism. It is now aware of
both itself and God, as separated beings. It now sees God as an object of desire
or of fear, and is no longer lost in Him as in a transcendent subject. Furthermore
it is aware of God as of an antagonistic and hostile being. And yet it is attracted
to Him as to its highest good. But the experience of itself becomes a "weight"
which gravitates away from God. Each act of self-affirmation increases the dualistic tension between self and God. Remember Augustine's dictum, *amor meus,*
pondus meum. "My love is a weight, a gravitational force." As one loves temporal things, one gains an illusory substantiality and a selfhood which gravitates
"downward," that is to say acquires a *need* for things lower in the scale of being
than itself. It depends on these things for its own self-affirmation. In the end
this gravitational pull becomes an enslavement to material and temporal cares,
and finally to sin. Yet this weight itself is an illusion, a result of the "puffing up"
of pride, a "swelling" without reality. The self that appears to be weighed down
by its love and carried away to material things is, in fact, an unreal thing. Yet it
retains an empirical existence of its own; it is what we think of as ourselves. And
this empirical existence is strengthened by every act of selfish desire or fear. It
is not the true self, the Christian person, the image of God stamped with the
likeness of Christ. It is the false self, the disfigured image, the caricature, the
emptiness that has swelled up and become full of itself, so as to create a kind of

fictional substantiality for itself. Such is Augustine's commentary on the phrase of St. Paul: *scientia inflat.* "Knowledge puffeth up."

These two passages from St. Augustine are sufficiently good parallels to the process which Dr. Suzuki describes in the sentence, "Out of the Emptiness of the Mind a thought mysteriously arises and we have the world of multiplicities." I do not of course insist that St. Augustine is teaching Zen. Far from it! There remain deep and significant divergences which we need not study at this point. Let it suffice to have said that there are also certain important similarities, due in great part to the Platonism of St. Augustine.

Once we find ourselves in the state of "knowledge of good and evil" we have to accept the fact and understand our position, see it in relation to the innocence for which we were created, which we have lost and which we can regain. But in the meantime it is a question of treating knowledge and innocence as complementary realities. This was the most delicate problem confronting the Desert Fathers, and for many of them it led to disaster. They recognized the difference between "knowledge of good and evil" on the one hand, and innocence or emptiness on the other. But, as Dr. Suzuki has wisely observed, they ran the risk of oversimplified and abstract solutions. Too many of them wanted to get along simply with innocence without knowledge. In our *Sayings*, John the Dwarf is a case in point. He wants to reach a state in which there is no temptation, no further stirring of the slightest passion.[1] All this is nothing but a refinement of "knowledge." Instead of leading to innocence, it leads to the most quintessentially pure love of self. It leads to the creation of a pseudo-emptiness, an exquisitely purified self that is so perfect that it can rest in itself without any trace of crude reflection. Yet this is not emptiness; there remains a "self" that is the subject of purity and the possessor of emptiness. And this, as the Desert Fathers saw, is the final triumph of the subtle tempter. It leaves a man rooted and imprisoned in his pure self, a clever discerner of good and evil, of self and nonself, purity and impurity. But he is not innocent. He is a master of spiritual knowledge. And as such, he is still subject to accusation from the devil. Since

---

1. "Abbot Pastor said that Abbot John the Dwarf had prayed to the Lord and the Lord had taken away all his passions, so that he became impassible. And in this condition he went to one of the elders and said: You see before you a man who is completely at rest and has no more temptations. The elder said: Go and pray to the Lord to command some struggle to be stirred up in you, for the soul is matured only in battles. And when the temptations started up again he did not pray that the struggle be taken away from him, but only said: Lord, give me strength to get through the fight" (*The Wisdom of the Desert*, XCI).

he is *perfect*, he is subject to the greatest deception of all. If he were *innocent*, he would be free from deception.

The man who has truly found his spiritual nakedness, who has realized he is empty, is not a self that has *acquired* emptiness or *become* empty. He just "is empty from the beginning," as Dr. Suzuki has observed. Or, to put it in the more affective terms of St. Augustine and St. Bernard, he "loves with a pure love." That is to say he loves with a purity and freedom that spring spontaneously and directly from the fact that he has fully recovered the divine likeness, and is now fully his true self because he is lost in God. He is one with God and identified with God and hence knows nothing of any ego in himself. All he knows is love. As St. Bernard says: "He who loves thus, simply loves, and knows nothing else but love." *Qui amat, amat et aliud novit nihil.*

Whether or not the Desert Fathers were fully articulate in expressing this kind of emptiness, they certainly strove for it. And their instrument in opening the subtle locks of spiritual deception was the virtue of *discretio*. It was discretion that St. Anthony called the most important of all the virtues in the desert. Discretion had taught him the value of simple manual labor. Discretion taught the fathers that purity of heart did not consist simply in fasting and self-maceration. Discretion—otherwise called the discernment of spirits—is indeed germane to the realm of knowledge, since it does distinguish between good and evil. But it exercises its functions in the light of innocence and in reference to emptiness. It judges not in terms of abstract standards so much as in terms of inner purity of heart. Discretion makes judgments and indicates choices, but the judgment and choice always point in the direction of emptiness, or purity of heart. Discretion is a function of humility, and therefore it is a branch of knowledge that lies beyond the reach of diabolical comment and perversion. (See Cassian, Conference II, *De Discretione*. Migne, PL 49:523ff.)

IV

JOHN CASSIAN, IN HIS reports of the "conferences" he heard among the Desert Fathers, lays down the fundamental rule of desert spirituality. What is the purpose and end of the monastic life? Such is the subject of the first conference.

The answer is that the monastic life has a twofold purpose. It must lead the monk first to an intermediate end, and then to an ultimate and final state of completion. The intermediate end, or *scopos*, is what we have been discussing as purity of heart, roughly corresponding to Dr. Suzuki's term "emptiness." That heart is pure which is *perfectum ac mundissimum* (perfect and most pure), that is to say completely free of alien thoughts and desires. The concept, in actual fact, corresponds rather to the Stoic *apatheia* than to Zen "suchness." But at any rate there is a close relationship. It is the *quies*, or rest, of contemplation—the state of being free from all images and concepts which disturb and occupy the soul. It is the favorable climate for *theologia*, the highest contemplation, which excludes even the purest and most spiritual of ideas and admits no concepts whatever. It knows God not by concepts or visions, but only by "unknowing." This is the language of Evagrius Ponticus, severely intellectual, a fact which brings him closer to Zen than the more affective theologians of prayer like St. Maximus and St. Gregory of Nyssa. Cassian himself, though close to Evagrius and sympathetic with him, nevertheless gives a characteristically Christian affective balance to the concept of purity of heart, and insists that it is to be defined simply as "perfect charity" or a love of God unmixed with any return upon self. This qualification might conceivably constitute a significant difference between Christian "purity of heart" and the "emptiness" of Zen, but the relations between the two concepts should be further studied.

One thing, and this is most important, remains to be said. Purity of heart is not the *ultimate end* of the monk's striving in the desert. It is only a step towards it. We have said above that Paradise is not yet heaven. Paradise is not the final goal of the spiritual life. It is, in fact, only a return to the true beginning. It is a "fresh start." The monk who has realized in himself purity of heart, and has been restored, in some measure, to the innocence lost by Adam, has still not ended his journey. He is only ready to begin. He is ready for a new work "which eye hath not seen, ear hath not heard, nor hath it entered into the heart of man to conceive." Purity of heart, says Cassian, is the intermediate end of the spiritual life. But the ultimate end is the Kingdom of God. This is a dimension which does not enter into the realm of Zen.

One might argue that this simply overturns all that has been said about emptiness, and brings us back into a state of dualism, and therefore to "knowledge of good and evil," duality between man and God, etc. Such is by no means the case. Purity of heart establishes man in a state of unity and emptiness in which he is one with God. But this is the necessary preparation not for further struggle between good and evil, but for the real work of God which is revealed in the Bible: the work of the *new creation*, the resurrection from the dead, the restoration of all things in Christ. This is the real dimension of Christianity, the eschatological dimension which is peculiar to it, and which has no parallel in Buddhism. The world was created without man, but the new creation which is the true Kingdom of God is to be the work of God in and through man. It is to be the great, mysterious, theandric work of the Mystical Christ, the New Adam, in whom all men as "one Person" or one "Son of God" will transfigure the cosmos and offer it resplendent to the Father. Here, in this transfiguration, will take place the apocalyptic marriage between God and His creation, the final and perfect consummation of which no mortal mysticism is able to dream and which is barely foreshadowed in the symbols and images of the last pages of the Apocalypse.

Here, of course, we are back in the realm of concept and image. To think about these things, to speculate on them, is, perhaps, to depart from "emptiness." But it is an activity of faith that belongs to our realm of knowledge, and conditions us for a superior and more vigilant innocence: the innocence of the wise virgins who wait with lighted lamps, with an emptiness that is enkindled by the glory of the Divine Word and enflamed with the presence of the Holy Spirit. That glory and that presence are not objects which "enter into" emptiness to "fill" it. They are nothing else but God's own "suchness."

6

*Notes for a Philosophy of Solitude**

This essay, which Merton himself called "very central" to his work (*Hidden Ground of Love*, 642) and written "from a kind of necessity" (*Dancing in the Water of Life*, 349), had a rather complex genesis and development (recounted in detail by William H. Shannon in "Reflections on Thomas Merton's Article 'Notes for a Philosophy of Solitude,'" *Cistercian Studies Quarterly* 29.1 [1994], 83-99). A brief version first appeared in French as "Dans le Désert de Dieu" in *Témoignages* 48 (March 1955), 132-36 (the presumed original English version of this material is no longer extant, but Shannon's translation from the French was published as "In God's Desert" in *The Merton Seasonal* 18.2 [Spring 1993], 4-6). An expanded version of this essay was published in April 1960 as *The Solitary Life*, in a limited edition of sixty copies, by Merton's friend Victor Hammer on his hand press (Lexington, KY: Stamperia del Santuccio) and later reprinted in *The Monastic Journey* (151-62). The final version, in which the first nine sections of Part I and the final section of Part III have been added, along with various alterations, some demanded by censors (see Merton's comments in his May 21, 1960, letter to Abbot General Gabriel Sortais [*School of Charity*, 131]), appeared in *Disputed Questions* (163-93). As Shannon notes in his article (see 88-89), this essay is less a systematically structured treatment of the topic (a "philosophy" of the solitary life) than a series of more loosely organized reflections, as signaled by the use of "Notes" in the title and

---

* This could also properly be called a "Philosophy of Monastic Life" if it be understood that a monk is, etymologically, a *monachos* or one who is isolated, alone. However since "monastic" now suggests not so much the man as the institution, I have seldom used the word "monk" in these pages. I am speaking of the solitary spirit which is really essential to the monastic view of life, but which is not confined to monasteries. Nor is it limited to men and women who have consecrated their lives to God by vow. Therefore, though I am treating the traditional concept of the *monachos*, or solitary, I am deliberately discarding everything that can conjure up the artificial image of the monk in a cowl, dwelling in a medieval cloister. In this way I intend obviously not to disparage or to reject the monastic institution, but to set aside all its accidentals and externals, so that they will not interfere with my view of what seems to me to be deepest and most essential. But by that same token, the "solitary" of these pages is never necessarily a "monk" (juridically) at all. He may well be a layman, and of the sort most remote from cloistered life, like Thoreau or Emily Dickinson.

by the arrangement in numbered sections. As the essay developed, its focus broadened from the monastic context to consider the "solitary spirit" wherever it might be found, as indicated by the references to Henry David Thoreau and Emily Dickinson in Merton's own introductory note. The essay's three major parts move from a recognition of the essentially solitary dimension of all human lives, which many people try to avoid through the distractions of superficial activity ("The Tyranny of Diversion"); through the difficulties of living out an authentic solitude that will serve the Church and society as a whole as a sign of contradiction to the illusion that one's value and significance depend on one's accomplishments ("In the Sea of Perils"); to the refusal to idealize or mythologize the solitary as a spiritually "superior" person, concluding with the magnificent final section identifying the "inner 'I,'" the true self, with all others and with Christ Himself ("Spiritual Poverty"). Merton commented on the essay in his journal, "The 'Notes on Solitude' is perhaps the best thing of the sort I have ever written. One reason being that the censors made me do it over five times at least. But this is something I must myself read and follow, for in it my deeper self is talking and I am obliged to listen" (*Turning Toward the World*, 40 [9/3/60]).

"*Un cri d'oiseau sur les récifs. . . .*"
St. John Perse

I. THE TYRANNY OF DIVERSION

1. WHY WRITE ABOUT solitude in the first place? Certainly not in order to preach it, to exhort people to become solitary. What could be more absurd? Those who are to become solitary are, as a rule, solitary already. At most they are not yet aware of their condition. In which case, all they need is to discover it. But in reality, all men are solitary. Only most of them are so averse to being alone, or to feeling alone, that they do everything they can to forget their solitude. How? Perhaps in large measure by what Pascal called "divertissement"—diversion, systematic distraction. By those occupations and recreations, so mercifully provided by society, which enable a man to avoid his own company for twenty-four hours a day.

Even the worst society has something about it that is not only good, but essential for human life. Man cannot live without society, obviously. Those who claim they would like to do so, or that they might be able to do so, are often those who depend most abjectly upon it. Their pretense of solitude is only an admission of their dependence. It is an individualistic illusion.

Besides protecting man's natural life, enabling him to care for himself, society gives each individual a chance to transcend himself in the service of others and thus to become a person. But no one becomes a person merely by diversion—in the sense of *divertissement*. For the function of diversion is simply to anesthetize the individual as individual, and to plunge him in the warm, apathetic stupor of a collectivity which, like himself, wishes to remain amused. The bread and circuses which fulfill this function may be blatant and absurd, or they may assume a hypocritical air of intense seriousness, for instance in a mass movement. Our own society prefers the absurd. But our absurdity is blended with a certain hard-headed, fully determined seriousness with which we devote ourselves to the acquisition of money, to the satisfaction of our appetite for status, and our justification of ourselves as contrasted with the totalitarian iniquity of our opposite number.

2. In a society like ours, there are obviously many people for whom solitude is a problem or even a temptation. I am perhaps in no position to resolve their problem or to exorcise their temptation. But it is possible that—knowing something at least of interior solitude—I might be able to say something of it which will reassure those tempted ones. At least I can suggest that if they have not been able to rest in the fervid consolations which are lavished upon them by society itself, that they do not need to seek such rest as that. They are perhaps perfectly capable of doing without such reassurance. They ought possibly to realize that they have less need of diversion than they are told, with such dogmatic self-complacency, by the organization men. They can confidently detach themselves from the engineers of the human soul whose talents are devoted to the cult of publicity. Such an influence in their life is truly, as they tend to suspect, as unnecessary as it is irritating. But I do not promise to make it unavoidable.

Nor do I promise to cheer anybody up with optimistic answers to all the sordid difficulties and uncertainties which attend the life of interior solitude. Perhaps in the course of these reflections, some of the difficulties will be mentioned. The first of them has to be taken note of from the very start: the disconcerting task of facing and accepting one's own absurdity. The anguish of realizing that underneath the apparently logical pattern of a more or less "well-organized" and rational life, there lies an abyss of irrationality, confusion, pointlessness, and indeed of apparent chaos. This is what immediately impresses itself upon the man who has renounced diversion. It cannot be otherwise: for in renouncing diversion, he renounces the seemingly harmless pleasure of building a tight, self-contained illusion about himself and about his little world. He accepts the difficulty of facing the million things in his life which are incomprehensible, instead of simply ignoring them. Incidentally it is only when the apparent absurdity of life is faced in all truth that faith really becomes possible. Otherwise, faith tends to be a kind of diversion, a spiritual amusement, in which one gathers up accepted, conventional formulas and arranges them in the approved mental patterns, without bothering to investigate their meaning, or asking if they have any practical consequences in one's life.

3. One of the first essentials of the interior solitude of which I speak is that it is the actualization of a faith in which a man takes responsibility for his own inner life. He faces its full mystery, in the presence of the invisible God. And he takes upon himself the lonely, barely comprehensible, incommunicable task of working his way through the darkness of his own mystery until he discovers that his mystery and the mystery of God merge into one reality, which is the only reality. That God lives in him and he in God—not precisely in the way that words seem to suggest (for words have no power to comprehend the reality) but in a way that makes words, and even attempts to communicate, seem utterly illusory.

The words of God, the words which unite in "One Body" the society of those who truly believe, have the power to signify the mystery of our loneliness and oneness in Christ, to point the way into its darkness. They have the power, also, to illuminate the darkness. But they do so by losing the shape of words and becoming—not thoughts, not things, but the unspeakable beating of a Heart within the heart of one's own life.

4. Every man is a solitary, held firmly by the inexorable limitations of his own aloneness. Death makes this very clear, for when a man dies, he dies alone. The only one for whom the bell tolls, in all literal truth, is the one who is dying. It tolls "for thee" insofar as death is common to all of us, but obviously we do not all die at one and the same moment. We die *like* one another. The presence of many living men around the deathbed of one who is in agony may unite them all in the mystery of death, but it also unites them in a mystery of living solitude. It paradoxically unites them while reminding them acutely—and beyond words—of their isolation. Each one will have to die, and die *alone*. And, at the same time (but this is what they do not want to see) each one must also *live* alone. For we must remember that the Church is at the same time community and solitude. The dying Christian is one with the Church, but he also suffers the loneliness of Christ's agony in Gethsemani.

Very few men are able to face this fact squarely. And very few are expected to do so. It is the special vocation of certain ones who dedicate their whole lives to wrestling with solitude. An "agony" is a "wrestling." The dying man in agony wrestles with solitude. But the wrestling with one's solitude is also a life-work— a "life agony." When a man is called to be a solitary—(even if only interiorly)— he does not need to be anything else, nor can anything else be demanded of him except that he remain physically or spiritually alone fighting his battle which few can understand. His function in the Church—a social function and a spiritual one—is to remain in the "cell" of his aloneness, whether it be a real cell in the desert, or simply the spiritual cell of his own incomprehensible emptiness; and, as the Desert Fathers used to say, his "cell will teach him all things."

5. The true solitary is not one who simply withdraws from society. Mere withdrawal, regression, leads to a sick solitude, without meaning and without fruit. The solitary of whom I speak is called not to leave society but to transcend it: not to withdraw from the fellowship with other men but to renounce the appearance, the myth of union in diversion in order to attain to union on a higher and more spiritual level—the mystical level of the Body of Christ. He renounces that union with his immediate neighbors which is apparently achieved through the medium of the aspirations, fictions, and conventions prevalent in his social group. But in so doing he attains to the basic, invisible, mysterious unity which makes all men "One Man" in Christ's Church beyond and in spite of natural social groups which, by their special myths and slogans, keep a man in a state of division.

The solitary, then, has a mysterious and apparently absurd vocation to supernatural unity. He seeks a spiritual and simple oneness in himself which, when it is found, paradoxically becomes the oneness of all men—a oneness beyond separation, conflict, and schism. For it is only when each man is one that mankind will once again become "One." But the solitary realizes that the images and myths of a particular group—projections of the interests, ideals, and sins of that group—can take possession of him and divide him against himself.

The illusions and fictions encouraged by the appetite for self-affirmation in certain restricted groups have much to be said for them and much to be said against them. They do in practice free a man from his individual limitations and help him, in some measure, to transcend himself. And if every society were ideal, then every society would help its members only to a fruitful and productive self-transcendence. But in fact societies tend to lift a man above himself only far enough to make him a useful and submissive instrument in whom the aspirations, lusts, and needs of the group can function unhindered by too delicate a personal conscience. Social life tends to form and educate a man, but generally at the price of a simultaneous deformation and perversion. This is because civil society is never ideal, always a mixture of good and evil, and always tending to present the evil in itself as a form of good.

6. There are crimes which no one would commit as an individual which he willingly and bravely commits when acting in the name of his society, because he has been (too easily) convinced that evil is entirely different when it is done "for the common good." As an example, one might point to the way in which

racial hatreds and even persecution are admitted by people who consider them-selves, and perhaps in some sense are, kind, tolerant, civilized, and even humane. But they have acquired a special deformity of conscience as a result of their identification with their group, their immersion in their particular society. This deformation is the price they pay to forget and to exorcise that solitude which seems to them to be a demon.

7. The solitary is one who is called to make one of the most terrible decisions possible to man: the decision to disagree completely with those who imagine that the call to diversion and self-deception is the voice of truth and who can summon the full authority of their own prejudice to prove it. He is therefore bound to sweat blood in anguish, in order to be loyal to God, to the Mystical Christ, and to humanity as a whole, rather than to the idol which is offered to him, for his homage, by a particular group. He must renounce the blessing of every convenient illusion that absolves him from responsibility when he is untrue to his deepest self and to his inmost truth—the image of God in his own soul.

The price of fidelity in such a task is a completely dedicated humility—an emptiness of heart in which self-assertion has no place. For if he is not empty and undivided in his own inmost soul, the solitary will be nothing more than an individualist. And in that case, his nonconformity is nothing but an act of rebel-lion: the substitution of idols and illusions of his own choosing for those chosen by society. And this, of course, is the greatest of dangers. It is both futility and madness. It leads only to ruin.

For to forget oneself, at least to the extent of preferring a social myth with a certain limited productiveness, is a lesser evil than clinging to a private myth which is only a sterile dream. And so, as Heraclitus said long ago, "We must not act and speak like sleepers. . . . The waking have one common world, but the sleeping turn aside each into a world of his own." Hence the vocation to solitude is not a vocation to the warm narcissistic dream of a private religion. It is a vocation to become *fully awake*, even more than the common somnolence permits one to be, with its arbitrary selection of approved dreams, mixed with a few really valid and fruitful conceptions.

8. It should be clear from the start then that the solitary worthy of the name lives not in a world of private fictions and self-constructed delusions, but in a world of emptiness, humility, and purity beyond the reach of slogans and beyond the gravitational pull of diversions that alienate him from God and from himself. He lives in unity. His solitude is neither an argument, an accusa-tion, a reproach, or a sermon. It is simply itself. It *is*. And therefore it not only

does not attract attention, or desire it, but it remains, for the most part, completely invisible.

9. It should be quite clear then, that there is no question in these pages of the eccentric and regressive solitude that clamors for recognition, and which seeks to focus more pleasurably and more intently on itself by stepping back from the crowd. But unfortunately, however often I may repeat this warning, it will not be heeded. Those who most need to hear it are incapable of doing so. They think that solitude is a heightening of self-consciousness, an intensification of pleasure in self. It is a more secret and more perfect diversion. What they want is not the hidden, metaphysical agony of the hermit but the noisy self-congratulations and self-pity of the infant in the cradle. Ultimately what they want is not the desert but the womb.

The individualist in practice completely accepts the social fictions around him, but accepts them in such a way that they provide a suitable background against which a few private and favored fictions of his own can make an appearance. Without the social background, his individual fictions would not be able to assert themselves, and he himself would no longer be able to fix his attention upon them.

II. IN THE SEA OF PERILS

1. THERE IS NO need to say that the call of solitude (even though only interior) is perilous. Everyone who knows what solitude means is aware of this. The essence of the solitary vocation is precisely the anguish of an almost infinite risk. Only the false solitary sees no danger in solitude. But his solitude is imaginary, that is to say built around an image. It is merely a social image stripped of its explicitly social elements. The false solitary is one who is able to imagine himself without companions while in reality he remains just as dependent on society as before—if not more dependent. He needs society as a ventriloquist needs a dummy. He projects his own voice to the group and it comes back to him admiring, approving, opposing, or at least adverting to his own separateness.

Even if society seems to condemn him, this pleases and diverts him for it is nothing but the sound of his own voice, reminding him of his separateness, which is his chosen diversion. True solitude is not mere separateness. It tends only to *unity*.

2. The true solitary does not renounce anything that is basic and human about his relationship to other men. He is deeply united to them—all the more deeply because he is no longer entranced by marginal concerns. What he renounces is the superficial imagery and the trite symbolism that pretend to

make the relationship more genuine and more fruitful. He gives up his lax self-abandonment to general diversion. He renounces vain pretenses of solidarity that tend to substitute themselves for real solidarity, while masking an inner spirit of irresponsibility and selfishness. He renounces illusory claims of collective achievement and fulfillment, by which society seeks to gratify and assuage the individual's need to feel that he amounts to something.

The man who is dominated by what I have called the "social image" is one who allows himself to see and to approve in himself only that which his society prescribes as beneficial and praiseworthy in its members. As a corollary he sees and disapproves (usually in *others*) mostly what his society disapproves. And yet he congratulates himself on "thinking for himself." In reality, this is only a game that he plays in his own mind—the game of substituting the words, slogans, and concepts he has received from society, for genuine experiences of his own. Or rather—the slogans of society are felt to rise up within him as if they were his own "spontaneous experience." How can such a man be really "social"? He is imprisoned in an illusion and cut off from real, living contact with his fellow man. Yet he does not feel himself to be in any way "alone"!

3. The solitary is first of all one who renounces this arbitrary social imagery. When his nation wins a war or sends a rocket to the moon, he can get along without feeling as if he personally had won the war or hit the moon with a rocket. When his nation is rich and arrogant, he does not feel that he himself is more fortunate and more honest, as well as more powerful than the citizens of other, more "backward" nations. More than this: he is able to despise war and to see the futility of rockets to the moon in a way quite different and more fundamental from the way in which his society may tolerate these negative views. That is to say, he despises the criminal, bloodthirsty arrogance of his own nation or class, as much as that of "the enemy." He despises his own self-seeking aggressivity as much as that of the politicians who hypocritically pretend they are fighting for peace.

4. Most men cannot live fruitfully without a large proportion of fiction in their thinking. If they do not have some efficacious mythology around which to organize their activities, they will regress into a less efficacious, more primitive, more chaotic set of illusions. When the ancients said that the solitary was likely to be either a god or a beast, they meant that he would either achieve a rare intellectual and spiritual independence, or sink into a more complete and brutish dependence. The solitary easily plunges into a cavern of darkness and of phantoms more horrible and more absurd than the most inane set of conventional social images. The suffering he must then face is neither salutary nor noble. It is catastrophic.

5. I do not pretend, in these pages, to establish a clear formula for discerning solitary vocations. But this much needs to be said: that one who is called to solitude is not called merely to imagine himself solitary, to live as if he were solitary, to cultivate the illusion that he is different, withdrawn, and elevated. He is called to emptiness. And in this emptiness he does not find points upon which to base a contrast between himself and others. On the contrary, he realizes, though perhaps confusedly, that he has entered into a *solitude that is really shared by everyone*. It is not that he is solitary while everybody else is social: but that everyone is solitary, in a solitude masked by that symbolism which they use to cheat and counteract their solitariness. What the solitary renounces is not his union with other men, but rather the deceptive fictions and inadequate symbols which tend to take the place of genuine social unity—to produce a façade of apparent unity without really uniting men on a deep level. Example— the excitement and fictitious engagement of a football crowd. This is to say, of course, that the Christian solitary is fully and perfectly a man of the Church.

Even though he may be physically alone the solitary remains united to others and lives in profound solidarity with them, but on a deeper and mystical level. They may think he is one with them in the vain interests and preoccupations of a superficial social existence. He realizes that he is one with them in the peril and anguish of their common solitude: not the solitude of the individual only, but the radical and essential *solitude of man*—a solitude which was assumed by Christ and which, in Christ, becomes mysteriously identified with the solitude of God.

6. The solitary is one who is aware of solitude in himself as a basic and inevitable human reality, not just as something which affects him as an isolated individual. Hence his solitude is the foundation of a deep, pure, and gentle sympathy with all other men, whether or not they are capable of realizing the tragedy of their plight. More—it is the doorway by which he enters into the mystery of God, and brings others into that mystery by the power of his love and his humility.

7. The emptiness of the true solitary is marked then by a great simplicity. This simplicity can be deceptive, because it may be hidden under a surface of apparent complexity, but it is there nevertheless, behind the outer contradictions of the man's life. It manifests itself in a kind of candor though he may be very reticent. There is in this lonely one a gentleness, a deep sympathy, though he may be apparently unsocial. There is a great purity of love, though he may hesitate to manifest his love in any way, or to commit himself openly to it. Underneath the complications that are produced in him by his uneasiness with social images, the man tends to live without images, without too much conceptual thought.

When you get to know him well—which is sometimes possible—you may find in him not so much a man who seeks solitude as one who has already found it, or been found by it. His problem then is not to find what he already has, but to discover what to do about it.

8. One who has made the discovery of his inner solitude, or is just about to make it, may need considerable spiritual help. A wise man, who knows the plight of the new solitary, may with the right word at the right time spare him the pain of seeking vainly some long and complex statement of his case. No such statement is necessary; he has simply discovered what it means to be a man. And he has begun to realize that what he sees in himself is not a spiritual luxury but a difficult, humiliating responsibility: the obligation to be spiritually mature.

9. The solitary condition also has its jargon and its conventions: these too are pitiful. There is no point in consoling one who has awakened to his solitude by teaching him to defile his emptiness with rationalizations. Solitude must not become a diversion to itself by too much self-justification. At least allow the lonely one to meet his emptiness and come to terms with it: for it is really his destiny and his joy. Too many people are ready to draw him back at any price from what they conceive to be the edge of the abyss. True, it is an abyss; but they do not realize that he who is called to solitude is called to walk across the air of the abyss without danger, because, after all, the abyss is only himself. He should not be forced to feel guilty about it, for in this solitude and emptiness of his heart there is another, more inexplicable solitude. Man's loneliness is, in fact, the loneliness of God. That is why it is such a great thing for a man to discover his solitude and learn to live in it. For there he finds that he and God are one: that God is alone as he himself is alone. That God wills to be alone in him.

When this is understood, then one sees that his duty is to be faithful to solitude because in this way he is faithful to God. Fidelity is everything. From it the solitary can expect truth and strength, light and wisdom at the right time. If he is not faithful to the inner anonymity and emptiness which are the secret of his whole life, then he can expect nothing but confusion.

10. Like everything else in the Christian life, the vocation to spiritual solitude can be understood only within the perspectives of God's mercy to man in the Incarnation of Christ. If there is any such thing as a Christian hermit, then he must be a man who has a special function in the mystical body of Christ—a hidden and spiritual function, and perhaps all the more vital because more hidden. But this social function of the solitary contemplative, precisely because it has to be invisible, cannot be allowed in any way to detract from his genuinely solitary character. On the contrary, his function in the Christian community is the paradoxical one of living outwardly separated from the community. And

this, whether he is conscious of it or not, is a witness to the completely transcendental character of the Christian mystery of our unity in Christ.

The hermit remains to put us on our guard against our natural obsession with the visible, social, and communal forms of Christian life which tend at times to be inordinately active, and often become deeply involved in the life of secular, non-Christian society. It is true to say of every Christian that he is in the world but not of it. But in case he might be likely to forget this—or worse still in case he might never come to know it at all—there must be men who have completely renounced the world: men who are neither in the world nor of it. In our day, when "the world" is everywhere, even in the desert where it makes and proves its secret weapons, the solitary retains his unique and mysterious function. But he will fulfill it perhaps in many paradoxical ways. Wherever he does so, even where he is unseen, he testifies to the essentially mystical bond of unity which binds Christians together in the Holy Spirit. Whether he is seen or not, he bears witness to the unity of Christ by possessing in himself the fullness of Christian charity.

In fact, the early Christians who went into the desert to see the hermits of Nitria and Scete admired in them not so much their extreme asceticism as their charity and discretion. The miracle of the Desert Fathers was precisely that a man could live entirely separate from the visible Christian community with its normal liturgical functions, and still be full of the charity of Christ. He was able to be so only because he was completely empty of himself. This vocation to solitude is therefore at the same time a vocation to silence, poverty, and emptiness. But the emptiness is for the sake of fullness: the purpose of the solitary life is, if you like, contemplation. But not contemplation in the pagan sense of an intellectual, esoteric enlightenment, achieved by ascetic technique. The contemplation of the Christian solitary is the awareness of the divine mercy transforming and elevating his own emptiness and turning it into the presence of perfect love, perfect fullness.

Hence a Christian can turn his back on society, even on the society of his fellow Christians, without necessarily hating society. This is because of the spiritual and mystical character of the Christian Church—the same spiritual character which accounts for the fact that one who renounces marriage in order to be a priest or a monk can thereby, if he is faithful, attain to a higher and more spiritual fruitfulness. So a Christian hermit can, by being alone, paradoxically live even closer to the heart of the Church than one who is in the midst of her apostolic activities. The life and unity of the Church are, and must be, visible. But that does not mean that the invisible and spiritual activities of men of prayer are not supremely important. On the contrary, the invisible and more mysterious life of prayer is *essential* to the Church. Solitaries, too, are essential to her!

11. Withdrawal from other men can be a special form of love for them. It should never be a rejection of man or of his society. But it may well be a quiet and humble refusal to accept the myths and fictions with which social life cannot help but be full—especially today. To despair of the illusions and façades which man builds around himself is certainly not to despair of man. On the contrary, it may be a sign of love and of hope. For when we love someone, we refuse to tolerate what destroys and maims his personality. If we love mankind, can we blind ourselves to man's predicament? You will say: we must do something about his predicament. But there are some whose vocation it is to realize that they, at least, cannot help in any overt social way. Their contribution is a mute witness, a secret and even invisible expression of love which takes the form of their own option for solitude in preference to the acceptance of social fictions. For is not our involvement in fiction, particularly in political and demagogic fiction, an implicit confession that we despair of man and even of God?

12. Christian hope in God and in the world to come is inevitably also hope in man, or at least *for* man. How can we despair of man when the Word of God was made man in order to save us all? But our Christian hope is, and must remain, inviolably pure. It must work and struggle in the chaos of conflicting policy which is the world of egotism; and in order to do so it must take on visible, symbolic forms by which to declare its message. But when these symbols become confused with other secular symbols, then there is danger that faith itself will be corrupted by fictions, and there is a consequent obligation, on the part of some Christians, to affirm their faith in all its intransigent purity.

At such a time, some men will seek clarity in isolation and silence, not because they think they know better than the rest, but because they want to see life in a different perspective. They want to withdraw from the babel of confusion in order to listen more patiently to the voice of their conscience and to the Holy Spirit. And by their prayers and their fidelity they will invisibly renew the life of the whole Church. This renewal will communicate itself to others who remain "in the world" and will help them also to regain a clearer vision, a sharper and more uncompromising appreciation of Christian truth. These will give themselves to apostolic work on a new level of seriousness and of faith. They will be able to discard fictitious gestures of zeal in favor of genuine self-sacrificing love. So when, as in our time, the whole world seems to have become one immense and idiotic fiction, and when the virus of mendacity creeps into every vein and organ of the social body, it would be abnormal and immoral if there were no reaction. It is even healthy that the reaction should sometimes take the form of outspoken protest, as long as we remember that solitude is no refuge for the rebellious. And if there is an element of protest in the solitary vocation, that element must be a matter of rigorous spirituality. It must be deep and interior, and intimately personal, so that the solitary is one who is critical, first of all, of himself. Otherwise he will divert himself with a fiction worse than that of all the others, becoming a more insane and self-opinionated liar than the worst of them, cheating no one more than himself. Solitude is not for rebels like this, and it promptly rejects them. The desert is for those who have felt a salutary despair of conventional and fictitious values, in order to hope in mercy and to be themselves merciful men to whom that mercy is promised. Such solitaries know the evils that are in other men because they experience these evils first of all in themselves.

Such men, out of pity for the universe, out of loyalty to mankind, and without a spirit of bitterness or of resentment, withdraw into the healing silence of the wilderness, or of poverty, or of obscurity, not in order to preach to others but to heal in themselves the wounds of the entire world.

13. The message of God's mercy to man must be preached. The word of truth must be proclaimed. No one can deny this. But there are not a few who are beginning to feel the futility of adding more words to the constant flood of language that pours meaninglessly over everybody, everywhere, from morning to night. For language to have meaning, there must be intervals of silence somewhere, to divide word from word and utterance from utterance. He who retires into silence does not necessarily hate language. Perhaps it is love and respect for language which impose silence upon him. For the mercy of God is not heard in words unless it is heard, both before and after the words are spoken, in silence.

14. There have always been, and always will be, men who are alone in the midst of society without realizing why. They are condemned to their strange isolation by temperament or circumstance, and they get used to it. It is not of these that I am speaking, but of those who having led active and articulate lives in the world of men, leave their old life behind, and go into the desert. The desert does not necessarily have to be physical—it can be found even in the midst of men. But it is not found by human aspirations or idealism. It is mysteriously designated by the finger of God.

15. There have always been solitaries who, by virtue of a special purity, and simplicity of heart, have been destined from their earliest youth to an eremitical and contemplative life, in some official form. These are the clear, uncomplicated vocations, and I do not speak explicitly of them here either. They have known from an early age that their destination was a Charterhouse or a Camaldolese cell. Or they have found their way, as though by unerring instinct, into the place

where they will be alone. The Church has welcomed these without question and without trouble into the "shadowy" (*umbratilis*) life of peace which she has reserved for her most favored children. There, in the peace and silence of a solitude fully recognized, protected, and approved by the Highest Authority of the Church, they live their lives, not without the sufferings and the complexities which in solitude are unavoidable, but in a peace and assurance which are a rare guarantee of a truly special vocation.

It is not of these that I speak but of the paradoxical, tormented solitaries for whom there is no real place; men and women who have not so much chosen solitude as been chosen by it. And these have not generally found their way into the desert either through simplicity or through innocence. Theirs is the solitude that is reached the hard way, through bitter suffering and disillusionment.

To say that they have been "found" and chosen by solitude is a metaphor that must not be taken to mean that they have been drawn into it entirely passively. The solitude of which I speak is not full grown and true until it has been elected by a deep interior decision. Solitude may choose and select a man for herself, but he is not hers unless he has accepted. On the other hand no amount of deciding will do any good, if one has not first been invited to make the decision. The door to solitude opens only from the inside. This is true of both solitudes, the exterior and the interior. No matter how alone one may be, if he has not been invited to interior solitude and accepted the invitation with full consciousness of what he is doing, he cannot be what I call a *monachos*, or solitary. But one who has made this choice and kept to it is always alone, no matter how many people there may be around him. Not that he is withdrawn from them, or that he is not one of them. His solitude is not of that order at all. It does not set him apart from them in contrast and self-affirmation. It affirms nothing. It is at the same time empty and universal. He is one, not by virtue of separation but by virtue of inner spiritual unity. And this inner unity is at the same time the inner unity of all. Needless to say, such unity is secret and unknown. Even those who enter it know it only, so to speak, by "unknowing."

It should therefore be clear that one who seeks to enter into this kind of solitude by affirming himself, and separating himself from others, and intensifying his awareness of his own individual being, is only travelling farther and farther away from it. But the one who has been found by solitude, and invited to enter it, and has entered freely, falls into the desert the way a ripe fruit falls out of a tree. It does not matter what kind of a desert it may be: in the midst of men or far from them. It is the one vast desert of emptiness which belongs to no one and to everyone. It is the place of silence where one word is spoken by God. And in that word are spoken both God Himself and all things.

16. Often the lonely and the empty have found their way into this pure silence only after many false starts. They have taken many wrong roads, even roads that were totally alien to their character and vocation. They have repeatedly contradicted themselves and their own inmost truth. Their very nature seems itself to be a contradiction. They have perhaps few "clear signs" of *any* vocation. But they end up nevertheless alone. Their way is to have no way. Their destiny is poverty, emptiness, anonymity.

17. Of course, everyone with any sense sees, from time to time, in a lucid moment, the folly and triviality of our conventionalized attitudes. It is possible for anyone to dream of liberty. But to undertake the wretched austerity of living in complete honesty, without convention and therefore without support, is quite another matter. That is why there exist communities of beatniks, of esoteric thinkers and cultists, of quasi-religious faddists, of Western followers of oriental religions. The break with the big group is compensated by enrollment in the little group. It is a flight not into solitude but into a protesting minority. Such a flight may be more or less honest, more or less honorable. Certainly it inspires the anger of those who believe themselves to be the "right thinking majority" and it necessarily comes in for its fair share of mockery on that account. Perhaps this mockery is so welcome as to contribute, negatively, to the process of falsification and corruption which these groups almost always undergo. They abandon one illusion which is forced on everyone and substitute for it another, more esoteric illusion, of their own making. They have the satisfaction of making a choice, but not the fulfillment of having chosen reality.

18. The true solitary is not called to an illusion, to the contemplation of himself as solitary. He is called to the nakedness and hunger of a more primitive and honest condition. The condition of a stranger (*xeniteia*) and a wanderer on the face of the earth, who has been called out of what was familiar to him in order to seek strangely and painfully after he knows not what.

And in demanding "honesty" of the hermit, let us not be too hypocritically exacting. He too may have his eccentricities. He may rely heavily on certain imperfect solutions to problems which his human weakness does not allow him to cope with fully. Let us not condemn him for failing to solve problems we have not even dared to face.

The solitary life is an arid, rugged purification of the heart. St. Jerome and St. Eucherius have written rhapsodies about the flowering desert, but Jerome was the busiest hermit that ever lived and Eucherius was a bishop who admired the hermit brethren of Lérins only from afar. The *eremi cultores*, the farmers of the desert sand, have had less to say about the experience. They have been washed out by dryness, and their burnt lips are weary of speech.

19. The solitary who no longer communicates with other men except for the bare necessities of life is a man with a special and difficult task. He is called to be, in some way, invisible. He soon loses all sense of his significance for the rest of the world. And yet that significance is great. The hermit has a very real place in a world like ours that has degraded the human person and lost all respect for that awesome loneliness in which each single spirit must confront the living God.

20. In the eyes of our conformist society, the hermit is nothing but a failure. He has to be a failure—we have absolutely no use for him, no place for him. He is outside all our projects, plans, assemblies, movements. We can countenance him as long as he remains only a fiction, or a dream. As soon as he becomes real, we are revolted by his insignificance, his poverty, his shabbiness, his total lack of status. Even those who consider themselves contemplatives often cherish a secret contempt for the solitary. For in the contemplative life of the hermit there is none of that noble security, that intelligent depth, that artistic finesse which the more academic contemplative seeks in his sedate respectability.

21. It has never been either practical or useful to leave all things and follow Christ. And yet it is spiritually prudent. Practical utility and supernatural prudence are sometimes flatly opposed to one another, as wisdom of the flesh and prudence of the spirit. Not that the spirit can never allow itself to accomplish things in a practical, temporal way. But it does not rest in purely temporal ends. Its accomplishments belong to a higher and more spiritual order—which is of course necessarily hidden. Practical utility has its roots in the present life. Supernatural prudence lives for the world to come. It weighs all things in the balance of eternity. Spiritual things have no weight for the "practical" man. The solitary life is something that cannot even tip his scales. It is "nothing," a non-entity. Yet St. Paul says: "The foolish things of the world hath God chosen that He may confound the wise, and the weak things of the world hath God chosen that He may confound the strong. And the base things of the world, and the things that are contemptible hath God chosen, and things that are not, that He might bring to nought things that are" (I Corinthians 1:27, 28).

And why is this? "That no flesh should glory in His sight." It is the invisible glory that is real. The empty horizons of the solitary life enable us to grow accustomed to a light that is not seen where the mirage of secular pursuits fascinates and deludes our gaze.

22. The hermit remains there to prove, by his lack of practical utility and the apparent sterility of his vocation, that cenobitic monks themselves ought to have little significance in the world, or indeed none at all. They are dead to the world, they should no longer cut a figure in it. And the world is dead to them. They are pilgrims in it, isolated witnesses of another kingdom. This of course is

the price they pay for universal compassion, for a sympathy that reaches all. The monk is compassionate in proportion as he is less practical and less successful, because the job of being a success in a competitive society leaves one no time for compassion.

The monk has all the more of a part to play in our world, because he has no proper place in it.

III. SPIRITUAL POVERTY

1. ONE OF THE most telling criticisms of the solitary may well be that even in his life of prayer he is less "productive." You would think that in his solitude he would quickly reach the level of visions, of mystical marriage, something dramatic at any rate. Yet he may well be poorer than the cenobite, *even in his life of prayer*. His is a weak and precarious existence, he has more cares, he is more insecure, he has to struggle to preserve himself from all kinds of petty annoyances, and often he fails to do so. His poverty is spiritual. It invades his whole soul as well as his body, and in the end his whole patrimony is one of insecurity. He enjoys the sorrow, the spiritual and intellectual indigence of the really poor. Obviously such a vocation has in it a grain of folly. Otherwise it is not what it is meant to be, a life of direct dependence on God, in darkness, insecurity, and pure faith. The life of the hermit is a life of material and physical poverty without visible support.

2. Of course, one must not exaggerate or be too absolute in this matter. Absolutism itself can become a kind of "fortune" and "honor." We must also face the fact that the average human being is incapable of a life in which austerity is without compromise. There comes a limit, beyond which human weakness cannot go, and where mitigation itself enters in as a subtle form of poverty. Maybe the hermit turns out, unaccountably, to have his ulcer just like the next man. No doubt he has to drink large quantities of milk and perhaps take medicines. This finally disposes of any hope of him becoming a legendary figure. He, too, worries. Perhaps he worries even more than others, for it is only in the minds of those who know nothing about it that the solitary life appears to be a life free from all care.

3. We must remember that Robinson Crusoe was one of the great myths of the middle class, commercial civilization of the eighteenth and nineteenth centuries: the myth not of eremitical solitude but of pragmatic individualism. Crusoe is a symbolical figure in an era when every man's house was his castle in the trees, but only because every man was a very prudent and resourceful citizen who knew how to make the best out of the least and could drive a hard bargain

with any competitor, even life itself. Carefree Crusoe was happy because he had an answer to everything. The real hermit is not so sure he has an answer.

4. It is true that the solitary life must also be a life of prayer and meditation, if it is to be authentically Christian. For the *monachos* in our context is purely and simply a man of God. This should be clear. But what prayer! What meditation! Nothing more like bread and water than this interior prayer of his! Utter poverty. Often an incapacity to pray, to see, to hope. Not the sweet passivity which the books extol, but a bitter, arid struggle to press forward through a blinding sandstorm. The solitary may well beat his head against a wall of doubt. That may be the full extent of his contemplation. Do not mistake my meaning. It is not a question of intellectual doubt, an analytical investigation of the theological, philosophical or some other truths. It is something else, a kind of unknowing of his own self, a kind of doubt that questions the very roots of his own existence, a doubt which undermines his very reasons for existing and for doing what he does. It is this doubt which reduces him finally to silence, and in the silence which ceases to ask questions, he receives the only certitude he knows: The presence of God in the midst of uncertainty and nothingness, as the only reality but as a reality which cannot be "placed" or identified.

Hence the solitary man says nothing, and does his work, and is patient (or perhaps impatient, I don't know), but generally he has peace. It is not the world's kind of peace. He is happy, but he never has a good time. He knows where he is going, but he is not "sure of his way," he just knows by going there. He does not see the way beforehand, and when he arrives, he arrives. His arrivals are usually departures from anything that resembles a "way." That is his way. But he cannot understand it. Neither can we.

5. Beyond and in all this, he possesses his solitude, the riches of his emptiness, his interior poverty but of course, it is not a possession. It is simply an established fact. It is there. It is assured. In fact, it is inescapable. It is everything. It contains God, surrounds him in God, plunges him in God. So great is his poverty that he does not even see God; so great are his riches that he is lost in God and lost to himself. He is never far enough away from God to see Him in perspective, or as an object. He is swallowed up in Him, and therefore so to speak, never sees Him at all.

6. All that we can say of this indigence of the lonely life must not make us forget the fact that this man is happy in his solitude, but especially because he has ceased to regard himself as a solitary in contradistinction to others who are not solitary. He simply is. And if he has been impoverished and set aside by the will of God, this is not a distinction, but purely and simply a fact. His solitude is sometimes frightening, sometimes a burden, yet it is more precious to him than

anything else because it is for him the will of God—not a thing willed by God, not an object decreed by a remote power, but simply the pressure, upon his own life, of that pure actuality which is the will of God, the reality of all that is real. His solitude is, for him, simply reality. He could not break away from this will even if he wanted to. To be prisoner of this love is to be free, and almost to be in paradise. Hence the life of solitude is a life of love without consolation, a life that is fruitful because it is pressed down and running over with the will of God; and all that has his will in it is full of significance, even when it appears to make no sense at all.

7. The terror of the lonely life is the mystery and uncertainty with which the will of God presses upon our soul. It is much easier, and gentler, and more secure to have the will of God filtered to us quietly through society, through decrees of men, through the orders of others. To take this will straight in all its incomprehensible, baffling mystery is not possible to one who is not secretly protected and guided by the Holy Spirit, and no one should try it unless he has some assurance that he really has been called to it by God. And this call, of course, should be made clear by Directors and Superiors. One has to be born into solitude carefully, patiently, and after long delay, out of the womb of society. One cannot rashly presume to become a solitary merely by his own will. This is no security outside the guidance of the Church.

8. The lone man remains in the world as a prophet to whom no one listens, as a voice crying in the desert, as a sign of contradiction. The world necessarily rejects him and in that act, rejects the dreaded solitude of God Himself. For that is what the world resents about God: His utter otherness, His absolute incapacity to be absorbed into the context of worldly and practical slogans, His mysterious transcendency which places Him infinitely beyond the reach of catchwords, advertisements, and politics. It is easier for the world to recreate a god in its own image, a god who justifies its own slogans, when there are no solitaries about to remind men of the solitude of God: the God Who cannot become a member of any purely human fellowship. And yet this Solitary God has called men to another fellowship, with Himself, through the passion and resurrection of Christ—through the solitude of Gethsemani and of Calvary, and the mystery of Easter, and the solitude of the Ascension: all of which precede the great communion of Pentecost.

9. The lonely man's function is to remain in existence as solitary, as poor and as unacceptable as God Himself in the souls of so many men. The solitary is there to tell them, in a way they can barely understand, that if they were able to discover and appreciate their own inner solitude they would immediately discover God and find out, from His word to them, that they are really persons.

10. It is often said that exterior solitude is not only dangerous, but totally unnecessary. Unnecessary because all that really matters is interior solitude. And this can be obtained without physical isolation.

There is in this statement a truth more terrible than can be imagined by those who make it, so readily and with so little awareness of the irony implicit in their words.

11. Indeed there is a special irony about solitude in community: that if you are called to solitude by God, even if you live in a community your solitude will be inescapable. Even if you are surrounded by the comfort and the assistance of others, the bonds that unite you with them on a trivial level break one by one so that you are no longer supported by them, that is, no longer sustained by the instinctive, automatic mechanisms of collective life. Their words, their enthusiasms become meaningless. Yet you do not despise them, or reject them. You try to find if there is not still some way to comprehend them and live by them. And you find that words have no value in such a situation. The only thing that can help you is the deep, wordless communion of genuine love.

At such a time it is a great relief to be put in contact with others by some simple task, some function of the ministry. Then you meet them not with your words or theirs, but with the words and sacramental gestures of God. The word of God takes on an ineffable purity and strength when it is seen as the only way in which a solitary can effectively reach the solitudes of others—the solitudes of which these others are unaware.

Then he realizes that he loves them more than ever: perhaps that he now loves them really for the first time. Made humble by his solitude, grateful for the work that brings him into contact with others, he still remains alone. There is no greater loneliness than that of an instrument of God who realizes that his words and his ministry, even though they be the words of God, can do nothing to change his loneliness: and yet that, beyond all distinction between mine and thine, they make him one with everyone he encounters.

12. What then is the conclusion? That this solitude of which we have been speaking, the solitude of the true *monachos*, of the lone one, is not and cannot be selfish. It is the opposite of selfish. It is the death and the forgetfulness of self. But what is self? The self that vanishes from this emptiness is the superficial, false social self, the image made up of the prejudices, the whimsy, the posturing, the pharisaic self-concern and the pseudo dedication which are the heritage of the individual in a limited and imperfect group.

There is another self, a true self, who comes to full maturity in emptiness and solitude—and who can, of course, begin to appear and grow in the valid, sacrificial, and creative self-dedication that belong to a genuine social existence. But note that even this social maturing of love implies at the same time the growth of a certain inner solitude.

Without solitude of some sort there is and can be no maturity. Unless one becomes empty and alone, he cannot give himself in love because he does not possess the deep self which is the only gift worthy of love. And this deep self, we immediately add, cannot be *possessed*. My deep self is not "something" which I acquire, or to which I "attain" after a long struggle. It is not mine, and cannot become mine. It is no "thing"—no object. It is "I."

The shallow "I" of individualism can be possessed, developed, cultivated, pandered to, satisfied: it is the center of all our strivings for gain and for satisfaction, whether material or spiritual. But the deep "I" of the spirit, of solitude, and of love cannot be "had," possessed, developed, perfected. It can only *be*, and *act* according to deep inner laws which are not of man's contriving, but which come from God. They are the Laws of the Spirit, who, like the wind, blows where He wills. This inner "I," who is always alone, is always universal; for in this inmost "I" my own solitude meets the solitude of every other man and the solitude of God. Hence it is beyond division, beyond limitation, beyond selfish affirmation. It is only this inmost and solitary "I" that truly loves with the love and the spirit of Christ. This "I" is Christ Himself, living in us: and we, in Him, living in the Father.

7

Theology of Creativity

This essay was first published in *The American Benedictine Review* 11 (September 1960), 197-213, as one segment of a three-part symposium entitled "The Catholic and Creativity," along with contributions by William Davidson, M.D., on "The Psychology of Creativity" and an interview with Brother Antoninus, OP (William Everson), on "The Artist and Religious Life." (The three pieces were also issued together as an offprint.) Merton's contribution was completed in July 1960, the date found in his own handwriting on the revised typescript. An excerpt was included in the original edition of *A Thomas Merton Reader* (527-30) but was omitted from the revised version; the complete essay was included in *Literary Essays* (355-70). In discussing the topic, Merton rejects both the superficial use of "creativity" to describe everything from slick advertising to eruptions of unfocused subconscious energy, and more thoughtful but still inadequate conceptions that equate creativity with spontaneous self-expression, or conformity to supposed "laws" of historical development, or mere productivity, or individual achievement of the artist-hero. Drawing on the insights of four contemporary religious aestheticians from a variety of traditions, Paul Tillich's charge to the artist to confront the threat of meaninglessness in an alienated world, D. T. Suzuki's Zen-influenced challenge to the "romantic" notion of the artist as isolated genius, Ananda Coomaraswamy's emphasis on discipline and craftsmanship, and Jacques Maritain's focus on the "creative intuition" that links the mystery in the depths of the authentic self with the mystery at the heart of creation, Merton proposes a theology of authentic creativity as a renunciation of spurious autonomy and a participation in the divine creativity, a vocation to renew the face of the earth not reserved to the artist but shared in some way by all humans made in the image of God.

T HE MOST OBVIOUS characteristic of our age is its destructiveness. This can hardly be doubted. We have developed an enormous capacity to build and to change our world, but far more enormous are our capacities for destruction. It is significant that the age of atomic war is the one in which man has become preoccupied with what he calls "creativity," and preoccupied with it almost to the point of obsession. The problem of creativity, when approached from the semantic viewpoint, reveals itself almost as a problem of guilt. The function of this paper is by no means the investigation of this admittedly fascinating and timely question. But the possibility has to be taken into account, otherwise a discussion of creativity, which is supposed, in the end, to be theological, will not make sense at all.

We must begin by facing the ambivalence which makes so much of our talk about creativity absurd because it is fundamentally insincere. Why insincere? Because it is so glib, so all-embracing. The popular use of the word creativity is so facile that one feels immediately that it is a pure evasion. It is a trick to avoid thought, and to avoid real communication. When everything is "creative," nothing is creative. But nowadays everything is called creative: we have creative salesmanship, meaning probably obnoxiously aggressive and vulgar salesmanship. We have creative advertising, which is merely outrageously whimsical or arbitrary. We have creative ways of doing everything under the sun, and in every case what is called "creative" is not even more original than what it is supposed to supersede; it implies nothing but a more ponderously stupid emphasis on what is already too familiar. In a word, being "creative" seems to mean little more than rushing forward with breakneck impetuosity into the conventional, the vulgar, or the absurd.

But there is a more serious complaint against our obsession with creativity. The inanity of the popular, commercialized degradation of this concept is merely an innocent "cover" for its self-contradictions when it is used on a deeper level. And here we come face to face with the implication of guilt.

The term "creativity" may be seen, if we observe carefully how it is used, to be in some cases nothing less than a justification of destructiveness. It is a negation, an un-making, justified by a positive-sounding name: "creation." There are, admittedly, almost infinitely interesting possibilities in broken pieces of machinery, ruined houses, even the smashed bodies of human beings. The revelation of these grim but arresting qualities in horrifying objects, contemplated from a certain detached viewpoint, is in fact a positive aesthetic value, and all the more positive by its implied contrast with empty and formalistic attempts at conventional "beauty." Nevertheless, it should be clear that to take delight in a symbolic, or represented, destruction is not far removed from taking delight in actual destruction. The artist may have a perfect right, perhaps even a duty, to protest as effectively and as vocally as he can against man's present state of alienation in a world that seems to be without meaning because of the moral, cultural, and economic crises of society. This protest certainly can be creative, and there is no doubt that it can bring forth great and living art. But when the protest has so taken possession of the artist that he is no longer articulate, and can only express it by gestures equivalent to dashing his brains out against the wall, then there is no longer question of creativity. What we have is destruction. It may be terribly pitiable, it may be a matter of urgent importance, but creativity is just not the honest word for tongue-tied frustration, helplessness, and self-hate. This means that not every expression of frustration and despair is creative, only such as are really articulate.

Our misuse of the word and concept of creativity has robbed us of a standard of judgment. We can no longer tell when an artist is expressing something human or merely screaming; we do not even try to interpret the noise, we just react to it one way or another, believing that the mere fact of having a reaction is somehow "creative." One reason for this seems to be that we have begun, out of resentment, to dissociate the creative from the human. We now tend to assume that a humanistic outlook frustrates the real creative urge, which is in some way subhuman, or even antihuman. But this makes our "creativity" nothing more than a destructive and negative reaction against that very element of life and spirit upon which true creativity depends.

At this point, though a partisan declaration is really not called for, it is necessary to make a personal statement in regard to modern art movements, including those that are most experimental and extreme. I want to say quite clearly and emphatically that I am for the people who experiment in modern art. I have in other places and contexts made known my admiration for Picasso, Matisse, Rouault, etc. In this I share the taste of my time and society. I do not intend to call into question the "creativity" of such great artists, though I must admit that the traditional, classic art of the past, especially primitive Italian, Byzantine, and Oriental sacred art, seem to me to be vastly more important and significant. I am interested in abstract art, surrealism, fauvism, action painting, and all the rest. It seems to me that the men who experiment in action painting have every right to do what they are doing, and that they have a claim upon our respectful attention, though I do not believe the publicity and money they receive are in proportion to their so far slight achievements. And though I am persuaded that they have every right to do what they are doing, I find it hard to get very excited about the results. Most action painting is to me little more than a pleasantly intriguing accident, no more worthy of insult than of praise. It is what it is. Comment on it would be absurd, and I suppose that is why the enormous amount of favorable comment that is actually made is couched in peculiarly earnest doubletalk which, if it were worth interpreting, would probably turn out to mean nothing whatever. Or perhaps it is simply a justification of its own meaninglessness.

When I reflect that the artistic history of the past decade recorded, among other things, the "first one-ape show" held in London, it becomes clear to me that the term "creativity" is all too likely to be used today as a pure cliché. There may well be a fortuitous design in the ape's "paintings," and one could probably find in them as many forms as in a Rorschach inkblot. But this applies to everything else under the sun: the grain in wood, stains on a damp wall, the fence of a vacant lot covered with tattered posters, and, for that matter, even the paintings of the most absurd and conventional academicians. If we include the ape, there is no reason for excluding the professional bootlickers who painted portraits of Hitler and Stalin, though doubtless in their case it is not the "art" that is creative but the "action painting" of the tongue on the leader's boot.

We find ourselves confronted with a situation where everything is creative. The sweaty palms of the frustrated businessman are "creating" for him a symbol of his frustration. But what does this mean? Frustration is due precisely to the incapacity for positive, constructive, creative activity. Creation in this sense is then nothing else but frustration failing to express itself freely and normally, calling desperately for help in a way that fails to be heard or understood. It is quite true that a neurotic symptom is a positive sign, but it is a sign of a negation, of a lack of creativity, or of a frustrated creativity. When everything is creative, nothing is creative. When nothing is creative, everything tends to be destructive, or at least to invite destruction. Our creativity is in great measure simply the expression of our destructiveness, the guarded, despairing admission of destructiveness that cries for help without admitting it. The only positive thing left in our destructiveness is its bitter anguish. This, at least, can claim to be. This has creative possibilities.

These initial reflections may seem to be unnecessarily pessimistic. They are not proposed as anything more than suggestions, or questions. I do not know how true they may be, but it seems to me they offer material for serious thought. I will not insist on the paradoxes I have proposed. Putting them aside, it can be said quite fairly and objectively that there are four misleading senses of creativity in current use. No doubt there are more than four, but these seem to be characteristic of our confusions on the subject.

In order to understand what is wrong with these conceptions we must first begin with what is right in them. They all seem to be a more or less vital reaction against lifeless formality and aesthetic cliché. Three of them are explicitly concerned with the sincerity and spontaneity of the artist and with the reality of his art. They encourage him to fight for the spiritual freedom he needs if he is to be a genuine artist who makes something new, something that lives with a life of its own, a new "creation." Creativity in this sense is a healthy reaction against conventionalism and academic inertia.

I. WE FIND THE word "creativity" quite often used to signify original and spontaneous self-expression, particularly in art. This meaning of the term is popular wherever men are concerned with the self-realization of the individual, with personalist values. Creativity is a fruit of personalism. The free and spontaneous person has something original to say, and he is able to say it in paint, in poetry, in music, in his house, in his work, or simply in his way of confronting life. Conversely, if his "creativity" can be allowed to develop without restraint when he is young, he will stand a better chance of growing into a well-rounded person.

I have used these clichés seriously and with respect. The need for spontaneity, for spiritual freedom, for personal growth, is certainly urgent: nothing more so. But when "creativity" and "personalism" slide into the context of popular mythology, they are not going to help us achieve this end. On the contrary, they may all too easily frustrate it. It should not be hard to see that this thoroughly understandable and commendable idea of personalist creativity has been corrupted by the mass media. Once corrupted, it is no longer creativity but mere wishful thinking. It is part of an optimistic myth, the myth that we can somehow escape the responsibilities of laboring, suffering, disciplining ourselves, sacrificing ourselves in order to carry out a difficult vocation. In the name of "life," creativity substitutes itself for responsibility and becomes an evasion of responsibility. But life is superficial and invalid as long as it is a mere evasion. The use of fine long words is no help. If "creativity" is mere laziness, narcissism, and self-display, then no amount of spontaneity can justify it, enliven it, or make it "original."

Hence the danger is apparent of a "creativity" that is merely a matter of relaxing and "doing what you want." This illusion is supported by the false idea that it is easy for us to know what we really want, and that as soon as we stop doing what someone else, what society demands of us, we can become "creative." One is tempted to say that this concept of creativity, when applied to primary education, has been notable above all for its effectiveness in producing juvenile delinquents. That might be unfair. But at any rate this concept is too tolerant, too vague, too dim, and by its light the artist cannot see his way to anything except doodling.

II. IF THE CHARACTERISTIC error of the capitalist world, in this matter, is to equate creativity with individualistic self-expression, Communists go to the other extreme. Creativity is not in the individual but in the party, or rather in history; but the party is the only infallible interpreter of the enigma of history. The party is creative because it is the midwife of history. Creative work is done only when the artist expresses the hidden dynamism of historical events and situations, and this means nothing more nor less than acting as the servant of a political program which is conceived to be based on a correct understanding of this hidden dynamism. The artist does not contemplate the inner creative spirit at work in history—this would be a noble and indeed a Christian conception. He merely paints pictures that make the worker happy about "creating" the new world which will be the inevitable result of overfulfilled production quotas. This concept of creativity really does not take art seriously. Art is only a superstructure whose creativity, if any, depends on the economic base upon which it stands. The worst art can be creative if its politics are correct, for then it is presumably built on a creative foundation.

There is no need to deplore what this sophistry has produced in art; everybody knows the story. However, it would be a mistake to suppose that this delusion is confined to Russia. Besides the personalist approach which is the more popular one here, there is a very widespread belief in American business and scientific circles that creativity is a matter of teamwork. It is not the individual who is creative but the team, and the more the individual submerges his originality and personal differences in the collective project, the more creative that project will turn out to be. This has been fully discussed in books like *Organization Man*.

III. A THIRD DELUSION would be to equate creativity with productiveness: a quantitative view which tempts everyone in a consumer society. An obsession with fecundity might well frustrate genuine creative potentialities in the artist. Once you get started, it is always easy to do too much, to keep on reproducing over and over again the one or two works the public has come to expect from you. Of course this makes money. It means popularity, a vulgar error. But the mass media give it such encouragement that it ruins very many. We ought to remember that an artist who paints only one or two pictures in his lifetime may well be more creative than one who paints one or two a week.

IV. THE FOURTH DELUSION brings us back, in some respects, to the first. We return to the idea of original self-expression, but this time we consider it on a deeper level. We find ourselves face to face with another myth, the myth of the genius as hero and as high priest in a cult of art that tends to substitute itself for religion. This delusion is serious, and it is here that "creativity" sometimes takes on a demonic quality which makes it one of the tragic temptations of our era. One of the most tragic of its aspects is the fact that the weaknesses of conventional religiosity are in some sense to blame for this apostasy of the artist. It is the inarticulateness of the preacher that moves the artist to assume a prophetic irresponsibility intended to justify not so much his art as his cult of himself. For here what matters is no longer art or the work of art as such. Here art stands out as the monument of genius, not as the symbol of a transcendent spiritual reality but as the ikon of the artist himself. The artist becomes fascinated by his own gifts and by their superhuman quality. He renounces everything else, including morality and sanity, in order to devote himself exclusively to their magic. His life becomes a deliberate cultivation of experience intended to open up new depths in his genius. Indeed it sometimes seems to him that a full, connatural acquaintance with evil and with despair has become a sacred obligation for him because only in this way can he fully assert his protest against the conventions and hypocrisies of a society he despises. His vocation is to devote his magic gifts as fully as possible to negation and to defiance, and if in saying "no" he can also explode with self-satisfaction, then all the better for him and for his art. He is a professional mystic-in-reverse.

It does not matter how somber or perverse his experiences may be; what matters is not their beauty, their significance, or even their reality, but the fact that they are his experiences. If they are sinful, degraded, subhuman, this makes no difference. Indeed it makes his experiences even more significant. The genius with his magic soul has descended into hell for a season of satanically detached lucidity which frightens ordinary men. This assures him of his own superiority and confirms him in his "prophetic" vocation.

Unfortunately this is a complacency that is no less complacent for being impure. It offers no escape from bourgeois smugness, for it is the same smugness turned inside out. This accounts for the dullness, the sameness, the conventionality, and the absurdity of all the second-rate followers of the few rare ones whose voices, speaking out of the shadows with Baudelaire and Rimbaud, impose upon the hearer the silence and the awe that are fitting in the presence of tragedy.

Here again, we cannot help being impressed by the inherent destructiveness of this kind of creativity, even when it is also genuinely creative.

As Jacques Maritain has pointed out, the artist who assumes this tragic role also takes upon himself the burden of forming the consciences of the lost, and guiding those who have not been able to find meaning or orientation in traditional philosophies.

In this cult of art, in which the artist is hero and high priest, and the work of art is an ikon or a fetish of the creative genius which produced it, we find a pitifully deluded hope of immortality. Though all must die and be forgotten, all must vanish into the void, the work of art remains as a monument to the options made by the unusually gifted one, the supersoul, the magic genius who dared to experience everything and who, in doing so, transcended everything—life, society, ethics, even his own art.

This is the religion of some modern intellectuals who are incapable of committing themselves to a religious, philosophical, or political ideal. They devote themselves to a cult of experience, a cult of "creativity" for its own sake. And creativity here becomes synonymous with despair. Hence it is not hard to see why a careful investigation of the word has been necessary.

In caricaturing the postures of those I believe to be deluded I have not intended in any way to minimize the residue of truth in their delusions. Of the various philosophical approaches to the problem four are chosen which have very much in common. They are all religious, and three of them are also existentialist. These existentialist and religious views all express a sympathy and respect for the real responsibility of the artist to his gifts. They take into account the importance of the aesthetic experience, its need for sincerity and depth. They well know art's exigencies for honesty at any price, even at the price of clarity, beauty, and so-called perfection of form. They pay full respect to the subjectivism which seems to be the only guarantee of honesty at the present moment. In a word they take into account the originality and genius of the artist, and they recognize his broadly "prophetic" role. But at the same time, in one way or another, they remind him of his responsibility toward the work done, and they introduce an element of salutary objectivity into the discussion. They strike a note which distracts the artist from complete obsession with himself and with his experience. They bring him back from the world of devils into the world of men and perhaps even of angels. Such things are still possible.

I. PAUL TILLICH HAS clearly seen the dialectic of creativity and destructivity which underlies the art of our time, a dialectic which expresses man's alienation from reality. Man is no longer able to preserve any depth in his encounter with reality, which has "lost its inner transcendence, . . . its transparency for the eternal."[1] Struggling to adjust himself in a world which becomes opaque and replaces God, man tries to endow himself with God's own creative powers. But in order to do so he has to forget his own limitations, his own essential reality. He lives in contradiction with himself. The reaction of religious thought and art against this demonic trend has been abortive: a feeble insistence on conventional symbols, expressed in a new style.

For Tillich, the only valid way out for the artist is to face squarely the very

---

1. Paul Tillich, *Theology of Culture* (New York: Oxford University Press, 1959), p. 43.

anxiety and meaninglessness inherent in contemporary technological culture and "live creatively, expressing the predicament of the most sensitive people of our time in cultural production."[2] A valid religious art in our time will then be a "creative expression of destructive trends." This is a sound justification of modern art when it is the expression of humility and anguish, not of pride and revolt. It is precisely pride that prevents modern man from achieving depth, even when he most seeks it.

II. THE BUDDHIST EXISTENTIALIST thinker Daisetz Suzuki, well known as the major modern spokesman of Zen, has profoundly significant pages on Japanese art, and these have the advantage of being lavishly illustrated.[3] Writing only of Japanese and Chinese art, Suzuki is interested in the work of art as an expression of Zen experience. The experience and its expression must not be separated, for, as he says, "In Zen, experience and expression are one."[4] What is this Zen experience? It is often explained by the term "self-realization," but this can easily be interpreted in a sense exactly contrary to its intended meaning. The "self" that is "realized" in Zen is by no means the "personality of the genius" discussed above. On the contrary, whereas the demonic experience of pseudo-creativity involves the affirmation of man's false, exterior self, the Zen experience is a deliverance from this false self. Rather it is an emptiness, an "original suchness" in which no such false and illusory self can be present at all. Zen tolerates no phenomenal ego that can be affirmed and placed over against other selves, other objects. Suzuki claims that the Zen experience is a leap out of relative, subject-object confrontations into pure "isness," in which there is no reflection upon self, no awareness of oneself as knower, or of one's own knowledge. There is simply "what is," an immediate grasp of existential fact, undimmed and undisturbed by mediate reflection or conceptual analysis. Is the "suchness" discovered by Zen a higher and more spiritual self? At times this is explicitly stated. Suzuki, at certain moments, talks like a Western personalist. But always behind his personalism we face the protean metaphysic of Buddhism. It is my own opinion that Buddhism is not as negative in its attitude to man's personality as is generally thought. The "ego" is not the "person" in the highest and most spiritual sense of the word. In abolishing the ego to discover the higher self, Zen, which Suzuki explicitly claims is "not pantheistic," asserts a peculiar, indefinable personalism of its own.

---

2. Ibid., p. 46.

3. Cf., *Zen and Japanese Culture* (Princeton, N.J.: Princeton University Press, 1959).

4. Ibid., p. 6.

The Zen artist does not "study Zen in order to paint." He does not, as is sometimes thought, practice meditation as a means to artistic experience and expression. Zen meditation is not a preliminary step to artistic creation. Indeed the Zen man does not strictly speaking practice meditation at all, in any sense familiar to us in the West. Rather he enters into a purifying struggle against conceptual knowledge, in which he "sweats out" his attachment to images, ideas, symbols, metaphors, analytic judgments, etc., as means for grasping, appreciating, and understanding reality. Instead of this, he seeks to recover an immediate, direct intuition: not so much an intuition "of" being as an intuition which is rooted in and identified with his very existence: an intuition in which the existent knows existence, or "isness," while completely losing sight of itself as a "knowing subject."

In the case of a Zen artist, there is then no artistic reflection. The work of art springs "out of emptiness" and is transferred in a flash, by a few brush strokes, to paper. It is not a "representation of" anything, but rather it is the subject itself, existing as light, as art, in a drawing which has, so to speak, "drawn itself." The work then is a concretized intuition: not however presented as a unique experience of a specially endowed soul, who can then claim it as his own. On the contrary, to make any such claim would instantly destroy the character of "emptiness" and suchness which the work might be imagined to have. For the Zen man to pretend to share with another "his" experience would be the height of absurdity. Whose experience? Shared with whom? The artist might well be brusquely invited to go home and consider the question: "Who do you think you are, anyway?" I do not know if this question is recorded among the traditional *koans*, but it deserves to be.

The chief thing about Zen in its relation to art is precisely that the "artist," the "genius as hero," completely vanishes from the scene. There is no self-display, because the "true self," which functions in Zen experience, is empty, invisible, and incapable of being displayed. A disciple once complained to a Zen master that he was unsettled in his mind. The master said: "All right, give me your mind and I will settle it for you." The disciple's helplessness to pick up his mind and hand it over to somebody else gave him some idea of the nature of his "problems." One cannot begin to be an artist, in Suzuki's sense, until he has become "empty," until he has disappeared.

These might seem like gratuitously confusing paradoxes. But fortunately Suzuki's numerous contacts with the West have given him the ability to explain himself in Christian terms. He translates his basic Zen idea of art into terms familiar to us:

When an art presents [the intuitively grasped mysteries of life] in a most profound and creative manner, it moves us to the depths of our being;

art then becomes a divine work. The greatest productions of art, whether painting, music, sculpture or poetry, have invariably this quality—something approaching the work of God. The artist, at the moment when his creativeness is at its height, is transformed into an agent of the creator. This supreme moment in the life of an artist, when expressed in Zen terms, is the experience of *satori*. To experience *satori* is to become conscious of the Unconscious [*mushin*, no-mind] psychologically speaking. Art has always something of the Unconscious about it. The *satori* experience cannot be attained by the ordinary means of teaching and learning. It has its own technique in pointing to the presence in us of a mystery that is beyond intellectual analysis. . . . Where *satori* flashes, there is the tapping of creative energy.[5]

This same Oriental concept of the artist was developed in a masterly way by the late Ananda Coomaraswamy, in various articles now buried in the files of art magazines. These articles ought to be gathered together and published. Speaking of Balinese dancers, Coomaraswamy alludes to their essentially passive and "limp" attitude, which enables them to respond to the will of an invisible master who, so to speak, moves them in the sacred dance.[6] Coomaraswamy quotes the Gospel, in which Christ says, "I do nothing of myself," and adds a beautifully significant line of Boehme: "Thou shalt do nothing but forsake thy own will, that which thou callest 'I' or 'thyself.' By which means all thy evil properties will grow weak, faint and ready to die; and then thou wilt sink down again into that from which thou art originally sprung."

Coomaraswamy comments:

The dancer is in fact not expressing "herself" but altogether an artist, inspired: her condition is quite properly described as one of trance or ecstasy. The whole procedure is a carrying over into art of the vital principle of resignation. Religion, and culture, sacred and profane, are [here] undivided.[7]

III. COOMARASWAMY JOINED WITH his friend Eric Gill in a vehement protest against the modern heresy of a pseudo-personalist art cult in which the genius is hero and high priest. Both Gill and Coomaraswamy derided this myth of our

---

5. Ibid., pp. 219-20.
6. Cf. Ananda Coomaraswamy, "Spiritual Paternity," *Psychiatry, Journal of the Biology and Pathology of Interpersonal Relations* 3 (August 1945), pp. 17-36.
7. Ibid., p. 28.

marketing society in which the artist, the practitioner of the "fine arts," is a very "special kind of man" whose "highly developed sensibility" is put on display. They protested against the dishonest use of the "fine arts" to justify the alienation of man in modern industrial society by providing him with a second-hand spirituality in art for art's sake. According to this view, we might describe the artist as the Orpheus in a kind of modern mystery cult. He immolates himself on the altar of art, and the devout public is saved from the Hades of industrialism in a vicariously salvific bath of "culture." Coomaraswamy and Gill declared that the artist is not a special kind of man, but every man is a special kind of artist. Both Coomaraswamy and Gill insisted with the greatest emphasis on the artist's responsibility to his work. He had to "make things right" irrespective of the quality of his artistic experience. In no circumstances was his experience to be exploited or displayed for its own sake. This strong and salutary reaction against the narcissistic cult of genius, with its false "creativity," can only be commended.

IV. JACQUES MARITAIN, WHILE clinging to St. Thomas as fervently as Eric Gill, has insisted more on the creative intuition of the artist and poet.[8] He proposes a reconciliation between Eastern and Western views. Whereas the Orient is utterly unconcerned with the artist's conscious "self," it nevertheless reveals his creative subjectivity. While Western art has in the last few centuries concentrated on the artist's subjectivity, it also tends to grasp and disclose the hidden mystery of things. However, Maritain takes account of the modern artist's tragic "craving for magical knowledge and his dismissal of beauty." He points out that certain modern art movements have consciously taken upon themselves a prophetic function precisely in the denial and rejection of beauty for the sake of the artist's own self-assertion or for the manifestation of his magic and prophetic gifts. In a more recent book,[9] Maritain stresses the artist's responsibility to his own gifts, to his subjectivity, to his creativity, which demands his complete, dedicated loyalty as artist. But he also shows that as a member of society the artist has other loyalties and obligations which cannot be "sacrificed" on the altar of his art.

Of the four views discussed, those of Maritain and Tillich are most sympathetic to the modern artist and the most ready to accept him on his own terms. True to the Western and personalist climate in which they write, these distinguished Christian thinkers are willing to excuse and accept very much

---

8. Cf., Jacques Maritain, *Creative Intuition in Art and Poetry* (New York: Pantheon, 1953).

9. *The Responsibility of the Artist* (New York: Scribner's, 1960).

that is negative, even much that is sick and decadent, in the name of the inherent dialectic between creativity and destruction in the modern world. Chiefly concerned with modern and Western art, Maritain and Tillich obviously have much to say about, and in favor of, the hidden spiritual possibilities in overtly secular creativities. More intent on modern nonreligious art, their viewpoint is generally less explicitly spiritual than that of the Orientals quoted. Our own Christian tradition is just as rich as the Oriental in examples of the higher "self-lessness" of the truly creative art. Maritain says of Dante:

> The ego of the man has disappeared in the creative Self of the poet. Theological faith itself, the most sacred belief, has entered the work through the instrumentality of creative emotion and poetic knowledge and passed through the lake of disinterestedness and of creative innocence.[10]

Having taken account of four religious philosophies of creativity and having carefully dismissed the main secular delusions on the subject, our conclusion can now be drawn. This conclusion will not be a fully developed theological statement, only a few hints and suggestions as to how some such statement might eventually be formulated. How shall we prepare ourselves to consider the theology of creativity?

The secular caricature is a futile and demonic attempt to squeeze divine powers out of man. Since there is no genuine creativity apart from God, the man who attempts to be a "creator" outside of God and independent of him is forced to fall back on magic. The sin of the wizard is not so much that he usurps and exercises a real preternatural power, but that his postures travesty the divine by degrading man's freedom in absurd and servile manipulations of reality. The dignity of man is to stand before God on his own feet, alive, conscious, alert to the light that has been placed in him, and perfectly obedient to that light. Wizardry and idolatry obscure the light, dim man's vision, and reduce him to a state of infatuated self-absorption in which he plays at unveiling and displaying powers that were meant to remain secret, not in the sense that they must be concealed from others, but in the sense that the artist ought not to be wasting his own attention upon them or calling the attention of others to them. He should be using them in an "empty" and disinterested manner for the good of others and for the glory of God instead of exploiting them to draw attention to himself. The commandment "to make no graven image" is designed first of all to protect man against his inveterate temptation to make gods in his own image, gods in which he can objectify and venerate the divinely given powers he finds

---

10. *Creative Intuition*, p. 379.

in himself. By this magic man seeks to enjoy in himself those powers that were given him as means to find fulfillment beyond and above himself. This bending back upon self, this fixation upon the exterior self was, for St. Augustine, one of the principal elements in the fall of Adam.[11]

Man's true creativity is lost, then, with his loss of innocence, selflessness, and simplicity. Oblivious of his external self and empty of self, man was originally one with God his creator. So intimate was their union that the creator could live and act with perfect freedom in his created instrument. Having fallen, and been redeemed in Christ, man is once again able to recover this state of innocence and union, in and through Christ. The Spirit of God, the *Creator Spiritus* who brooded over the waters before the world came into being, dwells in man and broods over the abyss of his human spirit, seeking to call forth from it a new world, a new spiritual creation, in union with the liberty of man redeemed in Christ. The theology of creativity will necessarily be the theology of the Holy Spirit re-forming us in the likeness of Christ, raising us from death to life with the very same power which raised Christ from the dead.[12] The theology of creativity will also be a theology of the image and likeness of God in man. The restoration of our creativity is simply one aspect of our recovery of our likeness to God in Christ. The image of God in man is his freedom, say St. Bernard and St. Gregory of Nyssa. The likeness of God in man is fully restored when man's freedom is perfectly united with the divine freedom, and when, consequently, man acts in all things as God acts. Or rather when God and man act purely and simply as one. Since "God is love" then for man to be restored to the likeness of God, all his acts must be pure and disinterested love, lacking all taint of that *proprium* which makes him aware of himself as a separate, insecure subject of inordinate needs which he seeks to satisfy at somebody else's expense. Creativity becomes possible insofar as man can forget his limitations and his selfhood and lose himself in abandonment to the immense creative power of a love too great to be seen or comprehended.

A theology of creativity might, then, meditate at some length on the first few chapters of Genesis, the narrative of the creation and the fall. Especially important is Genesis 2:15-24, in which Adam appears as God's collaborator in governing paradise and in which he is given the power to name the animals as he sees fit: "for whatsoever Adam called any living creature, the same is its name." The most significant part of this passage would be sought in the typical sense of verses 21-24, on the creation of Eve. The mystery of Christ and his Church

---

11. *De Trinitate*, xii, ii (PL 42:1007).
12. Ephesians 1:17-21.

would be the very heart of any fully developed theology of creativity. Patristic works like St. Gregory of Nyssa's *De Hominis Opificio* might furnish a rich variety of intuitions from which to start building a synthesis. We would, of course, have to ransack the works of Origen and St. Augustine. Among the scholastic sources, we ought not to neglect the magnificent *Collationes in Hexaemeron* of St. Bonaventure. Valuable materials for study can only be briefly indicated here.

It would above all be necessary to disentangle the various threads of thought about man's creativity as individual person and man's creativity in society. There can be no doubt that a theology of creativity would give an entirely new perspective to the distorted view produced by undue emphasis on the exceptional personality of the "genius" and his complete independence from all ethical and aesthetic norms by virtue of his talented personality. But the theological view would do nothing to diminish the value of the person; on the contrary, situating the person in his right place in relation to other men and to God, our theology would liberate in him the deepest potentialities of his nature and the highest, most secret endowments of divine grace.

The creativity of the Christian person must be seen in relation to the creative vocation of the new Adam, the mystical person of the "whole Christ." The creative will of God has been at work in the cosmos since he said: "Let there be light." This creative *fiat* was not uttered merely at the dawn of time. All time and all history are a continued, uninterrupted creative act, a stupendous, ineffable mystery in which God has signified his will to associate man with himself in his work of creation. The will and power of the Almighty Father were not satisfied simply to make the world and turn it over to man to run it as best he could. The creative love of God was met, at first, by the destructive and self-centered refusal of man: an act of such incalculable consequences that it would have amounted to a destruction of God's plan, if that were possible. But the creative work of God could not be frustrated by man's sin. On the contrary, sin itself entered into that plan. If man was first called to share in the creative work of his heavenly Father, he now became involved in the "new creation," the redemption of his own kind and the restoration of the cosmos, purified and transfigured, into the hands of the Father. God himself became man in order that in this way man could be most perfectly associated with him in this great work, the fullest manifestation of his eternal wisdom and mercy.

The Christian dimensions of creativity are then to be meditated in the light of such texts as Ephesians 1:8-10 (the re-establishment of all things in Christ); Colossians 1:9-29 (the work of God building the Church of saints united in Christ, the "firstborn of every creature," and through him reconciling all things to himself). In this text, particularly, we see the creative role of suffering. This is very important. It is the reply to the secular and demonic overemphasis on the individual, his self-fulfillment in art for its own sake. Here, on the contrary, we see that the cross is the center of the new creation: the tree of life, instead of the tree of the knowledge of good and evil. He who has approached the tree of the knowledge of good and evil has tasted the intoxicating fruit of his own special excellence but he dies the death of frustration. He becomes the prisoner of his own gifts and he sticks to his own excellence as if it were flypaper. There is no joy for him because he is alienated from life, love, and communion in creativity by his own demonic self-assertion, which automatically involves a rejection of suffering, of dependence, of charity, and of obedience.

On the contrary, it is the renunciation of our false self, the emptying of self in the likeness of Christ, that brings us to the threshold of that true creativity in which God himself, the creator, works in and through us. The fact that the Christian renounces his own limited ends and satisfactions in order to achieve something greater than he can see or understand means the sacrifice of immediate visible results. But it also means that the efficacy of his action becomes lasting as well as universal. Such creativity does not stop with a little ephemeral success here and there: it reaches out to the ends of time and to the limits of the universe.

This may sound like hyperbole; but this is creativity in a new and spiritual dimension, which is its full Christian dimension. And this applies not only to the artist, but to every Christian. To adapt Coomaraswamy's phrase, one might say "the creative Christian is not a special kind of Christian, but every Christian has his own creative work to do, his own part in the mystery of the 'new creation.'" Would that we were all more aware of this. Our awareness would produce a climate that would have a special meaning for the artist. The way for sacred art to become more "creative" is not just for the artist to study new and fashionable trends and try to apply them to sacred or symbolic themes. It is for the artist to enter deeply into his Christian vocation, his part in the work of restoring all things in Christ. But this is not his responsibility alone. This is the responsibility of the whole Church and everybody in it. We all have an obligation to open our eyes to the eschatological dimensions of Christian creativity, for, as St. Paul says, "all creation is groaning" for the final manifestation of this finished work, the only work that has an eternal importance: the full revelation of God by the restoration of all things in Christ.

8

Christian Culture Needs Oriental Wisdom

On June 16, 1961, Merton wrote in his journal, "Since it rained I stayed in and wrote the review of the 'Two Chinese Classics' sent by Paul Sih (*Tao Te Ching* and *Hsaio Ching*)" (*Turning Toward the World*, 128). The previous month, Sih, Director of the Center for Asian Studies at St. John's University in New York, had sent Merton new translations, published by the Center, of these two works (the first by John Wu, with whom Merton had begun corresponding in March 1961 and who would soon become a close friend and collaborator) (*Hidden Ground of Love*, 549). Merton intended the review for *Jubilee*, but having just published "Classic Chinese Thought," the first of Merton's essays on Oriental traditions, in January of that year, editor Ed Rice apparently decided this sequel might be a bit of "overkill" for his readers and returned it to Merton, as he relates in a January 28, 1962, letter to Sih, giving him carte blanche to place it elsewhere, making any necessary changes and corrections (*Hidden Ground of Love*, 551). The essay duly appeared as "Two Chinese Classics" in the Taiwanese journal *Chinese Culture Quarterly* 4 (June 1962), 34-41. Meanwhile, however, Merton himself sent it to *Catholic World* after having given it a new title, "Christian Culture Needs Oriental Wisdom," and adding an extensive conclusion commenting on the implications of this title (see *Hidden Ground of Love*, 552). But this version, which appeared a month previous to "Two Chinese Classics" (*Catholic World* 195 [May 1962], 72-79), is lacking seven substantial paragraphs toward the beginning of the essay, omitted perhaps for space reasons, or perhaps at least in part to deemphasize the article's origins as a review of these new translations. The *Catholic World* version was reprinted in *A Thomas Merton Reader* (319-26; rev. ed., 295-303), while the "Two Chinese Classics" version was included in *Mystics and Zen Masters* under the new title "Love and Tao" (69-80). The present "complete" version of the essay incorporates the five concluding paragraphs Merton added for *Catholic World*, along with the revised title, but also includes the paragraphs missing in this version but found in the other; it also retains from "Love and Tao" the helpful subheadings, and in the common material follows the text of this version, which is clearly superior in those few instances where there are substantial textual differences (e.g., "to grasp it is to lose it" vs. "to grasp it is to love it" in the *Tao Te Ching* quotation on page 108; "Europe and America" vs. "Europe" in the final common paragraph). The *Catholic World* title is both more evocative and more provocative, and with the additional paragraphs provides a helpful orientation for Merton's ongoing project of bringing the riches of Eastern thought to a Western, largely Christian, audience. His selection of the terms "culture" and "wisdom" makes clear that he does not believe that the Christian faith, or Christian doctrine, is somehow incomplete without an infusion from the East, but that the inevitably limited framework of Christian culture, the historical and geographical setting in which faith is embedded, could benefit greatly from an engagement with Eastern wisdom—not the belief systems *per se* but the experiential knowledge, the spiritual insights, of the great Asian religions. The analogy with the encounter with Greek thought both in the early Church and in the high Middle Ages supports Merton's call for a true "catholicity," and his overview of the two texts, the Taoist *Tao Te Ching* and the Confucian *Hsaio Ching*, exemplify, respectively, the contribution of these traditions to nurturing "a dimension of *wisdom* oriented to contemplation as well as to wise action" that Merton deems "essential" for "our spiritual and even our physical survival."

A HUNDRED YEARS AGO America began to discover the Orient and its philosophical tradition. The discovery was valid, it reached toward the inner truth of Oriental thought. The intuitions of Emerson and Thoreau were rich in promises that were not afterward fulfilled by successors. America did not have the patience to continue what was so happily begun. The door that had opened for an instant, closed again for a century. Now that the door seems to be opening again (and sometimes one wonders if it is the door of the same house), we have another chance. It is imperative for us to find out what is inside this fabulous edifice. From where we stand, we can descry the residents dressed in our kind of clothing and engaged in our kind of frantic gesturing. They are tearing the place apart and rebuilding it in the likeness of our own utilitarian dwellings, department stores, and factories. Not that there is anything wrong with industrial production, with its higher standard of living. Yet we know, or should know, by this time, that our material riches unfortunately imply a spiritual, cultural, and moral poverty that are perhaps far greater than we see.

In this quandary we cannot help regarding an effort such as that of the Institute of Asian Studies, at St. John's University, as a real, though seemingly modest, benefaction. Here, in contrast to some other institutions where zeal and organized efficiency go together with a lack of spiritual perspective, we find rather an emphasis on the primary and the sapiential. Under the direction of Dr. Paul K. T. Sih, a well-known Chinese Catholic scholar, two of the most fundamental and traditional Chinese philosophical texts have been handsomely published in excellent translations, with facing Chinese versions. No better choice of a translator could have been made for the *Tao Te Ching* than Dr. John C. H. Wu, whose rendering is superb. More than this, Dr. Wu is able not only to translate Lao Tzu's words but also to interpret his life. He is remarkable as a Catholic who has brought over into his fervent life of Christian faith all the humility, the sense of dependence on the unseen, and the sapiential awareness of the hidden patterns of life which, in Taoism, foreshadowed their fulfillment in the Gospel of Christ. The translator of the *Hsiao Ching* is a Maryknoll missionary sister with a profound knowledge and love of Chinese classical thought. She has done her task superlatively well.

Both these works are of such fundamental importance that a mere review calling attention, in stereotyped images, to their various qualities would hardly be adequate.

Everyone knows in a vague way that the *Tao Te Ching* is poetic, and indeed that it is great poetry. Most people know that it usually impresses Westerners as more than a little quietistic. Hence they treat it with condescension as a quaint impractical document of an ancient day when no one bothered much about progress. Perhaps they do not realize that some of the wisdom of the *Tao Te Ching*, which so often reminds one of the Sermon on the Mount, is absolutely necessary for us not only to progress but even to survive.

As for the *Hsiao Ching*: this is less well known in the West than the *Tao* classic. But it is no less characteristic of China. Here in this "Classic of Filial Love" we find not so much a Confucianism that is arbitrarily opposed to Taoism as what I would venture to call a *Confucian kind of Taoism*. We must not imagine that the classic Confucianism of the third century B.C. was something purely formalistic and external, without respect for the interior, the hidden mystery in which all life has its invisible roots. On the contrary, we shall see that filial love was, for these Confucians, the taproot which was sunk most deeply in the mystery of the ethical *Tao* and which, unless it was cut by selfishness, kept both the individual and society in living contact with the mysterious will of heaven.

CLASSICS AND MASTERS

THE WORD "CHING" WHICH is found in the titles of these and other celebrated Chinese texts, is roughly translated as "classic." It means something more than just "book," and yet it does not have the connotations that "classic" has come to have for us. In the West, a classical work is one of the "highest class" because it embodies the peculiar literary and stylistic excellence we find in the great writers of Greece and Rome. The classical writers of Greece and Rome are those whose style is most pure and admirable. But a "Ching" is not a classic in this sense. It might be more helpful to consider the word "Ching" as corresponding to "Bible." Remember that our word "Bible" comes from the Greek *ta biblia*, or "the books." And not simply "the books," but precisely the books as contrasted with some other vehicle of tradition; that is to say, with the oral tradition. Words like "Ching" and "Bible," then, far from referring to what we would now call "Great Books" as distinct from books of a lesser literary value, mean simply the ancient traditions as contained in books rather than as orally transmitted. Such books then are not so much the ornaments and jewels of a culture as its mind and its memory, though that is not accurate if we remember that oral transmission of wisdom is more important than transmission in writing.

Hence a "Ching" is an *authoritative* book. Not that it has been written by an authoritative man (a "classical scholar" or even a "philosopher"), but that it goes back to an authority higher than man. One hesitates to use the word supernatural in connection with Chinese thought, yet the fact that the *Tao Te Ching* distinguishes a *Tao* that can be known and spoken of from the *Tao* which is unknown and unable to be named authorizes us to find here something that corresponds with our notion of God above and beyond the cosmos. After all, did not Dr. Wu, when he translated the Gospel of St. John into Chinese thirty years ago, start out with the words: "In the beginning was Tao, and Tao was with God, and Tao was God"?

If we want to understand the position of writers like these ancient Chinese philosophers, we must compare them not only with Plato or Parmenides but also with the Hebrew scribes, the transmitters of the wisdom tradition in the so-called sapiential books of the Old Testament. The ideogram which represents Tzu, in Lao Tzu (Master Lao), means both "master" and "child." Indeed, we find this ideogram combined with another in the word *hsiao*, meaning filial love. There the "son" is seen bearing the "father" on his shoulders. A master is therefore a child of the ancient Fathers, who bears their tradition with him and transmits it to future generations. Or rather, to be much more accurate, a master is a child who, like Lao Tzu, knows how to draw secret nourishment in silence from his "mother" the Tao.

Hence, we see that a master is not merely one who learns and repeats authoritative forms of words passed on from the time of the ancients; he is one who has been born to his wisdom by the mysterious all-embracing and merciful love which is the mother of all being. He is one who knows the unknown not by intellectual penetration, or by a science that wrests for itself the secrets of heaven, but by the wisdom of "littleness" and silence which knows how to receive in secret a word that cannot be uttered except in an enigma. This enigma is not a verbal riddle but the existential mystery of life itself. The wisdom of the *Tao Te Ching* leads therefore to Zen, which is at least ideally a transmission without any "Ching," passed on unaccountably from master to disciple not by means of written words but by seemingly absurd *koans*, accompanied, on occasion, by kicks and clouts on the head.

THE CLASSIC OF TAO

THE LITERAL TRANSLATION OF the title *Tao Te Ching* is the "Book of the Way and Its (Hidden) Power." If there is a correct answer to the question: "What is the *Tao*?" it is: "I don't know."

> Tao *can be talked about but not the eternal* Tao,
> *Names can be named, but not the Eternal Name.*
> *As the origin of heaven and earth it is nameless:*
> *As "the Mother" of all things it is namable.*

It is like an "empty bowl that can never be filled." It is like the hole in the center of the hub of a wheel, upon which all the spokes converge.

> *We make doors and windows for a room;*
> *But it is these empty spaces that make the room livable.* . . .

> *Look at it but you cannot see it!*
> *Its name is* Formless.

> *Listen to it but you cannot hear it!*
> *Its name is* Soundless.

> *Grasp at it, but you cannot get it!*
> *Its name is* Incorporeal.

It is the formless form, the imageless image. It is a "fountain spirit" of inexhaustible life and yet never draws attention to itself. It does its work without remark and without recognition. It is utterly elusive: if you think you have seen it, what you have seen is not the *Tao*. Yet it is the source of all, and all things return to it "as to their home."

The whole secret of life lies in the discovery of this *Tao* which can never be discovered. This does not involve an intellectual quest, but rather a spiritual change of one's whole being. One "reaches" the *Tao* by "becoming like" the *Tao*, by acting, in some sense, according to the "way" (*Tao*). For the *Tao* is at once perfect activity and perfect rest. It is supreme act, *actus purissimus*. Hence human activity, even virtuous activity, is not enough to bring one into line with the *Tao*. Virtuous activity tends to be busy and showy, and even with the best intentions in the world it cannot avoid sounding the trumpet before itself in the marketplace.

> *He who cultivates the* Tao *is one with the* Tao;
> *He who practices Virtue is one with Virtue;*
> *And he who courts after Loss is one with Loss.*

The way of loss is the way of whirlwind activity, of rash endeavor, of ambition, the accumulation of "extraneous growths." It is the way of aggression, of success. The way of virtue is the Confucian way of self-conscious and professional goodness, which is, in fact, a less pure form of virtue. St. Thomas would say it works *humano modo* rather than with the divine and mysterious spontaneity of the gifts of the Holy Ghost. But the way of *Tao* is just that: the way of supreme spontaneity, which is virtuous in a transcendent sense because it "does not strive."

> *High virtue is non-virtuous;*
> *Therefore it has virtue.*
> *Low virtue never frees itself from virtuousness,*
> *Therefore, it has no virtue.*

The "sage," or the man who has discovered the secret of the *Tao*, has not acquired any special esoteric knowledge that sets him apart from others and makes him smarter than they are. On the contrary, he is from a certain point of view more stupid and exteriorly less remarkable. He is "dim and obscure." While everyone else exults over success as over a sacrificial ox, he alone is silent, "like a babe who has not yet smiled." Though he has in fact "returned to the root," the *Tao*, he appears to be the "only one who has no home to return to." He is very much like the One who has nowhere to lay His head, even though the foxes may have holes and the birds of the air their nests. He who has found the *Tao* has no local habitation and no name on the earth. He is "bland like the ocean, aimless as the wafting gale." Again we remember the Gospels: "The wind blows where it pleases . . . even so is every man who is born of the Spirit" (John 3:8).

The way of the sage is the way of not-attacking, not charging at his objective, not busying himself too intently about his goals. The Chinese ideogram for this is, unfortunately, hardly able to be translated. The "active" symbol in it looks like a charging horse. *Wu wei* is a Taoist and Zen technical expression, and perhaps it is better left as it stands. Dr. Wu coins an English expression for it: "non-ado," and one can see what is at the back of his mind. It recalls the Shakespeare title *Much Ado about Nothing.*

The Japanese Zen artist and poet Sengai has left us two Japanese characters, *Bu Ji*, which are a work of art in themselves and eloquent of the spirit of *Tao*. *Bu Ji* means "nothing doing." I can say that there is more energy, more creativity, more productiveness in these two powerful signs created by Sengai than in all the skyscrapers of New York, and yet he dashed them onto paper with four strokes of his brush.

Hence *wu wei* is far from being inactive. It is supreme activity, because it acts at rest, acts without effort. Its effortlessness is not a matter of inertia, but of harmony with the hidden power that drives the planets and the cosmos.

The sage, then, accomplishes very much indeed because it is the *Tao* that acts in him and through him. He does not act of and by himself, still less for himself alone. His action is not a violent manipulation of exterior reality, an "attack" on the outside world, bending it to his conquering will; on the contrary, he respects external reality by yielding to it, and his yielding is at once an act of worship, a recognition of sacredness, and a perfect accomplishment of what is demanded by the precise situation.

The world is a sacred vessel which must not be tampered with or grabbed after.

To tamper with it is to spoil it, and to grasp it is to lose it.

The power of the sage is then the very power which has been revealed in the Gospels as Pure Love. *Deus caritas est* is the full manifestation of the truth hidden in the nameless *Tao*, and yet it still leaves *Tao* nameless. For love is not a name, any more than *Tao* is. One must go beyond the word and enter into communion with the reality before he can know anything about it: and then, more likely than not, he will know "in the cloud of unknowing."

The sixty-seventh chapter of the *Tao Te Ching* is one of the most profound and the most akin to Christianity. In the *Tao*, "which is queer like nothing on earth," are found three treasures: mercy, frugality, and not wanting to be first in the world. And the extraordinarily profound statement is made

Because I am merciful, therefore I can be brave . . .
For heaven will come to the rescue of the merciful and protect him with its
  mercy.

Again one hears echoes of the Gospel: "Blessed are the merciful . . ."; "Perfect love casteth out fear." Comparing Dr. Wu's translation with that of Lin Yutang in the Modern Library edition of Lao Tzu (another extremely interesting translation, with parallel passages from the poet and sage Chuang Tzu), we find new perspectives. (It is often necessary to read a translated Chinese text in two or more versions.)

> *If one forsakes love and fearlessness,*
>   *forsakes restraint and reserve power,*
>   *forsakes following behind and rushes in front,*
> *He is doomed!*

> *For love is victorious in attack*
>   *And invulnerable in defense,*
> Heaven arms with love
>   Those it would not see destroyed.

The word which Lin Yutang translates as "love" and Dr. Wu as "mercy" is in fact the compassionate love of the mother for the child. Once again, the sage and the wise ruler are men who do not rush forward to aggrandize themselves, but cherish, with loving concern, the "sacred" reality of persons and things which have been entrusted to them by the *Tao*.

It must be remembered that the *Tao Te Ching* is basically not a manual for hermits but a treatise on government, and much is said there on war and peace. It is a manual that our leaders might be expected to read, and doubtless some of them might do so with profit. One of its most astute sayings is that in a war the winner is likely to be the side that enters the war with the most sorrow.

> *To rejoice over a victory is to rejoice over the slaughter of men!*
> *Hence a man who rejoices over the slaughter of men cannot expect to thrive in*
>   *the world of men.*
> *. . . Every victory is a funeral.*

THE CLASSIC OF FILIAL LOVE

THE PARADOXICAL BRILLIANCE OF the *Tao* classic contrasts with the simplicity of the *Hsiao Ching*, a primer of Chinese Confucian ethics and one of the first texts formerly studied by Chinese schoolboys. But this makes it even more interesting, in some respects, than the better-known *Tao Te Ching*. Many who would be secretly irritated by the apparent subtlety of the *Tao* classic might prefer to meditate on the "Classic of Filial Love." It is a revelation of the deepest natural wisdom, and its intuitions are surprisingly "modern." In fact, we are here on the same ground as Freud, and substantially the same conclusions that were reached by Freud more than twenty centuries later are here exposed in all simplicity and without benefit of the Oedipus complex.

One might be tempted to imagine that this treatise is designed merely to keep sons in subjection to their parents and hence to exalt parental authority for its own sake. It is doubtless true that the rigid formalism of Confucian ethics became, after two thousand years, a somewhat suffocating system. But, in its original purity, the Confucian ideal is basically *personalistic*. The fundamental justification for filial piety is that our person is received as a gift from our parents and is to be fully developed out of gratitude toward them. Hence, the astounding fact that this filial piety is not simply a cult of the parent as such, but a development of one's own gifts in honor of the parents who gave them to us. Then, when we reach manhood and our parents are old, we make a fitting return to them by loving support. This basic attitude is said to be "the foundation of virtue and the root of civilization."

If a child can enter fruitfully and lovingly into the five basic relationships, he will certainly develop into a good citizen and a worthy leader, supposing that to be his vocation. The five basic relationships are those of father to son, marked by *justice*; mother to son, marked by *compassion*, or merciful love; the son to his parents, marked by *filial love*; the elder brother to his younger brother, marked by *friendship*; and the younger to the elder, marked by *respect* for his senior.

Thus, we see a wonderful organic complex of strength from the father, warmth from the mother, gratitude from the son, and wholesome respectful friendship between brothers. "He who really loves his parents will not be proud in high station; he will not be insubordinate in an inferior position; among his equals he will not be contentious. To be proud in high station is to be ruined; to be insubordinate in an inferior position is to incur punishment; to be contentious among one's equals leads to physical violence. As long as these three evils are not uprooted, a son cannot be called filial even though he feast his parents daily on three kinds of choice meat." On such a ground grows up a love that reaches out through society and makes it the earthly image of the invisible order of heaven.

The *Hsiao Ching* then shows how this love has various ways of coming to fruitful development in all the levels of society, from the Son of Heaven down through the princes and scholars to the peasants. "From the Son of Heaven to the commoners, if filial piety is not pursued from beginning to end, disasters are sure to follow." The society of love (compare the works of Pseudo-Dionysius) is hierarchical. The lower depend on the higher in this exercise of love. The emperor is at the summit. All depends on him, and he should ideally be capable of the widest and most all-embracing love. For he must love all his subjects and care for their needs. In so doing, he embodies the "heavenly principle" on earth and imitates heaven, who loves all alike. He also has a duty to share with his subjects this knowledge of heavenly love, and this he does by means of *ritual and music*. In other words, the nation which lives by love grows in love by liturgical celebration of the mystery of love; such are the Christian terms in which we might expand this primitive intuition.

It is important to notice that in all this there is no such thing as blind subservience to age and to authority. On the contrary, one of the basic duties of filial love is to correct the father when he is wrong, and one of the basic duties of the minister is to correct his prince when he errs. This, of course, was the ideal. The pungent humor of Chuang Tzu shows us many occasions when in practice this kind of "filial love" was not appreciated.

CONCLUSIONS

CHRISTOPHER DAWSON HAS REMARKED on the "religious vacuum" in our education. It is absolutely essential to introduce into our study of the humanities a dimension of *wisdom* oriented to contemplation as well as to wise action. For this, it is no longer sufficient merely to go back over the Christian and European cultural traditions. The horizons of the world are no longer confined to Europe and America. We have to gain new perspectives, and on this our spiritual and even our physical survival may depend.

Does this mean that the suggestion given in our title is strictly true? Does Christian culture *need* Oriental wisdom? It would certainly be rash to state this without further qualification. Yet we may ask ourselves a few pertinent questions on the subject.

First of all, it is quite clear that no non-Christian religion or philosophy has anything that Christianity needs, insofar as it is a supernaturally revealed religion. Yet from the point of view of the "incarnation" of revealed Christian truth in a social and cultural context, in man's actual history, we know how much Greek philosophy and Roman law contributed to the actual formation of Christian culture and even Christian spirituality. We know too with what breadth of view and with what lofty freedom the scholastic doctors of the thirteenth century made use of Aristotle and his Arabian commentators. It can certainly be said that if a similar use had been made of Oriental philosophy and religious thought from the very start, the development of Christianity in Asia would have been a different story. Our Western Christian thought and culture would also have been immeasurably enriched and deepened.

Have we not been too ready to dismiss Oriental philosophy without really attempting to understand it? Do we not still shrug it off with a few easy generalizations? "Oh, that's all pantheism!" "The Buddhists are all quietists!" And so on?

Can we be content to leave the rich Asian heritage of wisdom on the level of "comparative religion," and subject it to a superficial and passing consideration, checking off concepts like "Tao" and "Dharma" and "Dhyana" as a bored tourist might saunter through the Louvre vaguely registering the famous masterpieces as he walked by them? Or can we simply study these Asian religions and philosophies from an apologetic or missiological standpoint, as "rival systems" which are known *a priori* to be "false," but which one must at least know how to refute? One cannot arrive at an understanding of any "wisdom," whether natural or supernatural, by arguing either for or against it. Wisdom is not penetrated by logical analysis. The values hidden in Oriental thought actually reveal themselves only on the plane of spiritual experience, or perhaps, if you like, of aesthetic experience. They belong, of course, to the natural order; but they certainly have deep affinities with supernatural wisdom itself. Surely we cannot doubt that they may be able, if properly grasped and appreciated, to lead us to a deeper and wiser understanding of our own magnificent mystical tradition, just as Platonism, without actually "influencing" the Greek Fathers, gave them a language and a sensibility that were equipped to penetrate in a specially significant way the depths of the revealed mystery of Christ.

At least this much can and must be said: the "universality" and "catholicity" which are essential to the Church necessarily imply an ability and a readiness to enter into dialogue with all that is pure, wise, profound, and humane in every kind of culture. In this one sense at least a dialogue with Oriental wisdom becomes necessary. A Christian culture that is not capable of such a dialogue would show, by that very fact, that it lacked catholicity.

9

A Letter to Pablo Antonio Cuadra concerning Giants

Though addressed to the Nicaraguan poet, editor, and social activist (and cousin to Merton's correspondent and former novice Ernesto Cardenal), some of whose poetry Merton would translate, this discussion of the Cold War and the role of the "third world" is clearly an essay rather than a personal letter. In a September 16, 1961, letter to Cuadra saying that the piece would follow in a day or two, Merton writes: "What I had to say took the form of a letter because I felt I could say it better if I knew the person I was addressing. Hence in speaking to you first of all I have said what I thought needed to be said to everyone else, especially in Latin America. The piece is really an article. . . . I felt that my position called for some kind of a statement of where I stand, morally, as a Christian writer" (*Courage for Truth*, 188-89). It was first published in English in *Black-friars* 43 (February 1962), 69-81, and a month later in Spanish translation in *El Pez y la Serpiente*, the magazine Cuadra edited (3 [March 1962], 9-30); this version was subsequently reprinted in El Salvador, Venezuela, and Argentina over the next two years. A substantial excerpt entitled "Conquistador, Tourist and Indian" appeared in *Good Work* 25 (Summer 1962), 90-94, and was included that same year in *A Thomas Merton Reader* (327-33; rev. ed., 304-10). The "letter" was included in Merton's 1963 book of verse, *Emblems of a Season of Fury* (70-89), as a kind of transition between Merton's original poems and his translations of mainly Latin American poets, among them Cuadra, and as a remnant of an earlier conception of the volume as including both poetry and prose. Though definitely not a poem, even a prose-poem, it was nevertheless included in Merton's *Collected Poems* (372-91). Merton himself was somewhat uncomfortable with what he considered the overly strident tone of the piece (see *Turning toward the World*, 162-63), but it is a major articulation of his views on the contemporary political situation and its moral and spiritual ramifications. Editor and critic David Cooper calls it "without question TM's most powerful political statement" (Thomas Merton and James Laughlin, *Selected Letters*, 137n). The "Giants" of the title are of course the superpowers of the day, the Soviet Union and the United States, referred to throughout the essay as Gog and Magog, names (originally found in Ezekiel 38–39) borrowed from the book of Revelation, which states that in the end times Satan "will go out to deceive the nations at the four corners of the earth, Gog and Magog, to gather them for battle" (Revelation 20:8). For Merton they become two opposing forces, one moved by love of power, the other by the cult of money, yet he links them as "the two faces of Janus looking inward, and dividing with critical fury the polluted sanctuary of dehumanized man." While "half-trust[ing] the strain of idealism in Magog" in whose land he himself lives, and grateful that Magog allows him to continue living where Gog might not, he is deeply suspicious of a distorted allegiance to these very ideals that might seem to justify the obliteration of the opponent. But the heart of the essay looks away from the giants, who seem to believe that they and their titanic struggle are all that matter, to the rest of humanity, who have been dominated and oppressed by the giants but have managed to retain "a spiritual outlook which is not abstract but concrete, not pragmatic but hieratic, intuitive and affective rather than rationalistic and aggressive." It is here, in the "global South," that Merton detects signs of hope that are ultimately less political than spiritual. The great sin of the West, he writes, has been its failure to perceive the divine image in every human being, its refusal to believe that "God speaks, and God is to be heard, not only on Sinai, not only in my own heart, but in the *voice of the stranger*." As a counterpoint to the distorted mirror-imaging of the giants, whose apparent differences mask a shared arrogance and a common demand for conformity, even if the patterns of that conformity differ radically, Merton calls for a respect for otherness, a recognition that the infinite God can and should be imaged in myriad ways: "We must, then, see the truth in the stranger, and the truth we see must be a newly living truth, not just a projection of a dead conventional idea of our own—a projection of our own self upon the stranger." While he is less than optimistic that Gog and Magog will at last come to their senses and humbly discover a brother in the stranger, he remains hopeful that it is not too late for the third world, represented by his friend Cuadra, to recall the lesson not to go and do likewise.

1

A T A MOMENT WHEN all the discordant voices of modern society attempt to exorcize the vertigo of man with scientific clichés or prophetic curses I come to share with you reflections that are neither tragic nor, I hope, fatuous. They are simply the thoughts of one civilized man to another, dictated by a spirit of sobriety and concern, and with no pretensions to exorcize anything. The vertigo of the twentieth century needs no permission of yours or mine to continue. The tornado has not consulted any of us, and will not do so. This does not mean that we are helpless. It only means that our salvation lies in understanding our exact position, not in flattering ourselves that we have brought the whirlwind into being by ourselves, or that we can calm it with a wave of the hand.

It is certainly true that the storm of history has arisen out of our own hearts. It has sprung unbidden out of the emptiness of technological man. It is the genie he has summoned out of the depths of his own confusion, this complacent sorcerer's apprentice who spends billions on weapons of destruction and space rockets when he cannot provide decent meals, shelter, and clothing for two-thirds of the human race. Is it improper to doubt the intelligence and sincerity of modern man? I know it is not accepted as a sign of progressive thinking to question the enlightenment of the twentieth-century barbarian. But I no longer have any desire to be considered enlightened by the standards of the stool pigeons and torturers whose most signal claim to success is that they have built so many extermination camps and operated them to the limit of their capacity.

These glorious characters, reveling in paroxysms of collective paranoia, have now aligned themselves in enormous power blocs of which the most striking feature is that they resemble one another like a pair of twins. I had not clearly understood from Ezekiel that Gog and Magog were to fight one another, although I knew that they were to be overcome. I knew that their ponderous brutality would exhaust itself on the mountains of Israel and provide a feast for the birds of the air. But I had not expected we would all be so intimately involved in their downfall. The truth is that there is a little of Gog and Magog even in the best of us.

We must be wary of ourselves when the worst that is in man becomes objectified in society, approved, acclaimed, and deified, when hatred becomes patriotism and murder a holy duty, when spying and delation are called love of truth and the stool pigeon is a public benefactor, when the gnawing and prurient resentments of frustrated bureaucrats become the conscience of the people and the gangster is enthroned in power, then we must fear the voice of our own heart, even when it denounces them. For are we not all tainted with the same poison?

That is why we must not be deceived by the giants, and by their thunderous denunciations of one another, their preparations for mutual destruction. The fact that they are powerful does not mean that they are sane, and the fact that they speak with intense conviction does not mean that they speak the truth. Nor is their size any proof that they possess a metaphysical solidity. Are they not perhaps specters without essence, emanations from the terrified and puny hearts of politicians, policemen, and millionaires?

We live in an age of bad dreams, in which the scientist and engineer possess the power to give external form to the phantasms of man's unconscious. The bright weapons that sing in the atmosphere, ready to pulverize the cities of the world, are the dreams of giants without a center. Their mathematical evolutions are hieratic rites devised by shamans without belief. One is permitted to wish their dreams had been less sordid!

But perhaps they are also the emanations of our own subliminal self!

2

I HAVE LEARNED THAT an age in which politicians talk about peace is an age in which everybody expects war; the great men of the earth would not talk of peace so much if they did not secretly believe it possible, with *one more war*, to annihilate their enemies forever. Always, "after just one more war" it will dawn, the new era of love; but first everybody who is hated must be eliminated. For hate, you see, is the mother of their kind of love.

Unfortunately the love that is to be born out of hate will never be born. Hatred is sterile; it breeds nothing but the image of its own empty fury, its own nothingness. Love cannot come of emptiness. It is full of reality. Hatred destroys the real being of man in fighting the fiction which it calls "the enemy." For man is concrete and alive, but "the enemy" is a subjective abstraction. A society that kills real men in order to deliver itself from the phantasm of a paranoid delusion is already possessed by the demon of destructiveness because it has made itself incapable of love. It refuses, *a priori*, to love. It is dedicated not to concrete relations of man with man, but only to abstractions about politics, economics, psychology, and even, sometimes, religion.

Gog is a lover of power, Magog is absorbed in the cult of money; their idols differ, and indeed their faces seem to be dead set against one another, but their madness is the same: they are the two faces of Janus looking inward, and dividing with critical fury the polluted sanctuary of dehumanized man.

Only names matter, to Gog and Magog, only labels, only numbers, symbols, slogans. For the sake of a name, a classification, you can be marched away with your pants off to be shot against a wall. For the sake of a name, a word, you can be gassed in a shower-bath and fed to the furnace to be turned into fertilizer. For the sake of a word or even a number they will tan your skin and make it into lampshades. If you want to get a job, make a living, have a home to live in, eat in restaurants, and ride in vehicles with other human beings, you have to have a right classification: depending perhaps on the shape of your nose, the color of your eyes, the kink in your hair, the degree to which you are sunburned, or the social status of your grandfather. Life and death today depend on everything except what you *are*. This is called humanism.

Condemnation or rehabilitation has no connection with what you happen to have done. There is no longer any question of ethical standards. We may have been liberated from idealistic objectivity about "right and wrong." This timely liberation from ethical norms and laws enables us to deal with an ever increasing population of undesirables in much more efficient fashion. Attach to each one an arbitrary label, which requires no action on his part and no effort of thought on the part of the accuser. This enables society to get rid of "criminals" without the latter putting anyone to any kind of inconvenience by committing an actual crime. A much more humane and efficient way of dealing with crime! You benevolently shoot a man for all the crimes he *might* commit before he has a chance to commit them.

3

I WRITE TO YOU today from Magog's country. The fact that Magog is to me more sympathetic than Gog does not, I think, affect my objectivity. Nor does it imply a choice of category, a self-classification. Magog and I seldom agree, which is one reason why I write this letter. I must however admit I feel indebted to Magog for allowing me to exist, which Gog perhaps might not. Perhaps it is not to my credit that I half-trust the strain of idealism in Magog, accepting it uncritically as a sign that, for all his blatant, materialistic gigantism, he is still human. Certainly he tolerates in his clients elements of human poignancy, together with an off-beat frivolity which Gog could never comprehend. (Yet Gog, in the right mood, weeps copiously into his vodka.) Magog, on the whole, is not demanding. A little lip service has been enough at least up to the present. He does not require the exorbitant public confessions which are a prelude to disappearance in the realm of Gog. The pressure of Magog is more subtle, more gently persuasive, but no less universal. Yet disagreement is still tolerated.

Magog is in confusion, an easier prey than Gog to panic and discouragement. He is less crafty as a politician, and he is handicapped by a vague and uncomplicated system of beliefs which everyone can understand. Hence the whole world can easily see discrepancies between his ideals and actualities. Magog is more often embarrassed than Gog who entertains no objective ideals but only pays homage to a dialectical process by which anything, however disconcerting, can quickly be justified.

Gog, I believe, is fondly hoping that Magog will be driven to despair and ruin himself in some way before it becomes necessary to destroy him. But in any case he is giving Magog every opportunity to discredit himself in the eyes of the rest of the world, so that if he cannot be persuaded to put his own head in the gas oven, his destruction can be made to appear as no crime but as a benefit conferred on the whole human race.

But let me turn from Gog and Magog to the rest of men. And by "the rest of men" I mean those who have not yet committed themselves to the cause of one or the other of the champions. There are many, even within the power groups, who hate wars and hate the slogans, the systems, and the official pronouncements of groups under whose dominance they live. But they seem to be able to do nothing about it. Their instinct to protest is restrained by the awareness that whatever they may say, however true, against one implacable power can be turned to good use by another that is even more inhuman. Even in protest one must be discreet, not only for the sake of saving one's skin, but above all for the sake of protecting the virginity of one's own protest against the salacious advances of the publicist, the agitator, or the political police.

4

LET ME ABANDON MY facetiousness, and consider the question of the world's future, if it has one. Gog and Magog are persuaded that it has: Gog thinks that the self-destruction of Magog will usher in the golden age of peace and love. Magog thinks that if he and Gog can somehow shoot the rapids of a Cold War waged with the chemically pure threat of nuclear weapons they will both emerge into a future of happiness, the nature and the possibility of which still remain to be explained.

I for my part believe in the very serious possibility that Gog and Magog may wake up one morning to find that they have burned and blasted each other off the map during the night, and nothing will remain but the spasmodic exercise of automatic weapons still in the throes of what has casually been termed overkill. The supererogatory retaliation may quite conceivably affect all the neutrals who have managed to escape the main event, but it is still possible that the southern hemisphere may make a dazed and painful comeback, and discover itself alone in a smaller, emptier, better-radiated but still habitable world.

In this new situation it is conceivable that Indonesia, Latin America, southern Africa, and Australia may find themselves heirs to the opportunities and objectives which Gog and Magog shrugged off with such careless abandon.

The largest, richest, and best developed single landmass south of the Equator is South America. The vast majority of its population is Indian, or of mixed Indian blood. The white minority in South Africa would quite probably disappear. A relic of European stock might survive in Australia and New Zealand. Let us also hopefully assume the partial survival of India and of some Moslem populations in central and northern Africa.

If this should happen it will be an event fraught with a rather extraordinary spiritual significance. It will mean that the more cerebral and mechanistic cultures, those which have tended to live more and more by abstractions and to isolate themselves more and more from the natural world by rationalization, will be succeeded by the sections of the human race which they oppressed and exploited without the slightest appreciation for or understanding of their human reality.

Characteristic of these races is a totally different outlook on life, a spiritual outlook which is not abstract but concrete, not pragmatic but hieratic, intuitive and affective rather than rationalistic and aggressive. The deepest springs of vitality in these races have been sealed up by the conqueror and colonizer, where they have not actually been poisoned by him. But if this stone is removed from the spring perhaps its waters will purify themselves by new life and regain their creative, fructifying power. Neither Gog nor Magog can accomplish this for them.

Let me be quite succinct: the greatest sin of the European-Russian-American complex which we call "the West" (and this sin has spread its own way to China) is not only greed and cruelty, not only moral dishonesty and infidelity to truth, but above all *its unmitigated arrogance towards the rest of the human race.* Western civilization is now in full decline into barbarism (a barbarism that springs *from within itself*) because it has been guilty of a twofold disloyalty: to God and to Man. To a Christian who believes in the mystery of the Incarnation, and who by that belief means something more than a pious theory without real humanistic implications, this is not two disloyalties but one. Since the Word was made Flesh, God is in man. God is in *all men.* All men are to be seen and treated as Christ. Failure to do this, the Lord tells us, involves condemnation for disloyalty to the most fundamental of revealed truths. "I was thirsty and you gave me not to drink. I was hungry and you gave me not to eat . . ." (Matthew 25:42). This could be extended in every possible sense, and is meant to be so extended, all over the entire area of human needs, not only for bread, for work, for liberty, for health, but also for truth, for belief, for love, for acceptance, for fellowship and understanding.

One of the great tragedies of the Christian West is the fact that for all the good will of the missionaries and colonizers (they certainly meant well, and behaved humanly, according to their lights which were somewhat brighter than ours), they could not recognize that *the races they conquered were essentially equal to themselves and in some ways superior.*

It was certainly right that Christian Europe should bring Christ to the Indians of Mexico and the Andes, as well as to the Hindus and the Chinese; but where they failed was in their inability to *encounter Christ* already potentially present in the Indians, the Hindus, and the Chinese.

Christians have too often forgotten the fact that Christianity found its way into Greek and Roman civilization partly by its spontaneous and creative adaptation of the pre-Christian natural values it found in that civilization. The martyrs rejected all the grossness, the cynicism and falsity of the cult of the state-gods which was simply a cult of secular power, but Clement of Alexandria, Justin, and Origen believed that Herakleitos and Socrates had been precursors of Christ. They thought that while God had manifested himself to the Jews through the Law and the Prophets he had also spoken to the Gentiles through their philosophers. Christianity made its way in the world of the first century not by imposing Jewish cultural and social standards on the rest of the world, but by abandoning them, getting free of them so as to be "all things to all men." This was the great drama and the supreme lesson of the Apostolic Age. By the end of the Middle Ages that lesson had been *forgotten*. The preachers of the Gospel to newly discovered continents became preachers and disseminators of European culture and power. They did not enter into dialogue with ancient civilizations; they imposed upon them their own monologue and in preaching Christ they also preached themselves. The very ardor of their self-sacrifice and of their humility enabled them to do this with a clean conscience. But they had omitted to listen to the voice of Christ in the unfamiliar accents of the Indian, as Clement had listened for it in the Pre-Socratics. And now, today, we have a Christianity of Magog.

It is a Christianity of money, of action, of passive crowds, an electronic Christianity of loudspeakers and parades. Magog is himself without belief, cynically tolerant of the athletic yet sentimental Christ devised by some of his clients, because this Christ is profitable to Magog. He is a progressive Christ who does not protest against Pharisees or moneychangers in the temple. He protests only against Gog.

It is my belief that we should not be too sure of having found Christ in ourselves until we have found him also in the part of humanity that is most remote from our own.

Christ is found not in loud and pompous declarations but in humble and fraternal dialogue. He is found less in a truth that is imposed than in a truth that is shared.

5

IF I INSIST ON giving you my truth, and never stop to receive your truth in return, then there can be no truth between us. Christ is present "where two or three are gathered in my name." But to be gathered in the name of Christ is to be gathered in the name of the Word made flesh, of God made man. It is therefore to be gathered in the faith that God has become man and can be seen in man, that he can speak in man and that he can enlighten and inspire love in and through any man I meet. It is true that the visible Church alone has the official mission to sanctify and teach all nations, but no man knows that the stranger he meets coming out of the forest in a new country is not already an invisible member of Christ and perhaps one who has some providential or prophetic message to utter.

Whatever India may have had to say to the West she was forced to remain silent. Whatever China had to say, though some of the first missionaries heard it and understood it, the message was generally ignored as irrelevant. Did anyone pay attention to the voices of the Maya and the Inca, who had deep things to say? By and large their witness was merely suppressed. No one considered that the children of the Sun might, after all, hold in their hearts a spiritual secret. On the contrary, abstract discussions were engaged in to determine whether, in terms of academic philosophy, the Indian was to be considered a rational animal. One shudders at the voice of cerebral Western arrogance even then eviscerated by the rationalism that is ours today, judging the living spiritual mystery of primitive man and condemning it to exclusion from the category on which love, friendship, respect, and communion were made to depend.

God speaks, and God is to be heard, not only on Sinai, not only in my own heart, but in the *voice of the stranger*. That is why the peoples of the Orient, and all primitive peoples in general, make so much of the mystery of hospitality.

God must be allowed the right to speak unpredictably. The Holy Spirit, the very voice of Divine Liberty, must always be like the wind in "blowing where he pleases" (John 3:8). In the mystery of the Old Testament there was already a tension between the Law and the Prophets. In the New Testament the Spirit himself is Law, and he is everywhere. He certainly inspires and protects the visible Church, but if we cannot see him unexpectedly in the stranger and the alien, we will not understand him even in the Church. We must find him in our enemy, or we may lose him even in our friend. We must find him in the pagan or we will lose him in our own selves, substituting for his living presence an empty abstraction. How can we reveal to others what we cannot discover in them ourselves? We must, then, see the truth in the stranger, and the truth we see must be a newly living truth, not just a projection of a dead conventional idea of our own—a projection of our own self upon the stranger.

The desecration, de-sacralization of the modern world is manifest above all by the fact that the stranger is of no account. As soon as he is "displaced" he is completely unacceptable. He fits into no familiar category, he is unexplained and therefore a threat to complacency. Everything not easy to account for must be wiped out, and mystery must be wiped out with it. An alien presence interferes with the superficial and faked clarity of our own rationalizations.

6

THERE IS MORE THAN one way of morally liquidating the "stranger" and the "alien." It is sufficient to destroy, in some way, that in him which is different and disconcerting. By pressure, persuasion, or force one can impose on him one's own ideas and attitudes towards life. One can indoctrinate him, brainwash him. He is no longer different. He has been reduced to conformity with one's own outlook. Gog, who does nothing if not thoroughly, believes in the thorough liquidation of differences, and the reduction of everyone else to a carbon copy of himself. Magog is somewhat more quixotic: the stranger becomes part of his own screen of fantasies, part of the collective dream life which is manufactured for him on Madison Avenue and in Hollywood. For all practical purposes, the stranger no longer exists. He is not even seen. He is replaced by a fantastic image. What is seen and approved, in a vague, superficial way, is the stereotype that has been created by the travel agency.

This accounts for the spurious cosmopolitanism of the naïve tourist and travelling businessman, who wanders everywhere with his camera, his exposure-meter, his spectacles, his sun glasses, his binoculars, and though gazing around him in all directions never sees what is there. He is not capable of doing so. He is too docile to his instructors, to those who have told him everything before-hand. He believes the advertisements of the travel agent at whose suggestion he bought the ticket that landed him wherever he may be. He has been told what he was going to see, and he thinks he is seeing it. Or, failing that, he at least wonders why he is not seeing what he has been led to expect. Under no circum-stances does it occur to him to become interested in what is actually there. Still less to enter into a fully human rapport with the human beings who are before him. He has not, of course, questioned their status as rational animals, as the scholastically trained colonists of an earlier age might have done. It just does not occur to him that they might have a life, a spirit, a thought, a culture of their own which has its own peculiar individual character.

He does not know why he is travelling in the first place; indeed he is travel-ling at somebody else's suggestion. Even at home he is alien from himself. He is doubly alienated when he is out of his own atmosphere. He cannot possibly realize that the stranger has something very valuable, something irreplaceable to give him: something that can never be bought with money, never estimated by publicists, never exploited by political agitators: the spiritual understanding of a friend who belongs to a different culture. The tourist lacks nothing except brothers. For him these do not exist.

The tourist never meets anyone, never encounters anyone, never finds the brother in the stranger. This is his tragedy, and it has been the tragedy of Gog and Magog, especially of Magog, in every part of the world.

If only North Americans had realized, after a hundred and fifty years, that Latin Americans really existed. That they were really people. That they spoke a different language. That they had a culture. That they had more than something to sell! Money has totally corrupted the brotherhood that should have united all the peoples of America. It has destroyed the sense of relationship, the spiritual community that had already begun to flourish in the years of Bolivar. But no! Most North Americans still don't know, and don't care, that Brazil speaks a language other than Spanish, that all Latin Americans do not live for the siesta, that all do not spend their days and nights playing the guitar and making love. They have never awakened to the fact that Latin America is by and large culturally superior to the United States, not only on the level of the wealthy minority which has absorbed more of the sophistication of Europe, but also among the desperately poor indigenous cultures, some of which are rooted in a past that has never yet been surpassed on this continent.

So the tourist drinks tequila, and thinks it is no good, and waits for the fiesta he has been told to wait for. How should he realize that the Indian who walks down the street with half a house on his head and a hole in his pants is Christ? All the tourist thinks is that it is odd for so many Indians to be called Jesus.

7

SO MUCH FOR THE modern scene: I am no prophet, no one is, for now we have learned to get along without prophets. But I would say that if Gog and Magog are to destroy one another, which they seem quite anxious to do, it would be a great pity if the survivors in the "third world" attempted to reproduce their collective alienation, horror, and insanity, and thus build up another corrupt world to be destroyed by another war. To the whole third world I would say there is one lesson to be learned from the present situation, one lesson of the greatest urgency: be unlike the giants, Gog and Magog. Mark what they do, and act differently. Mark their official pronouncements, their ideologies, and without any difficulty you will find them hollow. Mark their behavior: their bluster, their violence, their blandishments, their hypocrisy: by their fruits you shall know them. In all their boastfulness they have become the victims of their own terror, which is nothing but the emptiness of their own hearts. They claim to be humanists, they claim to know and love man. They have come to liberate man, they say. But they do not know what man is. They are themselves less human than their fathers were, less articulate, less sensitive, less profound, less capable of genuine concern. They are turning into giant insects. Their societies are becoming anthills, without purpose, without meaning, without spirit and joy.

What is wrong with their humanism? It is a humanism of termites, because without God man becomes an insect, a worm in the wood, and even if he can fly, so what? There are flying ants. Even if man flies all over the universe, he is still nothing but a flying ant until he recovers a human center and a human spirit in the depth of his own being.

Karl Marx? Yes, he was a humanist, with a humanist's concerns. He understood the roots of alienation and his understanding even had something spiritual about it. Marx unconsciously built his system on a basically religious pattern, on the Messianism of the Old Testament, and in his own myth Marx was Moses. He understood something of the meaning of liberation, because he had in his bones the typology of Exodus. To say that he built a "scientific" thought on a foundation of religious symbolism is not to say that he was wrong, but to justify what was basically right about his analysis. Marx did not think only with the top of his head, or reason on the surface of his intelligence. He did not simply verbalize or dogmatize as his followers have done. He was still human. And they?

Ultimately there is no humanism without God. Marx thought that humanism had to be atheistic, and this was because he did not understand God any better than the self-complacent formalists whom he criticized. He thought, as they did, that God was an idea, an abstract essence, forming part of an intellectual superstructure built to justify economic alienation. There is in God nothing abstract. He is not a static entity, an object of thought, a pure essence. The dynamism Marx looked for in history was something that the Bible itself would lead us in some sense to understand and to expect. And liberation from religious alienation was the central theme of the New Testament. But the theme has not been understood. It has too often been forgotten. Yet it is the very heart of the mystery of the Cross.

8

IT IS NOT WITH resignation that I wait for whatever may come, but with an acceptance and an understanding which cannot be confirmed within the limits of pragmatic realism. However meaningless Gog and Magog may be in themselves, the cataclysm they will undoubtedly let loose is full of meaning, full of light. Out of their negation and terror come certitude and peace for anyone who can fight his way free of their confusion. The worst they can do is bring death upon us and death is of little consequence. Destruction of the body cannot touch the deepest center of life.

When will the bombs fall? Who shall say? Perhaps Gog and Magog have yet to perfect their policies and their weapons. Perhaps they want to do a neat and masterly job, dropping "clean" bombs, without fallout. It sounds clinical to the point of humanitarian kindness. It is all a lovely, humane piece of surgery. Prompt, efficacious, sterile, pure. That of course was the ideal of the Nazis who conducted the extermination camps twenty years ago; but of course they had not progressed as far as we have. They devoted themselves dutifully to a disgusting job which could never be performed under perfect clinical conditions. Yet they did their best. Gog and Magog will develop the whole thing to its ultimate refinement. I hear they are working on a bomb that will destroy nothing but life. Men, animals, birds, perhaps also vegetation. But it will leave buildings, factories, railways, natural resources. Only one further step, and the weapon will be one of absolute perfection. It should destroy books, works of art, musical instruments, toys, tools, and gardens, but not destroy flags, weapons, gallows, electric chairs, gas chambers, instruments of torture or plenty of straitjackets in case someone should accidentally survive. Then the era of love can finally begin. Atheistic humanism can take over.

10

Peace: A Religious Responsibility

This essay was included in the anthology *Breakthrough to Peace: Twelve Views on the Threat of Thermonuclear Extermination* (New York: New Directions, [September] 1962), 88-116, which Merton edited (though anonymously because of censorship problems) and introduced. It is a further development and refinement of the essay "Nuclear War and Christian Responsibility" published in *Commonweal* 75.20 (February 9, 1962), 509-13, which Merton was somewhat uncomfortable with because of what he called its "rather sweeping statements" (see his February 4, 1962, letter to Msgr. John Tracy Ellis [*Hidden Ground of Love*, 176]); a somewhat earlier, less confrontational version, apparently never published during Merton's lifetime, was included by Gordon Zahn in his anthology *The Non-Violent Alternative* (originally titled *Thomas Merton on Peace*) as "Peace: Christian Duties and Perspectives" (12-19) (evidently completed in October 1961: see *Turning toward the World*, 174). A further revision appeared in two parts in *The Catholic Worker* as "We Have to Make Ourselves Heard" (28.10 [May 1962], 4-6 and 28.11 [June 1962], 4-5), which was then developed into the anthology article, subsequently included both in *Non-Violent Alternative* (107-28) and in William Shannon's anthology *Passion for Peace: The Social Essays* (99-123), which includes the *Commonweal* version (37-47) as well, along with helpful introductory headnotes tracing the evolution of the essay. This in turn served as the central core of Merton's book-length manuscript *Peace in the Post-Christian Era*, which he was not allowed to publish in his lifetime and appeared in print only in 2004, with a comprehensive introduction by editor Patricia Burton (xxv-lv) that traces its relationship to these earlier peace writings. In a December 17, 1962, letter to Jean and Hildegard Goss-Mayr, Merton calls this article "pretty much a summary of what I have had to say on the subject" (*Hidden Ground of Love*, 329). As such, it includes an overview of the inherently unstable nuclear situation in the early 1960s, with its increasing development of and reliance on ballistic missiles as a primary delivery system; the "complacent sophistry" of much of the current ethical reflection on atomic war, in which the theoretical licitness under natural law and just-war principles of a counter-force strike, combined with fear of communist domination, had given rise to totally unrealistic rationalizations claiming to legitimate the possibility of "limited nuclear war" and thus to justify the consequent "unintended" death of millions; the inadequacy of reliance on a policy of deterrence, the threat to carry out an immoral act that, if truly meant, is itself immoral; the demonization of the enemy, extended to include the entire population of a hostile nation, which would ignore the traditional obligation to avoid civilian casualties and fail even to take into account the presence of fellow believers among those attacked; the fatalistic passivity of the vast majority of citizens that allows "a largely anonymous power elite" to make decisions based not on sound moral principles but on a calculating *realpolitik* that would countenance massive retaliation and even preemptive attack; and the overwhelming failure of Christians to engage the issue in the context of recent authoritative teachings of the Church and the nonviolent witness of the life and death of Christ. While calling for practical, gradual steps moving in the direction of disarmament and the abolition of war, and for recognition and support of "a supra-national authority" to guide the process, Merton finds the fundamental motivation for the Christian's work for peace in the central Christian doctrine of the Incarnation, the full participation of God in human nature and existence, and the consequent "obligation to treat every other man as Christ Himself, respecting his life as if it were the life of Christ, his rights as if they were the rights of Christ." But this recognition is fully congruent with a respect for human dignity that should motivate believer and non-believer alike, what Merton calls in his preface to the anthology "a broad, tolerant, watchful and humanist outlook on the whole of life" shared by the authors of all the articles he has assembled (*Breakthrough to Peace*, 13). In the "Preamble" to his essay, Merton notes that relatively few people seem aware of the urgency of the problem; but within a month of the book's publication in September 1962, the Cuban Missile Crisis would jar the world into awareness and prompt the "religious opposition to war" called for and exemplified by the essay to become once again "articulate and widespread."

B ETWEEN 1918 AND 1939 religious opposition to war was articulate and widespread, all over Europe and America. Peace movements of significant proportions were active in Germany, Britain, and the United States. Yet they were crushed without difficulty and almost without protest by totalitarian regimes on the one hand, and silenced by the outbreak of a clearly defensive war on the other. Since 1945 there has been nothing to compare with the earlier movements of protest. Instead we have witnessed the enormous and crudely contrived fiction of the Communist Peace Movement which has been accepted with disillusioned resignation on one side of the Iron Curtain while, on the other, it has managed to make almost all efforts of independent civilian or religious groups to oppose nuclear war seem dishonest or subversive.

Yet never was opposition to war more urgent and more necessary than now. Never was religious protest so badly needed. Silence, passivity, or outright belligerence seem to be characteristic official and unofficial Christian reactions to the H-bomb. True, there has been some theological and ethical debate. This debate has been marked above all by a seemingly inordinate hesitation to characterize the uninhibited use of nuclear weapons as immoral. Of course the bomb has been condemned without equivocation by the "peace Churches" (Quakers, Mennonites, etc.). But the general tendency of Protestant and Catholic theologians has been to consider how far nuclear war could be reconciled with the traditional "just war" theory. In other words the discussion has been not so much a protest against nuclear war, still less a positive search for peaceful solutions to the problem of nuclear deterrence and ever increasing Cold-War obsessions, but rather an attempt to justify, under some limited form, a new type of war which is tacitly recognized as an imminent possibility. This theological thought has tended more and more to *accept* the evil of nuclear war, considering it a lesser evil than Communist domination, and looking for some practicable way to make use of the lesser evil in order to avoid the greater.

But it would seem that a genuinely religious perspective, especially a Christian perspective, should be totally different. Therefore the purpose of the present article is to stand back from the imminent risks of the Cold War crisis, seeking to judge the problem of nuclear war not in relation to what seems to be our own interests or even our own survival, but simply in the light of moral truth. A Christian ought to consider whether nuclear war is not in itself a moral evil so great that it *cannot* be justified even for the best of ends, even to defend the highest and most sacrosanct of values.

This does not imply a purely pacifist rejection of war as such. Assuming that a "just war" is at least a theoretical possibility and granting that in a just war Christians may be bound to defend their country, the question we want to examine here is whether or not the massive and unlimited use of nuclear weapons, or the use of them in a limited first strike which is foreseen as likely to set off a global cataclysm, can be considered under any circumstances just.

The great problem is in fact that both in the East and in the West nuclear weapons are taken for granted. Nuclear war is now assumed to be a rational option or at least nuclear deterrence is accepted as a reasonable and workable way of "preserving peace." The moral issue is generally set aside as irrelevant. But if in all these cases a use of nuclear weapons even to threaten total or quasi-total destruction of an enemy is immoral, then we are living in a completely noxious situation where most of our political, economic, and even religious thinking is inseparably bound up with assumptions that may ultimately prove criminal. And if this is so, we must be prepared to face terrible consequences. For moral truth is not a sentimental luxury. It is as much a necessity to man and his society as air, water, fire, food, and shelter.

This essay takes the stand that the *massive and uninhibited use of nuclear weapons*, either in attack or in retaliation, is contrary to Christian morality. And the arguments will be drawn particularly from Catholic sources. Recent Popes have declared ABC warfare (that is, atomic, biological, and chemical warfare) to be a "sin, an offense and an outrage" (Pius XII). It may be quite true that these Popes have also affirmed a nation's right to defend itself by *just means*, in a *just war*. It may also be true that a theological argument for the use of "tactical nuclear weapons" may be constructed on the basis of some of the Popes' statements. But when we remember that the twenty-kiloton A-bomb that was dropped on Hiroshima is now regarded as "small" and a "tactical device" and when we keep in mind that there is every probability that a force that is being beaten with small nuclear weapons will resort to big ones, we can easily see how little moral value can be found in these theorizings.

"Tactical nuclear weapons" and "limited war" with conventional forces are of course proposed with the best intentions: as a "realistic" way to avoid the horror of total nuclear warfare. Since it is claimed that men cannot get along without some kind of war, the least we can do is to insure that they will only destroy one another in thousands instead of in millions. Yet curiously enough, the restraint that would be required to keep within these limits (a restraint that was unknown on either side after the early phases of World War II), would seem to demand as much heroism and as much control as disarmament itself. It would therefore appear more realistic as well as more Christian and more humane to strive to think of total peace rather than of partial war. Why can we not do this? If disarmament were taken seriously, instead of being used as a pawn in the game of power politics, we could arrive at a workable agreement. It might not be ideal, but it would certainly be at once safer, saner, and more realistic than war, whether limited or total. But we make ourselves incapable of taking either disarmament or peace with total seriousness, because we are completely obsessed with the fury and the fantasies of the Cold War. The task of the Christian is to make the thought of peace once again seriously possible. A step towards this would be the rejection of nuclear deterrence as a basis for international policy. Nuclear war is totally unacceptable. It is immoral, inhuman, and absurd. It can lead nowhere but to the suicide of nations and of cultures, indeed to the destruction of human society itself.

We must now face the fact that we are moving closer and closer to war, not only as a result of blind social forces but also as the result of our own decisions and our own choice. The brutal reality is that, when all is said and done, we seem to *prefer* war, not that we want war itself, but we are blindly and hopelessly attached to all that makes war inevitable.

I. THE DANCE OF DEATH

NO ONE SERIOUSLY DOUBTS that it is now possible for man and his society to be completely destroyed in a nuclear war. This possibility must be soberly faced, even though it is so momentous in all its implications that we can hardly adjust ourselves to it in a fully rational manner. Indeed, this awful threat is the chief psychological weapon of the Cold War. America and Russia are playing the paranoid game of nuclear deterrence, each one desperately hoping to preserve peace by threatening the other with bigger bombs and total annihilation.

Every step in this political dance of death brings us inexorably closer to hot war. The closer we get to hot war, the more the theoretical possibility of our total destruction turns into a real probability.

There is no control over the arbitrary and belligerent self-determination of the great nations ruled by managerial power elites concerned chiefly with their own self-interest. The UN is proving itself unable to fulfill the role of international arbiter and powerless to control the pugnacity of the nuclear club. Indeed, the big powers have been content to use the UN as a forum for political and propagandist wrestling matches and have not hesitated to take independent action that led to the discrediting of the UN whenever this has been profitable to them. Hence the danger that the uncontrolled power of nuclear weapons may break loose whenever one of the belligerents feels himself sufficiently strong and sufficiently provoked to risk an all-out war. Repeated threats to use the bomb have doubtless been mostly bluff, but one day somebody's bluff is going to be called, perhaps in a very drastic fashion.

Meanwhile the United States alone possesses a stockpile of nuclear weapons estimated at 60,000 megatons. This is enough to wipe out the present civilized world and to permanently affect all life on the planet Earth. These nuclear bombs can be delivered by some 2,500 planes. It is no secret that such planes are constantly in the air, ready to strike. There are 200 missiles available to U.S. forces, mostly of intermediate range, and this does not suggest the immediate likelihood of a purely push-button war. But it is estimated that by 1963 there will be two thousand more of them, of which a large proportion will be intercontinental missiles based in "hard" installations. Attack on hard installations means ground bursts and therefore more fallout as well as more bombs. Hence even an attack concentrated on our missile bases is bound to have a destructive effect on many population centers.

An ICBM can carry an H-bomb warhead to a destination five thousand miles away, twenty times faster than the speed of sound. Intermediate-range missiles can be fired from submarines and deliver H-bombs which could reduce the eastern United States to a radioactive wasteland. H-bombs will soon be fitted to satellites and will be able to reach a target within a few minutes, without hope of interception.

It must be remembered that H-bombs are relatively cheap to produce, and it is not difficult to build and deliver big ones. Poison gas can also be delivered by long-range missiles. One such gas is manufactured in quantity by the U.S. Army Chemical Corps, and it can exterminate whole populations of men as if they were insects. A similar nerve gas, originally developed by the Nazis, is manufactured in Soviet Russia. This gas is considered to be more effective against civilian populations than any nuclear agent. It leaves industry and property intact and there is no fallout! Shelters offer no protection against chemical agents.

In a word, the logic of deterrence has proved to be singularly illogical, because of the fact that nuclear war is almost exclusively offensive. So far there is no indication that there can be any really effective defense against guided missiles. All the advantage goes to the force that strikes first, without warning. Hence the multiplication of "hard" weapon sites and of "deep shelters" becomes provocative, and instead of convincing the enemy of our invulnerability, it only invites a heavier preemptive attack by bigger bombs and more of them. The cost of moving a significant portion of industry, business, and the population underground is prohibitive, and the whole idea is in itself nonsensical, at least as a guarantee of "peace."

Far from producing the promised "nuclear stalemate" and the "balance of terror" on which we are trying to construct an improbable peace, these policies simply generate tension, confusion, suspicion, and paranoid hate. This is the climate most suited to the growth of totalitarianism. Indeed, the Cold War itself promises by itself to erode the last vestiges of true democratic freedom and responsibility even in the countries which claim to be defending these values. Those who think that they can preserve their independence, their civic and religious rights by ultimate recourse to the H-bomb do not seem to realize that the mere shadow of the bomb may end by reducing their religious and democratic beliefs to the level of mere words without meaning, veiling a state of rigid and totalitarian belligerency that will tolerate no opposition.

In a world where another Hitler and another Stalin are almost certain to appear on the scene, the existence of such destructive weapons and the moral paralysis of leaders and policy-makers combined with the passivity and confusion of mass societies which exist on both sides of the Iron Curtain constitute the gravest problem in the whole history of man. Our times can be called apocalyptic, in the sense that we seem to have come to a point at which all the hidden, mysterious dynamism of the "history of salvation" revealed in the Bible has flowered into final and decisive crisis. The term "end of the world" may or may not be one that we are capable of understanding. But at any rate we seem to be assisting at the unwrapping of the mysteriously vivid symbols in the last book of the New Testament. In their nakedness they reveal to us our own selves as the men whose lot it is to live in a time of possibly ultimate decision. In a word, the end of our civilized society is quite literally up to us and to our immediate descendants, if any. It is for us to decide whether we are going to give in to hatred, terror, and blind love of power for its own sake, and thus plunge our world into the abyss, or whether, restraining our savagery, we can patiently and humanely work together for interests which transcend the limits of any national or ideological community. We are challenged to prove we are rational, spiritual, and humane enough to deserve survival, by acting according to the highest ethical and spiritual norms we know. As Christians, we believe that these norms have been given to us in the Gospel and in the traditional theology of the Church.

II. THE CHRISTIAN AS PEACEMAKER

WE KNOW THAT CHRIST came into this world as the Prince of Peace. We know that Christ Himself is our peace (Ephesians 2:14). We believe that God has chosen for Himself, in the Mystical Body of Christ, an elect people, regenerated by the Blood of the Savior, and committed by their baptismal promise to wage war upon the evil and hatred that are in man, and help to establish the Kingdom of God and of peace.

This means a recognition that human nature, identical in all men, was assumed by the Logos in the Incarnation, and that Christ died out of love for all men, in order to live in all men. Consequently we have the obligation to treat every other man as Christ Himself, respecting his life as if it were the life of Christ, his rights as if they were the rights of Christ. Even if the other shows himself to be unjust, wicked, and odious to us, we cannot take upon ourselves a final and definitive judgment in his case. We still have an obligation to be patient, and to seek his highest spiritual interests. In other words, we are formally commanded to love our enemies, and this obligation cannot be met by a formula of words. It is not enough to press the button that will incinerate a city of five million people, saying in one's heart "this hurts me more than it hurts you," or declaring that it is all for love.

As Pope John XXIII pointed out in his first encyclical letter, *Ad Petri Cathedram*, Christians are obliged to strive for peace "with all the means at their disposal" and yet, as he continues, this peace cannot compromise with error or make concessions to it. Therefore it is by no means a matter of passive acquiescence in injustice, since this does not produce peace. However, the Christian struggle for peace depends first of all upon a free response of man to "God's call to the service of His Merciful designs" (Christmas message, 1958). Christ Our Lord did not come to bring peace to the world as a kind of spiritual tranquilizer. He brought to His disciples a vocation and a task, to struggle in the world of violence to establish His peace not only in their own hearts but in society itself. This was to be done not by wishing and fair words but by a total interior revolution in which we abandoned the human prudence that is subordinated to the quest for power, and followed the higher wisdom of love and of the Cross.

The Christian is and must be by his very adoption as a son of God, in Christ, a peacemaker (Matthew 5:9). He is bound to imitate the Savior who, instead of defending Himself with twelve legions of angels (Matthew 26:55), allowed Himself to be nailed to the Cross and died praying for His executioners. The Christian is one whose life has sprung from a particular spiritual seed: the blood of the martyrs who, without offering forcible resistance, laid down their lives rather than submit to the unjust laws that demanded an official religious cult of the emperor as God. That is to say, the Christian is bound, like the martyrs, to obey God rather than the state whenever the state tries to usurp powers that do not and cannot belong to it. We have repeatedly seen Christians in our time fulfilling this obligation in a heroic manner by their resistance to dictatorships that strove to interfere with the rights of their conscience and their religion.

Hence it must be stated quite clearly and without any compromise that the duty of the Christian as a peacemaker is not to be confused with a kind of quietistic inertia which is indifferent to injustice, accepts any kind of disorder, compromises with error and with evil, and gives in to every pressure in order to maintain "peace at any price." The Christian knows well, or should know well, that peace is not possible on such terms. Peace demands the most heroic labor and the most difficult sacrifice. It demands greater heroism than war. It demands greater fidelity to the truth and a much more perfect purity of conscience. The Christian fight for peace is not to be confused with defeatism. This has to be made clear because there is a certain complacent sophistry, given free currency by the theologians who want to justify war too easily, and who like to treat anyone who disagrees with them as if he were a practical apostate from the faith who had already surrendered implicitly to Communism by refusing to accept the morality of an all-out nuclear war. This, as anyone can easily see, is simply begging the question. And one feels that those who yield to this temptation are perhaps a little too much influenced by the pragmatism and opportunism of our affluent society.

There is a lot of talk, among some of the clergy, about the relative danger of nuclear war and a "Communist takeover." It is assumed, quite gratuitously, that the Communist is at the gates, and is just about to take over the United States, close all the churches, and brainwash all the good Catholics. Once this spectral assessment of the situation is accepted, then one is urged to agree that there is only one solution: to let the Reds have it before they get our government and our universities thoroughly infiltrated. This means a preemptive strike, based not on the fact that we ourselves are actually under military attack, but that we are so "provoked" and so "threatened" that even the most drastic measures are justified.

If it is argued that there can be no proportion between the awful destruction wrought by nuclear war and the good achieved by exorcising this specter of Communist domination, the argument comes back: "better dead than Red." And this, in turn, is justified by the contention that the destruction of cities, nations, populations is "only a physical evil" while Communist domination would be a "moral evil."

It must be said at once that this has no basis in logic, ethics, politics, or sound moral theology. Two quotations from Pope Pius XII will suffice to establish the true Catholic perspective on these points.

The destruction of cities and nations by nuclear war is *"only a physical evil"*? Pope Pius XII calls aggressive ABC warfare a "sin, an offense and an outrage against the majesty of God." And he adds: "It constitutes a crime worthy of the most severe national and international sanctions" (Address to the World Medical Congress, 1954). Fr. John Courtney Murray, S.J., whom no one can accuse of being a "pacifist" (he favors the licity of "limited nuclear war" and also believes that such a war would have practical value) has stated, "The extreme position of favoring a war . . . simply to kill off all Communists, cannot be a legitimate Catholic opinion."

The real issue here is not actually a moral principle so much as a state of mind. This state of mind is the one which we find in the American mass media. It is made up of a large number of very superficial assumptions about what is going on in the world and about what is likely to happen. We are in a sorry state, indeed, if our survival and indeed our Christian faith itself are left entirely at the mercy of such assumptions!

III. BEYOND EAST AND WEST

WE ARE NO LONGER living in a Christian world. The ages which we are pleased to call the "ages of faith" were certainly not ages of earthly paradise. But at least our forefathers officially recognized and favored the Christian ethic of love.

They fought some very bloody and unchristian wars, and in doing so, they also committed great crimes which remain in history as a permanent scandal. However, certain definite limits were recognized. Today a non-Christian world still retains a few vestiges of Christian morality, a few formulas and clichés, which serve on appropriate occasions to adorn indignant editorials and speeches. But otherwise we witness deliberate campaigns to oppose and eliminate all education in Christian truth and morality. Not only non-Christians but even Christians themselves tend to dismiss the Gospel ethic of nonviolence and love as "sentimental." As a matter of fact, the mere suggestion that Christ counseled nonviolent resistance to evil is enough to invite scathing ridicule.

It is therefore a serious error to imagine that because the West was once largely Christian, the cause of the Western nations is now to be identified, without further qualification, with the cause of God. The incentive to wipe out Bolshevism with H-bombs may well be one of the apocalyptic temptations of twentieth-century Christendom. It may indeed be the most effective way of destroying Christendom, even though man may survive. For who imagines that the Asians and Africans will respect Christianity and receive it after it has apparently triggered mass murder and destruction of cosmic proportions? It is pure madness to think that Christianity can defend itself by nuclear preemption. The mere fact that we now seem to accept nuclear war as reasonable and Christian is a universal scandal.

True, Christianity is not only opposed to Communism, but in a very real sense, at war with it. However this warfare is spiritual and ideological. "Devoid of material weapons," says Pope John, "the Church is the trustee of the highest spiritual power." If the Church has no military weapons of her own, it means that her wars are fought without violence, not that she intends to call upon the weapons of nations that were once Christian, in defense of the Gospel. Whatever we may think of the ethics of nuclear war, it is clear that the message of the H-bomb is neither salvation nor "good news."

But we believe, precisely, that an essential part of the "good news" is that spiritual weapons are stronger than material ones. Indeed, by spiritual arms, the early Church conquered the entire Roman world. Have we lost our faith in this "sword of the Spirit"? Have we perhaps lost all realization of its very existence?

Of course we must repudiate a tactic of inert passivity that purely and simply leaves man defenseless, without any recourse whatever to any means of protecting himself, his rights, or Christian truth. We repeat again and again that the right, and truth, are to be defended by the most efficacious possible means, and that the most efficacious of all are precisely the spiritual ones, which have always been the only ones that have effected a really lasting moral change in society and in man. The Church tolerates defensive use of weapons only insofar as men are unable to measure up to the stricter and more heroic demands of spiritual warfare. It is absolutely unchristian to adopt, in practice, a standard of judgment which practically rejects or ignores all recourse to the spiritual weapons, and relegates them entirely to the background as if they had no efficacy whatever, and as if material weapons (the bigger the better) were the ones that really counted.

It seems that a great deal of the moral discussion about nuclear war is based, in fact, on the assumption that spiritual weapons are quixotic and worthless and that material weapons alone are worthy of serious consideration. But this attitude is precisely what leads to a fundamental vitiation of the Church's traditionally accepted doctrine on the use of violence in war; it seeks in every possible way to evade the obligation to use war only as a last resort, purely in *defense*, and with the use of *just means only*.

Inevitably, as soon as the obsession with bigger and bigger weapons takes hold of us, we make it impossible for ourselves to consider the just rights of noncombatants. We twist and deform the truth in every possible way in order to convince ourselves that noncombatants are really combatants after all, and that our "attack" is in reality "defense," while the enemy's "defense" really constitutes an "attack." By such tactics we disqualify ourselves from receiving the guidance of light and grace which will enable us to judge as spiritual men and as members of Christ. Obviously, without this special gift of light, we remain utterly incapable of seeing or appreciating the superiority of spiritual weapons, prayer, sacrifice, negotiation, and nonviolent means in general.

This results in the unhappy situation that non-Christians with rather dubious doctrinal support in irreligious philosophies have been able to take over characteristically Christian spiritual methods, appropriating them to themselves and thus further discrediting them in the eyes of the orthodox believer who is already confused by the now instinctive justification of war and weapons as the "normal" Christian way of solving international problems.

We must remember that the Church does not belong to any political power bloc. Christianity exists on both sides of the Iron Curtain, and we should feel ourselves united by very special bonds with those Christians who, living under Communism, often suffer heroically for their principles.

Is it a valid defense of Christianity for us to wipe out those heroic Christians along with their oppressors, for the sake of "religious freedom"?

Let us stop and consider where the policy of massive retaliation and worse still of preemptive strike may lead us. Are we to annihilate huge population centers, at the same time showering vast areas around them with lethal fallout? Do we believe it is necessary to do this in order to protect ourselves against the menace of world Communism?

In these countries which we may perhaps be ready to annihilate, the vast majority is not Communist. On the contrary, while the people have resigned themselves passively to Communist domination, and have become quite convinced that there is no hope to be looked for from us because we are their declared enemies, and intend to wipe them out, they are by no means Communists. They do not want war. They have, in many cases, lived through the horrors and sacrifices of total war and experienced things which we are barely able to imagine. They do not want to go through this again.

We, in the name of liberty, of justice, of humanity, are pursuing a policy which promises to crush them with even greater horror, except that it may be perhaps "merciful" that millions of them will simply be blown out of existence in the twinkling of an eye. Merciful? When many of them have a Christian background, many are faithful Christians?

What good will our belligerent policy do us in those countries? None at all. It will only serve to reinforce the fatalistic conviction of the necessity of armament and of war that has been dinned into these populations by the Communist minority which dominates them.

How do we justify our readiness to wage a war of this kind? Let us face the fact that we feel ourselves terribly menaced by Communism. Certainly we believe we have to defend ourselves. Why are we menaced? Because, as time goes on, the Communists have gained a greater and greater advantage over us in the Cold War. Why have they been able to do this? This is a question of historic fact, which, however, is not absolutely clear, but anyone will admit that our very reliance on the massive power of the bomb has to a great extent crippled us and restricted our freedom to maneuver, and the Communists have been operating under the *protection* of this massive threat that is too enormous to let loose for any but the most serious causes. Hence, instead of the serious provocation, the massive attack, we are confronted with a multiplicity of little threats all over the world, little advances, little gains. They all add up, but even the total of all of them does not constitute a sufficient reason for nuclear war.

But we are getting mad, and we are beginning to be thoroughly impatient with the humiliation of constant defeat. The more humiliated we become, the worse we compromise our chances, the greater errors we make.

We used to have an unrivaled reputation among the backward peoples of the world. We were considered the true defenders of liberty, justice, and peace, the hope of the future. Our anger, our ignorance, and our frustration have made us forfeit this tremendous advantage.

IV. MORAL PASSIVITY AND DEMONIC ACTIVISM

ONE OF THE MOST disturbing things about the Western world of our time is that it is beginning to have much more in common with the Communist world than it has with the professedly Christian society of several centuries ago. On both sides of the Iron Curtain we find two pathological varieties of the same moral sickness: both of them rooted in the same basically materialistic view of life. Both are basically opportunistic and pragmatic in their own way. And both have the following characteristics in common. On the level of *morality* they are blindly passive in their submission to a determination which, in effect, leaves men completely irresponsible. Therefore moral obligations and decisions tend to become practically meaningless. At best they are only forms of words, rationalizations of pragmatic decisions that have already been dictated by the needs of the moment.

Naturally, since not everyone is an unprincipled materialist even in Russia, there is bound to be some moral sense at work, even if only as a guilt-feeling that produces uneasiness and hesitation, blocking the smooth efficiency of machine-like obedience to immoral commands. Yet the history of Nazi Germany shows us how appalling was the irresponsibility which would carry out even the most revolting of crimes under cover of "obedience" to "legitimately constituted authority" for the sake of a "good cause." This moral passivity is the most terrible danger of our time, as the American bishops have already pointed out in their joint letters of 1960 and 1961.

On the level of political, economic, and military activity, this moral passivity is balanced, or overbalanced, by a *demonic activism*, a frenzy of the most varied, versatile, complex, and even utterly brilliant technological improvisations, following one upon the other with an ever more bewildering and uncontrollable proliferation. Politics pretends to use this force as its servant, to harness it for social purposes, for the "good of man." The intention is good. The technological development of power in our time is certainly a risk and challenge, but it is by no means intrinsically evil. On the contrary, it can and should be a very great good. In actual fact, however, the furious speed with which our technological world is plunging toward disaster is evidence that no one is any longer fully in control—least of all, perhaps, the political leaders.

A simple study of the steps which led to the dropping of the first A-bomb on Hiroshima is devastating evidence of the way well-meaning men, the scientists, generals, and statesmen of a victorious nation, were guided step by step, without realizing it, by the inscrutable yet simple "logic of events" to fire the shot that was to make the Cold War inevitable and prepare the way inexorably for World War III. This they did purely and simply because they thought in all sincerity that the bomb was the simplest and most merciful way of ending World War II and perhaps all wars, forever.

The tragedy of our time is then not so much the malice of the wicked as the helpless futility of the best intentions of "the good." There are warmakers, war criminals, indeed. They are present and active on *both sides*. But all of us, in our very best efforts for peace, find ourselves maneuvered unconsciously into positions where we too can act as war criminals. For there can be no doubt that Hiroshima and Nagasaki were, though not fully deliberate crimes, nevertheless crimes. And who was responsible? No one. Or "history." We cannot go on playing with nuclear fire and shrugging off the results as "history." We are the ones concerned.

In plain words, in order to save ourselves from destruction we have to try to regain control of a world that is speeding downhill without brakes because of the combination of factors I have just mentioned: almost total passivity and irresponsibility on the moral level, plus demonic activism in social, political, and military life.

First of all we must seek some remedy in the technological sphere. We must try to achieve some control over the production and stockpiling of weapons. It is intolerable that such massive engines of destruction should be allowed to proliferate in all directions without any semblance of a long-range plan for anything, even for what is cynically called "defense." To allow governments to pour more and more billions into weapons that almost immediately become obsolete, thereby necessitating more billions for newer and bigger weapons, is one of the most colossal injustices in the long history of man. While we are doing this, two-thirds of the world is starving, or living in conditions of subhuman destitution.

Far from demanding that the lunatic race for destruction be stepped up, it seems to me that Christian morality imposes on every single one of us the obligation to protest against it and to work for the creation of an international authority with power and sanctions that will be able to control technology, and divert our amazing virtuosity into the service of man instead of against him.

It is not enough to say that we ought to try to work for a negotiated disarmament, or that one power bloc or the other ought to take the lead and disarm unilaterally. Methods and policies can and should be fairly considered. But what matters most is the obligation to travel in every feasible way in the direction of peace, using all the traditional and legitimate methods, while at the same time seeking to improvise new and original measures to achieve our end.

Long ago, even before the A-bomb, Pope Pius XII declared it was our supreme obligation to make "war on war" (1944). At that time he stressed our moral obligation to ban all wars of aggression, stating this duty was binding on *all* and that it "brooks no delay, no procrastination, no hesitation, no subterfuge." And what have we seen since then? The A-bomb, the H-bomb, the ICBM, the development of chemical and bacteriological weapons, and every possible evasion and subterfuge to justify their use without limitation as soon as one or the other nation decides that it may be expedient!

Therefore a Christian who is not willing to envisage the creation of an effective international authority to control the destinies of man for peace is not acting and thinking as a mature member of the Church. He does not have fully Christian perspectives. Such perspectives must, by their very nature, be "catholic," that is to say worldwide. They must consider the needs of mankind and not the temporary expediency and shortsighted policy of a particular nation.

To reject a "worldwide" outlook, to refuse to consider the good of mankind, and to remain satisfied with the affluence that flows from our war economy, is hardly a Christian attitude. Nor will our attachment to the current payoff accruing to us from weapons make it any easier for us to see and understand the need to take the hard road of sacrifice which alone leads to peace!

Equally important, and perhaps even more difficult than technological control, is the restoration of some moral sense and the resumption of genuine responsibility. Without this it is illusory for us to speak of freedom and "control." Unfortunately, even where moral principles are still regarded with some degree of respect, morality has lost touch with the realities of our situation. Modern warfare is fought as much by machines as by men. Even a great deal of the planning depends on the work of mechanical computers.

Hence it becomes more and more difficult to estimate the morality of an act leading to war because it is more and more difficult to know precisely what is going on. Not only is war increasingly a matter for pure specialists operating with fantastically complex machinery, but above all there is the question of absolute secrecy regarding everything that seriously affects defense policy. We may amuse ourselves by reading the reports in mass media and imagine that these "facts" provide sufficient basis for moral judgments for and against war. But in reality, we are simply elaborating moral fantasies in a vacuum. Whatever we may decide, we remain completely at the mercy of the governmental power, or rather the anonymous power of managers and generals who stand behind the facade of government. We have no way of directly influencing the decisions and policies taken by these people. In practice, we must fall back on a blinder and blinder faith which more and more resigns itself to trusting the "legitimately constituted authority" without having the vaguest notion what that authority is liable to do next. This condition of irresponsibility and passivity is extremely dangerous. It is hardly conducive to genuine morality.

An entirely new dimension is opened up by the fantastic processes and techniques involved in modern war. An American President can speak of warfare in outer space and nobody bursts out laughing—he is perfectly serious. Science fiction and the comic strip have all suddenly come true. When a missile armed with an H-bomb warhead is fired by the pressing of a button and its target is a whole city, the number of its victims is estimated in "megacorpses"—*millions* of dead human beings. A thousand or ten thousand more here and there are not even matter for comment. To what extent can we assume that the soldiers who exercise this terrible power are worthy of our confidence and actually realize what they are doing? To what extent can we assume that in passively following their lead and concurring in their decision—at least by default—we are acting as Christians?

V. THE MORAL PROBLEM

IN ALL-OUT NUCLEAR WAR, there is no longer question of simply permitting an evil, the destruction of a few civilian dwellings, in order to attain a legitimate end: the destruction of a military target. It is well understood on both sides that all-out nuclear war is purely and simply massive and indiscriminate destruction of targets chosen not for their military significance alone, but for their importance in a calculated project of terror and annihilation. Often the selection of the target is determined by some quite secondary and accidental circumstance that has not the remotest reference to morality. Hiroshima was selected for atomic attack, among other reasons, because it had never undergone any notable air bombing and was suitable as an intact target to give a good idea of the effectiveness of the bomb.

It must be frankly admitted that some of the military commanders of both sides in World War II simply disregarded all the traditional standards that were still effective. The Germans threw those standards overboard with the bombs they unloaded on Warsaw, Rotterdam, Coventry, and London. The Allies replied in kind with saturation bombing of Hamburg, Cologne, Dresden, and Berlin. Spokesmen were not wanting on either side to justify these crimes against humanity. And today, while "experts" calmly discuss the possibility of the United States being able to survive a war if "*only fifty millions*" (!) of the population are killed, when the Chinese speak of being able to *spare* "three hundred million" and "still get along," it is obvious that we are no longer in the realm where moral truth is conceivable.

The only sane course that remains is to work frankly and without compromise for a supranational authority and for the total abolition of war. The pronouncements of the Holy See all seem to point to this as the best ultimate solution.

The moral duty of the Christian is by no means simple. It is far from being a neat matter of ethical principle, clear cut, well defined, and backed by a lucid authoritative decision of the Church. To make the issue seem too simple is actually to do a great disservice to truth, to morality, and to man. And yet now more than ever we crave the simple and the clear solution. This very craving is dangerous, because the most tempting of all "simple" solutions are the ones which prescribe annihilation or submit to it without resistance. There is a grim joke underlying all this talk about "Red or dead." The inherent destructiveness of the frustrated mind is able to creep in here and distort the whole Christian view of life and of civilization by evading the difficult and complex way of negotiation and sacrifice, in order to resort, in frustrated desperation, to "magic" power and nuclear destruction. Let us not ignore this temptation, it is one of the deepest and most radical in man. It is the first of all temptations, and the root of all the others. "You shall be as gods . . ." (Genesis 3:5).

On the contrary, our Christian obligation consists in being and remaining men, believing in the Word Who emptied Himself and became man for our sakes. We have to look at the problem of nuclear war from the viewpoint of humanity and of God made man, from the viewpoint of the Mystical Body of Christ, and not merely from the viewpoint of abstract formulas. Here above all we need a reasoning that is informed with compassion and takes some account of flesh and blood, not a legalistic juggling with principles and precedents.

In the light of these deep Christian truths we will better understand the danger of fallacious justifications of every recourse to violence, as well as the peril of indifference, inertia, and passivity.

It is not a question of stating absolutely and infallibly that every Christian must renounce, under pain of mortal sin, any opinion that the use of the bomb might be legitimate. The H-bomb has not been formally and officially condemned, and doubtless it does not need to be condemned. There is no special point in condemning one weapon in order to give casuistical minds an opportunity to prove their skill in evasion by coming up with another, "licit" way of attaining the same destructive end. It is not just a matter of seeing how much destruction and murder we can justify without incurring the condemnation of the Church.

But I submit that at this time above all it is vitally important to avoid the "minimalist" approach. The issue of nuclear war is too grave and too general. It threatens everybody. It may affect the very survival of the human race. In such a case one is not allowed to take any but unavoidable risks. We are obliged to take the morally more secure alternative in guiding our choice. Let us remember too that while a doubt of the existence of an obligation leaves us with a certain freedom of choice, the doubt of an evil fact does not permit such freedom.

We may well dispute the legitimacy of nuclear war on principle; but when we face the *actual fact* that recourse to nuclear weapons may quite probably result in the quasi-total destruction of civilization, even possibly in the suicide of the entire human race, we *are absolutely obliged to take this fact into account and to avoid this terrible danger.*

It is certainly legitimate for a Catholic moralist to hold in theory that a limited nuclear war, in defense, is permitted by traditional Christian moral principles. He may even hold the opinion that the strategic use of nuclear, bacteriological, and chemical weapons is theoretically permissible for defense, provided that there is a possibility that what we are defending will continue to exist after it has been "defended."

But when we come face to face with the terrible doubt of fact, *dubium facti*, the absolutely real and imminent probability of massive and uncontrolled destruction with the annihilation of civilization and of life, then there is no such latitude of choice. We are most gravely and seriously bound by all norms of Christian morality, however minimal, to choose the safer course and to try at all costs to avoid so general a disaster.

Let us remember that even if one were to admit the theoretical legitimacy of nuclear weapons for purposes of defense, that use would become gravely unjust, without a shadow of doubt, as soon as the effects of nuclear destruction overflowed upon neutral or friendly nations. Even though we may feel justified in risking the destruction of our own cities and those of the enemy, we have no right whatever to bring destruction upon helpless small nations which have no interest whatever in the war and ask only to survive in peace. It is not up to us to choose that *they* should be dead rather than Red.

Pope Pius XII said in 1954 (concerning ABC warfare, described above as a sin, an offense, and an outrage against God): "Should the evil consequences of adopting this method of warfare *ever become so extensive as to pass entirely beyond the control of man, then indeed its use must be rejected as immoral.*" He adds that uncontrolled annihilation of life within a given area "IS NOT LAWFUL UNDER ANY TITLE."

Nor is it moral to overindulge in speculation on this dangerous point of "control." A lax interpretation of this principle would lead us to decide that a twenty-megaton H-bomb dropped on Leningrad is "fully under control" because all its effects are susceptible to measurement, and we know that the blast will annihilate Leningrad while the fallout will probably wipe out the population of Helsinki and Riga, depending on the wind. Obviously what the Pope meant was much more strict than that. He meant that if there was uncontrolled annihilation of everybody in Leningrad, without any discrimination between combatants and noncombatants, enemies, friends, women, children, infants, and old people, then the use of the bomb would be "not lawful under any title," especially in view of the "bonus" effects of fallout drifting over neutral territory, certainly without control. And I do not think "clean" bombs are going to get around this moral difficulty either.

Hence though nuclear warfare as such has not been entirely and formally condemned, the mind of the Church is obviously that every possible means should be taken to avoid it; and John XXIII made this abundantly clear in his Christmas Message of 1961 where he pleaded in most solemn terms with the rulers of all nations to "shun all thought of force" and remain at peace. The words of Pope John in this connection imply grave reservations even with regard to limited war which might possibly "escalate" and reach all-out proportions.

There can be no doubt whatever that the absence of formal condemnation cannot be twisted into a tacit official approval of all-out nuclear war. Yet it seems that this is what some of our theologians are trying to do.

On the contrary, out duty is to help emphasize with all the force at our disposal that the Church earnestly seeks the abolition of war; we must underscore declarations like those of Pope John XXIII pleading with world leaders to renounce force in the settlement of international disputes and confine themselves to negotiations.

Now let us suppose that the political leaders of the world, supported by the mass media in their various countries, and carried on by a tidal wave of greater and greater war preparations, see themselves swept inexorably into a war of cataclysmic proportions. Let us suppose that it becomes morally certain that these leaders are helpless to arrest the blind force of the process that has irresponsibly been set in motion. What then? Are the masses of the world, including you and me, to resign themselves to our fate and march to global suicide without resistance, simply bowing our heads and obeying our leaders as showing us the "will of God"? I think it should be evident to everyone that this can no longer, in the present situation, be accepted unequivocally as Christian obedience and civic duty.

It is true that Pope Pius XII in his Christmas Message of 1956 declared that a Catholic was bound in duty to help his country in a just war of defense. But to extend this to all-out nuclear war is begging the question because Papal pronouncements on nuclear war cast doubts upon its justice. No theologian, however broad, however lax, would insist that one was bound in conscience to participate in a war that was *evidently* leading to global suicide. Those who favor nuclear war can only do so by making all kinds of suppositions concerning the political and military facts: that it will be only a limited war or that the destructive effects of H-bombs are not as terrible as we have been told. However much they limit the score sheet of megacorpses, it is difficult for us to admit the morality of all-out nuclear war.

This brings us face to face with the greatest and most agonizing moral issue of our time. This issue is not merely nuclear war, not merely the possible destruction of the human race by a sudden explosion of violence. It is something more subtle and more demonic. If we continue to yield to theoretically irresistible determinism and to vague "historic forces" without striving to resist and control them, if we let these forces drive us to demonic activism in the realm of politics and technology, we face something more than the material evil of universal destruction. We face *moral responsibility for global suicide*. Much more than that, we are going to find ourselves gradually moving into a situation in which we are practically compelled by the "logic of circumstances" deliberately to *choose the course that leads to destruction*.

The great danger is then the savage and self-destructive commitment to a policy of nationalism and blind hate, and the refusal of all other policies more constructive and more in accordance with Christian ethical tradition. Let us realize that this is a matter of *choice*, not of pure blind determinism.

We all know the logic of temptation. We all know the confused, vague, hesitant irresponsibility which leads us into the situation where it is no longer possible to turn back, and how, arrived in that situation, we have a moment of clear-sighted desperation in which we freely commit ourselves to the course we recognize as evil. That may well be what is happening now to the whole world.

The free choice of global suicide, made in desperation by the world's leaders and ratified by the consent and cooperation of their citizens, would be a moral evil second only to the Crucifixion. The fact that such a choice might be made with the highest motives and the most urgent purpose would do nothing whatever to mitigate it. The fact that it might be made as a gamble, in the hope that some might escape, would never excuse it. After all, the purposes of Caiaphas were, in his own eyes, perfectly noble. He thought it was necessary to let "one man die for the people."

The most urgent necessity of our time is therefore not merely to prevent the destruction of the human race by nuclear war. Even if it should happen to be no longer possible to prevent the disaster (which God forbid), there is still a greater evil that can and must be prevented. It must be possible for every free man to refuse his consent and deny his cooperation to this greatest of crimes.

VI. THE CHRISTIAN CHOICE

IN WHAT DOES THIS effective and manifest refusal of consent consist? How does one "resist" the sin of genocide? Ideally speaking, in the imaginary case where all-out nuclear war seemed inevitable and the world's leaders were evidently incapable of preventing it, it would be legitimate and even obligatory for all sane and conscientious men everywhere in the world to lay down their weapons and their tools and starve and be shot rather than cooperate in the war effort. If such a mass movement should spontaneously arise in all parts of the world, in Russia and America, in China and France, in Africa and Germany, the human race could be saved from extinction. This is indeed an engaging hypothesis—but it is no more than that. It would be folly to suppose that men hitherto passive, inert, morally indifferent and irresponsible might suddenly recover their sense of obligation and their awareness of their own power when the world was on the very brink of war.

In any case, as has been said above, the ordinary man has no access to vital information. Indeed, even the politicians may know relatively little about what is really going on. How would it be possible to know when and how it was necessary to refuse cooperation? Can we draw a line clearly, and say precisely when nuclear war becomes so dangerous that it is suicidal? If a war of missiles breaks out, we will have at the most thirty minutes to come to our momentous conclusions—if we ever know what is happening at all. It seems to me that the time to form our conscience and to decide upon our course of action is *NOW*.

It is one thing to form one's conscience and another to adopt a specific policy or course of action. It is highly regrettable that this important distinction is overlooked and indeed deliberately obfuscated. To decide, in the forum of conscience, that one is obligated in every way, as a Christian, to avoid actions that would contribute to a worldwide disaster does not mean that one is necessarily committed to absolute and unqualified pacifism. One may start from this moral principle, which is repeatedly set before us by the Popes and which cannot be seriously challenged, and one may then go on to seek various means to preserve peace. About these different means, there may be considerable debate.

Yet it seems clear to me that the enormous danger represented by nuclear weapons, and the near impossibility of controlling them and limiting them to a scale that would fit the traditional ethical theory of a just war, makes it both logical and licit for a Catholic to proceed, from motives of conscience, to at least a relative pacifism, and to a policy of nuclear disarmament.

In so doing, however, he has a strict obligation to see that he does not take a naïve and oversimplified position which would permit him to be ruthlessly exploited by the politicians of another nuclear power. The logic of all serious efforts to preserve peace demands that our very endeavors themselves do not help the war effort of the "enemy," and thus precipitate war. There is sometimes a danger that our pacifism may be somewhat shortsighted and immature. It may consequently be more an expression of rebellion against the status quo in our own country than an effective opposition to war itself.

In a word, there are three things to be considered: (1) Christian moral principles, which by their very nature favor peace, and according to which nuclear war remains, if not absolutely forbidden, at least of exceedingly dubious morality; (2) the facts about weapons systems and defense policies. Our moral decision and the morality of our participation in the economic and political life of a society geared for nuclear war demand imperatively that we realize the real nature of the military policies to which we contribute by taxation and perhaps also by our work in industry. So much in our national life is today centered on the most intense and most overwhelming arms race in the history of man. Everything points to the fact that these frightful weapons of destruction may soon be used, most probably on the highest and most expanded scale; (3) we must finally consider factors by which these military policies are dictated.

The Christian moral principles are relatively clear. While there is still intense debate over details, no Christian moralist worthy of the name can seriously defend outright a nuclear war of unqualified aggression.

The facts about ABC warfare are also clear enough. There is no question of the immense destructiveness of the weapons available to us. There is no question that the destruction of civilization and even global suicide are both possible. There is no question that the policies of the nuclear powers are geared for an all-out war of incredible savagery and destructive force.

What remains to be explored by the Christian is the area that is least considered, which also happens to be the area that most needs to be examined and is perhaps the one place where something can be done.

By what are our policies of hatred and destructiveness dictated? What seems to drive us inexorably on to the fate which we all dread and seek to avoid? This question is not hard to answer. What started the First World War? What started the Second World War? The answer is, simply, the rabid, shortsighted, irrational, and stubborn forces which tend to come to a head in nationalism.

Christopher Dawson has said:

The defeat of Hitlerism does not mean that we have seen the end of such movements. In our modern democratic world, irrational forces lie very near the surface, and *their sudden eruption under the impulse of nationalist or revolutionary ideologies is the greatest of all the dangers that threaten the modern world.* . . . It is at this point that the need for a re-assertion of Christian principles becomes evident. In so far as nationalism denies the principle (of higher order and divine justice for all men) and sets up the nation and the national state as the final object of man's allegiance, *it represents the most retrograde movement the world has ever seen,* since it means a denial of the great central truth on which civilization was founded, and the return to the pagan idolatries of tribal barbarism.

Dawson then goes on to quote Pope Pius XII who distinguishes between "national life" and "nationalistic politics." National life is a combination of all the values which characterize a social group and enable it to contribute fruitfully to the whole policy of nations. Nationalistic politics on the other hand are divisive, destructive, and a perversion of genuine national values. They are "a principle of dissolution within the community of peoples."

This then is the conclusion: the Christian is bound to work for peace by working against global dissolution and anarchy. Due to nationalist and revolutionary ideologies (for Communism is in fact exploiting the intense nationalism of backward peoples), a worldwide spirit of confusion and disorder is breaking up the unity and the order of civilized society.

It is true that we live in an epoch of revolution, and that the breakup and reformation of society is inevitable. But the Christian must see that his mission is not to contribute to the blind forces of annihilation which tend to destroy civilization and mankind together. He must seek to build rather than to destroy. He must orient his efforts towards world unity and not towards world division. Anyone who promotes policies of hatred and of war is working for the division and the destruction of civilized mankind.

We have to be convinced that there are certain things already clearly forbidden to all men, such as the use of torture, the killing of hostages, genocide (or the mass extermination of racial, national, or other groups for no reason than that they belong to an "undesirable" category). The destruction of civilized centers by nuclear annihilation bombing is genocide.

We have to become aware of the poisonous effect of the mass media that keep violence, cruelty, and sadism constantly present to the minds of unformed and irresponsible people. We have to recognize the danger to the whole world in the fact that today the economic life of the more highly developed nations is in large part centered on the production of weapons, missiles, and other engines of destruction.

We have to consider that the hate propaganda, and the consistent heckling of one government by another, has always inevitably led to violent conflict. We have to recognize the implications of voting for politicians who promote policies of hate. We must never forget that our most ordinary decisions may have terrible consequences.

It is no longer reasonable or right to leave all decisions to a largely anonymous power elite that is driving us all, in our passivity, towards ruin. We have to make ourselves heard.

Every individual Christian has a grave responsibility to protest clearly and forcibly against trends that lead inevitably to crimes which the Church deplores and condemns. Ambiguity, hesitation, and compromise are no longer permissible. We must find some new and constructive way of settling international disputes. This may be extraordinarily difficult. Obviously war cannot be abolished by mere wishing. Severe sacrifices may be demanded and the results will hardly be visible in our day. We have still time to do something about it, but the time is rapidly running out.

11

The Humanity of Christ in Monastic Prayer

This essay was developed in the aftermath of Merton's discussion of John Cassian on prayer in his novitiate conferences of May 1963 (see *Pre-Benedictine Monasticism*, xxiv-xxv, for a discussion of its origins). The typescript is dated "June 1963" on its cover page, and in a June 10, 1963, letter to Dom Jean Leclercq, Merton mentions that he used material on Gregory the Great from Leclercq's section of the *Histoire de la Spiritualité Chrétienne* "in a long article I have done on the question of 'The Humanity of Christ in Prayer' as it was seen by the monastic Fathers" (*Survival or Prophecy?*, 96), though in a letter to Tarcisius [James] Conner on June 23 he writes: "I am doing a longish study . . . on Monastic Prayer (Humanity of Christ, acc. to Cassian, Gregory, Bede, Leo, Ambrose Autpert)" (*School of Charity*, 174), so apparently he was still at work on the article after writing to Leclercq. It was first published in *Monastic Studies* 2 (October 1964), 1-27, and included in *The Monastic Journey* (87-106). The essay is one of Merton's more scholarly articles, but it is motivated by a very practical concern, the question of the compatibility of apophatic prayer, prayer without forms, beyond words and concepts and images, with acceptance of Christ in his full humanity as the one mediator between the believer and the Father. Is it a matter of somehow "leaving behind" the humanity of Christ to contemplate the divinity, as sometimes seems to be proposed in Christian mystical teaching? The evidence Merton assembles from his examination of the patristic and early monastic tradition is consistent in its rejection of a theory or practice of prayer that would somehow relegate the humanity of Christ to a "lower" level, at the same time that it makes clear that such a position does not require an imaginative focus on the historical, corporeal Jesus. The living Christ to whom and with whom one prays is the resurrected and ascended Redeemer, dwelling eternally with the Father. "There is no question whatever of 'excluding' the humanity of Christ from contemplative prayer, in order to contemplate His divinity! On the contrary, humanity and divinity are contemplated in inseparable unity in the Person of the glorified Son of God." Authentic prayer as taught by the Fathers rejects any sort of quasi-Nestorian approach: "the Christ of monastic contemplation is neither the divinity alone nor the humanity alone, but the unity of the two natures in one Person." Moreover, through sharing in the Paschal Mystery, dying and rising with Christ, one does not simply become aware of the glorified presence of Christ within the divine life of the Trinity, but participates in that life and that love because one is united with Christ: "Christ in glory is more than 'the object' of *contemplatio*, since the contemplative experience is an ineffable sharing in the light that radiates spiritually from the glorified humanity of the savior," the free gift received by those "who, loving His cross, have emptied themselves in order to be one with Him."

A MODERN PROBLEM

REATERS OF ST. TERESA are familiar with a problem (or pseudo-problem) that was raised by illuminism and quietism in the sixteenth and seventeenth centuries. Mental prayer grows progressively simpler until it becomes "contemplation" in which there are few ideas or even none at all, and in which images play little or no part. But Christian prayer is obviously centered on the Person of Jesus Christ. Should contemplative prayer be understood as directed only to Christ as God, not as man? In other words, is there a time when the humanity of Christ no longer has any place in mental prayer? Or is there even a time when it becomes right and proper to deliberately *exclude* Christ the man from prayer, in order to be able to lose oneself entirely in His divinity? St. Teresa, with a healthy Catholic instinct, rejected the idea that the "one mediator" between God and men, the Man-God, should somehow become an obstacle instead of a mediator. She doubtless sensed the inner confusions and contradictions inherent in this abstract and arbitrary separation between the humanity and divinity of Christ. Let us recall briefly what she tells us of the "problem" as she experienced it.[1]

First she refers to writers "who advise us earnestly to put aside all corporeal imagination and to approach the contemplation of the divinity. For they say that anything else, even Christ's humanity, will hinder or impede those who have arrived so far from attaining to the most perfect contemplation. They quote the words of the Lord on this subject to the Apostles with regard to the coming of the Holy Spirit. . . ."[2]

Then she admits that she herself "when I began to gain some experience of supernatural prayer—I mean the prayer of quiet—I tried to put aside everything corporeal . . . I thought I was experiencing the presence of God, as proved to be true, and I contrived to remain with Him in a state of recollection." She found this so profitable that "no one could have made me return to meditation on the humanity," but afterwards she reproached herself for this as for "an act

---

1. St. Teresa of Avila, *Life*, chap. 22.

2. "It is better for you that I should go away; the Paraclete will not come to you unless I go," etc. (John 16:7ff.).

of high treason." She addresses Christ, saying: "Is it possible, my Lord, that for so much as an hour I should have entertained the thought that Thou couldst hinder my greatest good?" And she surmised, quite rightly, that there is a kind of pride and human self-conceit in wanting by deliberate effort and technique to attain to an "experience" of the "divine essence" while by-passing the Person of the Man-God as though He were an obstacle.

The problem, if it is really to be seen as a problem, arises when the *Person* of the God-Man is conceived as being an obstacle to "contemplation of the divine essence." So, in reality, what St. Teresa saw was that for a Christian there could be no contemplative experience of the divine essence except in and through the Person of Christ, the God-Man. However, she distinguished quite rightly between the state in which Christ lived and acted before His resurrection, and the glorified life in which He lives now after His resurrection and will live forever. Thus she says:

> I cannot bear the idea that we might withdraw ourselves entirely from Christ and *treat that divine Body of His as though it were on a level with our miseries.* . . . It may be that our temperament or some indisposition will not allow us always to think of His passion. . . . *But what can prevent us from being with Him and His resurrection body* since we have Him so near us in the sacrament, *where He is already glorified?*

Here we see that St. Teresa was in full accord with patristic and monastic tradition. A study of that tradition will enable us to appreciate more fully the real place of the humanity of Christ in monastic prayer.

What was the extreme and erroneous position against which St. Teresa reacted? Cardinal Casanata, preparing the condemnation of quietism by the Holy Office in 1687, summed up the error in these words: "True and perfect contemplation must fix itself upon the *pure essence of God stripped of Person and of attributes.*" "There can be no perfect contemplation *save only of the Divinity.*"[3] The Bull of 20 November 1687, condemning Molinos, listed this as the thirty-fifth condemned proposition: "Souls in the interior way must not elicit acts of love toward the Blessed Virgin, the saints, *or the humanity of Christ* because, since these are sensible objects, love for them is also sensible."[4] Without going into a detailed theological analysis of these statements, we can easily see what confusions they led to in "spirituality" and in "prayer," whether orthodox or

---

3. J. De Guibert, *Documenta Ecclesiastica Christianae Perfectionis Studium Spectantia* (Rome, 1931), nn. 445, 446.
4. Ibid., n. 461.

otherwise. To begin with, the terminology in which the controversy was some-times carried on created an impression that one could make an absolute and quasi-Nestorian separation between the "humanity" and the "divinity" of Christ. Forgetting or ignoring the concrete unity of the two natures in one Person, and forgetting that the object of all Christian prayer is union with the Father, through the *Person* of the Son, by the Holy Spirit, writers discussed the extent to which the "human nature of Christ," considered almost as if it were a self-subsisting entity, entered into pure contemplative prayer.

Sometimes, it is true, theologians who were more perspicacious referred not so much to "the humanity of Christ" as to "the *mysteries of the life of Christ*." For instance in drawing up the articles of Issy, Fenelon and Bossuet with their associates agreed that: "It is a dangerous error to exclude from the state of con-templation the attributes, the three divine Persons, the *mysteries of the incarnate Son of God*, especially that of the cross and that of the resurrection."[5]

For early monastic tradition there was no problem concerning the humanity and divinity of Christ in prayer, at least when that tradition was orthodox. It is true that some of the uneducated Coptic monks in Egypt were tempted to the heresy of anthropomorphism, as Cassian tells us. It is true also that the Fathers frequently quote and expound such texts as: "If we have known Christ accord-ing to the flesh we know Him so no longer" (II Corinthians 5:16) and "it is good for you that I go, for if I do not go away the Paraclete will not come to you" (John 16:7). But since the Fathers used these texts in the light of their context, and not torn out of context and applied more or less arbitrarily as "arguments," they did not miss the real and profound meaning of the biblical revelation con-cerning the Person of the Incarnate Word, and His promise: "Behold I am with you all days, even to the consummation of the world" (Matthew 28:20).

The purpose of this essay is to discuss some typical texts from early monastic tradition on this point, with a view to deepening and clarifying our theology of monastic and contemplative prayer.

JOHN CASSIAN

CASSIAN IS PERHAPS THE most important and influential writer in Western monasticism. It was he who, in the early fifth century, transmitted to the West the Origenist and Evagrian doctrines on monastic life and prayer which were, and remained, dominant in Hellenistic monachism. The ninth and tenth *Con-ferences* of Cassian represent not only what was probably the accepted doctrine

---

5. Ibid., n. 495.

on prayer in the monastic centers of lower Egypt, but also his own synthesis of the monastic ideology of Southern Gaul in the early fifth century. In any case, this teaching of Cassian on prayer, disseminated by the monastic Fathers of the West and by generations of Western monks, had a decisive influence on the whole of monastic theology, particularly that of the Cistercians. In these conferences on prayer we find a kind of early synthesis between the twin traditions of Eastern and Western monachism which later, after the tragic schism of 1054, split apart and developed separately. By returning to Cassian we are able to transcend some of the problems, or false problems, that developed in the later history of Western spirituality, and we are also able to obtain a vantage point from which to get a more intelligent and sympathetic view of Oriental monastic theology on prayer, including such movements as that of the Hesychasts of Sinai and Athos.

The whole monastic doctrine of Cassian is summed up in the equation: *perfecta caritas = puritas cordis = pura oratio*. The monk has left the world to seek the Kingdom of Heaven, which is union with God in contemplation. While Evagrius distinguishes the "Kingdom of God" and the "Kingdom of Christ," Cassian makes no such division. The monk fully enters the Kingdom of God when, through purity of heart, he receives the illumination of the Holy Spirit, the Spirit of Christ. His proximate end, as a monk, is to purify his heart by asceticism, thus attaining to a state of tranquility, or *puritas cordis*, in which his spirit recovers a natural "lightness" or freedom from material ties, and, like a dry feather in a light breeze, can be carried towards heaven by love. He is no longer weighed down by the cares and desires of a sinful or passionate existence. He is no longer distracted and dominated by earthly concerns, and hence he is able to pray without ceasing, thus fulfilling the Apostle's command in the most perfect manner (1 Thessalonians 5:17). It is for this end that men become monks.

Of course there are degrees in monastic prayer, and since the monastic ideal of Nitria and Scete was, as opposed to Pachomian cenobitism, explicitly contemplative and mystical, rather than merely ascetic, Cassian takes pains to make clear the nature of the highest kinds of contemplative prayer. In the first *Conference*[6] Cassian describes the many different kinds of contemplation of God. Contemplation assumes a variety of forms. For, he says, "God is not known *only in the wondering contemplation of His incomprehensible substance* which is *still hidden in the hope of the promise given to us*," but He is also contemplated in His creation, in His providential government of the world, in history, in our own life and vocation, and finally He is contemplated in the "dispensation of His incarna-

---

6. *Con.* I, 15; cf. *Con.* I, 18; *Con.* XIV, 9.

tion for our salvation." As we see, the contemplation of the "incomprehensible substance" is reserved for heaven, and we know from the Evagrian background that this contemplation means not merely the contemplation of the essence of God in unity, but above all the trinity of Persons. All the other objects of contemplation—providence, incarnation, etc.—"arise in our minds according to the quality of our life and the purity of our heart, and in these forms of contemplation *God is seen with pure vision or else is possessed* (i.e., by love)." The importance of this text is that it shows how the essence of God and the Trinity of Persons will be contemplated in heaven, while on earth we come, through meditation on the Incarnation and redemption, to a contemplative experience of God that is not, however, a vision of His essence. It also reminds us that for Cassian the way to contemplation is through meditative reading of the Bible. However these higher contemplations are described as intuitions of God alone: *solius Dei intuitus*, and *contemplatio solius Dei.*[7] Here there are no more words to utter, as the spirit is carried away beyond words and indeed beyond understanding into that *oratio ignita*, "burning prayer" or "prayer of fire," in which flame-like movements of love burst out from within the depths of the monk's being under the direct action of the Holy Spirit. This powerful surge of inner spiritual life and love is the pure gift of God, expressed in prayer of "most pure energy uttered within us by the Holy Spirit interceding *without our knowledge.*"[8]

Finally, Cassian quotes the celebrated statement attributed to St. Antony, in which the Father of Monasticism declared that the purest prayer was one in which the monk no longer knew that he was praying and was, indeed, no longer even aware of his own existence.[9]

---

7. *Haec itaque supplicationum genera sublimior adhuc status ac praecelsior subsequitur, qui contemplatione Dei solius et caritatis adore formatur, per quam mens in illius dilectionem resoluta atque rejecta, familiarissime Deo, velut Patri proprio, peculiari pietate colloquitur* (*Con.* IX, 18). Note that this is in no sense a Platonic contemplation of the divine essence. Here Cassian is commenting on the *Pater Noster* as the way to the highest contemplative prayer which is attained together with the *perfecta charitas filiorum*, the pure love which is inseparable from the "spirit of sonship." Hence there is implied that contemplation is union with the Father in and through Christ. In the next chapter when we pray for the coming of the Father's Kingdom we must realize also that this is "the Kingdom by which Christ reigns in His saints."

8. *In modum cujusdam incomprehensibilis ac rapacissimae flammae cuncta pervolitans, / mens coepit / ineffabiles ad Deum preces purissimi vigoris effundere, quas ipse Spiritus interpellans gemitibus inenarrabilibus, ignorantibus nobis, emittit ad Deum* (*Con.* IX, 15).

9. *Non est perfecta oratio in qua se monachus, vel hoc ipsum quod orat, intelligit* (*Con.* IX, 31).

The highest form of prayer is, then, a prayer "without forms," a pure prayer in which there are no longer any images or ideas, and in which the spirit does not take any initiative of its own, for all activity of the human mind and senses is here completely surpassed.

In a very important text,[10] which has rich implications for both Eastern and Western monastic theology, Cassian discusses the place of Christ in this pure prayer. And we must say at once Christ is, as we might obviously suppose, *at the very center* of this prayer, since all Christian prayer develops and becomes perfect by penetrating deeply, in the spirit, into the hidden mystery of Christ. How does Cassian explain this? By comparing it with the experience of the apostles who witnessed the Transfiguration of Christ on Tabor.

Now it is quite true that in this passage, Cassian says explicitly that the mature contemplative "with most pure eyes gazes UPON THE DIVINITY" of Christ: *illi soli purissimis oculis divinitatem ipsius speculantur. . . .* But he immediately adds an important qualification: the contemplative gazes upon the divinity of Christ only if he ascends, with Christ, the "high mountain of solitude": *qui cum illo secedunt in excelso solitudinis monte.*[11]

Here, of course, Cassian is expounding his characteristic doctrine: the pure contemplative life is that of the hermit who, having finished his active life of ascetic purification, departs into solitude with Christ. But note that the solitude is *with Christ.* To embrace the eremitical life is to ascend "the high mountain of solitude *with Christ.*" And to do this is to obey most perfectly Christ's monastic call to prayer. Indeed, it is to follow His example, for He Himself withdrew to pray on the mountain by night in order to give Christians an example of solitary prayer. Cassian says:

> He instructed us by the example of His withdrawal into solitude, showing that if we also wished to call upon God with a pure and complete love of our hearts (*puro et integro cordis affectu*) we too ought to go away from all the unquiet and confusion of the crowd.[12]

Hence, to ascend the mountain of solitude is to do what Christ asks of those who would be most perfect and uncompromising in following their monastic vocation to prayer. And the life of prayer which the monk will lead "on the mountain" will be the same kind of prayer that was Christ's own when He was on earth: a prayer free from images and concepts, free from distraction and care.

---

10. *Con.* X, 6 (the entire chapter should be read).
11. Ibid.
12. Ibid.

Not only that, but it is Christ Himself who purifies our prayer. That is to say, He purifies our hearts, making them tranquil and perfect in love, so that we may pray as He did on earth *qui universa polluta emundat atque sanctificat*.[13]

It is clear that Cassian, who, at St. Leo's request, wrote against Nestorianism,[14] was not going to fall into the error of treating the two natures in Christ in practice as if they were two separately subsisting persons. There is no question whatever of the slightest division in the unity of Christ, and no hint that the humanity of Christ might somehow get in the way of His divinity. On the contrary, all the emphasis is, as it should be, upon the Person of Christ, the God-Man, who is the utterly pure source of all holiness, *ipse fons inviolabilis sanctitatis*.[15]

However, it is quite true that in purifying our hearts, Christ does raise them above all bodily images in prayer. And it might even seem that in some sense Christ, as God, makes us forget Him as man. Indeed, Cassian seems at one point to be saying that this is so. He declares:

> They will not be able to see Jesus coming in His Kingdom, who still are held prisoners by a kind of Jewish infirmity and are unable to say with the Apostle: "even though we once knew Christ according to the flesh, we know Him so no longer."[16]

However, even the most casual glance at this text tells us there is all the difference in the world between Cassian and Molinos. It is not a question of "refusing to make acts of love for the humanity of Christ" or a captious division between His humanity and His divinity. There is certainly no equivalence between "Christ in the flesh" and the "humanity of Christ." It is, on the contrary, a much more fundamentally Christian distinction: that between Christ, God and Man, as He was *before His passion and resurrection*, and Christ, God and Man, *as He now is in the glory of the Father*. In one case, "Christ according to the flesh" or the Incarnate Word who no longer lives in that *forma servi* which marked His kenotic and hidden state before the resurrection. In the other, the Christ of glory, who reigns now in heaven, who is what He will always be, the supreme reality, the "pure source of all holiness" ever present to His faithful, acting upon their spirit through His spirit, and guiding their destinies toward that day in which He will appear manifestly before all men in glory to take to Himself those who have purified their hearts by love, in anticipation of His coming.

---

13. Ibid.
14. *De Incarnatione Christi* (PL 50:9-272).
15. *Con.* X, 6.
16. Ibid.

According to Cassian, then, the expressions *solius Dei intuitus* (the sight of God alone) and "contemplating the divinity of Christ" refer to the contemplation of the *glory of the risen God-Man.* This does not mean representing to ourselves, by an effort of imagination, what Christ must have looked like on Tabor, or trying to picture Him as He will come in judgment. The contemplative, in the highest form of prayer, the *oratio ignita* or prayer of fire, perceives in an ineffable and mystical fashion something of the light of divinity which has taken complete possession of the glorified humanity of Christ. Cassian comes near, then, to the Athonite theologians who taught that the light of contemplation was the same kind of light as that which shone in the humanity of Christ on Tabor. Experience of this light is, of course, a purely spiritual and mystical gift. There is no question whatever of "excluding" the humanity of Christ from contemplative prayer, in order to contemplate His divinity! On the contrary, humanity and divinity are contemplated in inseparable unity in the Person of the glorified Son of God.

PATRISTIC THEOLOGY: ST. LEO, ST. GREGORY, ST. BEDE

IN ORDER TO UNDERSTAND this doctrine of Cassian on the humanity of Christ in prayer, let us consider for a moment the dogmatic teaching of three Western Fathers, St. Leo the Great, St. Gregory, and St. Bede. We do not find these doctors of the Church concerned with a purely abstract division between the humanity and divinity of the Incarnate Word. Still less can we find anything that suggests a conflict or opposition between the Person of Christ and the divine essence "competing," as it were, for the attention of the monk at prayer.

Christian prayer goes to the Person of Christ and through Him to the Father. The monk does not contemplate abstract ideas of Christ, or form purely subjective images of Christ "in His humanity." Nor does the prayer of the monk lose itself in "the divine essence" without regard for the divine Persons. Monastic prayer is fully objective, at least in the sense that it goes to the Person of Christ as He now is, seated at the right hand of the Father in glory, though this does not necessarily imply *imagining* Him in glory. Nor does it necessarily imply a subject-object relationship in our prayer. St. Leo, in speaking of the human nature of Christ, emphasizes the fact that this human nature is really and concretely glorified and enthroned with the Father. Christ, he says, showed the disciples His wounds after the resurrection, that they might believe "that same nature which had lain in the sepulchre was to be enthroned together with the Father."[17]

At the ascension, in the sight of the disciples, "the nature of humankind soared above the dignity of all the creatures of heaven [the angels]" and "there was to be no limit to the advancement [of Christ's humanity] until, seated together with the eternal Father, it might share enthroned the glory of Him whose nature it shared in the Son": *illius gloriae sociaretur in throno cujus naturae copulabatur in Filio*.[18] And, of course, the Fathers never ceased to remind their hearers that this same manhood of Christ which was enthroned with the Father in the divine glory was to return and judge the world. "He set a limit to His bodily presence, and would remain at the right hand of the Father until He should return in the same flesh in which He had ascended."[19] Monastic prayer is eschatological and is centered on the expectation of the Parousia, the advent of the "immortal and invisible King of ages" who is both "God alone" and the Christ, our redeemer and liberator.

In the meantime it is *our nature* which is enthroned in heaven with Christ. It is our nature which shares the divinity of Christ and of the Father. Hence St. Leo puts these words into the mouth of the glorious redeemer: "I have united you to myself and *I became the son of man that you might become sons of God*."[20] St. Gregory adds that Christ has made us sons of God by taking us to heaven with Him: "He has led captivity captive because *he has swallowed up our corruption in the power of His incorruption*."[21] St. Leo says that with Christ's ascension into heaven we have recovered possession of paradise, and not only that, "we have even penetrated, in Christ, into the height of heaven,"[22] we have been enthroned with Him because we are "one body" with Him: *sibi concorporatos Dei Filius ad dexteram Patris collocavit*.[23] This is the reason why we should rejoice at His going to the Father: "above all the heavens, your lowliness is raised, in Me, to be placed at the right hand of the Father."[24] He is not separated from us unless we choose to remain bound to the earth by our passions. In contemplation we

---

17. *Eam naturam in Dei Patris consessuram throno quae jacuerat in sepulchro* (*Serm.* 73, PL 54:396).

18. PL 54:397.

19. PL 54:398.

20. *Serm.* 77 (PL 54:414). This last phrase, originating with St. Irenaeus, is constantly reiterated by the Fathers.

21. *Hom.* 29 (PL 76:1218).

22. *Serm.* 74 (PL 54:937). On "paradise" in patristic mysticism, see Dom A. Stolz, *The Doctrine of Spiritual Perfection* (St. Louis, 1946), pp. 17-36.

23. Ibid.

24. *Serm.* 77 (PL 54:414).

experience, at least obscurely, something of this mystery of our union with Him *now* in heaven.

This has important implications for the life of prayer. The life of the monk, being that of a perfect Christian, is a *conversatio in coelis*. While living bodily in exile and in his earthly pilgrimage, the monk is already spiritually in paradise and in heaven where he has ascended with Christ. That is to say, although he is not physically present in heaven, he is free to come and go there as he pleases, in spirit, in prayer, in faith, in thanksgiving, praise, and love, because he already "is" there mystically in Christ. "Let us therefore, my beloved, exult with a worthy and spiritual joy, happy before God in thanksgiving, and let us lift up the free eyes of our heart (*liberos oculos cordis*) to that height where Christ is."[25]

The Lord has already "made known to us all that He has heard from His Father" (John 15:15). St. Gregory, commenting on this line, says that Christ has made us His friends by making known to us "the joys of interior charity and *the festival of the heavenly country which He daily makes present in our minds by the desire of love.*" And St. Gregory explains that this loving knowledge of heavenly things is very real indeed, no mere fancy: "For when, hearing of heavenly things, we love them, we already know the things we love, for our love itself is a way of knowing—*amor ipse notitia est.*"[26] It is by the charity of Christ in our hearts that we "are in heaven" and know the things of heaven.

The source of our freedom and the power that raises our prayer to the height of heaven is the Holy Spirit Himself, sent by Christ and the Father after the God-Man ascended into heaven. And faith in Christ's presence in heaven *as man* merits for us the grace of the Holy Spirit.[27] The angels, says St. Gregory, already rejoice to have us as their companions, while they adore the humanity of the God-Man: *nec habere dedignantur hominem socium qui super se adorant hominem Deum.*[28]

While the Fathers do not draw a sharp contrast between the two abstract natures in Christ, still less between the Person of Christ and the divine essence, they are very aware of a contrast between the state of the God-Man before His passion and resurrection, and after His triumph over death. Before the passion, Christ was living "kenotically" in what St. Leo calls the *dispensatio humilitatis*. Here He worked miracles which were "signs of the divinity in the form of the

---

25. *Serm.* 74 (PL 54:399).
26. *Hom. 27 in Evang.* (PL 76:1207). Note this is the source for the famous principle used so frequently by William of St. Thierry.
27. See St. Leo, *Serm.* 76 (PL 54:397).
28. St. Gregory, *Hom. 8 in Evang.* (PL 76:1105).

servant."[29] But St. Leo adds: "After the passion, the chains of death having been broken ... weakness passed over into power, death into eternity, and humiliation into glory."[30] Note here the "paschal" implications of the idea of "passing over," or *transitus*. This is very important for the primitive teaching on monastic prayer, which is essentially centered in the Paschal Mystery.

The Word of God descended into the world, veiling His light in our frail human nature,[31] to "pass through" our mortal life, to die and rise from the dead and thus, having "taken captivity captive," to raise us with Him into heaven. Meditation on the life of Christ and on His passion belongs, then, to our participation in the Paschal Mystery and is necessary for our realization of the true objective of our monastic life and prayer. Dom Leclercq, summing up the doctrine of St. Gregory on this point, says: "In Christ, in this passage from a carnal condition to spiritual glory, was accomplished that which is the very aim of contemplation in man, the passage from the visible to the invisible, from the exterior to the interior, from faith to understanding, from humanity to divinity."[32] Meditation on the mysteries of the life and death of Christ is, then, to be seen as part of the *transitus* or *pascha* by which we "pass over" to contemplation of the invisible light shed in our hearts, through the Holy Spirit, by Christ in glory. In this *transitus* we ourselves pass from a human to a divine life, in Christ.

Here we must admit that we can find in St. Gregory some suggestion of the separation which was later to develop into a real split between the divinity and humanity of Christ. More precisely, we find St. Gregory saying that while the *more perfect* are able to contemplate the divinity, ordinary Christians are perhaps in some sense limited to the consideration of Christ in His humanity. But let us pay attention to the context. Actually, St. Gregory is speaking of St. Paul who has ascended to the "third heaven" and seen things which the tongue of man cannot repeat. Now this is something more than what is traditionally meant by "contemplation of the divinity of Christ." It was accepted by all the Fathers as a most extraordinary experience of divine vision, such as was granted perhaps to no one else except Moses. Obviously, then, this was not something that Paul could communicate to ordinary Christians. St. Gregory then comments that since the apostle could not convey to his hearers the glory of the divine majesty, he preached to them Christ crucified, and indeed himself boasted of knowing nothing among them but Christ, and Him crucified.[33]

---

29. *Serm.* 74 (PL 54:397).
30. Ibid.
31. St. Gregory, *Hom.* 34 *in Evang.* (PL 76:1249).
32. *La spiritualité du moyen âge* (Paris, 1961), p. 27.
33. Cf. *Moralia in Job*, XXXI, 51 (PL 76:630).

It is clear, then, that later medieval writers could find in St. Gregory a basis for their distinction between the contemplation of the humanity of Christ, which is for the humble and ignorant, and the contemplation of His divinity, which is reserved for great and mighty spirits. From this it was necessary to take only one more step, with St. Peter Damian, who exclaimed: "Let others have the majesty of the divinity; let us be content with the Cross alone."[34] We must not, however, exaggerate the import of this statement. It is a rhetorical trope rather than a firm declaration of theological principle.

It would certainly be anachronistic to imagine so strong a contrast in the early Fathers, or in St. Gregory. With the Benedictine pope, the allusion is only a passing remark, and it implies, as always, that the *memoria passionis*, or devout reflection on the life, suffering and death of Christ is a normal and natural preliminary to the knowledge (through contemplative faith) of His presence in mystery, as our glorified redeemer here and now. There is in St. Gregory no question of *preferring* the thought of the suffering Christ to that of the glorified Christ. In the paragraph immediately after the one we have just cited, he turns to Christ in glory, and, applying to His glorified humanity the text "where the body is, eagles will gather" (Matthew 24:28), St. Gregory puts these words on the lips of the risen Lord: "I, your incarnate redeemer, who sit in majesty upon the heavenly throne, will raise up the souls of the elect to heaven when I shall have delivered them from their flesh.[35] St. Gregory is always aware of Christ as a living and glorious presence, the source of holiness and divine life here and now, whereas the passion for him is a *memoria*, a past event whose sanctifying effect is mediated by the light of the risen and victorious savior.

It might, therefore, be closer to the spirit of the early Fathers to suggest that Christ in His earthly life and in His passion is the object of *meditatio* or *consideratio*, while Christ in glory is more than "the object" of *contemplatio*, since the contemplative experience is an ineffable sharing in the light that radiates spiritually from the glorified humanity of the savior. The Fathers meditated on the passion as a past event, in order to come to contemplation of Christ in His present glory. Hence monastic contemplation, according to the Fathers, is more than an effective and simple consideration, however loving and however intuitive, of an idea, thought, or image of Christ as He was before His victory. Meditative consideration of the life of Christ exercises our minds in faith and love, until we receive a special power to penetrate beyond ideas of the visible and to rest in love where the eye and even the intelligence cannot penetrate. "This is the

---

34. PL 145:557.
35. *Moralia in Job*, XXXI, 53 (PL 76:631).

strength of great minds," says St. Leo, "this is the light of truly faithful souls: to believe unhesitatingly what cannot be seen with the bodily eyes and to fix their desires where vision does not penetrate."[36] This "greatness" is not an elevation or assertion of the self to be feared and shunned. It is the power of faith, which is proportionate to humility. Contemplation of the glorified redeemer is for the humble who, loving His cross, have emptied themselves in order to be one with Him.

Thus the resurrection was the end of what St. Bede, following St. Gregory, calls the *dispensatio adsumptae mortalitatis*, and the ascension marks the triumphant return of the Man-God to the Father.[37] Our faith and our prayer follow Him in His journey and ascend with Him into heaven. We obviously cannot forget or ignore Christ in His *mortalitas* or in His *incarnationis sacramentum*. We do not neglect His passion in order to concentrate only on His glory. But the earthly life and the death of Christ have to be seen in their proper perspective in the *pascha* or passage out of this world to the Father. St. Bede, with his usual simplicity, speaks clearly and realistically of the part played in the monk's prayer by the thought of Christ's life on earth and of His passion. It is by trying to imitate the life of Christ and by sharing in His death that we pass with Him into the glory of heaven. Hence we meditate on His life and passion. The constant thought of the life, suffering, and death of Christ inspires and forms us in our active life of asceticism and virtue. The joy of His resurrection and of His life enthroned with the Father communicates itself to us in the light of contemplation. Note that St. Bede sees the liturgical mysteries as the point of contact where all these different aspects of Christ are brought into focus by His living presence among us in the celebration of the holy sacrifice. He also says that contemplatives see the light of the majesty of Christ in the *lectio divina* of Scripture. The *majestas Domini* is communicated to us in the *majestas Scripturae*. "*Soli qui mente superna petierint, maiestatem sacrae Scripturae quae in Domino est adimpleta perspicient.*"

St. Bede says we

> come early to the sepulchre of the Lord, bearing spices, when, being mindful of His passion and of the death He underwent for us, we show to others the light of good works exteriorly, and interiorly we burn in our hearts with the sweetness of pure compunction [note the reminiscence of Cassian and St. Gregory]. This we should do at all times, but above all when

---

36. *Serm.* 74 (PL 54:397).
37. St. Bede, *Hom.* II, 13 (*Corpus Christianorum* 122, p. 268).

we enter the church to pray, or when we approach the altar to partake in the mystery of the Lord's body and blood.[38]

However, St. Bede goes on to add a characteristic note: If the holy women showed such reverence for the (dead) Body of Christ, "how much more is it right that we who believe that He has risen from the dead, that He has ascended into heaven, we who have known the power of the divine majesty present everywhere, should stand in His presence with all reverence and celebrate His mystery."[39] Here, as always, there is emphasis on the realization by faith and love of the victorious savior as a living and infinitely life-giving presence, in the glory of the Father.

For St. Bede says that by our faith in the resurrection, we enter the sepulchre and find it empty. "With attentive hearts, going over the series of events in the incarnation and passion *we find that He has risen from the dead and is never to be seen again in His mortal flesh.*"[40] The "sacrament" of Christ's mortal life has reached a new dimension. It has passed over into the glory of the resurrection in order to pour itself out on us in grace and life.

In other words, the Fathers reflected on the life of Christ much as they reflected on the Old Testament: that is to say, as on something which has been radically changed in achieving its final fulfillment and perfection. So St. Bede says: "We must remember continually that we cannot find the body of our Lord on earth, and we must be all the more humbled as we see our need to cry out from the depths, to Him who dwells in heaven; we must be all the more saddened as we see that we are on pilgrimage, far away from Him in whose presence alone we can live happily."[41] However, this is to our advantage. "It was fitting that the form of the servant was taken away from us that the love of the divinity might be more firmly established in our minds."[42] To love "the divinity" means, here, simply to love the God-Man as He is now and will be forever, and to follow Him with all our desire, so as to be where He now is and thus share in His divine life.[43] We shall never see Him in mortal flesh, *mortali et carne corruptibili circumdatum*, but all must behold Him in majesty, coming to judge the world.[44]

According to St. Leo, when Christ told Mary Magdalen not to touch Him, on the morning of the resurrection, He was saying to the Church:

---

38. *Hom.* II, 10 (p. 247).
39. Ibid.
40. Ibid. (p. 248).
41. Ibid.
42. *Hom.* II, 111 (p. 254).
43. Ibid.
44. Ibid.

I do not want you to come to me in a bodily manner, or to know me with the senses of your flesh. I am making you wait for much higher realities and am preparing you for better things. WHEN I SHALL HAVE ASCENDED TO MY FATHER, THEN YOU WILL TOUCH ME IN A MUCH MORE PERFECT, MUCH MORE REAL MANNER. YOU WILL APPREHEND WHAT YOU CANNOT TOUCH AND YOU WILL BELIEVE WHAT YOU DO NOT SEE.[45]

In losing the *mortalitas* of Christ we have in reality lost nothing and gained everything. In passing over into a glorious state in which He cannot be seen, He is in reality not withdrawing Himself from us but giving Himself more perfectly both as God and as Man by mystically illuminating our hearts with the *lumen incircumscriptum*. "Then indeed, beloved, THE SON OF GOD, THE SON OF MAN, MAKES HIMSELF KNOWN IN A MORE EXCELLENT AND A MORE SACRED MANNER when He returns into the glory of the Father's majesty; and IN AN INEFFABLE WAY HE BEGAN TO BE MORE PRESENT IN HIS DIVINITY when He was more remote in His humanity."[46]

THE UNLIMITED LIGHT

IT IS CLEAR, THEN, that the meaning of the presence of Christ in prayer, as it was believed and understood by the early monastic tradition, cannot be grasped unless we are clear about the "more excellent and more sacred manner" in which the God-Man makes Himself known, now that He dwells in the glory of the Father. Note that in the last and most important text we have quoted from St. Leo, it is quite clear that Christ *both as man and as God* is now more intimately known since He has become "in an ineffable way more present." The fact that this more perfect presence is a presence "in His divinity" does not exclude the fact that in it He is also more perfectly present *as man*, though not according to the mode of presence which He had when He was on earth in His mortal flesh. It is clear, then, that the monastic Fathers are not merely setting aside the Person of the Incarnate Word and substituting the presence of the divine essence considered as "more perfect" and "more intimate" for this would be nothing but the substitution of the "God of the philosophers" for the "God of Abraham, Isaac, and Jacob"—an *essence* for a *Person*. The Fathers were not men who could be satisfied with prayer centered on an abstract essence.

According to St. Gregory, what we contemplate and love in the Person of the

---

45. *Serm.* 74 (PL 54:399).
46. Ibid. (PL 54:398).

Word is not purely and simply the divine essence as such, but rather the "unlimited light," the *lumen incircumscriptum* which is His personal prerogative as Man-God, the "glory" which He has received from the Father and which He communicates to us "in the Spirit" (cf. II Corinthians 3:17-18 and John 17:1-10). This is the light of contemplation that is poured out into our hearts by the Spirit of Christ, and which gives us an ineffable knowledge of God in the union of the two natures in the Person of Christ. The *lumen incircumscriptum* is none other than the *lumen Christi*, the light of the glorious and risen Christ, the light of which the Church sings exultantly in the Easter liturgy. It is the light of the divine, transcendent, and life-giving power which belongs to Christ not only as God but also as man, and to exclude the humanity of Christ from that light is to turn away in blindness from the true mystery of the one Christ. To know Christ *only* as a "divine essence" is little better than knowing Him only as a frail and mortal man. The Christian and monastic contemplation of Christ is that of a man who is God, who is totally transfigured in the light of God and who calls us, His brothers, out of darkness to a participation in that "admirable light" (1 Peter 2:9).

The true call to monastic contemplation is, then, a call to renounce all that opposes this "ineffable light" of God in Christ, to submit totally and without reservation to the *lumen Christi*, to accept one's own helplessness and one's own deficiency, indeed one's own impurity and darkness in the presence of His light, and yet to seek with all one's heart to become transformed by contemplation and love into the very purity of the light itself. The ineffable and indefinable light of Christ is a light of extreme simplicity and purity, but it is also a tender and merciful light which does not reject any darkness that is aware of itself and laments its alienation from His truth. The chief desire of the monk is, then, to surrender to the light of Christ, to remove all that acts as an obstacle between ourselves and that light. This presupposes a perfect honesty and a complete readiness to accept the light on its own terms, obedience to the light in total humility. It means, of course, first of all, the obedience of faith, the submission of our intelligence to God, and the acceptance of His way and His plan for us in the mystery of Christ. With this submission comes love, which gives us eyes with which to apprehend the invisible reality of the *lumen incircumscriptum*; this demands a supernatural gift of vision, since the "light" is invisible to a created intelligence as such.

Preaching on the parable of the woman who lost a groat, lit a lantern, and turned her whole house upside down until she found it,[47] St. Gregory says that the woman seeking the groat is like God seeking His image in man. God lit

---

47. *Hom. 34 in Evang.* (PL 76:1249).

a lantern to seek man when He enkindled the light of His wisdom in human nature. "For a lamp," says St. Gregory, "is a light burning in an earthenware vessel, and the light in the earthenware vessel is the divinity in flesh: *lumen in testa divinitas in carne.*"[48]

Now if we look a little closely at this expression, we will find that, as it stands, it does not give a fully satisfactory description of the union of the two natures in Christ. To describe the Incarnation as "divinity in flesh" is to make it not so much a *union* of the two natures as their *juxtaposition*. And objects that are merely set one within another can easily be separated again. The vessel that has been filled can also be emptied. But such is not the case with Christ. We must understand St. Gregory in his own terms, and we must take these comparisons in their context. St. Gregory adds: "An earthenware vessel is hardened in the fire, and the power [of Christ] was dried up like a potsherd (Psalm 21:16) because the flesh that He assumed, He made strong by the tribulation of the passion, for the glory of the resurrection." Here we have once again the paschal theme, the "passage" or "Passover" of Christ the man into the glory of the Father.

In these simple approximations and popular comparisons, St. Gregory is hinting at a deeper mystery: the fact that the distinct and inseparable natures united in the Person of Christ were manifested in an even more intimate and perfect unity after the resurrection so that the man Christ is now totally penetrated not only with hidden divinity but with the manifest and glorious light of His Godhead. Whereas before the resurrection the divine life of Christ was completely hidden, so that he could be thought of as a mere man, *this is no longer possible*. Christ the man is truly God of God and light of light, and can never be otherwise. Nor can His divinity and His humanity ever be separated except by the logical operations of our abstract thought. Our faith and our contemplation have absolutely no need for such a separation, since they are directed to the *Person of the God-Man in whom the two natures are perfectly united*. And this union makes the glorious Redeemer the source of all our spiritual illumination and our sanctification.

St. Gregory, therefore, goes on to say that when the light of glory is lit in the "lamp" of the risen Christ, it is able to strike directly into our conscience, and in the presence of this invisible light our conscience is shaken from top to bottom: *mox ut ejus divinitas per carnem claruit, omnis se conscientia nostra concussit.* The consequence is that the lost drachma, or man's likeness to God, is found when the *lumen incircumscriptum* enters the conscience, turning everything upside down and purifying the heart with tribulation.

---

48. Ibid.

In the twenty-second and twenty-third books of the *Moralia in Job*, St. Gregory gives one of his classical expositions on compunction, which is essential to true monastic prayer. Compunction is one of the first effects of the light of Christ in the soul, and it has a twofold character. First, sorrowful compunction, which springs from an experience of the contrast between our sinfulness and His love for us; secondly, a compunction which bursts out in tears of gladness at the recognition of God's mercy. "The light of truth, gliding into our hearts, sometimes moves us to sorrow by showing us the severe justice of God, at other times, opening up the springs of inward joy, it makes us serenely happy."[49] The *lumen incircumscriptum* thus enters our hearts as a purifying fire consuming our sins, and "then, when the eyes of our heart are cleansed, the joy of our heavenly homeland opens up to us. . . . First the burning ray of sorrow clears away from our interior vision (*mentis acie*) the darkness of our sins which stands in the way of sight. And then in a flash our mind is lit up with the dazzling blaze of indefinable light."[50] He goes on to describe the way in which our spirit, in this light, seems to be created anew, rapt out of itself into a totally new life which is the life of the world to come. At the same time (and this too is characteristic of the Gregorian teaching on contemplation) it apprehends its own complete incapacity to grasp the *lumen incircumscriptum*. Hence it is at the same time flooded with joy from the "immense source" of grace (Christ) and baffled by its own complete inability to grasp His light as it is in Himself. In the end, the spirit of man is blinded by the dazzling presence of His immensity all about us."[51]

This, then, is the light of Christ as it is poured out in monastic contemplation, the light of His personal presence, not the presence of the divine essence in its immensity, but the presence of the Man-God in His transcendent glory.

In these typical passages of St. Gregory we can see a profound development of the implications hidden in a simple phrase of the Prologue to St. Benedict's *Rule*: "with our eyes open to the deifying light: *apertis oculis ad deificum lumen*."

AMBROSE AUTPERT

IN CONCLUSION, AND in confirmation of what has been said, we may consider a text ascribed to a Benedictine master of the eighth century who is less well

---

49. *Moralia*, XXIII, 6 (PL 76:292).
50. *Tunc resplendente raptim coruscatione incircumscripti luminis illustratur* (ibid.).
51. *Immensitatis ejus coruscante circumstantia reverberatur.* Cf. *Hom. in Ez.* I, 5, 12 (PL 76:926).

known than he deserves to be, Ambrose Autpert,[52] Abbot of St. Vincent on the Volturno, one of the spiritual heirs of St. Gregory the Great. In a homily on the transfiguration he reminds us of the text of Cassian which we considered at the beginning of this study.

First he speaks of the body of the glorified Christ as being "new in glory but not new in nature": *alterius gloriae sed non alterius naturae.*[53] "He who was evident in His flesh suddenly blazed forth in majesty, full of glory."[54]

Yet as long as this glory is not manifested in the risen Lord, Autpert suggests that the human nature and actions of Christ tend to *hide* his real Person and His divine nature rather than reveal it. For instance, in the mystery of the Purification, Christ *hid* the sacrament (mystery) of His incarnation: *claudit impiis sacramentum divinae incarnationis.*[55] Mary, in keeping the law, hides the *majestas* of her Son, which is revealed by the spirit of prophecy to Simeon and Anna alone. In the same sermon, Ambrose Autpert calls the *caro redemptionis* before the passion a seal set upon the secret of the divinity: *Quoddam divinitatis ejus sigillum absconsionis.*[56] And yet Mary herself is fully aware both of the divinity and humanity in her Son.

> O how small, and a how great is He whom you have brought into the world! Small in His humanity, great in His divinity. Small in the kingdom of the Jews, great in the kingdom of the Gentiles. . . . You, beyond all others, recognized the immensity of Him whom you saw truly born of yourself; surely you adored with trembling the God whom you had brought into the world as an infant; but you suckled, cherished and nourished Him whom, according to His humanity, you recognized as your Son.[57]

Now obviously, though there is great tenderness toward the humanity of the savior in these lines, what Ambrose Autpert contemplates in adoring wonder is not the humanity as such, but *the union of humanity and divinity in the one Person of the Incarnate Word.* It is not the humanity of Christ that constitutes the mystery

---

52. Ambrose Autpert is probably the most original theologian in the Latin world in the eighth century. See Dom Berlière's "Ambroise Autpert" in the *Dictionnaire d'histoire et de géographie ecclésiastiques.* Dom J. Winandy has written a study of Autpert with some of his texts in Latin and French: *Ambroise Autpert, moine et théologien* (Paris, 1953). In an article on him in *La Vie Spirituelle,* 1950 (p. 149), Dom Winandy says of him: "Chez Autpert, la théologie est vraiment sagesse, elle ne fait qu'un avec elle."

53. PL 89:1308.

54. *Ut qui erat in carne conspicuus subito appareret in majestate coruscus.*

55. PL 89:293. Cf. Origen, *Hom. in Luc.* I, 4 (*Sources Chrétiennes* 87, p. 106).

56. PL 89:1300.

57. PL 89:1294.

of the incarnation, but the fact that this human nature has been assumed by a divine Person and subsists in an inseparable unity with His divine nature.

Returning to the transfiguration, we find in this mystery a certain inchoative manifestation of Christ's divinity in and through His humanity, but the manifestation is not yet perfect because the body of Christ has not yet won the complete victory over death. It has not yet "passed over" into the new state which is destined for His humanity. "He was as yet mortal and the very mortality of His body did not permit Him to show forth the light of His divinity as it really was."[58] At this point, Autpert advances a theory which is curiously reminiscent of the Christian Orient. He says that the light of the transfiguration was not the light of Christ's full glory as head of His Church, but the light which would be bestowed on the members of His mystical body in heaven.[59] The light of Tabor which came forth and transformed even His garments, making them "white as snow" was only a partial emanation of His inner and divine light: *ab illa interiore luce processit quam nullus humani generis corporeus oculus intueri potest.* He goes on to say that this inner light of Christ is the source of all visible light; from it comes the light of the sun and the stars, but it is also the light which illumines the minds of angels and men. Hence, while we consider in faith the miracle of the transfiguration, we should seek *to see in contemplation the light of Christ shining by His divinity within us: miremur potius hunc divinitate micantem interius.* At the last judgment, he continues, all, both sinners and just, will see the exterior glory of Christ as He was in the transfiguration, but only the just will see His inner glory, which will be hidden from the others. At the same time all the great contemplatives, both before Christ and after Him, were illumined by His inner and divine light. Moses, for instance, saw the light of the divine *majestas* in Christ, and it was this that gave him strength to fast for forty days and nights "without feeling hunger or thirst or darkness."[60]

Ambrose Autpert says that monks ought to seek with all their hearts, in perfect humility and unalterable desire, this inner light of the divine majesty shining in Christ, and sent by Him into our hearts. In order to do this, we must imitate Him (as Cassian said) by ascending the mountain to pray in solitude.

---

58. *Adhuc mortalis erat et ipsa carnis mortalitas claritatem divinitatis ejus, ut erat ostendere non sinebat* (PL 89:1309). In a very interesting article by G. Habra, "La signification de la Transfiguration dans la théologie byzantine," *Collectanea, O. C. R.* 25 (1963), we find several patristic quotations to this same effect (pp. 136-37).

59. *Figura membrorum suorum qualia . . . in futuro fulgebunt in sua claritate monstrabat* (ibid.). Cf. St. Bede, *Hom. in Luc.* III, 9 (*Corpus Christianorum* 120, p. 205).

60. PL 89:1319.

He went up on the mountain in order that He might pray; that is to say, He went in order that by this action of His He might show all who are to seek the sight of His *majestas* that they must pray without ceasing, and that they must not stay in the lowlands, but must always pray on the mountain. Those only can do this without obstacle who do not give in to earthly desires through the allurement of vices. But, with their eyes fixed on the heights, by love they gaze upon heavenly things.[61]

Then Bl. Ambrose, abbot as he was of a cenobium, added a note that is in strict accord with primitive monastic tradition: the lesson of Christ praying on the mountain is that the monk also, with his abbot's permission, should seek that degree of exterior solitude which is appropriate to his own spiritual maturity. "In this action [going up on the mountain to pray] the Lord shows that, if permission is given, exterior solitude itself should be sought for the sake of prayer, so that the monk may call upon God with all the more intimacy, when he is not surrounded by a tumult of other men."[62]

Our conclusion is evident. The patristic tradition distinguishes the humanity and divinity of Christ, not in order to separate but in order to unite them, because the Christ of monastic contemplation is neither the divinity alone nor the humanity alone, but the unity of the two natures in one Person. Ambrose Autpert sums up the tradition in these words:

In THE ONE PERSON OF OUR REDEEMER, GOD AND MAN, we confess there is the perfect nature of God and the perfect nature of man. By reason of one nature He is Lord, by virtue of the other, a servant . . . to be Lord is one thing, to be servant another (*aliud Dominus, aliud servus*), AND YET THE LORD IS NOT OTHER THAN THE SERVANT (*non tamen alius Dominus, alius servus*) AND FOR THERE IS BUT ONE AND THE SAME SON OF GOD AND MAN.[63]

It is precisely because this is so that the mysteries of Christ's human life on earth can become the object of our admiration and our love. But they are not, strictly speaking, the ultimate resting place of contemplation, which is a light received in the inner depths of our being from the risen savior, God and Man, reigning in the glory of the Father.

---

61. PL 89:1308.
62. Ibid.
63. PL 89:1299.

12

Message to Poets

As Merton's own headnote indicates, this essay was written for a gathering of young, mainly Latin American poets in Mexico City in February 1964. It was subsequently published twice in April of that year, in *Americas* 16 (1964), 29 and in *El Corno Emplumado* 10 (1964), 127-29. A Spanish translation by Merton's friend Miguel Grinberg, who had helped organize the event, appeared in Winter 1965 in the Argentinean journal *Eco Contemporaneo* 8 (Winter 1965), 60-63. It was then included in *Raids on the Unspeakable* (155-61). The essay is a kind of manifesto, encouraging the young writers to resist the temptation to exploit language for narrow ideological purposes. Merton opposes any "calculating" use of language for some predetermined end, and urges his audience to retain their "innocence," by which he means an immediacy of experience that cannot be expressed in formalities or abstractions or reductive slogans. He rejects the idea of words as "magical," able to produce effects on others without their inner consent, which is the technique of propaganda and advertising. He calls on the poets either to deride this incantatory use of language (i.e., through antipoetry) or to prophesy, by which he means to bring out the hidden meaning beneath the surface of everyday life. He calls for words that seek not to persuade but to point toward this silence beyond words. He encourages the poets to accept their marginality, the insecurity and abjection of a "dervish" existence, and concludes by urging them to strip away all secondhand ideas for the sake of the immediacy of an experience of the "water of life."

NOTE: *This message was read at a meeting of the "new" Latin-American poets— and a few young North Americans—Mexico City, February 1964. This was not a highly organized and well-financed international congress, but a spontaneous and inspired meeting of young poets from all over the hemisphere, most of whom could barely afford to be there. One, for instance, sold her piano to make the trip from Peru.*

W<small>E WHO ARE POETS</small> know that the reason for a poem is not discovered until the poem itself exists. The reason for a living act is realized only in the act itself. This meeting is a spontaneous explosion of hopes. That is why it is a venture in prophetic poverty, supported and financed by no foundation, organized and publicized by no official group, but a living expression of the belief that there are now in our world new people, new poets who are not in tutelage to established political systems or cultural structures—whether communist or capitalist—but who dare to hope in their own vision of reality and of the future. This meeting is united in a flame of hope whose temperature has not yet been taken and whose effects have not yet been estimated, because it is a new fire. The reason for the fire cannot be apparent to one who is not warmed by it. The reason for being here will not be found until all have walked together, without afterthought, into contradictions and possibilities.

We believe that our future will be made by love and hope, not by violence or calculation. The Spirit of Life that has brought us together, whether in space or only in agreement, will make our encounter an epiphany of certainties we could not know in isolation.

The solidarity of poets is not planned and welded together with tactical convictions or matters of policy, since these are affairs of prejudice, cunning, and design. Whatever his failures, the poet is not a cunning man. His art depends on an ingrained innocence which he would lose in business, in politics, or in too organized a form of academic life. The hope that rests on calculation has lost its innocence. We are banding together to defend our innocence.

All innocence is a matter of belief. I do not speak now of organized agreement, but of interior personal convictions "in the spirit." These convictions are as strong and undeniable as life itself. They are rooted in fidelity to *life* rather than to artificial systems. The solidarity of poets is an elemental fact like sunlight, like the seasons, like the rain. It is something that cannot be organized, it can only happen. It can only be "received." It is a gift to which we must remain open. No man can plan to make the sun rise or the rain fall. The sea is still wet in spite of all formal and abstract programs. Solidarity is not collectivity. The organizers of collective life will deride the seriousness or the reality of our hope. If they infect us with their doubt we shall lose our innocence and our solidarity along with it.

Collective life is often organized on the basis of cunning, doubt, and guilt. True solidarity is destroyed by the political art of pitting one man against another and the commercial art of estimating all men at a price. On these illusory measurements men build a world of arbitrary values without life and meaning, full of sterile agitation. To set one man against another, one life against another, one work against another, and to express the measurement in terms of cost or of economic privilege and moral honor is to infect everybody with the deepest metaphysical doubt. Divided and set up against one another for the purpose of evaluation, men immediately acquire the mentality of objects for sale in a slave market. They despair of themselves because they know they have been unfaithful to life and to being, and they no longer find anyone to forgive the infidelity.

Yet their despair condemns them to further infidelity: alienated from their own spiritual roots, they contrive to break, to humiliate, and to destroy the spirit of others. In such a situation there is no joy, only rage. Each man feels the deepest root of his being poisoned by suspicion, unbelief, and hate. Each man experiences his very existence as guilt and betrayal, and as a possibility of death: nothing more.

We stand together to denounce the shame and the imposture of all such calculations.

If we are to remain united against these falsehoods, against all power that poisons man, and subjects him to the mystifications of bureaucracy, commerce, and the police state, we must refuse the price tag. We must refuse academic classification. We must reject the seductions of publicity. We must not allow ourselves to be pitted one against another in mystical comparisons—political, literary, or cultural orthodoxies. We must not be made to devour and dismember one another for the amusement of their press. We must not let ourselves be eaten by them to assuage their own insatiable doubt. We must not merely be *for* something and *against* something else, even if we are for "ourselves" and against "them." Who are "they"? Let us not give them support by becoming an "opposition" which assumes they are definitively real.

Let us remain outside "their" categories. It is in this sense that we are all monks: for we remain innocent and invisible to publicists and bureaucrats. They cannot imagine what we are doing unless we betray ourselves to them, and even then they will never be able.

They understand nothing except what they themselves have decreed. They are crafty ones who weave words about life and then make life conform to what they themselves have declared. How can they trust anyone when they make life itself tell lies? It is the businessman, the propagandist, the politician, not the poet, who devoutly believes in "the magic of words."

For the poet there is precisely no magic. There is only life in all its unpredictability and all its freedom. All magic is a ruthless venture in manipulation, a vicious circle, a self-fulfilling prophecy.

Word-magic is an impurity of language and of spirit in which words, deliberately reduced to unintelligibility, appeal mindlessly to the vulnerable will. Let us deride and parody this magic with other variants of the unintelligible, if we want to. But it is better to prophesy than to deride. To prophesy is not to predict, but to seize upon reality in its moment of highest expectation and tension toward the new. This tension is discovered not in hypnotic elation but in the light of everyday existence. Poetry is innocent of prediction because it is itself the fulfillment of all the momentous predictions hidden in everyday life.

Poetry is the flowering of ordinary possibilities. It is the fruit of ordinary and natural choice. This is its innocence and dignity.

Let us not be like those who wish to make the tree bear its fruit first and the flower afterwards—a conjuring trick and an advertisement. We are content if the flower comes first and the fruit afterwards, in due time. Such is the poetic spirit.

Let us obey life, and the Spirit of Life that calls us to be poets, and we shall harvest many new fruits for which the world hungers—fruits of hope that have never been seen before. With these fruits we shall calm the resentments and the rage of man.

Let us be proud that we are not witch doctors, only ordinary men.

Let us be proud that we are not experts in anything.

Let us be proud of the words that are given to us for nothing; not to teach anyone, not to confute anyone, not to prove anyone absurd, but to point beyond all objects into the silence where nothing can be said.

We are not persuaders. We are the children of the Unknown. We are the ministers of silence that is needed to cure all victims of absurdity who lie dying of a contrived joy. Let us then recognize ourselves for who we are: dervishes mad with secret therapeutic love which cannot be bought or sold, and which the politician fears more than violent revolution, for violence changes nothing. But love changes everything.

We are stronger than the bomb.

Let us then say "yes" to our own nobility by embracing the insecurity and abjection that a dervish existence entails.

In the *Republic* of Plato there was already no place for poets and musicians, still less for dervishes and monks. As for the technological Platos who think they now run the world we live in, they imagine they can tempt us with banalities and abstractions. But we can elude them merely by stepping into the Heraklitean river which is never crossed twice.

When the poet puts his foot in that ever-moving river, poetry itself is born out of the flashing water. In that unique instant, the truth is manifest to all who are able to receive it.

No one can come near the river unless he walks on his own feet. He cannot come there carried in a vehicle.

No one can enter the river wearing the garments of public and collective ideas. He must feel the water on his skin. He must know that immediacy is for naked minds only, and for the innocent.

Come, dervishes: here is the water of life. Dance in it.

13

A Tribute to Gandhi

This essay was completed by April 1964, when Merton wrote to *Ramparts* editor Edward Keating to ask if it would be suitable for the magazine's planned issue on nonviolence (see *Passion for Peace*, 202). Though he was still unsure in late August if it would be used (see *Witness to Freedom*, 106; *Hidden Ground of Love*, 192), it appeared under the title "Gandhi: The Gentle Revolutionary" in the December 1964 issue of *Ramparts*, and almost simultaneously in *Seeds of Destruction* (221-34). It was later included in *The Non-Violent Alternative* (178-84) and in *Passion for Peace* (202-209). This was the first of two articles that Merton wrote about Gandhi in 1964, the second being "Gandhi and the One-Eyed Giant," which was published in *Jubilee* in January 1965 and served as the introduction to *Gandhi on Non-Violence* (1965), Merton's selections from the Mahatma's writings on peace and war. While the latter piece situates Gandhi in a broad religious and intellectual spectrum, from Aquinas to Hannah Arendt, Erasmus to Laurens Van Der Post, "A Tribute to Gandhi" is more immediately accessible, beginning with Merton's own experience of defending Gandhi and the cause of Indian independence at his school in 1931 and concluding with a prayer for the grace to follow Gandhi's example of sincerity and generosity. While Merton does not quote Gandhi's famous quip about being not a saint trying to be a politician, but rather a politician trying to be a saint, he stresses the spiritual and metaphysical foundations of Gandhi's political action, inspired both by the karma yoga of his own tradition, with its emphasis on *svadharma*, the Hindu equivalent of the traditional Western formula "the duties of one's state in life," and on detachment from the fruits of one's actions, from "results (which are in the hands of God)"; and by the Sermon on the Mount and the example of the nonviolent Jesus. Merton finds in Gandhi both a challenge and a model for professed disciples of Christ who take his teachings less seriously than this "outsider," and more generally for the secular democracies of the West in which pragmatism has too often replaced principle. Ultimately Merton finds Gandhi's vision of human nature summed up in the one sentence quoted in both of his Gandhi essays: "IF LOVE IS NOT THE LAW OF OUR BEING THE WHOLE OF MY ARGUMENT FALLS TO PIECES."

IN 1931 GANDHI, who had been released from prison a few months before, came to London for a conference. The campaign of civil disobedience which had begun with the Salt March had recently ended. Now there were to be negotiations. He walked through the autumn fogs of London in clothes that were good for the tropics, not for England. He lived in the slums of London, coming from there to more noble buildings in which he conferred with statesmen. The English smiled at his bald head, his naked brown legs, the thin underpinnings of an old man who ate very little, who prayed. This was Asia, wise, disconcerting, in many ways unlovely, but determined upon some inscrutable project and probably very holy. Yet was it practical for statesmen to have conferences with a man reputed to be holy? What was the meaning of the fact that one could be holy, and fast, and pray, and be in jail, and be opposed to England all at the same time?

Gandhi thus confronted the England of the depression as a small, disquieting question mark. Everybody knew him, and many jokes were made about him. He was also respected. But respect implied neither agreement nor comprehension. It indicated nothing except that the man had gained public attention, and this was regarded as an achievement. Then, as now, no one particularly bothered to ask if the achievement signified something.

Yet I remember arguing about Gandhi in my school dormitory: chiefly against the football captain, then head prefect, who had come to turn out the flickering gaslight, and who stood with one hand in his pocket and a frown on his face which was not illuminated with understanding. I insisted that Gandhi was right, that India was, with perfect justice, demanding that the British withdraw peacefully and go home; that the millions of people who lived in India had a perfect right to run their own country. Such sentiments were of course beyond comprehension. How could Gandhi be right when he was *odd*? And how could I be right if I was on the side of someone who had the wrong kind of skin, and left altogether too much of it exposed?

A counterargument was offered but it was not an argument. It was a basic and sweeping assumption that the people of India were political and moral infants, incapable of taking care of themselves, backward people, primitive, uncivilized, benighted pagan, who could not survive without the English to do their thinking and planning for them. The British Raj was, in fact, a purely benevolent, civilizing enterprise for which the Indians were not suitably grateful. . . .

Infuriated at the complacent idiocy of this argument, I tried to sleep and failed.

Certain events have taken place since that time. Within a dozen years after Gandhi's visit to London there were more hideous barbarities perpetuated in

Europe, with greater violence and more unmitigated fury than all that had ever been attributed by the wildest imaginations to the despots of Asia. The British Empire collapsed. India attained self-rule. It did so peacefully and with dignity. Gandhi paid with his life for the ideals in which he believed.

As one looks back over this period of confusion and decline in the West, the Cold War, and the chaos and struggle of the world that was once colonial, there is one political figure who stands out from all the rest as an extraordinary leader of men. He is radically different from the others. Not that the others did not on occasion bear witness to the tradition of which they were proud because it was Christian. They were often respectable, sometimes virtuous men, and many of them were sincerely devout. Others were at least genteel. Others, of course, were criminals. Judging by their speeches, their programs, their expressed motives were usually civilized. Yet the best that could be said of them may be that they sometimes combined genuine capability and subjective honesty. But apart from that they seemed to be the powerless victims of a social dynamic that they were able neither to control nor to understand. They never seemed to dominate events, only to rush breathlessly after the parade of cataclysms, explaining why these had happened, and not aware of how they themselves had helped precipitate the worst of disasters. Thus with all their good intentions, they were able at best to rescue themselves after plunging blindly in directions quite other than those in which they claimed to be going. In the name of peace, they wrought enormous violence and destruction. In the name of liberty they exploited and enslaved. In the name of man they engaged in genocide or tolerated it. In the name of truth they systematically falsified and perverted truth.

Gandhi on the other hand was dedicated to peace, and though he was engaged in a bitter struggle for national liberation, he achieved this by peaceful means. He believed in serving the truth by nonviolence, and his nonviolence was effective insofar as it began first within himself, as obedience to the deepest truth in himself.

It is certainly true that Gandhi is not above all criticism; no man is. But it is evident that he was unlike all the other world leaders of his time in that his life was marked by a wholeness and a wisdom, an integrity and a spiritual consistency that the others lacked, or manifested only in reverse, in consistent fidelity to a dynamism of evil and destruction. There may be limitations in Gandhi's thought, and his work has not borne all the fruit he himself would have hoped. These are factors which he himself sagely took into account, and having reckoned with them all, he continued to pursue the course he had chosen simply because he believed it to be true. His way was no secret: it was simply to follow conscience without regard for the consequences to himself, in the belief that this was demanded of him by God and that the results would be the work of God. Perhaps indeed for a long time these results would remain hidden as God's secret. But in the end the truth would manifest itself.

WHAT HAS GANDHI TO do with Christianity? Everyone knows that the Orient has venerated Christ and distrusted Christians since the first colonizers and missionaries came from the West.

Western Christians often assume without much examination that this oriental respect for Christ is simply a vague, syncretistic, and perhaps romantic evasion of the challenge of the Gospel: an attempt to absorb the Christian message into the confusion and inertia which are thought to be characteristic of Asia. The point does not need to be argued here. Gandhi certainly spoke often of Jesus, whom he had learned to know through Tolstoy. And Gandhi knew the New Testament thoroughly. Whether or not Gandhi "believed in" Jesus in the sense that he had genuine Christian faith in the Gospel would be very difficult to demonstrate, and it is not my business to prove it or disprove it. I think that the effort to do so would be irrelevant in any case. What is certainly true is that Gandhi not only understood the ethic of the Gospel as well, if not in some ways better, than many Christians, but he is one of the very few men of our time who applied Gospel principles to the problems of a political and social existence in such a way that his approach to these problems was *inseparably* religious and political at the same time.

He did this not because he thought that these principles were novel and interesting, or because they seemed expedient, or because of a compulsive need to feel spiritually secure. The religious basis of Gandhi's political action was not simply a program, in which politics were marshaled into the service of faith, and brought to bear on the charitable objectives of a religious institution. For Gandhi, strange as it may seem to us, political action had to be by its very nature "religious" in the sense that it had to be informed by principles of religious and philosophical wisdom. To separate religion and politics was in Gandhi's eyes "madness" because his politics rested on a thoroughly religious interpretation of reality, of life, and of man's place in the world. Gandhi's whole concept of man's relation to his own inner being and to the world of objects around him was informed by the contemplative heritage of Hinduism, together with the principles of Karma Yoga which blended, in his thought, with the ethic of the Synoptic Gospels and the Sermon on the Mount. In such a view, politics had to be understood in the context of service and worship in the ancient sense of *leitourgia* (liturgy, public work). Man's intervention in the active life of society was at the same time by its very nature *svadharma*, his own personal service (of

God and man) and worship, *yajna*. Political action therefore was not a means to acquire security and strength for one's self and one's party, but a means of witnessing to the truth and the reality of the cosmic structure by making one's own proper contribution to the order willed by God. One could thus preserve one's integrity and peace, being detached from results (which are in the hands of God) and being free from the inner violence that comes from division and untruth, the usurpation of someone else's *dharma* in place of one's own svadharma. These perspectives lent Gandhi's politics their extraordinary spiritual force and religious realism.

The success with which Gandhi applied this spiritual force to political action makes him uniquely important in our age. More than that, it gives him a very special importance for Christians. Our attitude to politics tends to be abstract, divisive, and often highly ambiguous. Political action is by definition secular and unspiritual. It has no really religious significance. Yet it is important to the Church as an institution in the world. It has therefore an official significance. We look to the Church to clarify principle and offer guidance, and in addition to that we are grateful if a Christian party of some sort comes to implement the program that has thus been outlined for us. This is all well and good. But Gandhi emphasized the importance of the individual person entering political action with a fully awakened and operative spiritual power in himself, the power of *Satyagraha*, nonviolent dedication to truth, a religious and spiritual force, a wisdom born of fasting and prayer. This is the charismatic and personal force of the saints, and we must admit that we have tended to regard it with mistrust and unbelief, as though it were mere "enthusiasm" and "fanaticism." This is a lamentable mistake, because for one thing it tends to short-circuit the power and light of grace, and it suggests that spiritual dedication is and must remain something entirely divorced from political action: something for the *prie dieu*, the sacristy or the study, but not for the marketplace. This in turn has estranged from the Church those whose idealism and generosity might have inspired a dedicated and creative intervention in political life. These have found refuge in groups dominated by a confused pseudo-spirituality, or by totalitarian messianism. Gandhi remains in our time as a sign of the genuine union of spiritual fervor and social action in the midst of a hundred pseudo-spiritual crypto-fascist, or communist movements in which the capacity for creative and spontaneous dedication is captured, debased, and exploited by the false prophets.

IN A TIME WHERE the unprincipled fabrication of lies and systematic violation of agreements has become a matter of course in power politics, Gandhi made this unconditional devotion to truth the mainspring of his social action. Once again, the radical difference between him and other leaders, even the most sincere and honest of them, becomes evident by the fact that Gandhi is chiefly concerned with truth and with service, *svadharma*, rather than with the possible success of his tactics upon other people; and paradoxically it was his religious conviction that made Gandhi a great politician rather than a mere tactician or operator. Note that *satyagraha* is matter for a vow, therefore of worship, adoration of the God of truth, so that his whole political structure is built on this and his other vows (*Ahimsa*, etc.) and becomes an entirely religious system. The vow of *satyagraha* is the vow to die rather than say what one does not mean.

The profound significance of *satyagraha* becomes apparent when one reflects that "truth" here implies much more than simply conforming one's words to one's inner thought. It is not by words only that we speak. Our aims, our plans of action, our outlook, or attitudes, our habitual response to the problems and challenges of life "speak" of our inner being and reveal our fidelity or infidelity to God and to ourselves. Our very existence, our life itself contains an implicit pretension to meaning, since all our free acts are implicit commitments, selections of "meanings" which we seem to find confronting us. Our very existence is "speech" interpreting reality. But the crisis of truth in the modern world comes from the bewildering complexity of the almost infinite contradictory propositions and claims to meaning uttered by millions of acts, movements, changes, decisions, attitudes, gestures, events, going on all around us. Most of all a crisis of truth is precipitated when men realize that almost all these claims to meaning and value are in fact without significance when they are not in great part entirely fraudulent.

The tragedy of modern society lies partly in the fact that it is condemned to utter an infinite proliferation of statements when it has nothing to reveal except its own meaninglessness, its dishonesty, its moral indigence, its inner divisions, its abject spiritual void, its radical and self-destructive spirit of violence.

Satyagraha for Gandhi meant first of all refusing to say "nonviolence" and "peace" when one meant "violence" and "destruction." However, his wisdom differed from ours in this: he knew that in order to speak truth he must rectify more than his inner *intention*. It was not enough to say "love" and *intend* love thereafter proving the sincerity of one's own intentions by demonstrating the insincerity of one's adversary. "Meaning" is not a mental and subjective adjustment. For Gandhi, a whole lifetime of sacrifice was barely enough to demonstrate the sincerity with which he made a few simple claims: that he was not lying, that he did not intend to use violence or deceit against the English, that he did not think that peace and justice could be attained through violent or selfish means, that he did genuinely believe they could be assured by nonviolence and self-sacrifice.

Gandhi's religio-political action was based on an ancient metaphysic of man, a philosophical wisdom which is common to Hinduism, Buddhism, Islam, Judaism, and Christianity: that "truth is the inner law of our being." Not that man is merely an abstract essence, and that our action must be based on logical fidelity to a certain definition of man. Gandhi's religious action is based on a religious intuition of *being* in man and in the world, and his vow of truth is a vow of fidelity to being in all its accessible dimensions. His wisdom is based on experience more than on logic. Hence the way of peace is the way of truth, of fidelity to wholeness and being, which implies a basic respect for life not as a concept, not as a sentimental figment of the imagination, but in its deepest, most secret and most fontal reality. The first and fundamental truth is to be sought in respect for our own inmost being, and this in turn implies the recollectedness and the awareness which attune us to that silence in which alone Being speaks to us in all its simplicity.

Therefore Gandhi recognized, as no other world leader of our time has done, the necessity to be free from the pressures, the exorbitant and tyrannical demands of a society that is violent because it is essentially greedy, lustful, and cruel. Therefore he fasted, observed days of silence, lived frequently in retreat, knew the value of solitude, as well as of the totally generous expenditure of his time and energy in listening to others and communicating with them. He recognized the impossibility of being a peaceful and nonviolent man if one submits passively to the insatiable requirements of a society maddened by overstimulation and obsessed with the demons of noise, voyeurism, and speed.

"Jesus died in vain," said Gandhi, "if he did not teach us to regulate the whole life by the eternal law of love." Strange that he should use this expression. It seems to imply at once concern and accusation. As Asians sometimes do, Gandhi did not hesitate to confront Christendom with the principles of Christ. Not that he judged Christianity, but he suggested that the professedly Christian civilization of the West was in fact judging itself by its own acts and its own fruits. There are certain Christian and humanitarian elements in democracy, and if they are absent, democracy finds itself on trial, weighed in the balance, and no amount of verbal protestations can prevent it from being found wanting. Events themselves will proceed inexorably to their conclusion. *Pacem in Terris* has suggested the same themes to the meditation of modern Europe, America, and Russia. "Civilization" must learn to prove its claims by a capacity for the peaceful and honest settlement of disputes, by genuine concern for justice toward people who have been shamelessly exploited and races that have been systematically oppressed, or the historical preeminence of the existing powers will be snatched from them by violence, perhaps in a disaster of cosmic proportions.

Gandhi believed that the central problem of our time was the acceptance or the rejection of a basic law of love and truth which had been made known to the world in traditional religions and most clearly by Jesus Christ. Gandhi himself expressly and very clearly declared himself an adherent of this one law. His whole life, his political action, finally even his death, were nothing but a witness to his commitment. "IF LOVE IS NOT THE LAW OF OUR BEING THE WHOLE OF MY ARGUMENT FALLS TO PIECES."

What remains to be said? It is true that Gandhi expressly dissociated himself from Christianity in any of its visible and institutional forms. But it is also true that he built his whole life and all his activity upon what he conceived to be the law of Christ. In fact, he died for this law which was at the heart of his belief. Gandhi was indisputably sincere and right in his moral commitment to the law of love and truth. A Christian can do nothing greater than follow his own conscience with a fidelity comparable to that with which Gandhi obeyed what he believed to be the voice of God. Gandhi is, it seems to me, a model of integrity whom we cannot afford to ignore, and the one basic duty we all owe to the world of our time is to imitate him in "dissociating ourselves from evil in total disregard of the consequences." May God mercifully grant us the grace to be half as sincere and half as generous as was this great leader, one of the noblest men of our century.

14

From Pilgrimage to Crusade

Merton speaks in his journal of completing this essay on August 2, 1964 (*Dancing in the Water of Life*, 132), though it is not until August 29 that he is "finishing off footnotes as an afterthought" (*Dancing in the Water of Life*, 139). Its origins are in part due to his discussion of Aetheria (Egeria) in novitiate conferences in January and February 1964 (see *Pre-Benedictine Monasticism*, xxix-xxxii, 169-87) as well as his increasing interest in the "new world" of Irish monasticism "that has waited until this time to open up" (*Dancing in the Water of Life*, 107), evidenced in numerous comments in his journal and letters during mid-1964 (see *Pre-Benedictine Monasticism*, xxxv-xxxvii for references; for an overview, see also Paul M. Pearson, "Merton and the Celtic Monastic Tradition: Search for the Promised Land," *The Merton Annual* 5 (1992), 263-77). The essay was first published in *Cithara* 4.1 (November 1964), 3-21, and subsequently in *Tomorrow: A Journal of Metaphysics, Cosmology and Traditional Studies* 13.2 (Spring 1965), 90-102; it is included in *Mystics and Zen Masters* (91-112). In a March 6, 1968, letter to June Yungblut, Merton calls this essay "central to my thought" (*Hidden Ground of Love*, 642), as is evident in the way it brings together so many strands of his mature "sapiential" perspective: his deep appreciation for the literature, especially the monastic literature, of early and medieval Christianity; his fascination with the archetype of the journey, in which "geographical pilgrimage is the symbolic acting out of an inner journey"—the quest for the promised land, the return to paradise, the search for the "place of resurrection" in the heart of the natural world, the enactment of true *metanoia*, a change of direction prompted by a change of heart; his awareness of the problematic, indeed catastrophic, dimensions of such journeys when made under the distorted influence of a faulty anthropology and a defective spirituality, exemplified both in the East during the Crusades and in the West in the conquest of the Americas; and the need to recover an authentic sense of pilgrimage that rediscovers paradise—personal, communal, even cosmic integration—not by driving out "the other" but by recognizing the same humanity, the same divine image, "in the aborigine who most differs from ourselves . . . the stranger who is Christ our fellow-pilgrim and our brother."

I

THE "SACRED JOURNEY" has origins in prehistoric religious cultures and myths. Man instinctively regards himself as a wanderer and wayfarer, and it is second nature for him to go on pilgrimage in search of a privileged and holy place, a center and source of indefectible life. This hope is built into his psychology, and whether he acts it out or simply dreams it, his heart seeks to return to a mythical source, a place of "origin," the "home" where the ancestors came from, the mountain where the ancient fathers were in direct communication with heaven, the place of the creation of the world, paradise itself, with its sacred tree of life.[1]

In the traditions of all the great religions, pilgrimage takes the faithful back to the source and center of the religion itself, the place of theophany, of cleansing, renewal, and salvation. For the Christian there is, of course, Jerusalem, the Holy Sepulchre, where the definitive victory of life over death, good over evil, was won. And there is Rome, the center of the Catholic Church, the See of Peter, the place of indulgence and forgiveness. There are also grottoes and springs blessed by visitations of the merciful Mother, sites of repentance and of healing. There are countless tombs of saints, places of hierophany and of joy.

Christian pilgrimages to Jerusalem, which simply followed the example and pattern of much older Jewish pilgrimages, began in the fourth century A.D. St. Helena's pilgrimage and the finding of the True Cross took place in 326. Less than ten years later, the splendid Basilica of the Holy Sepulchre was dedicated. It would attract thousands of pilgrims from the West. Already, in 333, a pilgrim from Bordeaux, in France, was writing about his visit to the Holy Places. One of the liveliest and most interesting of all written pilgrimages is that of the nun Aetheria,[2] who probably came from Spain and visited not only the Holy Places in Jerusalem but the monks of the Egyptian desert and of Palestine, even going through the Arabian desert to Mount Sinai, where there was as yet no monastery, but where there were colonies of hermits living in huts and caves. Large numbers of these anchorites escorted her enthusiastically to the summit of the mountain, where appropriate texts from the Bible were read, Mass was sung, *eulogiae* or spiritual gifts (consisting of fruits from the monks' orchard) were passed around, and the joys of the Christian life were generally celebrated in the very place where God had given the Law to Moses. Note that at this same time

---

1. Mircea Eliade: *Myths, Dreams and Mysteries* (London, 1960), pp. 59-72. See also, by the same author, *The Myth of the Eternal Return*.

2. *Le Pèlerinage d'Ethérie*, Latin text and French trans. by Hélène Petré (Sources Chrétiennes; Paris, 1948).

St. Gregory of Nyssa was writing his life of Moses,[3] which is in fact a description of the mystical itinerary and ascent of the monk to God in "dark contemplation." The geographical pilgrimage is the symbolic acting out of an inner journey. The inner journey is the interpolation of the meanings and signs of the outer pilgrimage. One can have one without the other. It is best to have both. History would show the fatality and doom that would attend on the external pilgrimage with no interior spiritual integration, a divisive and disintegrated wandering, without understanding and without the fulfillment of any humble inner quest. In such pilgrimage no blessing is found within, and so the outward journey is cursed with alienation. Historically, we find a progressive "interiorization" of the pilgrimage theme, until in monastic literature the "peregrinatio" of the monk is entirely spiritual and is in fact synonymous with monastic stability.[4]

Aetheria's account of her pilgrimage tells us much about the liturgy of fourth-century Jerusalem, where the Holy Sepulchre was regarded as the normal station for daily celebration of the Eucharist, and where the True Cross was set up under the roof of the same basilica, on what remained of the rock of Calvary (Aetheria calls it simply the *martyrium*—the place of martyrdom or of witness). Note that even though Calvary was there, the Eucharist was celebrated specifically at the Holy Sepulchre, not on Calvary. The sacred events of the New Testament were reenacted liturgically at the place where they actually happened. The liturgy of other places in the Christian world was simply intended to reproduce and remind the pilgrim of what he could see in its perfection at Jerusalem. Jerusalem was in every sense the "center of the world," not only in terms of ancient geography, but in the more important and sacred sense. It was the center par excellence of *Truth*, the place of the *True* Cross, of which all other crosses would be mementos and representations; the place of the true Holy Sepulchre, which would be recalled by the sepulchres of the martyrs in each altar of sacrifice: the place where the Savior had truly walked, spoken, preached, healed, suffered, risen, ascended. The places themselves in their reality bore witness to that truth; but they were, far more than that, sacraments of truth and of a special life-giving presence.[5] If Jerusalem was the place of the *anastasis*, the resurrection, the regions around it were filled with the *martyria*, where the apostles and

---

3. *La Vie de Moïse*, Greek text and French trans. by Jean Daniélou, 2nd ed. (Sources Chrétiennes; Paris, 1955).

4. Valerius of Vierzo, *Epistola de B. Echeria*, PL 87:424. See also the important article by Dom Jean Leclercq, "Monachisme et pérégrination du 9ᵉ au 12ᵉ siècles," *Studia Monastica* 3.1 (1961), pp. 33-52. This study traces the development from *stabilitas in peregrinatione* to *peregrinatio in stabilitate*.

5. For example, St. Silvinus, St. Ulric, etc., wished to venerate Christ in the very

saints had borne witness to the power of the resurrection. Finally, there were the monks in all the deserts of Syria, Palestine, Arabia, and Egypt who were living witnesses of the resurrection. The pilgrimage of Aetheria was, then, a sacred journey to the center from which the whole Christian world was charged with the true presence of the resurrection and glory of the Savior.

II

THE FALL OF ROME to the Barbarians in the beginning of the sixth century and the invasions that poured down over the East as well as over Western Europe temporarily cut off the Holy Land from the West. Though Jerusalem was then practically inaccessible to most European Christians, pilgrimages continued unabated elsewhere. But now they received a new character, imprinted upon them by the Celtic monks of Ireland.

Peregrinatio, or "going forth into strange countries," was a characteristically Irish form of asceticism. The Irish *peregrinus*, or pilgrim, set out on his journey, not in order to visit a sacred shrine, but in search of solitude and exile. His pilgrimage was an exercise in ascetic homelessness and wandering.[6] He entrusted himself to Providence, setting out with no definite aim, abandoning himself to the Lord of the universe. Since Ireland is an island, this meant entrusting oneself to the hazards of sea travel, and there are records of Irish *peregrini* who simply floated off aimlessly into the sea, abandoning themselves to wind and current, in the hope of being led to the place of solitude which God Himself would pick for them. In this way, some came to Wales or Cornwall or to the isles of western Scotland. Others, doubtless the majority, made use of their considerable skill in navigation and followed indications that had perhaps come down to them in years of seafaring tradition. Such were St. Columba, founder of the great monastic center at Iona,[7] and St. Brendan, whose legendary voyages[8] are

---

place where He had accomplished the mysteries of salvation. Leclercq, "Monachisme et pérégrination," pp. 37-39, 43.

6. H. Von Campenhausen, *Die asketische Heimatlösigkeit* (Tübingen, 1930); Dom L. Gougaud, *Christianity in Celtic Lands* (London, 1932), pp. 129ff.; N. K. Chadwick, *The Age of Saints in the Early Celtic Church* (London, 1961). Professor Chadwick calls this "one of the most important features of Irish asceticism and its chief legacy to after ages," p. 82.

7. *Adomnan's Life of Columba*, ed., with translation and notes, by the late Alan Orr Anderson and by Marjorie Ogilvie Anderson (Edinburgh, 1961), "de Scotia (Ireland) ad Britanniam *pro Christo peregrinari volens* enavigavit," p. 186.

8. *Navigatio Sancti Brendani abbatis*, ed. by Carl Selmer (Univ. Publication in Medieval Studies; Notre Dame, 1959).

thought, by some, to have brought him even to America. This has still to be convincingly proved. But there is historical evidence that Irish monks were in Iceland[9] before the coming of the Danes in the eighth century, and they had also visited the Faroe Islands, as well as the Shetlands and the Orkneys, not to mention Brittany, which was entirely populated by Welsh and Irish colonists, mostly monks, in the sixth century.

It is true, of course, that many of these pilgrimages brought Irish monks into inhabited places where the natives were willing and ready to receive the Christian message. The monks then became missionaries. The main reason for their journeys was not the missionary apostolate but the desire of voluntary exile.[10]

An *Old Irish Life of St. Columba* (a panegyric, not to be confused with the essentially historical life by Adomnan) describes the pilgrim spirit as belonging to the very essence of Christianity:

> God counselled Abraham to leave his own country and go in pilgrimage into the land which God had shown him, to wit the "Land of Promise." ... Now the good counsel which God enjoined here on the father of the faithful is incumbent on all the faithful; that is to leave their country and their land, their wealth and their worldly delight for the sake of the Lord of the Elements, and go in perfect pilgrimage in imitation of him.[11]

The example of Abraham inspired many other Irish pilgrims, including Saint Cadroe and his companions, who went forth to seek the land which the Lord "would show them."[12]

It was, of course, the vision of the "Land Promised to the Saints" that inspired the fabulous voyage of Brendan and his monks. In Celtic pilgrimages there is a reawakening of the archaic mythical theme of the "return to paradise"[13] under

---

9. See quotations from the Icelandic *Landnámbók* (eleventh or twelfth century) in *Christianity in Celtic Lands*, p. 132. Also a quote from *De Mensura Orbis* by Dicuil (ninth century) in L. Bieler, *Ireland the Harbinger of the Middle Ages* (London, 1963), p. 119.

10. Leclercq, "Monachisme et pérégrination," pp. 34, 36.

11. Quoted in Chadwick, *The Age of Saints in the Early Celtic Church,* p. 83. Cf. Leclercq, "Monachisme et pérégrination," p. 36. See also Leclercq, "La Séparation du monde dans le monachisme du moyen âge," in *La Séparation du Monde: Problèmes de la religieuse de d'aujourd'hui* (Paris, 1961), p. 77.

12. Leclercq, "Monachisme et pérégrination," passim, esp. pp. 37, 39, 41.

13. Mircea Eliade, *Myths, Dreams and Mysteries.* Cf. Anselm Stolz, O.S.B., *Théologie de la Mystique* (Chevetogne); Dom G.-M. Colombas, O.S.B., *Paraíso y vida angélica* (Monserrate, 1958).

the guidance of God or of His angels. But this is something more than "mere myth." The mystic spirituality of the Celtic monks is built on a charism of pilgrimage and navigation.

The objective of the monk's pilgrimage on earth may be imaginatively described as the quest of the "promised land" and "paradise," but more theologically this goal was described as the "place of resurrection"[14]—the place divinely appointed, in which the monk is to settle down, spend the rest of his days in solitude, doing penance, praying, waiting for the day of his death. To leave Ireland in search of this privileged place was to "go on pilgrimage for the love of God" (*peregrinari pro Dei amore*) or "in the name of God." If the pilgrimage were a "navigation," then the monk was seeking for a "desert in the sea."[15] The Irish had a predilection for lonely islands.[16] In the voyage of St. Brendan, one of the Faroe Islands covered with wild sea birds becomes transformed into a monastic and liturgical paradise, the place par excellence for the celebration of the Easter mystery.[17] The Holy Sepulchre has been replaced by the Desert Island. In any event, the object of pilgrimage is to take the monk to his peculiar and appointed place on the face of the earth, a place not determined by nature, race, and society, but by the free choice of God. Here he was to live, praise God, and finally die. His body would then be buried in this spot, and would there await the resurrection. The pilgrimage of the Celtic monk was not then just endless and aimless wandering for its own sake. It was a journey to a mysterious, unknown, but divinely appointed place, which was to be the place of the monk's ultimate meeting with God.

In the eighth and ninth centuries, when communication with the East was once again open, Irish monks went on pilgrimages to Egypt and the Holy Land, and in many cases their desire was either to settle at a Holy Place and die there, or else to find "the place of their resurrection" on the way back, and remain there, often as recluses, or solitaries living in completely enclosed cells built against the wall of a Church.[18] Thus, the ninth and tenth centuries record the

---

14. Chadwick, *The Age of Saints in the Early Celtic Church*, pp. 82-83. Kathleen Hughes, "The Irish Monks and Learning," *Los monjes y los estudios* (Poblet, 1963), pp. 66ff. Eleanor Shipley Duckett, *The Wandering Saints of the Early Middle Ages* (New York, 1959), pp. 24-25.

15. Adomnan, *Adomnan's Life of Columba*, I.6, "(Cormac) tribus vicibus herimum in ociano laboriose quaesivit . . ." pp. 222-24.

16. Bieler, *Ireland the Harbinger of the Middle Ages*, p. 119.

17. *Navigatio Brendani*, c. 11, pp. 22ff.

18. Dom H. Leclercq, O.S.B., "Celle," D.A.C.L., ii, 2870, and "Reclus," D.A.C.L., xiv, 2149ff. Rotha Mary Clay, *The Hermits and Anchorites of England* (London, 1914). P. McNulty and B. Hamilton, "Orientale Lumen et Magistra Latinitas—Greek Influences

presence of scores of Irish monks living in cities of Germany, Burgundy, Lorraine, etc., either as scholars teaching in schools or as recluses.[19]

Soon there were many secondary aims in the pilgrimage. Monks went to spend a time in *peregrinatio* with other monks and in monastic centers where they could find instruction and example. Or else they went to obtain liturgical and other books,[20] which they copied in their own monasteries. The five pilgrimages of St. Benedict Biscop to Rome are famous examples of this. Others went to Rome to obtain relics needed in the dedication of monastic churches or altars.[21] Some even went on pilgrimages in the hope of martyrdom;[22] others to escape death at the hands of invading Vikings.

Whatever one may think about some of the special forms taken by the Celtic *peregrinatio*, the records, historical as well as literary, bear witness to a profound spiritual integration in the culture from which this practice emerged. The external and geographic pilgrimage was evidently, in most cases, something more than the acting out of psychic obsessions and instabilities. It was in profound relationship with an inner experience of *continuity* between the natural and the supernatural, between the sacred and the profane, between this world and the next: a continuity both in time and in space.[23] For the Celt, as for archaic and primitive man, the true reality is that which is manifested obscurely and sacramentally in symbol, sacrament, and myth. The deepest and most mysterious potentialities of the physical and bodily world, potentialities essentially sacred, demanded to be worked out on a spiritual and human level.

The pilgrimage of the Irish monk was therefore not merely the restless search of an unsatisfied romantic heart. It was a profound and existential tribute to realities perceived in the very structure of the world, and of man, and of their being: a sense of ontological and spiritual dialogue between man and creation in which spiritual and bodily realities interweave and interlace themselves like manuscript illuminations in the Book of Kells. This resulted in an astounding

on Western Monasticism (900-1100)," *Le Millénaire du Mont Athos* (Chevetogne, 1963), esp. pp. 197-99, 216. Gougaud, *Ermites et Reclus* (Ligugé, 1928).

19. O. Doerr, *Das Institut der Inclusen in Suddeutschland* (Münster, 1934).

20. Chadwick, *The Age of Saints in the Early Celtic Church,* pp. 36, 37, 50-53.

21. See H. Leclercq, "Pèlerinages à Rome," D.A.C.L., xiv, 53-54. This applies more to Franks than to Celts, who were less enthusiastic about pilgrimages to Rome. Witness this ancient verse: "To go to Rome is great labor. The King you seek you will not find unless you bring Him with you." However, St. Moluca, disciple of St. Maedoc, pleaded with his master for permission to go to Rome: *Nisi videro Romam cito moriar.*

22. J. Leclercq, "Monachisme et pérégrination," pp. 42-43.

23. See M.-L. Soejstedt: *Dieux et héros des celtes,* quoted in R-Y Creston, *Journal de Bord de Saint Brendan* (Paris, 1957), p. 221.

spiritual creativity which made it impossible for the Celtic monk merely to accept his existence as something static and "given," or his monastic vocation as a juridically stabilized and sedentary existence. His vocation was to mystery and growth, to liberty and abandonment to God, in self-commitment to the apparent irrationality of the winds and the seas, in witness to the wisdom of God the Father and Lord of the elements. Better perhaps than the Greeks, some of the Celtic monks arrived at the purity of that *theoria physike* which sees God not in the essences or *logoi* of things, but in a hierophanic cosmos; hence the marvelous vernacular nature poetry of the sixth- and seventh-century Celtic hermits.[24]

As Dom Jean Leclercq points out,[25] pilgrimage was to remain a "form of hermit life" and a logical though exceptional constituent of the monastic vocation.

III

IN THE MEANTIME, QUITE a different concept of "pilgrimage" was growing up in Irish circles.

The penitential systems of Ireland and Anglo-Saxon England in the sixth to the tenth centuries completely transformed the old concept of ecclesiastical penance.[26] In primitive Christianity, the only formal penance imposed by the Church was public penance, and in the earliest times this could be performed only once. The transition to private and indefinitely repeatable penance was made under Celtic influence. One of the most important forms of penance was *peregrinatio*, pilgrimage, or exile, especially to an island, *relegatio in insulam*.[27] Instead of doing public penance in full view of the local church (for instance, by remaining outside the church in penitential garb, fasting and performing other prescribed works until reconciled), the penitent was sent off into exile, either

---

24. See Kenneth Jackson, *A Celtic Miscellany* (Cambridge, Mass., 1951), pp. 301ff. G. Murphy: *Early Irish Lyrics* (Oxford, 1956). Bieler, *Ireland the Harbinger of the Middle Ages*, p. 57.

25. Aussi la pérégrination continue-t-elle a être présentée comme un forme d'érémitisme, et, comme telle, dans la logique de la vie monastique. "Monachisme et pérégrination," p. 41.

26. L. Vogel, "Le Pèlerinage pénitentiel," *Revue des Sc. Rel.* XXXVIII.2 (1964), pp. 113ff. Poschmann, *Penance and the Anointing of the Sick* (New York, 1964). Chadwick, *The Age of Saints in the Early Celtic Church*, p. 103.

27. Chadwick notes that the Scilly Isles had been a penal settlement in Roman times and that some Priscillianist heretics had been sent there. She also cites the questionable tradition of St. Columba's exile for a sin of violence (*The Age of Saints in the Early Celtic Church*, p. 102). Vogel ("Le Pèlerinage pénitentiel," p. 127) does not think the medieval penitential practice of exile is traceable to Roman law.

perpetual or temporary. He might be sent to a lonely island, or simply turned out into the alien world to wander without a specified goal. The penitent just "peregrinated." Only after the eighth century is the penitent sent to a specific place, or perhaps to a distant bishop to *receive* a penance, and then when he returned to his own church, after giving proof that his penance was completed, he was absolved. We must always remember that at this time absolution was given only after the penance had been completed. After the ninth century, the goal of the penitent pilgrim was most often Rome, where he was sent to have the Pope decide his case and impose a suitable penance and send him back to his own bishop for absolution. Some penitents preferred to go direct to Rome, over the head of their own bishop, but this was reproved.[28]

It is not quite exact to regard this *peregrinatio* as a purely private and face-saving form of penance. On the contrary, it had a semi-public character[29] and was imposed for scandalous faults. The penitent pilgrim was driven forth as an outcast, dressed in rags or sackcloth, barefoot, perhaps even wearing a chain.[30] He was under strict obligation to keep moving, for he was a "wanderer" ("Let him not spend the night twice in the same place," said one of the Penitentials).[31] He was not allowed to bear arms, and was therefore sent totally defenseless among strangers who might be barbarians and pagans (for instance, the Picts in Scotland or many of the inhabitants of lands east of the Rhine). The pilgrim who was carrying out a canonical penance wore a distinctive garb and badge. The pilgrim thus became a familiar figure in the Europe of the Dark Ages, and he was easily recognizable as a sacred person. If he were a canonical penitent, he was, like Cain, one on whom the curse of God rested, one who was being punished and healed, whom *man might not touch* (Genesis 4:13-15). He was, so to speak, a holy outcast, a consecrated tramp, living under a mystery of execration and protection, overshadowed by inscrutable love, a mystery and portent to every man. It was a sacred duty to protect him, feed him, give him shelter, and show him his way. Failure to shelter and protect pilgrims was declared to be the reason for punishment by an invasion of Lombards in southern France.[32] Since one could not count even on the faithful to respect the pilgrim and peni-

---

28. Council of Seligenstadt, 1022/23. Vogel, "Le Pèlerinage pénitentiel," pp. 143-44.

29. Vogel, "Le Pèlerinage pénitentiel," p. 118.

30. Numerous references given in Vogel, "Le Pèlerinage pénitentiel," pp. 130-31.

31. *Canones sub Edgaro Rege*, England, tenth century, quoted by Vogel, "Le Pèlerinage pénitentiel," p. 127.

32. St. Gregory of Tours: *Hist. Franc.*, VI, 6. H. Leclercq, "Pèlerinages à Rome," D.A.C.L., xiv, p. 52.

tent, these travelers were sometimes provided with official letters of identification.[33] Special hostelries for the numerous Irish and Anglo-Saxon pilgrims were
provided both at the chief places of pilgrimage and on the way there, and the
Anglo-Saxon hostelry in Rome was supported by taxation in England.[34] Thus
the penitent pilgrim, though cast out, had a very definite and indeed privileged
place in the Church.

Pilgrimage or perpetual exile was usually given as penances for the worst
crimes:[35] murder, incest, sacrilegious sins of violence or lust; and if the penitent
was convinced of his need for penance and forgiveness, there is no question that
he would take his penance seriously. Unfortunately, when it became common
to send the worst offenders on pilgrimage as penance for grave crimes, large
numbers of criminals were in effect turned loose, to live an irresponsible and
wandering existence in common.[36] They naturally tended to band together, and
when they did, their influence on each other was perhaps not much help in carrying forward their repentance and conversion.

Alcuin complained, in a letter,[37] of the dangers that came from associating
with the riffraff of the roads, the jugglers, the thieves, and the pilgrims of various shades and dispositions who were met everywhere. Even genuine pilgrims
who fell in with these others tended to suffer grave damage from their contact,
and St. Boniface lamented that there was hardly a city on the way from England to Rome that did not have a few fallen Anglo-Saxon women living there
as whores.[38] They were among the many for whom pilgrimage, on the Continent, was hardly a spiritual success. Note that on the Continent especially, pilgrimage was imposed as penance on clerics and monks who were considered
scandalous and even incorrigible, doubtless as a last resort.[39] In fact, since the
monk was already living in a public state of penance, he was not able to perform
the ordinary public penance according to the ancient and solemn discipline.

---

33. D.A.C.L. One penitent even carried an identification in Latin verse by
Venantius Fortunatus, id. 52, on *litterae tractoriae*. See Vogel, "Le Pèlerinage pénitentiel,"
p. 133.

34. D.A.C.L., xiv., p. 60.

35. See penitential of Vinnian, n. 23, quoted in Bieler, *Ireland the Harbinger of
the Middle Ages,* p. 52. Chadwick, *The Age of Saints in the Early Celtic Church,* p. 102.

36. Le Pèlerinage pénitential aboutit en fait à sélectionner les pires criminels et à
les lancer sur les chemins. Vogel, "Le Pèlerinage pénitentiel," p. 130.

37. Ep. 289.

38. See the famous letter of St. Boniface to Cuthbert of Canterbury (MGH. Epp.
III, 78, p. 354), of which Vogel says that it "constitutes a sociological document of the
highest order" ("Le Pèlerinage pénitentiel," p. 140).

39. Rule of St. Benedict, C. 38; cf. the quotation of I Cor. 5:5 in the Rule, C. 25.

The paradoxical result of the penitential pilgrimage in the Middle Ages was to *increase* scandal by turning loose clerics and monks of disordered life to wander in public in situations that invited them to further sins that could hardly be kept hidden.[40] There was consequently a strong reaction on the part of the eleventh-century reformers against the "gyrovagues" or wandering monks.[41]

We have seen that pilgrimages were originally intended as expiation, by a defenseless and nonviolent, wandering existence, of the worst crimes of violence. Now in the ninth and tenth centuries, even killing in war was regarded as a sin requiring expiation.[42] In the Anglo-Saxon penitential of Theodore of Canterbury, a soldier who killed a man in war was obliged to a forty-day fast even though he might have killed his enemy in the "ordinary line of duty," under obedience to his officer. Later penitentials distinguished between offensive and defensive killing. One who attacked an enemy and killed him was obliged to do penance. One who killed another in self-defense was not obliged to do penance, but was *counseled* to do so for the good of his soul. Burchard of Worms, in the eleventh century, equated killing in war with ordinary homicide and assigned seven years of penance, without distinction as to offense or defense.[43]

Pilgrimage was not usually given as a penance for killing in war. But persons who had accumulated many penances for various sins might find themselves faced with a staggering burden of penitential "tariffs" to pay off. In order not to have to fast and do penance for scores of years, they had their multiple penance commuted to a single pilgrimage, which took care of everything.

With this, the systematization of pilgrimage began, and pilgrimages were imposed by the Inquisition as afflictive punishments.[44] The Church recognized places of major pilgrimage, such as Jerusalem and Rome, Canterbury and Compostela. There were also minor places of pilgrimage such as Le Puy, St. Gilles, Rocamadour, in France.[45] Ponce de Léras, a twelfth-century brigand in the central mountains of France, abandoned his life of brigandage, made restitution, went on pilgrimage to Compostela, and returned to settle down in a Cistercian

---

40. Vogel, "Le Pèlerinage pénitentiel," p. 126.

41. St. Peter Damian, Opusc. XII., 9-14, 20-25. PL 145:260ff. G. Penco, "Il Capitulo de Generibus Monachorum nella Traditione Medievale," *Studia Monastica* (1961),41f. J. Leclercq, "Le Poème de Payen Belotin contre les faux ermites," *Rev. Ben.* (1958), pp. 52ff.

42. Vogel, "Le Pèlerinage pénitentiel," p. 145.

43. Ibid., p. 146. Cf. PL 140:952.

44. Vogel, "Le Pèlerinage pénitentiel," p. 135.

45. For a complete list of places of pilgrimage, see Vogel, "Le Pèlerinage pénitentiel," p. 135.

monastery he had founded.[46] This was a standard medieval pattern for a successful conversion of life. As a matter of fact, it introduces us to a new pattern, in which "wandering eremitism" is no longer favored as an ascetic ideal, and in which the *peregrinatio* of Abraham is imitated by the monk who leaves "the world" for the cloister and stability of the monastery. In the eleventh and twelfth centuries we find frequent attacks upon "false hermits" who wander about. The monk who has entered the cloister will no longer leave to wander further afield. His perfection will consist in his stability.[47] However, as Dom Leclercq points out,[48] the monk in the cloister will read the narratives of saintly pilgrims as his "adventure stories." He will also take a passionate interest in the Crusades. As a matter of fact, in the case of the Crusades, an exception will be made. Many Cistercians accompanied the Crusades as chaplains, and Cistercian foundations were made in the Near East. In any case, the same spiritual crisis which led to monastic reforms in the eleventh and twelfth centuries led at the same time to a revival of itinerant eremitism and also, above all, to the great mass-*peregrinatio* of the Crusade.[49]

IV

IT IS OFTEN THOUGHT that the sole or chief reason for the Crusades was the fact that Christian pilgrims suffered harassment from the Moslems who were masters of Jerusalem.[50] It is certain that the popular enthusiasm that drove thousands of knights and common soldiers to the East in 1095 was an eruption of zeal for the liberation of the Holy Sepulchre. But it must be remembered that the first idea of the Crusade, which goes back to Gregory VII in 1074, was a project for the defense of Constantinople, an essentially "ecumenical" venture, by which it was hoped that the union of Greek and Latin against the Turk

---

46. *Hagiologium Cisterciense*, Aug. 1.

47. Texts quoted by J. Leclercq, "Monachisme et pérégrination," pp. 40-49.

48. On ne peut s'empêcher de penser que de tels récits étaient, en quelque sorte, les romans d'aventures des moines du moyen âge. J. Leclercq, "Monachisme et pérégrination," p. 40.

49. J. Leclercq, in Leclercq, Vandenbroucke, Bouyer, *Histoire de la Spiritualité Chrétienne*, Vol. II, p. 165.

50. Pilgrims, being foreigners, were naturally suspect, but Moslems usually understood the idea of pilgrimage, which plays a central part in the religion of Islam. St. Willibald was arrested in Edessa in 723 but released when an aged Moslem assured the police that he had many times seen Christians like this one "fulfilling their law." H. Leclercq, D.A.C.L., xiv, p. 163.

would heal the schism that had begun in 1054. Actually Constantinople was a holy city and a place of pilgrimage. The First Crusade was itself an enormous pilgrimage, a holy war preached and organized by the Church, led by an armed bishop, Adhemar, ordinary of Le Puy, one of the "minor" places of pilgrimage in France. The various armies converged on Constantinople, and then went on to take Jerusalem.

Pilgrimages to Jerusalem had opened a familiar way to the armies of the Cross. In the first half of the eleventh century, Robert II, Duke of Normandy, had to make a barefoot pilgrimage to Jerusalem to expiate the murder of his brother, Duke Richard III.[51] In 1073, Count Theodore, murderer of Conrad, Archbishop of Trier, went to Jerusalem. These two examples among many[52] show that the Crusaders were not all launching out into the unknown. Noblemen who had done penance and visited the Holy Sepulchre were now also attracted by the prospect of settling in this most sacred of lands, and having castles of their own in Judea or Galilee, there to await the second coming of Christ and the resurrection.

In the mind of Pope Urban II, the Holy Crusade was to be not only a great unification of Christendom against the Turk, but a magnificent and general act of repentant faith that would culminate in the moral reform and total renewal of Christendom. The "land of promise" which the Holy Father envisioned was a general state of holiness, unity, and perfection in the whole Church, East and West, a Christendom united and renewed in peace at the Holy Sepulchre.

Since the ninth century, very serious and sustained efforts had been made to limit wars among Christians. While promulgating the Crusade, the Council of Clermont (1095) also made the "Truce of God" of general obligation. This prohibition of fighting, from Septuagesima to Trinity Sunday and from Wednesday to Monday all year, had previously been imposed by local councils. Pope Urban was seeking a paradise of peace in Christendom, united in defense of the Holy Land, which symbolized the peace promised to all men of good will. As a Catholic historian observes,[53] "he commanded Christians to make a truce to all hostility that sprang from private interests. Thus the very notion of war was altered under the influence of the Roman Pontiff." War was now to be waged only in obedience to the Church, which was intent upon restricting the use of violence to what was absolutely necessary for the defense of Christendom. In the sense that the Crusade was expected to unify Christendom and consolidate

---

51. Vogel, "Le Pèlerinage pénitentiel," pp. 128-29.

52. Ibid., p. 129; see references.

53. Mourret-Thompson, *History of the Catholic Church* (St. Louis, 1941), Vol. IV, p. 282.

Christian power in a way that would permanently subdue Islam and hold off all future aggression from without, it was explicitly considered a "war to end wars." This eschatological hope accounted in part for the tremendous expectation and enthusiasm of the first Crusaders.[54] War against the infidel now became a sacred duty for all because it was the pledge of unity and peace within Christendom as well as of permanent peace for the Christian world. Hence, the Crusade was considered one of the greatest and most meritorious good works. There was no "Truce of God" in killing Turks, because the sooner the great work was accomplished, the better it would be for all.

But above all, in the intentions of the Popes, the Crusade remained essentially a pilgrimage, but a mass pilgrimage of all Christians united in the expectation of the imminent return of Christ. The eschatological hope was expressed in the hymns and marching songs of the Crusaders.[55] Just as pilgrimage had been the commutation of all other penances, so now the Crusade, the super-pilgrimage, amply satisfied for the sins of a whole lifetime, even a lifetime of brigandage, lechery, murder, blasphemy, impiety, anything. The Crusade became the *epitome of all penance*. In fact, there was a great deal of penitential ardor among the first Crusaders. They fasted and prayed before battles and multiplied processions and acts of devotion. They were in general dedicated to a true spirit of poverty and austerity befitting pilgrims. The proof of one's profound and sincere conversion and loyalty to Christ and His Church was one's readiness to undergo hardship and privation, and do battle against an enemy who, quite naturally, came to be regarded as the incarnation of all the forces of evil. St. Bernard emphasized that the presence of infidels at the Holy Sepulchre was an outrage and insult to the Savior.[56] Urban II at Clermont urged the faithful to take up arms against an "abominable . . . impure people . . . [who had] ravaged and stained the holy places."[57] He had barely uttered his call when the cry went up everywhere: *Deus vult!* "God wills it!" The same cry, "It is written!," had launched the Moslems, a people of pilgrimage, upon the holy war.

It has been noted about St. Bernard (who preached the Second Crusade) that a deep vein of Augustinian pessimism about fallen man in a world of sin colored his ideas.[58] For St. Bernard, salvation outside a monastery was, to say the

54. J. Leclercq, *Histoire de la Spiritualité Chrétienne*, Vol. II, p. 166. See references to Dupront, Rousset, etc.

55. Ibid., p. 167.

56. St. Bernard, Letter 458 and *De Laude Novae Militiae*.

57. Mourret-Thompson, *History of the Catholic Church*, p. 283.

58. Cf. E. Delaruelle, "L'Idée de croisade chez S. Bernard," *Mélanges S. Bernard* (Dijon, 1953), p. 57.

least, extremely difficult and doubtful. Though he was himself not friendly to pilgrimages for monks, he felt that the Crusade offered a unique opportunity for penance and salvation for multitudes of Christians who would otherwise most certainly be damned. "I call blessed the generation that can seize an opportunity of such rich indulgence as this blessed, to be alive in this year of God's choice. The blessing is spread throughout the whole world and all the world is called to receive the badge of immortality."[59] But if this is the case, then the Crusade is a Jubilee open to everyone—not only to an elite but to all sinners. It is not merely a question of a challenge to noble knights; there is a terrible moral risk for anyone who refuses to take this unique opportunity.[60]

St. Bernard even more than Urban II believed that the Crusade was a providential opportunity for the total renewal of feudal society.

With exaltation and immense relief, the first great army of repentant sinners started for the East, assured by Pope Urban himself that if they died on the expedition they would possess eternal life without further delay. "The robbers and pirates," said Oderic Vital, "criminals of every sort, moved by grace, came forth from the abyss of their wretchedness, disavowed their crimes and forsook them, and departed for the far-off country."[61]

Thus we see that in the course of time the peaceful and defenseless pilgrimage, the humble and meek "return to the source" of all life and grace, became the organized martial expedition to liberate the land promised to Abraham and his sons. It is surely significant that in the Middle Ages this conception of the Christian life became deeply embedded in European man; the "center," the "source," the "holy place," the "promised land," the "place of resurrection" becomes something to be attained, conquered, and preserved by politics and by force of arms. The whole Christian life and all Christian virtue then take on a certain martial and embattled character. The true life of Christian virtue now becomes a struggle to death with pagan adversaries who are wickedly standing in the way of one's divinely appointed goal and perversely preventing fulfillment of a "manifest destiny."

Meanwhile, of course, certain ambiguities appeared in this conception of the Christian life as a mystique of martial and political organization. In the Second Crusade these ambiguities made themselves decisively felt: if the Crusade is a war to annihilate the enemy, then strategy comes first and the army should besiege Aleppo. If it is primarily a pilgrimage, then the crusading pilgrims should

---

59. St. Bernard, Letter 363. Cf. Bruno James, *Letters of St. Bernard* (Chicago, 1953).

60. Delaruelle, "L'Idée de croisade chez S. Bernard," p. 58.

61. Oderic Vital, *Historia Ecclesiastica*, ix, PL 188:652.

go up to Jerusalem. Yet the king had not made a vow to conquer Aleppo, only to go to Jerusalem.[62] Thus, the concept of an essentially embattled Christian society tended to become inseparable from the Christian outlook, one might almost say the Christian faith. Christian eschatology in the West took on a very precise historical and social coloring in centuries of combat against the Turk. It was defense of Western Christendom against Eastern and pagan autocracy and power.

It would be naïve to underestimate the sincerity and the deep spiritual motivation of the Crusades, just as it would be naïve to ignore the fact that the violence, the greed, the lust, and the continued depravity of the worst elements continued unchanged. In point of fact, the Crusades had an immense effect on European and Christian society in the West. They certainly opened the way to renaissance and modern Christendom. But the paradise of spiritual benefits that had been hoped for was never attained. On the contrary, from the point of view of East-West relations in Christendom, the Crusades were a disaster. They certainly made all reunion between Rome and Constantinople unthinkable.

Above all, the Crusades introduced a note of fatal ambiguity into the concept of pilgrimage and penance. What was intended as a remedy for sins of violence, particularly murder, now became a consecration of violence. There is, of course, a distinction between war and murder, and the sacrifice entailed by warfare can certainly be regarded as "penitential." But a man prone to violence and passion, a potential or actual murderer and sadist, is not likely to make too many fine distinctions when he discovers that he can now not only kill people legitimately, but even offer his acts to God as "good works" and as "penance," provided he concentrates on infidels, regarded as the embodiment of all evil.

We know that the Crusaders did not confine their warlike activities to what was juridically "holy." The sack of Christian Constantinople and the internecine battles among the Crusaders themselves are there to prove it.

Finally, a very interesting development took place in the Crusades. The mystique of sacred love was, in the twelfth century, very close to the courtly love of the troubadours. But we find, curiously enough, that a typical troubadour, Jaufré Rudel, who took part in the Second Crusade, could sing in the same breath of the love for little Jesus in Bethlehem and of a more secular love for the "distant lady" in whose "service" the loyal knight will risk death and imprisonment. The Crusade becomes merged with the romance of courtly love. At the same

---

62. Delaruelle, "L'Idée de croisade chez S. Bernard," p. 54.

time the sacred element tends to be neglected by those who, like Bertrand de Born, are engrossed in the martial glory and exploits of the knights.[63]

V

So MUCH FOR THE East. There remained the fabulous paradise of the West. It is curious that in the folklore tradition of Spain, the "Lost Island" of the West, identified with the Brendan legend to the point that it was given Brendan's own name, remained the paradisiacal refuge to which the kings of Spain and Portugal might flee from Moorish invasions,[64] just as in the Celtic legend the "land of promise" in the western ocean was evidently regarded as a place of refuge from the Norsemen.

Christopher Columbus was most probably aware of the Brendan legend[65] as well as of such classic medieval descriptions of the "Lost Island," or Perdita, as that of Honorius of Autun (or more exactly, William of Conches):

> There is a certain island of the Ocean called Perdita, and it excels all the lands of the earth in the beauty and fertility of all things. Found once by chance, it was later sought again and not found, whence it is called Perdita. To this isle, Brendan is said to have come.[66]

The description has all the mythical qualities of the lost paradise, and Columbus's idyllic description of his landfall on Hispaniola showed that the new land appeared to him to be in every way an earthly paradise. He did not believe he had discovered Perdita, however, and Spanish expeditions in search of the "Lost Island" continued even after the discovery of the American mainland.

Brendan's Island was marked ("tentatively") on maps as late as the eighteenth century.[67] It was even formally renounced by Portugal in the Treaty of Evora (1519), so that if it ever were found it was already assigned in advance (by the Apostolic See) to his Catholic majesty of Spain.

In one word, the Renaissance explorers, the conquistadors, the Puritans, the

---

63. Delaruelle, "L'Idée de croisade chez S. Bernard," p. 66.

64. C. Selmer, "The Vernacular Translations of the *Navigatio Brendani*," *Medieval Studies*, xvii, 1956, p. 150.

65. H. B. Workman, *Evolution of the Monastic Ideal*, reprint (Boston, 1962), p. 196 n.

66. *De Imagine Mundi*, I.36, PL 172:132.

67. W. H. Babcock, "St. Brendan's Explorations and Islands," *Geographical Review* (July 1919), pp. 37-46.

missionaries, the colonizers, and doubtless also the slave traders and pirates, were in their own way deeply influenced by the mythical paradisiacal aspect of the Americas. But it was a paradise into which they could not penetrate without the most profound ambiguities.

They came, in a way, as "penitents" or as men seeking renewal, deliverance from the past, the gift to begin again. But at the same time the pattern of this renewal forbade neither self-enrichment nor the free enjoyment of the opportunities which the "paradise" so generously offered (native women). And it prescribed, above all, as a sort of vestige of crusading ardor and as an earnest of absolution, an uncompromising zeal in the subjection of the infidel—and, of course, in his conversion. It was also a good thing to build churches at home with Inca gold. While St. Theresa of Avila was following her interior and mystic itinerary (not without some very energetic peregrination about Spain, founding Carmels[68]), her brother was in the Kingdom of Quito getting rich. When he returned to Spain, he financed the Carmel of Seville (where St. Theresa enjoyed the view of the river with the gallant ships of the Armada back from the Indies). And there is no reason to doubt the depth and sincerity of his inner life, troubled only by certain violent reactions, which his sister, though she had never experienced such things, did not find surprising.

There was in the Indies the lush and tempting beauty and fantastic opulence of nature. There were the true and legendary riches, from the mines of San Luis Potosí to the lake of Eldorado and the fountain of eternal youth. There were the Indians and their cities, appearing now as idyllic "noble savages" in utopian communities, now as treacherous devils indulging in infernal tricks and sunk in the worst forms of heathenism.

Thus, the European white man set foot on the shores of America with the conflicting feelings of an Adam newly restored to paradise and of a Crusader about to scale the walls of Acre.

The mentality of the pilgrim and that of the Crusader had fused together to create a singular form of alienation: that of the Puritan "pilgrim father" and that of the conquistador. Centuries of ardent, unconscious desire for the Lost Island had established a kind of right to paradise once it was found. It never occurred to the sixteenth-century Spaniard or Englishman to doubt for a moment that the new world was entirely and rightly his. It had been promised and given to him by God. It was the end of centuries of pilgrimage. It was the long-sought land of promise and renewal, where the old deficiencies and limitations no lon-

68. *The Book of the Foundations*, in the *Complete Works of St. Theresa*, translated by E. Allison Peers (New York, 1946), Vol. III.

ger existed: the land of the new beginning not only for the individual but for society itself. The land of refuge from persecution. The land of peace and plenty, where all the iniquities and oppressions of the old world were forgotten. Here peace and unity were bought at the price of Christian courage in battling with the wilderness and with the infidel. To conquer and subjugate the native population was not regarded as an unjust aggression, as usurpation or as robbery and tyranny but on the contrary as proof of one's loyalty to all the values dear to the European and Christian heart since Charlemagne.

It is true, however, that some of the missioners had a different and more mystical view of paradise. But their solution was only more logically and consistently paradisiacal; as in the primitive and religious Jesuit utopias in Paraguay, or the communities of Vasco de Quiroga in Mexico.

These were, indeed, admirable and virtuous efforts. But for the greater part, the pilgrims were rushing upon the Lost Island with a combative ferocity and a wasteful irresponsibility that have tainted the fruits of the paradise tree with bitterness ever since.

Somehow it has been forgotten that a paradise that can be conquered and acquired by force is not paradise at all.

So the story of man's pilgrimage and search has reached the end of a cycle and is starting on another: now that it is clear that there is no paradise on earth that is not defiled as well as limited, now that there are no lost islands, there is perhaps some dry existentialist paradise of clean ashes to be discovered and colonized in outer space: a "new beginning" that initiates nothing and is little more than a sign of our irreversible decision to be disgusted with the paradises and pilgrimages of earth. Disgust with paradise, but not with crusades! The new planet is apparently to be the base for a more definitive extermination of infidels, together with the mass of less agile pilgrims so occupied in keeping body and soul together that they cannot be singled out as pilgrims to a promised land.

And yet the pilgrimage must continue, because it is an inescapable part of man's structure and program. The problem is for his pilgrimage to make sense—it must represent a complete integration of his inner and outer life, of his relation to himself and to other men.

The Bible has always taken man in the concrete, never in the abstract. The world has been given by God not to a theoretical man but to the actual beings that we are. If we instinctively seek a paradisiacal and special place on earth, it is because we know in our inmost hearts that the earth was given us in order that we might find meaning, order, truth, and salvation in it. The world is not only a vale of tears. There is joy in it somewhere. Joy is to be sought, for the glory of God.

But the joy is not for mere tourists. Our pilgrimage is more than the synthetic happy-making of a vacation cruise. Our journey is from the limitations and routines of "the given"—the *Dasein* which confronts us as we are born into it without choice—to the creative freedom of that love which is personal choice and commitment. Paradise symbolizes this freedom and creativity, but in reality this must be worked out in the human and personal encounter with the stranger seen as our other self.

As long as the Inca, the Maya, the Mestizo, the Negro, the Jew, or what have you, confronts us as *Dasein*, as a lump of limited and nonnegotiable *en-soi*, he will seem to stand in the way of our fulfillment. "*L'enfer, c'est les autres*,"[69] and we will seek paradise by combating his presence, subduing him, enslaving him, eliminating him.

Our task now is to learn that if we can voyage to the ends of the earth and there find *ourselves* in the aborigine who most differs from ourselves, we will have made a fruitful pilgrimage. That is why pilgrimage is necessary, in some shape or other. Mere sitting at home and meditating on the divine presence is not enough for our time. We have to come to the end of a long journey and see that the stranger we meet there is no other than ourselves—which is the same as saying that we find Christ in him.

For if the Lord is risen, as He said, He is actually or potentially alive in every man. Our pilgrimage to the Holy Sepulchre is our pilgrimage to the stranger who is Christ our fellow-pilgrim and our brother. There is no lost island merely for the individual. We are all pieces of the paradise isle, and we can find our Brendan's island only when we all realize ourselves together as the paradise which is Christ and His Bride, God, man, and Church.

It was in this spirit that St. Francis went on pilgrimage—on his own original kind of "crusade"—to meet the Soldan: as a messenger not of violence, not of arrogant power, but of humility, simplicity, and love.[70]

And it was in this spirit that Pope John XXIII wrote *Pacem in Terris*.

---

69. Jean-Paul Sartre: *No Exit*. This expression sums up the existentialist's meditation on hell.

70. G. Basetti-Sani, O.F.M., *Mohammed et Saint François* (Ottawa, 1959).

15

Religion and Race in the United States

On July 14, 1964, Merton mentions in his journal that he is writing "a short article for Père Hervé Chaigne, O.F.M.—a French Franciscan interested in nonviolence" (*Dancing in the Water of Life*, 127); on August 2, he notes that "my article on race" has been sent to Chaigne in Bordeaux (*Dancing in the Water of Life*, 132). The essay was published in French translation as "Christianisme et Question Raciale aux États-Unis" in Chaigne's journal *Frères du Monde* 31 (1964), 50-65. Excerpts from a somewhat revised version of the piece, entitled "The Extremists, Black & White: A Mystique of Violence," appeared in *Peace News* (September 18, 1964), 6, while the English version of the complete essay was published in the British Dominican journal *New Blackfriars* 46 (January 1965), 218-25. It was included in a slightly different form in *Faith & Violence* (130-44) and reprinted in *Passion for Peace* (217-27). "Religion and Race" is the second of Merton's three major discussions of the American civil rights struggle, following "Letters to a White Liberal" (November 1963) and preceding "The Hot Summer of Sixty-Seven." In this article he follows up on the idea first voiced in his review of William Melvin Kelley's novel *A Different Drummer* (see *Seeds of Destruction*, 76) and in "Letters" that the nonviolent and deeply Christian movement for racial liberation led by Martin Luther King constituted a "providential 'hour,' the *kairos* not merely of the Negro, but of the white man" (*Seeds of Destruction*, 65). While praising the movement led by King as "the greatest example of Christian faith in action in the social history of the United States," he now considers that the moment of *kairos* has passed, and foresees that a more destructive ethos will predominate in the next phase of the black freedom struggle. Nevertheless, he considers that the failure of white Christianity to respond adequately to the invitation to conversion offered by the call for racial liberation can actually be a purificatory experience, a dispelling of triumphalist illusions, a humbling admission that "we are not a special kind of privileged being, that our faith does not exempt us from facing the mysterious realities of the world with the same limitations as everybody else, and with the same capacity for human failure." If the turn to violence on the part of blacks can lead to an awareness of the structural violence built into the social fabric of American institutions, Merton tells his European audience, then ultimately it can bring about authentic social transformation, though he is far from certain when or how this could happen.

THE IDEA OF *KAIROS*—the time of urgent and providential decision—is
something characteristic of Christianity, a religion of decisions in time
and in history. Can Christians recognize their *kairos*? Is it possible that
when the majority of Christians become aware that "the time has come" for a
decisive and urgent commitment, the time has, in fact, already run out?

There can be no question now that the time for a certain kind of crucial
Christian decision in America has come and gone. In 1962, and finally in 1963,
there were "moments of truth" which have now passed, and the scene is becoming one of darkness, anarchy, and moral collapse. These, of course, still call for a
Christian response, a Christian decision. But it might seem that the responses
and decisions of Christians will necessarily be less clear and more tragic because
it is now apparent that there is little left for Christians as such to do to shape
the events—or forestall the tragedies—that are to come. At best they can pray,
and patiently suffer the consequences of past indecision, blindness, and evasion.
They cannot lead and guide the nation through this crisis, but they can still help
others, if they choose, to understand and accept the sufferings involved in order
to make a creative and constructive use of the situation for the future. Are they
really likely to do this? Who can say?

In the Negro Christian nonviolent movement, under Martin Luther King,
the *kairos*, the "providential time," met with a courageous and enlightened
response. The nonviolent-Negro civil rights drive has been one of the most positive and successful expressions of Christian social action that has been seen anywhere in the twentieth century. It is certainly the greatest example of Christian
faith in action in the social history of the United States. It has come almost
entirely from the Negroes, with a few white Christians and liberals in support.
There can be no question that the Christian heroism manifested by the Negroes
in the Birmingham demonstrations, or the massive tranquility and order of the
March on Washington in August of 1963, had a great deal to do with the passage of the Civil Rights Bill. It must also be admitted, as Bayard Rustin, a Negro
nonviolent leader, has pointed out, that without the Christian intervention of
white Protestants and Catholics all over America, the bill would not have been
passed. The fact that there is now a Civil Rights Law guaranteeing, at least *de
jure*, the freedom of all citizens to enjoy the facilities of the country equally is
due to what one might call a Christian as well as a humanitarian and liberal
conscience in the United States. However the Northern Negro is, generally
speaking, disillusioned with the Churches and with the Christian preaching
of moderation and nonviolence. His feeling is that the Churches are part of
the establishment (which in fact they are!). They support the power structure

and therefore (he believes) keep the Negro deluded and passive, preventing him from fighting for his rights.

The passage of the Civil Rights Bill has only brought the real problem to a head. The struggle for rights now enters a new and more difficult phase.

Hitherto the well-intentioned and the idealistic have assumed that if the needed legislation were passed, the two races would "integrate" more or less naturally, not without a certain amount of difficulty, of course, but nonetheless effectively in the end. They have also assumed as axiomatic that if something is morally right and good, it will come to pass all by itself as soon as obstacles are removed. Everyone seemed to believe with simple faith that law and order, morality, the "American way of life" and Christianity are all very much the same thing. Now it is becoming quite clear that they are not so at all. Many Christians, who have confused "Americanism" with "Christianity," are in fact contributing to the painful contradictions and even injustices of the racial crisis. For the one thing that has been made most evident by the long and bitter struggle of the South, and now of the North, to prevent civil rights legislation from being passed or enforced or made effective is that the legislators and the police themselves, along with some ministers and indeed all those whom one can call "the establishment," seem to be the first to defy the law or set it aside when their own interests are threatened. In other words we are living in a society that is not exactly moral, a society which misuses Christian clichés to justify its lawlessness and immorality.

And so there are many who think that nonviolence has not proved itself a success. It is considered naïve and over-simple and it does not get real results. Certainly nonviolence postulates a belief in the fundamental goodness of human nature. But this attitude of optimism can come to be confused with shallow confidence in the morality and intrinsic goodness of a society which is proving itself torn by vicious internal contradictions. Nonviolence still continues to be used as a tactic, but the days of its real effectiveness are apparently over. It will probably never again convey the message it conveyed in Montgomery, Birmingham, and Selma. Those days are over, and it seems that people who believed in all that was implied by nonviolence will look back upon those days with a certain nostalgia. For nonviolence apparently presupposed a sense of justice, of humaneness, of liberality, of generosity that were not to be found in the white people to whom the Negroes made their stirring appeal. The problem of American racism turned out to be far deeper, far more stubborn, infinitely more complex. It is also part of a much greater problem: one that divides the whole world into what may one day turn into a huge revolutionary interracial war of two camps: the affluent whites and the impoverished nonwhites.

One reason why nonviolence apparently cannot continue to be a really effective instrument for the vindication of Negro rights is this: it seems that the willingness to take punishment and suffering, which is essential to nonviolent resistance, cannot mean the same thing to the Negro minority in the United States as it meant to the Hindus in their vast majority facing English colonialism in India. There, Hindu nonviolence bore witness to overwhelming strength. In the Negro ghettoes of America it has turned out to mean, to Negroes and to whites in general, another admission of Negro inferiority and helplessness. The Negro is always the one who lets his head be bashed in. Whether or not this is what nonviolence really means, the confused image of it has now become unacceptable to many activists in the struggle for civil rights, while resentful whites, north and south, are not willing to see its true meaning in any case. The Negroes, on the other hand, more and more disillusioned not only with white reactionaries but also with ambiguous liberals, have tended to take a more desperate course. On the one hand there has been an increasing trend toward unsystematic and spontaneous violence, and on the other there has been the systematic campaign for "Black Power" which, not properly understood and not always clearly explained, has managed to frighten white people not a little. We will discuss this further on.

In any case there is more and more violent action on both sides, as it becomes increasingly clear that the Civil Rights Law has not really solved the racial problem and that in actual fact the ghetto existence of the Negro has only become better and more inexorably defined by his inability to take advantage of the rights that have been granted him only on paper and too late.

The Negro is integrated by law into a society in which there really is no place for him—not that a place could not be made for him, if the white majority were capable of wanting him as a brother and a fellow-citizen. But even those who have been theoretically in favor of civil rights are turning out to be concretely reluctant to have the Negro as next-door neighbor. The so-called "white backlash" manifests a change from tolerant indifference to bitter hatred on the part of some Northern whites. It is virulent and passionate and one hears the word "nigger" spat out with a venom which one had thought belonged to the past. And there are reasons, for violence and gratuitous attacks on white people by Negroes are common everywhere in the North. The Negro's clear awareness that he is still despised and rejected, after years of bitter struggle and deception, has destroyed his confidence in legal and peaceful methods. Perhaps he is beginning to want something besides "rights" that are purely Platonic—an opportunity to unburden himself of his bitterness by violent protest, that will disrupt a social "order" that seems to him to have proved itself meaningless and fraudulent.

The problem is much more complex, much more tragic, than people have imagined. To begin with, it is something that extends beyond America. It affects the whole world. The race problem of America has been analyzed (by such writers as William Faulkner, for example) as a problem of deep guilt for the sin of slavery. The guilt of white America toward the Negro is simply another version of the guilt of the European colonizer toward all the other races of the world, whether in Asia, Africa, America, or Polynesia. The racial crisis in the United States has rightly been diagnosed as a "colonial crisis" within the country itself rather than on a distant continent. But it is nevertheless closely related to the United States' problems in Southeast Asia and in Latin America, particularly with Cuba.

The fact that nonviolent resistance did not fully succeed and the fact that its partial failure clearly disclosed the refusal of white America to really integrate the Negro into its social framework has radically altered the Negro's evaluation of himself and of his struggle. Whereas before he might have been willing to believe it possible for him to find a place in white society, he has now largely ceased to find real integration either credible or desirable. True, there are probably countless middle-class Negroes who are able to find life tolerable and who seek only to avoid further trouble and violence. But there are far more numerous Negroes for whom the present situation spells nothing but despair and total rejection from a society which to them has no real meaning. To these Negroes, if any political self-awareness makes sense at all, it is one in which they begin dimly to recognize themselves as identified with the colored races in all parts of the world which are struggling to assert themselves and find their proper place in it. The slogan "Black Power" implies not only the intent to use political means in order to gain what is granted the Negro by law and refused him in fact. It implies a consciousness of revolutionary solidarity with the colored in other parts of the world. This has been brought sharply to attention by the fact, for example, of Negro protest against fighting against "other colored people" in Vietnam, and fighting them for the interests of the white United States. Thus the Vietnam War, ostensibly being fought for "freedom" and "against communist oppression" is seen to be fraught with its own very unpleasant ambiguities. And this in turn brings into focus all the doubts which radicals, white and Negro alike, are raising about the sincerity of our claim to be the most democratic society on earth.

The civil rights struggle has therefore, in largely abandoning its reliance on nonviolence, made a very significant shift in its position. It has changed its basic assumptions. It no longer takes for granted that American society is just, freedom loving, and democratic and that the ways to satisfy the just claims of the

Negro are built into our system. On the contrary, it takes for granted that our society is basically racist, that it is inclined toward fascism and violence, and that the rights of Negroes cannot be guaranteed without real political power.

When a nation is torn by contradictions, the problem can be apparently "simplified" and "clarified" if unpleasant choices are excluded and if one falls back on primitive positions—on crude and satisfying myths—for instance the myth that "it was all started by the commies." If the whites insist on attributing to Communism the responsibility for every protest which releases the frustrated energies of the Negro, the Negroes in the end will begin to respect and trust Communism. Up to the present they have been supremely indifferent towards it. Their new international consciousness will dispose them more and more to look with respect toward Red China which claims to lead the colored people of the world in revolution.

In one of the big riots of 1964, the one in Harlem in mid-July, when the streets were filled with people in confusion, running from the police; when bricks and bottles were pelting down from the rooftops and the police were firing into the air (not without killing one man and wounding many others), the police captain tried to disperse the rioters by shouting through a megaphone: "Go home! Go home!"

A voice from the crowd answered: "We are home, baby!"

The irony of this statement, and its humor, sums up the American problem. There is no "where" for the Negro to go. He is where he is. White America has put him where he is. The tendency has been to act as if he were not there, or as if he might possibly go somewhere else, and to beat him over the head if he makes his collective presence too manifest. The American Negro himself has tried to return to Africa, but the plan was farcical. The Black Nationalists are even now agitating for a part of the country to be turned over to the Negroes—so they can live by themselves. One of the purposes of the violence which those Negro racists actively foment is to make white society willing and happy to get rid of them. The fact remains that the Negro is now in the home the white man has given him: the three square miles of broken-down tenements which form the ghetto of Harlem, the biggest Negro city in the world, type of all the Negro ghettoes in America, full of crime, misery, squalor, dope addiction, prostitution, gang warfare, hatred, and despair. And yet, though Harlem is a problem, it will not become less of a problem if we consider only the negative side. For those who think only of the prostitutes and criminals, Harlem becomes part of the general obsessive national myth of the "bad Negro." The majority of the people in Harlem are good, peaceable, gentle, long-suffering men and women, socially insecure but more sinned against than sinning.

What is to be wondered at is not the occasional mass demonstrations and rioting, not the juvenile delinquency, and not the more and more deliberate excursions of small violent groups into other areas of the city to beat up white people and rob them. What is to be wondered at is the persistence of courage, irony, humor, patience, and hope in Harlem!

In a spiritual crisis of the individual, the truth and authenticity of the person's spiritual identity are called into question. He is placed in confrontation with reality and judged by his ability to bring himself into a valid and living relationship with the demands of his new situation. In the spiritual, social, historic crises of civilizations—and of religious institutions—the same principle applies. Growth, survival, and even salvation may depend on the ability to sacrifice what is fictitious and unauthentic in the construction of one's moral, religious, or national identity. One must then enter upon a different creative task of reconstruction and renewal. This task can be carried out only in the climate of faith, of hope, and of love; these three must be present in some form, even if they amount only to a natural belief in the validity and significance of human choice, a decision to invest human life with some shadow of meaning, a willingness to treat other men as other selves.

Gandhi long ago pointed out that Western democracy was on trial. There is no need for me here to show in how many ways the American concepts of democracy and Christianity are here being weighed in the balance.

THE PROBLEM OF AMERICAN Christianity is the same as the problem of Christianity everywhere else: Christianity is suffering a crisis of identity and authenticity, and is being judged by the ability of Christians themselves to abandon unauthentic, anachronistic images and securities, in order to find a new place in the world by a new evaluation of the world and a new commitment in it.

In the American crisis the Christian faces a typical choice. The choice is not interior and secret, but public, political, and social. He is perhaps not used to regarding his crucial choices in the light of politics. He can now either find security and order by falling back on antique and basically feudal (or perhaps fascist) conceptions, or go forward into the unknown future, identifying himself with the forces that will inevitably create a new society. The choice is between "safety," based on negation of the new and the reaffirmation of the familiar, or the creative risk of love and grace in new and untried solutions, which justice nevertheless demands.

Those who are anxious to discover whether Christianity has had any positive effect on the civil rights struggle seldom ask an equally important question: has the struggle had an effect on Christianity? It has certainly had an effect on the Catholic Church. The case of Father William Du Bay, a young assistant in a Los Angeles Negro parish, is a direct outcome of the racial crisis. His protest was an admitted attempt not only to defend the rights of his Negro parishioners, but also to assert his own right to break through the absolutely ironbound restrictions of clerical submission to canonical authority, not as an act of willful disobedience but as a protest that the priest owes a higher obedience—to the demands of charity and justice—which cannot be shrugged off by simply leaving all responsibility to rest upon superiors. Whatever may have been the rights and wrongs of the case, which was a rude shock to Catholic authority, Father Du Bay was clearly trying to say that he did not believe that the inaction of his bishop entitled him to be passive himself, and that there is such a thing as public opinion in the Church. Not all Catholics have agreed, but all have taken note of this assertion!

The mystique of American Christian rightism, a mystique of violence, of apocalyptic threats, of hatred, and of judgment is perhaps only a more exaggerated and more irrational manifestation of a rather universal attitude common to Christians in many countries. The conviction that the great evil in the world today can be identified with Communism, and that to be a Christian is simply to be an anti-Communist. Communism is the antichrist. Communism is the source of all other problems, all conflicts. All the evils in the world can be traced to the machinations of Communists. The apocalyptic fear of Communism which plays so great a part in the Christianity of some Americans—and some Europeans—resolves itself into a fear of revolution and indeed a fear of any form of social change that would disturb the status quo.

This mentality which we have summarized as "Christian violence" becomes more and more irrational in proportion as it implies both an absolute conviction of one's own rightness and a capacity to approve the use of any means, however violent, however extreme, in order to defend what one feels, subjectively, to be right. This is an axiom. This totalism admits no distinctions, no shades of meaning. "Our side" is totally right, everyone else is diabolically wicked.

Naturally, this synthetic and sweeping "rightness" is compounded of many unconscious doubts and repressed fears. Nor are all the fears repressed. But they take a more or less symbolic form. There is no question that the white racists of the South willingly admit a certain fear of the Negro. The fear is part of their mystique and indeed accounts for a great deal of its emotional power. It is the quasi-mystical obsession with the black demon waiting in the bushes to rape the virginal white daughters of the old South.

The literal truth outdoes all caricature, and it gives us a clue to the mentality and mystique of the "Christian violence" which is coming into being here and there all over the United States, not only among fanatical sects and not only in the South. The intensity of emotion, the sacred and obsessional fear, rising from subliminal levels and reaching consciousness in a panic conviction of spiritual danger, judges all that seems menacing and calls it diabolical. But everything seems menacing and therefore the most innocent of oppositions, the slightest dissenting opinions, calls for the most extreme, the most violent, and the most ruthless repressions. At the present time, the Southern pseudo-mystique of sexual and racist obsessions (and of course there have been rapes, and seductions, of whites by Negroes, as well as infinitely more rapes and seductions of Negroes by whites) now joins with the deeper and more universal fear of revolution. This combination results in a peculiarly potent climate of aggressive intolerance, suspiciousness, hatred, and fear. When we consider that this self-righteous, pseudo-religious faith has its finger terribly close to the button that launches intercontinental ballistic missiles, it gives us food for thought.

The American Negro is well aware of all these obsessions in his regard. He realizes better than the benevolent white liberal to what extent these subliminal fears exist in all white Americans. The tensions created by this dangerous situation are going to increase as the Negro, consciously or otherwise, renounces his hopeful and friendly expectations and begins to test his capacity to shake the foundations of white society by threats of violence.

Well then: what of the *kairos*? Shall we say that it has passed and left the Christian Churches only half awake? It depends upon the sense the Christian gives to his *kairos*. It is certainly possible for us to recognize that we have missed a chance for significant social action. We can edify the world with those subtle and contrite self-examinations which we often substitute for purposeful activity. Or we can do worse, and involve ourselves in the righteous and apocalyptic fury of those whose "Christianity" has emptied itself of serious meaning in order to become a fanatical negation, a refusal of reality, and a ritual hunting of Communist witches.

For those whose Christianity is still a religion of truth and love, not of hate and fear, I think the first thing to do is to admit that our *kairos* is perhaps not always likely to be what we expect. Are we, for example, justified in assuming so complacently that *kairos*, in race crisis, means an opportunity for us as Christians to step in and settle everything with a few wise answers and the adoption of the right attitudes? Are we not called upon to re-evaluate our own notions and see that "right attitudes" are not enough and that it is not sufficient merely to have goodwill, or even to go to jail gloriously for an honest cause? We need a little more depth and a keener sense of the tragedy (or perhaps the comedy) of our situation: we are living in a world which is in many ways "post-Christian" and acting as if we were still running things, still in a position to solve all the world's problems and tell everybody what to do next. It might help if we realized that in fact most people have lost interest in our official pronouncements, and while the fanatical type of Christian still thrives on the belief that he is hated, the rest of us are beginning to realize that the wicked world can no longer take the trouble to do even that. It is simply not interested.

This, as a matter of fact, is no disaster. It is really a liberation. We no longer have to take ourselves so abominably seriously as "Christians" with a public and capital "C." We can give a little more thought to the reality of our vocation and bother less with the image which we show to the world.

If there is a *kairos*, and perhaps there still is, it is not a "time" in which once again we will convince the world that we are right, but perhaps rather a time in which the crisis of man will teach us to see a few sobering truths about our own Christian calling and our place in the world—a place no longer exalted and mighty, or perhaps even influential.

In fact we are learning that we are as other men are, that we are not a special kind of privileged being, that our faith does not exempt us from facing the mysterious realities of the world with the same limitations as everybody else, and with the same capacity for human failure. Our Christian calling does not make us superior to other men, does not entitle us to judge everyone and decide everything for everybody. We do not have answers to every social problem, and all conflicts have not been decided beforehand in favor of our side. Our job is to struggle along with everybody else and collaborate with them in the difficult, frustrating task of seeking a solution to common problems, which are entirely new and strange to us all.

The American racial crisis which grows more serious every day offers the American Christian a chance to face reality about himself and recover his fidelity to Christian truth, not merely in institutional loyalties and doctrinal orthodoxies (in which no one has taken the trouble to accuse him of failing) but in recanting a more basic heresy: the loss of that Christian sense which sees every other man as Christ and treats him as Christ. For, as St. John said: "We know what love is by this: that he laid down his life for us so that we ought to lay down our lives for the brotherhood. But whoever possesses this world's goods and notices his brother in need and shuts his heart against him, how can the love of God remain in him? Dear children, let us put our love not into words or into talk but into deeds, and make it real" (1 John 3:16-18).

We do indeed have a message for the world, and the Word of God is still as alive and penetrating today "as any two-edged sword." But we have perhaps taken the edge off the sword by our short-sightedness and our complacency.

The Christian failure in American racial justice has been all too real, but it is not the fault of the few dedicated and nonviolent followers of Christ. It is due much more to the fact that so few Christians have been able to face the fact that nonviolence comes very close to the heart of the Gospel ethic, and is perhaps essential to it.

But nonviolence is not simply a matter of marching with signs and placards under the eyes of unfriendly policemen. The partial failure of liberal nonviolence has brought out the stark reality that our society itself is radically violent and that violence is built into its very structure. We live in a society which, while appealing to Christian ethical ideals, violently negates its Christian pretensions and in so doing drives a radical minority to desperation and violence. The white Christian cannot in such a situation be content merely to march with his black brother at the risk of getting his head broken or of being shot. The problem is to eradicate this basic violence and unjustice from white society. Can it be done? How?

16

Rain and the Rhinoceros

Merton first refers to this, one of his best-known essays, in a December 19, 1964, letter to Mark Van Doren, as "an article I was asked for, and wrote in the hermitage. As one can easily tell" (*Road to Joy*, 49). On the following day he notes in his journal, "Finished article for *Holiday*," the popular magazine that had requested it, "and sent it yesterday" (*Dancing in the Water of Life*, 180-81); a revised version was mailed off on January 30, 1965 (*Dancing in the Water of Life*, 197), and on March 4 he notes that the magazine paid a thousand dollars for the article, temporarily retitled "The Art of Solitude" (*Dancing in the Water of Life*, 214). It was published with its original title in *Holiday* 37 (May 1965) 8, 10, 12, 15-16 (accompanied by a bizarrely whimsical cartoon of a clothed rhinoceros inserting a coin into a rain machine, a sort of combination of parking meter and shower head!), and then as the opening piece in *Raids on the Unspeakable* (9-23). In this meditation, written from his hermitage during the period when he was not yet living there permanently but had received permission to stay overnight, Merton presents the rain as an image of natural renewal and a countersymbol to the world of quantity and consumption that has intruded even into the hermitage itself in the slogan of the Coleman lantern he had bought the month before (see *Dancing in the Water of Life*, 162): "*Stretches days to give more hours of fun.*" The insights of the sixth-century Syrian hermit Philoxenos, who writes of solitude as essential for the discovery of a true self not defined by social myths and prejudices, are compared to those of the absurdist playwright Ionesco in *Rhinoceros*, in which the difficulty of maintaining one's own identity in the face of totalitarian demands for conformity and obedience is dramatized. (The material on Philoxenos is drawn from his reading in preparation for conferences on the hermit given to his novices from March through August 1965, when he began living in the hermitage full-time: see *Pre-Benedictine Monasticism*, xliii-li for the background). The conclusion applies the theme to the contemporary political situation, as seen and heard from the hermitage: "Even here the earth shakes. Over at Fort Knox the Rhinoceros is having fun."

L ET ME SAY THIS before rain becomes a utility that they can plan and distribute for money. By "they" I mean the people who cannot understand that rain is a festival, who do not appreciate its gratuity, who think that

216

what has no price has no value, that what cannot be sold is not real, so that the only way to make something *actual* is to place it on the market. The time will come when they will sell you even your rain. At the moment it is still free, and I am in it. I celebrate its gratuity and its meaninglessness.

The rain I am in is not like the rain of cities. It fills the woods with an immense and confused sound. It covers the flat roof of the cabin and its porch with insistent and controlled rhythms. And I listen, because it reminds me again and again that the whole world runs by rhythms I have not yet learned to recognize, rhythms that are not those of the engineer.

I came up here from the monastery last night, sloshing through the cornfield, said Vespers, and put some oatmeal on the Coleman stove for supper. It boiled over while I was listening to the rain and toasting a piece of bread at the log fire. The night became very dark. The rain surrounded the whole cabin with its enormous virginal myth, a whole world of meaning, of secrecy, of silence, of rumor. Think of it: all that speech pouring down, selling nothing, judging nobody, drenching the thick mulch of dead leaves, soaking the trees, filling the gullies and crannies of the wood with water, washing out the places where men have stripped the hillside! What a thing it is to sit absolutely alone, in the forest, at night, cherished by this wonderful, unintelligible, perfectly innocent speech, the most comforting speech in the world, the talk that rain makes by itself all over the ridges, and the talk of the watercourses everywhere in the hollows!

Nobody started it, nobody is going to stop it. It will talk as long as it wants, this rain. As long as it talks I am going to listen.

But I am also going to sleep, because here in this wilderness I have learned how to sleep again. Here I am not alien. The trees I know, the night I know, the rain I know. I close my eyes and instantly sink into the whole rainy world of which I am a part, and the world goes on with me in it, for I am not alien to it. I am alien to the noises of cities, of people, to the greed of machinery that does not sleep, the hum of power that eats up the night. Where rain, sunlight, and darkness are contemned, I cannot sleep. I do not trust anything that has been fabricated to replace the climate of woods or prairies. I can have no confidence in places where the air is first fouled and then cleansed, where the water is first made deadly and then made safe with other poisons. There is nothing in the world of buildings that is not fabricated, and if a tree gets in among the apartment houses by mistake it is taught to grow chemically. It is given a precise reason for existing. They put a sign on it saying it is for health, beauty, perspective; that it is for peace, for prosperity; that it was planted by the mayor's daughter. All of this is mystification. The city itself lives on its own myth. Instead of waking up and silently existing, the city people prefer a stubborn and fabricated dream; they do not care to be a part of the night, or to be merely of the world. They have constructed a world outside the world, against the world, a world of mechanical fictions which contemn nature and seek only to use it up, thus preventing it from renewing itself and man.

OF COURSE THE FESTIVAL of rain cannot be stopped, even in the city. The woman from the delicatessen scampers along the sidewalk with a newspaper over her head. The streets, suddenly washed, became transparent and alive, and the noise of traffic becomes a plashing of fountains. One would think that urban man in a rainstorm would *have* to take account of nature in its wetness and freshness, its baptism and its renewal. But the rain brings no renewal to the city, only to tomorrow's weather, and the glint of windows in tall buildings will then have nothing to do with the new sky. All "reality" will remain somewhere inside those walls, counting itself and selling itself with fantastically complex determination. Meanwhile the obsessed citizens plunge through the rain bearing the load of their obsessions, slightly more vulnerable than before, but still only barely aware of external realities. They do not see that the streets shine beautifully, that they themselves are walking on stars and water, that they are running in skies to catch a bus or a taxi, to shelter somewhere in the press of irritated humans, the faces of advertisements and the dim, cretinous sound of unidentified music. But they must know that there is wetness abroad. Perhaps they even *feel* it. I cannot say. Their complaints are mechanical and without spirit.

Naturally no one can believe the things they say about the rain. It all implies one basic lie: *only the city is real.* That weather, not being planned, not being fabricated, is an impertinence, a wen on the visage of progress. (Just a simple little operation, and the whole mess may become relatively tolerable. Let business *make* the rain. This will give it meaning.)

THOREAU SAT IN *HIS* cabin and criticized the railways. I sit in mine and wonder about a world that has, well, progressed. I must read *Walden* again, and see if Thoreau already guessed that he was part of what he thought he could escape. But it is not a matter of "escaping." It is not even a matter of protesting very audibly. Technology is here, even in the cabin. True, the utility line is not here yet, and so G.E. is not here yet either. When the utilities and G.E. enter my cabin arm in arm it will be nobody's fault but my own. I admit it. I am not kidding anybody, even myself. I will suffer their bluff and patronizing complacencies in silence. I will let them think they know what I am doing here.

They are convinced that *I am having fun.*

This has already been brought home to me with a wallop by my Coleman lantern. Beautiful lamp: It burns white gas and sings viciously but gives out a splendid green light in which I read Philoxenos, a sixth-century Syrian hermit. Philoxenos fits in with the rain and the festival of night. Of this, more later. Meanwhile: what does my Coleman lantern tell me? (Coleman's philosophy is printed on the cardboard box which I have (guiltily) not shellacked as I was supposed to, and which I have tossed in the woodshed behind the hickory chunks.) Coleman says that the light is good, and has a reason: it *"Stretches days to give more hours of fun."*

Can't I just be in the woods without any special reason? Just being in the woods, at night, in the cabin, is something too excellent to be justified or explained! It just *is*. There are always a few people who are in the woods at night, in the rain (because if there were not the world would have ended), and I am one of them. We are not having fun, we are not "having" anything, we are not *"stretching our days,"* and if we had fun it would not be measured by hours. Though as a matter of fact that is what fun seems to be: a state of diffuse excitation that can be measured by the clock and "stretched" by an appliance.

There is no clock that can measure the speech of this rain that falls all night on the drowned and lonely forest.

Of course at three-thirty A.M. the SAC plane goes over, red light winking low under the clouds, skimming the wooded summits on the south side of the valley, loaded with strong medicine. Very strong. Strong enough to burn up all these woods and stretch our hours of fun into eternities.

AND THAT BRINGS ME to Philoxenos, a Syrian who had fun in the sixth century, without benefit of appliances, still less of nuclear deterrents.

Philoxenos in his ninth *memra* (on poverty) to dwellers in solitude, says that there is no explanation and no justification for the solitary life, since it is without a law. To be a contemplative is therefore to be an outlaw. As was Christ. As was Paul.

One who is not "alone," says Philoxenos, has not discovered his identity. He seems to be alone, perhaps, for he experiences himself as "individual." But because he is willingly enclosed and limited by the laws and illusions of collective existence, he has no more identity than an unborn child in the womb. He is not yet conscious. He is alien to his own truth. He has senses, but he cannot use them. He has life, but no identity. To have an identity, he has to be awake, and aware. But to be awake, he has to accept vulnerability and death. Not for their own sake: not out of stoicism or despair—only for the sake of the invulnerable inner reality which we cannot recognize (which we can only *be*) but to which we awaken only when we see the unreality of our vulnerable shell. The discovery of this inner self is an act and affirmation of solitude.

Now if we take our vulnerable shell to be our true identity, if we think our mask is our true face, we will protect it with fabrications even at the cost of violating our own truth. This seems to be the collective endeavor of society: the more busily men dedicate themselves to it, the more certainly it becomes a collective illusion, until in the end we have the enormous, obsessive, uncontrollable dynamic of fabrications designed to protect mere fictitious identities—"selves," that is to say, regarded as objects. Selves that can stand back and see themselves having fun (an illusion which reassures them that they are real).

SUCH IS THE IGNORANCE which is taken to be the axiomatic foundation of all knowledge in the human collectivity: in order to experience yourself as real, you have to suppress the awareness of your contingency, your unreality, your state of radical need. This you do by creating an awareness of yourself as *one who has no needs that he cannot immediately fulfill.* Basically, this is an illusion of omnipotence: an illusion which the collectivity arrogates to itself, and consents to share with its individual members in proportion as they submit to its more central and more rigid fabrications.

You have needs; but if you behave and conform you can participate in the collective power. You can then satisfy all your needs. Meanwhile, in order to increase its power over you, the collectivity increases your needs. It also tightens its demand for conformity. Thus you can become all the more committed to the collective illusion in proportion to becoming more hopelessly mortgaged to collective power.

How does this work? The collectivity informs and shapes your will to happiness ("have fun") by presenting you with irresistible images of yourself as you would like to be: having *fun that is so perfectly credible that it allows no interference of conscious doubt.* In theory such a good time can be so convincing that you are no longer aware of even a remote possibility that it might change into something less satisfying. In practice, expensive fun always admits of a doubt, which blossoms out into another full-blown need, which then calls for a still more credible and more costly refinement of satisfaction, which again fails you. The end of the cycle is despair.

Because we live in a womb of collective illusion, our freedom remains abortive. Our capacities for joy, peace, and truth are never liberated. They can never be used. We are prisoners of a process, a dialectic of false promises and real deceptions ending in futility.

"The unborn child," says Philoxenos, "is already perfect and fully constituted in his nature, with all his senses, and limbs, but he cannot make use of them in their natural functions, because, in the womb, he cannot strengthen or develop them for such use."

Now, since all things have their season, there is a time to be unborn. We must begin, indeed, in the social womb. There is a time for warmth in the collective myth. But there is also a time to be born. He who is spiritually "born" as a mature identity is liberated from the enclosing womb of myth and prejudice. He learns to think for himself, guided no longer by the dictates of need and by the systems and processes designed to create artificial needs and then "satisfy" them.

This emancipation can take two forms: first that of the active life, which liberates itself from enslavement to necessity by considering and serving the needs of others, without thought of personal interest or return. And second, the contemplative life, which must not be construed as an escape from time and matter, from social responsibility and from the life of sense, but rather, as an advance into solitude and the desert, a confrontation with poverty and the void, a renunciation of the empirical self, in the presence of death, and nothingness, in order to overcome the ignorance and error that spring from the fear of "being nothing." The man who dares to be alone can come to see that the "emptiness" and "uselessness" which the collective mind fears and condemns are necessary conditions for the encounter with truth.

It is in the desert of loneliness and emptiness that the fear of death and the need for self-affirmation are seen to be illusory. When this is faced, then anguish is not necessarily overcome, but it can be accepted and understood. Thus, in the heart of anguish are found the gifts of peace and understanding: not simply in personal illumination and liberation, but by commitment and empathy, for the contemplative must assume the universal anguish and the inescapable condition of mortal man. The solitary, far from enclosing himself in himself, becomes every man. He dwells in the solitude, the poverty, the indigence of every man.

It is in this sense that the hermit, according to Philoxenos, imitates Christ. For in Christ, God takes to Himself the solitude and dereliction of man: every man. From the moment Christ went out into the desert to be tempted, the loneliness, the temptation, and the hunger of every man became the loneliness, temptation, and hunger of Christ. But in return, the gift of truth with which Christ dispelled the three kinds of illusion offered him in his temptation (security, reputation, and power) can become also our own truth, if we can only accept it. It is offered to us also in temptation. "You too go out into the desert," said Philoxenos, "having with you nothing of the world, and the Holy Spirit will go with you. See the freedom with which Jesus has gone forth, and go forth like

Him—see where he has left the rule of men; leave the rule of the world where he has left the law, and go out with him to fight the power of error."

And where is the power of error? We find it was after all not in the city, but in *ourselves*.

TODAY THE INSIGHTS OF a Philoxenos are to be sought less in the tracts of theologians than in the meditations of the existentialists and in the Theater of the Absurd. The problem of Berenger, in Ionesco's *Rhinoceros*, is the problem of the human person stranded and alone in what threatens to become a society of monsters. In the sixth century Berenger might perhaps have walked off into the desert of Scete, without too much concern over the fact that all his fellow citizens, all his friends, and even his girl Daisy, had turned into rhinoceroses.

The problem today is that there are no deserts, only dude ranches.

The desert islands are places where the wicked little characters in the *Lord of the Flies* come face to face with the Lord of the Flies, form a small, tight, ferocious collectivity of painted faces, and arm themselves with spears to hunt down the last member of their group who still remembers with nostalgia the possibilities of rational discourse.

When Berenger finds himself suddenly the last human in a rhinoceros herd he looks into the mirror and says, humbly enough, "After all, man is not as bad as all that, is he?" But his world now shakes mightily with the stampede of his metamorphosed fellow citizens, and he soon becomes aware that the very stampede itself is the most telling and tragic of all arguments. For when he considers going out into the street "to try to convince them," he realizes that he "would have to learn their language." He looks in the mirror and sees that *he no longer resembles anyone*. He searches madly for a photograph of people as they were before the big change. But now humanity itself has become incredible, as well as hideous. To be the last man in the rhinoceros herd is, in fact, to be a monster.

Such is the problem which Ionesco sets us in his tragic irony; solitude and dissent become more and more impossible, more and more absurd. That Berenger finally accepts his absurdity and rushes out to challenge the whole herd only points up the futility of a commitment to rebellion. At the same time in *The New Tenant* (*Le Nouveau Locataire*) Ionesco portrays the absurdity of a logically consistent individualism which, in fact, is a self-isolation by the pseudo-logic of proliferating needs and possessions.

Ionesco protested that the New York production of *Rhinoceros* as a farce was a complete misunderstanding of his intention. It is a play not merely against *conformism* but about *totalitarianism*. The rhinoceros is not an amiable beast, and with him around the fun ceases and things begin to get serious. Everything has to make sense and be totally useful to the totally obsessive operation. At the same time Ionesco was criticized for not giving the audience "something positive" to take away with them, instead of just "refusing the human adventure." (Presumably "rhinoceritis" is the latest in human adventure!) He replied: "They [the spectators] leave in a void—and that was my intention. It is the business of a free man to pull himself out of this void by his own power and not by the power of other people!" In this Ionesco comes very close to Zen and to Christian eremitism.

"IN ALL THE CITIES of the world, it is the same," says Ionesco. "The universal and modern man is the man in a rush (i.e., a rhinoceros), a man who has no time, who is a prisoner of necessity, who cannot understand that *a thing might perhaps be without usefulness*; nor does he understand that, at bottom, it is the useful that may be a useless and back-breaking burden. If one does not understand the usefulness of the useless and the uselessness of the useful, one cannot understand art. And a country where art is not understood is a country of slaves and robots . . ." (*Notes et Contre Notes*, p. 129). Rhinoceritis, he adds, is the sickness that lies in wait "for those who *have lost the sense and the taste for solitude*."

The love of solitude is sometimes condemned as "hatred of our fellow men." But is this true? If we push our analysis of collective thinking a little further we will find that the dialectic of power and need, of submission and satisfaction, ends by being a dialectic of hate. Collectivity needs not only to absorb everyone it can, but also implicitly to hate and destroy whoever cannot be absorbed. Paradoxically, one of the needs of collectivity is to reject certain classes, or races, or groups, in order to strengthen its own self-awareness by hating them instead of absorbing them.

Thus the solitary cannot survive unless he is capable of loving everyone, without concern for the fact that he is likely to be regarded by all of them as a traitor. Only the man who has fully attained his own spiritual identity can live without the need to kill, and without the need of a doctrine that permits him to do so with a good conscience. There will always be a place, says Ionesco, "*for those isolated consciences who have stood up for the universal conscience*" as against the mass mind. But their place is solitude. They have no other. Hence it is the solitary person (whether in the city or in the desert) who does mankind the inestimable favor of reminding it of its true capacity for maturity, liberty, and peace.

It sounds very much like Philoxenos to me.

And it sounds like what the rain says. We still carry this burden of illusion because we do not dare to lay it down. We suffer all the needs that society demands we suffer, because if we do not have these needs we lose our "usefulness" in society—the usefulness of suckers. We fear to be alone, and to be ourselves, and so to remind others of the truth that is in them.

"I will not make you such rich men as have need of many things," said Philoxenos (putting the words on the lips of Christ), "but I will make you true rich men who have need of nothing. Since it is not he who has many possessions that is rich, but he who has no needs." Obviously, we shall always have *some* needs. But only he who has the simplest and most natural needs can be considered to be without needs, since the only needs he has are real ones, and the real ones are not hard to fulfill if one is a free man!

THE RAIN HAS STOPPED. The afternoon sun slants through the pine trees: and how those useless needles smell in the clear air!

A dandelion, long out of season, has pushed itself into bloom between the smashed leaves of last summer's day lilies. The valley resounds with the totally uninformative talk of creeks and wild water.

Then the quails begin their sweet whistling in the wet bushes. Their noise is absolutely useless, and so is the delight I take in it. There is nothing I would rather hear, not because it is a better noise than other noises, but because it is the voice of the present moment, the present festival.

Yet even here the earth shakes. Over at Fort Knox the Rhinoceros is having fun.

17

The Contemplative Life in the Modern World

The original version of this essay was written in March 1965 as the preface for a Japanese translation of *Seeds of Contemplation* (published in *"Honorable Reader"*, 83-92, with a helpful headnote by editor Robert Daggy). Merton subsequently reworked and expanded the piece and published it as "The Contemplative Life in the Modern World" in the Indian journal *Mountain Path* 2 (October 1965), 223-27; this version, with slight alterations and the addition of two paragraphs on the pseudo-mysticism of hallucinogenic drugs (the third and fourth in the present text), was included in *Faith and Violence* (215-24). It is perhaps Merton's most incisive articulation of his belief in the crucial necessity to preserve and foster the way of wisdom in an era of technological hubris and a reductively positivist scientism. Without contemplative awareness, human life "has lost the spiritual orientation upon which everything else—order, peace, happiness, sanity—must depend." A wisdom "that seeks truth for its own sake, that seeks the fullness of being, that seeks to rest in an intuition of the very ground of all being" has been throughout human history, Merton maintains, the integrating factor essential for personal and communal wholeness, uniting action and contemplation, commitment and detachment, in a synthesis that transcends superficial oppositions and dualities. To reclaim this perspective is not an evasion of the challenges and opportunities of contemporary culture but an engagement that brings resources which the culture itself too often does not recognize or understand, and for which it too often substitutes the ersatz unity of a coercive or seductive conformity that inevitably degenerates into hatreds, conflicts, and irrationality. For the Christian, Merton explains to his primary audience of non-Christian Asians, this path of contemplative wisdom is simply "a way of emptiness and transcendence in union with the crucified Christ," the process of dying to the illusory self so as to be reborn with and in and as Christ, able to declare, as St. Paul did to the Galatians, in a passage to which Merton returns repeatedly throughout his writing, "I live, now not I, but Christ lives in me."

CAN CONTEMPLATION STILL FIND a place in the world of technology and conflict which is ours? Does it belong only to the past? The answer to this is that, since the direct and pure experience of reality in its ultimate root is man's deepest need, contemplation must be possible if man is to remain human. If contemplation is no longer possible, then man's life has lost the spiritual orientation upon which everything else—order, peace, happiness, sanity—must depend. But true contemplation is an austere and exacting vocation. Those who seek it are few and those who find it fewer still. Nevertheless, their presence witnesses to the fact that contemplation remains both necessary and possible.

Man has an instinctive need for harmony and peace, for tranquility, order, and meaning. None of these seem to be the most salient characteristics of modern society. Life in a monastery, where the traditions and rites of a more contemplative age are still alive and still practiced, cannot help but remind men that there once existed a more leisurely and more spiritual way of life—and that this was the way of their ancestors. Thus even into the confused activism of Western life is woven a certain memory of contemplation. It is a memory so vague and so remote that it is hardly understood, and yet it can awaken the hope of recovering inner vision. In this hope, modern man can perhaps entertain, for a brief time, the dream of a contemplative life and of a higher spiritual state of quiet, of rest, of untroubled joy. But a sense of self-deception and guilt immediately awakens in Western man a reaction of despair, disgust, rejection of the dream, and commitment to total activism. We must face the fact that the mere thought of contemplation is one which deeply troubles the modern person who takes it seriously. It is so contrary to the modern way of life, so apparently alien, so seemingly impossible, that the modern man who even considers it finds, at first, that his whole being rebels against it. If the ideal of inner peace remains attractive the demands of the way to peace seem to be so exacting and so extreme that they can no longer be met. We would like to be quiet, but our restlessness will not allow it. Hence we believe that for us there can be no peace except in a life filled up with movement and activity, with speech, news, communication, recreation, distraction. We seek the meaning of our life in activity for its own sake, activity without objective, efficacy without fruit, scientism, the cult of unlimited power, the service of the machine as an end in itself. And in all these a certain dynamism is imagined. The life of frantic activity is invested with the noblest of qualities, as if it were the whole end and happiness of man: or rather as if the life of man had no inherent meaning whatever and had to be given a meaning from some external source, from a society engaged in a gigantic communal effort to raise man above himself. Man is indeed called to transcend himself. But do his own efforts suffice for this?

At this point it would be tempting to analyze the complex new situation that has arisen due to the popularity of hallucinogenic drugs. It is not possible for me to attempt such an analysis. Yet the fact that these drugs exist and are so widely used does require at least a passing mention. The most obvious thing about them is that they are short cuts to "inner vision." They promise contemplative experience without any need to practice the disciplines of the contemplative life. In other words they offer just the sort of thing modern man most wants, the opportunity to eat his cake and have it, to have the best of both worlds, to become a "mystic" without making any sacrifices. Unfortunately, this situation is not one that can be casually blamed on beatniks and irresponsible juveniles. It seems to me that it is only another aspect of that affluence to which official religion has contributed its own measure of confusion and bad faith. It has after all been the claim of official religion—more or less in all the Churches—that religion would act as a happiness pill, would help people to solve their problems, would make life easier and more jolly, and so on. If religion is enthusiastically advertised as a happiness pill, and then a real happiness pill comes along, then I see no justification for religious people complaining that the public likes the competitor's product better. After all, it is cheaper and more effective.

What needs to be made clear, however, is that contemplation is not a deepening of experience only, but a radical change in one's way of being and living, and the essence of this change is precisely a liberation from *dependence on external means to external ends*. Of course one may say that an opening of the "doors of perception" is not entirely "external," and yet it is a satisfaction for which one may develop a habitual need and on which one may become dependent. True contemplation delivers one from all such forms of dependence. In that sense it seems to me that a contemplative life that depends on the use of drugs is essentially different from one which implies complete liberation from all dependence on anything but freedom and divine grace. I realize that these few remarks do not answer the real question but they express a doubt in my own mind.

In any event I believe the reason for the inner confusion of Western man is that our technological society has no longer any place in it for wisdom that seeks truth for its own sake, that seeks the fullness of being, that seeks to rest in an intuition of the very ground of all being. Without wisdom, the apparent opposition of action and contemplation, of work and rest, of involvement and detachment, can never be resolved. Ancient and traditional societies, whether of Asia or of the West, always specifically recognized "the way" of the wise, the way of spiritual discipline in which there was at once wisdom and method, and by which, whether in art, in philosophy, in religion, or in the monastic life, some men would attain to the inner meaning of being; they would experience this meaning for all their brothers; they would so to speak bring together in themselves the divisions or complications that confused the life of their fellows. By healing the divisions in themselves they would help heal the divisions of the whole world. They would realize in themselves that unity which is at the same time the highest action and the purest rest, true knowledge and selfless love, a knowledge beyond knowledge in emptiness and unknowing; a willing beyond will in apparent non-activity. They would attain to the highest striving in the absence of striving and of contention.

This way of wisdom is no dream, no temptation, and no evasion, for it is on the contrary a return to reality in its very root. It is not an escape from contradiction and confusion for it finds unity and clarity only by plunging into the very midst of contradiction, by the acceptance of emptiness and suffering, by the renunciation of the passions and obsessions with which the whole world is "on fire." It does not withdraw from the fire. It is in the very heart of the fire, yet remains cool, because it has the gentleness and humility that come from self-abandonment, and hence does not seek to assert the illusion of the exterior self.

Once a man has set his foot on this way, there is no excuse for abandoning it, for to be actually on the way is to recognize without doubt or hesitation that only the way is fully real and that everything else is deception, except insofar as it may in some secret and hidden manner be connected with "the way."

Thus, far from wishing to abandon this way, the contemplative seeks only to travel farther and farther along it. This journey without maps leads him into rugged mountainous country where there are often mists and storms and where he is more and more alone. Yet at the same time, ascending the slopes in darkness, feeling more and more keenly his own emptiness, and with the winter wind blowing cruelly through his now tattered garments, he meets at times other travelers on the way, poor pilgrims as he is, and as solitary as he, belonging perhaps to other lands and other traditions. There are of course great differences between them, and yet they have much in common. Indeed, the Western contemplative can say that he feels himself much closer to the Zen monks of ancient Japan than to the busy and impatient men of the West, of his own country, who think in terms of money, power, publicity, machines, business, political advantage, military strategy—who seek, in a word, the triumphant affirmation of their own will, their own power, considered as the end for which they exist. Is not this perhaps the most foolish of all dreams, the most tenacious and damaging of illusions?

In any event, it is certain that the way of wisdom is not an evasion. Simply to evade modern life would be a futile attempt to abdicate from its responsibilities and a renunciation of advantages—and illusions. The contemplative way requires first of all and above all renunciation of this obsession with the triumph of the individual or collective will to power. For this aggressive and self-assertive drive to possess and to exert power implies a totally different view of reality than that which is seen when one travels the contemplative way. The aggressive and dominative view of reality places at the center the individual self with its bodily form, its feelings and emotions, its appetites and needs, its loves and hates, its actions and reactions. All these are seen as forming together a basic and indubitable reality to which everything else must be referred, so that all other things are also estimated in their individuality, their actions and reactions, and all the ways in which they impinge upon the interests of the individual self. The world is then seen as a multiplicity of conflicting and limited beings, all enclosed in the prisons of their own individuality, all therefore complete in a permanent and vulnerable incompleteness, all seeking to find a certain completeness by asserting themselves at the expense of others, dominating and using others. This world becomes, then, an immense conflict in which the only peace is that which is accorded to the victory of the strong, and in order to taste the joy of this peace, the weak must submit to the strong and join him in his adventures so that they may share in his power. Thus there arises a spurious, inconclusive unity: the unity of the massive aggregate, the unity of those thrown together without love and without understanding by the accidents of the power struggle. Seen from the point of view of "the way" this unity is nothing but a collective monstrosity because it has no real reason for existing and is not a unity at all. However insistently it may claim for itself the dignities of a truly communal and human existence, it does not elevate man by a truly communal and interpersonal cooperation. It only drives him with mad and irresistible demands, exploiting him, alienating him from reality and demanding from him a blind, irrational, and total subjection. The life of the collective mass is such that it destroys in man the inmost need and capacity for contemplation. It dries up the living springs of compassion and understanding. It perverts the creative genius and destroys the innocent vision that is proper to man in communion with nature. Finally the collective mass becomes a vast aggregate of organized hatred, a huge and organized death-wish, threatening its own existence and that of the entire human race.

The mission of the contemplative in this world of massive conflict and collective unreason is to seek the true way of unity and peace, without succumbing to the illusion of withdrawal into a realm of abstraction from which unpleasant realities are simply excluded by the force of will. In facing the world with a totally different viewpoint, he maintains alive in the world the presence of a spiritual and intelligent consciousness which is the root of true peace and true unity among men. This consciousness certainly accepts the fact of our empirical and individual existence, but refuses to take this as the basic reality. The basic reality is neither the individual, empirical self nor an abstract and ideal entity which can exist only in reason. The basic reality is being itself, which is one in all concrete existents, which shares itself among them and manifests itself through them. The goal of the contemplative is, on its lowest level, the recognition of this splendor of being and unity—a splendor in which he is one with all that is. But on a higher level still, it is the transcendent ground and source of being, the not-being and the emptiness that is so called because it is absolutely beyond all definition and limitation. This ground and source is not simply an inert and passive emptiness, but for the Christian it is pure act, pure freedom, pure light. The emptiness which is "pure being" is the light of God which, as St. John's Gospel says, "gives light to every man who comes into the world." Specifically, the Gospel sees all being coming forth from the Father, God, in His Word, who is the light of the world. "In Him (the Word) was life, and this life was Light for all men, and the Light shone in darkness and the darkness could not understand it" (John 1:4-5).

Now very often the ordinary active and ethical preoccupations of Christians make them forget this deeper and more contemplative dimension of the Christian way. So active, in fact, has been the face presented by Christianity to the Asian world that the hidden contemplative element of Christianity is often not even suspected at all by Asians. But without the deep root of wisdom and contemplation, Christian action would have no meaning and no purpose.

The Christian is then not simply a man of goodwill, who commits himself to a certain set of beliefs, who has a definite dogmatic conception of the universe, of man, and of man's reason for existing. He is not simply one who follows a moral code of brotherhood and benevolence with strong emphasis on certain rewards and punishments dealt out to the individual. Underlying Christianity is not simply a set of doctrines about God considered as dwelling remotely in heaven, and man struggling on earth, far from heaven, trying to appease a distant God by means of virtuous acts. On the contrary Christians themselves too often fail to realize that the infinite God is dwelling within them, so that He is in them and they are in Him. They remain unaware of the presence of the infinite source of being right in the midst of the world and of men. True Christian wisdom is therefore oriented to the experience of the divine Light which is present in the world, the Light in whom all things are, and which is nevertheless unknown to the world because no mind can see or grasp its infinity. "He was in the world and the world was made by Him and the world did not know Him. He came into His own and His own did not receive Him" (John 1:10-11).

Contemplative wisdom is then not simply an aesthetic extrapolation of certain intellectual or dogmatic principles, but a living contact with the Infinite Source of all being, a contact not only of minds and hearts, not only of "I and Thou," but a transcendent union of consciousness in which man and God become, according to the expression of St. Paul, "one spirit."

Though this contemplative union is an extreme intensification of conscious awareness, a kind of total awareness, it is not properly contained or signified in any particular vision, but rather in nonvision, which attains the totality of meaning beyond all limited conceptions, by the surrender of love. God Himself is not only pure being but also pure love, and to know Him is to become one with Him in love. In this dimension of Christian experience, the Cross of Christ means more than the juridical redemption of man from the guilt of evil-doing. It means the passage from death to life and from nothingness to fullness, or to fullness in nothingness. Thus the contemplative way of ancient Christian monastic tradition is not simply a way of good works and of loving devotion, fine as these are, but also a way of emptiness and transcendence in union with the crucified Christ. The Cross signified that the sacrificial death which is the end of all lust for earthly power and all indulgence of passion is in fact the liberation of those who have renounced their exterior self in order to dedicate their lives to love and to truth. Christ is not simply an object of love and contemplation whom the Christian considers with devout attention: He is also "the way, the truth, and the life" so that for the Christian to be "on the way" is to be "in Christ" and to seek truth is to walk in the light of Christ. "For me to live," says St. Paul, "is Christ. I live, now not I, but Christ lives in me."

This is a summary outline of the meaning of Christian contemplation, a meaning which calls for much greater development particularly in all that concerns the sacramental and liturgical life of the Church. Such is the way of contemplation.

One need not be a monk to turn this way. It is sufficient to be a child of God, a human person. It is enough that one has in oneself the instinct for truth, the desire of that freedom from limitation and from servitude to external things which St. Paul calls the "servitude of corruption" and which, in fact, holds the whole world of man in bondage by passion, greed, the lust for sensation and for individual survival, as though one could become rich enough, powerful enough, and clever enough to cheat death.

Unfortunately, this passion for unreality and for the impossible fills the world today with violence, hatred, and indeed with a kind of insane and cunning fury which threatens our very existence.

Science and technology are indeed admirable in many respects, and if they fulfill their promises they can do much for man. But they can never solve his deepest problems. On the contrary, without wisdom, without the intuition and freedom that enable man to return to the root of his being, science can only precipitate him still farther into the centrifugal flight that flings him, in all his compact and uncomprehending isolation, into the darkness of outer space without purpose and without objective.

18

Day of a Stranger

This essay on Merton's life in the hermitage, written at the request of a South American editor, is dated May 1965 in its earliest version (*Dancing in the Water of Life*, 237-42), some three months before he took up permanent residence there on August 20. It was first published in a Spanish translation by Merton's friend Ludovico Silva (see *Courage for Truth*, 226) as "Día de un Extraño" in the July-September 1965 issue of the Venezuelan journal *Papeles* (41-45), and appeared in its original English in *Hudson Review* 20 (Summer 1967), 211-18. Merton's correspondence in the latter part of 1968 with New Directions publisher James Laughlin makes clear that they planned to publish the essay, illustrated with Merton's photographs, in tandem with *Woods, Shore, Desert*, the journal of his May 1968 trip to the West Coast, in the fall of 1969 (see Merton/Laughlin, *Selected Letters*, 355, 357, 366, 367), but after Merton's death the project was shelved. It finally appeared in an illustrated edition published by Gibbs M. Smith in 1981, with a lengthy introduction by Robert E. Daggy that is the best guide to its genesis and development (*Woods, Shore, Desert* was published separately the following year). The essay is also included in *A Thomas Merton Reader* (rev. ed., 431-38) and in *Thomas Merton: Spiritual Master* (214-22) (with a helpful headnote by editor Lawrence Cunningham). The essay reveals the essential elements of the life of solitude as Merton had already begun to experience it at the hermitage. It is simply structured, in two main sections. The first part provides an overview of Merton's new way of life, in which his hermit vocation is experienced as a sign of contradiction to the pervasive power of technology, an assertion of an identity that cannot be reduced to a number, and as a participation both in the "ecological balance" of the natural world in which he is immersed and in "a mental ecology, a living balance of spirits in this corner of the woods" that includes the voices of poets and prophets, Eastern and Western sages, men and women artists and visionaries. The second section moves chronologically through the day, beginning with the chanting of psalms "at two-fifteen in the morning, when the night is darkest and most silent," charged with an awareness of the broken, suffering world in which he lives, moving through the coming of the dawn, the performance of the ordinary "rituals" of housekeeping, his descent to the monastery where he still carries out the responsibilities of novice master, and his return to the silence of the hermitage where he is in harmony with the *consonantia* of nature and with the deeper, unheard "central tonic note" that is the source of all meaning, while the return of the nuclear-armed plane seen earlier in the day is a reminder that living alone provides no escape from the perils and follies of contemporary life. He is a "stranger" not because he lives an exotic existence apart from others, but only in the sense that he is aware that his identity, like that of everyone, is a mystery that cannot be defined by a role or function. At the heart of the meditation is the sense of wonder at the invitation to attend to "the secret that is heard only in silence," to be present at "the virginal point of pure nothingness which is at the center of all other loves," to embrace "the primordial paradise tree, the *axis mundi*, the cosmic axle, ... the Cross."

THE HILLS ARE blue and hot. There is a brown, dusty field in the bottom of the valley. I hear a machine, a bird, a clock. The clouds are high and enormous. Through them the inevitable jet plane passes: this time probably full of passengers from Miami to Chicago. What passengers? This I have no need to decide. They are out of my world, up there, busy sitting in their small, isolated, arbitrary lounge that does not even seem to be moving—the lounge that somehow unaccountably picked them up off the earth in Florida to suspend them for a while with timeless cocktails and then let them down in Illinois. The suspension of modern life in contemplation that *gets you somewhere!*

There are also other worlds above me. Other jets will pass over, with other contemplations and other modalities of intentness.

I have seen the SAC plane, with the bomb in it, fly low over me, and I have looked up out of the woods directly at the closed bay of the metal bird with a scientific egg in its breast! A womb easily and mechanically opened! I do not consider this technological mother to be the friend of anything I believe in. However, like everyone else, I live in the shadow of the apocalyptic cherub. I am surveyed by it, impersonally. Its number recognizes my number. Are these numbers preparing at some moment to coincide in the benevolent mind of a computer? This does not concern me, for I live in the woods as a reminder that I am free not to be a number.

There is, in fact, a choice.

IN AN AGE WHERE there is much talk about "being yourself" I reserve to myself the right to forget about being myself, since in any case there is very little chance of my being anybody else. Rather it seems to me that when one is too intent on "being himself" he runs the risk of impersonating a shadow.

Yet I cannot pride myself on special freedom, simply because I am living in the woods. I am accused of living in the woods like Thoreau instead of living in the desert like St. John the Baptist. All I can answer is that I am not living "like anybody." Or "unlike anybody." We all live somehow or other, and that's that. It is a compelling necessity for me to be free to embrace the necessity of my own nature.

I exist under trees. I walk in the woods out of necessity. I am both a prisoner and an escaped prisoner. I cannot tell you why, born in France, my journey ended here in Kentucky. I have considered going farther, but it is not practical. It makes no difference. Do I have a "day"? Do I spend my "day" in a "place"? I know there are trees here. I know there are birds here. I know the birds in fact very well, for there are precise pairs of birds (two each of fifteen or twenty species) living in the immediate area of my cabin. I share this particular place with them: we form an ecological balance. This harmony gives the idea of "place" a new configuration.

As to the crows, they form part of a different pattern. They are vociferous and self-justifying, like humans. They are not two, they are many. They fight each other and the other birds, in a constant state of war.

THERE IS A MENTAL ecology, too, a living balance of spirits in this corner of the woods. There is room here for many other songs besides those of birds. Of Vallejo, for instance. Or Rilke, or René Char, Montale, Zukofsky, Ungaretti, Edwin Muir, Quasimodo, or some Greeks. Or the dry, disconcerting voice of Nicanor Parra, the poet of the sneeze. Here also is Chuang Tzu whose climate is perhaps most the climate of this silent corner of woods. A climate in which there is no need for explanation. Here is the reassuring companionship of many silent Tzu's and Fu's; Kung Tzu, Lao Tzu, Meng Tzu, Tu Fu. And Hui Neng. And Chao-Chu. And the drawings of Sengai. And a big graceful scroll from Suzuki. Here also is a Syrian hermit called Philoxenus. An Algerian cenobite called Camus. Here is heard the clanging prose of Tertullian, with the dry catarrh of Sartre. Here the voluble dissonances of Auden, with the golden sounds of John of Salisbury. Here is the deep vegetation of that more ancient forest in which the angry birds, Isaias and Jeremias, sing. Here should be, and are, feminine voices from Angela of Foligno to Flannery O'Connor, Theresa of Avila, Juliana of Norwich, and, more personally and warmly still, Raissa Maritain. It is good to choose the voices that will be heard in these woods, but they also choose themselves, and send themselves here to be present in this silence. In any case, there is no lack of voices.

THE HERMIT LIFE IS cool. It is a life of low definition in which there is little to decide, in which there are few transactions or none, in which there are no packages to be delivered. In which I do not bundle up packages and deliver them to myself. It is not intense. There is no give and take of questions and answers, problems and solutions. Problems begin down the hill. Over there under the water tower are the solutions. Here there are woods, foxes. Here there is no need for dark glasses. "Here" does not even warm itself up with references to "there." It is just a "here" for which there is no "there." The hermit life is that cool.

The monastic life as a whole is a hot medium. Hot with words like "must," "ought," and "should." Communities are devoted to high-definition projects: "making it all clear!" The clearer it gets the clearer it has to be made. It branches out. You have to keep clearing the branches. The more branches you cut back the more branches grow. For one you cut you get three more. On the end of each branch is a big bushy question mark. People are running all around with packages of meaning. Each is very anxious to know whether all the others have received the latest messages. Has someone else received a message that he has not received? Will they be willing to pass it on to him? Will he understand it when it is passed on? Will he have to argue about it? Will he be expected to clear his throat and stand up and say "Well the way I look at it St. Benedict said . . ."? Saint Benedict saw that the best thing to do with the monastic life was to cool it but today everybody is heating it up. Maybe to cool it you have to be a hermit. But then they will keep thinking that *you* have got a special message. When they find out you haven't. . . . Well, that's their worry, not mine.

THIS IS NOT A hermitage—it is a house. ("Who was that hermitage I seen you with last night? . . .") What I wear is pants. What I do is live. How I pray is breathe. Who said Zen? Wash out your mouth if you said Zen. If you see a meditation going by, shoot it. Who said "Love"? Love is in the movies. The spiritual life is something that people worry about when they are so busy with something else they think they ought to be spiritual. Spiritual life is guilt. Up here in the woods is seen the New Testament: that is to say, the wind comes through the trees and you breathe it. Is it supposed to be clear? I am not inviting anybody to try it. Or suggesting that one day the message will come saying NOW. That is none of my business.

I AM OUT OF bed at two-fifteen in the morning, when the night is darkest and most silent. Perhaps this is due to some ailment or other. I find myself in the primordial lostness of night, solitude, forest, peace, a mind awake in the dark, looking for a light, not totally reconciled to being out of bed. A light appears, and in the light an ikon. There is now in the large darkness a small room of radiance with psalms in it. The psalms grow up silently by themselves without effort like plants in this light which is favorable to them. The plants hold themselves up on stems which have a single consistency, that of mercy, or rather great mercy. *Magna misericordia.* In the formlessness of night and silence a word then pronounces itself: Mercy. It is surrounded by other words of lesser consequence: "destroy iniquity" "wash me" "purify" "I know my iniquity." *Peccavi.* Concepts without interest in the world of business, war, politics, culture, etc. Concepts also often without interest to ecclesiastics.

Other words: Blood. Guile. Anger. The way that is not good. The way of blood, guile, anger, war.

Out there the hills in the dark lie southward. The way over the hills is blood, guile, dark, anger, death: Selma, Birmingham, Mississippi. Nearer than these, the atomic city, from which each day a freight car of fissionable material is brought to be laid carefully beside the gold in the underground vault which is at the heart of this nation.

"Their mouth is the opening of the grave; their tongues are set in motion by lies; their heart is void."

Blood, lies, fire, hate, the opening of the grave, void. Mercy, great mercy.

THE BIRDS BEGIN TO wake. It will soon be dawn. In an hour or two the towns will wake, and men will enjoy everywhere the great luminous smiles of production and business.

—Why live in the woods?
—Well, you have to live somewhere.
—Do you get lonely?
—Yes, sometimes.
—Are you mad at people?
—No.
—Are you mad at the monastery?
—No.
—What do you think about the future of monasticism?
—Nothing. I don't think about it.
—Is it true that your bad back is due to Yoga?
—No.
—Is it true that you are practicing Zen in secret?
—Pardon me, I don't speak English.

ALL MONKS, AS IS well known, are unmarried, and hermits more unmarried than the rest of them. Not that I have anything against women. I see no reason why a man can't love God and a woman at the same time. If God was going to regard women with a jealous eye, why did he go and make them in the first place? There is a lot of talk about a married clergy. Interesting. So far there has not been a great deal said about married hermits. Well, anyway, I have the place full of ikons of the Holy Virgin.

One might say I had decided to marry the silence of the forest. The sweet dark warmth of the whole world will have to be my wife. Out of the heart of that dark warmth comes the secret that is heard only in silence, but it is the root of all the secrets that are whispered by all the lovers in their beds all over the world. So perhaps I have an obligation to preserve the stillness, the silence, the poverty, the virginal point of pure nothingness which is at the center of all other loves. I attempt to cultivate this plant without comment in the middle of the night and water it with psalms and prophecies in silence. It becomes the most rare of all the trees in the garden, at once the primordial paradise tree, the *axis mundi*, the cosmic axle, and the Cross. *Nulla silva talem profert.* There is only one such tree. It cannot be multiplied. It is not interesting.

IT IS NECESSARY FOR me to see the first point of light which begins to be dawn. It is necessary to be present alone at the resurrection of Day, in the blank silence when the sun appears. In this completely neutral instant I receive from the Eastern woods, the tall oaks, the one word "DAY," which is never the same. It is never spoken in any known language.

SERMON TO THE BIRDS: "Esteemed friends, birds of noble lineage, I have no message to you except this: be what you are: be *birds*. Thus you will be your own sermon to yourselves!"

Reply: "Even this is one sermon too many!"

RITUALS. WASHING OUT THE coffee pot in the rain bucket. Approaching the outhouse with circumspection on account of the king snake who likes to curl up on one of the beams inside. Addressing the possible king snake in the outhouse and informing him that he should not be there. Asking the formal ritual question that is asked at this time every morning: "Are you in there, you bastard?"

MORE RITUALS. SPRAY BEDROOM (cockroaches and mosquitoes). Close all the windows on south side (heat). Leave windows open on north and east sides (cool). Leave windows open on west side until maybe June when it gets very hot on all sides. Pull down shades. Get water bottle. Rosary. Watch. Library book to be returned.

It is time to visit the human race.

I START OUT UNDER the pines. The valley is already hot. Machines out there in the bottoms, perhaps planting corn. Fragrance of the woods. Cool west wind under the oaks. Here is the place on the path where I killed a copperhead. There is the place where I saw the fox run daintily and carefully for cover carrying a rabbit in his mouth. And there is the cement cross that, for no reason, the novices rescued from the corner of a destroyed wall and put up in the woods; people imagine someone is buried there. It is just a cross. Why should there not be a cement cross by itself in the middle of the woods?

A squirrel is kidding around somewhere overhead in midair. Tree to tree. The coquetry of flight.

I come out into the open over the hot hollow and the old sheep barn. Over there is the monastery, bugging with windows, humming with action.

The long yellow side of the monastery faces the sun on a sharp rise with fruit trees and beehives. This is without question one of the least interesting buildings on the face of the earth. However, in spite of the most earnest efforts to deprive it of all character and keep it ugly, it is surpassed in this respect by the vast majority of other monasteries. It is so completely plain that it ends, in spite of itself, by being at least simple. A lamentable failure of religious architecture—to come so close to non-entity and yet not fully succeed! I climb sweating into the novitiate, and put down my water bottle on the cement floor. The bell is ringing. I have duties, obligations, since here I am a monk. When I have accomplished these, I return to the woods where I am nobody. In the choir are the young monks, patient, serene, with very clear eyes, then, reflective, gentle, confused. Today perhaps I tell them of Eliot's *Little Gidding*, analyzing the first movement of the poem ("Midwinter spring is its own season"). They will listen with attention thinking that some other person is talking to them about some other poem.

CHANTING THE *ALLELUIA* in the second mode: strength and solidity of the Latin, seriousness of the second mode, built on the *Re* as though on a sacrament, a presence. One keeps returning to the *re* as to an inevitable center. *Sol-Re, Fa-Re, Sol-Re, Do-Re*. Many other notes in between, but suddenly one hears only the one note. *Consonantia*: all notes, in their perfect distinctness, are yet blended in one. (Through a curious oversight Gregorian chant has continued to be sung in this monastery. But not for long.)

IN THE REFECTORY IS read a message of the Pope, denouncing war, denouncing the bombing of civilians, reprisals on civilians, killing of hostages, torturing of prisoners (all in Vietnam). Do the people of this country realize who the Pope is talking about? They have by now become so solidly convinced that the Pope never denounces anybody but Communists that they have long since ceased to listen. The monks seem to know. The voice of the reader trembles.

IN THE HEAT OF noon I return with the water bottle freshly filled, through the cornfield, past the barn under the oaks, up the hill, under the pines, to the hot cabin. Larks rise out of the long grass singing. A bumblebee hums under the wide shady eaves.

I sit in the cool back room, where words cease to resound, where all meanings are absorbed in the *consonantia* of heat, fragrant pine, quiet wind, bird song, and one central tonic note that is unheard and unuttered. This is no longer a time of obligations. In the silence of the afternoon all is present and all is inscrutable in one central tonic note to which every other sound ascends or descends, to which every other meaning aspires, in order to find its true fulfillment. To ask when the note will sound is to lose the afternoon: it has already sounded, and all things now hum with the resonance of its sounding.

I SWEEP. I SPREAD a blanket out in the sun. I cut grass behind the cabin. I write in the heat of the afternoon. Soon I will bring the blanket in again and make the bed. The sun is over-clouded. The day declines. Perhaps there will be rain. A bell rings in the monastery. A devout Cistercian tractor growls in the valley. Soon I will cut bread, eat supper, say psalms, sit in the back room as the sun sets, as the birds sing outside the window, as night descends on the valley. I become surrounded once again by all the silent Tzu's and Fu's (men without office and without obligation). The birds draw closer to their nests. I sit on the cool straw mat on the floor, considering the bed in which I will presently sleep alone under the ikon of the Nativity.

Meanwhile the metal cherub of the apocalypse passes over me in the clouds, treasuring its egg and its message.

19

Symbolism: Communication or Communion?

In his journal for June 18, 1965, Merton wrote, "Ought to get on to the article on symbolism today" (*Dancing in the Water of Life*, 257), and by the end of the month he
informs a correspondent that "a new essay on symbolism . . . written originally for a magazine in India" is presently being typed (*Courage for Truth*, 175). The article appeared
in the October 1966 issue of *The Mountain Path* (3: 339-48), which Merton tells James
Laughlin was "published at the ashram of one of the former great Indian saints of our
time, Ramana Maharshi" (Merton/Laughlin, *Selected Letters*, 331), the same journal
in which "The Contemplative Life in the Modern World" had appeared the previous
year. Though Laughlin himself planned to reprint what he called this "wonderful essay
. . . since it says so much, so well and forcefully, that I myself believe" (Merton/Laugh-
lin, *Selected Letters*, 328), as the lead piece in a subsequent *New Directions Annual*,
this did not in fact happen. Its first American publication was its posthumous appearance in the journal *Monastic Exchange* 2 (Summer 1970), 1-10; it was later included
in *Love and Living* (54-79). The essay articulates Merton's conviction that authentic
symbolism is an irreplaceable vehicle of a participatory, holistic way of knowing that
is largely disregarded and threatened by the rise of a culture based on quantification
and a pseudo-scientific objectivity predicated on the exclusive epistemological validity of the indicative sign. For Merton the symbol, unlike the sign, has the capacity to
mediate a contemplative awareness, a recognition of Being transcending the distinction
between subject and object—a *via positiva* experience of wisdom that complements
the apophatic way of darkness and emptiness. Hence the crucial importance of art and
myth and ritual that enable humans to surrender their empirical selves, their individual
egos, and so to enter into communion with the Center of all reality (and the danger
of the degeneration of symbols into idols, which posit a unity with an illusory center).
Merton will echo the key insight of this essay in the well-known final words of his talk
at the Temple of Understanding Conference in Calcutta in October 1968, less than two
months before his death: "And the deepest level of communication is not communication, but communion. It is wordless. It is beyond words, and it is beyond speech, and it
is beyond concept. Not that we discover a new unity. We discover an older unity. My
dear brothers, we are already one. But we imagine that we are not. And what we have to
recover is our original unity. What we have to be is what we are" (*Asian Journal*, 308).

THE TOPIC ANNOUNCED in this title could easily lend itself to a detailed, long-winded academic treatment. In order to avoid the disadvantages of such an approach, the author will permit himself to set down, in a more spontaneous and less organized form, a few bare intuitions. These may suggest further lines of thought in the mind of the reader.

In dealing with symbolism one enters an area where reflection, synthesis, and contemplation are more important than investigation, analysis, and science. One cannot apprehend a symbol unless one is able to awaken, in one's own being, the spiritual resonances which respond to the symbol not only as *sign* but as "sacrament" and "presence." Needless to say, when we speak of symbol here we are interested only in the full and true sense of the word. Mere conventional symbols, more or less arbitrarily taken to represent something else, concrete images which stand for abstract qualities, are not symbols in the highest sense. The true symbol does not merely point to some hidden object. It contains in itself a structure which in some way makes us aware of the inner meaning of life and of reality itself. A true symbol takes us to the center of the circle, not to another point on the circumference. A true symbol points to the very heart of all being, not to an incident in the flow of becoming.

ONE MIGHT BEGIN BY asking whether one can even attempt such reflections, in the Western world of the twentieth century, without a certain note of urgency, accompanied by a sense of conflict and confusion. In other words, the reader must be prepared to find these remarks somewhat lacking in serenity. The tension in the West, especially in America, between a naïve surface optimism (belief in scientific progress as an end in itself) and the deep, savage destructive tendencies of a technology and an economy in which man becomes the instrument of blind inhuman forces makes us realize that the *degradation of the sense of symbolism* in the modern world is one of its many alarming symptoms of spiritual decay.

The most unique and disturbing feature of this spiritual degeneration is that it finds itself armed with a colossal will-to-power and with almost unlimited facilities for implementing its brutal aspirations. Thus twentieth-century man who mistakenly imagines himself to be standing on a peak of civilized development (since he confuses technology with civilization) does not realize that he has in reality reached a critical point of moral and spiritual disorganization. He is a savage armed not with a club or a spear but with the most sophisticated arsenal of diabolical engines, to which new inventions are added every week.

NIETZSCHE'S DECLARATION THAT "GOD is dead" is one that is now taken up, not without seriousness, by the prophets of the most "progressive" tendencies in

Western religion, which now seems, in some quarters, eager to prove its sincerity, in the eyes of a godless society, by an act of spiritual self-destruction.

Meanwhile, artists, poets, and others who might be expected to have some concern with the inner life of man are declaring that the reason why God has ceased to be present to man (therefore "dead") is that man has ceased to be present to himself, and that consequently the true significance of the statement "God is dead" is really that "MAN is dead." The obvious fact of man's material agitation and external frenzy serves only to emphasize his lack of spiritual life.

Since it is by symbolism that man is spiritually and consciously in contact with his own deepest self, with other men, and with God, then both the "death of God" and the "death of man" are to be accounted for by the fact that symbolism is dead. The death of symbolism is itself the most eloquent and significant symbol in our modern cultural life. Since man cannot live without signs of the invisible, and since his capacity to apprehend the visible and the invisible as a meaningful unity depends on the creative vitality of his symbols, then, even though he may claim to have no further interest in this "bringing together" (which is the etymological sense of "symbol"), man will nevertheless persist in spite of himself in making symbols. If they are not living signs of creative integration and inner life, then they will become morbid, decaying, and pathogenic signs of his own inner disruption. The solemn vulgarity, indeed the spiritually hideous and sometimes unconsciously obscene nature of some of the "symbols" that are still held worthy of respect by the establishment and by the masses (whether in the capitalist West or in socialist countries), has naturally aroused the total protest of the modern artist who now creates only anti-art and non-symbol, or else contemplates without tremor and without comment the ultimate spiritual affront of those forms and presences which marketing and affluence have made "normal" and "ordinary" everywhere.

THE LOSS OF THE sense of symbol in scientific and technological society is due in part to an incapacity to distinguish between the *symbol* and the *indicative sign*. The function of the sign is communication, and first of all, the communication of factual or practical knowledge. The function of the symbol is not the statement of facts or the conveyance of information, even of spiritual information about absolute or religiously revealed truths. A symbol does not merely teach and inform. Nor does it *explain*.

It is quite true that the content of a religious symbol is usually rich with spiritual or revealed truth. Nevertheless, revelation and spiritual vision are contained in symbols not in order that one may extract them from the symbol and study them or appropriate them intellectually apart from the symbol itself. Revealed truth is made present concretely and existentially in symbols, and is grasped in and with the symbol by a living response of the subject. This response defies exact analysis and cannot be accurately described to one who does not experience it authentically in himself. The capacity for such experience is developed by living spiritual traditions and by contact with a spiritual master (*guru*), or at least with a vital and creative liturgy and a traditional doctrine. So, to demand that a symbol should fulfill the function of informing and explaining, or clarifying and scientifically verifying all the most intimate facts of the cosmos, of man, of man's place in the cosmos, of man's relation to God, of man's relation to himself, and so on, is to demand that the symbol should do what indicative or quantitative signs do. As soon as one makes such a demand, he immediately becomes convinced that the symbol is of far less practical value than the sign. In a world where practical use and quantitative scientific information are highly prized, the symbol quickly becomes meaningless.

When the symbol is called upon to *communicate*, it necessarily restricts itself to conveying the most trivial kind of idea or information. The symbol is then reduced to the *trademark* or the *political badge*, a mere sign of identification. Identification is not identity. "Rubber stamp" identification is actually a diminution or loss of identity, a submersion of identity in the generalized class. The pseudo-symbols of the mass movement become signs of the pseudo-mystique in which the mass man loses his individual self in the false, indeed the demonic void, the general pseudo-self of the Mass Society. The symbols of the Mass Society are crude and barbaric rallying points for emotion, fanaticism, and exalted forms of hatred masking as moral indignation. The symbols of Mass Society are ciphers on the face of a moral and spiritual void.

WERNER HEISENBERG, THE PHYSICIST, has discussed the revolutionary change in man's attitude toward nature in an age of science and technology.* In the pre-scientific era man sought even in his "scientific" investigations to arrive at the most living and most qualitatively significant apprehension of nature as a whole. Such an apprehension, even when it contained elements of experiment and objective observation, remained essentially poetic, philosophical, and even religious.

Modern science does not seek to create a "living representation" but to acquire and coordinate quantitative data from which to construct explanations or simply working hypotheses with a practical orientation. Where reli-

---

*All quotations from Werner Heisenberg in this section are from his essay "The Representation of Nature in Contemporary Physics" (1954).

gion, philosophy, and poetry use the power of the creative symbol to attain a synthetic apprehension of life in its ultimate metaphysical roots, science uses technical instruments to gather quantitative data about the physical universe, and those data are reduced to mathematical formulas, which can then serve the practical needs of technology.

What is not generally realized yet is that modern science itself has undermined the worldview of naïve materialism which believed that "ultimate reality" could be found in the elementary particles of matter. Science has above all destroyed the materialistic idea of a purely objective knowledge in which we can, with absolute certitude, make statements about "reality" based on our observations of matter, as if we ourselves were observing everything from a platform of "science" in a pure realm of truth. Actually, as Heisenberg says, we cannot observe the particles of matter as pure objects, since the fact of our observation itself enters into the interaction and behavior of the entities we observe. Hence it is that the formulas of the atomic physicist represent *"no longer the behavior of the elementary particles but rather our knowledge of this behavior."* At the same time, technology as it develops and apparently "penetrates" the "mysteries of nature," in so doing *"transforms our environment and impresses our image upon it."* This use of technology and science to transform nature and bring it under man's power appears to Heisenberg an extension of biological processes, so that man's technology becomes part of him as the spider's web is inseparable from the biology of the spider. The result of this is that man no longer stands in opposition to nature; he confronts no adversary in the world in which he is alone with himself and which he will soon completely transform in his own image. But the problem arises: there does remain one adversary, *man himself,* and as Heisenberg says, in this situation man's technology, instead of broadening and expanding man's capacities for life, suddenly threatens to contract them and even destroy them altogether. "In such a confrontation, the extension of technology need no longer be an indication of progress."

Now symbolism exercises its vital and creative function in a cosmos where man had to come to terms with a nature in which he was struggling to maintain a place of his own—albeit a place of spiritual preeminence. Symbolism strives to "bring together" man, nature, and God in a living and sacred synthesis. But technological man finds himself in another artificial synthesis in which he has no longer any knowledge of anything except himself, his machines, and his knowledge that he knows what he knows. This knowledge is not a knowledge of reality but a knowledge of knowledge. That is to say—man no longer is "in contact with nature" but is only well situated in the context of his own experiments. He can say with certainty how an experiment will turn out, but he cannot find any ultimate meaning for this. Man is, therefore, cut off from any reality except that of his own processes—that is to say, in fact, of his own inner chaos—and that of the extraordinary new world of his machines. As the knowledge of his own disruption is unpalatable, he turns more and more to his machines. But through the power of his machines he acts out the uncomprehended tragedy of his inner disruption. As Heisenberg says, in the arresting comparison, "man finds himself in the position of a captain whose ship has been so securely built of iron and steel that his compass no longer points to the north but only towards the ship's mass of iron."

Heisenberg quotes the Chinese sage Chuang Tzu, who, twenty-five hundred years ago, discovered that dependence even on a simple kind of machine caused man to become "uncertain in his inner impulses." Naturally, the advance of science and technology is irreversible and man now has to come to terms with himself in his new situation. He cannot do so if he builds an irrational and unscientific faith on the absolute and final objectivity of scientific knowledge of nature. The limits of science must be recognized, and blind faith in an uncontrolled proliferation in technology must be abjured.

To return to the ship's captain, Heisenberg says that his danger will be less if he recognizes what has gone wrong and tries to navigate by some other means— for instance, by the stars. To "navigate by the stars" he needs to go beyond the limitation of a scientific worldview and recover his sense of the symbol.

ALFRED NORTH WHITEHEAD, WHO, as a scientist, took a cool and detached view of symbolism, declared that society needed to defend itself against the proliferation of symbols which "have a tendency to run wild like the vegetation of a tropical forest." It is certainly true that a mass of obscure symbols that have ceased to illuminate and invigorate may end by stifling social and personal life. Therefore, "an occasional revolution in symbolism is required," says Whitehead, in a rather offhand way, as if symbols could be created anew by act of Parliament. Nevertheless, Whitehead is quite definite in saying, "Symbolism is no mere idle fancy or corrupt degeneration: it is inherent in the very texture of human life." He sees clearly that symbolism does not seek merely to convey information but to enhance the importance and value of what it symbolizes (see his *Symbolism, Its Meaning and Efficacy*). He points out how in social life symbolism replaces "the force of instinct which suppresses individuality" and creates instead a dynamism of thought and action in which the individual person can integrate his own free activity into the work of the commonweal, without simply submitting, in passive and automatic fashion, to external directives of authority.

By means of the social symbol, the person can make the common good really his own. By means of the religious symbol, the person can enter into commu- nion, not only with his fellow man and with all creation, but with God. Sym- bolism is powerful, says Whitehead, because of its "enveloping suggestiveness and emotional efficacy." However, the symbol is not merely emotional, and "it affords a foothold for reason by its delineation of the particular instinct which it expresses."

Whitehead, however, thinking in terms of the mass movement and of blind political prejudice, points to the danger of those (political) symbols which evoke a *direct (reflex) response* without reference to any meaning whatever. The effect of such symbols becomes hypnotic—certain responses, usually violent, are elicited without thought and without moral judgment.

Thus, in certain unhealthy situations, the political or military symbol can produce the automatic obedience of storm troopers and political policemen who are ready for any savagery and any abomination. The symbol, in this case, has the effect of suppressing conscience and reasoned judgment and bringing about a demonic communion in evil.

But is this the fault of symbolism as such? Certainly not. It is due to the deg- radation of symbols. A man who is trained to respond to higher, more creative, and more spiritual symbols will *instantly react in revulsion* against the crude barbarity of the totalist symbol. His reaction, too, is instinctive and, as it were, automatic. What matters, then, is not that the symbol tends to concentrate around itself man's instinctive forces for action and self-dedication, but that liv- ing and creative symbols elevate and direct that action in a good sense, while pathogenic and depraved symbols divert man's energies to evil and destruction.

The point is to educate men so that they can discern one from the other.

But if in our education we assume that all symbolism is mere fantasy and illu- sion, we no longer teach people to make this distinction. Hence, while imagin- ing they have risen above the "childishness" of symbolism, they will easily and uncritically submit, in fact, to the fascination of the perverse and destructive symbols which are actually obsessing the whole society in which they live.

In our modern world the fascination of violence has become, through TV, magazines, movies, radio, etc., almost irresistible. There is now so much free- floating terror and hatred in the moral climate of the world that the slightest and most ridiculous of actions can be interpreted symbolically and instantly unleash mass hysteria on a global scale. The only remedy for this is in a return to the level of spiritual wisdom on which the higher symbols operate. This is easy enough to say; but is it actually possible today? Have we, in fact, simply fallen away from our capacity for "symbolically conditioned action" in the higher sense (guidance by the *meaning* and *wisdom* of the higher symbol) and relapsed into purely reflex and instinctive action without reference to meaning, and above all *without any rational sense of causality and responsibility*?

At the end of his suggestive essay, without perhaps fully intending to do so, Whitehead speaks of the community life of ants governed (probably) by pure instinct rather than by meaningful symbol.

It is no new idea to say that if man does survive in his cybernetic society without blowing himself up, it may well be that, renouncing the creative symbol and living mechanically, he learns to make his world into a vast anthill. If mere survival is all we desire, this may seem a satisfactory prospect. But if our vocation is to share creatively in the spiritualization of our existence, then the anthill concept is somewhat less than desirable.

OBVIOUSLY THE DIRECTION THAT symbolism must take is that of expressing union, understanding, and love among men—what Paul Tillich has called a "communal eros." But the crude symbolism of violence has gained its power precisely from the fact that the symbolism of love has been so terribly debased, cheapened, and dehumanized. There is something very frightening about the awful caricature of love and beauty which has manifested itself for several centuries, growing progressively worse, in Western literature and art, including religious literature and art, until today the sensitive mind recoils entirely from the attempt to see and portray "the beautiful" and concentrates on the hideous, the meaningless, the formless, in a sincere attempt to clear the desecrated sanctuary of the rubbish which fills it.

IN TECHNOLOGICAL SOCIETY, IN which the means of communication and signification have become fabulously versatile, and are at the point of an even more prolific development, thanks to the computer with its inexhaustible memory and its capacity for immediate absorption and organization of facts, the very nature and use of communication itself becomes unconsciously symbolic. Though he now has the capacity to communicate anything, anywhere, instantly, man finds himself with *nothing to say*. Not that there are not many things he could communicate, or should attempt to communicate. He should, for instance, be able to meet with his fellow man and discuss ways of building a peaceful world. He is incapable of this kind of confrontation. Instead of this, he has intercontinental ballistic missiles which can deliver nuclear death to tens of millions of people in a few moments. This is the most sophisticated message modern man has, apparently, to convey to his fellow man. It is, of course, a message about himself, his alienation from himself, and his inability to come to terms with life.

The vital role of the symbol is precisely this: to express and to encourage man's acceptance of his own center, his own ontological roots in a mystery of being that transcends his individual ego. But when man is reduced to his empirical self and confined within its limits, he is, so to speak, excluded from himself, cut off from his own roots, condemned to spiritual death by thirst and starvation in a wilderness of externals. In this wilderness there can be no living symbols, only the dead symbols of dryness and destruction which bear witness to man's own inner ruin. But he cannot "see" these symbols, since he is incapable of interior response.

IN A RECENT ESSAY, of a rather esoteric yet popular nature, an American theoretician of nuclear war devised an elaborate "ladder of escalation" in which his avowed purpose was to construct a *rudimentary language*. It is a language of destruction, in which each rung on the "ladder" (including massive exchanges of nuclear weapons, destruction of cities, missile sites, etc.) was a way of "saying something" and of "conveying information" to the enemy. One feels that millennia ago, in the early Stone Age, communication among men must have been more basic, more articulate, and more humane. The "ladder" (itself an ancient symbol, as in Genesis 28:12, as in Babylonian religion, as in the cosmic tree, the *axis mundi* of Asian myths, etc.) has now become a symbol of the total and negative futility of a huge technological machine organized primarily for destruction. At the top of the ladder is not God but "Spasm." But "spasm" is on every rung. All rungs of escalation are "insensate war."

OF COURSE, THE MORE constant and more public claim made by the salesmen of communication is that our modern media are still interested, first of all, in rapidly conveying messages of love. This, of course, is another way of affirming what is, in fact, so universally doubted: that men still have messages of genuine love to convey. Let us, for a moment, not dispute this. Here is one instance of such "communication."

A busy physician in an American city has a telephone in his car, so that even when he is not in his office, at the hospital, or at home, he can receive urgent calls. While he is driving through the city, his phone rings and he picks it up. It is a call from Africa, via shortwave radio. He listens. It is a friend who has recently gone to Africa. What does he have to say? Nothing. "I had a chance to make this call for nothing so I thought I would say 'Hello.'" They exchange greetings, they assure each other that they are well, their families are well, and so on. They indulge in the same completely inconsequential kind of talk as in any other casual phone call. One can reflect on this and recognize that even some of the seemingly "important" matters that occupy the communications media are perhaps almost as trivial as this.

Someone will argue: what does it matter if they had no really serious information to communicate? This was something more than communication. It was an expression of friendship, therefore of love. Is not love more important than factual information? Were these friends not seeking *communion* even more than communication?

To this one can only answer that love and communion are indeed most important and far outweigh mere "communication." But the fact remains that where communion is no longer understood, and where, in fact, communication is regarded as primary, because "practical," then people are reduced to making a *symbolically useless* use of expensive means of communication, in an effort to achieve communion. But the symbolic uselessness remains self-frustrating, since, in the code of a technological culture, to carry out such useless acts is to become guilty of a sin against the basic virtue: practicality.

Yet even here there are most curious ambiguities, for while the extraordinary efficacy of technological instruments increases every day, one is obliged to admit that the uses to which they are put are increasingly useless and even destructive. What is the uselessness of a friendly phone call from Africa to America compared to the titanic uselessness of space travel and moon flights? One suddenly realizes that, in point of fact, technology at present is built entirely on uselessness rather than on use, and this uselessness is in fact symbolic. (It is a symptom. And in a sickness, a symptom is a symbol. Right understanding of the symptom can lead to restoration of health. Wrong response aggravates the illness.) The one great usefulness technology might have for us is precisely what no one sees: its symbolic uselessness, which no amount of sermons on progress can manage to justify.

TRADITIONALLY, THE VALUE OF the symbol is precisely in its apparent uselessness as a means of simple communication. *Because it is not an efficient mode of communicating information, the symbol can achieve a higher purpose, the purpose of going beyond practicality and purpose, beyond cause and effect.* Instead of establishing a new contact by a meeting of minds in the sharing of news, the symbol tells nothing new: it revives our awareness of what we already know, but deepens that awareness. What is "new" in the symbol is the ever new discovery of a new depth and a new actuality in what IS and always has been. The function of the symbol is not merely to *bring about* a union of minds and wills, as a cause produces an effect; the function of the symbol is to manifest a union that *already exists but is not fully realized*. The symbol awakens awareness, or restores it. Therefore, it aims not at communication but at communion. Communion is the awareness of participation in an ontological or religious reality: in the mystery of being, of human love, of redemptive mystery, of contemplative truth.

The purpose of the symbol, if it can be said to have a "purpose," is not to increase the quantity of our knowledge and information but to deepen and enrich the *quality* of life itself by bringing man into communion with the mysterious sources of vitality and meaning, of creativity, love, and truth, to which he cannot have direct access by means of science and technique. The realm of symbol is the realm of wisdom in which man finds truth not only in and through objects but in himself and in his life, lived in accordance with the deepest principles of divine wisdom. Naturally, such wisdom does not exclude knowledge of objects. It gives a new dimension to science. What would our world of science be, if only we had wisdom?

APPRECIATION OF THE SYMBOL necessarily implies a certain view of reality itself, a certain cosmology and a religious metaphysic of being, above all a spiritual view of man. Symbols begin to have a living and creative significance only when man is understood to be a sacred being. The "desecration" of man begins when symbols are emptied of meaning and are allowed to survive precisely insofar as they are patronizingly admitted to be misleading but still "necessary for the ignorant."

The symbol is then regarded only as a politically or religiously "useful lie," insofar as it seems to communicate information on a childish level, information which is inadequate but acceptable to those to whom "objective truth" is not yet clear. The "sacredness" of man consists, however, precisely in the fact that the truth for which and by which he lives is primarily within himself, and therefore prime importance belongs to the symbol which directs him to this truth, not as an external object, but as a spiritual and personal fulfillment. Without this interior fulfillment, the mind of man is not equipped to cope with objective truth, and the spirit that has no interior roots will find that its "scientific" knowledge of objects turns out to be "a lie" even when it is materially correct. It completely misleads him as to the meaning of his own existence.

Thus, in order that man be profoundly secularized and "desecrated," symbols themselves must be discredited and excluded from art, culture, and religion. For Marx, the symbol (above all, the religious symbol) is nothing but an instrument of alienation. Yet how many pseudoreligious symbols have sprung up in Marxist society, equaling in vulgarity and in triviality those of the capitalist and fascist societies? The emptiness of these symbols bears witness to the alienation of man in these societies.

THE DESECRATION OF SYMBOLS has been systematically proceeding for two centuries and more, especially in semiscientific theories of anthropology, archaeology, comparative religion, and so on. For example, consider the totally unrealistic theory that the art of primitive man had its origin in a utilitarian concept, the supposed magic efficacy of an artistic image. To paint a picture of a bison on the wall of a cave was supposedly primitive man's way of saying that he was desperately hungry and had not tasted bison meat for a long time. He painted a bison on the theory that the image gave him power over a real bison. The painting constituted a "virtual capture" of the desired prey. Once again, the symbol is seen only as an efficacious sign, an attempt to exercise causality, to produce a practical and useful effect in the world of objects. This means that primitive art is understood only in modern commercial and technological terms.

A symbol is thought, like other signs, to have only a practical reference. It is supposed to claim a certain kind of efficacy, to pretend to a definite causal influence: it provides a mode of control over objects. It is part of a technique. It is to be seen in a context of magic and archaic pre-technology which is now discarded as totally inefficacious. Art is, then, seen only as an imitation of objects, as a substitute for the possession of a desired object. What is important is not the art but the object to which it points. This is the basic axiom of advertising, which *suggests* a need, awakens a need, and keeps it awake, in the prospective consumer, by means of "art." This is also the principle governing political propaganda art.

This crude theory of the origin of primitive art lacks, first of all, any appreciation for the *extraordinary creative power* of these amazing symbols made by prehistoric man. The most elementary familiarity with modern psychology ought to be enough to show that such creative power could not normally proceed from a naked physical desire. It could only come from a sublimated transformation of desire.

Acquaintance with primitive religion shows us that primitive man had a deep sense of kinship with the animals among which he lived, including those on which he depended for his existence. His "love" for the bison or the reindeer was something far deeper and more complex than a modern city dweller's craving for this or that kind of meat, derived from an animal never seen in its natural state. This primitive "love" of the animals was embodied in a very complex religious relationship, hedged in with severe ritual limitations which prohibited useless and irresponsible killing and all kinds of misuse. Primitive art was far from being merely a weak, inefficacious, half-despairing attempt of an inept hunter to bring down good luck on his spear. It was also an acknowledgment of a deep communion with all living beings, with the animals among which man lived on terms of familiarity that are no longer imaginable to us.

Hence, the symbols of primitive art are vitally significant on more than one level. There is, of course, the representation of the everyday level, the hunt for food. But there is also another level, that of kinship, of religious fellowship with the animal regarded from one point of view as superior to man, as "divine."

The Biblical polemic against the deification of natural beings and forces comes relatively late in man's cultural development, and doubtless by that time primitive religion had, in fact, become deeply degenerate. But a study of the philosophical ideas of the Bantu in Africa still shows that primitive man's reverence for life and for the sacred, creative dynamism of life, expressed in his art and in his symbolism, could be extremely deep and pure. Modern man's misinterpretation of his primitive ancestors' thought and culture reflects discredit on our own blind complacency and sense of superiority.

Primitive art undoubtedly draws a great deal of its power from the *ambivalence of love and guilt*, due to the fact that man had to slay a loved, admired, and mysterious object in order to keep alive himself. This became so strong that, eventually, in certain highly developed religious cultures, such as those of India, the killing of animals and the eating of meat were eventually prohibited. Here one encounters an even deeper level of communion: the level of *being itself.* Man and the animal are finally seen as sharing in the ontological mystery of being; they are somehow one "in God the Creator." Or as Hinduism would say, the Atman is one in them both.

Primitive art cannot be comprehended unless the implications of these different levels of symbolic meaning are somehow apprehended. Merely to declare that primitive art had a magic or utilitarian purpose, aimed at a limited, practical result, is to ignore this symbolic quality and attach oneself exclusively to a supposed causal signification which is then shown to be so naïve and preposterous that it cannot be taken seriously. Thus, substituting the practical sign for the religious symbol, the theorist manages to call into question all forms of culture—religious, philosophical, artistic, mystical—which make use of the symbol. All instantly become incomprehensible.

PAUL TILLICH, THE AMERICAN Protestant theologian I have already mentioned, has rightly seen that "a real symbol points to an object that can never become an object." This is a profound and intriguing declaration. The symbol cannot possibly convey *information about an object* if it is true to its nature as symbol. Only when it is debased does a symbol point exclusively to an object other than itself. *The symbol is an object pointing to the subject.* The symbol is not an object for its own sake: it is a reminder that we are summoned to a deeper spiritual awareness, far beyond the level of subject and object.

It would, however, be a great mistake to think that the symbol merely reminds the subject to become aware of himself as object, after the Western manner of introspection and self-examination. We must repeat, the symbol is an object which leads beyond the realm of division where subject and object stand over against one another. That is why the symbol goes beyond communication to communion. Communication takes place between subject and object, but communion is beyond the division: it is a sharing in basic unity. This does not necessarily imply a "pantheist metaphysic." Whether or not they may be strictly monistic, the higher religions all point to this deeper unity, because they all strive after the experience of this unity. They differ, sometimes widely, in ways of explaining what this unity is and how one may attain to it.

Christianity sees this unity as a special gift of God, a work of grace, which brings us to unity with God and one another in the Holy Spirit. The religions of Asia tend to see this unity in an ontological and natural principle in which all beings are metaphysically one. The experience of unity for the Christian is unity "in the Holy Spirit." For Asian religions it is unity in Absolute Being (Atman) or in the Void (Sunyata). The difference between the two approaches is the difference between an ontologist mysticism and a theological revelation: between a return to an Absolute Nature and surrender to a Divine Person.

The symbols of the higher religions may at first sight seem to have little in common. But when one comes to a better understanding of those religions, and when one sees that the experiences which are the fulfillment of religious belief and practice are most clearly expressed in symbols, one may come to recognize that often the symbols of different religions may have more in common than the abstractly formulated official doctrines.

The Chinese ideogram *Chung* (中) bears more than a superficial resemblance to the Cross. It is also a picture of the five cosmic points, the four cardinal points centered on the "pivot" of Tao. This is analogous to the traditional Christian cosmic interpretation of the Cross symbol, the "picture" of the new creation and of the recapitulation of all in Christ (Ephesians 1:12). One might pursue these analogies in studying the traditional Buddhist stupas, and so on. It is sufficient to suggest those lines of thought which the reader can investigate for himself.

A SYMBOL IS, THEN, not simply an indicative sign conveying information about a religious object, a revelation, a theological truth, a mystery of faith. It is an *embodiment* of that truth, a "sacrament," by which one participates in the religious presence of the saving and illuminating One. It does not merely point the way to the One as object. As long as the One is regarded as object, it is not the One, it is dual or multiple, since there is a division between It and the one (or ones) seeking to attain it. Hence, the question of a Zen master: "If all things return to the one, where does the one return to?" To such a question there can be no answer, since the question itself is contradictory. Reason might seek a way to get around the contradiction and resolve it. Symbol tends rather to accept the contradiction in order to point beyond it. It seems to take the One as if it were an object, but, in fact, it reveals the One as present within our own subjective and interior entity. It reveals that the subjectivity of the subject is, in fact, now, deeply rooted in the infinite God, the Father, the Word, the Spirit, or in Hindu terms Atman, *sat-cit-ananda*. The symbol does not merely bridge the distance and cause the believer to become united with God. It proclaims that, in one way or another, according to the diversity of religions, the believer can and does even now return to Him from Whom he first came. It does not simply promise a new and effective communication by which the believer can make himself heard by the Deity and can even exercise a certain persuasive force upon Him. It does much more: it opens the believer's inner eye, the eye of the heart, to the realization that he must come to be centered in God because that, in fact, is where his center is. He must become what he is, a "son of God," "seeking only his Father's will," abandoned to the invisible Presence and Nearness of Him Who Is, for there is no reality anywhere else but in Him.

But the symbol also speaks to many believers in one: it awakens them to their communion with one another in God. It does not merely bring their minds into communication with one another, in a common worship, for instance. Worship itself is symbolic, and as such it is communion rather than communication. (Hence the great pity of a certain type of Christianity, which has become in great measure mere communication of information, a meeting where the audience is entertained by an inspiring lecture.) Worship is symbolic communion in mystery, the mystery of the actual presence of Him Who is Being, Light, and Blessedness of Love. It is recognition of the fact that, in reality, we cannot be without Him, that we are centered in Him, that He dwells in us, and that because He is in us and we in Him, we are one with one another in Him.

> ... that all may be one, even as thou, Father, in me and I in thee; that they also may be one in us, that the world may believe that thou hast sent me. And the glory that thou hast given me, I have given to them, that they may be one, even as we are one: I in them and thou in me; that they may be perfected in unity, and that the world may know that thou hast sent me, and that thou hast loved them even as thou hast loved me.

Father, I will that where I am, they also whom thou has given me may
be with me; in order that they may behold my glory, which thou hast
given me, because thou hast loved me before the creation of the world.

John 17:21-24.

THE DESECRATION OF SYMBOLS cannot be blamed exclusively on the forces
of secularism and atheism. On the contrary, it unfortunately began in religious
circles themselves. When a tradition loses its contemplative vitality and wisdom, its symbolism gradually loses its meaning and ceases to be a point of contact with "the center." Symbolism degenerates into allegorism. The symbol has
no life of its own, it merely designates an abstraction. In the system of allego-
ries, everything points to everything else and nothing conclusively ends in real
meaning. There is nothing but a circle of references without end. "A" points to
"B," which points to "C," which points to "A." The center is forgotten.

All that matters is to have a key to the hidden meanings and to know that "A"
really stands for "B," so that when you say "A" you really mean "B." But then a
scientific critic comes along and says that "A" does not mean "B"; that there is no
way of knowing that "A" means anything at all; and all we can say is, that in 500
B.C. "A" was thought to mean "B," while today science shows this interpretation
to be impossible.

When the symbol degenerates into a mere means of communication and
ceases to be a sign of communion, it becomes an idol, insofar as it seems to
point to an object with which it brings the subject into effective, quasi-magical,
psychological, or parapsychological communication. It would be pointless here
to go into the ancient Biblical polemic against "idols of wood and stone." There
are much more dangerous and much more potent idols in the world today:
signs of cosmic and technological power, political and scientific idols, idols of
the nation, the party, the race. These are evident enough, but the fact that they
are evident in themselves does not mean that people do not submit more and
more blindly, more and more despairingly to their complete power. The idol of
national military strength was never more powerful than today, even though
men claim to desire peace. In fact, though they pay lip service to the love of life
and of humanity, they obscurely recognize that in submitting to the demon of
total war they are, in fact, releasing themselves from the anxieties and perplexi-
ties of a "peace" that is fraught with too many ambiguities for comfort. Can man
resist the temptation to sacrifice himself utterly and irrevocably to this idol?

ANOTHER IDOL THAT IS not so obvious is that of supposed "spiritual experience" sought as an object and as an end in itself. Here, too, the temptation that offers itself is one of escape from anxiety and limitation, and an *affirmation of the individual self as object*, but as a special kind of object, *to be experienced as free from all limitations*.

The temptation of modern pseudomysticism is perhaps one of the gravest and most subtle, precisely because of the confusion it causes in the minds and hearts of those who might conceivably be drawn to authentic communion with God and with their fellow men by the austere traditional ways of obedience, humility, sacrifice, love, knowledge, worship, meditation, and contemplation. All these ancient ways demand the control and the surrender, the ultimate "loss" of the empirical self in order that we may be "found" again in God. But pseudomysticism centers upon the individualistic enjoyment of experience, that is, upon *the individual self experienced as without limitation*. This is a sublime subtlety by which one can eat one's cake and have it. It is the discovery of a spiritual trick (which is sought as a supremely valuable "object") in which, while seeming to renounce and deny oneself, one, in fact, definitively affirms the ego as a center of indefinite and angelic enjoyments. One rests in the joy of the spiritualized self, very much aware of one's individual identity and of one's clever achievement in breaking through to a paradise of delights without having had to present one's ticket at the entrance. The ticket that must be surrendered is one's individual, empirical ego. Pseudomysticism, on the contrary, seeks the permanent delight of the ego in its own spirituality, its own purity, as if it were itself absolute and infinite.

And this explains the success and the danger of the current Western fad for producing "spiritual experience" by means of drugs.

SHALL WE CONCLUDE ON a note of pessimism? Not necessarily. The present crisis of man is something for which we have no adequate historical standard of comparison. Our risks are extreme. The hopes which we have based on our technological skill are very probably illusory. But there remain other dimensions. The fact that we are not able to grasp these dimensions is not necessarily cause for despair. If our destiny is not entirely in our own hands, we can still believe, as did our fathers, that our lives are mysteriously guided by a wisdom and a love which can draw the greatest good out of the greatest evil. The fact remains that man needs to recognize something of this mysterious guidance and enter into active cooperation with it. But such recognition and cooperation cannot really exist without the sense of symbolism. This sense is now to a great extent corrupted and degenerate. Man cannot help making symbols of one sort or another; he is a being of symbols. But at present his symbols are not the product of spiritual creativity and vitality; they are the symptoms of a violent illness, a technological cancer, from which he may not recover.

Meanwhile, the final answer does not remain entirely and exclusively in the hands of those who are still equipped to interpret ancient religious traditions. Nor is it in the hands of the scientist and technician. The artist and the poet seem to be the ones most aware of the disastrous situation, but they are for that very reason the closest to despair. If man is to recover his sanity and spiritual balance, there must be a renewal of communion between the traditional, contemplative disciplines and those of science, between the poet and the physicist, the priest and the depth psychologist, the monk and the politician.

Certainly the mere rejection of modern technology as an absolute and irremediable evil will not solve any problems. The harm done by technology is attributable more to its excessive and inordinately hasty development than to technology itself. It is possible that in the future a technological society *might* conceivably be a tranquil and contemplative one. In any case, it will do no good for us to remain specialists, enclosed in our respective fields, viewing with suspicion and disdain the efforts of others to make sense out of our world. We must try, together, to bring about a renewal of wisdom that must be more than a return to the past, however glorious. We need a wisdom appropriate to our own predicament; and such wisdom cannot help but begin in sorrow.

But one thing is certain: if the contemplative, the monk, the priest, and the poet merely forsake their vestiges of wisdom and join in the triumphant, empty-headed crowing of advertising men and engineers of opinion, then there is nothing left in store for us but total madness.

20

The Other Side of Despair:
Notes on Christian Existentialism

On June 27, 1965, Merton wrote in his journal, "The *Critic* has asked for an article on Existentialism and I think I will do it" (*Dancing in the Water of Life*, 261); two months later, on August 27, he noted, "Finished first draft of the existentialism article for the *Critic*—thank God I have that one out of the way" (*Dancing in the Water of Life*, 276). The article in question was "The Other Side of Despair," which appeared soon afterward in the Catholic monthly *The Critic* 24 (October-November 1965), 12-23, and was included in *Mystics and Zen Masters* (255-80). In his March 1968 letter to June Yungblut, Merton includes this "existentialism piece" as "central, I think"—though almost as an afterthought to the list he was providing (*Hidden Ground of Love*, 642). While he never explains the meaning of the title, it seems to refer to his conviction that unlike the atheist existentialism that had attracted such attention a decade earlier but had now largely run its course, the Christian existentialist stance that he considers to be of perennial value and with which he identifies himself leads not to but through despair to a spiritually grounded hope that does not avoid but confronts and transcends "dread" (a term borrowed from Kierkegaard that will feature prominently in *The Climate of Monastic Prayer*). Merton's attraction to existentialism, not as a movement, still less as a "system," but as a way of thought and a way of life, is due to its focus on the concrete and the personal dimensions of existence, an undermining of abstractions and mystifications that he considers to be a recovery of a fundamentally biblical perspective and that he discovers in the dark comedy of Flannery O'Connor and in the call to conversion and community articulated by the Second Vatican Council, coming to a close at the very time the essay appeared. The existentialist attack on alienation and on the mass society that institutionalizes such alienation reinforces Merton's own distinction between false and true self and his call for a prophetic religious commitment that defends and promotes the human dignity of every person. In its rejection of a static and overly theoretical and intellectualized worldview in favor of the dynamism of immediate experience, Merton likens existentialism to Zen and to apophatic Christian mysticism, incapable of being reduced to verbal formulas and reductive labels because it is "hidden in life itself."

∞

TEN YEARS AGO, conservative writers were already engaged in a definitive summing up of the "existentialist revolt." What had begun, they said, in the eccentric religiosity of Kierkegaard had ended in the open rebellion of Sartre against all that was decent and sane; and now it had even penetrated Catholic thought with the contagion of situation ethics. But the Church was on the watch, the warning had been sounded. Indeed, the encyclical *Humani Generis* may have been the reason why Gabriel Marcel repudiated the title "existentialist." After a short and competent mopping-up operation in the theological reviews, another victory would be enshrined in the revised editions of the theological manuals, and all would continue in good order. And there can be no question that the existentialism of the forties and fifties was dangerous to Catholicism in many ways. Atheistic existentialism still is!

Outside the Church, even the existentialist philosophers were tending to close up accounts. In 1949, F. H. Heinemann was already asking, "What is alive and what is dead in existentialism?" He was concluding, not without some justification, that existentialism regarded *as a philosophical system* is a contradiction in terms, and was therefore dead even before it tried to live. He added that what was alive in existentialism was the metaphysical problem it raised. However, in asking a somewhat tedious question Heinemann gave us further reason to complain, as Mounier had done, that "a philosophy whose purpose is to drag us away from our idle gossiping" itself tends to degenerate into gossip.

The question Heinemann asked was: "Are the existentialists the spiritual leaders of our time?" This is resolved into another question: "Are they leading us out of our crisis or into a blind alley?" The answers were respectively no and yes. Sartre, the most influential of the existentialists, is for Heinemann at best a pseudo-leader. On the other hand, he does not concern himself with Camus, who, he says, is "not an existentialist." But by 1965 Camus was exercising a very positive influence in America, especially on those concerned with civil rights and avant-garde political positions. And his influence was certainly as "existentialist" as Kierkegaard's, for instance.

However, since these questions belong to the realm of journalism and of academic gossip, I do not intend to get sidetracked into a discussion of them. The fact that existentialism is *less discussed* today than it was in 1950 or 1955 does not mean that it has ceased to be active. However, its activities, I would say, can be soberly estimated today as far less nefarious and perhaps a great deal more useful than they were then thought to be. We can now safely admit the existence of a Christian existentialism active not only in philosophy but also in the renewed Biblical theology which has been so eloquent and so salutary in the years of Vatican II.

If, in talking about existentialism, we distinguish between the "movement," the gossip about the movement, and the cogent reality of existentialist thinking, we can perhaps say that both the movement and the gossip about it are a great deal less actual now than they were ten, fifteen, or twenty years ago.

The "existentialist movement" ("revolt") is associated in the popular mind with the French literary existentialists, especially the austere and ironic genius of Camus, lost to us in death, and the bitter Sartre of World War II, also to a great extent lost, or transformed, in his own current brand of Marxism. It is true that, in canonizing Genet, Sartre has shown an undiminished aspiration to meet the popular need for existentialism to be scandalous, and, in refusing the Nobel Prize, he has improvised a hasty defense against being identified, himself, with the French literary establishment.

Is Sartre perhaps caught in his own vicious circle? He is probably right in saying that society *needs* people like Genet to be what they are. But is he right in assuming that the free acceptance of this evil lot, and the total commitment to evil as an act of revenge, is the way to authenticity and liberation? Is it not the logical fulfillment of society's perverse demand that the criminal be totally evil? Is it not then a final capitulation? Sartre should have accepted the reward which our confused and distraught society offered him! He earned it, in his own way.

The existentialism which is most active and of most vital interest to the Church today is neither as well publicized nor as thoroughly discussed as the literature of those earlier days: it is the existentialist theology, both Protestant and Catholic, which owes so much to Heidegger.

We must at once admit that the loaded word "existentialist" must here be used with great circumspection. It is still a term of opprobrium among Catholics, and people are still in the habit of blaming everything they fear or dislike upon it. To suggest that Karl Rahner, for instance, might be tinged with "existentialism" (he is to some extent a disciple of Heidegger) would in some circles be quite enough to damn him, but it would hardly be enough to convict him of being nothing more than a Catholic Sartre. That is the trouble with gossip. Since for various good reasons existentialism is still regarded as "dangerous," and since the function of gossip is, among other things, to permit people to enjoy danger vicariously, at no greater risk than that of being misled, we shall try in this article neither to excite nor to mislead.

Existentialism is still in the air. It influences the climate of theology, and before we dismiss it as completely pestilential, let us at least try to find out what it is.

Of course this is both difficult and deceptive. Existentialism is an experience and an attitude, rather than a system of thought. As soon as it begins to present itself as a system, it denies and destroys itself. Non-objective, elusive, concrete, dynamic, always in movement and always seeking to renew itself in the newness of the present situation, genuine existentialism is, like Zen Buddhism and like apophatic Christian mysticism, hidden in life itself. It cannot be distilled out in verbal formulas. Above all, the journalistic clichés about existentialist nihilism, pessimism, anarchism, and so on, are totally irrelevant, even though they may have some foundation in certain existentialist writings. It is my contention that these writings cannot fairly be taken as representative of genuine existentialism.

RATHER THAN ATTEMPT STILL another abstract and technical definition of something which, in itself, is neither abstract nor technical, let us begin with a concrete example. Existentialism has expressed itself most unambiguously in literature, where it is free from technicalities and quasi-official formulas. Literature offers us an example quite close to home, in the novels and short stories of Flannery O'Connor. I can think of no American writer who has made a more devastating use of existential intuition. She does so, of course, without declamation, without program, without distributing manifestoes, and without leading a parade. Current existentialism is, in fact, neither partisan nor programmatic. It is content with the austere task of minding its own literary, philosophical, or theological business.

A casual consideration of the "good" and the "bad" people in Flannery O'Connor will help us to appreciate the existentialist point of view—that point of view which is so easily obscured when it presents itself in terms of a program. For example, in her story "A Good Man Is Hard to Find," evil is not so much in the gangsters, so fatally and so easily "found," as in the garrulous, empty-headed, folksy, sentimental old fool of a grandmother. Not that she is deliberately wicked, but the fact is, she does get everybody killed. It is her absurd and arbitrary fantasy that leads them directly to the "good man" and five deaths. She is a kind of blank, a void through which there speaks and acts the peculiar nemesis that inhabits (or haunts) the world of Flannery O'Connor—and doubtless ours too, if we could but see it as she did. This frightening action of Sophoclean nemesis in and through the right-thinking man who is null and void is spelled out in its full and public identity in types like Rayber, the positivist schoolteacher in *The Violent Bear It Away.*

The first thing that anyone notices in reading Flannery O'Connor is that her moral evaluations seem to be strangely scrambled. The good people are bad and the bad people tend to be less bad than they seem. This is not in itself unusual. But her crazy people, while remaining as crazy as they can possibly be, turn out to be governed by a strange kind of sanity. In the end, it is the sane ones who are incurable lunatics. The "good," the "right," the "kind" do all the harm. "Love" is a force for destruction, and "truth" is the best way to tell a lie.

Rayber is, by all standards, the kind of person our society accepts as normal, not only a sane man but a kind one. A teacher, a man with forward-looking and optimistic perspectives, illuminated and blessed with a scientific worldview, he is acquainted with all the best methods for helping people to become happy and well adjusted in the best of all possible societies.

It is he who sees through nonsense, prejudice, and myth. It is he who gets the Bible student to sleep with the frustrated girl from the woods, to relieve her tensions and open her up to a more joyous and fulfilled mode of life. It is he who, when their child is born, wants to protect him against the fanatic uncle, the prophet and believer. It is he who suffers permanent damage (deafness) trying to liberate the boy from the awful trammels of obscurantism and superstition. Rayber is our kind of man, is he not? A sound and practical positivist, well adjusted in a scientific age. True, he is not a Catholic, but we have plenty of Catholics who think more or less as he does, and he could perhaps be persuaded that we too are reasonable.

Yet as we read Flannery O'Connor we find an uncomfortable feeling creeping over us: we are on the side of the fanatic and the mad boy, and we are against this reasonable zombie. We are against everything he stands for. We find ourselves nauseated by the reasonable, objective, "scientific" answers he has for everything. In him, science is so right that it is a disaster.

Such is the dire effect of reading an existentialist.

Rayber wants to help the wild boy to find himself, to forget the madness he learned from the prophet, to become a docile and useful citizen in a world of opportunity where he can at last have everything. Rayber will not count the cost in sacrifice that must be paid. "Now I can make up for all the time we've lost. I can help correct what he's done to you, help you to correct it yourself... This is our problem together."

It was perhaps not kind of the boy, Tarwater, to be so suspicious of the world of reason, psychiatry, and togetherness, or to look with such an ugly glint upon the teacher's hearing aid. ("What you wired for?" he drawled. "Does your head light up?")

Alas, we share his cruel satisfaction. We have come to agree that the positivist Mephistopheles from Teachers College is a pure void, a mouthpiece for demons.

> "I forget what color eyes he's got," the old man would say, irked. "What difference does the color make when I know the look? I know what's behind it."

"What's behind it?"

"Nothing. He's full of nothing."

"He knows a heap," the boy said. "I don't reckon it's anything he don't know."

"He don't know it's anything he can't know," the old man said. "That's his trouble. He thinks if it's something he can't know then somebody smarter than him can tell him about it and he can know it just the same. And if you were to go there, the first thing he would do would be to test your head and tell you what you were thinking and how come you were thinking it and what you ought to be thinking instead. And before long you wouldn't belong to yourself no more, you would belong to him."

This, in brief, is the existentialist case against the scientism and sociologism of positivist society. It is a brief for the person and for personal, spiritual liberty against determinism and curtailment.

The old man was doing Rayber no injustice. This is precisely what his *hubris* consists in: the conviction that the infinite rightness and leveling power of "scientific method" has given him a mandate to transform other people into his own image: which is the image of nothing. And though he is "nothing," yet others, he knows it well, must do things his way since he has science on his side.

If, for Flannery O'Connor, the mild, agnostic, and objective teacher is not so much evil as pure void, and if this is what it means to be a villain—this will to reduce everyone else by an infallible process to the same void as oneself—we begin to understand existentialism in its passionate resistance against the positivist outlook. We also begin to see why, after all, existentialism is no immediate danger in a society almost entirely inclined to the consolations of sociometric methods.

Existentialism offers neither attractions nor peril to people who are perfectly convinced that they are headed in the right direction, that they possess the means to attain a reasonably perfect happiness, that they have a divine mandate to remove anyone who seems inclined to interfere with this aim. Existentialism calls into question the validity, indeed the very possibility, of such an aim. But, for positivism, its rightness is never in question. Nor, indeed, is its nature. The positivist does not even need to be quite sure where he is going. The direction must be the right one, since it is determined by his processes and by his scientific method. For him, the only question that really matters is *how* to keep on moving faster and faster in the same direction. Philosophy reduces itself to knowing how: *know-how*. The question *what* is relatively insignificant. As long as one knows *how*, the *what* will take care of itself. You just initiate the process, and keep it going. The *what* follows. In fact, the *how* tends more and more to determine the *what*.

The question *who* also turns out to be irrelevant except insofar as it is reducible to a *how*. That is to say that what matters is not the person so much as the position he occupies, the influence he wields, the money he makes, and his general usefulness in getting things done, or at least his place in the machinery of society. Thus, a man is identified not by his character but by his function or by his income, not by what he is but by what he has. If he has nothing, he does not count, and what is done to him or with him ceases to be a matter of ethical concern.

Pragmatism and positivism are therefore interested in the question *how*. Traditional metaphysics, whether scholastic (realist) or idealist, is interested in the question *what* (the essence). Existentialism wants to know *who*. It is interested in the authentic use of freedom by the concrete personal subject.

The objective truth of science remains only half the truth—or even less than that—if the subjective truth, the true-being (*Wahrsein*), of the subject is left out of account. This true-being is not found by examining the subject as if it were another object. It is found in personal self-realization, that is to say, in freedom, in responsibility, in dialogue (with man and God), and in love. Existentialism is, in other words, concerned with authentic personal identity, and concerned with it in a way that behaviorist methods and psychometry can never be. (The tests are neither interested in nor capable of finding out *who* thinks, only with describing *how* he reacts.) The chief complaint that sets existentialism over against positivism in diametric opposition is this: the claim of science and technology to expand the capacity of the human person for life and happiness is basically fraudulent, because technological society is not the least interested in values, still less in persons: it is concerned purely and simply with the functioning of its own processes. Human beings are used merely as means to this end, and the one significant question it asks in their regard is not *who* they are but *how* they can be most efficiently used.

At this point, we might go back a hundred years to consider a prophetic page of Kierkegaard's, from *The Present Age*. Here he describes the process of "leveling" and of "reflection," related to what has come to be called "alienation" and "estrangement" in more recent existential thought.

The process which Kierkegaard calls "leveling" is that by which the individual person loses himself in the vast emptiness of a public mind. Because he identifies this abstraction with objective reality, or simply with "the truth," he abdicates his own experience and intuition. He renounces conscience and is lost. But the public mind is a pure abstraction, a nonentity. "For," says Kierkegaard, "the public is made up of individuals at the moments when they are nothing," that is to say, when they have abdicated conscience, personal decision, choice, and responsibility, and yielded themselves to the joy of being part of a pure myth. The mythical being which thinks and acts for everybody, and does the most shameful of deeds without a moment of hesitation or of shame, is actually no being at all. Those who take part in its acts can do so insofar as they have abstracted themselves from themselves and have surrendered to the public void, which they believe to be fully and objectively real: this collective self whose will is the will of nobody, whose mind is the mind of nobody, which can contradict itself and remain consistent with itself. "More and more individuals, owing to their bloodless indolence, will aspire to be nothing at all—in order to become the public." Therefore, Kierkegaard concludes, the public is an "abstract whole formed in the most ludicrous way by all the participants becoming a third party (an onlooker)." This process of leveling, of self-abandonment, of abdication of identity, in order to dare what nobody dares and to participate in the unthinkable as though one were an innocent bystander, sweeps through the world as a "hopeless forest fire of abstraction." "The individual no longer belongs to God, to himself, to his beloved, to his art or his science; he is conscious of belonging in all things to an abstraction to which he is subjected by reflection (estrangement) just as a serf belongs to an estate. . . . The abstract leveling process, that self-combustion of the human race produced by the friction which arises when the individual ceases to exist as singled out by religion, is bound to continue like a trade wind until it consumes everything."

The existentialist is aware of this danger above all. He tirelessly insists that it is the great danger of our time, since it is completely prevalent both in the capitalist positivism of America and in the Marxist positivism of the Communist countries. For this reason, the existentialist is condemned everywhere for a wide variety of reasons which usually boil down to this one: he is a rebel, an individualist, who, because he withdraws from the common endeavor of technological society to brood on his own dissatisfactions, condemns himself to futility, sterility, and despair. Since he refuses to participate in the glorious and affluent togetherness of mass society, he must pay the price of fruitless isolation. He is a masochist. He gets no better than he deserves.

Of course, this criticism implies considerable overemphasis on one particular kind of existentialism—that of Sartre, for instance—which lends itself to facile caricature as lawless, negative, profligate, and generally beat. The moral conclusion drawn from this by the mass media, for example, is that nonconformity is, today more than ever, fatal. Not to submit to "leveling" is to become a weirdie. Only the public is fully human. The private sphere can no longer be human except at the price of admitting the abstract and the general into its own intimacy.

To prove your docility, you have to be totally invaded by the public image and the public voice. If you do this, however, you will be repaid by a certain negative privacy: you will not be forced into a disturbing *personal* confrontation with other human beings. You will meet them as strangers and as objects that make no direct demand for love—or, if they do, the demand is easily evaded. So you play it safe by never turning off the TV, and never, under any circumstances, entertaining a thought, a desire, or a decision that is authentically your own. It is in the general void, the universal noise, that you remain alone.

All the existentialists have protested against this state of affairs. To cite two typical works: Karl Jaspers's *Man in the Modern World* and Gabriel Marcel's *Man Against Mass Society*. Authentic "existence" (in defense of which one becomes an "existentialist") is contrasted with the bare inert *Dasein*, the "being there" of the lumplike object which is alienated man in the mass, man in the neuter, *das Mann*. *Dasein* is the passive, motiveless mode of being of the individual who simply finds himself thrown arbitrarily, by inscrutable fate, into a world of objects. He is a die in a crap game. He neither accepts nor rejects himself, he is incapable of authentically willing to be what he is, he submits to the process. It is the only reality he knows. He is intent on one thing above all: the mental and social gymnastics by which he remains at the same time a participant and a spectator, public and private, passively involved and emotionally distant in the amorphous public mass in which we are spectators and yet all somehow inexorably perform the enormities which the public "does." All see, all participate as though vicariously in the collective excitement (sometimes even the collective ecstasy) without really "being there" except as things, as fragments of the scene. All are aware, all consent, but consent safely because they are neutral. That is to say, they consent passively, they do not choose, they do not decide. They accept what has been decided by the public, that is, by nobody.

From the moment one elects to exist truly and freely, all this comes to an end. Decision begins with the acceptance of one's own finiteness, one's own limitations, in fact, one's own nothingness; but when one's own nothingness is seen as a matter of personal choice, of free acceptance, and not as part of the vast, formless void of the anonymous mass, it acquires a name, a presence, a voice, an option in the actions of the real world—not the abstract world of the public but the concrete world of living men.

Here we come upon a point that requires immediate clarification. Existentialism is not a withdrawal into unworldliness. It is not "monastic." Quite the contrary, it is a frankly worldly philosophy in the sense that it conceives no other realistic option than that of being a live man in the world of men. But the authentic world of men is, precisely, not the fictitious and arbitrary collective illusion of "the public."

The real contest between existentialism and its opponents is precisely about this: existentialism always claims in one way or another that the accepted, conventional forms of thought and life have in fact attempted to substitute a fraudulent world of unauthentic and illusory relationships for the real community of man with man. This, they would say, is obvious. A system which demands the abdication of personality by that very fact destroys all possibility of community. What we have then is a conflict between two concepts of community: on one hand, a false and arbitrary fiction, collectivist togetherness, in which all possibility of authentic personal existence is surrendered and one remains content with one's neutral quasi-objectified presence in the public mass; on the other, a genuine community of persons who have first of all accepted their own fragile lot, who have chosen to exist contingently, and thereby have accepted the solitude of the person who must think and decide for himself without the warm support of collective fictions. Only between such free persons is true communication possible. At the same time, such communication is absolutely necessary if there are to be free and mature persons, authentically existing, with faces, identities, and histories of their own. The authentic person is not born in stoic isolation but in the openness and dialogue of love.

The clue to this concept of community is found in the word *openness*. The world of *Dasein* is a world where all possibilities are closed to the individual who has *a priori* renounced his choice. As individual he is indifferent: he has surrendered his options, his capacity to determine the future by turning to this possibility or that. He has submitted to the abstract leveling force of "the public," "the party," "science," "business," or what you will. In this case, instead of open communication between personal freedoms, we have the submersion of atomized individuals in a general mass. We have a comforting routine of merely mechanical responses.

True openness means the acceptance of one's own existence and one's own possibilities in confrontation with, and in free, vital relation with, the existence and potentialities of the other. It means genuine acceptance, response, participation. It is here that the famous "I-Thou" of the Jewish existentialist Martin Buber has contributed so much to Christian personalism in our day. The world of *Dasein* and of objects is defined only by the "I-it" relationship. The "I" who regards itself as a purely isolated subject surrounded by objects also inevitably regards itself implicitly as an object. In a world where no one else, no "other," is willingly identified, the "I" also loses its own identity. In practice, the collective life of mass society is a mere aggregate of spurious and fictitious identities. On the one hand, we see the leaders or heroes who sum up in themselves the collective nonentity of the mass and become, so to speak, icons of the public void (see Max Picard's book *Hitler in Ourselves*); on the other, the alienated individuals who fabricate for themselves crude identities by contemplating themselves in the typological hero. Note that the word "alienation" is used by non-existentialists to support the fictions of collective life. For them, the "alienated" man is the one who is not at peace in the general myth. He is the nonconformist: the oddball who does not agree with everybody else and who disturbs the pleasant sense of collective rightness. For the existentialist, the alienated man is one who, though "adjusted" to society, is alienated *from himself.* The inner life of the mass man, alienated and leveled in the existential sense, is a dull, collective routine of popular fantasies maintained in existence by the collective dream that goes on, without interruption, in the mass media.

The freedom by which one delivers oneself from the tyranny of the void is the freedom to choose oneself without being determined beforehand by the public, either in its typological fantasies or in its sociological pressures. What then is the basis of this choice? In what sense can it be called unconditional? In the sense that it is made in and proceeds from the inviolate sanctuary of the personal conscience.

It is precisely here that atheistic existentialism proves itself to be so unsatisfactory and so inconsistent. According to Jaspers, Marcel, and all the other basically religious existentialists, conscience is incomprehensible except as the voice of a transcendent Ground of being and freedom—in other words, of God Himself. Hence, the basic choice by which one elects to have one's own personal, autonomous existence is a choice *of oneself as a freedom that has been gratuitously given by God.* It is acceptance of one's existence and one's freedom as pure gift.

In religious existentialism the blank, godless nothingness of freedom and of the person, Sartre's *néant*, becomes the luminous abyss of divine gift. The self is "void" indeed, but void in the sense of the apophatic mystics like St. John of the Cross, in whom the *nada*, or nothingness of the self that is entirely empty of fictitious images, projects, and desires, becomes the *todo*, the All, in which the freedom of personal love discovers itself in its transcendent Ground and Source which we are accustomed to call the Love of God and which no human name can ever account for or explain.

When this becomes clear, we immediately see why even nonreligious existentialism is unconsciously oriented toward a religious view of life (if the word "religious" is qualified, as we shall soon see). For this reason also it can be said both that the religious existentialists probably outnumber the atheists and that even those who make no religious claims are, like Heidegger, spontaneously oriented to a religious view of man's destiny.

Taking a broad, random view of the field of existentialism, we see on the one hand Camus and Sartre, both of whom explicitly class themselves as atheists. We have Heidegger, who is nonreligious. On the other hand, we have Jaspers, whose thought is basically theistic and even Christian; we have the Jewish existentialism of Buber, the Orthodox and gnostic existentialism of Berdyaev, the Buddhist existentialism of Suzuki and Nishida, the Protestant existentialism of Bultmann, Tillich, and others, the Catholic existentialism of Gabriel Marcel and Louis Lavelle. It is true of course that both Marcel and Lavelle, and some others we have named here, have renounced the existentialist label. The fact remains that the most significant religious thought of our day, whether in philosophy or in theology, has been marked by "existentialist" insights into man's current situation. We remember also that Maritain and Gilson, while remaining faithful to St. Thomas and criticizing existentialism from a Thomist viewpoint, have themselves contributed in no small measure to a broadly existentialist Christian perspective (see Maritain's *Existence and the Existent*).

Here we must repeat that the popular connotations of the term are altogether misleading, and we must be quite clear that what we must understand by this is not some supposed infiltration into Catholic thought of negativism, disillusionment, and moral license. Christian existentialism is, on the contrary, associated with the return to a Biblical mode of thought which is entirely concrete and personal and, in fact, much more fundamentally Christian than the rather abstract and intellectualist approach that has been accepted as the "only" Catholic approach for almost seven hundred years.

Let us then consider the basic elements of the new existential theology in its implications for human freedom.

YEARS AGO, KARL ADAM, whom no one would think of calling an existentialist, protested against the routine Catholic notion of faith as an intellectual assent to dogmatic propositions, nothing more. Faith, he said, could never be reduced to "a purely intellectual and therefore shallow awareness of the teaching of the Church, and to a mere assent of the mind." Then he added this, which strikes the exact tone of the new Catholic theology and, we may add, the renewed perspective of faith as seen in the light of the Second Vatican Council.

Every "Credo," if said in the spirit of the Church, ought to be an act of complete dedication of the entire man to God, an assent springing from the great and ineffable distress of our finite nature and our sin.

Here we already see formulated the awareness which has been made completely explicit by Vatican II. We see the difference between two concepts of faith and of the Church. On one hand, there is the idea that the Church is primarily an official and authoritative public organization and the act of faith is the intellectual acceptance by the individual of what this organization publicly and officially teaches. Thus, the act of faith becomes a profession of orthodoxy and of regularity, a protestation of conformity (backed no doubt by sincere good will) in order to merit, so to speak, a religious security clearance. One's act of faith is then a declaration that one is a reliable member of the organization, willing to abide by everything that is publicly held by it, and to attack everything that opposes it. Such dogmatic professions of faith are of course necessary and right in certain circumstances. They have their proper place. But, as Karl Adam says, they do not exhaust the possibilities of true Christian faith.

To begin with, they do not take sufficient account of man's "existential situation." It is here that insights such as those of Jaspers and Heidegger can serve the theologian.

One can certainly subscribe in all sincerity to correct dogmatic formulas without the intimate spiritual ground of one's own existence being called into question. One can formally acknowledge that one is created and redeemed by God without showing any deep sense of being personally involved in a religious relationship with Him. Indeed, and this is always tragic both for the individual and for the Church, the mere formal acknowledgment of these truths can come to substitute in practice for any kind of intimate and personal surrender to God. Religion thus becomes a matter of formalities and gestures. "This people honors me with its lips and not with its heart."

In this case, we find ourselves confronted with the kind of Christianity which Kierkegaard attacked precisely because it transferred into the religious sphere all the facticity, the routine, and the falsity of "abstract leveling." Instead of obeying the Word and Spirit of God living and active in His Church, the body of those who love one another precisely insofar as they have been freed from facticity and routine, one surrenders at the same time one's human and one's religious integrity. In effect, this is a spiritual disaster if we consider that the Church should be the one hope of alienated man recovering himself and his freedom. The Bible shows us, without equivocation, that human society itself is "fallen" and alienated. It estranges man from himself and enslaves him to delusion. The word of God calls man back out of this delusion to his true self. The Church has, as her first function of all, to disturb man and unsettle him in the world of facticity by challenging him to return to himself. *Metanoiete*, repent, change your heart, is the inexhaustibly repeated message of God's word to man in fallen society. He who hears this word cannot rest content with the "leveling" routine of mass society. Unfortunately, we see that, in fact, mass society is more and more curtailing the area of good ground on which the seed of the Gospel can germinate. At best, the soul of mass-man is a plot of thorns. Most of the time he is simply a wayside trampled by a restless and unmotivated multitude.

It is here that the Church, in her anxiety to enter into a dialogue with the modern world, must not hastily and unawares overlook the problem of evil and evade the challenge of atheist existentialism. If in trying to reply to the Marxists we take an exclusively optimistic view of man, of the world of science and progress, and of man's chances of solving all his problems here on earth, we find ourselves accused, by the existentialists, of consenting to certain mystifications that ignore the evils which actually confront man and the despair which meets him at every turn. Seeing this danger, one of the best modern Russian theologians, Father P. Evdokimov, of the Russian Orthodox Seminary in Paris, has written:

We must pay close attention to the existentialist questionings, which have considerable philosophical strength. They overturn the naïvely joyous optimism of a religious philosophy in which evil serves as a good and hence ceases to exist as evil—a fact which makes the death of God on a Cross incomprehensible. It is precisely Sartre's claim that "God" diminishes the radical character of evil, of unhappiness, and of guilt.

The important thing, therefore, is not for Christians to be found ready, once again, with a glib religious answer for another modern question, but for us to reaffirm, in terms at once contemporary and deeply serious, the Christian message to man's liberty. We must reemphasize the call of the Gospel to healing and to hope, not merely reaffirm that everything is going to be all right because man is smart and will meet the challenge of evil with the best possible solutions.

IT IS AT THIS point that the current concept of "religion" must be seriously examined and qualified.

If in practice the function of organized religion turns out to be nothing more than to justify and to canonize the routines of mass society; if organized religion abdicates its mission to disturb man in the depths of his conscience, and seeks instead simply to "make converts" that will smilingly adjust to the status quo, then it deserves the most serious and uncompromising criticism. Such criticism is not a disloyalty. On the contrary, fidelity to truth and to God demands it. One of the most important aspects of our current biblical-existentialist theology is precisely the prophetic consciousness of a duty to question the claims of any religious practice that collaborates with the "process of leveling" and alienation.

This means that such theology will manifest a definite social concern and will, in the light of the Bible, identify and reject anything that compromises the standards of justice and mercy demanded by the word of God. It will identify these precisely by the measure of authentic respect and love for the human person. Thus, for instance, any claim that this or that policy or strategy deserves a "Christian" sanction and the blessing of the Church must be examined in the light of the principles we have seen. If in actual fact it amounts to the support of the abstract organization, granting or blessing a destructive power to coerce the individual conscience, it is to be rejected as fraudulent, as incompatible with Christian truth, and as disobedience to the Gospel commandment of love. In one word, the Church must not implicitly betray man into the power of the irresponsible and anonymous "public." If it does so, it will destroy itself in destroying true freedom and authentic human community.

We must certainly recognize the danger of individualism, but we must also be fully aware of where this danger really lies.

The false community of mass society is in fact *more individualistic* than the personalist community envisaged by the Gospels, the *koinonia* of intersubjective love among persons, which is the Church. Mass society is individualistic in the sense that it isolates each individual subject from his immediate neighbor, reducing him to a state of impersonal, purely formal, and abstract relationship with other objectified individuals. In dissolving the more intimate and personal bonds of life in the family and of the small sub-group (the farm, the shop of the artisan, the village, the town, the small business), mass society segregates the individual from the concrete and human "other" and leaves him alone and unaided in the presence of the Faceless, the collective void, the public. Thus, as was said above, mass-man finds himself related not to flesh-and-blood human beings with the same freedom, responsibility, and conflicts as himself, but with idealized typological images: the Führer, the president, the sports star, the teen singer, the space man.

It is by rigorously confining him within the limits of his own individual nonentity that mass society completely integrates the individual into the mass. The function of the Church is, then, not to intensify this process, giving it an inviolable religious sanction and tranquilizing the anguish of the alienated mind by injunctions to obey the state. It is precisely to strengthen the individual person against the one great temptation to surrender, to abdicate his personality, to fall and disappear in the void. "Man," says Heidegger, "wants to surrender to the world. He tempts himself. He flees from himself and desires to fall into the world. In his everyday talking and curiosity he prepares for himself a permanent temptation to fallenness." There is in this of course an inescapable element of existentialist jargon, but in substance it recalls the eschatological message of the New Testament.

IF IN FACT THE Church does nothing to counter this "temptation to fallenness" except call man to subscribe to a few intellectual formulas and then go his way with the rest of the crowd, she will have failed in her gravest responsibility. If, on the other hand, she misunderstands the seriousness of modern theology and lets herself be carried away with a specious enthusiasm for a space-age image of herself, she will equally fail.

While it is popularly supposed that "existentialism" has no other function than to allow man to do as he pleases, leaving him at the mercy of subjective fantasy and passion, removing him from the protective surveillance of social authority, we see that in fact the shoe is on the other foot. If existential theology is properly understood, we see that it unmasks the spurious social responsibility by means of which man flees from his true self and takes cover in the neutral, fallen world of alienation. The true rebellion against God today is not merely that of the defiant and promethean individual, but much rather that of the massive and abstract collectivity in which man in the neuter, *das Mann*, man in the anonymous mass, becomes serenely convinced of his inviolable security as master of his own destiny and of his world. In finding her place in the modern world, the Church must take care not to embrace or even canonize the *hubris* of technological society.

Where some forms of existentialism fail is in their inability to get beyond the individual's discovery and affirmation of himself standing outside of and apart from the neutral mass, and obliged to defend himself with all his power against exploitation or invasion by others. This is particularly true in the early Sartre, for whom "*L'enfer c'est les autres.*" Neither his doctrinaire political positions nor his "cool" relationship with Simone de Beauvoir can do anything to modify this judgment of Sartrian existentialism as closed to dialogue and genuine communion.

With Camus the problem is much more subtle and profound. One feels that few men in our time, Christian or not, were at once more soberly aware of the limitation of man in mass society and more open, in compassion and understanding, to his plight. *The Plague* is a novel of crisis and alienation in which a few men manage to prove themselves authentic persons by openness and availability in a mass of thoughtless, stupefied human beings. Here, incidentally, the Church is examined and found somewhat wanting in the person of a Jesuit priest who, in spite of a certain degree of heroism and self-sacrifice, remains insulated from human realities and from other men by the "official answers" with which he has already solved all problems in advance.

An existential theology is not one that claims to know all the answers in advance. It is concerned not with answers or with statements ("what," "how"), but with man's authentic existence (*who*). This depends on his capacity for dialogue with his fellow man, his ability to respond to the need of another, to waive his own anterior rights and claims in order to meet the other on a common ground. In a word, it depends on freedom and on love. Hence, it is by no means concerned (as Sartre appears to be) merely with the cool assertion of one's privacy. However, in existential *theology*, more is at stake than openness to others. Man cannot be genuinely open to others unless he first admits his capacity to hear and obey the word of God, to bear and to understand the inevitable anxiety of an estrangement from God and from his own inner truth. Since this call to authenticity is heard in the depths of the conscience, existential theology emphasizes the formation of conscience. It seeks at all costs to defend the personal conscience against distortion by the all-pervading influence of collective illusion. It is all too easy for conscience to be twisted out of shape by merely attending to the claims of worldly care. The care of one's own privacy and one's own liberty can be included as "worldly."

Existential theology focuses on grace and on love, rather than on nature and on law. It tends to view grace less as a supernatural quality modifying our human nature than as an event, an eschatological encounter with God, who, by His word, restores to us the capacity for authentic personal freedom, and the power to love in a "new creation." Far from being a further development in liberal and rationalistic dilution of the Gospel message, existential theology, because of its Biblical content, strongly emphasizes the obedience of faith, the surrender of the free person to Christ. Far from being a justification of disobedience, existential theology insists that it is only in the obedience of faith that we truly discover our authentic existence, our true selves. Though Heidegger is never explicitly Christian, this element of openness to grace, this capacity for obedience, is implicit in his philosophy, of which John Macquarrie has said: "Although Heidegger does not acknowledge it, his understanding of man brings us to the place where either the divine grace must intervene or all thought of an authentic existence must be given up entirely."

Existential theology is concerned with man in his world and in his time. The word of God, the dialogue of man and God, is not confined to a meditation on the Bible written two thousand years ago. In the light of Biblical revelation, the Christian feels himself challenged, summoned, addressed by God here and now in the events of our own confused and sometimes alarming history. But the Christian existentialist knows precisely that he cannot evade the present and fly from it into a safe and static past, preserved for him in a realm of ideal essences, to which he can withdraw in silent recollection. His recollection will be of no use to him if it merely serves him as a pretext for not being open to his brother here and now. The existential insistence on grace as event, as an ever renewed encounter with God and one's fellow man *now*, in present reality, in dynamic acceptance and availability, disturbs the idealistic and static outlook which treats grace as a "thing," a "commodity," to which one gains access by virtue of a spiritual secret, a ritual formula, or a technique of meditation.

Whatever one may say about it, Christian existentialism is not gnostic. It does not regard grace as a "supply" of light and fuel for the spiritual mansion in which one dwells in complacent isolation. It sees grace as an eschatological encounter and response, an opening of the heart to God, a reply of the Spirit within us to God our Father (Romans 8:15-16), in obedience of faith, in humility and openness to all men. Grace is sonship and dialogue, from which obstacles and limitations, whether of law, of nature, of sin, of selfishness, of fear, and even of death, have all been taken away by the death and resurrection of Christ. Grace is perfect and total reconciliation, in Christ, with one's true self, one's neighbor, and with God.

Writing in *New Blackfriars* (July 1965), John Dalrymple (not a professed "existentialist") sums this up by saying: "The question is whether we today offer Christ to the world as a liberating person or an agent of restriction. If we are to show forth Christ as a liberating agent then we must first have entered into that liberation ourselves; we must have conquered our primal fears; we must first have prayed. This is the level at which modern theology has its greatest significance spiritually. Its insights draw us powerfully to prayer." This is important to remember because a superficial understanding of modern theology seems to end in restless activism, itself an illusion and an evasion.

Rudolf Bultmann has done much to bring out the Christian implications which he found to be latent in the existentialist philosophy of Heidegger, and Macquarrie says of him: "The whole aim of Bultmann's theology, including his views on demythologizing, is to spotlight the essential kerygma of the New Testament for men and women of our time and to bring it before them as the one relevant possibility that is still open for a bewildered world."

Hence, though the existentialism of Heidegger may seem to end up with stoic heroism in the presence of unavoidable death, Bultmann and other Christian theologians influenced by Heidegger have gone much further. They have convincingly restructured the classic theology of Christian and Gospel hope in the categories of existentialist freedom. This does not mean, however, that the revelation of God in Christ the Incarnate Word means the same to Bultmann as it does to the Catholic Church. Here we would indeed find serious divergences on the level of dogma. But, from the point of view of freedom and grace of *lived* experience, Bultmann's insights have their value for Catholics.

Far from being a negative cult of life-denying despair, existential theology challenges the sterility and the inner hopelessness, the spurious optimism and the real despair which masks itself in the secular and positivist illusion. For the fallen world there can be no genuine future: only death. But for Christian freedom there is an authentic future indeed. In fact, for the existentialists freedom would be worth nothing if it were not constituted by openness to a genuine future—a future liberated from the facticity of life in a depersonalized mass, free from the care and concern with mere "objects," free at last even from death.

At the same time, however, existential theology is recognizing that it must move further and further from the characteristic subjectivity of the early existentialism in order to achieve a genuine relatedness to and full participation in the world of nature and above all the world of man. Where the earlier existentialists regard "the other" with suspicion as a hostile force, and even tended to consider *all* communal life as a threat to individual integrity, the existential theologians look rather for a transformation of communal life by the leaven of Christian freedom and agape. This implies willingness to renounce suspiciousness, to be open to man and to his world, to freely participate in all the most cogent concerns of the world, but with a freedom of spirit which is immune to the forces of "leveling." This, it must be admitted, demands a certain maturity! But maturity cannot be acquired in withdrawal and subjective isolation, in fear and in suspicion. Maturity is the capacity for free and authentic *response*. Once again, this demands something more than psychological adjustment. It calls for divine grace. And our openness to grace is proportionate to our sense of our *need* for it. This in turn depends on our awareness of the reality of the crisis we are in.

The most serious claim to consideration which the existential theologian can offer is the cogent diagnosis of our trouble, and the complete sincerity, the total frankness with which he faces the basic Christian problems of death, sin, the wrath of God, grace, faith, freedom, and love. Where he is still admittedly weak is perhaps in his sense of Christian communion and of the Church. But let us not forget that in his sensitivity to the danger of an alienated and unfaithful Church organization, the existentialist has done us a service, and warned us against the ever present peril of institutional complacency. There is no greater danger than this for the Church in the modern world, and we are daily reminded of the fact when we see how easily the faithful, even some of the hierarchy, yield to the temptation to identify the Church with the status quo, the public establishment, and to submerge the Christian conscience in the complex and dubious cares of an existence that is inauthentic because it is sociological rather than Christian.

21

The Time of the End Is the Time of No Room

In an August 31, 1965, letter to his friend and agent Naomi Burton Stone, Merton refers to "[t]he bit for *Motive*, a magazine you don't know, I imagine, mostly Protestant, published in Nashville" (*Witness to Freedom*, 147); three days later, in a letter to James Laughlin, he identifies this "article of which Naomi has a copy" as "The Time of the End Is the Time of No Room" (Merton/Laughlin, *Selected Letters*, 266), a Christmas essay which did appear at the end of the year in *Motive* 26 (December 1965), 4-9. It was included, as Merton's two letters propose, in *Raids on the Unspeakable* (65-75), and was subsequently reprinted in *A Thomas Merton Reader* (rev. ed., 360-67). In this meditation on the meaning of the Incarnation, Christ's identity with the excluded is recognized as an eschatological sign that signals the end of the old world and the arrival of a radically different vision of justice and love, a time both "of great tribulation" and "certainly and above all the time of The Great Joy" announced by the angelic choir. It is a recognition that the good news is proclaimed not to the powerful, the comfortable, the complacent, but to those living "in silence, loneliness and darkness," the descendants of the desert-dwellers, the faithful but neglected remnant, the *anawim*. And the good news is precisely that the Lord God Himself has come to share their lot, to be born and to live and even to die as an outsider, excluded from the frenetic, aimless, demonic busyness of the faceless crowds. "Into this world, this demented inn, in which there is absolutely no room for Him at all, Christ has come uninvited. But because He cannot be at home in it, because He is out of place in it, and yet He must be in it, His place is with those others for whom there is no room." For Merton the birth of Christ is the inbreaking of a disruptive power that shatters the presumptive order of a world that no longer has room for the divine presence, a terrifying prospect for those invested in the present age and implicated in its duplicities; only for those willing to take the risk of hope, Merton concludes, is the time of the end "not the last gasp of exhausted possibilities but the first taste of all that is beyond conceiving as actual."

NOTE: *In its Biblical sense, the expression "the End" does not necessarily mean only "the violent, sudden and bad end." Biblical eschatology must not be confused with the vague and anxious eschatology of human foreboding. We live in an age of two*

superimposed eschatologies: that of secular anxieties and hopes, and that of revealed fulfillment. Sometimes the first is merely mistaken for the second, sometimes it results from complete denial and despair of the second. In point of fact the pathological fear of the violent end which, when sufficiently aroused, actually becomes a thinly disguised hope for the violent end, provides something of the climate of confusion and despair in which the more profound hopes of Biblical eschatology are realized—for everyone is forced to confront the possibility, and to accept or reject them. This definitive confrontation is precisely what Biblical eschatology announces to us. In speaking of "the time of the End," we keep in mind both these levels of meaning. But it should be clear that for the author, there is no question of prognostication or Apocalypse—only a sober statement about the climate of our time, a time of finality and of fulfillment.

WHEN THE PERFECT and ultimate message, the joy which is *The Great Joy*, explodes silently upon the world, there is no longer any room for sadness. Therefore no circumstance in the Christmas Gospel, however trivial it may seem, is to be left out of The Great Joy. In the special and heavenly light which shines around the coming of the Word into the world, all ordinary things are transfigured. In the mystery of Peace which is proclaimed to a world that cannot believe in peace, a world of suspicion, hatred, and distrust, even the rejection of the Prince of Peace takes on something of the color and atmosphere of peace.

So there was no room at the inn? True! But that is simply mentioned in passing, in a matter-of-fact sort of way, as the Evangelist points to what he really means us to see—the picture of pure peace, pure joy: "She wrapped her firstborn Son in swaddling clothes and laid him in the manger" (Luke 2:7). By now we know it well, and yet we all might still be questioning it—except that a reason was given for an act that might otherwise have seemed strange: "there was no room for them at the inn." Well, then, they obviously found some other place!

But when we read the Gospels and come to know them thoroughly, we realize there are other reasons why it was necessary that there be no room at the inn, and why there had to be some other place. In fact, the inn was the last place in the world for the birth of the Lord.

The Evangelists, preparing us for the announcement of the birth of the Lord, remind us that the fullness of time has come. Now is the time of final decision, the time of mercy, the "acceptable time," the time of settlement, the time of the end. It is the time of repentance, the time for the fulfillment of all promises, for the Promised One has come. But with the coming of the end, a great bustle and business begins to shake the nations of the world. The time of the end is the time of massed armies, "wars and rumors of wars," of huge crowds moving this way and that, of "men withering away for fear," of flaming cities and sinking fleets, of smoking lands laid waste, of technicians planning grandiose acts of destruction. The time of the end is the time of the Crowd: and the eschatological message is spoken in a world where, precisely because of the vast indefinite roar of armies on the move and the restlessness of turbulent mobs, the message can be heard only with difficulty. Yet it is heard by those who are aware that the display of power, *hubris,* and destruction is part of the *kerygma.* That which is to be judged announces itself, introduces itself by its sinister and arrogant claim to absolute power. Thus it is identified, and those who decide in favor of this claim are numbered, marked with the sign of power, aligned with power, and destroyed with it.

Why then was the inn crowded? Because of the census, the eschatological massing of the "*whole world*" in centers of registration, to be numbered, to be identified with the structure of imperial power. The purpose of the census: to discover those who were to be taxed. To find out those who were eligible for service in the armies of the empire.

The Bible had not been friendly to a census in the days when God was the ruler of Israel (II Samuel 24). The numbering of the people of God by an alien emperor and their full consent to it was itself an eschatological sign, preparing those who could understand it to meet judgment with repentance. After all, in the apocalyptic literature of the Bible, this "summoning together" or convocation of the powers of the earth to do battle is the great sign of "the end." For then "the demon spirits that work wonders go out to the Kings all over the world to muster them for battle on the great Day of God Almighty" (Revelation 16:14). And "the Beasts and the Kings of the earth and their armies gathered to make war upon him who was mounted on the horse and on his army" (Revelation 19:19). Then all the birds of prey gather from all sides in response to the angel's cry: "Gather for God's great banquet, and eat the bodies of Kings, commanders and mighty men, of horses and their riders ..." (Revelation 19:18).

It was therefore impossible that the Word should lose Himself by being born into shapeless and passive mass. He had indeed emptied Himself, taken the form of God's servant, man. But he did not empty Himself to the point of becoming mass man, faceless man. It was therefore right that there should be no room for him in a crowd that had been called together as an eschatological sign. His being born outside that crowd is even more of a sign. That there is no room for Him is a sign of the end.

Nor are the tidings of great joy announced in the crowded inn. In the massed crowd there are always new tidings of joy and disaster. Where each new announcement is the greatest of announcements, where every day's disaster is beyond compare, every day's danger demands the ultimate sacrifice, all news and all judgment is reduced to zero. News becomes merely a new noise in the mind, briefly replacing the noise that went before it and yielding to the noise that comes after it, so that eventually everything blends into the same monotonous and meaningless rumor. News? There is so much news that there is no room left for the true tidings, the "Good News," *The Great Joy*.

Hence The Great Joy is announced, after all, in silence, loneliness, and darkness, to shepherds "living in the fields" or "living in the countryside" and apparently unmoved by the rumors or massed crowds. These are the remnant of the desert-dwellers, the nomads, the true Israel.

Even though "the whole world" is ordered to be inscribed, they do not seem to be affected. Doubtless they have registered, as Joseph and Mary will register, but they remain outside the agitation, and untouched by the vast movement, the massing of hundreds and thousands of people everywhere in the towns and cities.

They are therefore quite otherwise signed. They are designated, surrounded by a great light, they receive the message of The Great Joy, and they believe it with joy. They see the Shekinah over them, recognize themselves for what they are. They are the remnant, the people of no account, who are therefore chosen— the *anawim*. And they obey the light. Nor was anything else asked of them.

They go and they see not a prophet, not a spirit, but the Flesh in which the glory of the Lord will be revealed and by which all men will be delivered from the power that is in the world, the power that seeks to destroy the world because the world is God's creation, the power that mimics creation, and in doing so, pillages and exhausts the resources of a bounteous God-given earth.

WE LIVE IN THE time of no room, which is the time of the end. The time when everyone is obsessed with lack of time, lack of space, with saving time, conquering space, projecting into time and space the anguish produced within them by the technological furies of size, volume, quantity, speed, number, price, power, and acceleration.

The primordial blessing, "increase and multiply," has suddenly become a hemorrhage of terror. We are numbered in billions, and massed together, marshaled, numbered, marched here and there, taxed, drilled, armed, worked to the point of insensibility, dazed by information, drugged by entertainment, surfeited with everything, nauseated with the human race and with ourselves, nauseated with life.

As the end approaches, there is no room for nature. The cities crowd it off the face of the earth.

As the end approaches, there is no room for quiet. There is no room for solitude. There is no room for thought. There is no room for attention, for the awareness of our state.

In the time of the ultimate end, there is no room for man.

Those that lament the fact that there is no room for God must also be called to account for this. Have they perhaps added to the general crush by preaching a solid marble God that makes man alien to himself, a God that settles himself grimly like an implacable object in the inner heart of man and drives man out of himself in despair?

The time of the end is the time of demons who occupy the heart (pretending to be gods) so that man himself finds no room for himself in himself. He finds no space to rest in his own heart, not because it is full, but because it is void. Yet if he knew that the void itself, when hovered over by the Spirit, is an abyss of creativity. . . . He cannot believe it. There is no room for belief.

There is no room for him in the massed crowds of the eschatological society, the society of the end, in which all those for whom there is no room are thrown together, thrust, pitched out bodily into a whirlpool of empty forms, human specters, swirling aimlessly through their cities, *all wishing they had never been born.*

In the time of the end there is no longer room for the desire to go on living. The time of the end is the time when men call upon the mountains to fall upon them, because they wish they did not exist.

Why? Because they are part of a proliferation of life that is not fully alive, it is programmed for death. A life that has not been chosen, and can hardly be accepted, has no more room for hope. Yet it must pretend to go on hoping. It is haunted by the demon of emptiness. And out of this unutterable void come the armies, the missiles, the weapons, the bombs, the concentration camps, the race riots, the racist murders, and all the other crimes of mass society.

Is this pessimism? Is this the unforgivable sin of admitting what everybody really feels? Is it pessimism to diagnose cancer as cancer? Or should one simply go on pretending that everything is getting better every day, because the time of the end is also—for some at any rate—the time of great prosperity? ("The Kings of the earth have joined in her idolatry and the traders of the earth have grown rich from her excessive luxury" [Revelation 18:3]).

INTO THIS WORLD, THIS demented inn, in which there is absolutely no room for Him at all, Christ has come uninvited. But because He cannot be at home in it, because He is out of place in it, and yet He must be in it, His place is with those others for whom there is no room. His place is with those who do not belong, who are rejected by power because they are regarded as weak, those who are discredited, who are denied the status of persons, tortured, exterminated. With those for whom there is no room, Christ is present in this world. He is mysteriously present in those for whom there seems to be nothing but the world at its worst. For them, there is no escape even in imagination. They cannot identify with the power structure of a crowded humanity which seeks to project itself outward, anywhere, in a centrifugal flight into the void, to get *out there* where there is no God, no man, no name, no identity, no weight, no self, nothing but the bright, self-directed, perfectly obedient and infinitely expensive machine.

For those who are stubborn enough, devoted enough to power, there remains this last apocalyptic myth of machinery propagating its own kind in the eschatological wilderness of space—while on earth the bombs make room!

But the others: they remain imprisoned in other hopes, and in more pedestrian despairs, despairs and hopes which are held down to earth, down to street level, and to the pavement only: desire to be at least half-human, to taste a little human joy, to do a fairly decent job of productive work, to come home to the family . . . desires for which there is no room. It is in these that He hides Himself, for whom there is no room.

The time of the end? All right: when?
That is not the question.

To say it is the time of the end is to answer all the questions, for if it is the time of the end, and of great tribulation, then it is certainly and above all the time of The Great Joy. It is the time to "lift up your heads for your redemption is at hand." It is the time when the promise will be manifestly fulfilled, and no longer kept secret from anyone. It is the time for the joy that is given not as the world gives, and that no man can take away.

For the true eschatological banquet is not that of the birds on the bodies of the slain. It is the feast of the living, the wedding banquet of the Lamb. The true eschatological convocation is not the crowding of armies on the field of battle, but the summons of The Great Joy, the cry of deliverance: "Come out of her my people that you may not share in her sins and suffer from her plagues!" (Revelation 18:4). The cry of the time of the end was uttered also in the beginning by Lot in Sodom to his sons-in-law: "Come, get out of this city, for the Lord will destroy it. But he seemed to them to be jesting" (Genesis 19:14).

To leave the city of death and imprisonment is surely not bad news except to those who have so identified themselves with their captivity that they can conceive no other reality and no other condition. In such a case, there is nothing but tribulation: for while to stay in captivity is tragic, to break away from it is unthinkable—and so more tragic still.

What is needed then is the grace and courage to see that "The Great Tribulation" and "The Great Joy" are really inseparable, and that the "Tribulation" becomes "Joy" when it is seen as the Victory of Life over Death.

True, there is a sense in which there is no room for Joy in this tribulation. To say there is "no room" for The Great Joy in the tribulation of "the end" is to say that the Evangelical joy must not be confused with the joys proposed by the world in the time of the end—and, we must admit it, these are no longer convincing as joys. They become now stoic duties and sacrifices to be offered without question for ends that cannot be descried just now, since there is too much smoke and the visibility is rather poor. In the last analysis, the "joy" proposed by the time of the end is simply the satisfaction and the relief of getting it all over with. . . .

That is the demonic temptation of "the end." For eschatology is not *finis* and punishment, the winding up of accounts and the closing of books: it is the final beginning, the definitive birth into a new creation. It is not the last gasp of exhausted possibilities but the first taste of all that is beyond conceiving as actual.

But can we believe it? ("He seemed to them to be jesting!")

22

Blessed Are the Meek

This essay was written in response to a request by Hildegard Goss-Mayr, the nonviolent activist Merton had been writing to since early 1962 (see *Hidden Ground of Love*, 325) and had met at Gethsemani in October 1965; in a letter that arrived on December 7, 1965, she had requested from Merton an essay on humility to be published in the German journal *Der Christ in der Welt* (see *Hidden Ground of Love*, 336). On January 2, 1966, Merton notes in his journal that he is "[w]orking on an essay for Hildegard Goss-Mayr" (*Learning to Love*, 3), and he sent the completed article, "which turned out to be really an essay on the beatitude of the Meek, as applied to Christian nonviolence" (*Hidden Ground of Love*, 337), on January 14. It first appeared in German translation in the April 1966 issue of *Der Christ in der Welt* [*Christ in the World*], and in English in *Fellowship* 33 (May 1967), 18-22. It was issued two months later as a Catholic Peace Fellowship pamphlet, dedicated to Joan Baez, and was included in *Faith and Violence* (14-29); it was reprinted in *The Nonviolent Alternative* (208-18) and in *Passion for Peace* (248-59), with an informative headnote. This essay is Merton's most developed and most comprehensive discussion of the centrality of nonviolence to Christian discipleship. It is rooted specifically in Merton's understanding of and commitment to the principle of realized eschatology, the recognition that with the life, death, and resurrection of Christ, the reign of God has been definitively established, and the vocation of the Church and of each Christian is to incarnate that reality in the present moment. As he wrote in his journal in March 1964, "'realized eschatology'—the transformation of life and of human relations by Christ *now* . . . is the heart of genuine Christian humanism and hence its tremendous importance for the Christian peace effort" (*Dancing in the Water of Life*, 87). This belief receives classic expression in this essay in Merton's declaration that the "great historical event, the coming of the Kingdom, is made clear and is 'realized' in proportion as Christians themselves live the life of the Kingdom in the circumstances of their own place and time" and that "Christian nonviolence is nothing if not first of all a formal profession of faith in the Gospel message that the Kingdom has been established and that the Lord of truth is indeed risen and reigning over his Kingdom, defending the deepest values of those who dwell in it." For Merton, then, nonviolence must not be reduced to a tactic aimed simply at achieving practical results. It is intrinsic to the theological and spiritual essence of the Christian life, embodied in the total self-gift of Christ's *kenosis* in the incarnation and in the cross. The meek are blessed because they are invited, and commanded, to share in the humility, the self-emptying, of Christ himself, and so to share as well in his victory over all sources of human broken-ness, over the divisive power of sin, over death itself. Thus the principles of Christian nonviolence that Merton sets out in the essay, with their emphasis on purity of inten-tion, purity of means, a commitment to truth, and a recognition of the divine image in even the most intransigent enemy, flow from the conviction that authentic action for peace and justice, whether it shows any immediate results or not, is truly sacramental, a sign and instrument of the reconciliation effected once for all by the crucified and risen Lord. As Merton will say in a later essay, "Nonviolence is not primarily the language of efficacy, but the language of *kairos*. It does not say 'We shall overcome' so much as 'This is the day of the Lord, and whatever may happen to us, *He* shall overcome'" (*Nonviolent Alternative*, 75).

I T WOULD BE a serious mistake to regard Christian nonviolence simply as a novel tactic which is at once efficacious and even edifying, and which enables the sensitive man to participate in the struggles of the world with-out being dirtied with blood. Nonviolence is not simply a way of proving one's point and getting what one wants without being involved in behavior that one considers ugly and evil. Nor is it, for that matter, a means which anyone can legitimately make use of according to his fancy for any purpose whatever. To practice nonviolence for a purely selfish or arbitrary end would in fact discredit and distort the truth of nonviolent resistance. To use nonviolence merely in order to gain political advantage at the expense of the opponent's violent mis-takes would also be an abuse of this tactic.

Nonviolence is perhaps the most exacting of all forms of struggle, not only because it demands first of all that one be ready to suffer evil and even face the threat of death without violent retaliation, but because it excludes mere tran-sient self-interest, even political, from its considerations. In a very real sense, he who practices nonviolent resistance must commit himself not to the defense of his own interests or even those of a particular group: he must commit himself to the defense of objective truth and right and above all of *man*. His aim is then not simply to "prevail" or to prove that he is right and the adversary wrong, or to make the adversary give in and yield what is demanded of him.

Nor should the nonviolent resister be content to prove *to himself* that *he* is virtuous and right, that *his* hands and heart are pure even though the adversary's may be evil and defiled. Still less should he seek for himself the psychological gratification of upsetting the adversary's conscience and perhaps driving him to an act of bad faith and refusal of the truth. We know that our unconscious motives may, at times, make our nonviolence a form of moral aggression and even a subtle provocation designed (without our awareness) to bring out the evil we hope to find in the adversary, and thus to justify ourselves in our own eyes and in the eyes of "decent people." Wherever there is a high moral ideal there is an attendant risk of pharisaism and nonviolence is no exception. The basis of pharisaism is division: on one hand this morally or socially privileged self and the elite to which it belongs. On the other, the "others," the wicked, the unenlightened, whoever they may be, communists, capitalists, colonialists, traitors, international Jewry, racists, and so forth.

Christian nonviolence is not built on a presupposed division, but on the basic unity of man. It is not out for the conversion of the wicked to the ideas of the good, but for the healing and reconciliation of man with himself, man the person and man the human family.

The nonviolent resister is not fighting simply for "his" truth or for "his" pure conscience, or for the right that is on "his side." On the contrary, both his strength and his weakness come from the fact that he is fighting for *the* truth, common to him and to the adversary, *the* right which is objective and universal. He is fighting for *everybody*.

For this very reason, as Gandhi saw, the fully consistent practice of nonviolence demands a solid metaphysical and religious basis both in being and in God. This comes before subjective good intentions and sincerity. For the Hindu this metaphysical basis was provided by the Vedantist doctrine of the Atman, the true transcendent Self which alone is absolutely real, and before which the empirical self of the individual must be effaced in the faithful practice of *dharma*. For the Christian, the basis of nonviolence is the Gospel message of salvation for *all men* and of the Kingdom of God to which *all* are summoned. The disciple of Christ, he who has heard the good news, the announcement of the Lord's coming and of His victory, and is aware of the definitive establishment of the Kingdom, proves his faith by the gift of his whole self to the Lord in order that *all* may enter the Kingdom. This Christian discipleship entails a certain way of acting, a *politeia*, a *conversatio*, which is proper to the Kingdom.

The great historical event, the coming of the Kingdom, is made clear and is "realized" in proportion as Christians themselves live the life of the Kingdom in the circumstances of their own place and time. The saving grace of God in the Lord Jesus is proclaimed to man existentially in the love, the openness, the simplicity, the humility and the self-sacrifice of Christians. By their example of a truly Christian understanding of the world, expressed in a living and active application of the Christian faith to the human problems of their own time, Christians manifest the love of Christ for men (John 13:35; 17:21), and by that fact make him visibly present in the world. The religious basis of Christian nonviolence is then faith in Christ the Redeemer and obedience to his demand to love and manifest himself in us by a certain manner of acting in the world and in relation to other men. This obedience enables us to live as true citizens of the Kingdom, in which the divine mercy, the grace, favor, and redeeming love of God are active in our lives. Then the Holy Spirit will indeed "rest upon us" and act in us, not for our own good alone but for God and his Kingdom. And if the Spirit dwells in us and works in us, our lives will be a continuous and progressive conversion and transformation in which we also, in some measure, help to transform others and allow ourselves to be transformed by and with others, in Christ.

The chief place in which this new mode of life is set forth in detail is the Sermon on the Mount. At the very beginning of this great inaugural discourse, the Lord numbers the beatitudes, which are the theological foundation of Christian nonviolence: Blessed are the poor in spirit . . . blessed are the meek (Matthew 5:3-4).

This does not mean "blessed are they who are endowed with a tranquil natural temperament, who are not easily moved to anger, who are always quiet and obedient, who do not naturally resist!" Still less does it mean "blessed are they who passively submit without protest to unjust oppression." On the contrary, we know that the "poor in spirit" are those of whom the prophets spoke, those who in the last days will be the "humble of the earth," that is to say the oppressed who have no human weapons to rely on and who nevertheless resist evil. They are true to the commandments of Yahweh, and who hear the voice that tells them: "Seek justice, seek humility, perhaps you will find shelter on the day of the Lord's wrath" (Zephaniah 2:3). In other words they seek justice in the power of truth and of God, not by the power of man. Note that Christian meekness, which is essential to true nonviolence, has this eschatological quality about it. It refrains from self-assertion and from violent aggression because it sees all things in the light of the great judgment. Hence it does not struggle and fight merely for this or that ephemeral gain. It struggles for the truth and the right which alone will stand in that day when all is to be tried by fire (I Corinthians 3:10-15).

Furthermore, Christian nonviolence and meekness imply a particular understanding of the power of human poverty and powerlessness when they are united with the invisible strength of Christ. The beatitudes indeed convey a profound existential understanding of the dynamic of the Kingdom of God—a dynamic made clear in the parables of the mustard seed and of the yeast. This is a dynamism of patient and secret growth, in belief that out of the smallest, weakest, and most insignificant seed the greatest tree will come. This is not merely a matter of blind and arbitrary faith. The early history of the Church, the record of the apostles and martyrs remains to testify to this inherent and mysterious dynamism of the ecclesial "event" in the world of history and time. Christian nonviolence is rooted in this consciousness and this faith.

THIS ASPECT OF CHRISTIAN nonviolence is extremely important and it gives us the key to a proper understanding of the meekness which accepts being "without strength" (*gewaltlos*) not out of masochism, quietism, defeatism, or false passivity, but trusting in the strength of the Lord of truth. Indeed, we repeat, Christian nonviolence is nothing if not first of all a formal profession of faith in the Gospel message that the Kingdom has been established and that the Lord of truth is indeed risen and reigning over his Kingdom, defending the deepest values of those who dwell in it.

Faith of course tells us that we live in a time of eschatological struggle, facing a fierce combat which marshals all the forces of evil and darkness against the still invisible truth, yet this combat is already decided by the victory of Christ over death and over sin. The Christian can renounce the protection of violence and risk being humble, therefore *vulnerable*, not because he trusts in the supposed efficacy of a gentle and persuasive tactic that will disarm hatred and tame cruelty, but because he believes that the hidden power of the Gospel is demanding to be manifested in and through his own poor person. Hence in perfect obedience to the Gospel, he effaces himself and his own interests and even risks his life in order to testify not simply to "the truth" in a sweeping, idealistic, and purely platonic sense, but to the truth that is incarnate in a concrete human situation, involving living persons whose rights are denied or whose lives are threatened.

Here it must be remarked that a holy zeal for the cause of humanity in the abstract may sometimes be mere lovelessness and indifference for concrete and living human beings. When we appeal to the highest and most noble ideals, we are more easily tempted to hate and condemn those who, so we believe, are perversely standing in the way of their realization.

Christian nonviolence does not encourage or excuse hatred of a special class, nation, or social group. It is not merely *anti*-this or that. In other words, the Evangelical realism which is demanded of the Christian should make it impossible for him to generalize about "the wicked" against whom he takes up moral arms in a struggle for righteousness. He will not let himself be persuaded that the adversary is totally wicked and can therefore never be reasonable or well intentioned, and hence need never be listened to. This attitude, which defeats the very purpose of nonviolence—openness, communication, dialogue—often accounts for the fact that some acts of civil disobedience merely antagonize the adversary without making him willing to communicate in any way whatever, except with bullets or missiles. Thomas à Becket, in Eliot's play *Murder in the*

Cathedral, debated with himself, fearing that he might be seeking martyrdom merely in order to demonstrate his own righteousness and the king's injustice: "This is the greatest treason, to do the right thing for the wrong reason."

Instead of trying to use the adversary as leverage for one's own effort to realize one's ends however ideal, nonviolence seeks only to enter into a dialogue with him in order to attain, together with him, the common good of *man*. Nonviolence must be realistic and concrete. Like ordinary political action, it is no more than the "art of the possible." But precisely the advantage of nonviolence is that it lays claim to a *more Christian and more humane notion of what is possible*. Where the powerful believe that only power is efficacious, the nonviolent resister is persuaded of the superior efficacy of love, openness, peaceful negotiation, and above all of truth. For power can guarantee the interests of *some men* but it can never foster the good of *man*. Power always protects the good of some at the expense of all the others. Only love can attain and preserve the good of all. Any claim to build the security of *all* on force is a manifest imposture.

Now all these principles are fine and they accord with our Christian faith. But once we view the principles in the light of current *facts*, a practical difficulty confronts us. If the "Gospel is preached to the poor," if the Christian message is essentially a message of hope and redemption for the poor, the oppressed, the underprivileged, and those who have no power humanly speaking, how are we to reconcile ourselves to the fact that Christians belong for the most part to the rich and powerful nations of the earth? Seventeen percent of the world's population control 80 percent of the world's wealth, and most of these 17 percent are supposedly Christian. Admittedly those Christians who are interested in nonviolence are not ordinarily the wealthy ones. Nevertheless, like it or not, they share in the power and privilege of the most wealthy and mighty society the world has ever known. Even with the best subjective intentions in the world, how can they avoid a certain ambiguity in preaching nonviolence? Is this not a mystification?

We must remember Marx's accusation that, "The social principles of Christianity encourage dullness, lack of self-respect, submissiveness, self-abasement, in short all the characteristics of the proletariat." We must frankly face the possibility that the nonviolence of the European or American preaching Christian meekness may conceivably be adulterated by bourgeois feelings and by an unconscious desire to preserve the status quo against violent upheaval.

On the other hand, Marx's view of Christianity is obviously tendentious and distorted. A real understanding of Christian nonviolence (backed up by the evidence of history in the Apostolic Age) shows not only that it is a *power*, but that it remains perhaps the only really effective way of transforming man and human society. After nearly fifty years of communist revolution, we find little evidence that the world is improved by violence. Let us however seriously consider at least the *conditions* for relative honesty in the practice of Christian nonviolence:

1. Nonviolence must be aimed above all at the transformation of the present state of the world, and it must therefore be free from all occult, unconscious connivance with an unjust and established abuse of power. This poses enormous problems—for if nonviolence is too political it becomes drawn into the power struggle and identified with one side or another in that struggle, while if it is totally a-political it runs the risk of being ineffective or at best merely symbolic.

2. The nonviolent resistance of the Christian who belongs to one of the powerful nations and who is himself in some sense a privileged member of world society will have to be clearly not *for himself* but *for others*, that is for the poor and underprivileged. (Obviously in the case of Negroes in the United States, though they may be citizens of a privileged nation their case is different. They are clearly entitled to wage a nonviolent struggle for their rights, but even for them this struggle should be primarily for *truth itself*—this being the source of their power.)

3. In the case of nonviolent struggle for peace—the threat of nuclear war abolishes all privileges. Under the bomb there is not much distinction between rich and poor. In fact the richest nations are usually the most threatened. Nonviolence must simply avoid the ambiguity of an unclear and *confusing protest* that hardens the warmakers in their self-righteous blindness. This means in fact that *in this case above all nonviolence must avoid a facile and fanatical self-righteousness*, and refrain from being satisfied with dramatic self-justifying gestures.

4. Perhaps the most insidious temptation to be avoided is one which is characteristic of the power structure itself—this fetishism of immediate visible results. Modern society understands "possibilities" and "results" in terms of a superficial and quantitative idea of efficacy. One of the missions of Christian nonviolence is to restore a different standard of practical judgment in social conflicts. This means that the Christian humility of nonviolent action must establish itself in the minds and memories of modern man not only as *conceivable* and possible, but as a *desirable alternative* to what he now considers the only realistic possibility, namely political manipulation backed by force. Here the human dignity of nonviolence must manifest itself clearly in terms of a freedom and a nobility which are able to resist political manipulation and brute force and show them up as arbitrary, barbarous, and irrational. This will not be easy. The temptation to get publicity and quick results by spectacular tricks or by forms of protest that are merely odd and provocative but whose human meaning is not clear may defeat this purpose.

The realism of nonviolence must be made evident by humility and self-restraint which clearly show frankness and open-mindedness and invite the adversary to serious and reasonable discussion.

It is here that genuine humility is of the greatest importance. Such humility, united with true Christian courage (because it is based on trust in God and not in one's own ingenuity and tenacity), is itself a way of communicating the message that one is interested only in truth and in the genuine rights of others. Conversely, our authentic interest in the common good above all will help us to be humble, and to distrust our own hidden drive to self-assertion.

5. Christian nonviolence, therefore, is convinced that the manner in which the conflict for truth is waged will itself manifest or obscure the truth. To fight for truth by dishonest, violent, inhuman, or unreasonable means would simply betray the truth one is trying to vindicate. The absolute refusal of evil or suspect means is a necessary element in the witness of nonviolence.

As Pope Paul said before the United Nations Assembly: "Men cannot be brothers if they are not humble. No matter how justified it may appear, pride provokes tensions and struggles for prestige, domination, colonialism, and egoism. In a word *pride shatters brotherhood.*" He went on to say that attempts to establish peace on the basis of violence were in fact a manifestation of human pride. "If you wish to be brothers, let the weapons fall from your hands. You cannot love with offensive weapons in your hands."

6. A test of our sincerity in the practice of nonviolence is this: are we willing to *learn something from the adversary*? If a *new truth* is made known to us by him or through him, will we admit it? Are we willing to admit that he is not totally inhumane, wrong, unreasonable, cruel? This is important. If he sees that we are completely incapable of listening to him with an open mind, our nonviolence will have nothing to say to him except that we distrust him and seek to outwit him. Our readiness to see some good in him and to agree with some of his ideas (though tactically this might look like a weakness on our part) actually gives us power, the power of sincerity and of truth. On the other hand, if we are obviously unwilling to accept any truth that we have not first discovered and declared ourselves, we show by that very fact that we are interested not in the truth so much as in "being right." Since the adversary is presumably interested in being right also, and in proving himself right by what he considers the superior argument of force, we end up where we started. Nonviolence has great power, provided that it really witnesses to truth and not just to self-righteousness.

The dread of being open to the ideas of others generally comes from our hidden insecurity about our own convictions. We fear that we may be "convicted"— or perverted—by a pernicious doctrine. On the other hand, if we are mature and objective in our open-mindedness, we may find that in viewing things from a basically different perspective—that of our adversary—we discover our own truth in a new light and are able to understand our own ideal more realistically.

Our willingness to take *an alternative approach* to a problem will perhaps relax the obsessive fixation of the adversary on his view, which he believes is the only reasonable possibility and which he is determined to impose on everyone else by coercion.

It is the refusal of alternatives—a compulsive state of mind which one might call the "ultimatum complex"—which makes wars in order to force the unconditional acceptance of one oversimplified interpretation of reality. The mission of Christian humility in social life is not merely to edify, but *to keep minds open to many alternatives*. The rigidity of a certain type of Christian thought has seriously impaired this capacity, which nonviolence must recover.

Needless to say, Christian humility must not be confused with a mere desire to win approval and to find reassurance by conciliating others superficially.

7. Christian hope and Christian humility are inseparable. The quality of nonviolence is decided largely by the purity of the Christian hope behind it. In its insistence on certain human values, the Second Vatican Council, following *Pacem in Terris*, displayed a basically optimistic trust *in man himself*. Not that there is not wickedness in the world, but today trust in God cannot be completely divorced from a certain trust in man. The Christian knows that there are radically sound possibilities in every man, and he believes that love and grace always have power to bring out those possibilities at the most unexpected moments. Therefore if he has hopes that God will grant peace to the world it is because he also trusts that man, God's creature, is not basically evil: that there is in man a potentiality for peace and order which can be realized provided the right conditions are there. The Christian will do his part in creating these conditions by preferring love and trust to hate and suspiciousness. Obviously, once again, this "hope in man" must not be naïve. But experience itself has shown, in the last few years, how much an attitude of simplicity and openness can do to break down barriers of suspicion that had divided men for centuries.

It is therefore very important to understand that Christian humility implies not only a certain wise reserve in regard to one's own judgments—a good sense which sees that we are not always necessarily infallible in our ideas—but it also cherishes positive and trustful expectations of others. A supposed "humility" which is simply depressed about itself and about the world is usually a false humility. This negative, self-pitying "humility" may cling desperately to dark and apocalyptic expectations, and refuse to let go of them. It is secretly convinced that only tragedy and evil can possibly come from our present world situation. This secret conviction cannot be kept hidden. It will manifest itself in our attitudes, in our social action, and in our protest. It will show that in fact we despair of reasonable dialogue with anyone. It will show that we expect only the worst. Our action therefore seeks only to block or frustrate the adversary in some way. A protest that from the start declares itself to be in despair is hardly likely to have positive or constructive results. At best it provides an outlet for the personal frustrations of the one protesting. It enables him to articulate his despair in public. This is not the function of Christian nonviolence. This pseudo-prophetic desperation has nothing to do with the beatitudes, even the third. No blessedness has been promised to those who are merely sorry for themselves.

In résumé, the meekness and humility which Christ extolled in the Sermon on the Mount and which are the basis of true Christian nonviolence, are inseparable from an eschatological Christian hope which is completely open to the presence of God in the world and therefore to the presence of our brother who is always seen, no matter who he may be, in the perspectives of the Kingdom. Despair is not permitted to the meek, the humble, the afflicted, the ones famished for justice, the merciful, the clean of heart, and the peacemakers. All the beatitudes "hope against hope," "bear everything, believe everything, hope for everything, endure everything" (I Corinthians 13:7). The beatitudes are simply aspects of love. They refuse to despair of the world and abandon it to a supposedly evil fate which it has brought upon itself. Instead, like Christ himself, the Christian takes upon his own shoulders the yoke of the Savior, meek and humble of heart. This yoke is the burden of the world's sin with all its confusions and all its problems. These sins, confusions, and problems are our very own. We do not disown them.

Christian nonviolence derives its hope from the promise of Christ: "Fear not, little flock, for the Father has prepared for you a Kingdom" (Luke 12:32).

The hope of the Christian must be, like the hope of a child, pure and full of trust. The child is totally available in the present because he has relatively little to remember, his experience of evil is as yet brief, and his anticipation of the future does not extend very far. The Christian, in his humility and faith, must be as totally available to his brother, to his world, in the present, as the child is. But he cannot see the world with childlike innocence and simplicity unless his memory is cleared of past evils by forgiveness, and his anticipation of the future is hopefully free of craft and calculation. For this reason, the humility of Christian nonviolence is at once patient and uncalculating. The chief difference between nonviolence and violence is that the latter depends entirely on its own calculations. The former depends entirely on God and on his Word.

At the same time the violent or coercive approach to the solution of human problems considers man in general, in the abstract, and according to various notions about the laws that govern his nature. In other words, it is concerned with man as subject to necessity, and it seeks out the points at which his nature is consistently vulnerable in order to coerce him physically or psychologically. Nonviolence on the other hand is based on that respect for the human person without which there is no deep and genuine Christianity. It is concerned with an appeal to the liberty and intelligence of the person insofar as he is able to transcend nature and natural necessity. Instead of forcing a decision upon him from the outside, it invites him to arrive freely at a decision of his own, in dialogue and cooperation, and in the presence of that truth which Christian nonviolence brings into full view by its sacrificial witness. The key to nonviolence is the willingness of the nonviolent resister to suffer a certain amount of accidental evil in order to bring about a change of mind in the oppressor and awaken him to personal openness and to dialogue. A nonviolent protest that merely seeks to gain publicity and to show up the oppressor for what he is, without opening his eyes to new values, can be said to be in large part a failure. At the same time, a nonviolence which does not rise to the level of the personal, and remains confined to the consideration of nature and natural necessity, may perhaps make a deal but it cannot really make sense.

The distinction suggested here, between two types of thought—one oriented to nature and necessity, the other to person and freedom—calls for further study at another time. It seems to be helpful. The "nature oriented" mind treats other human beings as objects to be manipulated in order to control the course of events and make the future conform to certain rather rigidly determined expectations. "Person-oriented" thinking does not lay down these draconian demands, does not seek so much to *control* as to *respond*, and to *awaken response*. It is not set on determining anyone or anything, and does not insistently demand that persons and events correspond to our own abstract ideal. All it seeks is the openness of free exchange in which reason and love have freedom of action. In such a situation the future will take care of itself. This is the truly Christian outlook. Needless to say that many otherwise serious and sincere Christians are unfortunately dominated by this "nature-thinking" which is basically legalistic and technical. They never rise to the level of authentic interpersonal relationships outside their own intimate circle. For them, even today, the idea of building peace on a foundation of war and coercion is not incongruous—it seems perfectly reasonable!

It is understandable that the Second Vatican Council, which placed such strong emphasis on the dignity of the human person and the freedom of the individual conscience, should also have strongly approved, "those who renounce the use of violence in the vindication of their rights and who resort to methods of defense which are otherwise available to weaker parties too" (Constitution on the Church in the Modern World, no. 78) In such a confrontation between conflicting parties, on the level of personality, intelligence, and freedom, instead of with massive weapons or with trickery and deceit, a fully human solution becomes possible. Conflict will never be abolished but a new way of solving it can become habitual. Man can then act according to the dignity of that adulthood which he is now said to have reached—and which yet remains, perhaps, to be conclusively demonstrated. One of the ways in which it can, without doubt, be proved is precisely this: man's ability to settle conflicts by reason and arbitration instead of by slaughter and destruction.

23

Events and Pseudo-Events
Letter to a Southern Churchman

On February 10, 1966, Merton wrote in his journal, "Today I finished a first draft of an article for *Katallagete* which was difficult to write. They insist on my writing something and I do not really know the South. So it is general! . . . They are just starting—it is one of the only really articulate voices in the South and so deserves support" (*Learning to Love*, 18). Published by the progressive Committee of Southern Churchmen, founded by Merton's friend, the maverick Baptist preacher Will Campbell, *Katallagete* ("Be reconciled" in Greek) became a significant religious advocate for racial justice and social transformation. The essay appeared in the Summer 1966 issue (10-17), and then in *Faith and Violence* (145-64). Merton struggled with the article, noting in his journal two days later that he was tired from "writing under pressure to finish the article for *Katallagete*—very aware of my incompetence to say what needs to be said, not knowing where to begin. I ended with an ambiguous sort of letter that took great labor and much rewriting and I am still not at all satisfied, but there is no point in fooling with it any more. It has brought me close to a nervous crisis—tension yesterday, and last night, interrupted sleep, nightmares, etc. All to the good. I have to sweat it all out and try to find my way forward" (*Learning to Love*, 359-60). Writing as a monk for a largely Protestant audience, Merton freely draws upon the language of that tradition of being "under judgment," rejecting the facile optimism of the then-fashionable "religionless religion" movement while citing the words and example of Dietrich Bonhoeffer, whose use of such terminology had much more depth and complexity than was to be found in the work of his contemporary followers. Unnuanced "world-affirmation," Merton maintains, risks becoming simply another form of the primal sin of idolatry, a choice of the *simulacrum*, the plausible, seductive illusion that one's own partial and distorted perspective is the objective, absolute truth. In his prescient analysis of the power of the media and the political elite to manipulate and manufacture "news," to demand "correct" interpretations of essentially meaningless but potentially dangerous "pseudo-events" as prerequisites for acceptance and inclusion in nation, party, class, or race, Merton foresees much of the demand for conformism as well as the eventual social and political fragmentation of the decades to follow. Returning repeatedly to the scriptural basis of the magazine's title, he warns that if the Church is to fulfill its vocation to share Christ's mission of reconciliation, it must resist the temptation to proclaim an ideology rather than the Gospel and to protect its own institutional image by preferring a comforting but mythical version of its passage through history to the challenging, often unattractive, but always liberating truth.

I HAVE PUBLICLY STATED that I would no longer comment on current events. People ask why. There are many reasons, and I might as well say at once that they are reasons which may possibly be valid for me only, not for others. In any case I did not make this decision for anyone but myself. Nor would I have made it unless I had previously made my position clear in the areas of greatest urgency—race and peace.

First of all, I mistrust an obsession with declarations and pronouncements. While silence can constitute guilt and complicity, once one has taken a stand he is not necessarily obliged to come out with a new answer and a new solution to insoluble problems every third day.

After all, was it not Bonhoeffer himself who said it was an "Anglo-Saxon failing" to imagine that the Church was supposed to have a ready answer for every social problem?

When one has too many answers, and when one joins a chorus of others chanting the same slogans, there is, it seems to me, a danger that one is trying to evade the loneliness of a conscience that realizes itself to be in an inescapably evil situation. We are all under judgment. None of us is free from contamination. Our choice is not that of being pure and whole at the mere cost of formulating a just and honest opinion. Mere commitment to a decent program of action does not lift the curse. Our real choice is between being like Job, who knew he was stricken, and Job's friends who did not know that they were stricken too— though less obviously than he. (So they had answers!)

If we *know* that we are all under judgment, we will cease to make the obvious wickedness of "the others" a fulcrum for our own supposed righteousness to exert itself upon the world. On the contrary, we will be willing to admit that we are "right-wised" not by condemning others according to our law or ethical ideal, but by seeing that the real sinner whom we find abominable and frightening (because he threatens our very life) still has in himself the ground for God's love, the same ground that is in our own sinful and deluded hearts.

To justify ourselves is to justify our sin and to call God a liar.

Second, there is the nature of my own vocation to the monastic, solitary, contemplative life—the vocation of Job! Of course this monastic life does not necessarily imply a total refusal to have anything to do with the world. Such a refusal would, in any case, be illusory. It would deceive no one but the monk himself. It is not possible for anyone, however isolated from the world, to say "I will no longer concern myself with the affairs of the world." We cannot help being implicated. We can be guilty even by default. But the monastic and contemplative life does certainly imply a very special perspective, a viewpoint which others do not share, the viewpoint of one who is not directly engaged in the struggles and controversies of the world. Now it seems to me that if a monk is permitted to be detached from these struggles over particular interests, it is only in order that he may give more thought to the interests of all, to the whole question of the reconciliation of all men with one another in Christ. One is permitted, it seems to me, to stand back from parochial and partisan concerns, if one can thereby hope to get a better view of the whole problem and mystery of man.

A contemplative will, then, concern himself with the same problems as other people, but he will try to get to the spiritual and metaphysical roots of these problems—not by analysis but by simplicity. This of course is no easy task, and I cannot claim that I have discovered anything worth saying. Yet since I have been asked to say something, I will at least hazard a few conjectures. Take them for what they may be worth: they are subjective, they are provisional, they are mere intuitions, they will certainly need to be completed by the thinking of others. If they suggest a few useful perspectives to others, then I am satisfied.

I am more and more impressed by the fact that it is largely futile to get up and make statements about current problems. At the same time, I know that silent acquiescence in evil is also out of the question. I know too that there are times when protest is inescapable, even when it seems as useless as beating your head up against a brick wall. At the same time, when protest simply becomes an act of desperation, it loses its power to communicate anything to anyone who does not share the same feelings of despair.

There is of course no need to comment on the uselessness of false optimism, or to waste any attentions on the sunlit absurdities of those who consistently refuse to face reality. One cannot be a Christian today without having a deeply afflicted conscience. I say it again: we are all under judgment. And it seems to me that our gestures of repentance, though they may be individually sincere, are collectively hollow and even meaningless. Why?

This is the question that plagues me.

The reason seems to be, to some extent, a deep failure of communication.

THERE IS A GREAT deal of talk today about the Church and the world, about secular Christianity, religionless religion and so on. It seems to me that religionless religion is certainly a result of this failure of communication. (Here I am distinguishing Bonhoeffer's disciples from Bonhoeffer himself.) Seeing that traditional and biblical language simply does not ring any bells in the minds of modern men, the apostles of religionless religion have discarded that language and decided thereby to avoid the problem of communication altogether. Having done so, however, they seem to have also gotten rid of any recognizable Christian message. To reconcile man with man and not with God is to reconcile no one at all. It is the old problem of the social Gospel over again. When the life expectancy of the average secular ideology today is about five years (barring a few notable exceptions that have become orthodoxies, like Marxism and Freudianism) it seems rather irresponsible to identify the Gospel with one or the other of them.

Assuming then that the Church has something to communicate to the world that the world does not already know, what does this imply? First of all, we must try to clarify the relation of the Church to the world. It seems to me false simply to say that the Church and the world should be considered as perfectly identified, as indistinguishable, and leave it at that. After all, there is still 1 John 2:15-16 to be considered.

This judgment of the world as by definition *closed in upon itself* and therefore *closed to any revelation that demands to break through its defensive shell* is surely one of the key ideas of the New Testament. By the Incarnation and Cross Christ does in fact *break through* the defensive shell not only of sin and passionate attachment, but of all ethical and religious systems that strive to make man self-sufficient in his own worldly realm.

The Church and the world are related in a dialectic of identity and non-identity, yes and no, nearness and distance. The Church is Christ present in the world to reconcile the world to Himself. The world is therefore not purely and simply Christ. There is a question of acceptance or refusal. If we are dealing with the self-revelation of a cosmic Christ who is gradually becoming visible in man, simply as *man*, the decision for this Christ becomes a kind of poetic commitment to pantheistic vitalism or something of the sort, not an acceptance of the Gospel in the obedience of faith. In other words "Christ" is then only a symbol for the world as a closed-system. Such a symbol may seem inspiring; but it is idolatrous. Further, if Christ is simply manifesting himself in man's history, whether we do anything about it or not, then there is no need either of dialogue or of dialectic between the Church and the world. By this dialectic of challenge, faith and love, word and response, we break out of the closed system. If we forsake this forward movement toward eschatological fulfillment, then we plunge into the interminable circling of the world upon itself. No amount of religious clichés can make this encapsulation a true "freedom."

It seems to me that one of the great obligations of the Christian is to keep the eyes of his faith clear of such confusions. And the monk above all has to keep free from this circling-in-desperation, this closed system, which is essentially pagan and which implies a hidden servitude to the elements and the powers of the air in St. Paul's sense (Galatians 4:3, 9). (I readily admit, with Luther, that in practice the monk who makes monasticism a "law" automatically fails in his primal obligation.)

Though there are certainly more ways than one of preserving the freedom of the sons of God, the way to which I was called and which I have chosen is that of the monastic life.

Paul's view of the "elements" and the "powers of the air" was couched in the language of the cosmology of his day. Translated into the language of our own time, I would say these mysterious realities are to be sought where we least expect them, not in what is most remote and mysterious, but in what is most familiar, what is near at hand, what is at our elbow all day long—what speaks or sings in our ear, and practically does our thinking for us. The "powers" and "elements" are precisely what stand between the world and Christ. It is they who stand in the way of reconciliation. It is they who, by influencing all our thinking and behavior in so many unsuspected ways, dispose us to decide *for* the world *as against* Christ, thus making reconciliation impossible.

Clearly, the "powers" and "elements" which in Paul's day dominated men's minds through pagan religion or through religious legalism today dominate us in the confusion and the ambiguity of the Babel of tongues that we call mass-society. Certainly I do not condemn everything in the mass-media. But how does one stop to separate the truth from the half-truth, the event from the pseudo-event, reality from the manufactured image? It is in this confusion of images and myths, superstitions and ideologies that the "powers of the air" govern our thinking—even our thinking about religion! Where there is no critical perspective, no detached observation, no time to ask the pertinent questions, how can one avoid being deluded and confused? Someone has to try to keep his head clear of static and preserve the interior solitude and silence that are essential for independent thought.

A monk loses his reason for existing if he simply submits to all the routines that govern the thinking of everybody else. He loses his reason for existing if he simply substitutes other routines of his own! He is obliged by his vocation to have his *own mind* if not to speak it. He has got to be a free man.

What did the radio say this evening? I don't know.

What was on TV? I have watched TV twice in my life. I am frankly not terribly interested in TV anyway. Certainly I do not pretend that by simply refusing to keep up with the latest news I am therefore unaffected by what goes on, or *free* of it all. Certainly events happen and they affect me as they do other people. It is important for me to know about them too; but I refrain from trying to know them in their fresh condition as "news." When they reach me they have become slightly stale. I eat the same tragedies as others, but in the form of tasteless crusts. The news reaches me in the long run through books and magazines, and no longer as a stimulant. Living without news is like living without cigarettes (another peculiarity of the monastic life). The need for this habitual indulgence quickly disappears. So, when you hear news without the "need" to hear it, it treats you differently. And you treat it differently too.

In this perspective you are perhaps able to distinguish the real happening from the pseudo-event. Nine-tenths of the news, as printed in the papers, is pseudo-news, manufactured events. Some days ten-tenths. The ritual morning trance, in which one scans columns of newsprint, creates a peculiar form of generalized pseudo-attention to a pseudo-reality. This experience is taken seriously. It is one's daily immersion in "reality." One's orientation to the rest of the world. One's way of reassuring himself that he has not fallen behind. That he is still there. That he still counts!

My own experience has been that renunciation of this self-hypnosis, of this participation in the unquiet universal trance, is no sacrifice of reality at all. To "fall behind" in this sense is to get out of the big cloud of dust that everybody is kicking up, to breathe and to see a little more clearly.

When you get a clearer picture you can understand why so many want to stand in the dust cloud, where there is comfort in confusion.

The things that actually happen are sometimes incredibly horrible.

The fog of semi-rational verbiage with which the events are surrounded is also terrible, but in a different way.

And then, beside the few real horrors, there are the countless pseudo-events, the come-on's, the releases, the statements, the surmises, the slanders, the quarrels, the insults, and the interminable self-advertising of the image-makers.

We believe that the "news" has a strange metaphysical status outside us: it "happens" by itself. Actually, it is something we fabricate. Those who are poor artisans make only pseudo-events. These are the tired politicians and businessmen, the educators, writers, intellectuals, and tiredest of all, the Churchmen.

Others are better at it: they know how to make real bad news!

READING THE VULGATE I run across the Latin word *simulacrum* which has implications of a mask-like deceptiveness, of intellectual cheating, of an ideological shell-game. The word *simulacrum*, it seems to me, presents itself as a very suggestive one to describe an advertisement, or an over-inflated political presence, or that face on the TV screen. The word shimmers, grins, cajoles. It is a fine word for something monumentally phony. It occurs for instance in the last line of the First Epistle of John. But there it is usually translated as "idols" . . . "Little Children, watch out for the simulacra!"—watch out for the national, the regional, the institutional images!

Does it not occur to us that if, in fact, we live in a society which is par excellence that of the *simulacrum*, we are the champion idolaters of all history? No, it does not occur to us, because for us an idol is nothing more than a harmless Greek statue, complete with a figleaf, in the corner of the museum. We have given up worrying about idols—as well as devils. And we are living in the age of science. How could we, the most emancipated of men, be guilty of superstition? Could science itself be our number one superstition?

You see where my rambling has brought me. To this: we are under judgment. And what for? For the primal sin. We are idolaters. We make *simulacra* and we hypnotize ourselves with our skill in creating these mental movies that do not appear to be idols because they are so alive! Because we are idolaters, because we have "exchanged the glory of the immortal God for the semblance of the likeness of mortal man, of birds, of quadrupeds, of reptiles . . ." we fulfill all the other requirements of those who are under God's wrath, as catalogued by Paul in Romans 1:24-32.

Our idols are by no means dumb and powerless. The sardonic diatribes of the prophets against images of wood and stone do not apply to our images that live, and speak, and smile, and dance, and allure us and lead us off to kill. Not only are we idolaters, but we are likely to carry out point by point the harlotries of the Apocalypse. And if we do, we will do so innocently, decently, with clean hands, for the blood is always shed somewhere else! The smoke of the victims is always justified by some clean sociological explanation, and of course it is not superstition because we are by definition the most enlightened people that ever happened.

The things that we do, the things that make our news, the things that are contemporary, are abominations of superstition, of idolatry, proceeding from minds that are full of myths, distortions, half-truths, prejudices, evasions, illusions, lies: in a word—*simulacra*. Ideas and conceptions that look good but aren't. Ideals that claim to be humane and prove themselves, in their effects, to be callous, cruel, cynical, sometimes even criminal.

We have no trouble at all detecting all this in the ideologies of *other* nations, other social groups. That is at least something! But it is not enough. We cannot begin to face our real problems until we admit that these evils are universal.

We see them in others because they are in ourselves. Until we admit that we are subject to the same risks and the same follies, the same evils and the same fanaticisms, only in different forms, under different appearances (*simulacra*) we will continue to propose solutions that make our problems insoluble. We will continue to be deadlocked with adversaries who happen to be our own mirror image.

MY THESIS IS NOW clear: in my opinion the root of our trouble is that our habits of thought and the drives that proceed from them are basically idolatrous and mythical. We are all the more inclined to idolatry because we imagine that we are of all generations the most enlightened, the most objective, the most scientific, the most progressive, and the most humane. This, in fact, is an "image" of ourselves—an image which is false and is also the object of a cult. We worship ourselves in this image. The nature of our acts is determined in large measure by the demands of our worship. Because we have an image (*simulacrum*) of ourselves as fair, objective, practical, and humane, we actually make it more difficult for ourselves to be what we think we are. Since our "objectivity" for instance is in fact an image of ourselves as "objective," we soon take our objectivity for granted, and instead of checking the facts, we simply manipulate the facts to fit our pious conviction. In other words, instead of taking care to examine the realities of our political or social problems, we simply bring out the idols in solemn procession. "We are the ones who are right, *they* are the ones who are wrong. We are the good guys, *they* are the bad guys. We are honest, *they* are crooks." In this confrontation of images, "objectivity" ceases to be a consistent attention to fact and becomes a devout and blind fidelity to myth. If the adversary is by definition wicked, then objectivity consists simply in refusing to believe that he can possibly be honest in any circumstances whatever. If facts seem to conflict with images, then we feel that we are being tempted by the devil, and we determine that we will be all the more blindly loyal to our images. To debate with the devil would be to yield! Thus in support of realism and objectivity we simply determine beforehand that we will be swayed by no fact whatever that does not accord perfectly with our own preconceived judgment. Objectivity becomes simple dogmatism.

As I say, we can see this mechanism at work in the Communists. We cannot see it in ourselves. True, of course, our dogmatism is not as blatant, as rigid, as bureaucratically dense, as monolithic. It is nonetheless real. That is to say, it is based on *refusals* that are just as categorical and just as absolute.

These refusals are made necessary by a primary commitment to a false image which is the object of superstitious worship. The fact that the image is not made of stone or metal, but of ideas, slogans and pseudo-events only makes it all the more dangerous.

A MORE COMPLEX SYNDROME in our mythical thinking. I shall call it "justification by snake-handling."

Let me say at once that I am not trying to ridicule the good, simple people in the Tennessee mountains or in North Carolina who every once in a while gather in their little Churches, work themselves up into a state of exaltation and then pass around a live rattlesnake from hand to hand. There is a kind of rugged starkness about this primitive fundamentalism that calls for a certain respect, and I am reminded that in the novels of Flannery O'Connor due honor was not denied to primitives. The people Flannery O'Connor despised were those whose mental snake-handling was more polite and less risky, more sophisticated and adroit, more complacent and much less honest, based on the invocation not of Mark 16:18, but of something at once more sinister, more modern, and more obscure.

I take the mountain people as my starting point simply because in them the cycle is stark and clinically clear. And they are aware of what they are doing.

The rest of us do it without recognizing the analogy.

I do not say we do it every day. Snake-handling is reserved for moments of crisis, when we feel ourselves and our myths called into question. It is our reaction to deep stirring of guilt about ourselves and our images. We handle snakes in order to restore the image to a place of perfect security.

In Christian terms, the mental snake-handling is an attempt to evade judgment when our conscience obscurely tells us that we are under judgment. It represents recourse to a daring and ritual act, a magic gesture that is visible and recognized by others, which proves to us that we are right, that the image is right, that our rightness cannot be contested, and whoever contests it is a minion of the devil.

Here is the scenario.

First, a drab, uninteresting or over-organized, bored existence. Or at least an obscure feeling that your life is not quite as meaningful as it ought to be. That there is not only something lacking, but probably *everything* lacking. The more obscure and diffuse the feeling, the better. If you are hardly aware of it at all, fine. Most Americans on any day of the week can, if they reflect a little on it, see that they easily meet these qualifications. Even if one has all he needs in material goods, he can still feel as if he lacked *everything*!

Second, you have to connive with a group of other people who feel the same way, at least implicitly. You may perhaps come to an agreement with them in actual discussion together, or you may simply (more often than not) find that you and a lot of other people have all seen the same thing on TV or somewhere and are all reacting to it in the same way. I will not go into bizarre details about snake-handling in small fanatical groups of adepts and snake-handling on the national level. Let's keep it simple. First, you are bored and dissatisfied. Second, you find yourself in collusion with others who react as you do to some event.

Implicitly or explicitly you agree on some course of action which is at the same time *symbolic, arbitrary, and dangerous.* These three characteristics are essential. There may be others. But at least the act has to be symbolic. If the symbolism is unconscious, so much the better. The act or event has to be arbitrary, irrational, and in a sense provocative. It must not only be more or less unreasonable, it should, if possible, even openly *defy* reason. Indeed it may be totally irrelevant. If at the same time it is an act which defies morality, public or private, this may enhance its value. But that is not essential. It must at least be basically irrational. If it is completely useless and irrelevant, so much the better. And it must be dangerous, if not physically then at least socially or morally. The event brings one face to face with destruction or grave harm, if not danger to life and limb, then a danger to reputation, to one's social acceptability, one's future.

However, while the event may implicitly defy ostracism or hatred on the part of an out-group, it strengthens the bonds of the in-group, those who have agreed to engage in the symbolic and arbitrary activity together. At this point, we recognize characteristic adolescent behavior, but teenagers have no monopoly on it, except insofar as we are in fact a teenage society—a society that likes to play "chicken" not with fast cars, but with ballistic missiles.

The symbolic, irrational, and perilous event must prove something, at least to those who perform it. The thing it attempts to prove must be some basic value in themselves: that they are *alive*, that they are *real*, that they *count*, or (as in the case of the authentic snake-handlers) that they are *the Chosen*. In fact, it is a *substitute for divine judgment*. Instead of waiting around in uncertainty, one forces the issue. One does something drastic and "conclusive."

Naturally, not all who enact such events are necessarily believers. One does not have to believe in God—one merely needs to have an "image"! This mental ritual is a component in our contemporary idolatries.

Finally, and this is the point, those who have come together, who have agreed, who have performed the irrational, quasi-initiatory act, who have "proved themselves" thereby, who have stabilized their common image, *are now in a position to judge others*. By creating this situation of challenge, by constructing this "event," they have proved themselves to be "the ones who are right." They have not done this by thinking or reasoning, nor by discussion, dialogue, investigation: they have done it by a ritual and initiatory action in which they enjoyed the sense of self-transcendence, of escape from the monotony and the affront of a meaning-less existence. And note that it is a cycle that is all the more easily set in motion when existence is in fact more really drab, when the mentality of the partici-pants is more genuinely desperate, when the inner contradictions they seek to escape are all the more inexorable.

Though by its nature this event is arbitrary, unnecessary, and in some sense fabricated, if it is sufficiently drastic it can become far more than a pseudo-event. It can become an act of genuine horror. It can lead to incalculably tragic consequences. If, in handing the rattlesnake around, somebody gets bitten, it is no longer a pseudo-event. Yet nevertheless, in its origin, the event was artificial, fabricated, and indeed uncalled for.

Some examples: on the international level, a paradigm of snake-handling and pseudo-event was the Berlin crisis, turned on and off periodically, for the sake of effect. It reached its paroxysm in Cuba, and shortly after that Khrushchev's snake-handling days were over.

The big fuss about fallout shelters in this country was another episode of the same kind, and it was our reaction to the Berlin crisis. A purely symbolic and irrational exercise.

The philosophy of escalation, with its mystical degrees and esoteric mean-ings, is a form of intellectual snake-handling. To "think of the unthinkable" is to display one's prowess in handling a cosmic copperhead without dismay. Since the copperhead is only abstract at the time the feat is not uncomfortable. But in this area myths can suddenly and without warning turn into unpleasant reali-ties. In point of fact, our snake-handling in Southeast Asia is not abstract—but, as I said before, I am not commenting on events.

On another level, we all participate in one way or another in this national or international snake-handling when we get into the act in some more or less dramatic way. A lot of our protests and demonstrations, even when they are perfectly valid and reasonable in themselves, take the form of political snake-handling. This, I submit, robs them of their real value, because it isolates our action and protest in a closed realm of images and idols which mean one thing to us and another to our adversaries. *We no longer communicate. We abandon communication in order to celebrate our own favorite group-myths in a ritual pseudo-event.* "News" is largely made up of this liturgy of pseudo-events and irrelevant witness. Let us realize that "ideals" and "purity of heart" may easily cover a snake-handling approach to political reality.

Everywhere, from extreme right to extreme left, we find people in our society who become "sanctified," set apart, chosen, sealed off in a ritual game of some sort by reason of events enacted in honor of images. They move step by step, taking the nation with them, into realms of commitment and of absurdity, areas where, by virtue of the fact that one has agreed to face some very select irrationality, *one is quarantined from the ordinary world of right and wrong.*

The man who has agreed with his peers in the enactment of a symbolic, dangerous, and arbitrary event has thereby put himself and them beyond good and evil. They have all entered together into the realm of the gods, and in that realm they find that their action has had amazing consequences: it changes the whole meaning of truth and falsity; it imposes on life an entirely new logic; one must follow on from one irrationality to the next in a demonic consistency dictated by machines.

But here of course, I am speaking of mental snake-handling only at the highest and most mystical echelons of the technological elite. Down on our pedestrian level there is no such mystical security, no such permanent election. We are not initiated into a whole new kingdom of sacred irresponsibilities. We have to repeat some crude fanatical stunt again and again because it never quite takes. However, we have the privilege of remotely participating in the snake-handling exploits of the high-priests of policy and strategy.

On this liturgy of pseudo-events the survival of the human race—or at least its sanity and dignity—are now made to depend.

Our salvation, on the contrary, cannot be sought in this realm of images and idols, of fabricated events and unclear meanings.

AFTER ALL THIS RAMBLING and conjecturing, it is time to draw a few conclusions. Should the Church turn to the world of modern man and identify with him completely? In all his legitimate aspirations, in all his authentic human hopes and aspirations, obviously it must. If not it betrays him and betrays the Gospel. "Insofar as you did it to one of the least of these my brothers, you did it unto me" (Matthew 25:40). But the Church betrays herself and modern man if she simply identifies with his superstitions, his image-making, his political snake-handling, and his idolatries of nation, party, class, and race.

The Church has an obligation *not* to join in the incantation of political slogans and in the concoction of pseudo-events, *but to cut clear through the deviousness and ambiguity of both slogans and events by her simplicity and her love.*

"To be simple," says Bonhoeffer, "is to fix one's eye solely on the simple truth of God at a time when all concepts are being confused, distorted, and turned upside-down. It is to be single-hearted and not a man of two souls. . . . *Not fettered by principles but bound by love for God.* The simple man has been set free from the problems and conflicts of ethical decision."

It is unfortunately true that the Church has to repent of remaining enclosed in parochial concerns, and turn to the outside world. To turn to the world is to recognize our mission and service to man and man's world. We are not in the world for ourselves, for our own spiritual advantage, but for Christ and for the world. We have a mission to reconcile the world with Christ. How can we do this if we do not "turn to the world"? At the same time, in turning to our fellow-man and loving him, we will ourselves be reconciled with Christ. What other point has there ever been in preaching the Gospel? Unfortunately the simple business of "making converts" has sometimes obscured all deep understanding of what this turning to the world really means as *event*.

The Church is indeed concerned with news: the Good News. The Church is concerned with real events: saving events, the encounter of man and Christ in the reconciliation of man with man. In a sense, there is no other kind of event that matters and there is no other news that matters. To abandon this news, and become implicated in the manufacturing of pseudo-events in order to create an "image" that will then attract converts. . . . This is an affront to the world and to Christ. Can it be entirely avoided? I do not know, but one thing must be said about it now: *it has ceased to have any meaning whatever to modern man*.

If *image* means *idol*—and it does—then the Church too can unfortunately make an idol of itself, or identify itself too closely with other idols: nations, region, race, political theory.

Obviously the Church is present in history and is responsible to man in his historical predicament. But let us not take too superficial and too distorted a view of history. Our over-sensitive awareness of ourselves as responsible for "making history" is a grotesque illusion, and it leads us into the morass of pseudo-events. Those who are obsessed with "making history" are responsible for the banality of the bad news which comes more and more to constitute our "history." The Church that takes all this too literally and too seriously needs to go back and read the New Testament, not omitting the book of *Revelation*.

The genuine saving event, the encounter of man with Christ in his encounter of love and reconciliation with his fellowman, is generally *not newsworthy*. Not because there is an ingrained malice in journalists but because such events are not sufficiently visible. In trying to make them newsworthy, or visible, in trying to put them on TV, we often make them altogether incredible—or else reduce them to the common level of banality at which they can no longer be distinguished from pseudo-events.

Finally, no matter how you doctor it, *the pseudo-event cannot be turned into a saving and reconciling event*. Whether it is a display of political snake-handling, or some other demonstration of man's intent to justify his existence by seeing himself in the morning paper, no matter how noble and how Christian the intention may be, no man is ever going to come to the truth through pseudo-events, or be reconciled with his fellow man as a result of pseudo-events. On the contrary, by its very nature the pseudo-event arouses anxiety, suspicion, fear of deception, and a full awareness of the inherent weakness of the position which it is supposed to justify.

The great question then is how *do* we communicate with the modern world? If in fact communication has been reduced to pseudo-communication, to the celebration of pseudo-events and the irate clashing of incompatible myth-systems, how are we to avoid falling into this predicament? How are we to avoid the common obsession with pseudo-events in order to construct what seems to us to be a credible idol?

It is a nasty question, but it needs to he considered, for in it is contained the mystery of the evil of our time.

I do not have an answer to the question, but I suspect the root of it is this: if we love our own ideology and our own opinion instead of loving our brother, we will seek only to glorify our ideas and our institutions and by that fact we will make real communication impossible.

I think Bonhoeffer was absolutely right when he said our real task is to bear in ourselves the fury of the world against Christ in order to reconcile the world with Christ (a statement that does not accord with the superficial worldliness of some of Bonhoeffer's disciples). But let us take care that the fury of the world is not merely directed against our own ethical or political ideals, worse still our image of ourselves incarnated in our particular mode of symbolic protest.

When I began this letter I did not promise an answer, I only promised a question. Our own lifetime will not suffice to bring us close to the answer. But the root of the answer is the love of Christ and the ground is the sinful heart of sinful man as he really is—as we really are, you, and I, and our disconcerting neighbor.

24

The Spiritual Father in the Desert Tradition

Though this essay appeared almost simultaneously in *Cistercian Studies* 3 (April 1968), 3-23, *Monastic Studies* 5 (Easter 1968), 87-111, and *R. M. Bucke Society Newsletter-Review* 3 (Spring 1968), 7-21 (and was included in Part II of *Contemplation in a World of Action* [269-93]), the original typescript is dated February 1966. It was apparently intended originally for *Monastic Studies*, since Merton's January 1966 "to-do" list includes: "Eremitism for *Mon Studies*" (*Learning to Love*, 351). In a journal entry of February 7, Merton mentions his discovery of the work of the Syrian monk John the Solitary, which had "remained practically unknown" but which he finds "extremely interesting" and useful for "the article I am writing now on Spiritual Direction in the Desert Fathers" (*Learning to Love*, 17). As the notes attest, Merton incorporated numerous early monastic sources in the essay, relying particularly on *The Paradise of the Fathers*, E. A. Wallis Budge's two-volume compilation and translation of Syriac versions of the sayings of the Desert Fathers, lives of the early hermits, and similar material, which had arrived at Gethsemani while Merton was in the midst of his novitiate conferences on *Pre-Benedictine Monasticism* a couple of years earlier. The essay is a culminating exploration both of Merton's long-standing theoretical and practical interest in spiritual direction (evident in his previous discussions in *Spiritual Direction and Meditation* [3-42]; the essay "Spiritual Direction in the Monastic Setting" included as an appendix to his novitiate conferences on *Monastic Observances* [251-78]; the lengthy section on "The Spiritual Direction of Contemplatives" in his *Introduction to Christian Mysticism* conferences [251-332]; and his article on spiritual direction written for, though not included in, *The New Catholic Encyclopedia* [*The Merton Seasonal* 32.1 (Spring 1997), 3-17]) and of his love for and fascination with the teaching and example of the earliest monks (seen in *The Wisdom of the Desert*; his dialogue with D. T. Suzuki on the sayings included there; his novitiate conferences on *Cassian and the Fathers* and *Pre-Benedictine Monasticism*; as well as in the briefer essay "The Cell" [*Contemplation in a World of Action*, 252-59], written a month after this one). It also implicitly reflects his awareness of the importance of direct personal guidance in oriental spiritual traditions, the role of the roshi in Zen and of the guru in Hinduism. Shortly before departing for Asia he told his hosts at the Center for the Study of Democratic Institutions in Santa Barbara, California, that "the real essence of monasticism is the handing down from master to disciple of an incommunicable experience. That is to say, an experience that cannot be communicated in terms of philosophy, that cannot be communicated in words. It can only be communicated on the deepest possible level. And this . . . to me is the most important thing. This is the only thing in which I am really interested" (*Preview of the Asian Journey*, 34-35). This interest is clearly apparent in the sayings, stories, and commentary assembled here, focused on the traditional role of the spiritual father in providing wise counsel aimed at assisting the disciple to overcome the "worship of the self . . . the last and most difficult of idolatries to detect and get rid of," and so to encounter "in the center of one's nothingness . . . the infinitely real."

THE PLACE OF THE "Director of Conscience" or "Spiritual Director" in modern Catholic practice since the Council of Trent need not be treated here in detail, but it must at least be mentioned as the term of a long evolution of which we wish to discuss the beginning.[1] The "Director of Conscience" as his title suggests is usually a confessor and also by implication a "specialist" with an appropriate theological and spiritual training. If he is called a "Director of Conscience" this suggests that he is adept in settling *casus conscientiae*, or special cases and problems, for which he provides professional solutions. But this imposes rather unfortunate juridical limitations upon the traditional concept. The term "Spiritual Director" is broader, and suggests one who, by virtue of his learning and experience, is equipped to help others make progress in the spiritual life. Ideally speaking, the "spiritual director" will help others to reach the heights of spiritual and mystical perfection. In the lives of saints since the Middle Ages, for instance St. Teresa of Avila,[2] the importance of the spiritual director is sufficiently underlined. His influence may be positive or negative. He may prove to be a great obstacle to progress, or he may remove obstacles and help one to attain to the liberty of spirit which is necessary in order to obey the mysterious action of the Holy Spirit and attain to union with God. But in any case the director, if not essential for the spiritual life, is considered in practice to have had a decisive part to play in the lives of saints and mystics, with a few notable exceptions. St. Francis de Sales may be taken as the

---

1. For an excellent survey of the whole history of spiritual direction in the Christian context, see the article "Direction Spirituelle" in the *Dictionnaire de Spiritualité*, Vol. III, cols. 1002-1214.

2. See the *Life*, St. Teresa's autobiography, where for instance in C. 28 she speaks of the great help she received from Fr. Balthasar Alvarez. In her *Interior Castle*, VI Mansion, she speaks of the injury done to mystics, during their time of purifying trial, by bad directors, and how the fears and scruples of confessors can add to the suffering of one who is already disconcerted by inexplicable experiences.

typical saintly "director," who by his prudence, learning, experience, good sense, and intuitive understanding of others helped many to find their spiritual path, leading them safely to high contemplation and mystical union. Such directors have clearly exercised a providential function in the lives not only of individuals but also of religious congregations and of certain social milieux, indeed of the Church herself.

However, it is not of these modern directors that we are writing here. Rather we wish to return to the *archetypal* figure of the "spiritual Father" as depicted in the literature of early monasticism, that is to say, the monasticism of Egypt, Palestine, and Syria in the fourth and fifth centuries. Particularly valuable as source material are the *Apophthegmata* or sayings of the Desert Fathers.[3] Even though these are "typical" stories of figures that have become quasi-legendary, we need not question the fact that they represent an authentic spirit and indeed a historical attitude, a view of life that was so profound and so real that it exercised a permanent influence on centuries of Christian spirituality.

The Abba or spiritual Father was first of all one who by long experience in the desert and in solitude had learned the secrets of desert life. He was, by reason of his holiness, endowed with charismatic gifts which enabled him to detect and dispel the illusions that would inevitably tempt the beginner—or even the experienced monk who had not yet attained to the full maturity and perfection of the monastic life. But the function implied by the name "Father" is not fully accounted for in spiritual advice and instruction. The spiritual Father exercised a genuine "paternity"—in the name of God—engendering the life of the Spirit in the disciple. Of course, this concept must not be exaggerated (as it has sometimes been in later monastic circles, for instance in Byzantine cenobitism). The only source of the spiritual life is the Holy Spirit. The spiritual life does not come from men. The Holy Spirit is given in Baptism. However, as we know too well, the seeds of the spiritual life planted in Baptism too often remain dormant or die altogether. The Abba or "spiritual Father" was one who was recognized as a charismatic and "life-giving" influence, under whose care these mysterious seeds would truly grow and flourish. The Fathers attracted disciples who came not only for lectures and counsel, but seeking *life* and *growth* in a special relationship of filial love and devotion—indeed, in later times, of actual veneration.

The sayings of the Fathers show us in simple, often naïve terms, the arche-

<hr>

3. The *Apophthegmata* are to be found in Migne's Greek Patrology, Vol. 65, and many of the same stories are reproduced in the *Verba Seniorum* in the Latin Patrology, Vol. 73, col. 739ff. For the sake of convenience the excellent English version of E. Wallis Budge, in the *Paradise of the Fathers* (from Syriac) 2 vols. (London, 1907), will be used here.

typal life-giving charismata of these quiet, humble, often very humorous, always human figures. To such experienced and spiritually gifted *seniores* or "elders," even though they might not be priests, the young would spontaneously direct themselves with their questions, asking for those "words of salvation" that would awaken new life and growth in their hearts.

In the *Apophthegmata* we are concerned chiefly with the desert hermits, rather than with the cenobites. In fact the distinction is important, for though the heads of cenobitic communities, like St. Pachomius and Theodore, were also spiritual Fathers with great experience and wisdom, the large cenobitic communities tended to receive their guidance first of all by a Rule and observances which doubtless implemented a spiritual doctrine, but which were by their nature general rather than personal. The *Apophthegmata* on the other hand represent the direct and personal answers to the question of individuals. The "word" becomes, in each case, endowed with a general validity for "everyone" in the same or in analogous circumstances. Among the hermits these individual directives tended to take the place of general written rules; or rather they were intended to help the monk discover his own rule of life, or God's will *for him* in particular.

In order to understand these directives, we must first understand the objective of the solitary in the desert. It would be an oversimplification to say that the Egyptian and Syrian hermits went into the desert "to find solitude and lead the contemplative life." It is true that many of them were Greeks, or had a Greek outlook on life (acquired in Constantinople, Rome, or Alexandria); and for these the search for a primarily intellectual intuition of God was the most important thing about desert life. This particular tradition is represented in the writings of Evagrius Ponticus[4] and was doubtless prevalent at Nitria and Scete. But the term contemplation, *theoria*, is not prominent in the *apophthegmata* or other popular stories of the Fathers, though we read of them "seeing the glory of God" or having prophetic visions. There is, then, another term which is at once simpler, more profound, and more general, and which embraces all the different modes of desert spirituality—whether the intellectual or the volitional, the Platonic or the Biblical: that term is "tranquility," in Greek *hesychia* and in Latin *quies*. This repose is essentially "contemplative" if you like, but it is more: in its deepest meaning it implies perfect sonship of God, union with God by a complete renunciation of self, and total surrender to the word and will of God

---

4. The most characteristic work of Evagrius—as well as the most influential—is his treatise on prayer, *De Oratione*, long ascribed to St. Nilus, and available in a French translation by Père I. Hausherr, S.J.

in faith and love. This is exemplified in a classic anecdote about the vocation of the Desert Father St. Arsenius.

> When Abba Arsenius was in the palace, he prayed to God and said, "O Lord, direct me how to live" and a voice came to him, saying, "Arsenius, flee from men and thou shall live." And when Arsenius was living the ascetic life in the monastery, he prayed to God the same prayer, and again he heard a voice saying to him, "Arsenius, flee, keep silence and lead a life of silent contemplation, for these are the fundamental causes which prevent a man from committing sin."[5]

The *fuge, tace, quiesce* of Arsenius became a classical trope of the contemplative life. The "flight" was of course from the monastery into complete desert solitude as a hermit. The silence is self-explanatory, and the *quies* as we have said above is the real goal of the solitary life: the rest and "purity of heart" which comes from complete liberation from worldly care, from the concerns of a life devoted to the assertion of a social ego, and from the illusions consequent upon such a life. John Cassian, in his first conference, defining the whole purpose of the monastic life, brings together three things which he identifies with monastic perfection. These three are simply aspects of the same spiritual reality. Perfection does *not* consist merely in solitude, asceticism, prayer, or other practices. All these may be sought for basically selfish motives, and they may in the end be simply more subtle and more stubborn ways of affirming one's own ego. True perfection is found only when one renounces the "self" that seems to be the subject of perfection, and that "has" or "possesses" perfection. For Cassian this perfection is "charity ... which consists in purity of heart alone" and which he identifies with *quies*, since it consists in "always offering to God a perfect and most pure heart, and in keeping that heart untouched by all perturbations."[6] Behind this formula we must recognize the doctrine of Evagrius, for whom the monastic life was a purification first from all passionate desires, then from all disturbing thoughts, then finally from all conceptualization, leading thus to the attainment of *theologia*. The highest "rest" is in direct intuition of the Trinity.

---

5. *Paradise of the Fathers*, II, 3. This saying is the first in the entire series and thus acquires a certain importance as a paradigm for the whole monastic ascesis.

6. Cassian, *Collatio* I. 6. Migne PL 49:488. Cf. St. Peter Damian: "As the proper office of the priest is to apply himself completely to offer sacrifice, and the doctor's function is to preach, so no less is the hermit's office to rest in fasting and silence—*in jejunio silentioque quiescere*." Opus xv.5. PL 145:339. Dom J. Leclercq, O.S.B., has developed the theme of *quies* in *Otia Monastica*, Studia Anselmiana (Rome, 1963).

If the Greek tradition gave this *quies* some sophisticated and intellectual implications which the simple Coptic hermits never knew, the fact remains that all sought this tranquility and liberty of spirit in one form or other and all identified it with love of God. In all the different traditions—Greek, Coptic, Palestinian, and Syriac—we find a common agreement in this: that in the desert the monk renounces his own illusory ego-self, he "dies" to his worldly and empirical existence, in order to surrender completely to the transcendent reality which, though described in various terms, is always best expressed in the simple Biblical expression: "the will of God." In his surrender of himself and of his own will, his "death" to his worldly identity, the monk is renewed in the image and likeness of God, and becomes like a mirror filled with the divine light.

This doctrine of man finding his true reality in his remembrance of God in whose image he was created is basically Biblical and was developed by the Church Fathers in connection with the theology of grace, the sacraments, and the indwelling of the Holy Spirit. In fact, the surrender of our own will, the "death" of our selfish ego, in order to live in pure love and liberty of spirit, is effected not by our own will (this would be a contradiction in terms!) but by the Holy Spirit. To "recover the divine likeness," to "surrender to the will of God," to "live by pure love," and thus to find peace, is summed up as "union with God in the Spirit," or "receiving, possessing the Holy Spirit." This, as the nineteenth-century Russian hermit St. Seraphim of Sarov declared, is the whole purpose of the Christian (therefore *a fortiori* the monastic) life. St. John Chrysostom says: "As polished silver illumined by the rays of the sun radiates light not only from its own nature but also from the radiance of the sun, so a soul purified by the Divine Spirit becomes more brilliant than silver; it both receives the ray of Divine Glory and from itself reflects the ray of this same glory."[7] Our true rest, love, purity, vision, and *quies* is not something in ourselves, it is God the Divine Spirit. Thus we do not "possess" rest, but go out of ourselves into him who is our true rest.

In the Coptic life of St. Pachomius we read a touching episode in which Pachomius, not yet founder of his community, but living as a hermit with his brother, is praying to know the "will of God." He and his brother are living in an abandoned village, Tabbenese, and they are occupied in harvesting for neighboring farmers, thus earning their bread. One night, after their common prayers, Pachomius goes apart and "he was desolate and broken hearted about the will of God which he desired to learn." A luminous personage appears before

---

7. Serm. VII on II Epist. to Corinthians. Quoted by Callistus and Ignatius in *Writings from the Philokalia on Prayer of the Heart*, edited by Kadloubovsky and Palmer (London, 1951), p. 166.

him and asks, "Why are you desolate and broken hearted?" "Because I seek the will of God," Pachomius replies. The personage tells him: "It is the will of God that you serve the human race, in order to reconcile it with him." Pachomius is at first shocked: "I ask about the will of God and you tell me to serve men?" The personage repeats three times: "It is God's will that you serve men in order to bring them to him."[8]

The story is interesting from many points of view. First of all it contrasts in some respects with the *fuge, tace, quiesce* of Arsenius. The spirituality of the Pachomian communities was more active than contemplative, and in any case Pachomius is here being called to the task of being a Father and Founder of cenobitism. It is characteristic of St. Pachomius's thought that in the cenobitic life the monk is brought to perfection not so much by an isolated ascetic struggle directed by an enlightened spiritual master, as by participation in the life of the holy community, the brotherhood of those gathered together "in the spirit." Pachomius is said by his disciple Theodore to have declared: "This Congregation . . . is the model for all those who wish to gather together souls according to God, in order to help them until they become perfect."[9]

But in the Pachomian system too the goal is peace, *quies*, the spiritual security that comes from complete detachment and self-renunciation. The Abba regulates the life and work of the monks in the way that seems to him best for their spiritual advancement, and they in turn, trusting completely in him as God's instrument, find peace in following his regulations.[10]

Meanwhile, however, we find Pachomius himself seeking peace, tranquility, and *quies* in the clear perception of and surrender to God's will. What is important for us in the story we have quoted is the fact that in "desolation and with a broken heart" Pachomius is seeking the *ultimate meaning of his life*. This is characteristic of all the desert monks. They have come out into the desert tormented by a need to know the inner meaning of their own existence, which to them has lost all significance and purpose in the cities of men. And though the individual answers may take different and even contradictory forms, yet they all have this one thing in common: all authentic answers come from God and are the expression of his will, manifested in his word, and when one receives and obeys this word one has peace, *quies*. These answers are not easily come by. One must seek them in repentance, suffering, and patience, for no one can demand an answer as by right, and each one must be prepared to accept an answer that may be in many ways disconcerting. The suffering and solitude of the desert life are, in the

---

8. L. Th. Lefort, *Les Vies Coptes de Saint Pachôme* (Louvain, 1943), pp. 60, 61.
9. Lefort, *Les Vies Coptes, Avant Propos*, p. 1.
10. Lefort, *Les Vies Coptes*, p. 74.

eyes of the Egyptian monks, the price that has to be paid for such an ultimate solution to the question of existence. The price is not too high.

Meanwhile, though the stories may tell us that some of the pioneers, like Arsenius, Pachomius, Anthony, received their answers by interior inspiration or from "luminous personages," the other Desert Fathers had to be content with a more prosaic and ultimately more secure source of information: they had to ask other monks who had found their answer. They had to approach a "spiritual Father."

Anecdotes about the Desert Fathers are more often than not direct and succinct reports of spiritual consultations; and the "sayings" (*Apophthegmata*) of the Fathers are generally solutions of problems or difficulties. These may have been presented by a disciple living in the same cell as the Master or in a neighboring cell, in order to be taught and formed by him; or they may be posed by a stranger who has travelled a long distance with the precise purpose of getting this answer from a famous Abba. Sometimes the questions are general and fundamental, involving what we would call today a vocational decision, changing the entire course of the questioner's life. In the terminology of the "sayings" such questions are formulated: "What ought I to do?" "Speak to me a word" (i.e., "a word of salvation," manifesting the will of God and thereby showing the way to the goal of my existence). The answer to such a question is a program of life in the desert, or, if you like, a "Rule" expressed in three or four words appropriate to the needs of the one asking. In each case, the reply of the Master is intended to meet the personal need of the inquirer, but it is also a fundamental statement about the monastic life.

One of the best examples of this kind of statement is found in the Coptic life of St. Pachomius. It is the story of Pachomius's first encounter with the hermit Abba Palemon, his request to become the old man's disciple, and Abba Palemon's reply.[11]

Pachomius knocks at the cell door. The old man cries out rudely, "Why are you knocking?" The youth says, "Father, I desire you to let me be a monk with you."

The old man then launches on a sobering, if not discouraging, account of the solitary vocation: "Many have come here for that very purpose and were not able to stand it; they turned back shamefully...." Nevertheless, he briefly exposes the purpose of the monastic life ("Scripture orders us to pray and fast in order that we may be saved"), and the actual Rule that is followed by the monks. "The Rule of monasticism, as we have been taught by our predecessors, is as follows: at all

---

11. Lefort, *Les Vies Coptes*, pp. 84-85.

times we spend half the night—and often from evening to morning—in vigils, reciting the words of God, and doing much manual work, with thread, hair or palm-fiber, so as not to be importuned by sleep and to provide for our bodily needs; whatever remains over and above what we need, we give to the poor." He continues with details about the fasting and prayers, and concludes: "Now that I have taught you the law of monasticism, go and examine yourself on all these points. See if you are capable of doing what I have said. . . ." He also says, "go to your own house, stay there and hold fast to what you have received. See . . . if you are capable of enduring."

This passage is a paradigm for monastic formation and the deciding of vocations.[12]

Other simpler examples:

A cenobite comes to the hermit Abba Bessarion and asks advice about how to live in his community: "The old man said unto him, 'Keep silence and consider thyself to be nothing.'"[13]

"A brother asked Abba Muthues saying: 'Speak a word to me'; and the old man replied, 'Cut off from thee contention concerning every matter whatsoever, and weep and mourn, for the time hath come.'"[14]

This "compunction," and the eschatological perspective which saw all things in the light of their end, was sufficient to revolutionize a man's whole outlook on himself and on life.

Notice that in these two examples, chosen at random, emphasis is laid on being at peace with others, "not contending" with them, even in thought. This is a very common theme in the sayings of the Fathers. Retirement into solitude is of no use if the hermit is to live alone with aggressive and hostile fantasies. A prerequisite for this tranquility (*quies*) of the true solitary is the renunciation of all judgments, all criticisms of others, and all interior argumentation. Living in the presence of the divine judge of all was the beginner's way to reduce all these things to their true dimensions.

Sometimes the question concerns a particular problem in the ascetic life. The solution given constitutes a principle which has a certain importance in analogous cases.

A brother to Abba Poemen: "My body is weak and I am not able to perform ascetic labors; speak to me a word whereby I may live." And the old

---

12. See *Rule of St. Benedict*, chapter 58.
13. *Paradise,* II, 13.
14. Ibid., p. 32.

man said unto him: "Art thou able to rule thy thought and not to permit it to go to thy neighbor in guile?"[15]

A brother asked the same Abbot Poemen:

"What shall I do, for I am troubled when I am sitting in my cell?" The old man said unto him, "Think lightly of no man; think no evil in thy heart; condemn no man and curse no man; then shall God give thee rest, and thy habitation shall be without trouble."[16]

There are some sayings in which the Master is, so to speak, certifying that the disciple has reached a certain state of perfection and that he is now able, with spiritual freedom, to go forth and help others. Thus Theodore, himself an "old man" and therefore experienced,

asked Abba Pambo saying, "Tell me a word." And with much labor he said to him, "Theodore, get thee gone and let thy mercy be poured out on every man, for thy loving-kindness hath found freedom of speech before God."[17]

An answer of an anonymous Abba covers the whole field of monastic asceticism, according to his view of it:

In my opinion the work of the soul is as follows: to live in silence, persistent endurance, self denial, labor, humility of body, and constant prayer. And a man should not consider the shortcomings of men, but his own lapses; if now a man will persist in these things the soul will after no great time make manifest the fruits of spiritual excellence.[18]

If the Fathers answered different questioners to their needs, it followed that sometimes they solved the same problem in different ways or gave seemingly contradictory answers to identical questions. Once Abba Joseph was reproached with this. When asked how to deal with tempting thoughts, he told one monk to resist them forcefully and thrust them out, and another to pay no attention to them. It was this second who complained of the contradiction. The answer of the Abba was: "I spoke to *you* as I would have spoken to myself"[19]—in other words he knew that his questioner was experienced, and that forceful resistance

---

15. Ibid., p. 83.
16. Ibid.
17. Ibid., p. 97.
18. Ibid., p. 199.
19. Ibid., p. 198.

was not necessary as the tempting thoughts made no real appeal to his will, while direct resistance would only cause him to be unnecessarily concerned with them, devoting his attention to them when it would be better occupied elsewhere.

This purpose is well stated in a Syrian work of the fifth or sixth century, outside the context of Egyptian monasticism, and more speculative than the practical "sayings" of the Fathers. Yet the gist of it is much the same.

> A disciple asks the question: "What is the beginning of the conduct of the interior man?"
>
> Master: Renunciation of the love of money. After renunciation of the love of money, it is necessarily required of him that he strip himself of the love of praise. Then after that it is possible for him to be in the virtue of understanding: in humility and in patience, in quietude and lucidity of spirit, in the joy of his hope, in the vigilance of noble concerns, in the perfect love of God and of men: by these things he will come to purity of soul which is the crowning of all the conduct God has enjoined upon man to attain in this life.[20]

This fact will help us to understand the various statements of principle which are made by the Fathers: all must be understood in the light of concrete situations. At one moment stern asceticism is declared essential, at another nonessential. Everything depends on the concrete case. In a word, the sayings of the Fathers are not to be taken as hard and fast rules which apply in the same way in every situation: they are applications of broad general principles, which we have already considered. The most fundamental of them is stated clearly in the first Conference of Cassian: every practice, every decision, every change in one's mode of life is to be judged in terms of the purpose of the solitary life. That purpose is purity of heart, perfect charity, and *quies*, or the tranquility of the selfless and detached spirit.

The worth and meaning of every ascetic practice are to be estimated in terms of quietude, lucidity of spirit, love, and purity of heart. Anything that does not lead to these is worthless, for instead of liberating us from self-preoccupation, it only reinforces our illusory and obsessive concern with our own ego and its victory over the "not-I." True quietude and purity of heart are impossible where this division of the "I" (considered as right and good) and the "not-I" (considered as threatening) governs our conduct and our decisions.

---

20. John the Solitary, *Dialogue sur l'Âme et les Passions*, trans. by I. Hausherr, S.J., Orientalia Christiana Analecta 120 (Rome, 1939), pp. 31-32.

When one has been liberated from this obsession with self, says the same text, one attains to *integrity*, to the "conduct of the new man." This is the "beginning" of the true life, the life of the interior or spiritual man who lives entirely as a son of God and not as a slave.

Is THERE ONE PRINCIPLE above all which can be said to cover almost every case, a basic norm of the solitary life? Yes, there is one. Its observance is practically synonymous with *quies* because it is the essential condition for tranquility. It is the key principle of the solitary life and is sometimes stated with such finality that it even seems to dispense with further advice. Here is a classic statement of it:

> A certain brother went to Abba Moses in Scete, and asked him to speak a word; and the old man said, "*Get thee gone, and sit in thy cell, and thy cell shall teach thee all things.*"[21]

This saying has obvious implications for the practice of spiritual direction. As stated here, it clearly implies that there is no use in the monk leaving his cell and running about asking advice, if he is not first prepared to *face his own solitude in all its naked reality*.

Though we cannot go into all the depth of this idea at present, let us at least say this much: it is in solitude that the monk most completely comes to discover the true inner dimensions of his own being, at once "real" and "unreal." The conviction of one's "self" as a static, absolute, and invariable reality undergoes a profound transformation and dissolves in the burning light of an altogether new and unsuspected awareness. In this awareness we see that our "reality" is not a firmly established ego-self already attained that merely has to be perfected, but rather that we are a "nothing," a "possibility" in which the gift of creative freedom can realize itself by its response to the free gift of love and grace. This response means accepting our loneliness and our "potentiality" as a gift and a commission, as a *trust* to be used—as a "talent," in the language of the parables. Our existence is then at once terrible and precious because radically it belongs not to us but to God. Yet it will not be fully "His" unless we freely make it "ours" and then offer it to Him in praise. This is what Christian tradition means by "obedience to the Word of God." The monk must learn this for himself.

Of course he needs the assistance of others but he cannot be helped by others if he is not first determined to help himself. Others will be of little use as mediators between himself and God if he does not have enough faith to give first place

---

21. *Paradise*, II, 16.

to prayer and solitude in his own eremitical life. In other words, it is the solitude of the cell itself that teaches one how to face illusion, how to resist temptation, how to pray. All other advice and direction is first of all contingent upon the young hermit's willingness to accept this basic principle. One might say that all other advice assumes that one is ready and willing to sustain the purifying silence and loneliness of the cell, in which one is stripped of his illusory image of himself and forced to come to terms with the nothingness, the limitation, the infidelity, the defectibility, or as we might say today the "void" of his own life.

St. Anthony, who knew better than anyone the meaning of this solitary combat with thoughts ("demons"),[22] said that life in the cell was at times like being in a fiery furnace. Yet in that furnace one came face to face with God. The saying recalls that of a modern monk of Mount Athos, Staretz Silouan, who lived "as though in hell" but did not despair.[23] Anthony left us a most important saying, with deep implications about the mystical life (of which little is said explicitly in the *Apophthegmata*): "The cell of the monk is the furnace of Babylon wherein the three children found the Son of God, and it is also the pillar of cloud wherefrom God spoke with Moses."[24]

The monk who faces this fire and darkness will not be able to continue in the cell at all unless he lives as a man of faith and prayer. A monastic saying has it that when you do not live worthily in your cell, the cell of its own accord vomits you out. This accounts, perhaps, for the fact that the Desert Fathers were not carried away with enthusiasm over the specious zeal to convert others which often presented itself as an honorable evasion from the solitude of the cell and from the *acedia* caused by the "noonday demon."[25]

A young monk, tormented by this kind of problem, confesses to Abba Arsenius:

My thoughts vex me and say: "thou canst not fast; and thou art not able to labour; therefore visit the sick which is a great commandment." Then Abba Arsenius, after the manner of one who was well acquainted with

22. In all spiritual traditions there is recognized a stage in which thoughts and desires, whether good or bad, are projected and objectified as external beings or persons. This stage has to be transcended, but the experiences that belong to it have to be taken into account even if "illusory." The question of the metaphysical reality of angels or demons is another matter.

23. See *The Undistorted Image*, by Archimandrite Sophrony (London, 1962).

24. *Paradise*, II, 14, for the pillar of cloud as a mystical symbol. See St. Gregory of Nyssa, *De Vita Moysis*, French trans. by J. Daniélou, S.J., *Sources Chrétiennes*, 2nd edition (Paris, 1955).

25. See Cassian, *De Cenobiorum Institutis*, Lib. X, PL 49:359ff.

the war of devils said to him: "Eat, drink and sleep and toil not but on no account go out of thy cell," for the old man knew that dwelling constantly in the cell induceth all the habits of the solitary life.[26]

The rest of this charming story tells how the young monk, remaining in the cell, gradually found himself working and praying more and more steadily and finally won the ascetic battle—the great battle of the solitary—against all his "thoughts." (That is to say he found *quies* by resolving the division caused in himself by useless interior activity and self-projection into words and ideas which were obstacles between himself and his life.)

Another old man discussed the problem of wandering thoughts in the following terms:

The matter is like unto that of a she-ass which hath a sucking foal. If she be tied up, however much the foal may gambol about or wander hither and thither, he will come back to her eventually, either because he is hungry or because of other reasons which drive him to her; but if it happen that his mother be also roaming about loose, both animals will go to destruction. And thus is it in the matter of the monk. If the body remain continually in its cell the mind thereof will certainly come back to it after all its wanderings, for many reasons which will come upon it, but if the body as well as the soul wander outside the cell both will become a prey and a thing of joy to the enemy.[27]

If the Fathers place so much emphasis on staying in the cell, this does not mean that there are no other rules to follow and that the beginner, provided he stays out of sight, can do anything he pleases. "Become not a lawgiver to thyself," said one of the elders.[28] Another saying of monastic tradition is, "those who are not under the law of the governors shall fall like leaves."[29] The reason for this is not only that the beginner is inexperienced and needs to be instructed and helped. Everywhere in the sayings of the Fathers we find men who are themselves experienced and yet follow the guidance of others, not trusting their own judgment. Though the solitary must certainly develop a certain ability to

---

26. *Paradise,* II, 4.

27. Ibid., p. 12. Here we see that the importance of "staying in the cell" is analogous to the emphasis on *Zazen* (sitting in meditation) in Zen Buddhism. Dom J. Leclercq has an important essay, "Sedere" (sitting), in the volume *Le Millénaire du Mont Athos* (Chevetogne, 1963).

28. Ibid., p. 161.

29. Palladius, *Historia Lausiaca* 24. *Paradise,* I, 136.

take care of himself, this does not mean that he trusts in his own strength or in his own ideas. His search in the desert is not merely for solitude in which he can simply do as he pleases and admire himself as a great contemplative. There would be no real *quies* in such an exploit, or if there were peace, it would be the false peace of self-assurance and self-complacency.

Hence we have another story which qualifies the saying: "Stay in thy cell and it shall teach thee all things." One must be in the cell for the right reasons.

> A certain brother had recently received the garb of a monk and he went and shut himself up in a cell and said, "I am a desert monk." And when the Fathers heard this, they came and took him out of his place and made him to go about the cells of the brethren and to make apologies to them saying, "I am not a desert monk, and I have only just begun to be a disciple."[30]

The monk does not come into the desert to reinforce his own ego-image, but to be delivered from it. After all, this worship of the self is the last and most difficult of idolatries to detect and get rid of. The monk knows this, and therefore he determines to take the proper means to destroy instead of reinforcing the image. For this purpose he renounces his own will in order to be taught and guided by another, even though he may live alone. Still he consults a spiritual Father, and as we have seen above in the story of Abbot Theodore, he may be an old man himself before he is told, by the spiritual Father, that he can now go out on his own because he has obtained the freedom and confidence not of the self-opinionated proud man who believes in his own ascetic prowess, but of the humble man who has perfect trust in God.

A brother confessed to an elder:

> "In my cell I do all that one is counseled to do there, and I find no consolation from God." The elder said: "This happens to you because you want your own will to be fulfilled." The brother said: "What then do you order me to do, Father?" The elder said: "Go, attach yourself to a man who fears God, humble yourself before him, give up your will to him, and then you will receive consolation from God."[31]

The term "consolation from God" is not explained. In the normal context of monastic spirituality it means "compunction." Now, compunction is a sign

---

30. *Paradise,* II, 240.

31. Paul Evergetinos. See I. Hausherr, S.J., *Direction Spirituelle en Orient autrefois,* Orientalia Christiana Analecta 144 (Rome, 1955), p. 162.

of valid and authentic repentance, that is to say of *metanoia* or *conversatio*. This means much more than simply a "feeling" of sorrow for sin expressed in the "gift of tears." It is, more basically, a sense of *truth*, a sense of having reached the ground of one's being (or, if you prefer, of one's "nothingness") in the crucial realization that one is completely defectible, that one is *"he who is not"* in the presence of "him who is." The heart of "consolation" lies precisely in this sense that in the center of one's nothingness one meets the infinitely real. In a word, humility and consolation go together, for humility is truth experienced in its concrete and existential factuality in our own life. One who simply "runs his own life" by putting into effect ideal projects designed to establish his own ego-image more and more firmly cannot possibly taste "consolation from God." He is not debarred from other consolations—those which come from the image he has constructed for himself! But these consolations are laborious fabrications, ambivalent and nauseating to anyone with a sense of truth.

MERELY READING BOOKS AND following the written instructions of past masters is no substitute for direct contact with a living teacher.[32] The Master does not merely lecture or instruct. He has to know and to analyze the inmost thoughts of the disciple. The most important part of direction is the openness with which the disciple manifests to the spiritual Father not only all his acts but all his thoughts.

An apothegm attributed to St. Anthony declares: "The monk must make known to the elders every step he takes and every drop of water he drinks in his cell, to see if he is not doing wrong."[33]

Since the real "work of the cell" is not a matter of bodily acts and observances, but of interior struggle with "thoughts" (that is, in the last analysis, with the ego-thinking-centered passion and pride), it is most important for the disciple to be able to make known to the spiritual Father all that is going on in his heart. The purpose of this is to learn *diacrisis*, or the discernment of spirits, which identi-fies these motions in their very beginning and does not mistake proud, vain, illusory, or obsessive drives for "the will of God" and "inspirations of the Spirit." The stories of the Desert Fathers abound in examples of monks who were stern ascetics but who, for lack of discernment (*diacrisis*) went to fantastic extremes or completely wrecked their lives.

Cassian, using an expression which had become current in monastic cir-cles because it had even been attributed to Christ in a *logion*, said that monks

---

32. Ibid., pp. 167-68 (quoting St. Gregory of Nyssa).
33. *Apophthegmata*, Alpha Antonii, n. 8, Migne PG 65:88.

should, "according to the commandment of the Lord become as wise money-changers,"[34] able to distinguish gold from brass, and to accept only genuine coin. Cassian applies this to the testing of thoughts.

Seemingly spiritual thoughts may indeed be only illusions or superstitions. Or they may be merely superficial. Sometimes monks are dazzled by words, or by subtle-sounding methods that promise to bring them to a new kind of illumination. Or else they are too ready to follow a train of thought that, in the end, is entirely contrary to the true purpose of the monastic life (i.e., detachment from self and *quies*).

Since the appetite for novel doctrines and for curious new methods provides an outlet for self-will, which can defeat the monk's own purpose, or at best induce him to waste his time in trivialities, the spiritual Father will not tolerate any such fantasies. He severely demands the renunciation of all these subterfuges by which the disciple is merely trying to flatter his own ego. Conversely, a monk who takes pains to avoid having a master shows by that fact that he prefers his own will and his own illusions.

> Is it therefore possible to think a man leads a Divine life, in accordance with the Word of God, if he lives without a guide, pandering to himself and obeying his own self-will? Naturally not. . . . [To such monks St. John of the Ladder says] "know that you are attempting a short but hard way which has only one road, leading into error."[35]

The monk should of course be free to choose his own spiritual Father, but he will only deceive himself if, in making the choice, he seeks out a Master who will never tell him anything except what he wants to hear, and never commands him anything against his own will. In fact the spiritual Father must if necessary be uncompromisingly severe, and make extremely difficult demands upon the disciple in order to test his vocation to solitude and help him make rapid progress. It was naturally of the greatest importance for the disciple to accept these trials and face them squarely. The young monk was expected to give uncompromising and complete obedience to the demands and advice of the spiritual Father no matter how disconcerting some might appear. In this hard school of training—and here alone—the monk would learn to "get rid of three things: self-will, self-justification and the desire to please."[36] If he can put up with rough treatment, realizing that the Spiritual Father knows what he is doing, he will rapidly come

---

34. Cassian, Conference I, c. 20. Migne PL 49:514-16.
35. Callistus and Ignatius in *Writings from the Philokalia*, p. 175.
36. Barsanuphius, quoted in Hausherr, *Direction Spirituelle*, p. 165.

to a state of detachment from his own will and his own ego. He will then enter a state of spiritual liberty in which, instead of being guided by his own subjective fantasies and desires, he completely accepts objective reality and conforms to it with no other purpose than to "walk in truth." This implies a state of complete indifference to his own subjective preferences, to the desire to be praised and accepted by others, to have a respected place in the society of men. In the language of the Fathers, this transformation was the result of a complete substitution of God's will for the will of the individual ego.[37]

SUCH IS THE SPIRITUAL freedom without which there is no tranquility, no *quies*, no purity of heart. In other words, the purpose of the spiritual training given by the Fathers was to bring their disciples as quickly as possible to this state of inner liberty which made them able to live as sons of God.

Nevertheless, a loose and irresponsible reading of the Fathers has sometimes led less discerning ascetics of a later age to place undue emphasis on arbitrary and unreasonable commands, systematically insulting the intelligence and the essential human dignity of the subject, as if the sole purpose of ascetic training were to break down his personal integrity by so-called blind obedience. Fr. Hausherr points out that the term "blind obedience" is not found in the *Vitae Patrum*, and that the Fathers in any case would certainly not have thought that one who was following a guide endowed with a charismatic gift of understanding was obeying blindly.[38] A more accurate expression would be "uncritical" or "unquestioning" obedience. This is not blind, unreasoning, and passive obedience of one who obeys merely in order to let himself be "broken," but the clear-sighted trusting obedience of one who firmly believes that his guide knows the true way to peace and purity of heart and is an interpreter of God's will for him. Such obedience is "blind" only in the sense that it puts aside its own limited and biased judgment, but it does so precisely because it sees that to follow one's own judgment in things one does not properly understand is indeed to walk in darkness.

At this point, passing from the viewpoint of the disciple to that of the Master, we see that the Master must be extraordinarily humble, discerning, kind, and in no sense a despotic character. The "hard sayings" which he administers must spring from genuine kindness and concern for the interests of the disciples and not from a secret desire to dominate and exploit them for his own egotistic ends. The Master must, in other words, be himself one who is no longer in the

---

37. Hausherr, *Direction Spirituelle*.
38. Ibid., p. 197.

least attracted by "superiority" or by the desire to rule and teach others. In fact, we find many of the apothegms devoted to stories of monks who refused to take on the role of Abba, or who fled from those who attempted to gather around them as disciples. However, as in the case of St. Pachomius and the other great Masters, they eventually gave in and accepted, realizing that this service of others was a further step in their own self-renunciation. But they always taught first by example, and only after that by their words.

> A brother said to Abba Poemen: "Some brothers are living with me: do you wish me to command them?" The old man replied: "Not at all. Act first, and if they wish to 'live,' they will put the lesson into effect themselves." The brother said: "Abba, they themselves want me to command them." The old man said: "No, become a model for them, and not a lawgiver."[39]

One remarkable characteristic of the Desert hermits as reflected in the "sayings" is their great respect for the variety of personal vocations and "ways." They did not seek to impose hard and fast rules, reducing all to an arbitrary uniformity. Far from seeking security in a kind of servile conformism, they were able to appreciate the diversity of gifts which manifested the One Spirit dwelling in them all (I Corinthians 12:4):

> Abba John used to say: "The whole company of the holy men is like unto a garden which is full of fruit-bearing trees of various kinds, and wherein the trees are planted in one earth and all of them drink from one fountain; and thus it is with all the holy men, for they have not one rule only, but several varieties, and one man laboureth in one way and another man in another, but it is one Spirit which operateth and worketh in them."[40]

Finally, to sum up, we can say that the spiritual Father must indeed be "spiritual" in the technical sense of *pneumatikos*, a man entirely guided and illuminated by the Divine Spirit, one who has totally surrendered himself to God, and who is therefore guided by love and not by merely external or logical norms. John the Solitary distinguishes the "spiritual man" (*pneumatikos*) from the merely rational and virtuous man whom he calls *psychicos*. Actually he is simply following the terminology of St. Paul (I Corinthians 2:14) where the *psychicos*

---

39. *Apophthegmata*, Alph. Poemen, 174, PG 65:364; see Hausherr, *Direction Spirituelle*, p. 190.
40. *Paradise*, II, 148.

is sometimes translated the "natural man," and where the Apostle says: "The *psychicos* does not receive what comes from the Spirit of God, for it is folly to him." The spiritual man is he who has received the Spirit of God and knows the "things of the Spirit" (see I Corinthians 2:6-13).

For John the Solitary, transferring the Pauline teaching into the monastic context, the *psychicos* is the well-meaning but literal-minded monk who seeks to gain much merit by his good works, and estimates everything by the yardstick of human respect. "If his good works are eclipsed (by the superior action of the Spirit) he falls into a kind of despair."[41] He is unable to give genuine spiritual guidance, for all he knows about are the externals of asceticism and cult, which are good in themselves, but which he does not know how to relate to their true end.

We can sum up the teaching of the Fathers on spiritual direction by saying that the monk who is merely a *psychicos* lacks the wisdom required to make a true spiritual Father. He cannot liberate minds and heart, he cannot open them to the secret action of the Spirit. He trusts entirely in an external and legalistic knowledge of mere rudiments, and does not "give life" or open up the way to genuine development. On the contrary, by an insistence on non-essentials and by consistent neglect of the living needs of the disciple, he tends to stifle life and to "extinguish the Spirit" (1 Thessalonians 5:19).

John the Solitary observes very acutely that while the *psychicos* has overcome his grosser passions and lives virtuously, he does not really love God and men. He is in a kind of intermediate state in which he has ceased to be moved by passion and crude self-interest (which would make him "love" those who accorded with his own interests), and he has not attained to the spiritual freedom which loves all men perfectly in and for God. "The love of God is not acquired by bodily asceticism but by insight into the mysteries; and since he has not attained to this he fails to love all men."[42] He does indeed have love for some men, but what is the basis of this love? It is, says John, his love *for his own doctrine*, his own ascetic system, "his rule, his way." He is capable of loving *only those who acquiesce in his teaching.* Hence this charity is not authentic. He loves his disciples *for the sake of his own doctrine*, that is to say he makes use of the disciple to affirm the truth and rightness of his own system, or in the end, to show that he himself is a good director!

On the contrary, a truly spiritual Father is sought out not only by beginners but by those who are themselves advanced, because he has the "words of life,"

---

41. John the Solitary, *Dialogue sur l'Âme et les Passions*, p. 34. Compare St. John of the Cross, *Living Flame of Love*, III, 29ff.

42. *Dialogue sur l'Âme et les Passions*, p. 43.

and loves men as God does. They see that he loves not a doctrine, not a method, but men. Since he loves not his ideal but them, they say to him:

> We have hastened to come to you . . . because we have found in your words so many things that had never even entered our minds. For although for many years we had never gone out of our cell, the fact of coming to see you has been of much greater profit to us than our stability. We had fixed certain customs for ourselves but we have now set them aside as trivial on account of the knowledge you have shown us. We feel as St. Paul must have felt . . . who at first gained credit for himself and took satisfaction in living according to the law, thinking that there was no other way of perfection until he received the knowledge of Christ. So we also thought that what we had was perfection. . . .[43]

Since in fact one of the pitfalls of the strictly regulated ascetic life of the monks was this spirit of legalism and trust in external works, the true spiritual Father was necessary to insure that the solitaries did not forget the "freedom of the sons of God" which was so ardently preached by Paul and is at the very heart of the New Testament. It was in this freedom alone that they could find authentic purity of heart and true *quies*. This freedom and tranquility are the "good ground" in which the seed of grace and wisdom can bring forth fruit a hundredfold. This state of purity and rest is not what one can call the "summit of perfection," whatever that may mean. It is simply the last stage of development that can be observed and discussed in logical terms. It is what John the Solitary calls "integrity," but his integrity is not the end, it is really only the *beginning* of the true spiritual (*pneumatikos*) life. "Beyond integrity is mystery which cannot be defined."[44]

> They used to say that one of the old men asked God that he might see the Fathers, and he saw them all with the exception of Abba Anthony; and he said to him that showed them to him: "Where is Abba Anthony?" And he said to him, "Wheresoever God is, there is Anthony."[45]

---

43. John the Solitary, *Dialogue sur l'Âme et les Passions*, p. 39.
44. Ibid., p. 46.
45. Paradise, II, 165.

25

Is the World a Problem?[*]

On April 30, 1966, Merton noted in his journal, "yesterday—wrote an article *Commonweal* asked for, about 'the World'" (*Learning to Love*, 48-49). The article was published in *Commonweal* as "Is the World a Problem? Ambiguities in the Secular" (84 [June 3, 1966], 305-9), and without its subtitle in *Contemplation in a World of Action* (143-56). It is perhaps the most familiar and almost certainly the most often quoted of Merton's later essays, with its vivid opening self-description of the author as "the stereotype of the world-denying contemplative," its declaration, much beloved of undergraduates, that "I love beer, and, by that very fact, the world," its recognition of his inescapable involvement, as "the contemporary of Auschwitz, Hiroshima, Vietnam and the Watts riots," in the concrete circumstances of current human crises, and its measured and nuanced endorsement of the Church's "turning to the world" in the wake of the Second Vatican Council. With its combination of autobiographical reflection (including the inadvertent dating of the composition of his autobiography a full decade too early!), astute historical analysis (the true meaning of world-denial and the clear presence of world-affirmation in medieval Christianity), humorous asides (a pair of references to Harpo Marx's antics in *A Night at the Opera*, which not by chance, we may assume, frame a brief initial discussion of his namesake Karl), and its skepticism about "all obligatory answers," whatever their source, this is widely regarded as one of Merton's most accessible and attractive essays. In its refusal to exchange the outworn stereotypes of world-rejection for "a collection of equally empty stereotypes of world affirmation" that fail to engage the most profound challenges of contemporary human existence, in its warnings against a dualistic bifurcation that fails to acknowledge the interpenetration of self and world, and above all in its concluding affirmation that one is not called to choose either Christ or the world (properly understood), but both at once, its recognition that if love is "the deepest ground of my being, ... then in that very love itself and nowhere else will I find myself, and the world, and my brother and Christ," this essay articulates Merton's profoundly Catholic, and catholic, vision of authentic engagement with a world formed

---

[*] On the original title page the author had written:
*Et quand donc suis-je plus vrai
que lorsque je suis le monde?*
—Camus

by God yet too often deformed by futile human efforts to place oneself at the center of reality.

IS THE WORLD a problem? I type the question. I am tempted to type it over again, with asterisks between the letters, the way H*y*m*a*n K*a*p*l*a*n used to type his name in *The New Yorker* thirty years ago. And as far as I am concerned that would dispose of the question. But the subject is doubtless too "serious" for a chapter title heading a page with "Is the world a problem" running down the middle, full of asterisks. So I have to be serious too, and develop it.

Maybe I can spell this question out politely, admitting that there are still cogent reasons why it should be asked and answered. Perhaps, too, I am personally involved in the absurdity of the question; due to a book I wrote thirty years ago, I have myself become a sort of stereotype of the world-denying contemplative—the man who spurned New York, spat on Chicago, and tromped on Louisville, heading for the woods with Thoreau in one pocket, John of the Cross in another, and holding the Bible open at the Apocalypse. This personal stereotype is probably my own fault, and it is something I have to try to demolish on occasion.

Now that we are all concerned about the Church and the World, the Secular City, and the values of secular society, it was to be expected that someone would turn quizzically to me and ask: "What about you, Father Merton? What do *you* think?"—and then duck as if I were St. Jerome with a rock in my fist.

First of all, the whole question of the world, the secular world, has become extremely ambiguous. It becomes even more ambiguous when it is set up over against another entity, the world of the sacred. The old duality of time-eternity, matter-spirit, natural-supernatural, and so on (which makes sense in a very limited and definite context) is suddenly transposed into a totally different context in which it creates nothing but confusion. This confusion is certainly a problem. Whether or not "the world" is a problem, a confused idea of what the world might possibly be is quite definitely a problem, and it is that confusion I want to talk about. I want to make clear that I speak not as the author of *The Seven Storey Mountain*, which seemingly a lot of people have read, but as the author of more recent essays and poems which apparently very few people have read. This is not the official voice of Trappist silence, the monk with his hood up and his back to the camera, brooding over the waters of an artificial lake. This is not the petulant and uncanonizable modern Jerome who never got over the fact that he could give up beer. (I drink beer whenever I can lay my hands on any. I love beer, and, by that very fact, the world.) This is simply the voice of a self-questioning human person who, like all his brothers, struggles to cope with turbulent, mysterious, demanding, exciting, frustrating, confused existence in which almost nothing is really predictable, in which most definitions, explanations, and justifications become incredible even before they are uttered, in which people suffer together and are sometimes utterly beautiful, at other times impossibly pathetic. In which there is much that is frightening, in which almost everything public is patently phony, and in which there is at the same time an immense ground of personal authenticity that is right there and so obvious that no one can talk about it and most cannot even believe that it is there.

I am, in other words, a man in the modern world. In fact, I am the world just as you are! Where am I going to look for the world first of all if not in myself?

As long as I assume that the world is something I discover by turning on the radio or looking out the window I am deceived from the start. As long as I imagine that the world is something to be "escaped" in a monastery—that wearing a special costume and following a quaint observance takes me "out of this world," I am dedicating my life to an illusion. Of course, I hasten to qualify this. I said a moment ago that in a certain historic context of thought and of life, this kind of thought and action once made perfect sense. But the moment you change the context, then the whole thing has to be completely transposed. Otherwise you are left like the orchestra in the Marx Brothers' *Night at the Opera* where Harpo had inserted "Take Me Out to the Ball Game" in the middle of the operatic score.

The confusion lies in this: on one hand there is a primitive Christian conception of the world as an object of choice. On the other there is the obvious fact that the world is also something about which there is and can be no choice. And, historically, these notions have sometimes got mixed up, so that what is simply "given" appears to have been chosen, and what is there to be chosen, decided for or against, is simply evaded as if no decision were licit or even possible.

That I should have been born in 1915, that I should be the contemporary of Auschwitz, Hiroshima, Vietnam, and the Watts riots, are things about which I was not first consulted. Yet they are also events in which, whether I like it or not, I am deeply and personally involved. The "world" is not just a physical space traversed by jet planes and full of people running in all directions. It is a complex of responsibilities and options made out of the loves, the hates, the fears, the joys, the hopes, the greed, the cruelty, the kindness, the faith, the trust, the suspicion of all. In the last analysis, if there is war because nobody trusts anybody, this is in part because I myself am defensive, suspicious, untrusting, and intent on making other people conform themselves to my particular brand of death wish.

Put in these terms, the world both is and is not a problem. The world is a "problem" insofar as everybody in it is a problem to himself. The world is a problem insofar as we all add up to a big collective question. Starting then from this concept of a world which is essentially problematic because it is full of problematic and self-doubting freedoms, there have been various suggestions made as to what to do about it.

At present the Church is outgrowing what one might call the Carolingian suggestion. This is a worldview which was rooted in the official acceptance of the Church into the world of imperial Rome, the world of Constantine and of Augustine, of Charlemagne in the West and of Byzantium in the East. In crude, simple strokes, this worldview can be sketched as follows: We are living in the last age of salvation history. A world radically evil and doomed to hell has been ransomed from the devil by the Cross of Christ and is now simply marking time until the message of salvation can be preached to everyone. Then will come the judgment. Meanwhile, men, being evil and prone to sin at every moment, must be prevented by authority from following their base instincts and getting lost.

They cannot be left to their own freedom or even to God's loving grace. They have to have their freedom taken away from them because it is their greatest peril. They have to be told at every step what to do, and it is better if what they are told to do is displeasing to their corrupt natures, for this will keep them out of further subtle forms of mischief. Meanwhile the Empire has become, provisionally at least, holy. As figure of the eschatological kingdom, worldly power consecrated to Christ becomes Christ's reign on earth. In spite of its human limitations the authority of the Christian prince is a guarantee against complete chaos and disorder and must be submitted to—to resist established authority is equivalent to resisting Christ. Thus we have a rigid and stable order in which all values are fixed and have to be preserved, protected, defended against dark forces of impulse and violent passion. War on behalf of the Christian prince and his power becomes a holy war for Christ against the devil. War too becomes a sacred duty.

The dark strokes in the picture have their historical explanation in the crisis of the barbarian invasions. But there are also brighter strokes, and we find in the thought of Aquinas, Scotus, Bonaventure, Dante a basically world-affirming and optimistic view of man, of his world and his work, in the perspective of the Christian redemption. Here in the more peaceful and flourishing years of the twelfth and thirteenth centuries we see a harmonious synthesis of nature and grace, in which the created world itself is an epiphany of divine wisdom and love, and, redeemed in and by Christ, will return to God with all its beauty restored by the transforming power of grace, which reaches down to material creation through man and his work. Already in St. Thomas we find the groundwork for an optimistic Christian affirmation of natural and worldly values in the perspective of an eschatological love. However, this view too is static rather than dynamic, hierarchic, layer upon layer, rather than ongoing and self-creating, the fulfillment of a predetermined intellectual plan rather than the creative project of a free and self-building love.

In the Carolingian worldview it somehow happened that the idea of the world as an object of choice tended to be frozen. The "world" was identified simply with the sinful, the perilous, the unpredictable (therefore in many cases the new, and even worse the free), and this was what one automatically rejected. Or, if one had the misfortune to choose it, one went at once to confession. The world was therefore what one did not choose. Since society itself was constructed on this concept of the world, Christian society ("Christendom") conceived itself as a world-denying society in the midst of the world. A pilgrim society on the way to another world. It was fitting that there should be in the midst of that society, and in a place of special prominence and choice, certain people who were professional world-deniers, whose very existence was a sign of *contemptus mundi* and of otherworldly aspirations. Thus from a certain point of view this renunciation and unworldliness of monks became a justification of worldly power and of the established social and economic structures. The society that, by its respect for consecrated unworldliness, confessed its own heavenly aspirations, was certainly the realm of Christ on earth; its kings and its mighty were all alike pilgrims with the poor and humble. If all kept their proper place in the procession the pilgrimage would continue to go well. This is all obvious to everyone who has ever read a line about the Middle Ages, and its obviousness is presently being run into the ground by critics of monasticism. What these critics overlook is that though the theory was austere and negative, in practice the "sacred" and basically "clerical" and "monastic" Christendom produced a world-affirming, nature-respecting, life-loving, love-oriented, fruitful, and rich culture. It had its limitations and its grave flaws. But the monastic and contemplative ideal of the Middle Ages, based on an ideological rejection of the world, actually recovered and rediscovered the values of the world on a deeper and more imperishable level, not merely somewhere aloft in a card file of Platonic ideas, but in the world itself, its life, its work, its people, its strivings, its hopes, and its existential day-to-day reality. The world-denying monastic ethos found itself willy-nilly incorporated in a life-affirming and humanistic climate. No one who has really read Anselm, Thomas, John of Salisbury, Scotus, Bonaventure, Eckhart, and the rest can seriously doubt this.

Nevertheless, this stereotyped hierarchic idea of the world's structure eventually ceased to be really fruitful and productive. It was already sterile and unreal as early as the fifteenth century. And the fact that the Church of the Second Vatican Council has finally admitted that the old immobilism will no longer serve is a bit too overdue to be regarded as a monumental triumph. The Constitution on the Church in the Modern World is salted with phrases which suggest that the Fathers were, at least some of them, fully aware of this.

In any case, one of the essential tasks of *aggiornamento* is that of renewing the whole perspective of theology in such a way that our ideas of God, man, and the world are no longer dominated by the Carolingian-medieval imagery of the sacred and hierarchical cosmos, in which everything is decided beforehand and in which the only choice is to accept gladly what is imposed as part of an immobile and established social structure.

In "turning to the world" the contemporary Church is first of all admitting that the world can once again become an object of choice. Not only can it be chosen, but in fact it must be chosen. How? If I had no choice about the age in which I was to live, I nevertheless have a choice about the attitude I take and about the way and the extent of my participation in its living ongoing events. To choose the world is not then merely a pious admission that the world is acceptable because it comes from the hand of God. It is first of all an acceptance of a task and a vocation in the world, in history and in time. In my time, which is the present. To choose the world is to choose to do the work I am capable of doing, in collaboration with my brother, to make the world better, more free, more just, more livable, more human. And it has now become transparently obvious that mere automatic "rejection of the world" and "contempt for the world" is in fact not a choice but the evasion of choice. The man who pretends that he can turn his back on Auschwitz or Vietnam and act as if they were not there is simply bluffing. I think this is getting to be generally admitted, even by monks.

On the other hand the stereotype of world rejection is now being firmly replaced by a collection of equally empty stereotypes of world affirmation in which I, for one, have very little confidence. They often seem to be gestures, charades, mummery designed to make the ones participating in them feel secure, to make them feel precisely that they are "like participating" and really doing something. So precisely at the moment when it becomes vitally important for the destiny of man that man should learn to choose for himself a peaceful, equitable, sane, and humane world the whole question of choice itself becomes a stark and dreadful one. We talk about choosing, yet everything seems more grimly determined than ever before. We are caught in an enormous web of con-sequences, a net of erroneous and even pathological effects of other men's deci-sions. After Hitler, how can Germany be anything but a danger to world peace? To choose the world therefore is to choose the anguish of being hampered and frustrated in a situation fraught with frightful difficulties. We can affirm the world and its values all we like, but the complexity of events responds too often with a cold negation of our hopes.

In the old days when everyone compulsively rejected the world it was really not hard at all to secretly make quite a few healthy and positive affirmations of a worldly existence in the best sense of the word, in praise of God and for the good of all men. Nowadays when we talk so much of freedom, commitment, "engagement" and so on, it becomes imperative to ask whether the choices we are making have any meaning whatever. Do they change anything? Do they get us anywhere? Do we really choose to alter the direction of our lives or do we simply comfort ourselves with the choice of making another choice? Can we really decide effectively for a better world?

The "suggestion" that has now most obviously replaced that of the Carolin-gians is that of Karl Marx. In this view, history is not finished; it has just reached the point where it may, if we are smart, begin. There is no predetermined divine plan (although frankly the messianism in Marx is basically Biblical and eschato-logical). After a long precarious evolution matter has reached the point, in man, where it can become fully aware of itself, take itself in hand, control its own destiny. And now at last that great seething mass of material forces, the world, will enter upon its true destiny by being raised to a human level. The instru-ments by which this can be accomplished—technology, cybernetics—are now in our power. But are we in our own power? No, we are still determined by the illusions of thought patterns, superstructures, devised to justify antiquated and destructive economic patterns. Hence if man is to choose to make himself, if he is to become free at last, his duty can be narrowed down to one simple option, one basic commitment: the struggle against the (imperialist) world.

With a shock we find ourselves in a familiar pattern: a predetermined strug-gle against evil in which personal freedom is viewed with intolerance and sus-picion. The world must be changed because it is unacceptable as it is. But the change must be guided by authority and political power. The forces of good are all incarnate in this authority. The forces of evil are on the contrary incarnate in the power of the enemy system. Man cannot be left to himself. He must submit entirely to the control of the collectivity for which he exists. "Man" is not the person but the collective animal. Though he may eventually become free, now is not the time of freedom but of obedience, authority, power, control. Man does not choose to make himself except in the sense that he submits to a choice dictated by the authority of science and the messianic collective—the party which represents the chosen eschatological class. Hence though in theory there are all kinds of possible choices, in reality the only basic choice is that of rejecting and destroying the evil "world"—namely capitalist imperialism and, in the present juncture, the United States. Hence the ambiguities of Communist dogma at the moment: the choice of peace is of course nothing else than the choice of war against the United States. In other words, we have turned the page of *Aïda* and we are now playing "Take Me Out to the Ball Game," but it is the same crazy Marx Brothers' opera. Freedom, humanism, peace, plenty, and joy are all enthusiastically invoked, but prove on closer examination to be their opposites. There is only one choice, to submit to the decision handed down from on high by an authoritarian power which defines good and evil in political terms.

This, as I see it, is the present state of the question. The Church has finally realized officially that the classic worldview, which began to develop serious flaws five hundred years ago, is no longer viable at all. There is something of a stampede for security in a new worldview.

In this endeavor the dialogue with Marxism is going to be of crucial importance not only for Christians but for Marxists. For if it is a true dialogue it will possibly involve some softening and adjustment of doctrinaire positions and an opening to new perspectives and possibilities of collaboration. Obviously, however, the dialogue with official and established Marxism—the Soviets or Red China—is not to be considered yet as a meaningful possibility. But the conversations that have begun with the type of revisionist Marxism represented by the French thinker Roger Garaudy may certainly have some effects. But what effects? Good or bad? It is all too easy for enthusiastic Catholics, having tasted a little of the new wine, to convince themselves that "turning to the world" and "choosing the world" means simply turning to Marx and choosing some variation—Maoist, Soviet, Castroist—of the Communist political line. There is no question that since the Council a few Catholic thinkers and publicists in Europe and South America are tending in this direction. Their tendency is understandable, but I do not find it altogether hopeful.

The majority of Catholic thinkers today are, however, working in the direction of a modern worldview in which the demands of the new humanism of Marx, Freud, Teilhard, Bonhoeffer, and others are fully respected and often heartily endorsed. For them, the tendency is no longer to regard God as enthroned "out there" at the summit of the cosmos, but as the "absolute future" who will manifest Himself in and through man, by the transformation of man and the world by science oriented to Christ. Though this certainly is not a view which conservative theologians find comforting, it represents a serious attempt to re-express Christian truths in terms more familiar to modern man. It demands that we take a more dynamic view of man and of society. It requires openness, freedom, the willingness to face risks. It also postulates respect for the human person in the human community. But at the same time it seems to me that it may have serious deficiencies insofar as it may ignore the really deep problems of collective technological and cybernetic society. To assume, for instance, that just because scientific and technological humanism can theoretically be seen as "perfectly biblical" ("nothing is more biblical than technology," says Père Daniélou) does not alter the profound dehumanization that can in fact take place in technological society (as Daniélou also clearly sees). The fact that man can now theoretically control and direct his own destiny does nothing to mitigate the awful determinism which in practice makes a mockery of the most realistic plans and turns all men's projects diametrically against their professed humanistic aims. The demonic gap between expressed aims and concrete achievements in the conduct of the Vietnam War, for instance, should be an object lesson in the impotence of technology to come to grips with the human needs and realities of our time.

I have a profound mistrust of all obligatory answers. The great problem of our time is not to formulate clear answers to neat theoretical questions but to tackle the self-destructive alienation of man in a society dedicated in theory to human values and in practice to the pursuit of power for its own sake. All the new and fresh answers in the world, all the bright official confidence in the collectivity of the secular city, will do nothing to change the reality of this alienation. The Marxist worldview is the one really coherent and systematic one that has so far come forward to replace the old medieval Christian and classic synthesis. It has in fact got itself accepted, for better or for worse, by more than half the human race. And yet, while claiming to offer man hope of deliverance from alienation, it has demanded a more unquestioning, a more irrational, and a more submissive obedience than ever to its obligatory answers, even when these are manifestly self-contradictory and destructive of the very values they claim to defend.

The dialogue with Marxism is an obvious necessity. But if in the course of it we simply create a vapid brew of neo-modernist and pseudoscientific optimism I do not see what has been gained, especially if it leaves people passive and helpless in the presence of dehumanizing forces that no one seems quite able to identify exactly and cope with effectively. In this sense, the world is certainly a problem. Its idea of itself is extremely ambiguous. Its claims to pinpoint and to solve its own greatest problems are, in my opinion, not very convincing. Its obligatory answers are hardly acceptable. I am not in love with them!

When "the world" is hypostatized (and it inevitably is) it becomes another of those dangerous and destructive fictions with which we are trying vainly to grapple. And for anyone who has seriously entered into the medieval Christian, or the Hindu, or the Buddhist conceptions of *contemptus mundi, Mara,* and the *"emptiness of the world,"* it will be evident that this means not the rejection of a reality, but the unmasking of an illusion. The world as pure object is something that is not there. It is not a reality outside us for which we exist. It is not a firm and absolute objective structure which has to be accepted on its own inexorable terms. The world has in fact no terms of its own. It dictates no terms to man. We and our world interpenetrate. If anything, the world exists for us, and we exist for ourselves. It is only in assuming full responsibility for our world, for our lives, and for ourselves that we can be said to live really for God. The whole human reality, which of course transcends us as individuals and as a collectivity, nevertheless interpenetrates the world of nature (which is obviously "real") and the world of history (also "real" insofar as it is made up of the total effect of all our decisions and actions). But this reality, though "external" and "objective," is not something entirely independent of us, which dominates us inexorably from without through the medium of certain fixed laws which science alone can discover and use. It is an extension and a projection of ourselves and of our lives, and if we attend to it respectfully, while attending also to our own freedom and our own integrity, we can learn to obey its ways and coordinate our lives with its mysterious movements. The way to find the real "world" is not merely to measure and observe what is outside us, but to discover our own inner ground. For that is where the world is, first of all: in my deepest self. But there I find the world to be quite different from the "obligatory answers." This "ground," this "world" where I am mysteriously present at once to my own self and to the freedoms of all other men, is not a visible objective and determined structure with fixed laws and demands. It is a living and self-creating mystery of which I am myself a part, to which I am myself my own unique door. When I find the world in my own ground, it is impossible for me to be alienated by it. It is precisely the obligatory answers which insist on showing me the world as totally other than myself and my brother, which alienate me from myself and from my brother. Hence I see no reason for our compulsion to manufacture ever newer and more shiny sets of obligatory answers.

The questions and the answers surely have their purpose. We are rational and dialectical beings. But even the best answers are themselves not final. They point to something further which cannot be embodied in a verbal ground. They point to life itself in its inalienable and personal ground. They point to that realm of values which, in the eyes of scientific and positivistic thought, has no meaning.

But how can we come to grips with the world except insofar as it is a value, that is to say, insofar as it exists for us?

There remains a profound wisdom in the traditional Christian approach to the world as to an object of choice. But we have to admit that the habitual and mechanical compulsions of a certain limited type of Christian thought have falsified the true value-perspective in which the world can be discovered and chosen as it is. To treat the world merely as an agglomeration of material goods and objects outside ourselves, and to reject these goods and objects in order to seek others which are "interior" and "spiritual," is in fact to miss the whole point of the challenging confrontation of the world and Christ. Do we really choose between the world and Christ as between two conflicting realities absolutely opposed? Or do we choose Christ by choosing the world as it really is in him, that is to say created and redeemed by him, and encountered in the ground of our own personal freedom and of our love? Do we really renounce ourselves and the world in order to find Christ, or do we renounce our alienated and false selves in order to choose our own deepest truth in choosing both the world and Christ at the same time? If the deepest ground of my being is love, then in that very love itself and nowhere else will I find myself, and the world, and my brother and Christ. It is not a question of either-or but of all-in-one. It is not a matter of exclusivism and "purity" but of wholeness, wholeheartedness, unity, and Meister Eckhart's *Gleichheit* (equality) which finds the same ground of love in everything.

The world cannot be a problem to anyone who sees that ultimately Christ, the world, his brother, and his own inmost ground are made one and the same in grace and redemptive love. If all the current talk about the world helps people to discover this, then it is fine. But if it produces nothing but a whole new divisive gamut of obligatory positions and "contemporary answers" we might as well forget it. The world itself is no problem, but we are a problem to ourselves because we are alienated from ourselves, and this alienation is due precisely to an inveterate habit of division by which we break reality into pieces and then wonder why, after we have manipulated the pieces until they fall apart, we find ourselves out of touch with life, with reality, with the world, and most of all with ourselves.

26

A Christian Looks at Zen[1]

In late November 1965, John Wu, diplomat, scholar, Catholic convert, and Merton's chief supporter and advisor for his book *The Way of Chuang Tzu*, wrote to ask if Merton would provide an introduction for a book Wu was writing about the great Chinese Zen (or Ch'an) masters. Merton replied on December 3: "if you are not afraid that I will ruin the book and take away the readers' appetite, and afflict them with permanent allergies to Zen and all things related to it, I will gladly try my hand, though I have been forbidden to write any more prefaces by my publisher, who says I write too many" (*Hidden Ground of Love*, 631). While the preface was included in Merton's "to-do" list in January 1966 (*Learning to Love*, 351), Merton's July 11 letter to Wu reveals that it was still unwritten: "You are probably wondering about the preface. I am still in the long stage of preparation. I simply cannot rush into a thing like this, but I think that by next week I will be ready to try getting something on paper. I want to treat the question of Christianity and Zen: in what are they alike, in what they are not alike, and so on. A brief simple contribution to East-West understanding. But that is exactly the hardest thing to do well" (*Hidden Ground of Love*, 634). On July 20 Merton noted in his journal, "Yesterday, though it was very hot in the hermitage, forced myself to begin the long delayed introduction to John Wu's book. But I still don't feel I am ready yet" (*Learning to Love*, 97); two days later, he wrote, "Finished the first draft for my preface to John Wu's book on Zen. It is a great relief to get this out of the way" (*Learning to Love*, 99). In the event, there was no need to hurry; Wu evidently had difficulty finding a publisher, and it was more than a year later that *The Golden Age of Zen* appeared, with Merton's preface (1-27), in Taiwan (Taipei: National War College/Committee on the Compilation of the Chinese Library, 1967) (an American edition had to wait until the Doubleday Image paperback in 1996). In slightly different form, less closely tied to the book, the essay was included in *Zen and the Birds of Appetite* (33-58), the version reprinted here. While not particularly brief or notably simple, the essay does achieve Merton's aim to contribute to East-West understanding, and is probably his most compelling statement both of the reasons for his own attraction to Zen and of his conviction of Zen's compatibility with, even enhancement of, his own Christian faith. He emphasizes that the priority in Zen, and in Buddhism generally, of immediate

---

1. First published as preface to John C. H. Wu's *The Golden Age of Zen*, Committee on Compilation of the Chinese Library.

experience over verbal formulation and abstract explanation means that it can be quite readily approached not as a competing source of revelation but as a way of paying attention, of become aware of and participating in the unitive ground of being beyond the distinction of subject and object. Such an intuitive awareness not only does not contradict the Christian kerygma, the revelation of the saving power of Christ, but can serve as a catalyst for the Christian to move beyond the intellectual acceptance of doctrinal formulations to the lived experience of participating in the redemptive pattern such formulations describe, of sharing in the Paschal Mystery of unitive love described by St. Paul in Galatians and echoed by Christian contemplatives throughout the history of the Church: "I have been crucified with Christ; it is no longer I who live but Christ lives in me." For Merton, this *Kenosis*, this emptying of self to be reborn in Christ, is at the heart of the Christian mystery, and puts Christians in touch with the heart of the mystery of nondualism in Zen that is expressed as "having the Buddha mind." The wisdom of Zen, Merton suggests, can reawaken in Christians long accustomed to a highly intellectualized and moralistic conception of their faith a recognition that "the full inner life of the Church . . . includes not only access to an authoritative teaching but above all to a deep personal experience which is at once unique and yet shared by the whole Body of Christ in the Spirit of Christ." Zen's "intuitive affinity for Christian mysticism" provides both a point of contact for understanding and appreciating a different religious tradition, and also an opportunity to rediscover a crucial yet largely neglected dimension of one's own spiritual heritage.

D
R. JOHN C. H. WU is in a uniquely favorable position to interpret Zen for the West. He has given courses on Zen in Chinese and in American universities. An eminent jurist and diplomat, a Chinese convert to Catholicism, a scholar but also a man of profoundly humorous simplicity and spiritual freedom, he is able to write of Buddhism not from hearsay or study alone, but from within. Dr. Wu is not afraid to admit that he brought Zen, Taoism, and Confucianism with him into Christianity. In fact in his well-known Chinese translation of the New Testament he opens the Gospel of St. John with the words, "In the beginning was the Tao."

He nowhere feels himself obliged to pretend that Zen causes him to have dizzy spells or palpitations of the heart. Nor does he attempt the complex and frustrating task of trying to conciliate Zen insights with Christian doctrine. He simply takes hold of Zen and presents it without comment. Anyone who has any familiarity with Zen will immediately admit that this is the only way to talk about it. To approach the subject with an intellectual or theological chip on the shoulder would end only in confusion. The truth of the matter is that you can hardly set Christianity and Zen side by side and compare them. This would almost be like trying to compare mathematics and tennis. And if you are writing a book on tennis which might conceivably be read by many mathematicians, there is little point in bringing mathematics into the discussion—best to stick to the tennis. That is what Dr. Wu has done with Zen.

On the other hand, Zen is deliberately cryptic and disconcerting. It seems to say the most outrageous things about the life of the spirit. It seems to jolt even the Buddhist mind out of its familiar thought routines and devout imaginings, and no doubt it will be even more shocking to those whose religious outlook is remote from Buddhism. Zen can sound, at times, frankly and avowedly irreligious. And it is, in the sense that it makes a direct attack on formalism and myth, and regards conventional religiosity as a hindrance to mature spiritual development. On the other hand, in what sense is Zen, as such, "religious" at all? Yet where do we ever find "pure Zen" dissociated from a religious and cultural matrix of some sort? Some of the Zen Masters were iconoclasts. But the life of an ordinary Zen temple is full of Buddhist piety and ritual, and some Zen literature abounds in devotionalism and in conventional Buddhist religious concepts. The Zen of D. T. Suzuki is completely free from all this. But can it be called "typical"? One of the advantages of Dr. Wu's Christian treatment is that he, too, is able to see Zen apart from this accidental setting. It is like seeing the mystical doctrine of St. John of the Cross apart from the somewhat irrelevant backdrop of Spanish baroque. However, the whole study of Zen can bristle with questions like these, and when the well-meaning inquirer receives answers to his questions, then hundreds of other questions arise to take the place of the two or three that have been "answered."

Though much has been said, written, and published in the West about Zen, the general reader is probably not much the wiser for most of it. And unless he has some idea of what Zen is all about he may be mystified by Dr. Wu's book, which is full of the classic Zen material: curious anecdotes, strange happenings, cryptic declarations, explosions of illogical humor, not to mention contradictions, inconsistencies, eccentric and even absurd behavior, and all for what? For some apparently esoteric purpose which is never made clear to the satisfaction of the logical Western mind.

Now the reader with a Judeo-Christian background of some sort (and who in the West does not still have some such background?) will naturally be predisposed to misinterpret Zen because he will instinctively take up the position of one who is confronting a "rival system of thought" or a "competing ideology" or an "alien worldview" or more simply "a false religion." Anyone who adopts such a position makes it impossible for himself to see what Zen is, because he assumes in advance that it must be something that it expressly refuses to be. Zen is not a systematic explanation of life, it is not an ideology, it is not a worldview, it is not a theology of revelation and salvation, it is not a mystique, it is not a way of ascetic perfection, it is not mysticism as this is understood in the West, in fact it fits no convenient category of ours. Hence all our attempts to tag it and dispose of it with labels like "pantheism," "quietism," "illuminism," "Pelagianism," must be completely incongruous, and proceed from a naïve assumption that Zen pretends to justify the ways of God to man and to do so falsely. Zen is not concerned with God in the way Christianity is, though one is entitled to discover sophisticated analogies between the Zen experience of the Void (*Sunyata*) and the experience of God in the "unknowing" of apophatic Christian mysticism. However, Zen cannot be properly judged as a mere doctrine, for though there are in it implicit doctrinal elements, they are entirely secondary to the inexpressible Zen experience.

True, we cannot really understand Chinese Zen if we do not grasp the implicit Buddhist metaphysic which it so to speak acts out. But the Buddhist metaphysic itself is hardly doctrinal in our elaborate philosophical and theological sense: Buddhist philosophy is an interpretation of ordinary human experience, but an interpretation which is not revealed by God nor discovered in the access of inspiration nor seen in a mystical light. Basically, Buddhist metaphysics is a very simple and natural elaboration of the implications of Buddha's own experience of enlightenment. Buddhism does not seek primarily to understand or to "believe in" the enlightenment of Buddha as the solution to all human problems, but seeks an existential and empirical participation in that enlightenment experience. It is conceivable that one might have the "enlightenment" without being aware of any discursive philosophical implications at all. These implications are not seen as having any theological bearing whatever, and they point only to the ordinary natural condition of man. It is true that they arrive at certain fundamental deductions which were in the course of time elaborated into complex religious and philosophical systems. But the chief characteristic of Zen is that it rejects all these systematic elaborations in order to get back, as far as possible, to the pure unarticulated and unexplained ground of direct experience. The direct experience of what? Life itself. What it means that I exist, that I live: who is this "I" that exists and lives? What is the difference between an authentic and an illusory awareness of the self that exists and lives? What are and are not the basic facts of existence?

When we in the West speak of "basic facts of existence" we tend immediately to conceive these facts as reducible to certain austere and foolproof propositions—logical statements that are guaranteed to have meaning because they are empirically verifiable. These are what Bertrand Russell called "atomic facts."

Now for Zen it is inconceivable that the basic facts of existence should be able to be stated in any proposition however atomic. For Zen, from the moment fact is transferred to a statement it is falsified. One ceases to grasp the naked reality of experience and one grasps a form of words instead. The *verification* that Zen seeks is not to be found in a dialectical transaction involving the reduction of fact to logical statement and the reflective verification of statement by fact. It may be said that long before Bertrand Russell spoke of "atomic facts" Zen had split the atom and made its own kind of statement in the explosion of logic into *Satori* (enlightenment). The whole aim of Zen is not to make foolproof statements about experience, but to come to direct grips with reality without the mediation of logical verbalizing.

But *what* reality? There is certainly a kind of living and nonverbal dialectic in Zen between the ordinary everyday experience of the senses (which is by no means arbitrarily repudiated) and the experience of enlightenment. Zen is not an idealistic rejection of sense and matter in order to ascend to a supposedly invisible reality which alone is real. The Zen experience is a direct grasp of the *unity* of the invisible and the visible, the noumenal and the phenomenal, or, if you prefer, an experiential realization that any such division is bound to be pure imagination.

D. T. Suzuki says: "Tasting, seeing, experiencing, living—all these demonstrate that there is something common to enlightenment-experience and our sense-experience; the one takes place in our innermost being, the other on the periphery of our consciousness. Personal experience thus seems to be the foundation of Buddhist philosophy. In this sense Buddhism is radical empiricism or experientialism, whatever dialectic later developed to probe the meaning of the enlightenment experience" (D. T. Suzuki, *Mysticism: Christian and Buddhist* [New York, 1957], p. 48).

Now the great obstacle to mutual understanding between Christianity and Buddhism lies in the Western tendency to focus not on the Buddhist *experience*, which is essential, but on the *explanation*, which is accidental and which indeed Zen often regards as completely trivial and even misleading.

Buddhist meditation, but above all that of Zen, seeks not to *explain* but to *pay attention*, to *become aware*, to *be mindful*, in other words to develop a certain *kind of consciousness that is above and beyond deception* by verbal formulas—or by emotional excitement. Deception in what? Deception in its grasp of itself as it really is. Deception due to diversion and distraction from what is right there—consciousness itself.

Zen, then, aims at a kind of certainty: but it is not the logical certainty of philosophical proof, still less the religious certainty that comes with the acceptance of the word of God by the obedience of faith. It is rather the certainty that goes with an authentic metaphysical intuition which is also existential and empirical. The purpose of all Buddhism is to refine the consciousness until this kind of insight is attained, and the religious implications of the insight are then variously worked out and applied to life in the different Buddhist traditions.

In the *Mahayana* tradition, which includes Zen, the chief implication of this insight into the human condition is *Karuna* or compassion, which leads to a paradoxical reversal of what the insight itself might seem to imply. Instead of rejoicing in his escape from the phenomenal world of suffering, the Bodhisattva elects to remain in it and finds in it his *Nirvana*, by reason not only of the metaphysic which identifies the phenomenal and the noumenal, but also of the compassionate love which identifies all the sufferers in the round of birth and death with the Buddha, whose enlightenment they potentially share. Though there are a heaven and a hell for Buddhists, these are not ultimate, and in fact it would be entirely ambiguous to assume that Buddha is regarded as a Savior who leads his faithful disciples to *Nirvana* as to a kind of negative heaven. (Pure Land Buddhism or Amidism is, however, distinctly a salvation religion.)

It cannot be repeated too often: in understanding Buddhism it would be a great mistake to concentrate on the "doctrine," the formulated philosophy of life, and to neglect the experience, which is absolutely essential, the very heart of Buddhism. This is in a sense the exact opposite of the situation in Christianity. For Christianity begins with revelation. Though it would be misleading to classify this revelation simply as a "doctrine" and an "explanation" (it is far more than that—the revelation of God Himself in the mystery of Christ) it is nevertheless communicated to us in words, in statements, and everything depends on the believer's accepting the truth of these statements.

Therefore Christianity has always been profoundly concerned with these statements: with the accuracy of their transmission from the original sources, with the precise understanding of their exact meaning, with the elimination and indeed the condemnation of false interpretations. At times this concern has been exaggerated almost to the point of an obsession, accompanied by arbitrary and fanatical insistence on hairsplitting distinctions and the purest niceties of theological detail.

This obsession with doctrinal formulas, juridical order, and ritual exactitude has often made people forget that the heart of Catholicism, too, is a *living experience* of unity in Christ which far transcends all conceptual formulations. What too often has been overlooked, in consequence, is that Catholicism is the taste and experience of eternal life: "We announce to you the eternal life which was with the Father and has appeared to us. What we have seen and have heard we announce to you, in order that you also may have fellowship with us and that our fellowship may be with the Father and with His Son Jesus Christ" (1 John 1:2-3). Too often the Catholic has imagined himself obliged to stop short at a mere correct and external belief expressed in good moral behavior, instead of entering fully into the life of hope and love consummated by union with the invisible God "in Christ and in the Spirit," thus fully sharing in the Divine Nature (Ephesians 2:18; 2 Peter 1:4; Colossians 1:9-17; 1 John 4:12-13).

The Second Vatican Council has (we hope) happily put an end to this obsessive tendency in Catholic theological investigation. But the fact remains that for Christianity, a religion of the Word, the understanding of the statements which embody God's revelation of Himself remains a primary concern. Christian experience is a fruit of this understanding, a development of it, a deepening of it.

At the same time, Christian experience itself will be profoundly affected by the idea of revelation that the Christian himself will entertain. For example, if revelation is regarded simply as a system of truths *about* God and an explanation of how the universe came into existence, what will eventually happen to it, what is the purpose of Christian life, what are its moral norms, what will be the rewards of the virtuous, and so on, then Christianity is in effect reduced to a worldview, at times a religious philosophy and little more, sustained by a more or less elaborate cult, by a moral discipline, and a strict code of Law. "Experience" of the inner meaning of Christian revelation will necessarily be distorted and diminished in such a theological setting. What will such experience be? Not so much a living theological experience of the presence of God in the world and in mankind through the mystery of Christ, but rather a sense of security in one's own correctness: a feeling of confidence that one has been saved, a confidence which is based on the reflex awareness that one holds the correct view of the creation and purpose of the world and that one's behavior is of a kind to be rewarded in the next life. Or, perhaps, since few can attain this level of self-assurance, then the Christian experience becomes one of anxious hope—a struggle with occasional doubt of the "right answers," a painful and constant effort to meet the severe demands of morality and law, and a somewhat desperate recourse to the sacraments which are there to help the weak who must constantly fall and rise again.

This of course is a sadly deficient account of true Christian experience, based on a distortion of the true import of Christian revelation. Yet it is the impression non-Christians often get of Christianity from the outside, and when one proceeds to compare, say, Zen experience in its purity with this diminished and distorted type of "Christian experience," then one's comparison is just as meaningless and misleading as a comparison of Christian philosophy and theology on their highest and most sophisticated level with the myths of a popular and decadent Buddhism.

When we set Christianity and Buddhism side by side, we must try to find the points where a genuinely common ground between the two exists. At the present moment, this is no easy task. In fact it is still practically impossible, as suggested above, to really find any such common ground except in a very schematic and artificial way. After all, what do we mean by Christianity, and what do we mean by Buddhism? Is Christianity Christian Theology? Ethics? Mysticism? Worship? Is our idea of Christianity to be taken without further qualification as the Roman Catholic Church? Or does it include Protestant Christianity? The Protestantism of Luther or that of Bonhoeffer? The Protestantism of the God-is-dead school? The Catholicism of St. Thomas? Of St. Augustine and the Western Church Fathers? A supposedly "pure" Christianity of the Gospels? A demythologized Christianity? A "social Gospel"? And what do we mean by Buddhism? The Theravada Buddhism of Ceylon, or that of Burma? Tibetan Buddhism? Tantric Buddhism? Pure Land Buddhism? Speculative and scholastic Indian Buddhism of the Middle Ages? Or Zen?

The immense variety of forms taken by thought, experience, worship, moral practice, in both Buddhism and Christianity make all comparisons haphazard, and in the end, when someone like the late Dr. Suzuki announced a study on *Mysticism: Christian and Buddhist*, it turned out to be, rather practically in fact, a comparison between Meister Eckhart and Zen. To narrow the field in this way is at least relevant, though to take Meister Eckhart as representative of Christian mysticism is hazardous. At the same time we must remark that Dr. Suzuki was much too convinced that Eckhart was unusual in his time, and that his statements must have shocked most of his contemporaries. Eckhart's condemnation was in fact due in some measure to rivalry between Dominicans and Franciscans, and his teaching, bold and in some points unable to avoid condemnation, was nevertheless based on St. Thomas to a great extent and belonged to a mystical tradition that was very much alive and was, in fact, the most vital religious force in the Catholicism of his time. Yet to identify Christianity with Eckhart would be completely misleading. That was not what Suzuki intended. He was not comparing the *mystical theology* of Eckhart with the Buddhist philosophy of the Zen Masters, but the *experience* of Eckhart, ontologically and psychologically, with the *experience* of the Zen Masters. This is a reasonable enterprise, offering some small hope of interesting and valid results.

But can one distill from religious or mystical experience certain pure elements which are common everywhere in all religions? Or is the basic understanding of the nature and meaning of experience so determined by the variety of doctrines that a comparison of experiences involves us inevitably in a comparison of metaphysical or religious beliefs? This is no easy question either. If a Christian mystic has an experience which can be phenomenologically compared with a Zen experience, does it matter that the Christian in fact believes he is personally united with God and the Zen-man interprets his experience as *Sunyata* or the Void being aware of itself? In what sense can these two experiences be called "mystical"? Suppose that the Zen Masters forcefully repudiate any attempt on the part of Christians to grace them with the titles of "mystics"?

It must certainly be said that a certain type of concordist thought today too easily assumes as a basic dogma that "the mystics" in all religions are all experiencing the same thing and are all alike in their liberation from the various doctrines and explanations and creeds of their less fortunate co-religionists. All religions thus "meet at the top," and their various theologies and philosophies become irrelevant when we see that they were merely means for arriving at the same end, and all means are alike efficacious. This has never been demonstrated with any kind of rigor, and though it has been persuasively advanced by talented and experienced minds, we must say that a great deal of study and investigation must be done before much can be said on this very complex question which, once again, seems to imply a purely formalistic view of theological and philosophical doctrines, as if a fundamental belief were something that a mystic could throw off like a suit of clothes and as if his very experience itself were not in some sense modified by the fact that he held this belief.

At the same time, since the personal experience of the mystic remains inaccessible to us and can only be evaluated indirectly through texts and other testimonials—perhaps written and given by others—it is never easy to say with any security that what a Christian mystic and a Sufi and a Zen Master experience is really "the same thing." What does such a claim really mean? Can it be made at all, without implying (quite falsely) that these higher experiences are "experiences of something"? It therefore remains a very serious problem to distinguish in all these higher forms of religious and metaphysical consciousness what is "pure experience" and what is to some extent determined by language, symbol, or indeed by the "grace of a sacrament." We have hardly reached the point where we know enough about these different states of consciousness and about their metaphysical implications to compare them in accurate detail. But there are nevertheless certain analogies and correspondence which are evident even now, and which may perhaps point out the way to a better mutual understanding. Let us not rashly take them as "proofs" but only as significant clues.

Is it therefore possible to say that both Christians and Buddhists can equally well practice Zen? Yes, if by Zen we mean precisely the quest for direct and pure experience on a metaphysical level, liberated from verbal formulas and linguistic preconceptions. On the theological level the question becomes more complex. It will be touched on at the end of this essay.

The best we can say is that in certain religions, Buddhism for instance, the philosophical or religious framework is of a kind that *can* more easily be discarded, because it has in itself a built-in "ejector," so to speak, by which the meditator is at a certain point flung out from the conceptual apparatus into the Void. It is possible for a Zen Master to say nonchalantly to his disciple, "If you meet the Buddha, kill him!" But in Christian mysticism the question whether or not the mystic can get along without the human "form" (*Gestalt*) or the sacred Humanity of Christ is still hotly debated, with the majority opinion definitely maintaining the necessity for the Christ of faith to be present as ikon at the center of Christian contemplation. Here again, the question is confused by the failure to distinguish between the objective theology of Christian experience and the actual psychological facts of Christian mysticism in certain cases. And then one must ask, at what point do the abstract demands of theory take precedence over the psychological facts of experience? Or, to what extent does the theology of a theologian without experience claim to interpret correctly the "experienced theology" of the mystic who is perhaps not able to articulate the meaning of his experience in a satisfactory way?

We keep returning to one central question in two forms: the relation of objective doctrine to subjective mystic (or metaphysical) experience, and the difference in this relationship between Christianity and Zen. In Christianity the objective doctrine retains priority both in time and in eminence. In Zen the experience is always prior, not in time but in importance. This is because Christianity is based on supernatural revelation, and Zen, discarding all idea of any revelation and even taking a very independent view of sacred tradition (at least written), seeks to penetrate the natural ontological ground of being. Christianity is a religion of grace and divine gift, hence of total dependence on God. Zen is not easily classified as "a religion" (it is in fact easily separable from any religious matrix and can supposedly flourish in the soil either of non-Buddhist religions or no religion at all), and in any event it strives, like all Buddhism, to make man completely free and independent even in his striving for salvation and enlightenment. Independent of what? Of merely external supports and authorities which keep him from having access to and making use of the deep resources in his own nature and psyche. (Note that Chinese and Japanese Zen both in fact flourished in extremely disciplined and authoritarian cultures. Hence their emphasis on "autonomy" meant in fact an ultimate and humble discovery of inner freedom after one had exhausted all the possibilities of an intensely strict and austere authoritarian training—as the methods of the Zen Masters make abundantly clear!)

On the other hand, let us repeat that we must not neglect the great importance of experience in Christianity. But Christian experience always has a special modality, due to the fact that it is inseparable from the mystery of Christ and the collective life of the Church, the Body of Christ. To experience the mystery of Christ mystically or otherwise is always to transcend the merely individual psychological level and to "experience theologically with the Church" (*sentire cum Ecclesia*). In other words, this experience must always be in some way reducible to a theological form that can be shared by the rest of the Church or that shows that it is a sharing of what the rest of the Church experiences. There is therefore in the recording of Christian experiences a natural tendency to set them down in language and symbols that are easily accessible to other Christians. This may perhaps sometimes mean an unconscious translation of the inexpressible into familiar symbols that are always at hand ready for immediate use.

Zen on the other hand resolutely resists any temptation to be easily communicable, and a great deal of the paradox and violence of Zen teaching and practice is aimed at blasting the foundation of ready explanation and comforting symbol out from under the disciple's supposed "experience." The Christian experience is acceptable insofar as it accords with an established theological and symbolic pattern. The Zen experience is only acceptable on the basis of its absolute singularity, and yet it must be in some way communicable. How?

We cannot begin to understand how the Zen experience is manifested and communicated between master and disciple unless we realize *what* is communicated. If we do not know *what* is supposed to be signified, the strange method of signification will leave us totally disconcerted and more in the dark than we were when we started. Now in Zen, what is communicated is not a message. It is not simply a "word," even though it might be the "word of the Lord." It is not a "what." It does not bring "news" which the receiver did not already have, about something the one informed did not yet know. What Zen communicates is an awareness that is potentially already there but is not conscious of itself. Zen is then not *Kerygma* but realization, not revelation but consciousness, not news from the Father who sends His Son into this world, but awareness of the ontological ground of our own being here and now, right in the midst of the world. We will see later that the supernatural *Kerygma* and the metaphysical intuition of the ground of being are far from being incompatible. One may be said to prepare the way for the other. They can well complement each other, and for this reason Zen is perfectly compatible with Christian belief and indeed with Christian mysticism (if we understand Zen in its pure state, as metaphysical intuition).

If this is true, then we must admit it is perfectly logical to admit, with the Zen Masters, that "Zen teaches nothing." One of the greatest of the Chinese Zen Masters, the Patriarch, Hui Neng (seventh century A.D.), was asked a leading question by a disciple: "Who has inherited the spirit of the Fifth Patriarch?" (i.e., who is Patriarch now?):

Hui Neng replied: "One who understands Buddhism."

The monk pressed his point: "Have you then inherited it?"

Hui Neng said: "No."

"Why not?" asked the monk.

"Because I do not understand Buddhism."

This story is meant precisely to illustrate the fact that Hui Neng *had* inherited the role of Patriarch, or the charism of teaching the purest Zen. He was qualified to transmit the enlightenment of the Buddha himself to disciples. If he had laid claim to an authoritative teaching that made this enlightenment understandable to those who did not possess it, then he would have been teaching *something else*, that is to say a doctrine *about* enlightenment. He would be disseminating the message of his own understanding of Zen, and in that case he would not be awakening others to Zen in themselves, but imposing on them the imprint of his own understanding and teaching. Zen does not tolerate this kind of thing, since this would be incompatible with the true purpose of Zen: awakening a deep ontological awareness, a wisdom-intuition (*Prajna*) in the ground of the being of the one awakened. And in fact, the pure consciousness of *Prajna* would not be pure and immediate if it were a consciousness that one understands *Prajna*.

The language used by Zen is therefore in some sense an anti-language, and the "logic" of Zen is a radical reversal of philosophical logic. The human dilemma of communication is that we cannot communicate ordinarily without words and signs, but even ordinary experience tends to be falsified by our habits of verbalization and rationalization. The convenient tools of language enable us to decide beforehand what we think things mean, and tempt us all too easily to see things only in a way that fits our logical preconceptions and our verbal formulas. Instead of seeing *things* and *facts* as they are we see them as reflections and verifications of the sentences we have previously made up in our minds. We quickly forget how to simply *see* things and substitute our words and our formulas for the things themselves, manipulating facts so that we see only what conveniently fits our prejudices. Zen uses language against itself to blast out these preconceptions and to destroy the specious "reality" in our minds so that we can *see directly*. Zen is saying, as Wittgenstein said, "Don't think: Look!"

Since the Zen intuition seeks to awaken a direct metaphysical consciousness beyond the empirical, reflecting, knowing, willing, and talking ego, this awareness must be immediately present to itself and not mediated by either conceptual or reflexive or imaginative knowledge. And yet far from being mere negation, Zen is also entirely positive. Let us hear D. T. Suzuki on the subject:

> Zen always aims at grasping the central fact of life, which can never be brought to the dissecting table of the intellect. To grasp the central fact of life, Zen is forced to propose a series of negations. Mere negation however is not the spirit of Zen. . . . [Hence, he says, the Zen Masters neither affirm nor negate, they simply act or speak in such a way that the action or speech itself is a plain fact bursting with Zen. . . . Suzuki continues:] When the spirit of Zen is grasped in its purity, it will be seen what a real thing that (act—in this case a slap) is. For here is no negation, no affirmation, but a plain fact, a pure experience, the very foundation of our being and thought. All the quietness and emptiness one might desire in the midst of most active meditation lies therein. Do not be carried away by anything outward or conventional. Zen must be seized with bare hands, with no gloves on. (D. T. Suzuki, *Introduction to Zen Buddhism* [London, 1960], p. 51)

It is in this sense that "Zen teaches nothing; it merely enables us to wake up and become aware. It does not teach, it points." (Suzuki, *Introduction*, p. 38) The acts and gestures of a Zen Master are no more "statements" than is the ringing of an alarm clock.

All the words and actions of the Zen Masters and of their disciples are to be understood in this context. Usually the Master is simply "producing facts" which the disciple either sees or does not see.

Many of the Zen stories, which are almost always incomprehensible in rational terms, are simply the ringing of an alarm clock, and the reaction of the sleeper. Usually the misguided sleeper makes a response which in effect turns off the alarm so that he can go back to sleep. Sometimes he jumps out of bed with a shout of astonishment that it is so late. Sometimes he just sleeps and does not hear the alarm at all!

Insofar as the disciple takes the fact to be a sign of something else, he is misled by it. The Master may (by means of some other fact) try to make him aware of this. Often it is precisely at the point where the disciple realizes himself to be utterly misled that he also realizes everything else along with it: chiefly, of course, that there was nothing to realize in the first place except the fact. What *fact*? If you know the answer you are awake. You hear the alarm!

But we in the West, living in a tradition of stubborn ego-centered practicality and geared entirely for the use and manipulation of everything, always pass from one thing to another, from cause to effect, from the first to the next and to the last and then back to the first. Everything always points to something else, and hence we never stop anywhere because we cannot: as soon as we pause, the escalator reaches the end of the ride and we have to get off and find another one. Nothing is allowed just to be and to mean itself: everything has to mysteriously signify something else. Zen is especially designed to frustrate the mind that thinks in such terms. The Zen "fact," whatever it may be, always lands across our road like a fallen tree beyond which we cannot pass.

Nor are such facts lacking in Christianity—the Cross for example. Just as the Buddha's "Fire Sermon" radically transforms the Buddhist's awareness of all that is around him, so the "word of the Cross" in very much the same way gives the Christian a radically new consciousness of the meaning of his life and of his relationship with other men and with the world around him.

In both cases, the "facts" are not merely impersonal and objective, but facts of personal experience. Both Buddhism and Christianity are alike in making use of ordinary everyday human existence as material for a radical transformation of consciousness. Since ordinary everyday human existence is full of confusion and suffering, then obviously one will make good use of both of these in order to transform one's awareness and one's understanding, and to go beyond both to attain "wisdom" in love. It would be a grave error to suppose that Buddhism and Christianity merely offer various *explanations* of suffering, or worse, justifications and mystifications built on this ineluctable fact. On the contrary both show that suffering remains inexplicable most of all for the man who attempts *to explain it in order to evade it*, or who thinks explanation itself is an escape. Suffering is not a "problem" as if it were something we could stand outside and control. Suffering, as both Christianity and Buddhism see, each in its own way, is part of our very ego-identity and empirical existence, and the only thing to do about it is to plunge right into the middle of contradiction and confusion in order to be transformed by what Zen calls the "Great Death" and Christianity calls "dying and rising with Christ."

Let us now return to the obscure and tantalizing "facts" in which Zen deals. In the relation between Zen Master and disciple, the most usually encountered "fact" is the disciple's frustration, his inability to get somewhere by the use of his own will and his own reasoning. Most sayings of the Zen Masters deal with this situation, and try to convey to the disciple that he has a fundamentally misleading experience of himself and of his capacities.

"When the cart stops," said Huai-Jang, the Master of Ma-Tsu, "do you whip the cart or whip the ox?" And he added, "If one sees the Tao from the standpoint of making and unmaking, or gathering and scattering, one does not really see the Tao."

If this remark about whipping the cart or the ox is obscure, perhaps another *Mondo* (question and answer) will suggest the same fact in a different way.

A monk asks Pai-Chang, "Who is the Buddha?"
Pai-Chang answers: "Who are you?"

A monk wants to know what is *Prajna* (the metaphysical wisdom-intuition of Zen). Not only that, but *Mahaprajna*, Great or Absolute Wisdom. The whole works.

The Master answers without concern:

"The snow is falling fast and all is enveloped in mist."
The monk remains silent.
The Master asks: "Do you understand?"
"No, Master, I do not."
Thereupon the Master composed a verse for him:
    Mahaprajna
    It is neither taking in nor giving up.
    If one understands it not,
    The wind is cold, the snow is falling.
      (Suzuki, *Introduction*, pp. 99-100)

The monk is "trying to understand" when in fact he ought to try to *look*. The apparently mysterious and cryptic sayings of Zen become much simpler when we see them in the whole context of Buddhist "mindfulness" or awareness, which in its most elementary form consists in that "bare attention" which simply *sees* what is right there and does not add any comment, any interpretation, any judgment, any conclusion. It just *sees*. Learning to see in this manner is the basic and fundamental exercise of Buddhist meditation (See Nyanaponika Thera, *The Heart of Buddhist Meditation* [Colombo, Ceylon, 1956]).

If one reaches the point where understanding fails, this is not a tragedy: it is simply a reminder to stop thinking and start looking. Perhaps there is nothing to figure out after all: perhaps we only need to wake up.

A monk said: "I have been with you (Master), for a long time, and yet I am unable to understand your way. How is this?"

The Master said: "Where you do not understand, there is the point for your understanding."

"How is understanding possible when it is impossible?"

The Master said: "The cow gives birth to a baby elephant; clouds of dust rise over the ocean." (Suzuki, *Introduction*, p. 116)

In more technical language, and therefore perhaps more comprehensibly for us, Suzuki says: "*Prajna* is pure act, pure experience . . . it has a distinct noetic quality . . . but it is not rationalistic . . . it is characterized by immediacy . . . it must not be identified with ordinary intuition . . . for in the case of *prajna* intuition there is no definable object to be intuited. . . . In *prajna* intuition the object of intuition is never a concept postulated by an elaborate process of reasoning; it is never 'this' or 'that'; it does not want to attach itself to one particular object" (D. T. Suzuki, *Studies in Zen* [London, 1957], p]. 87-89). For this reason, Suzuki concludes that *Prajna* intuition is different from "the kind of intuition we have generally in religious and philosophical discourses" in which God or the Absolute are objects of intuition and "the act of intuition is considered complete when a state of identification takes place between the object and the subject" (Suzuki, *Studies,* p. 89).

This is not the place to discuss the very interesting and complex question raised here. Let us only say that it is by no means certain that the religious, or at any rate mystical, intuition always sees God "as object." And in fact we shall see that Suzuki qualifies this opinion quite radically by admitting that the mystical intuition of Eckhart is the same as *Prajna*.

Leaving this question aside, it must be said here that if anyone tries to spell out a philosophical or doctrinal interpretation for the Zen sayings like those we have quoted above, he is mistaken. If he seeks to argue that when Pai Chang points to the falling snow as answer to a question about the Absolute, as though to say that the falling snow were identified with the Absolute, in other words that this intuition was a reflexive pantheistic awareness of the *Absolute as object*, seen in the falling snow, then he has entirely missed the point of Zen. To imagine that Zen is "teaching pantheism" is to imagine that it is trying to explain something. We repeat: Zen explains nothing. It just sees. Sees what? Not an Absolute Object but Absolute Seeing.

Though this may seem very remote from Christianity, which is definitely a message, we must nevertheless remember the importance of *direct experience* in the Bible. All forms of "knowing," especially in the religious sphere, and especially where God is concerned, are valid in proportion as they are a matter of experience and of intimate contact. We are all familiar with the Biblical expression "to know" in the sense of to possess in the act of love. This is not the place to examine the possible Zenlike analogies in the experiences of the Old Testament prophets. They were certainly as factual, as existential, and as disconcerting as any fact of Zen! Nor can we more than indicate briefly here the well-known importance of direct experience in the New Testament. This is of course to be sought above all in the revelation of the Holy Spirit, the mysterious Gift in which God becomes one with the Believer in order to know and love Himself in the Believer.

In the first two chapters of the first Epistle to the Corinthians St. Paul distinguishes between two kinds of wisdom: one which consists in the knowledge of words and statements, a rational, dialectical wisdom, and another which is at once a matter of paradox and of experience, and goes beyond the reach of reason. To attain to this spiritual wisdom, one must first be liberated from servile dependence on the "wisdom of speech" (I Corinthians 1:17). This liberation is effected by the "word of the Cross" which makes no sense to those who cling to their own familiar views and habits of thought and is a means by which God "destroys the wisdom of the wise" (I Corinthians 1:18-23). The word of the Cross is in fact completely baffling and disconcerting both to the Greeks with their philosophy and to the Jews with their well-interpreted Law. But when one has been freed from dependence on verbal formulas and conceptual structures, the Cross becomes a source of "power." This power emanates from the "foolishness of God" and it also makes use of "foolish instruments" (the Apostles) (I Corinthians 1:27ff.). On the other hand, he who can accept this paradoxical "foolishness" experiences in himself a secret and mysterious power, which is the power of Christ living in him as the ground of a totally new life and a new being (I Corinthians 2:1-4; cf. Ephesians 1:18-23; Galatians 6:14-16).

Here it is essential to remember that for a Christian "the word of the Cross" is nothing theoretical, but a stark and existential experience of union with Christ in His death in order to share in His resurrection. To fully "hear" and "receive" the word of the Cross means much more than simple assent to the dogmatic proposition that Christ died for our sins. It means to be "nailed to the Cross with Christ," so that the ego-self is no longer the principle of our deepest actions, which now proceed from Christ living in us. "I live, now not I, but Christ lives in me" (Galatians 2:19-20; see also Romans 8:5-17). To receive the word of the Cross means the acceptance of a complete self-emptying, a *Kenosis*, in union with the self-emptying of Christ "obedient unto death" (Philippians 2:5-11). It is essential to true Christianity that this experience of the Cross and of self-emptying be central in the life of the Christian so that he may fully receive the Holy Spirit and know (again by experience) all the riches of God in and through Christ (John 14:16-17, 26; 15:26-27; 16:7-15).

When Gabriel Marcel says: "There are thresholds which thought alone, left to itself, can never permit us to cross. An experience is required—an experience of poverty and sickness . . . ." (quoted, A. Gelin, *Les Pauvres de Yahvé* [Paris, 1954], p. 57) he is stating a simple Christian truth in terms familiar to Zen.

We must never forget that Christianity is much more than the intellectual acceptance of a religious message by a blind and submissive faith which never understands what the message means except in terms of authoritative interpretations handed down externally by experts in the name of the Church. On the contrary, faith is the door to the full inner life of the Church, a life which includes not only access to an authoritative teaching but above all to a deep personal experience which is at once unique and yet shared by the whole Body of Christ, in the Spirit of Christ. St. Paul compares this knowledge of God, in the Spirit, to the subjective knowledge that a man has of himself. Just as no one can know my inner self except my own "spirit," so no one can know God except God's Spirit; yet this Holy Spirit is given to us, in such a way that God knows Himself in us, and this experience is utterly real, though it cannot be communicated in terms understandable to those who do not share it (see I Corinthians 2:7-15). Consequently, St. Paul concludes, "we have the mind of Christ" (I Corinthians 2:16).

Now when we see that for Buddhism *Prajna* is describable as "having the Buddha mind" we understand that there must surely be some possibility of finding an analogy somewhere between Buddhist and Christian experience, though we are now speaking more in terms of doctrine than of pure experience. Yet the doctrine is about the experience. We cannot push our investigation further here, but it is significant that Suzuki, reading the following lines from Eckhart (which are perfectly orthodox and traditional Catholic theology), said they were "*the same as Prajna intuition*" (D. T. Suzuki, *Mysticism: East and West*, p. 40; the quotation from C. de B. Evans's translation of Eckhart [London, 1924], p. 147). "In giving us His love God has given us the Holy Ghost so that we can love Him with the love wherewith He loves Himself." The Son Who, in us, loves the Father, in the Spirit, is translated thus by Suzuki into Zen terms: "one mirror reflecting another with no shadow between them" (Suzuki, *Mysticism: East and West*, p. 41).

Suzuki also frequently quotes a sentence of Eckhart's: "The eye wherein I see God is the same eye wherein God sees me" (Suzuki, *Mysticism: East and West*, p. 50) as an exact expression of what Zen means by *Prajna*.

Whether or not Dr. Suzuki's interpretation of the text in Zen terms is theologically perfect in every way remains to be seen, though at first sight there seems to be no reason why it should not be thoroughly acceptable. What is important for us here is that the interpretation is highly suggestive and interesting in itself, reflecting a kind of intuitive affinity for Christian mysticism. Furthermore it is highly significant that a Japanese thinker schooled in Zen should be so open to what is basically the most obscure and difficult mystery of Christian theology: the dogma of the Trinity and the mission of the Divine Persons in the Christian and in the Church. This would seem to indicate that the real area for investigation of analogies and correspondences between Christianity and Zen might after all be theology rather than psychology or asceticism. At least theology is not excluded, but it must be theology as experienced in Christian contemplation, not the speculative theology of textbooks and disputations.

The few words that have been written in this introduction, and the brief, bare suggestions it contains, are by no means intended as an adequate "comparison" between Christian experience and Zen experience. Obviously, we have done little more than express a pious hope that a common ground can some day be found. But at least this should make the Western and Christian reader more ready to enter this book with an open mind, and perhaps help him to suspend judgment for a while, and not decide immediately that Zen is so esoteric and so outlandish that it has no interest or importance for us. On the contrary, Zen has much to teach the West, and recently Dom Aelred Graham, in a book which became deservedly popular (Graham, *Zen Catholicism* [New York, 1963]), pointed out that there was not a little in Zen that was pertinent to our own ascetic and religious practice. It is quite possible for Zen to be adapted and used to clear the air of ascetic irrelevancies and help us to regain a healthy natural balance in our understanding of the spiritual life.

But Zen must be grasped in its simple reality, not rationalized or imagined in terms of some fantastic and esoteric interpretation of human existence.

Though few Westerners will ever actually come to a real understanding of Zen, it is still worth their while to be exposed to its brisk and heady atmosphere.

27

Terror and the Absurd: Violence and Nonviolence in Albert Camus

This essay is dated August 1966 on the mimeographed copy, confirmed by Merton's August 14 letter to Gloria Bennett mentioning that he had "just finished a study of Camus on violence" and would send along a copy when one became available (*Road to Joy*, 342). It is the first of seven studies on various aspects of Camus' work that Merton would write, four of them in late summer and early fall of 1966, the others in mid-1967 and early 1968. (For a fine overview of the first phase, including this essay, see David Joseph Belcastro, "Merton and Camus on Christian Dialogue with a Postmodern World," *The Merton Annual* 10 [1997], 223-33.) It first appeared in India in *Gandhi Marg* 42 (April 1967), 85-101, but was not published in America until after Merton's death, in *Motive* 29 (February 1969), 4-15. The *Motive* version is considerably shorter than the original, almost certainly abridged for publication purposes, first by cancellations on the mimeograph and then in a retyped version of the shortened text, with some minor alterations but no significant additions, a reversal of Merton's usual practice of revision and expansion. The *Motive* text has been shortened even further, presumably by the editors at the time of printing. An editor's note accompanying the printed text states that the article had been requested more than a year before and that a "final version" had been sent the previous summer. The longer version was included, along with Merton's six other essays on Camus, in *Literary Essays* (232-51), and is the one reprinted here; it is virtually identical with the *Gandhi Marg* text, except that the latter lacks the introductory author's note. Merton's interest in Camus dates back to the late 1950s, when he began reading the French writer's novels, essays, and plays as part of his quest for a "third way" between communist totalitarianism and laissez-faire capitalist idolatry of individualistic self-interest. He was particularly impressed by Camus' refusal to subordinate the rights and needs of concrete human persons to the demands of abstract ideology of whatever political stripe, and his commitment to a rigorous yet generous humanism not grounded in theistic belief. Merton finds his own adherence to religious nonviolence both challenged and reinforced by Camus' nuanced discussion of the ethic of revolt in *The Rebel*, in which he rejects both the "rigid and totalist revolution" that is willing to sacrifice as many lives as are considered necessary to realize its ideal, and the stance of "passive resignation" that is willing to countenance injustice, to oneself and especially toward others, that permits the forces of oppression and death to prevail—a position he associates, in Merton's view somewhat simplistically, with traditional Christian preaching of the consolations of eternal life in the face of earthly suffering. While Camus accepts the logic of a nonviolence rooted in "a philosophy of eternity," belief in a transcendent God, he finds himself blocked from such a belief by the pervasive reality of human suffering. He chooses instead an ethic of revolt that is in his view at once more modest in its rejection of transcendence and more dynamic in its demand for active resistance to evil. While Merton questions the accuracy of Camus' association of nonviolence "with silence, submission, and passivity when authentic nonviolent resistance is *active* and should be highly articulate, since, if it is understood in the Gandhian sense, it demands much more lucidity and courage than the use of force does," he values Camus' warning against "preach[ing] an abstract and ideal nonviolence" that is not grounded in a disciplined and committed praxis but subject to unfocused experimentation that could "simply play into the hands of the violent." As a sympathetic yet challenging critic whose position on human dignity and human weakness is in many ways remarkably close to the religious vision he cannot accept, Camus is revealed in this essay as a significant dialogue partner for Merton, a role that he will continue to play throughout the series of subsequent essays on Camus.

Author's Note

The purpose of these notes is to examine sympathetically some features of an ethic which is basically atheistic and characteristically modern. The examination is not apologetic in intent and confines itself to being expository rather than critical. With this approach, it is hoped that we can more clearly see those elements in Camus' thought which, though radically in accord with the Gospel, suggest possibilities too often neglected or overlooked by Christians. The weakness of Camus is by no means in the integrity of his moral feeling but in the obstinate refusal to integrate that feeling into the solidity of a consistent rational structure. This is the price he pays in order to preserve the purity of his intuition of the absurd, the importance of which he doubtless overestimates. The absurd can hardly be a firm basis for logical argumentation. It is rather the occasion of an existential wager. If we can provisionally respect the gambler in Camus we can also profit by his practical conclusions.

ALBERT CAMUS, the French-Algerian novelist, playwright, and essayist, was perhaps one of the most serious and articulate ethical thinkers of the mid-twentieth century. Active in the French resistance, associated with the existentialist movement in literature, though he repudiated the title of existentialist philosopher, Camus declared himself an atheist and yet spoke as the moral conscience of an embattled generation. In reality he is typical of that secular and nonreligious thought of the so-called "post-Christian era" which seeks to defend values that are essentially those of Western and Christian tradition against the nihilism and violence that have arisen out of the breakdown of Western civilization. Though considered a revolutionary, Camus turns out in the end to be conservative in the sense that he preaches the recovery of a basic and primordial humanism, the seeds of which are implanted in man's own nature and which was favored, he thought, by the ancient cultural climate of pre-Christian Mediterranean culture.

One of the tragedies of Western civilization, for Camus, is its infidelity to the Greek sense of measure, beauty, harmony, and natural limits. Modern Europe, in totalist frenzy, is the child of unreason and of extremes. "We light up in a drunken sky any suns that we please." And yet the limits remain. Those who sin against reason and measure will be pursued and found out by Nemesis. What is our Nemesis? We are delivered over to the god of power that we adore—our punishment is to have what we want. "God being dead there remain only history and power." And power is incarnate in the secular city. Camus disagrees very strongly with Hegel's declaration: "Only the modern city offers to the spirit a ground in which it can achieve consciousness of itself." For Camus, the alienated life of the dark and northern city is a life in which consciousness gets lost (he has a different idea of the Mediterranean city, as evident in his luminous essay on Algiers in summer). When Camus rejects the modern idea that values are to be created by the dynamism of history and realized in the future and returns instead to the Greek idea of eternal and essential values which are ontological and natural and provide a norm for rational conduct, we see how like an existentialist he really is! Yet he will not turn away from our world—it is the only one we learn to live in! And we cannot live in it by hating one another. Friendship, loyalty to man, lucidity, courage in accepting the absurd but only as the starting point of a new creation—these are the elements with which the creative and "rebel" spirit can reaffirm the wisdom of Greece in the face of police states and the new Inquisition.[1]

We are not concerned here with Camus' so called "neo-paganism" except to say that it accounts for a certain life-affirming and optimistic outlook in all his writing. It is true that his first novel, *The Stranger*, may have seemed morbid and bizarre in its description of an "absurd" and alienated character—or rather an absurd and alienated culture: our own. Because of this book Camus was labeled a pessimist from the start. No one can question the sense of the tragic and his keen eye for all that tempts us to despair. Yet actually, though he was not patient

---

1. Quotations so far from the essay "L'Exil d'Hélène," in *L'Eté* (Pléiade edition), vol. II, pp. 853-57.

with the illusory optimism of the naïve or of organization men, his was one of the more hopeful voices of his generation. It has been said of him, and quite rightly, that "his need to establish a passionately loved life on intellectual foundations that seemed valid to him [was] the strongest driving force behind his work and made a writer of him."[2]

As is well known, Camus was deeply concerned with politics but determined to remain a nonpartisan and in some sense to keep out of the more bitter and complex struggle of those who had completely committed themselves to this or that revolutionary cause. This led to his open break with Sartre, who committed himself to a broadly Marxist position and to collaboration with the Communists. Camus chose the more difficult and less consoling course: that of continuing to hope for a third position between the capitalist bourgeois establishment of the West and the rigid totalist establishment of the Communists. He saw that the world had reached a deadlock between these two forces and that there was nothing to be hoped for in merely supporting one of these against the other. No matter which side one chose, both were wrong, both were corrupt, both were sterile. In the end the struggle between them could only end in an intensification of nihilism and terror.

The "two imperialisms"—Eastern and Western—were for Camus a pair of twins "who grow up together and *cannot get along without each other*."[3] When it was objected that this confrontation was a reality he replied that cancer is also a reality, but that is no reason for not trying to cure it. He rejected the two systems along with their rival ideologies, which "born with the steam engine and naïve scientific optimism a century ago, are today obsolete and incapable in their present form of solving the problems posed in the age of the atom and of relativity."[4]

The only hope he saw was in a difficult and genuinely dialectical struggle to pass beyond either of these positions, and in the last analysis the success of such a struggle depended on the lucidity and integrity of individuals, "Rebels" in the special sense in which, as we shall see, he uses the word. Rebels both against a stagnant and ineffectual bourgeois culture and against a fanatical and arbitrary totalism. In an interview in 1952, Camus said: "We can no longer live without positive values. Bourgeois morality repels us by its hypocrisies and its cruelties. We find equally repugnant the political cynicism that reigns in the revolution-

---

2. Germaine Brée, *Camus,* rev. ed. (New York: Harbinger Books, 1964), p. 27.

3. An interview, December 1948, in Camus, *Essais* (Pléiade edition), vol. II, pp. 1587-88.

4. Quoted in Brée, *Camus,* p. 57.

ary movement. As for the independent left (Sartre, etc.) it is in fact fascinated by Communist power and entangled in a Marxism of which it is ashamed."[5]

At this point we may remark that though Camus remained resolutely un-Christian and indeed never concealed his scorn for the religious façade and sham of pseudo-Christianity, he retained a deep respect for authentic Catholicism. Though his own philosophy demanded of him a "passionate unbelief" he wrote in a letter of August 1943, "I have Catholic friends and for those among them who are truly Catholic I have more than sympathy: I have the feeling we are fighting for the same things. In fact, they are interested in the same things I am. In their eyes, the solution is evident, in mine it is not. . . ."[6]

Elsewhere he spoke of having deep respect for the person of Christ and of not believing in the resurrection—a standard "good pagan" posture. However, though he clung with total loyalty to the ideals and values of Greece, and though he tended to blame Christianity in part for the loss of those ideals, he still respected true Christian values. Were they the specifically *Hellenic* elements in Christianity? At any rate we remember he wrote a philosophical thesis at the University of Algiers on "Plotinus and St. Augustine."

In his most difficult book, *The Rebel* (*L'Homme révolté*), Camus examines the great problem and scandal of modern revolutions which, starting out with the affirmation of absolute liberty, have speedily consummated their efforts in absolute tyranny, and having pleaded for a more abundant life, have ended in hecatombs of political victims. Though himself an atheist (perhaps more accurately, an agnostic) Camus views with concern the fact that revolutions which began with the "death of God" and put man in the place of God were unable to work out a morality worthy of man. Having rejected the Kingdom of God and the realm of grace, having put the realm of justice in its place, the revolution proceeded from justice to the reign of terror, demanding the complete suspension of all liberty in view of a perfect consummation postponed to the future. Having rejected God it proceeded to reject man in the concrete, in favor of man in the abstract. In the name of this abstraction every violence, every cruelty, every inhumanity became permissible and even logically necessary. Though in this book Camus is speaking for the Rebel, he is speaking against "the revolution" in its historic forms. The Rebel is, in fact, in rebellion not only against a static and conservative establishment but also against a rigid and totalist revolution that has crystallized into a police state and maintains itself in existence by violence.

The key idea of *The Rebel* is that revolution nullifies itself when it resorts to

---

5. "Réponse à E. d'Astier," *Actuelles*, I, (Pléiade edition), vol. II, p. 358.
6. *Essais*, p. 1596.

massive killing. The need for the revolution to kill in order to maintain itself in power means that it no longer has the right to be in power. When the love of life that is at the root of revolution turns into a need for the death of hundreds and thousands of other men, then the "love of life" becomes a contradiction and a denial of itself, and revolution turns into absurdity and nihilism. To reject the Kingdom of God and of grace is to build a society on the abstract concept of "justice," and this leads inexorably to the concentration camp. "Absolute liberty becomes a prison of absolute duties"—including the duty to exterminate thousands of one's fellow men in the name not of a happy and life-affirming present but of a hypothetical happiness in the future. The "death of God" means in the end an imperialism of the spirit that seeks world hegemony and total control at the price of unlimited murder and terror. Note that this same logic operates not only in the death camps of a Hitler, the labor camps of the Soviets or Red Chinese, but also where the power of unlimited destruction is concentrated in nuclear and other weapons. It is the same logic of power and terror that grows out of a radical godlessness which leaves man to build his world alone. This is what happens to man when "refusing God, he chooses history" and seeks (with Hegel, Nietzsche, and Marx) the eschatological unity of the human race "deified" by its own exercise of absolute political power. Once God is dead, the vacuum caused by His "death" sucks into itself this huge drive toward total human political power. To accept the death of God in some sense means to accept passively the awful force of this drag and suction into the emptiness created by His absence.

Camus grants all this without ceasing to hold his atheist position. Why? In common with those who more truly merit the name of existentialists, he considers that to accept the idea of God as the explanation and justification of an otherwise absurd life is a kind of "cheating."

The man who resorts to God to give sense to an otherwise senseless life is, according to Camus, evading the austere and stoical duty of facing up to "the absurd" and deciding to live with it. It has been said that Camus makes Pascal's wager—but in reverse. Instead of gambling on the possibility of God, he gambles on his impossibility and accepts the resulting absurdity of the universe with all its consequences—violence, ruthlessness, terror. For Camus as for Sartre, theological faith is a temptation. It is "bad faith" by definition. But what is faith anyway? Camus as a typical modern starts with the assumption that the world is absurd and that God then becomes necessary for some minds to explain the absurdity. God is regarded somehow as a *need* of man's mind and heart; and indeed a certain kind of apologetic in the past has been all too ready to advance this distorted and inadequate view of God. Here God is seen simply as the projection of man's need for clarity, for rationality. The act of faith then becomes a determination to convince oneself that no matter how absurd things may *look*, they are in fact quite reasonable because God must make them reasonable. One believes because one refuses to despair of an absolute and infallible reason.

But this assumes that God is merely called in to our lives as a kind of logical *Deus ex machina* and that he is little more than a convenient hypothesis. Is this what is really meant by God in Christianity?

Camus, with Ivan Karamazov, examines the classic problem of evil in the world and rejects a hypothesis of a God whose rule may have to be justified at the price of the suffering of one innocent child. Camus, like Ivan Karamazov, says that if this is the case he will turn in his ticket to heaven. But then, resolutely facing a world that has become frankly absurd, he has to watch dry-eyed the suffering not of one innocent child but of millions of innocents: a suffering that is demanded by the logic of a world without God. Camus may realize the contradiction implied in this position: he shrugs it off. He does not bother to argue. He merely assumes that one cannot save the millions by bringing God back to life.

In spite of all this, one of the root problems of *The Rebel* (hence one of the root problems of our world in revolutionary crisis) is the problem of God. This problem as stated by Camus remains insoluble, and Camus simply bypasses it, not on the basis of any reasoning in metaphysics or theodicy, but simply because the historical forms of Christianity—and other religions—seem to him to demand of man a futile and degrading resignation that solves nothing and merely leaves him at the mercy of blind social forces that push him this way and that.

Yet Camus recognizes that the problem of God arises in another inexorable form as the problem of murder. If the most critical problem of our time is the problem of (mass) murder and if human life has been reduced to an entity without value, this is because "God is dead." Camus admits it, without feeling any need for God to be other than dead—bringing him back to life may no longer mean a recovery of the sense of man as a value. Those who claim to represent God have often done much to cheapen man. If conventional and institutional religious establishments have taught man to hold human life cheap, if they have trivialized death, exalted nationalist or political abstractions, and given a blanket permission to kill without practical limit in the name of patriotism or of revolution, then they have contributed their share to the "death of God" in the experience of twentieth-century man. When the problem of God necessarily reappears as the problem of the sacredness of life and prohibition of limitless killing, then Camus must grapple with it. The most tragic thing, the root of crime, is the *silence* and complicity which accept the supposed rightness and necessity for man-killing, whether in war or in prison camps.

> We live in terror because persuasion is no longer possible; because man has been wholly submerged in history, because he can no longer tap that part of his nature, as real as the historical part, which he recaptures in contemplating the beauty of nature and of human faces; because we live in a world of abstractions, of bureaus and machines, of absolute ideas and crude messianism. We suffocate among people who think they are absolutely right, whether in their machines or in their ideas. And for all who can live only in an atmosphere of human dialogue and sociability, this silence is the end of the world.[7]

The face of Camus' "Rebel" now begins to appear in its true character. He is a man who protests, but protests not against abstract injustice, nor in the name of a theoretical program. He protests in the name of man, individual and concrete man of flesh and blood, against the war-making arrogance of total power, against the abstractions on which power bases its claim to an absolute right to kill. The Rebel moreover refuses to be silent and insists on an open dialogue which will help others like himself to arrive at a lucid and common decision to oppose absurdity and death and to affirm man against all abstractions.

In a certain sense, the starting point of Camus' ethic of revolt is a protest against passive resignation. In 1937, visiting the famous Campo Santo of Pisa, he was revolted by the pious and conventional sentiments of the epitaphs and mortuary art he saw all around him. For him they were in fact a mockery of the awful seriousness and mystery of man's contingency, an evasion of the inscrutable reality of death. So too, the "black" first chapter of *The Stranger* in all its apparent indifference and heartlessness is a protest against the utter inadequacy of formal social rituals surrounding death. All social forms tend, in Camus' eyes, to cheat and play obscene tricks with the mystery of death.

The Campo Santo of Pisa and the tombs in the cloister of the Annunziata were after all noble compared to those in the city cemetery of Algiers. Of this he wrote: "Everything that touches on death is here made ridiculous or hateful. This people living without religion and without idols dies alone after living in a mob. I know no more hideous place than the cemetery of Bru Boulevard, facing one of the finest landscapes in the world. . . ." He goes on to speak of the revolting vulgarity of tombs on which angels fly in stucco airplanes, of hearts

---

7. "Neither Victims nor Executioners," in *The Pacifist Conscience*, ed. Peter Mayer (New York: Holt, 1966), p. 424.

inscribed with words like "Our memory will never abandon you"—or clusters of stucco flowers accompanied by the declaration: "Your tomb will never be without flowers." Here it is not religion that he derides but the awful religionless and godless secularity that has crept in behind a collapsing religious façade. What is the façade? Resignation. And Camus, speaking now as a pure "Rebel," declines to be resigned. Even in Italy, where there was still some religious substance in the renaissance monuments to honor the dead, he said: "None of this convinces me. All of them . . . had become resigned, doubtless because they accepted their other duties. I shall not grow resigned. With all my silence I shall protest to the very end. There is no reason to say: 'It had to be.' It is my revolt which is right, and it must follow this joy which is like a pilgrim on earth, follow it step by step."[8]

The Rebel of Camus is therefore first of all the man who refuses to accept, with passive and unreasoning resignation, a diminution or falsification of authentic and living possibilities. The Rebel is one who is not resigned to letting his life be destroyed or mutilated in the name of something else, whether it be business, or politics, or money, or revolution—or religion. He is, in a word, the man who refuses alienation. It is interesting to notice that a few pages later in the same notebook Camus speaks with approval of the early Franciscans. He describes their religious poverty as a liberating force. It is clear that in Camus' eyes, Franciscan poverty was an enrichment of life and not a mutilation. Meditating in a cloister in Fiesole he recognizes in himself a deep affinity with the early Franciscans, for they too are Rebels in his sense of the word:

> Sitting on the ground I think of the Franciscans whose cells I have just visited and whose sources of inspiration I can now see. I feel clearly that if they are right then it is in the same way that I am. This splendor of the world [he alludes to the view from the monastery] seems to justify these men. I put all my pride in a belief that it also justifies me and all the men of my race who know that there is an extreme point at which poverty always rejoins the luxury and richness of the world. . . . Being naked always has associations of physical liberty, of harmony between the hand and the flowers it touches, of loving understanding between the earth and men who have been freed from human things. Ah, I should become a convert to this if it were not already my religion.[9]

---

8. Albert Camus, *Notebooks 1935-1942* (New York: Alfred A. Knopf, 1963), p. 64.

9. Ibid., p. 57.

If we consider all the implications of this passage we will be tempted to think that Camus has ended by standing Franciscanism on its head. Camus' own neo-pagan and naïve atheism rests on a refusal to trust anything that is not directly accessible to the senses. He knows and loves the world as he sees it, directly in front of his nose: it is for him a unique and inexhaustible value, though it also confronts him with an absurd and enigmatic silence. For there remains death, and Camus will not play around with any "explanation" that evades or minimizes the seemingly utter finality of death. His refusal is not metaphysical or logical but aesthetic. Life and death are realities directly accessible to experience. The immediacy with which they sometimes confront us may be so stark as to be absurd. No matter. The absurd too is real. But for Camus the religious and metaphysical arguments for another life, for Providence, and so on are not accessible. They are not a matter of experience or of immediate grasp. They are therefore, he thinks, arbitrary fabrications.

On the other hand, his approval of the Franciscans in the passage quoted is based on the fact that he thinks they see things his way. They have gambled as he has: not on reasonings and ideas but on immediate facts: the burnt hills of Tuscany, the vineyards, the poverty of the people, the poverty of Franciscan life. All these are immediately experienced. They are directly present in the Franciscan consciousness, they are not mere objects of rationalization.

There is something to this intuition. The vision of a St. Francis is not the vision of an abstract and purely transcendent God dwelling in eternity, but the immediate, overwhelming, direct, tangible confrontation of "God who is" simply in the "is-ness" of everyday reality. The belief of a Franciscan in eternal life does not determine how he lives—it flows from his life and is part and parcel of that life. If Camus had been able to follow this through he would have realized that the abstract God he could not believe in was not, and never had been, the living God of authentic Christianity.

Camus contrasts the peace and joy of life-affirming love with the frenzy born of abstractions which followed the French Revolution. Reason, disincarnated by godless revolution, "floated off like a balloon into the empty sky of the great principles," and therefore it needed the support of force: "To adore theorems for any length of time, faith is not enough: one also needs a police."[10]

The root of Camus' ethic is then not a fanatically reasoned nihilism but on the contrary an affirmation of life which, we have seen, he spontaneously correlates with Franciscan poverty. In fact, the root of his ethic is love. In his notebooks we find this:

---

10. Albert Camus, *L'Homme révolté* (Pléiade edition), pp. 154, 155.

If someone here told me to write a book on morality, it would have a hundred pages and ninety-nine would be blank. On the last page I should write "I recognize only one duty, and that is to love." And as far as everything else is concerned I say *no*.[11]

We have so far seen that Camus' Rebel refuses the resignation of a life submissive to cynical travesty in a decadent postreligious culture, or a life obedient to the dictates of totalist police in a godless revolutionary state, and that the paradigm of the Rebel is strangely enough the poverty-loving, therefore liberated, Franciscan. Will he pursue his idea further? If the godless revolution denies itself and cancels itself out in the blood of human victims, will Camus turn to a nonviolent revolution in the name of God and of love? No, for since to him God is only an inadmissible logical hypothesis, he has to engage in an intricate dialectic between godless violence and religious nonviolence in order to reach a different synthesis.

It is interesting to see how he arrives at this synthesis. His thought in this matter has certain positive implications even for the Christianity that he rejects. But while we admit that his conclusions are somewhat different from those of an ideally Christian nonviolence, they are at the same time a more strict and rigorous rejection of force than we find in the traditional Christian "just war" theory. In practice, we can say that Camus, while admitting that violence may be necessary, speaks and writes as a pacifist not only in the face of global war but also in the face of world revolution. He contends that the power struggle of our time, whether on the side of capitalism or on that of communism, is essentially nihilistic and therefore starts from the implicit or explicit proposition that God is dead in order to justify in practice (if not in theory) torture, genocide, the police state, the death camps, and the obliteration of nations by nuclear war. All this in the name of a humanism postponed to an indefinite future when full justice will have been carried out on the adversary.

At this point, we can let Camus explain himself succinctly in statements or notes from the *Carnets* during the period after World War II when he finally broke with Sartre and Merleau-Ponty on this issue of humanism and terror.

In 1946 Camus said: "*There is only one problem today, which is that of murder. All our disputes are vain. One thing alone matters: peace.*"[12]

This problem faces everybody, and not just politicians, businessmen, military strategists, manufacturers of armaments, or revolutionists. All men confront

---

11. *Notebooks 1935-1942*, p. 54.
12. *Essais*, p. 1569.

372 • *Thomas Merton: Selected Essays*

the problem of co-operation in murder, perhaps even in genocide. "We are in a world in which one must choose between being a victim or an executioner."[13]

To face such a world and such a choice means to confront the absurd. Either we know it or we do not. If we accept the absurd choice as perfectly reasonable or at least as an inevitable necessity, we resign our human dignity and freedom, we surrender to unreason and unfreedom in the name of abstractions which ignore our human measure and inexorably lead to our own destruction. There is only one answer: to become a Rebel—*un homme révolté*. The Rebel is distinguished on the one hand from the conformist who accepts a conservative establishment and its injustices and on the other from the revolutionary who in the name of an ideology and an abstract humanism consents to the alienation and destruction of his fellow man, and indeed of his own human honor and integrity, for the sake of a future utopia. This precise sense of the Rebel must be remembered. The Rebel is one who squarely faces the absurdity and risk of a choice that may in fact be meaningless and inefficacious because it is in fact nullified and set aside by the ruthless dynamism of the power struggle that grinds on inexorably toward global suicide or the establishment of a nihilist and totalist police state. The Rebel refuses to be an executioner, and if he has to be a victim he will at least know why. But as soon as he takes up this position of refusal, autonomy, and self-determination in the presence of the absurd, as soon as he resolves to confront the absurd and work within the limits that it necessarily imposes, he finds himself in solidarity with other Rebels who have made the same commitment. Camus says that revolt gives the Rebel an identity and a viewpoint analogous to the Cartesian self-awareness, "I think therefore I am," which is the starting point of modern epistemology. The Rebel finds his identity in the Revolt which places him side by side with other Rebels in their common lucidity: "I revolt, therefore *we are*." The Rebel is then not simply the disgruntled individual—certainly not the alienated and seemingly apathetic individualist like Meursault, the hero of *The Stranger*, that classic of the absurd. The true Rebels portrayed by Camus are Rieux and Tarrou in *The Plague*, men who decide in the face of the tragic absurdity of the plague to affirm life and human solidarity as best they can, for the best motives they can muster.

Solidarity in revolt is the only thing that balances and nullifies the absurd. From this solidarity and from the compassion it implies emerge the reasons by which one can decide for or against violence.

---

13. Ibid., p. 1567.

The aim of revolt is the pacification of men. Any revolt reaches the ultimate and reverberates in the assertion of human limits—and of a community of all men, whoever they are, within those limits. Humility and genius.[14]

The nature of revolt, as opposed to the rigid authoritarianism of a totalist revolution directed from above by "the Party," is that it springs from the warmth and authenticity of human solidarity and compassion. Revolt is based on love, revolution on a political abstraction. Revolt is therefore real, and its reality is defined by risk, limitation, uncertainty, vulnerability. It has to be constantly created anew by a renewal of fervor, intelligence, and love. Revolution is abstract, and it seeks to guarantee itself indefinitely by the exercise of power, therefore by murder, and it is by this resort to force in the name of justice directed from above that it cancels itself out and makes renewal impossible. Revolt is the only thing that can give to revolution the renewal and lucidity it needs. Hence one can see that Camus was *persona non grata* with the Communists since he demanded revolt against Communism itself as well as against capitalism. Revolt strikes at every form of power that relies on blood.

> My effort: to show that the logic of revolt rejects blood and selfish motives. And that a dialogue carried to the absurd gives a chance of purity. Through compassion? (suffer together)[15]

The logic of revolt demands dialogue, openness, speech. Therefore revolt protests against the conspiracy of silence which, everywhere, both under totalism and under capitalism, seals men's lips so that they do not protest against organized murder but approve it.

> What balances the absurd is the community of men fighting against it. And if we choose to serve that community we choose to serve the dialogue carried to the absurd against any policy of falsehood or of silence. That's the way one is free with others. . . .[16]
>
> The universal order cannot be built from above, in other words through an idea; but rather from below, in other words through the common basis which. . . .[17]

---

14. *Notebooks 1942-1951* (New York: Alfred A. Knopf, 1965), p. 144.
15. Ibid., p. 125.
16. Ibid., p. 126.
17. Ibid., p. 147.

The phrase is unfinished, but we can easily reconstruct the rest of Camus' idea from other passages in the notebooks: when men resolve to speak out, they define for one another the absurd. When they find themselves in the presence of the absurd and recognize the need for revolt against it, in affirmation of life against death, they undertake a struggle against absurdity, in solidarity with one another. In this struggle their own lives acquire the meaning and the direction which alone overcome the absurd. This is Love.

> Thus starting from the absurd it is not possible to live revolt without reaching at some point or other an experience of love that is still undefined.[18]

In *The Myth of Sisyphus*, man who has come to terms with the absurd does not yield to the temptation of suicide—a form of "resignation" or demission. On the contrary, man makes something out of the absurd by not agreeing to it. "The absurd has meaning only insofar as it is not agreed to."[19]

But this "not agreeing" is in fact a constant and very exacting discipline. Faith, for one thing, is rigorously excluded. One must not forget the absurd, or dismiss it, or explain it away, or give it a good reason. One must spend the rest of his life rubbing his nose in it.

> Once he has reached the absurd and tries to live *accordingly*, a man always perceives that consciousness is the hardest thing in the world to maintain. Circumstances are almost always against it. He must live his lucidity in a world where dispersion is the rule.[20]

This would be an intolerable exercise of solipsism if Camus went no further. Fortunately he does. The confrontation with the absurd, and the ability to be undistractedly, unflinchingly aware of it, is not final. It is purely provisional, it is only a beginning. It must under no conditions become a dead end. The experience of the absurd is not suggested as an absolute value in itself (or if you prefer an absolute nonvalue). It is a clearing of the ground for something else. This something else is not mere individual lucidity and purity of heart, but solidarity in creative revolt—ultimately it is solidarity in love.

The refusal to agree to the absurd and to accept "the unreasonable silence of the world" opens up a new possibility: the possibility of a difficult and dialectical choice between a passive and religious resignation (the yogi) and active revo-

---

18. Ibid., p. 138.
19. *The Myth of Sisyphus* (New York: Vintage Books, 1959), p. 24.
20. *Notebooks 1942-1951*, p. 10.

lutionary commitment (the commissar)—a choice which Camus also describes as being "between God and history." The Rebel chooses neither the absolute and transcendent God who "explains everything" and gets rid of the absurd, nor a historical dynamic which promises to wipe out all absurdity in the future, while in the present it wipes out the people who are responsible for all the absurdity. In his refusal of either of these consolations, the absurd man maintains the possibility of a vocation to revolt. On the basis of a lucid indifference which "lives without appeal" (to systematic explanations which justify one's experiences and give them an appearance of quality) revolt acts without concern for quality. This, as Camus puts it, sounds a bit hard-boiled, but we can perhaps understand it by correlating it with the Oriental idea of concentrating on the act itself and not on its results or on the merit accruing from it.

More exactly, the moral value of an act, for Camus, depends not so much on the object and intuition, the will behind the act, as on the lucidity of the act. To appeal to some other standard which lucidity does not verify, to call upon a quality which lucidity cannot vouch for, is to abandon and muddle lucidity itself. The will to destroy one's enemies automatically involves sins against lucidity since it seeks abstract and impossible justifications for murder—reasons why, for the time being, death is more important than life. These illusory reasons can, it is thought, be maintained if one's acts are carried out with a certain quality of ruthlessness, or heroism, or patriotism, or self-sacrifice, and so on. Camus has no patience with any of this language, though the facts of heroism and self-sacrifice are not absent from his ethic. They are simply not preached, because for him preaching is irrelevant. At the same time the purely "quantitative ethic" suggested as a consequence of the absurd in *The Myth of Sisyphus* must not be taken too seriously. It obviously was repudiated by Camus himself when he joined the French resistance, and is repudiated in his ideas on murder and in the stoic generosity of the heroes in *The Plague*.

> Relation of the absurd to revolt. If the final decision is to reject suicide in order to maintain the confrontation, this amounts implicitly to admitting life as the only factual value, the one that allows the confrontation, "the value without which nothing." Whence it is clear that to obey that absolute value, whoever rejects suicide likewise rejects murder, or the justification of murder. Ours is the era which having carried nihilism to its extreme conclusions has accepted suicide. This can be verified in the ease with which we accept murder or the justification of murder. The man who kills himself alone still maintains one value, which is the life of others. . . . But the men of Terror have carried the values of suicide to their extreme

consequence, which is legitimate murder, in other words collective suicide. Illustration: the Nazi apocalypse in 1945.[21]

In other words, it is the men of terror who have fully implemented a "quantitative ethic." In *The Myth of Sisyphus*, the hero of the absurd by not agreeing to
the absurd, yet confronting it in lucidity and without any spurious hopes, gives
it meaning and affirms the value which enables him to give it meaning. Revolt
repeats the process collectively and in solidarity. Revolt is the refusal to agree
with an absurd and self-destroying social system. Revolt affirms the life which
that system negates and destroys in the name of an abstraction. Revolt is also, *a
fortiori*, the negation of this idolized abstraction.

The great danger to lucidity and to revolt is the silent acquiescence in absurdity: the homage of unquestioning acceptance which the majority of men offer
to the idol. Hence the obligation to speak.

> Mankind's dialogue has just come to an end. And naturally a man with
> whom one cannot reason is a man to be feared. The result is that—besides
> those who have not spoken out because they thought it useless—a vast
> conspiracy of silence has spread all about us, a conspiracy accepted by
> those who are frightened and who rationalize their fears in order to hide
> them from themselves, a conspiracy fostered by those whose interest it is
> to do so . . .[22]

The obligation is not so much to formulate a direct accusation of injustice and
level it against this or that economic system or power structure. The purpose of
speech in the presence of the absurd political situation is to point to the fact that
abuse of power is in fact a denial of life and an affirmation of death insofar as it
depends on the killing of so many thousands or millions of human beings and
implements policies which sooner or later will demand and exact these deaths.
Note that there are innumerable ways of inflicting death on man. A rich nation
can in effect "kill" thousands of people in a poorer nation without even firing
a shot or dropping a bomb, simply by keeping the poorer nation in a state of
dependence in which the reasonable development of its resources is blocked
(in favor of the exploitation which is profitable to the rich nation) and consequently people starve.

> [We confront a world] where murder is legitimate, and where human life
> is considered trifling. This is the great political question of our times, and

---

21. Ibid., p. 149.
22. "Neither Victims nor Executioners," in *The Pacifist Conscience*, p. 424.

before dealing with other issues one must take a position on it. Before anything can be done, two questions must be put: "Do you or do you not, directly or indirectly, want to be killed or assaulted? Do you or do you not, directly or indirectly, want to kill or assault?" All who say No to both these questions are automatically committed to a series of consequences which must modify their way of posing the problem.[23]

It is obvious that neither side in the power struggle really claims to want death or killing. But Camus believes that the power struggle is essentially a dilemma in which both sides must in the end, in spite of all their professed humanistic and peaceful aims, be committed to unlimited killing because of their implicit or explicit justification of mass murder, a justification which is of the very essence of their absurdity. Camus cites with approval Simone Weil's remark that official history is a matter of believing the self-justifications of murderers. Simone Weil was for him an example of "authentic Christianity" (she refused to join the Church) and, in fact, of a genuine Rebel in her integrity, her solitude, and her capacity for renunciation.

But can one escape implication in a murderous power struggle? Is there another choice? What about the choice of religious nonviolence?

Since in fact Camus did at times speak like a pacifist and came so close to the nonviolent position, his adversaries thought that to refute Camus it was enough to refute nonviolence. To one of these critics (a Marxist) Camus replied in 1948:

> I have never argued for nonviolence . . . I do not believe that we ought to answer blows with blessings. I believe that violence is inevitable, and the years of the [Nazi] occupation have convinced me of it . . . I do not say that one must suppress all violence, which would be desirable but, in fact, uto-pian. I only say that we must refuse all legitimation of violence, whether this legitimation comes from an absolute *raison d'état* or from a totalitar-ian philosophy. *Violence is at the same time unavoidable and unjustifiable.*[24]

Hence violence must always be confined to the strictest possible limits. In an age of nuclear war, to canonize violence and force is an intolerable and criminal absurdity, and hence Camus is, in practice, a "nuclear pacifist." In the face of the disastrous consequences of atomic war, he has no other choice but

---

23. Ibid., p. 425.
24. "Réponse à E. d'Astier," p. 355.

"the fight against war and the very long effort to establish a true international democracy."[25]

If a "scientific" historicism starts from the denial of God and proceeds to build a world unity without God, the consequence will be nihilism, totalism, the deification of force and the police state. It is the world of justice and history instead of the world of God and grace. In effect, Camus lumps capitalism and Communism together under this heading, since in fact the religious motives which are so conveniently advertised by the capitalist West do not convince him as being very serious. On the other hand, what of an authentic Christian non-violence? Camus admits that such a philosophy is possible and reasonable. In fact: "In today's world a philosophy of eternity alone can justify nonviolence."[26] He agrees here with Gandhi, for whom *ahimsa* was not really possible without faith in God. Unfortunately, to solve the problem of killing by a resort to God is, for Camus, no solution. It merely raises once again the whole question of the metaphysic of evil, and Camus stands by the side of Ivan Karamazov. If the suffering of one child . . . For this reason the lucid Rebel cannot choose a non-violence based on faith in God because he cannot choose God. To choose God is, for Camus, to choose an *explanation* and hence to evade the bitter honesty of a full confrontation with the absurd without hope and "without appeal" to any force other than that of human honesty and courage within the confines of human limitation.

Camus does not argue against God. The absurd is not a denial of God. Like the radical Protestant "death of God" theologians who often appeal to him, Camus simply discards the whole notion of God as irrelevant because it is *inaccessible* to the mind and experience of so many modern people. He does not go so far as to make a basic act of faith that God *cannot* be accessible to any modern believer as some of the radical theologians seem to. He simply says: "If today one could neither live nor act outside of God, a great number of Westerners would perhaps be condemned to sterility."[27]

In Camus' eyes religious nonviolence is doomed to failure because it is in fact unfaithful to the actual condition of (unbelieving) man. It is based on presuppositions which most men simply no longer find acceptable or even conceivable. Thus in fact, in his eyes, the choice of religious nonviolence based on an appeal to God and to eternity would end only in political quietism, in silence, in resignation, in acceptance of injustice, in final submission to one or other side in the worldly power struggle.

---

25. Ibid., p. 359.
26. *L'Homme révolté*, p. 354.
27. *Essais*, p. 1426.

At the same time, religious nonviolence is to him suspect because it savors of the futile desire of the bourgeois to convince himself of his perfect innocence. Christianity itself is suspect to Camus, as it is to many moderns since Marx, for this reason. A religious nonviolence produces in its devotee a pure and virtuous conscience and therefore a sense of subjective righteousness which may blind him to the fact that he is still deeply involved in collective guilt and violence. We must be very careful not to impute this desire of moral unassailability to Camus' Rebel. If the Rebel rejects a purely religious nonviolence it is because he insists on not regarding himself as any more innocent and "pure" than anyone else. True revolt is not clothed in virtuous justification: it has nothing to be proud of but its own naked lucidity and anguish in the presence of the absurd—and its love of man who is caught in absurdity. Revolt is not reducible to a mere cult of integrity and sincerity without efficacy. This is another complaint against religious nonviolence. It is, Camus suggests, inclined to accept defeat virtuously rather than to engage in efficacious combat. For him, nonviolence in the pure state is demission, resignation, or simply illusion. The true Rebel, according to Camus, is allowed to choose neither terror and murder on one hand nor resignation, nonviolence, and silence on the other. The question arises why Camus so easily identifies nonviolence with silence, submission, and passivity when authentic nonviolent resistance is *active* and should be highly articulate, since, if it is understood in the Gandhian sense, it demands much more lucidity and courage than the use of force does.

In any case, Camus refuses to accept absolute nonviolence. His Rebel may take up arms, and may indeed be compelled by duty to do so, but with one most important reservation:

> Authentic action in revolt will consent to arm itself only for institutions which limit violence, not for those that give it the force of law.[28]

This is all very fine—but what war-making institution does not in practice claim to be limiting violence and fighting for peace? The escalation of the Vietnam War by the Pentagon is all, allegedly, in order to *limit* violence!

Camus does, however, come in practice very close to the nonviolent position. While admitting that violence and killing may in certain circumstances be necessary he lays down one ideal condition which is supposed to close the door to all unnecessary violence: he who kills must do so only on the understanding that

---

28. *L'Homme révolté*, p. 360.

he is willing to pay for the adversaries' life with his own. In this, Camus points with approval to the revolutionaries of the 1905 uprising in Russia.[29]

In this example Camus is suggesting a paradigm that is perhaps aesthetically satisfying but has no real application in politics. It may remain as a symbolic and edifying instance, and it may help us to take a more reserved view of the efficacy and legitimacy of force. The rebels of 1905 are there, he says, to restore an authentic perspective to the twentieth-century revolution.[30] The real meaning of Camus' position is to be sought elsewhere. He was not a man of precise and doctrinaire solutions. It was for this reason that he rejected a mystique of nonviolence although he was in practice aware of the possibly fatal consequences of escalating violence. He did not want to dictate absolute formulas in the realm of political and historical action, where situations and circumstances are always new. Therefore he left the way open for the use of force, in a situation where there might be no other way of liberating oneself from intolerable oppression. He did not declare *a priori* that nonviolence was necessarily more efficacious in the long run than force, when he doubted that most people would be capable of understanding and practicing nonviolence in its highest religious sense. To preach an abstract and ideal nonviolence and deliver this doctrine into the hands of people who do not understand it, leaving them to improvise and experiment with it, would simply play into the hands of the violent. Perhaps, too, he was thinking of the problem that arises when the illuminated moralist, speaking from the Olympian heights of privilege, presumes to make choices for others whose situation is far from privileged. Camus then, at the risk of seeming inconclusive, does not prescribe a *method* or a *tactic*. He is concerned only with one thing: the integrity and the lucidity of revolt, or in other words the moral climate of insight, loyalty, and courage without which no tactic can be humanly fruitful or creative.

In conclusion, then, the Camusian Rebel "is not only [in rebellion] as slave against master, but *he is man against the world of master and slave.*"[31] The logic of Revolt is not that of destruction but of creation.[32] It is basically "a protest against death."[33] The Rebel cannot take refuge in self-righteousness: he recognizes in himself the same universal tendencies toward murder and despair. "The value that keeps him on his feet is never given him once for all, he must constantly

29. *L'Homme révolté*, p. 207ff.
30. "Défense de l'homme révolté," *Essais*, p. 1707.
31. Ibid., p. 351.
32. Ibid., p. 352.
33. Ibid., p. 352.

maintain it in existence."[34] He cannot take refuge, either, in the self-assurance provided by a religious or political system that guarantees infallible knowledge. He must admit a "calculated ignorance" and never affirm more than he actually knows. He must be faithful to "human limits" and the "human measure," and he must be ready to risk even inevitable violence, because to pretend exemption from this would seem to be a denial of the human condition and an attempted evasion from practical reality.

Yet the basic choice remains this: *the refusal to be a murderer or the accomplice of murderers*, and this demands above all the resolute refusal to accept any system which rests directly and essentially on the justification of killing, especially mass killing, whether by war or by more subtle forms of destructive domination.

Over the expanse of five continents throughout the coming years an endless struggle is going to be pursued between violence and friendly persuasion, a struggle in which, granted, the former has a thousand times the chances of success than that of the latter. But I have always held that, if he who bases his hopes on human nature is a fool, he who gives up in the face of circumstances is a coward. And henceforth the only honorable course will be to stake everything on a formidable gamble: that words are more powerful than munitions.[35]

34. Ibid., p. 353.
35. "Neither Victims nor Executioners," p. 438.

28

The Monastic Renewal:
Problems and Prospects

The first version of this essay, entitled "The Monastic Renewal: Problems and Prospects for Ed Rice," is a sixteen-page multigraphed (spirit master) text dated December 1966; it was evidently intended for publication in *Jubilee*, the magazine Rice edited, which would cease publication less than a year later; the typescript of a longer, twenty-six-page version, with the same title but no mention of Rice, is dated January 1967. Whether due to *Jubilee's* woes or for some other reason, it was never published there (the expanded version was probably too long for *Jubilee*, so Merton may have already known in January that Rice wouldn't use it), nor did it appear in any other periodical. It became the introductory chapter in the posthumous essay collection *Contemplation in a World of Action* (3-25), with the main title omitted (as "Monastic Renewal" was made the section title for the first and longest section of the book); it has been restored for this printing. This essay is a characteristic and comprehensive reflection on an area of major concern in Merton's writing from "The Monk in the Diaspora" of 1964 (*Seeds of Destruction*, 199-213) through the Bangkok talk "Marxism and Monastic Perspectives" (*Asian Journal*, 326-43), delivered hours before his death, and evident in his discussion of various aspects of the topic in the other essays collected in Part I of *Contemplation in a World of Action*. Merton's central point about the renewal of monastic life in the wake of the Second Vatican Council is that "the radical reshaping of institutional structures," while necessary, is by no means sufficient. Authentic renewal entails the recovery of the authentic charism of monasticism, a recognition that the monk is not defined by a particular function or task but by a vocation "to a life of freedom and detachment, a 'desert life' outside normal social structures." It is from this marginal position that the monk is able to be of service to the wider Church and world as a prophetic witness to the value of silence and solitude for authentic human existence, a sign of contradiction to all systems and worldviews that define human worth according to status or accomplishments, by what one does or what one has rather than who one is. Therefore Merton insists that a renewed monasticism must be open to and engaged with the struggles and problems of all humanity, but sufficiently distanced from secular society as to be able to identify and resist "the routines, the clichés, the disguised idolatries and empty formalities" that characterize so much of contemporary life. Such a life must be free from the obsessions of "the world" in order to model for the world the truth and love and communion that flow from participation in the mystery of Christ's death and resurrection. Monks owe it not only to themselves but to the world, Merton maintains, to reject any program of renewal that settles for structural readjustments rather than a radical reappropriation of "the mystical and prophetic dimension" of the monastic charism.

BEFORE THE SECOND VATICAN COUNCIL the monastic orders had begun to consider the question of renewal. Some efforts at renewal were already under way. But these efforts mostly presupposed that existing institutions would continue as they already were and had been for centuries. Changes in the horarium, in the liturgical celebration offices, in the formation and recruitment of new members, in the size and character of the community, in the understanding and observance of the vows would suffice to meet the requirements of *aggiornamento*. After the Council, even though the decree *Perfectae Caritatis* was very general and in no sense revolutionary, religious as a whole have begun to question the basic institutional structures of the religious life. Though this is not what the Council formally enjoined upon them, it has been an inevitable result of the investigations and self-questioning which the Council demanded.

The monastic Orders have hitherto proved themselves among the most conservative in the Church in the sense that they have tended more than the active institutes to preserve a traditional and somewhat archaic style of life. Before the Council, even those who were in favor of the most sweeping changes still seem to have thought of the monastic community as permanently established on medieval foundations. The renewal of the monastic life has seemed, to many monks and to General Chapters, to demand merely a modernization and adaptation of familiar medieval patterns, freeing them of all that was most obviously feudal and antique, but maintaining their structure, since that structure is conceived to be essential to the monastic way of life.

This is obviously not enough. The monks have been under fire from critics outside the monastic Orders. Many have openly questioned the right of the monastic Orders to continue in existence. It is a bit ironic to see that when Protestants themselves have begun to rediscover monastic values, the Lutheran arguments against monasticism have been adopted and turned against the monks by some Catholic publicists. Thus the very essence of the monastic life itself is attacked, as if the very nature of monasticism made all renewal and adaptation to the present needs of the Church impossible. This presupposes, however, that the monastic life is *essentially* medieval, and that if the medieval formalities, ritualism, observances, and conceptions of the vowed life are discarded, there will be nothing left. What complicates matters is that the conservative element in monasticism does, to a great extent, accept this challenge on their critics' terms, assuming that the medieval forms are of the essence, and must therefore be preserved. This incites the younger and more radical element to side with those who demand that the monks leave the cloister, come out into the world, join in the labor of evangelization, and justify their existence by active and secular lives. This sweeping attack takes for granted that "the contemplative life" is sterile, foolish, wasteful, selfish and that it serves no purpose but to keep monks immature, walled off from contemporary reality, in a state of self-delusion, dedicated to childish formalities.

Some monks are quite willing to accept this diagnosis, and they also maintain that the only remedy is active work in the world. In effect, however, this extreme solution does not differ from the anti-monastic view in any way. It amounts to an abandonment of the monastic vocation—a capitulation to the arguments of those who deny that there is any place left for a life which "leaves the world." Indeed, the vagaries of a theology and spirituality which overemphasized "contempt for the world" have all been blamed on the monks. Some critics even seem to think that all the aberrations in the theology and devotionalism of an entrenched and defensive Christianity, suspicious of the world and excessively clerical in its outlook, are to be traced to monasticism. It is true that medieval monasticism did exercise an enormous influence on post-medieval spirituality, but, once again, must we assume that medieval monasticism is the *only* possible form?

Medieval monasticism was feudal, aristocratic, highly ritualized, thoroughly organized. The medieval monk might indeed lead a personally austere life, and the atmosphere of the monasteries was often not only highly cultured and spiritual but often genuinely mystical. Contemplative *otium* (leisure) was paid for by hard sacrifice, but the monk (while no doubt seriously concerning himself with the Benedictine ladder of humility) found himself at the top of society in a privileged kind of existence. This air of aristocratic leisure, of privilege and of lordly isolation from the common run of men became more frankly questionable when monasteries were, in fact, places of easy and comfortable retirement from the responsibilities of secular existence. There is, then, plenty of historical warrant for the suspicion that the monastic life can become merely a refuge for the inadequate. On the other hand, the struggle to restore monasticism, after the French Revolution had almost swept it out of existence, certainly modified this. There are, it is true, a few highly aristocratic communities still in existence. No one seriously considers them ready for renewal. Everyone recognizes that these do indeed belong to the feudal past. Nevertheless this suspicion has caused many to question all large and manifestly prosperous monasteries as if they were as feudal as twelfth-century Cluny. This is by no means true. Nevertheless, it must be admitted that the nineteenth-century restorers of monasticism were not only traditionalists in theology and spirituality but even at times royalists and feudalists in politics. They deliberately attempted to restore the medieval structures of monasticism in Europe as models for a reformation of medieval society. Those who came from Europe to make new foundations in America were seldom tempted to question this concept until very recent years.

The fact that this "triumphalist" monasticism is seriously undermined today means that all the arguments which it advanced to justify its existence are now questionable.

Is it enough to wall the monk off in a little contemplative enclave, and there allow him to ignore the problems and crises of the world, should he forget the way other men have to struggle for a living, and simply let his existence be justified by the fact that he punctually recites the hours in choir, attends conventual Mass, strives for interior perfection and makes an honest effort to "live a life of prayer"? Do these innocuous occupations make him a "contemplative"? Or do they make of the monastery a dynamo which "generates spiritual power" for those who are too busy to pray? The famous argument of Pius XI in *Umbratilem* (praising the Carthusians) has been twisted out of shape by decades of routine monastic self-justification, and the sound, traditional theology of that document has been gradually distorted into a quaint superstition, a kind of magic prayer-wheel concept which has lost all power to convince anyone.

On the other hand, no one who is familiar with authentic monastic theology will be seriously disturbed by these arguments, which are all based on the false premise that monasticism is and can only be the sham gothic stereotype re-created a hundred and fifty years ago. The monastic community does not have to be a museum or a liturgical showplace with a college or brewery attached. There are other possibilities, and the monk can justify his existence without rushing back to join in the apostolic life which is, in fact, just as seriously questioned as the monastic life itself.

The essence of the monastic vocation is positive, not negative. It is more than a matter of turning one's back on the world and then doing something or other that can be effectively carried on behind walls—saying prayers, painting pictures, brewing beer, navel-gazing, or what have you.

The monk is (at least ideally) a man who has responded to an authentic call of God to a life of freedom and detachment, a "desert life" outside normal social structures. He is liberated from certain particular concerns in order that he may belong entirely to God. His life is one dedicated completely to love, the love of God and man, but a love that is not determined by the requirements of a special task. The monk is, or should be, a Christian who is mature enough and decided enough to live without the support and consolation of family, job, ambition, social position, or even active mission in the apostolate. He is also mature enough and determined enough to use this freedom for one thing only: the love and praise of God and the love of other men. He is mature and free enough to exercise a love of other men that is not confined to this or that apostolic routine, this or that particular form of work.

The monk is not defined by his task, his usefulness. In a certain sense he is supposed to be "useless" because his mission is not to *do* this or that job but to *be* a man of God. He does not live in order to exercise a specific function: his business is life itself. This means that monasticism aims at the cultivation of a certain *quality* of life, a level of awareness, a depth of consciousness, an area of transcendence and of adoration which are not usually possible in an active secular existence. This does not imply that the secular level is entirely godless and reprobate, or that there can be no real awareness of God in the world. Nor does it mean that worldly life is to be considered wicked or even inferior. But it does mean that more immersion and total absorption in worldly business end by robbing one of a certain necessary perspective. The monk seeks to be free from what William Faulkner called "the same frantic steeplechase toward nothing" which is the essence of "worldliness" everywhere.

Teilhard de Chardin has developed a remarkable mystique of secularity which is certainly necessary for our time when the vast majority of men have no choice but to seek and find God in the busy world. But where did Teilhard acquire this perspective? In the deserts of Asia, in vast solitudes which were in many ways more "monastic" than the cloisters of our monastic institutions. So too Bonhoeffer, regarded as an opponent of all that monasticism stands for, himself realized the need for certain "monastic" conditions in order to maintain a true perspective in and on the world. He developed these ideas when he was awaiting his execution in a Nazi prison.

What the monastic life should provide, then, is a special awareness and perspective, an authentic understanding of God's presence in the world and His intentions for man. A merely fictitious and abstract isolation does not provide this awareness. The symbol of medieval monasticism is the wall and the cloister. Instead of merely being self-enclosed, the modern monk might perhaps emulate Teilhard in the desert of Mongolia or Bonhoeffer in prison. These are more primitive and more authentic examples of what a charismatic solitude can mean!

The need for a certain *distance* from the world does not make the monk love the world less. Nor does it imply that he never has any contact with the outside world. Certainly the monastic community has the right and duty to create a certain solitude for the monks: it is no sin to live a silent life. But at the same time the monastic community owes other men a share in that quiet and that solitude. Obviously the balance must be very delicate, for quiet and solitude are destroyed by the movement of crowds. But the fact remains all the more true: the monk has a quiet, relatively isolated existence in which it is possible to concentrate more on the *quality* of life and its mystery, and thus to escape in some measure from the senseless tyranny of quantity.

IT IS CERTAINLY TRUE, then, that this special perspective necessarily implies that the monk will be in some sense critical of the world, of its routines, its confusions, and its sometimes tragic failures to provide other men with lives that are fully sane and human. The monk can and must be open to the world, but at the same time he must be able to get along without a naive and uncritical "secularity" which blandly assumes that everything in the world is at every moment getting better and better for everybody. This critical balance is no doubt difficult to achieve. But it is something which the monk *owes to the world*. For the monastic life has a certain prophetic character about it: not that the monk should be able to tell what is about to happen in the Kingdom of God, but in the sense that he is a living witness to the freedom of the sons of God and to the essential difference between that freedom and the spirit of the world. While admitting that God "so loved the world that he gave his only begotten Son" (John 3:16), the monk does not forget that when the Son of God came into the world it did not receive him because it *could* not. It was bound to oppose and reject him (John 1:10-11; 7:7; 15:18; 14:17, etc.).

The monastic life then must maintain this prophetic seriousness, this wilderness perspective, this mistrust of any shallow optimism which overlooks the ambiguity and the potential tragedy of "the world" in its response to the Word. And there is only one way for the monk to do this: to live as a man of God who has been manifestly "called out of the world" to an existence that differs radically from that of other men, however sincere, however Christian, however holy, who have remained "in the world."

In other words, the problem of monastic renewal is this: though it must obviously involve a radical reshaping of institutional structures, the renewal is by no means merely an institutional concern. It would be a great mistake to assume that renewal is nothing but *reorganization* or even juridical reform. What is needed is not only new rules but new structures and new life. The new life stirs, but faintly, incoherently. It does not know if it can exist without the old structures. What is also needed is a new outlook and a new faith in the capacities of modern men to be monks in a new way. Then the organization of monastic life can perhaps become less cramped, less obsessive, less narcissistic, and new life can develop with creative spontaneity. This spontaneity should be rooted in living tradition. But living tradition must not be confused with dead conventionalism and futile routine, as it so often has been. The situation of monasticism in America is now such that a genuine renewal, and not merely a few new rules, is imperative if American monasticism is to continue a fruitful existence.

Authentic renewal is going to demand a great deal of variety and originality in experimentation. Obviously, the mere issuing of decrees and ordinances from the top down, carried out mechanically on a massive scale, will simply stifle what life is left in monasticism. On the other hand the danger of irresponsibility and levity in ill-considered innovation remains real. But renewal must be bought at the price of risk. Undoubtedly a juncture obsession with novelty for its own sake will cause the ruin of some monastic communities. The winds are blowing and a lot of dead wood is going to fall. The true strength of monasticism is to be sought in its capacity for renunciation, silence, prayer, faith, and its realization of the cross in our life. All genuine renewal must seek life at the source of life: the cross and resurrection of Jesus.

Fortunately there are signs that such a renewal, though perhaps still tentative and painful, is trying to get under way.

THE MONASTIC ORDERS CAME to America in the nineteenth century. On one hand the Cistercians (Trappists) brought with them a strictly enclosed penitential form of common life which disconcerted Americans more than it inspired them. The Benedictines brought missionary and apostolic abbeys which maintained schools, colleges, parishes, and seminaries on the frontier, thus fulfilling an urgent need, but tending to depart from the ancient contemplative tradition of monasticism.

One of the most curious phenomena in the life of the American Church after World War II was the sudden interest in the strict contemplative life of the Cistercians and the rush of vocations to the three Cistercian abbeys, which rapidly made foundations in all parts of North America and even in the Southern Hemisphere. Those of us who lived through this minor explosion took it more or less as it came, but now we look back on it aghast, realizing that we cannot really account for it, and soberly aware that it was not an unequivocal success. On the contrary, most of those who entered Cistercian monasteries by the scores and even by the hundreds (there were in all about two thousand postulants received into the Gethesmani community over a period of some ten years in the forties and fifties), later took their departure. Most of those who left went during their novitiate. Others were dispensed from simple and even solemn vows.

It is perhaps too soon to decide what this commotion signified. But this much can certainly be said: there was a sincere interest in monastic ideals and a genuinely experienced *need* for what the monastic life offered. There were many authentic monastic vocations and they were *lost*. Men who clearly demonstrated their ability to live as excellent monks found themselves defeated and confused by a system that apparently frustrated their development. They discovered two things: first, that they wanted what the monastic life had to offer; second, that the monastic life was now built in such a way that what it offered remained, for many monks, a dream or an impossibility. In effect, one could live fruitfully enough as a novice, but after that one became caught in a complex and fatal machinery in which one was finally exhorted to renounce even what he had come to the monastery to find. This does not mean that the values of monasticism no longer existed, but that they were present in a form that made them morally, psychologically, or spiritually inaccessible to many modern men and women. The Cistercians themselves recognized this, and already in the early fifties considerable changes began to be made in the daily schedule and in the various observances. These changes have continued to be made and the whole shape of the life has been significantly altered in the last fifteen years. But the problem of renewal remains just as real and just as perplexing as before, since changes in schedule and in details of observance do not seem to have got right down to the root of the matter. Nor will they ever do so as long as medieval or baroque attitudes prevail.

Meanwhile monastic foundations of a new type began to be made, in the fifties, more than ten years before the Council. Already the "Primitive Benedictine" monasteries like Mount Saviour and Weston felt that monasticism had to get off to a new start. Pioneering efforts were attempted, especially in the vernacular liturgy. The community structure of two classes, lay brothers and priests, was modified to create a community of simple monks in one class, only a few of whom were priests. At the same time the Primitive Benedictines applied themselves to a more serious study of monastic tradition and of the Bible, while experimenting in more flexible and simple formulas of monastic observance than those which had been imported from Europe by the big monasteries a century before. The keynote of the new monasticism was a simple, natural, more or less hard life in contact with nature, nourished by the Bible, the monastic fathers and the liturgy, and faithful to the ancient ideal of prayer, silence, and that "holy leisure" (*otium sanctum*) necessary for a pure and tranquil heart in which God could be experienced, tasted, in the silence and freedom of the monk's inner peace. It can be said that though the Primitive Benedictines were at first criticized (doubtless because they were envied), the older monasteries soon began in various ways to imitate them and attempt changes along lines which the Primitive Benedictine experiments had suggested. Thus even before the Council decree *Perfectae Caritatis* all the monks were working more or less at renewal.

The ferment produced by the Council resulted in increased and unexpected activity among the Cistercians. Monks of the larger abbeys or even of their small foundations began to question the existing formula as such, and to seek opportunities to make a new beginning of their own. Several small experimental foundations have therefore been made by Cistercians in various parts of the United States. These have generally not managed to get a high degree of official backing. Their state is still, at the time of writing [1967], too uncertain for any kind of comment, particularly since detailed information has not been readily available.

Finally, the question of a completely solitary life in hermitages has been admitted back into the full light of the monastic consciousness, after centuries of burial in the darkness of suppressed fantasies. This was made possible and even necessary by the fact that Dom Jacques Winandy, a retired Benedictine abbot from Luxembourg, who had lived as a hermit in Switzerland and then Martinique, formed a colony of hermits in British Columbia. This colony was recruited largely from Cistercian and Benedictine abbeys in the United States, where there have always been a few monks attracted to complete solitude. Taking stock of the situation, the Cistercians realized that a place might be made for hermit vocations within the Order itself. It is now possible for Cistercians to obtain permission to live as hermits in the woods near their monasteries—a solution which had also been arrived at ten years before by the Primitive Benedictines. This in fact is nothing radically new: there exists a long tradition of Benedictine hermits going back to the time of Benedict himself. It is admittedly a good solution but it affects only a few individuals. These have the advantage of a solitary life and of freedom to develop according to their own needs and personal vocation. They have a minimum of concern about temporalities, and they are able to continue their monastic life as members of the community where they made profession. Normally, however, monks have neither the desire nor the grace to live this particular kind of life, and the real problems remain to be solved in the context of common living.

All that has been attempted so far is a provisional beginning, and we cannot yet safely predict what will happen to the monastic movement in this country. One thing is certain: the destinies of the big monasteries are not what they were thought to be a decade ago, and the large new buildings put up to accommodate the many who are no longer there may one day seem a bit bleak and void. But things are certainly a lot quieter—and more peaceful. Life in a big Cistercian monastery may be far from the perfect ideal, but monastically there is still a lot to be said for it, and many of the monks may grudgingly admit that they never had it so good. The admission is, however, no sign of complete satisfaction, because all eyes are on the future, and the present state of affairs is not accepted by anyone as final. How good do they expect to have it?

Speaking as one who has more or less retired to a marginal existence, I am inclined to think they are not yet quite sure themselves. Nor is anyone quite sure just what direction the monastic renewal will take. It may go in different directions in different places: one monastery may be concerned with more openness to the world, another with a return to the desert wilderness and solitude. There is room for variety and for original solutions, provided always that the essence of the monastic vocation is respected. But there is uncertainty because, even to the monks themselves, that essence has seemingly never been quite clear.

IN ORDER TO UNDERSTAND monasticism, it is important to concentrate on the *charism of the monastic vocation* rather than on the *structure of monastic institutions or the patterns of monastic observance.*

Most of the ambiguities and distresses of the current renewal seem to come from the fact that there is too much concern with changing the observances or adapting the institution and not enough awareness of the charism which the institution is meant to serve and protect. Indeed, one sometimes feels that too many monks have got the cart before the horse, and assume that the vocation or charism exists for the sake of the institution, and that men who are called by God to the peace and inner freedom of the monastic life can be regarded as material to be exploited for the good of the monastic institution, its prestige, its money-making projects, and so on.

Obviously, in a community life each monk will want to do an honest job of work and earn his share of the bread that is placed on the common table. But we must be fully aware of the fact that men do not come to a monastery today in order to live the routine busy life of an employee in a big business corporation. The mere fact that a busy life is lived in a monastic enclosure does not make it "contemplative." There are certain forms of exhausting and meaningless servitude which are characteristic of "the world." It is of the very essence of the monastic life to protest, by its simplicity and its liberty, against these servitudes. Of course there is obedience in the monastic life: it is the very heart of that life. Obedience is, paradoxically, the one guarantee of the monk's charismatic inner liberty. But obedience must always be consciously oriented to the fulfillment of the monastic vocation in the monk's own person and not *merely* to the impersonal success of some business project. Not only is there serious danger of monastic obedience being used today to frustrate the true purpose of monastic life, but the renewal may be carried out in such a way that this deformity is carefully protected and preserved. Indeed, one sometimes feels that all sorts of token changes are made on a superficial level, with care being taken to see that in no case the priority of the institution over the person will ever be threatened. In such conditions, "renewal" can never be anything but futile.

The whole question of monastic work, and of the support of the monastic community, is, today, an extremely vexed one. On the one hand there are monks who are claiming that the only honest way for a monk to earn his living is to go out and be a wage earner and then return at night to his community (in this case a small group) and his life of contemplation. Others are for a more complete return to nature and to primitive forms of farm work and handicrafts, etc. Still others think that a highly mechanized monastic "plant" will guarantee enough leisure for reading and contemplation. All these solutions have clear disadvantages, and they all seem to suffer from distorted perspectives and even from a kind of pragmatism that is concerned not with the essence of monasticism but with one or another aspect of it. The ones who want to go and work in factories are concerned with being and appearing poor and also with sharing the lot of the workman in the modern world. Poverty and work are, it is true, essential to the monastic life: but so too is a certain authentic solitude and isolation from the world, a certain protest against the organized and dehumanizing routines of a worldly life built around gain for its own sake. The danger is that the witness of monastic poverty will simply get lost in the mammoth machinery geared for one thing only: profit. The same thing happens when the monastery itself becomes a prosperous industrial unit with the monks working in offices and living on a comfortable income. As to the primitive and ideally agrarian setup: this tends to become a self-consciously arty-and-crafty venture in archaism which, in practice, has to be supported by benefactions from the mammon of iniquity.

When the concern for institutional adjustment is uppermost, then all monastic problems tend to fall into this kind of pattern. It becomes a struggle to adjust the institution in order to emphasize some one aspect, *some particular value*, which an individual or a group appreciates over all the others. When everything is centered on liturgy and on the harmonious, aesthetic decorum of traditional monasticity, then poverty and work may suffer. When everything is centered on poverty and labor, then the community may be overworked and lose interest in reading, prayer, and contemplation. When everything is centered on "openness to the world" the monks may become agitated and self-complacent gossips and under the pretext of "charity" forget that love which originally drew them to the monastery. In the past an excessive Trappist rigorism produced communities of well-meaning and devout men who sometimes bordered on the boorish or the fanatical.

Actually, the renewal of monasticism cannot have any real meaning until it is seen as a renewal of the *wholeness* of monasticism in its *charismatic* authenticity. Instead of concentrating on this or that means, we need first of all to look more attentively at the end. And here, while we must certainly focus accurately on the traditional ideal, a little realism and common sense will not be out of place. These were, after all, characteristic of that Benedictine Rule on which, whatever may be our time and its problems, renewal will normally be based.

The charism of the monastic life is the freedom and peace of a wilderness existence, a return to the desert that is also a recovery of (inner) paradise. This is the secret of monastic "renunciation of the world." Not a *denunciation*, not a denigration, not a precipitous flight, a resentful withdrawal, but a liberation, a kind of permanent "vacation" in the original sense of "emptying." The monk simply discards the useless and tedious baggage of vain concerns and devotes himself henceforth to the one thing really necessary—the one thing that he really wants: the quest for *meaning* and for *love*, the quest for his own identity, his secret name promised him by God (Apocalypse 2:17), and for the peace of Christ which the world cannot give (John 14:27). In other words the monk renounces a life of agitation and confusion for one of order and clarity. But the order and clarity are not his own making; nor are they, so to speak, an institutional product, an effect of exterior regularity. They are the fruit of the Spirit. The monastic life is a response to the call of the Spirit to espousals and to peace in the wilderness (Hosea 2:19-20).

The monastic charism is not, however, one of pure solitude without any community. It is also a charism of brotherhood in the wilderness: for the monk, even though he may eventually, in an exceptional case, live as a hermit, is prepared for solitude by living in close brotherly relationship with his fellow monks in the monastic community. This closeness is understood as being at least ideally a very human and warm relationship, and the charism of the monastic life is, and has been from the beginning, a grace of *communion* in a shared quest and a participated light. It is then a charism of special love and of mutual aid in the attainment of a difficult end, in the living of a hazardous and austere life. The monk is close to his brother insofar as he realizes him to be a fellow pilgrim in the spiritual "desert." Monastic work, obedience, poverty, chastity, are all in some way colored and tempered by the communal charism of brotherhood in pilgrimage and in hope.

Obviously the monastic life is not purely charismatic. Nothing could be more ruinous for monasticism than to turn a lot of inexperienced monks loose to live without any institutional structures and without organization—or to assume them capable of improvising new institutions overnight. Though the monastic life today is too rigidly institutionalized and too hidebound with senseless traditions, the basic lines of a monastic communal structure must be preserved, and the authentic wisdom, drawn from the experience of ages in which monasticism was fully *lived*, must not be lost. The new monastic communities will need to be much more democratic than in the past. The abbot will have to be a spiritual father, not a prelate, a police chief and a corporation president rolled into one. The monks will have to have much more initiative in running their own lives, and the abbot will have to concern himself more with genuine spiritual guidance than with institutional control. The spiritual role of the superior presupposes a certain freedom and discretion in the subject. The superior can no longer arrogate to himself the right to do all his subjects' thinking for them and to make all their decisions for them. Obviously, in the period of transition, mistakes will be made. But with the grace of God these mistakes themselves will be more fruitful than the stifling inertia of over-control. The monks will learn for themselves some lessons that they could never learn any other way.

The charism of the monastic vocation is one of simplicity and truth. The monk, whether as hermit or as cenobite, is one who abandons the routines, the clichés, the disguised idolatries and empty formalities of "the world" in order to seek the most authentic and essential meaning of the dedicated life on earth. Ideally speaking, then, the monastery should be a place of utter sincerity, without empty and deceptive formalities, without evasions, without pretenses.

Often, the rules and disciplines of community life have merely created an atmosphere of formalism and artificiality which, instead of helping the monks to live in close rapport as true brothers, served only to estrange them from one another. It is tragic that in the name of discipline and obedience monastic silence has been exploited as a means of keeping the monks out of touch with each other, indeed fearful and suspicious of one another. Monastic enclosure has at times become nothing more than a means of keeping the monks ignorant of the outside world in the hope that they would become indifferent to its tragic conflicts and not create any bother by having problems of conscience over things like war, poverty, race, and revolution.

There is no question that one of the most disturbing things about the monastic institution for most of those moderns who have come seeking to give themselves to God in solitude, prayer, and love, has been the current interpretation of religious vows, especially obedience. One who dedicates himself to God by vows today finds himself committed for life to a massively organized, rigidly formalistic institutional existence. Here everything is decided for him beforehand. Everything is provided for by rule and system. Initiative is not only discouraged, it becomes useless. Questions cease to have any point, for you already know the answers by heart in advance. But the trouble is that they are not answers, since they imply a firm decision to ignore your questions. Obedience then no longer consists in dedicating one's will and love to the service of God, but almost the renunciation of all human rights, needs, and feelings in order to conform to the rigid demands of an institution. The institution is identified with God, and becomes an end in itself. And the monk is given to understand from the start that there is no *alternative* for him but to regard this institutional life in all its details, however arbitrary, however archaic, however meaningless to him, as the *only way* for him to be perfect in love and sincere in his quest for God. This has been impressed upon him not only as a most solemn religious duty but almost as an article of faith: indeed, the young monk who has serious problems with a life that may seem to him increasingly fruitless and even absurd may be forcefully told that he is failing in Christian faith and verging on apostasy!

It is here that we see how far the perversion of the "spiritual dynamo" idea can sometimes be carried. The monastic institution, with its constant prayer, its regularity, its impeccable observance, its obedient and submissive monks, is implicitly regarded as a beautiful machine which, as long as it runs smoothly, obtains infallible results from God. The object of the monastic order, of the superiors, chapters, and so on, is to make sure that the machine is well oiled and keeps running exactly as it should. Faith assures us that the monastic machine is exerting an irresistible influence on God who, it is assumed, takes a mysterious pleasure in the operation of this ingenious toy. The legal clockwork of monasticism has been specially devised by the Church to enchant the Almighty and to cunningly manipulate His power. For what? For the institutional benefit of the rest of the Church—its manifold projects, the conversion of infidels, the return of heretics and apostates to humble submission, the humiliation and destruction of the Church's enemies, and so on. Obviously such a valuable machine must not be tampered with in any way. "Renewal" simply means a cleaning and oiling that will make the clock run more perfectly than before!

The most tragic misunderstandings have arisen from this attitude which, in some cases, one must frankly admit it, savors of gross superstition and arrogance. In any event, it has led to the ruin of many monastic vocations which seemed to be in every respect serious and genuine. One feels that if there had been a little flexibility, a little humaneness shown—if the monk, when he began to have trouble with the life, had been allowed a change of scene or a more genuinely human relationship with his brothers—he might have adjusted to the life after all. Unfortunately, there still exists such a grave fear of the austere institutional image being tarnished by concessions that vocations are sacrificed in order to preserve a monastic façade.

As everywhere else in American life, there has been an enormous amount of neurotic anxiety in monasteries. The tendency has been, in each case, to blame the individual. Sometimes, however, one wonders if a certain neurotic pattern has not finally got built into the system itself. Indeed one might at times wonder if the system does not require and favor neurotic insecurity, both in subjects and in superiors, in order to continue functioning as it does. Certainly neurosis is not endemic in monasticism as such. But a particular concept of monastic regularity and obedience does seem to encourage neuroses while loudly deploring them and advocating therapy—which then becomes part of the process.

Monks are human in their needs, their frailties, and also in their unconscious efforts to compensate for what they have given up by leaving the world. The man who has renounced family life and the love of children may, without realizing it himself, seek compensation in some other way—for instance by dominating other people. Men and women in the cloister have sometimes been notoriously aggressive, ambitious, given to a bitter and thoroughly worldly struggle for political power in their community. Those who lack the forcefulness required to exercise power themselves are content to live as monastic Peter Pans, in passive dependence on those whom they flatter and try to manipulate. In the long run, they find that this passivity too implies a certain power, for by subservience and manipulation they can get their own will incorporated into the system and have their ideas imposed by a superior.

The man who loves power can, with most idealistic motives, seek to gratify this love not only by exercising his power over his contemporaries, but even by building his will into the structure of the institution so that later generations will go on being dominated by him long after his death. In the current effort at renewal, it may happen that this kind of underground power struggle is being carried on without the monks realizing it too clearly. Many of those who are most enthusiastic and active in the work of "renewal" seem to be going about it in such a way as to make sure that *their* ideas and plans will not be seriously contested, and that in the end it will be *their* reforms that will win out. It also unfortunately happens that the adjustment these people advocate is superficial only: and if they have their way, they will hand on the *status quo*, embellished with a few trimmings of their own, and it will be a monument to themselves. This "monumental," "massive," and basically static concept of the monastic life is certainly to blame for the institutional rigidities that prevent true adjustment today. But such monasticism as this cannot survive. It is doomed. The sense of outrage, protest, and refusal is too evident in monastic communities. Unfortunately there is also a growing impatience, and those who allow themselves to become obsessed with the problem may forget that monastic renewal is God's work and not theirs, and they too may be tempted, in a basically selfish desperation, to abandon the effort that the Church asks of them.

The monastic movement needs leaders who must come from the new generation. These must have the patience to undergo the testing and formation without which their ability cannot be proved. No one will entrust himself to the guidance of men who have never had to suffer anything and have never really faced the problems of life in all their bitter seriousness. The young must not be too ready to give up in despair. They have work to do! Fortunately there are creative forces at work. There are communities and superiors who are fully aware of the real nature of the monastic vocation not simply as a summons to become a cog in an institutional machine, but as a charismatic breakthrough to liberation and love. It is more and more clearly realized that fidelity to monastic tradition no longer means simply dictating pre-formulated answers to all the questions of the young monk, and forcing him to look at his life through somebody else's glasses. Tradition is not passive submission to the obsessions of former generations but a living assent to a current of uninterrupted vitality. What was once real in other times and places becomes real in us today. And its reality is not an official parade of externals. It is a living spirit marked by freedom and by a certain *originality*. Fidelity to tradition does not mean the renunciation of all initiative, but a new initiative that is faithful to a certain spirit of freedom and of vision which demands to be incarnated in a new and unique situation. True monasticism is nothing if not creative.

The creativity in monastic life springs from pure love: the natural desire of man for truth and for communion first of all, and the supernatural gift of grace in the spirit of the Risen Lord, calling man to the highest truth and most perfect communion in the Mystery of Christ. Love is not mere emotion or sentiment. It is the lucid and ardent response of the whole man to a value that is revealed to him as perfect, appropriate, and urgent in the providential context of his own life. Hence there are innumerable ways in which man can be awakened from the sleep of a mechanical existence and summoned to give himself totally in the clarity of love. To restrict vocations to this or that narrow area, as if there were only one way to love, is to stifle the spirit and fetter the freedom of the Christian heart. Why are people so intent on refusing others the right to see a special value in a life apart from the world, a life dedicated to God in prayer "on the mountain alone" when the New Testament itself repeatedly shows Christ retiring to the solitary prayer which he himself loved? Certainly one can find God "in the world" and in an active life but this is not the only way, any more than the monastic life is the only way. There are varieties of graces and vocations in the Church and these varieties must always be respected. The specific value that draws a Christian into the "desert" and "solitude" (whether or not he remains physically "in the world") is a deep sense that *God alone suffices.* The need to win the approval of society, to find a recognized place in the world, to achieve a temporal ambition, to "be somebody" even in the Church seems to them irrelevant. They realize themselves to be called to a totally different mode of existence, outside of secular categories and *outside of the religious establishment.* This is the very heart of monasticism; hence a firmly "established" monasticism is a self-contradiction.

The creative spirit of initiative in monasticism is bound to be killed by an exaggerated emphasis on a well-established monastic "presence," an undue concern with law and ritual and with the externals of observance. The true creative spirit must be fired with love and with *an authentic desire of God.* This means, in so many words, that the monastic vocation is one which implicitly, if not explicitly, seeks *the experience of union with God.* True, the humility and obedience which are essential to the monastic life are absolutely necessary to purge this desire from all elements of self-will and of spiritual ambition. But the need for spiritual liberation, the need for vision, the hunger and thirst for that perfect "justice" which is found in total surrender to God as love to the Beloved: these are the only real justifications for the monk's wilderness life and his desert pilgrimage. If these are systematically frustrated, and if institutional formalities are everywhere substituted for the inner desire of holiness and union, monks will not remain in the monastery. If they are true to themselves and to God they will be compelled to look elsewhere. This is the real problem of monastic renewal: not a surrender to the "secular city" but a recovery of the deep desire of God that draws a man to seek a *totally new way of being in the world.*

This is perhaps a better way of envisaging the monastic vocation. There is no longer any place for the idea that monasticism is mere *repudiation* of the world. It is not enough to "say no," to develop "contempt" for the world, and to spend one's life in a walled-up existence which simply rejects all the pleasures, interests, and struggles of the world as suspect or as sinful. This negative idea of monasticism has caused it to be completely misunderstood by its critics because it has so often been misunderstood by the monks themselves. And that is why, when the young monk in quest of renewal looks for something to say "yes" to, he comes up with the same "yes" as the world itself. In either case, there is no real awareness of what monasticism is all about.

The monastic life is neither worldly nor unworldly. It is not artificially "otherworldly." It is merely intended to be liberated and simple. The purpose of monastic detachment—which demands genuine sacrifice—is simply to leave the monk unencumbered, free to move, in possession of his spiritual senses and of his right mind, capable of living a charismatic life in freedom of spirit. To love, one must be free, and while the apostolic life implies one mode of freedom in the world, the monastic life has its own freedom which is that of the wilderness. The two are not opposed or mutually exclusive. They are complementary, and, on the highest level, they turn out to be one and the same: union with God in the mystery of total love, in the oneness of His Spirit.

In the solitude of the monastic life, the monk begins obscurely to sense that great depths are opened up within him, and that the charism of his monastic vocation demands an obedience that is carried out in an abyss too deep for him to understand. It is an obedience that permeates the very roots of his being. Such obedience is far more difficult than any compliance with the will of man, but it must be tested by rule, by discipline, and by submission to the wills of other men. Otherwise it is sheer illusion. Nevertheless, for rule and command to retain their worth in the monastic life, they must be seen in their right relation to the ultimate purpose of that life. Monastic obedience exists not to make yes-men and efficient bureaucrats who can be used in institutional politics, but to liberate the hearts and minds into the lucid and terrible darkness of a contemplation that no tongue can explain and no rationalization can account for. And it must always be remembered that this contemplative liberation is a gift of God, granted not necessarily to the perfect only, and certainly not as a prize for political collaboration with the schemes and ambitions of others.

It remains to speak one word to the monks themselves, that is to those who now, at this time, are persevering in monasteries and hermitages. That word is: *do not be impatient and do not be afraid.* Do not imagine that everything depends on some instant magic transformation of constitutions and of laws. You already have what you need right in your hands! You have the grace of your vocation and of your love. No earthly situation has ever been ideal. God does not need an ideal situation in order to carry out His work in our hearts. If we do what we can with the means and grace at our disposal, if we sincerely take advantage of our genuine opportunities, the Spirit will be there and His love will not fail us. Our liberation, our solitude, our vision, our understanding, and our salvation do not depend on anything remote from us or beyond our reach. Grace has been given us along with our good desires. What is needed is the faith to accept it and the energy to put our faith to work in situations that may not seem to us to be promising. The Holy Spirit will do the rest. There will continue to be monasteries in the mountains and the forests of this continent. And they will be good monasteries, places of silence, of peace, of austerity, of simplicity, of prayer, and of love. They will house communities of men who love one another and share with the world the light they have received, though in a silent and obscure way. They will open out on to the desert solitude in which every monk, at one time or another, whether for a short time or for life, seeks to be alone in the silence and the mystery of his God, liberated from the images of Egypt and from the Babel of tongues.

Yet there is no such thing as a purely charismatic monasticism without any institution. There will always be laws and Rules. And Christ must always be especially present in the person of an abbot, a spiritual father. Indeed spiritual fatherhood itself is a charism and one of the greatest. Not only is it a signal blessing for any monastic community, but it is essential for the work of genuine renewal. Without experienced guides who are completely open to the full dimension—the mystical and prophetic dimension—of love in Christ, renewal will mean little more than the replacement of old rules by new ones and of old traditions by novel frenzies.

29

"Baptism in the Forest":
Wisdom and Initiation in William Faulkner

At the end of 1966 Merton had embarked on an intensive reading of William Faulkner, and began to speak about the Southern novelist at the Sunday afternoon conferences he gave to the monastic community, his most regular ongoing contact with his fellow monks after moving full-time into his hermitage in August of the previous year. (For a helpful overview of Merton on Faulkner, see Ross Labrie, "Thomas Merton on Art and Religion in William Faulkner," *Religion and the Arts* 14 [2010], 401-17.) On December 2 he writes in his journal of the long story "The Bear" as "Shattering, cleansing, a mind-changing and transforming myth that makes you stop to think about re-evaluating everything" (*Learning to Love*, 165). Two weeks later he calls Faulkner "The American prophet of the twentieth century (or at least the first half of it)—too great to be heeded by the nation" (*Learning to Love*, 178). On December 22 he writes of "another tremendous bout with Faulkner," this time the encounter with the story "Old Man," and its "fantastic myth, the void, the great power of evil, the alone man, the woman, their relationship, the ark—paradise—hell of snakes where the child is born" (*Learning to Love*, 173). On January 2, 1967, he writes Ernesto Cardenal about giving conferences on "The Bear" and adds, "Perhaps I will write something about it if I get time" (*Courage for Truth*, 158). The time apparently came sooner than expected when George Panichas asked Merton to write an introduction for a collection of essays he was editing to be entitled *Mansions of the Spirit*. On January 24 Merton mentions "writing my piece" for the book (*Learning to Love*, 187), and five days later notes both that he is "finishing the ms. of the book of essays" and that his own piece on Faulkner "is being typed now" (*Learning to Love*, 188). He reports on February 19 that Panichas "liked the Faulkner essay" (*Learning to Love*, 200), which was published in the book later in the year ([New York: Hawthorn Books, 1967], 19-44); it later appeared in abbreviated form in *Catholic World* 207 (June 1968), 124-30, and was included in full in *Literary Essays* (92-116). While Merton does mention and briefly comment on some of the other essays in the volume, his article functions less as an introduction to the other contributors' work than as a sustained reflection on his own reading of "The Bear" and of *The Wild Palms*, the Faulkner book in which "Old Man" is juxtaposed in alternating sections with the apparently unrelated title story. The rationale Merton uses to position this essay as introductory to the volume as a whole is to begin with a reflection on the problematic nature of "religious" literature in the contemporary world, and to suggest much imaginative writing wrestling with ultimate questions, like that of Faulkner, is better described as "sapiential," wisdom-oriented, than as "religious." This sapiential perspective is evident in "the wisdom of the Indian in the wilderness" found in "The Bear," "a kind of knowledge by identification, an intersubjective knowledge, a communion in cosmic awareness and in nature. . . a wisdom based on love." It is also embedded in the mythic structure of "Old Man," with its affirmation of life through self-sacrifice and its revelation of "an authentic and saving balance, an order and integrity" found in the mutual respect and support of man and woman, and completely missing in the desacralized passion of the lovers in *The Wild Palms*, in which wisdom is discovered only in the wake of tragedy. This focus on *sapientia*, wisdom, holistic, participatory knowledge, expressed most memorably in his prose poem *Hagia Sophia* (*Collected Poems*, 363-71), is a unifying thread that brings together much of Merton's mature writing on contemplation, interreligious dialogue, Gandhian nonviolence, protecting the environment, and here and elsewhere, imaginative literature, for as Merton suggests, in a culture that has largely lost touch with traditional sources of sacred vision, "creative writing and imaginative criticism provide a privileged area for wisdom in the modern world."

PERHAPS THE BEST WAY to approach the rather troublesome question of literature and religion today is to begin with a typical case, an example not of "religious literature" but rather of the confusions surrounding it. When Camus undertook to adapt Faulkner's *Requiem for a Nun* for the French stage, there was a certain amount of gossip in the press: "Camus has been converted!" Why? Because the work of Faulkner was "religious." (Anything with the word "nun" in the title has to be Roman Catholic, you know.) In an interview published in *Le Monde*[1] Camus had to go through the usual tiresome business of explaining the fairly obvious. He was fascinated by Faulkner, "the greatest American novelist." To Camus, Faulkner was one of the few modern writers who possessed the "keys of ancient tragedy" and who was able to discover in the back pages of the newspapers myths embodying the essential tragedy of our time. Faulkner could place modern characters in conflict with their destiny and could resolve that conflict in the way classic tragedy had done. In a word, Faulkner made it possible to hope that the "tragique de notre histoire" would one day be made credible on the stage.[2] In Faulkner the theme of suffer-

---

1. See the texts assembled by Roger Quilliot in Camus' *Théâtre, récits, nouvelles* (Paris, 1963), pp. 1855ff.

2. In his hope for a return of true tragedy Camus was influenced by the ideas of Antonin Artaud's manifestoes on "Le Théâtre de la cruauté." See Artaud, *Oeuvres*

ing was treated in a tragic, therefore (Camus thought) in a basically religious manner. Faulkner combined and concentrated in himself the "universe of Dostoevski and, besides that, Protestant rigorism." This was not at all a question of conventional moral sermons, which (Camus admitted) bored him to death, but of the mystery of suffering as a dark abyss into which Faulkner saw a possibility of a little light sometimes filtering. Without being "converted," Camus was certainly fascinated by the "étrange religion de Faulkner," readily suggesting that it contained the secret of Faulkner's tragic power.

In a preface to the regular French edition of *Requiem*, translated by Maurice-Edgar Coindreau, Camus roundly asserted that the paradoxical religious outlook of Faulkner, which made a saint of the prostitute Nancy and "invested brothels and prisons with the dignity of the cloister," could not be dispensed with in an adaptation. "Ce paradoxe essentiel il fallait le conserver." Nonetheless, Camus admitted that he had shortened the meditative passages on God and faith.

Camus added sardonically, "If I translated and staged a Greek tragedy, no one would ask me if I believed in Zeus." At the same time, in the aforementioned interview, Camus repudiated a superficial "godlessness" which he considered "vulgar and threadbare." "I do not believe in God," he said, "but I am not for all that an atheist."

The purpose of these quotations is not to approve or to disapprove of Camus' evaluation of Faulkner or of "Faulkner's religion." The case is adduced as evidence of two facts: namely, that there does exist a consensus which admits the existence even today of "religious literature" and that there is also a disquieting, even annoying, popular tendency to look for "conversions" in connection with this literature. I do not say that these popular beliefs substantiate all that critics sometimes say about literature and religion. I am merely showing what seems to me to be the source of the problem with which the present book attempts to deal. Far from taking these popular opinions as proof of "Faulkner's religion," I will merely use them as a starting point for a more pedestrian investigation of themes in Faulkner which might conceivably be called "religious" but which, I think, can better be classified by another term.

Meanwhile, let us firmly repudiate those vices which make this whole question of "religious literature" so distasteful and so confusing. First, there is the often morbid curiosity about conversions and apostasies associated with the writing or the reading of this or that literary work. This curiosity is every bit as

---

complètes, Tome IV (Paris, 1964), p. 101ff. A reading of these helps us to appreciate what Camus saw in Faulkner.

vulgar and tiresome as the aggressive religion and irreligion which often go with it. In large part the blame may well lie with the prevalence of another critical vice, that of "claiming for the faith" (see, in this connection, the essay by Hyatt Waggoner). This is the habit of searching authors for symptoms of belief—whether Christian, Marxist, or any other—and of forthwith enrolling them in one's own sect. John Cruickshank would call this "intellectual imperialism," and we can join him in finding it repugnant, especially when it claims to be "Christian." Unfortunately, the embattled inferiority complex of much nineteenth-century thought made this tendency almost second nature in some quarters. The dead, whose hash was definitely settled and who could not be discovered to have been deathbed converts, were nevertheless shown to have been secret believers in one way or another. The living were always rumored to be about to bow their heads over the font. Aldous Huxley, for instance, was repeatedly rumored to be on the verge of becoming a Catholic, perhaps because (as Milton Birnbaum shows) he once said that he disliked Catholics less than Puritans! Nor is there any need to recall the fury of conversions and apostasies which thirty years ago kept a ceaseless procession of intellectuals moving in and out of the Communist Party.

Further refinements in these matters can be left to the very competent treatment of the essayists in the first part of this volume. Is there such a thing as religious literature at all? What is meant here by "religious"? Does "religious literature" imply the author's orthodoxy, his belonging to a Church, or his commitment to a recognizable set of beliefs? The writers in this volume do not agree in their terminology, although they do in fact come to pretty much the same conclusions. "Literary" and "religious" values must not be confused. Obviously, religious orthodoxy or sincerity is no guarantee that a work is artistically valid. If, on the other hand, an understanding of the work implies some awareness of religious values, then one must be able to identify oneself to some extent with the author in holding these values to be "real." Otherwise, it becomes impossible to enjoy the work in question. But, again, what are "religious values"? Father Blehl, for instance, says that Graham Greene's whisky priest displays religious values, whereas in Faulkner's "The Bear" "the experiences have almost no intrinsic religious significance at all." Here, by "religious" Father Blehl evidently means "Christian" and "theological." The "religious" is "sacerdotal and spiritually redemptive" and "shows the operation of God in a world of sin." I would like to suggest later that Faulkner (at least in "The Bear") does have a "spiritually redemptive" view of the world, though it is not necessarily the orthodox Christian view.

Thomas L. Hanna would also like the range of "religion" in this regard severely restricted. For Hanna, a work is religious only if God is in the cast of characters. The fact that an author happens to have a coherent view of the world and of man's struggle with destiny in the world does not mean that he is giving "religious" answers. Perhaps, Hanna suggests, we should call his outlook a "metaphysic" rather than "religion." In such a case Camus' statement about the "étrange religion de Faulkner" should be emended to read "l'étrange métaphysique de Faulkner." I submit that the idea is subtly transformed as soon as it gets into French. Hanna is undoubtedly right in protesting against the naïveté of disoriented Christians who, having no metaphysic and needing one badly, assume that when they find a few ingredients for one, they have rediscovered "Christianity." Still, this deficiency and this naïveté are perhaps more apparent in America than in Europe. When in the very next essay Edwin M. Moseley can speak calmly of "the essentially religious content of serious drama in every age," he seems to be contradicting Hanna; yet he is not. Moseley's statement is much more plausible in his own context, since he starts out from Greek tragedy and talks the language of people like F. M. Cornford. Here again our allusions to Camus come in handy. Everyone can still respond to the great religious and mythical motifs of Greek tragedy without being converted to a belief in Zeus. As a matter of fact, Greek tragedy could imply a very definite ambiguity toward the gods. Faith in the Olympians did not necessarily imply a personal commitment to their service, and devotion to one of them might bring the devotee into strained relations with another (as Homer brings out). Aeschylus was not at all convinced that Zeus' rule was beneficial or even fully justified. And the Zeus of *Prometheus* is regarded as a usurper against whom Prometheus has a very plausible case.

Nevertheless, there is no getting around the facts that Greek tragedy deals religiously with the great basic problems of human destiny and that one can accept this without committing oneself to a particular dogmatic faith. The "religious" elements in Greek tragedy are of the same nature as the "essential paradox" which Camus found in Faulkner's *Requiem*. They lie embedded in different ground from that in which the revealed truths of Christianity are found. They are embedded in human nature itself, or, if that expression is no longer acceptable to some readers, then in the very constitution of man's psyche, whether his collective unconscious or his individual character structure.

In this connection we can readily understand why the neopositivism of Alain Robbe-Grillet rejects all tragedy as sentimental and false because it inevitably implies certain basic religious postulates about the value of life. But he assumes that these religious postulates are something *added* to reality, not inherent in it. In his suppression of values he suppresses something of reality itself. Hence his people are, as Father Jarrett-Kerr says, like insects. Such is the fruit of a method which has triumphantly "made tragedy impossible" and has, at the same time, rejected as irrelevant the idea of human nature and, even more, that of the human person. But Father Jarrett-Kerr also raises the question whether there can be "Christian tragedy" in any context where the resurrection of the dead is taken for granted. "Theology," in I. A. Richards' words, "is fatal to tragedy."

But redemption is not automatic. "Salvation" can never be taken for granted. All the good potentialities in man can be irretrievably wasted and destroyed through his own fault. The Christian concept of damnation, whether one believes in it or not, is supremely tragic. When Camus (out of the bitterness of his experience under the Nazis and during the Algerian war) spoke of our time as "tragic," he was aware of the aspect of its *destruction of man*. And Camus excels in portraying the damned.

Greek tragedy is comprehensible irrespective of whether we "believe in" the Greek gods. It is so because it is not in fact concerned with truth about the gods but with truths about man. It is concerned with them in such a "classical," such a universal way that we, too, find ourselves involved in them without passing through the medium of a doctrinal explanation. This immediacy of Attic tragedy may be more obvious to us in the West because our whole culture is built on the basis of Greek and Hebrew literature and thought. But I think that with very little initiation the Nō drama of Japan, for instance, or the religious drama of Bali[3] can have the same awe-inspiring and cathartic impact on a Western audience. In other words, once the ritual and symbolic language of gesture is grasped, one can participate in Oriental drama almost as well as in Greek tragedy. In either case, what is happening is not just that we are spelling out for ourselves a religious or a metaphysical message. Rather, the drama is having a direct impact on the deepest center of our human nature, at a level beyond language, where our most fundamental human conflicts find themselves not *explained*, not *analyzed*, but *enacted* in the artistic way which Aristotle tried to account for in his theory of catharsis, of pity and terror in tragedy.

In this way tragedy does not merely convince us that we ought to be resigned. Above all, it does not merely propose suitable reasons for resignation. Through its therapeutic effect it enables us to rise above evil, to liberate ourselves from it by a return to a more real evaluation of ourselves, a change of heart analogous to Christian "repentance." As we know, the mechanism of Greek tragedy is centered on *hubris*, that fundamentally false and arrogant estimate of one's self and of its capacities. The catharsis of pity and terror delivers the participant from *hubris* and restores him to an awareness of his place in the scheme of things—of

---

3. See Artaud, "Sur le théâtre balinais," *Oeuvres complètes*, 64ff.

his limitations as well as of his true nobility. It enables him to realize that "Puny Man," as Father Jarrett-Kerr says, "is still valuable for his freedom."

Now it is quite obvious that both Greek tragedy and Oriental ritual dance-drama were not merely presentations which an audience sat and watched. They were religious celebrations, liturgies, in which the audience participated. Thus, although we can still be immediately stirred by the impact of these archaic dramas even when we read them in translation, it does not take much imagination for us to represent to ourselves what would be the effect of our being present *then*, in those days, for instance in the theater at Delphi during the festival of Apollo. (Note what Father Jarrett-Kerr says about a recent performance of *Medea* before an African audience in Johannesburg.) We—our twentieth-century selves—might possibly have found the experience too powerful to bear. Or perhaps we would have undergone the sort of thing that happens now to the people who take LSD, which is presumably why they take it and why the taking of it has been invested with a quasi-religious ritual atmosphere.

The point is, I think, to realize that something of the same excitement and discovery remains accessible to us today in reading not only ancient tragedies but works of our own time. Faulkner is certainly one of those writers who possess this power to *evoke* in us an experience of meaning and of direction or a catharsis of pity and terror which can be called "religious" in the same sense as Greek tragedy was religious.

Unfortunately, as we have seen, the term "religious" is also very ambiguous, insofar as it is associated with many other things that have nothing to do with this basic experience. For example, the idea of religion today is mixed up with confessionalism, with belonging to this or that religious institution, with making and advertising a particular kind of religious commitment, with a special style in devotion or piety, or even with a certain exclusiveness in the quest for an experience which has to be sacred and not secular. In spite of all the talk of believers about breaking down the limits between the sacred and the secular, one still feels that there is a very obsessive insistence that one's whole experience of life has to be dominated *from without* by a system of acquired beliefs and attitudes and that every other experience (for instance, that of reading a novel) has first to be tested by this system of beliefs. Thus one has to read Faulkner with suspicion and enjoy only what conforms to one's own moral and religious code.

In order to make this simple and easy, one just proceeds to codify the novelists themselves. What did they believe? What was the preferred system of each? What in fact were "their messages"? But I submit that if you sit down to codify the "strange religion of Faulkner" and if you do so in terms of some other no doubt less strange religion of your own, you are likely to miss the real "religious" impact of Faulkner. His impact has all the directness of Greek tragedy because, although he works in words, he produces an effect that is somehow not explicable by an investigation of the words alone. He has a power of "enactment" which, if you are open to it, brings you into living participation with an experience of basic and universal human values on a level which words can *point* to but cannot fully attain. Faulkner is typical of the creative genius who can associate his reader in the same experience of creation which brought forth his book. Such a book is filled with efficacious sign-situations, symbols, and myths which release in the reader the imaginative power to experience what the author really means to convey. And what he means to convey is not a system of truths which explain life but a certain depth of awareness in which life itself is lived more intensely and with a more meaningful direction. The "symbolic" in this sense is not a matter of contrived signification in which things point arbitrarily to something else. Symbols are signs which release the power of imaginative communion.

The power of symbols is, I think, fully explicable only if you accept the theory that symbols are something more than mere artifacts of a few human minds. They are basic archetypal forms anterior to any operation of the mind, forms which have risen spontaneously with awareness in all religions and which have everywhere provided patterns for the myths in which man has striven to express his search for ultimate meaning and for union with God. Needless to say, these myths retain their power and their seminal creativity in the unconscious even after conscious minds have agreed that "God is dead." The myth of the death of God and of the void consequent upon it springs from the same archaic source as other myths. The conscious determination to deny that there is any void and to suppress all anxiety about it is another matter.

At the same time it must be quite clear that this imaginative and symbol-making capacity in man must not be confused with theological faith. But, because faith implies communication and language, the language of symbols is most appropriate in activating the deepest centers of decision which faith calls into play.

I would submit that the term "religious" no longer conveys the idea of an imaginative awareness of basic meaning. As D. H. Lawrence asserted, "It's not religious to be religious." And I would also say that the word "metaphysical" is not quite adequate to convey these values. There are other possibilities. One of them is the term *sapiential*.

Sapientia is the Latin word for "wisdom." And wisdom in the classic, as well as the Biblical, tradition is something quite definite. It is the highest level of cognition. It goes beyond *scientia*, which is systematic knowledge, beyond *intellec-*

tus, which is intuitive understanding. It has deeper penetration and wider range than either of these. It embraces the entire scope of man's life and all its meaning. It grasps the ultimate truths to which science and intuition only point. In ancient terms, it seeks the "ultimate causes," not simply efficient causes which make things happen, but the ultimate reasons why they happen and the ultimate values which their happening reveals to us. Wisdom is not only speculative, but also practical: that is to say, it is "lived." And unless one "lives" it, one cannot "have" it. It is not only speculative but creative. It is expressed in living signs and symbols. It proceeds, then, not merely from knowledge *about* ultimate values, but from an actual possession and awareness of these values as incorporated in one's own existence.

But *sapientia* is not inborn. True, the seeds of it are there, but they must be cultivated. Hence wisdom develops not by itself but in a hard discipline of traditional training, under the expert guidance of one who himself possesses it and who therefore is qualified to teach it. For wisdom cannot be learned from a book. It is acquired only in a living formation; and it is tested by the master himself in certain critical situations.

I might say at once that creative writing and imaginative criticism provide a privileged area for wisdom in the modern world. At times one feels they do so even more than current philosophy and theology. The literary and creative current of thought that has been enriched and stimulated by depth psychology, comparative religion, social anthropology, existentialism, and the renewal of classical, patristic, Biblical, and mystical studies has brought in a sapiential harvest which is not to be despised. Let me mention some of the more obvious examples: T. S. Eliot both as critic and as poet, Boris Pasternak, St.-John Perse, D. H. Lawrence,[4] and William Butler Yeats. Jacques Maritain's *Creative Intuition in Art and Poetry* illustrates what I mean, as do D. T. Suzuki's *Zen and Japanese Culture* and William Carlos Williams's *In the American Grain*. A great deal of what I call "sapiential" thinking has come out in studies of Melville and of the American novel in general, as well as in some of the recent Milton and Shakespeare criticism. I was fortunate to study in college under "sapiential" teachers like Mark Van Doren and Joseph Wood Krutch. In the classics Jane Harrison, Werner Jaeger, and F. M. Cornford have left us "sapiential" material.

The "wisdom" approach to man seeks to apprehend man's value and destiny in their global and even ultimate significance. Since fragmentation and objectivity do not suffice for this and since quantitative analysis will not serve, either, sapiential thought resorts to poetic myth and to religious or archetypal symbol.

---

4. Vivian de Sola Pinto's essay in *Mansions of the Spirit* brings this out well.

These must not be mistaken for *scientific* propositions. Symbols are not, here, ciphers pointing to hidden sources of information. They are not directed so much at the understanding and control of things as at man's own understanding of himself. They seek to help man liberate in himself life forces which are inhibited by dead social routine, by the ordinary involvement of the mind in trivial objects, by the conflicts of needs and of material interests on a limited level. Obviously, we do live in a world of things and institutions. We need to eat and to manage our everyday lives. But we also need an overall perspective to liberate us from enslavement to the immediate without taking us altogether outside the "real world." Sapiential awareness deepens our communion with the concrete: It is not an initiation into a world of abstractions and ideals. The poetic and contemplative awareness is sapiential—and it used to be, normally, religious. In fact, there is a relation between all "wisdoms." Greek wisdom was not out of harmony with that of the Bible. "Pythagoras and his disciples, and also Plato, followed that inward vision of theirs which was aimed at the truth, and this they did not without the help of God; and so in certain things they were in agreement with the words of the prophets."[5] So said Clement of Alexandria, hinting that all wisdom opened out upon true religion.

Wisdom, in any case, has two aspects. One is metaphysical and speculative, an apprehension of the radical structure of human life, an intellectual appreciation of man in his human potentialities and in their fruition. The other is moral, practical, and religious, an awareness of man's life as a task to be undertaken at great risk, in which tragic failure and creative transcendence are both possible. Another aspect of this moral and religious wisdom is a peculiar understanding of conflict, of the drama of human existence, and especially of the typical causes and signs of moral disaster. I might add that one of the characteristic qualities of this wisdom is that it goes beyond the conscious and systematic moral principles which may be embodied in an ethical doctrine and which guide our conscious activity. Wisdom also supposes a certain intuitive grasp of *unconscious motivations*, at least insofar as these are embodied in archetypes and symbolic configurations of the psyche.

Sapiential thinking has, as another of its characteristics, the capacity to bridge the cognitive gap between our minds and the realm of the transcendent and the unknown, so that without "understanding" what lies beyond the limit of human vision, we nevertheless enter into an intuitive affinity with it, or seem to experience some such affinity. At any rate, religious wisdoms often claim not only to teach us truths that are beyond rational knowledge but also to *initiate* us

---

5. *Stromata* V. 14.116.1.

into higher states of awareness. Such forms of wisdom are called mystical. I do not pause here to discuss the validity of various claims to mystical wisdom. It is sufficient to say that certain types of wisdom do in fact lay claim to an awareness that goes beyond the aesthetic, moral, and liturgical levels and penetrates so far as to give the initiate a direct, though perhaps incommunicable, intuition of the ultimate values of life, of the Absolute Ground of life, or even of the invisible Godhead. Christian wisdom is essentially theological, Christological, and mystical. It implies a deepening of Christian faith to the point where faith becomes an experiential awareness of the realities and values of man's life in Christ and "in the Spirit" when he has been raised to divine sonship.

In this collection of essays only the last two raise the question of Christian wisdom in modern life. Robert Detweiler's study of Flannery O'Connor introduces us to the radically new character of a wisdom that is "from above" and is based on a Word which is an offense, breaking through the hierarchical orders of cosmic sapience and overturning every other form of knowledge in order to bring man into confrontation with a whole new kind of destiny, a destiny to freedom in Christ. (Flannery O'Connor well knew how to exploit the ironies of this shocking situation!) The essay by George A. Panichas, on the other hand, brings us into contact with the ancient contemplative tradition of the Eastern Church, which represents a much more peaceful approach to a Christian wisdom from which Hellenic elements have not been driven out. The story of the Russian Pilgrim that so impressed Salinger's Franny informs us of a sapiential technique first devised by the monks of Sinai and transmitted from there to Mount Athos and then to Rumania and Russia. The purpose of this elementary technique was to dispose the contemplative to a possibility of direct illumination by God in the *theoria* described by the Greek Fathers and further developed by Athonite hesychasm in the fourteenth century.

FOR MY PART, I am not concerned in this essay with specifically Christian wisdom. I want to discuss two examples of what I would call the natural sapiential outlook in Faulkner: in other words, two examples of a conscious and deliberate construction of myth in order to convey a sense of initiatory awakening into the deeper meaning of life in terms of a tradition of natural wisdom. In the two works I take as examples, *Go Down, Moses* and *The Wild Palms*, it seems to me that this sapiential use of myth and of symbolic narrative, culminating in a new awareness of the meaning of life in a historical situation, has to be appreciated and accepted if one is to understand what the author is trying to say.

Let me be clear about what I mean by "myth." A myth is a tale with an archetypal pattern capable of suggesting and of implying that man's life in the cosmos has a hidden meaning which can be sought and found by one who somehow religiously identifies his own life with that of the hero in the story. For example, the *Odyssey* shows life as a journey with many trials and perils typified by symbolic test situations, a journey of return to one's home and one's place in the scheme of things. The ironic epic journey of the tall convict on the flooded river in *The Wild Palms* is a mystical *navigation* of this kind, but other important mythical elements enter into it. The flood is indeed seen as an eschatological deluge. It is not only a mystical journey for the tall convict (whose name we never know and who is a kind of archetypal man), but also a parable of judgment and a revelation of the meaning or un-meaning of human destiny. But the journey of the convict is a spiritual one, and its goal is a deeper sense of his own identity and his own "vocation." What he finds is a more definite, and more ironic, certitude of his own measure and of his place in the world which, in this story, is absurd and void.

The part of *Go Down, Moses* that interests me most is, of course, "The Bear." There has been a great deal of exciting criticism written about this exploitation of the "Paradise theme" and the "Lost Wilderness,"[6] but I would add that the story of Ike McCaslin's novitiate and initiation in the wilderness life has to be seen in the context of the whole book, *Go Down, Moses*, since in fact Part IV of "The Bear" does not reveal its full meaning when "The Bear" is printed and read apart from the rest of the McCaslin story. The violation of the wilderness, symbolic of a certain predatory and ferocious attitude toward the natural world, is for Faulkner an especially Southern phenomenon here, because it is connected with slavery. Ike McCaslin's initiation, his "baptism in the forest,"[7] culminating

---

6. For example, R. W. B. Lewis, "The Hero in the New World: William Faulkner's 'The Bear,'" *The Kenyon Review* 13 (1951), pp. 458-74. This essay was reprinted in *Interpretations of American Literature*, ed. Charles Feidelson, Jr., and Paul Brodtkorb, Jr. (New York, 1959), pp. 332-48. For Lewis, "The Bear" is "Faulkner's first sustained venture towards the more hopeful liberated world after the Incarnation," a canticle celebrating the new life "not lacking in dimly seen miraculous events." He sees in Ike McCaslin's renunciation an intimation of "conscious Christ-likeness," and the wisdom of "The Bear" is "the transmutation of power into charity." It is true that there is a definite and perhaps intended Christ-likeness in Ike McCaslin; but it seems to me that the forces of "redemption" and "renewal" in "The Bear" are more on the order of a wilderness cult and identification with cosmic spirits than explicit Christianity.

7. The words are those of an interviewer who admired Ike "because he underwent the baptism in the forest, because he rejected his inheritance." Faulkner replied that rejecting one's inheritance was not enough: "He should have been more affirmative instead of just shunning people." Quoted in Michael Millgate, *The Achievement of William Faulkner* (London, 1966), p. 208.

in a "revelatory vision" followed by the death of the Bear and of Ike's spiritual "Father" and "Guru," Sam Fathers, leads to a religious decision, a monastic act of renunciation, by which Ike attempts to cleanse himself of the guilt that he believes to have become associated, like a classic "miasma," with the Southern earth. He renounces his ownership of land which, as he sees it, belongs to God and cannot be "owned" by anyone. But he finds that monastic poverty alone is not enough (note that he remains on his land but works as a carpenter, "like the Nazarene").

Poverty without chastity remains in some sense ambiguous and ineffective, as Ike's wife intuitively senses in the scene where she tries to bind him again, by erotic ecstasy and the generation of a child, to the earth he has tried to renounce. It is almost as if she has instinctively sensed the power of a counter-mysticism, another more elemental "wisdom," to cancel out the spiritual vision in the wilderness. And perhaps she succeeds, for after this Ike McCaslin remains an ambiguous personage. At the end of *Go Down, Moses* (in "Delta Autumn") he reveals the almost total loss of any prophetic charisma that might once have been supposed his. We must not then forget that in spite of his initiation and vision Ike McCaslin remains a failed saint and only half a monk. (Speaking after twenty-five years in a monastery, I would like to add that it is extraordinarily difficult for *anyone* to be more than that, and most of us are not even that far along.)

However, it is the account of the spiritual initiation that seems to me to be a particularly good, because evidently deliberate, use of the sapiential in Faulkner. It is clearly the story of a disciple being taught and formed in a traditional and archaic wisdom by a charismatic spiritual Father who is especially qualified for the task and who hands on not only a set of skills or a body of knowledge, but a *mastery of life*, a certain way of being aware, of being in touch not just with natural objects, with living things, but with the cosmic spirit, with the wilderness itself regarded almost as a supernatural being, a "person." Indeed, the Bear, Old Ben, is treated as a quasi-transcendent being, like Sam Fathers and like Lion, the fabulous brute of a hound that finally (when Old Ben has himself more or less consented) brings the Bear down into death. It is as if the wilderness spirit were somehow incarnated in Old Ben—as if he were a wilderness god. The annual autumn hunting party of Major de Spain becomes a more or less ritual performance in which Old Ben is ceremoniously hunted; it is "the yearly pageant of Old Ben's furious immortality." He is never seen and never expected to be caught, until the end comes for the whole wilderness and Old Ben, we are led to believe, is ready to surrender himself and the woods to the portentous ritual of desecration that awaits them. This desecration signals the beginning of a new age, not of gold or silver but of iron.

Thus the initiation of Ike McCaslin takes place precisely at a crucial moment of religious history, a turning point when all that he has learned and seen is to become obsolete. He will learn to be not only a wonderful hunter but a contemplative and prophet, a wise man who has beheld the real ground of mystery and value which is concealed in the Edenic wilderness and which others can only guess at. But his skill and his vision remain useless aristocratic luxuries. They are anachronisms in the modern world, and he is helpless when, as an old man, he sees a young relative getting involved in the ancient tragedy of miscegenation and injustice. He has seen the inner meaning of the wilderness as an epiphany of the cosmic mystery. He has encountered the Bear and had his "illumination." In the light of this he has seen into the religious and historic mystery of the South which lies under judgment and under a curse. Yet there is nothing he can do about it apart from his monastic gesture, which remains ambiguous and abortive.

Worst of all, Ike McCaslin seems to have become oblivious of the one vital, indestructible force that remains in the world—the force of human love. "Old man," says the Negro mistress of Ike's nephew, "have you lived so long and forgotten so much that you don't remember anything you knew or felt or even heard about love?" The failure is typically monastic. Ike is concerned exclusively with the ritual handing on of General Compson's hunting horn, which belongs by right to the illegitimate son. Thus, there is after all a fruitful ambiguity in Faulkner's treatment of this wilderness-paradise wisdom which no longer has any real application in the world of our time, any more than the romantic gallantry of the Sartoris family has.

Nevertheless, the story of the boy's formation by Sam Fathers, his growing awareness of the Bear as spiritual reality and as "presence," his experience of the numinous mystery of the Bear as quasi-transcendent being, his decision to make the sacrifice which is necessary to see the Bear, and his consequent entering into a quasi-mystical relationship with the Bear: all this is told with an inspired mastery that betrays Faulkner's own enthusiasm, another evidence of "his strange religion." The story has Old Testament resonances characteristic of Faulkner everywhere, and the gradual ascent of the disciple to vision suggests the mystery cults of Greece; but what Faulkner actually celebrates is the primitive wisdom of the American Indian, the man who was *par excellence* the wilderness hunter and the free wanderer in the unspoiled garden of Paradise.

Countless mythical themes have been discovered in "The Bear." Everything is said to be there, from the Great Mother to the Holy Grail. There is no need to go into all that. I am primarily interested in Ike McCaslin's introduction to the wisdom of the wilderness and his initiation into it as spiritual mystery. This has the deepest possible resonances. It is not just a matter of knowledge or even of maturity. It is a question of *salvation*. This is not, of course, salvation and redemption in any Christian or theological sense, but rather a natural analogue of supernatural salvation: a man justifying his existence and liberating his soul from blindness and captivity by acquiring a deep and definitive understanding of his life's purpose and deciding to live in accordance with this understanding. This is not mere solipsism, but an illuminating and mysterious communion with cosmic reality explicated in mythical and symbolic terms. Though Ike becomes in the end ambiguous as a charismatic figure (and this is perhaps necessary because the wilderness itself, which would be the very ground and source of his charism, has all but vanished), there is no question, at least in my mind, that Faulkner intended him to be one of "the saved."

This limited concept of salvation is not new, though it may seem so to most of us who have forgotten the classic tradition. It is a humanistic as well as basically a religious concept with an essentially ethical component, the same "old verities" which Faulkner said in his Nobel Prize acceptance speech he had always been writing about: "The old verities and truths of the heart, the universal truths lacking which any story is ephemeral and doomed—love and honor and pity and pride and compassion and sacrifice." These Ike learns from Sam Fathers in the wilderness, along with humility and courage ("Be scared but don't be afraid. . . . A bear or a deer has got to be scared of a coward the same as a brave man has to be"). His wilderness life is essentially an education and a spiritual formation: "The wilderness the old bear ran was his college, and the old male bear himself . . . was his alma mater." The term "alma mater" is not a mere cliché. It is to be taken seriously enough here (with all its irony), for Ike is *regenerated*, twice born; he enters into a new life because of the death of the Bear and of Sam Fathers. He becomes the "child" and "heir" of the wilderness spirit which was in them and which is passed on to him. (Note that there is another, less profound way of participating in the wilderness spirit. To hunters, whisky—not women— is a "condensation of the wild immortal spirit." This magic elixir is also well known to have played a part in Faulkner's "étrange religion.") This experience makes up not only an education but a spiritual and religious formation—Ike's "novitiate to the true wilderness."

To understand fully this novitiate, we need to read "The Old People," another section of *Go Down, Moses*, in which Sam Fathers is shown introducing him into a kind of timeless contemporaneousness with a largely vanished race. "Gradually to the boy those old times would cease to be old times and would become a part of the boy's present, not only as if they had happened yesterday but as if they were still happening and more—as if some of them had not come into existence yet." This extraordinary shift in consciousness makes Ike McCaslin aware that there is a whole new dimension of being which is obscured by civilized assumptions and that in order to find himself truly he has to make an existential leap into this mysterious other order, into the dimension of a primitive wilderness experience. He will do so by "seeing" the Bear, an act of initiation in which his own identity will be fully established.

The successive experiences of closer and closer awareness of the Bear are described almost like degrees of mystical elevation in which the Bear (acting not without a certain suggestion of spiritual initiative of his own) becomes more and more a real and finally almost a personal presence. The Bear is first experienced as an insurmountable void and absence, apprehended negatively in relation to the curious barking of the hysterically frightened hounds and then again in the silence created when a woodpecker suddenly stops drumming and then starts again. "There had been nothing except the solitude. . . ." The Bear has passed invisibly. Then Ike realizes that he is *seen* by the Bear without seeing anything himself. The Bear, he feels, now knows and recognizes him. In the end he resolves to go out into the woods without a gun and "prove" to the Bear that he is not an ordinary hunter. When this is not enough, he leaves his watch and compass hanging on a branch and lets himself get lost in the virgin forest. It is then that he finally sees the Bear in an instant of peaceful and Edenic revelation in which the Bear, incidentally, also brings him back to the place where his watch and compass are waiting. It is a description of the kind of "existential leap" which Kierkegaard demanded for any passage to a higher level of awareness or of existence. But what makes it possible for some critics to see the Bear as a symbol of Christ is the fact that in becoming *visible*, then *personal*, in manifesting himself to men, the Bear yields to a kind of weakness in his "supernatural" being, a kind of divine and *kenotic* flaw which will eventually make him vulnerable, destructible, mortal, and which will ultimately bring about his destruction. Hence I have no doubt that some will want to read "The Bear" as a fable of the death of God. Certainly there is good reason to see how Faulkner's myth *does* tell us something of the critical change in intellectual and spiritual climate, the irreversible mental revolution that has apparently made religious faith an impossibility for so many people. This could have been part of Faulkner's intention.

The wilderness-paradise in which Ike McCaslin receives his "baptism in the forest" is the archaic world of religious myth and traditional wisdom. Wisdom is perfectly at home in such a world. Initiation leads to a definite enlightenment which sets the seal of authenticity upon the communion of the initiate with the "gods" and "spirits" of the cosmic order which he now knows as a privileged and conscious participant. He has found his place in the hierarchy of being as a hunter who is worthy, who has earned his position by proving his respect and love for the other living beings in the forest, even those he must kill. In other words, the wisdom to which Ike McCaslin is initiated presupposes a traditional metaphysic, a structure which man can intuitively understand, which he can lovingly accept, and which is basically reasonable and right, with its own inner laws. The "wise man" knows these laws, knows the penalties for violating them, and knows how to avoid violating them. He lives in harmony with the world around him because he is in harmony with its spirits and with the Providence of God Who rules over it all. That Ike could pay homage to this underlying "will" by renouncing his property is, to him, a perfectly logical consequence of his enlightenment and a basically religious act of worship, though precisely *how* it has this religious character is not fully explained. Nor need it be. We know it to be more or less in the natural order, akin to the religious wisdom of primitive peoples and to classic stoicism. There may be Biblical allusions here and there, but it is essentially a pre-Christian type of wisdom in an archaic and classic scheme of things which is supplanted as soon as Ike is initiated.

IN *THE WILD PALMS* we are in a totally different world: the world of Pascal with its vast emptiness, its terrifying void, the world in which, in the words of Nietzsche's madman, someone has provided us with a sponge that has wiped away the horizon. This, in fact, is precisely the image we get in Faulkner's masterly description of the convicts arriving on the levee and seeing for the first time the vast expanse of the flooded Mississippi on which one of their number is about to be carried away on a helpless and fantastic odyssey. As J. Hillis Miller points out in the present volume, it is the world where God is not merely dead but murdered, and murdered not so much by willful malice as by a new code of consciousness. The specific characteristic of this new consciousness, which if not *the* scientific consciousness is nonetheless a scientific consciousness, is that it excludes the kind of wisdom and initiation we have discovered in "The Bear." The wisdom of the Indian in the wilderness is a kind of knowledge by identification, an intersubjective knowledge, a communion in cosmic awareness and in nature. Faulkner has described it as a wisdom based on love: love for the wilderness and for its secret laws; love for the paradise mystery apprehended almost unconsciously in the forest; love for the "spirits" of the wilderness and of the cosmic parent (both Mother and Father) conceived as symbolically incarnate in the great Old Bear. But there is nothing of the kind in the new world. "This Anno Domini 1938," says Wilbourne in *The Wild Palms*, "has no place in it for love." "If Jesus returned today we would have to crucify him quick in our own defense to justify and preserve the civilization we have worked and suffered and died shrieking and cursing in rage and impotence and terror for two thousand years to create and perfect in man's own image: if Venus returned she would be a soiled man in a subway lavatory with a palm full of French post-cards."

The new consciousness which isolates man in his own knowing mind and separates him from the world around him (which he does not know as it is in itself but only as it is in his mind) makes wisdom impossible because it severs the communion between subject and object, man and nature, upon which wisdom depends. In the new consciousness man is as radically cut off from the ground of his own being, which is also the ground of all being, as the struggling convict is cut off from a foothold on the solid earth of cottonfields by ten or fifteen feet of raging flood water.

Space does not permit us here to go fully into the problem of the person and society which is central in *The Wild Palms*. Faulkner faces a radical dilemma in modern life. Speaking of Sam Fathers and his wisdom in *Go Down, Moses*, Cass Edmonds says: "His blood . . . knew things that had been tamed out of our blood so long ago that we have not only forgotten them, *we have to live together in herds to protect ourselves from our own sources*" (my italics). But this does not imply that in order to return to vital contact with our own sources we need merely leave society. If people who have had the wisdom "tamed out of their blood" by civilization simply relinquish civilized society without being trained in the difficult work of recovering another wisdom, they will be as helpless as the convict in the flood and will be destroyed, in spite of themselves, like Charlotte and her lover.

But if the characters in *The Wild Palms* find themselves blind, helpless, and without wisdom, Faulkner, their creator, wants us to see them still from the point of view of classic tragedy and of an implicit wisdom. *The Wild Palms* is a mysterious pattern of fateful ironies which the characters themselves never see, or do not see until it is too late. Hence these characters remain starkly lonely and forlorn, struggling pitiably, full of determination and even of outrage, in a world they see to be absurd and against forces they cannot comprehend or manage in any way whatever, no matter how hard they try. The two "heroes," the lover Wilbourne and the tall convict, do end with a kind of dim and partially adequate illumination. But can we say that they have been initiated into wisdom, or that they have been reborn, or that they understand and fully accept their destinies? They do the best they can in their circumstances. Their best is not much. In one case it is a kind of comic return to a beginning which the convict never wanted to leave anyway—with an absurd bonus of ten more years of prison for "attempting to escape." In the other story the lover goes without resistance and without comment to the same prison, in a resignation that is not without nobility. In either case, the prison is the last refuge of provisional meaning in an otherwise meaningless world. And prison itself means little more than a place in which to "do time." The one thing this book has in common with "The Bear" is that the solution is ironically "monastic." The tall convict likes the peace and order of his secluded existence, and Wilbourne is determined at least to continue to exist and to grieve, rather than simply to let go and fall into total nothingness. To grieve, be it remembered, is the traditional function of the monk.

It is true that the saga of the tall convict, the story sometimes printed by itself as "Old Man," is able to stand apart from the other half of the novel, "The Wild Palms." But in actual fact the author's intention to play one against the other in counterpoint is not to be lightly dismissed. On the contrary, each section gains immensely in power when this counterpoint is perceived and appreciated. And it is precisely in the counterpoint of the two sections that the sapiential structure of the book is revealed.

It is true that the cosmos itself in *The Wild Palms* does not reveal a mysterious inner meaning. It remains a terrifying and inscrutable void speaking through its elements of water and air with no message that man can interpret. Yet man himself is still capable of giving his own life a meaning if he can grasp "the old verities" and be faithful to them. These "verities" are not arbitrary. One cannot simply select a value one feels to be appropriate and neglect everything else. Life is a balance of values and verities, and the true secret is in achieving wholeness and integrity. The two parts of *The Wild Palms* complete each other in a diptych which gives us the whole picture of man. Neither half is complete in itself. The wholeness of man is in the paradisal and integral union of man and woman, and in each half of the book *one* aspect of that union is sketched out. Charlotte and Wilbourne have erotic fulfillment, a passionately reciprocated love. The convict and the woman have no emotional relationship at all; in fact, they behave completely impersonally toward each other. They are pure archetypes. But what they do have is the complete moral responsibility toward each other and toward a basic truth of their relationship which is almost entirely lacking in Charlotte and Wilbourne. It is almost as if the convict and the woman were the mystical embodiment of what was morally lacking in the two lovers, acting itself out on a mysterious transcendent plane. But there is a positive conclusion: Man does not necessarily have to be overwhelmed by the tragic forces which are let loose within him. There is an authentic and saving balance, an order and an integrity which he can discover and live by, in his right relation with woman; and this integrity is sapiential, in a sense salvific. It is centered on life, not on death. It is an affirmation of life, but an affirmation of a peculiar kind: "He that would save his life must lose it."

The saga of the convict with the nameless woman on the flooded river is a mythical and symbolic counterpart of the moral and psychological disaster of the lovers in "The Wild Palms." All the peril and evil are external to the man and the woman in the boat. Here we have an archetypal, larger than life, eschatological myth—the Deluge in fact—as commentary on the Judgment under which the lovers stand without knowing it at all because it is taking place within themselves. An explicit correspondence is suggested between the immanent will of Charlotte to seek an "absolute" love and the blind exterior force of the river that sweeps away the convict and the woman. As Wilbourne meets Charlotte on the train, which carries them away together, he is struck by her poise and by "that instinctive proficiency in and *rapport* for the mechanics of cohabitation even of innocent and unpracticed women—that serene confidence in their amorous destinies like that of birds in their wings—that tranquil ruthless belief in an imminent deserved personal happiness which fledges them instantaneous and full-winged from the haven of respectability *into untried and supportive space where no shore is visible*" (my italics). Here, of course, the "supportive" element is air, not water. Maurice-Edgar Coindreau, the French translator and critic of Faulkner, has pointed out the evident balancing of mythical functions between "air" and "wind" in "The Wild Palms" and "water" in "Old Man."[8] But the sea as the mythical element of death plays an important part in "The Wild Palms" too. The lovers end like driftwood cast up on an evil-smelling, low-tide beach, helpless, exhausted, one of them about to die. They have been destroyed, in contrast with the completely unsinkable and indestructible pair in their rowboat, without oars on the worst flood in Mississippi history, who bounce off every danger unharmed and return to "normal life" with a healthy newborn baby.

In each story a man and a woman are more or less completely isolated from the rest of the world in situations that still somehow explicitly recall the paradise myth, though only in tragic or comic irony. For the convict, it is a daydream situation come true, and yet everything prevents him from taking advantage of it. First of all, the woman is pregnant. Besides, she repels him. Second, he has an obsessive sense of responsibility for her and for the boat which has been entrusted to him, and he still thinks he can rescue a man stranded on the roof of a cotton house and get back to the group of convicts with whom he belongs.

---

8. Maurice-Edgar Coindreau, "Préface aux *Palmiers sauvages*," *Les Temps modernes* 7 (January 1952), pp. 1187-96.

As far as the woman is concerned, he wants only to get rid of her and the baby as soon as he decently and humanly can.

For the two lovers, Charlotte Rittenmeyer and Harry Wilbourne, there is also a daydream situation which has been made to come true by her determination (that determination which ultimately destroys her). Their love comes before everything else. Wilbourne cannot be persuaded to leave her even to save his own life. They live in order to make love together, alone, away from everyone else. They work only as much as is necessary to keep themselves alive and capable of making love. They intend explicitly to be *lovers* and not married people; hence they flee from any situation in which they find themselves settling down and living like secure and comfortable spouses. They accept absurd hardships in order to be left alone to their ritual erotic dream. Their life is consciously planned and patterned according to what one might call a certain level of wisdom, a certain understanding of man and of human destiny, in which sexual fulfillment is seen as the only real value worth living for. An erotic relationship between two passionately devoted partners then becomes an absolute, an end for which everything else can and should be sacrificed. There is nothing very esoteric about this "wisdom." It would probably be accepted as more or less axiomatic by a rather large proportion of Americans and Europeans today. You have one life to live; you might as well get as much out of it as you can. The best way to do this is to find someone with whom you really get on nicely in bed. And many would accept, in theory, the conclusion which these two carried out together in practice: you then spend as much time as humanly possible in bed together.

Wilbourne and Charlotte were able to do this because of her unwavering determination to sacrifice respectability, security, comfort, and all that is socially acceptable in order that they might give themselves with complete single-mindedness to their love. What remains a daydream for others became their life. Yet the blind force of cosmic tragedy bore down on them as the flood bore down on the convict and the woman in the drifting rowboat. Only here the force of tragedy was the destructive power of their own myth, or rather the inscrutable polarization set up between their personal myth and the trivial dreams which society has substituted for wisdom. Though they withdraw to a marginal life and try to construct for themselves a world of values which cannot be found in society, they do not succeed because it is not possible for man to get along without society. What is destructive is not their eros, but their determination to ignore an insoluble dilemma.

The judgment of Faulkner goes a little deeper than the general erotic daydream. "The Wild Palms" is neither homily nor casuistry. It is not a lesson in ethics. It is tragedy and myth, in a highly sophisticated artistic and sapiential pattern. The tragic death of Charlotte, as the result of an abortion which she forced her own lover to perform on her, is seen to be a consequence of the same passionate forces which drove her to run away and live with him. The seed of tragedy was present in the very nature of their love, in its psychology, in the strange disordered relationship between this willful, deeply erotic woman and the passive male she drew into a destructive and symbiotic relationship with herself.

Faulkner everywhere plays the deep, archaic, archetypal sapiential myths against the shallow and trifling mythology of modern society. This is explicit in "Old Man," where the convict realizes that he is in jail because he let himself be seduced and deceived by cheap crime stories. Wilbourne, at one point in his liaison with Charlotte, works by writing *True Confession* stories. He feeds daydreams to others and is aware of his bad faith in doing so. Yet he and Charlotte are dominated by the popular myth that when man and woman satisfy each other sexually, they have no problems. Everything is taken care of. This, as any analyst knows, is a gross oversimplification. But, for a vast number of people in the so-called civilized world, it is the most basic of all articles of faith. It is easy to confuse this superficial notion with the more profound mystique of sexuality which Vivian de Sola Pinto analyzes in his essay on D. H. Lawrence. But even in Lawrence's terms Charlotte, for all her sexual freedom, is "fallen" through willfulness and through the modern consciousness "into herself alone . . . a god-lost creature turning upon herself."

In "The Wild Palms" the love of Charlotte and Wilbourne is perfectly gratifying and in a sense happy. Yet their relationship is essentially destructive and death-oriented. From the beginning we are disturbed by the "bad smell," the classic miasma, which plays such an important symbolic part in their story and which is much more than unconscious guilt. It is the willfulness which is the direct result of that new consciousness which has isolated modern man from the world around him and from other human beings as an atom in the great void. The utter moral isolation of the modern character—Tillich and others would stress it as alienation, estrangement—leaves it no other way than to assert itself by pure will. In the void where there are no standards left (once one has broken away from the purely external and artificial ones imposed by society and which the characters of Victorian fiction could still take seriously) what is there left but to try to "get what you want"? But what do you want? How do you know what you want? You simply follow the incline down which you are already rolling. In other days one called it the "dominant passion," which you could accept or resist. But now who knows? Maybe it is your very identity which speaks, not just a tendency in you. When a person arbitrarily decides that a part of himself or herself is henceforth, for all practical purposes, *the whole self*, life will necessarily be lived destructively because of its radical bad faith. The power at work in Charlotte becomes as capricious, as arbitrary, and finally as devastating in its own order as the cosmic power of the flooding river. The tall convict saves himself and the woman by pitting all his strength against this power and by having miraculously good luck from beginning to end. Wilbourne has no strength to pit against anything, and his instinctive respect for love and for life that would have saved Charlotte is too weak to resist her will. He destroys her and in so doing destroys himself. Or rather, he completes the work of destruction which she has already made irreversible. Only in the end does he manage to salvage something from his own ruins by his refusal to escape or to commit suicide and by his determination to "grieve." Indeed, there finally emerges in him a kind of limited greatness, a tragic quietism, as if, sinking into his own nullity, he at last becomes united with the blind Tao of wind and finds in himself the acceptance of unbornness and unbeing which is for him his "salvation" and his entry into apophatic wisdom. Thus even Wilbourne is an "initiate" in a genuine traditional sense if we accept the idea that the devotee, as a Greek fragment says, is "not to learn but to suffer and to be made worthy by suffering."[9] The power of the last section of "The Wild Palms," the eerie sound of wind in hospital and jail, makes it one of the most impressive things Faulkner ever wrote.

The wisdom of *The Wild Palms* is barely what one would call "religious" wisdom. The "gods" dealt with, if one could call them that, are malignant spirits, bent on destroying or at least frustrating man. The convict who wants nothing but to surrender to the police and get back to the prison farm which is "his place" is repeatedly thrust back, with all brutality and incomprehension, into the wild and hostile chaos of the flood. He feels himself to be up against "the old, primal, faithless manipulator of all the lust and folly and injustice," and his highest virtue consists in the cry of "final and irrevocable repudiation" of any such evil force. Here the "strange religion of Faulkner" becomes identical with the philosophy of Camus, his ethic of the absurd and of rebellion. But there is more to Faulkner's religion than this. It might be possible to interpret the voyage of the convict and the woman as a mythical "journey," like the medieval *Navigatio Brendani* with its visits to strange islands symbolizing spiritual states. The Indian mound where the baby is born is described as an "earthen Ark out of Genesis"; and its "cypress choked life-teeming constricted desolation," where

---

9. Quoted in Hugo Rahner, *Greek Myths and Christian Mystery* (New York, 1963), p. 22.

the snakes respect the convict and the woman and where nothing harms anything else, is a kind of eschatological paradise in reverse. But one would still have to stretch Faulkner's symbols a long way to find in this "deluge" an unquestionably Christian meaning.

However, the wisdom of *The Wild Palms* and of *Go Down, Moses* is not all of Faulkner, and it can be played in counterpoint to more explicitly Christian themes in his other works. That exercise does not concern us here. What matters is to show that a *sapiential* reading of Faulkner's works is both possible and rewarding. Such a reading protects the Christian against the temptation to claim Faulkner for the faith on the basis of a mythical development like that in "The Bear." At the same time it shows Faulkner's concern with the "old verities and truths of the heart" which flow from his classic view of the world as endowed with basic meaning and value. He embodies this view in symbols of a kind that man has always spontaneously recognized to be "religious" in a sense that is not confessional but sapiential.

What is the position of a believing Christian before the sick and bewildering gnosticism of modern literature? First of all, while respecting the truth and accuracy of his own religious belief, the Christian realizes that today he lives in a world where most people find Christian doctrine incomprehensible or irrelevant. Most modern literature speaks a language that is neither Christian nor unchristian. It seeks to explore reality in terms that are often symbolic, mythical, sapiential, vaguely religious. The modern reader is intolerant of dogmatism, whether it be Christian, Marxist, behaviorist, or any other; and he demands of the novelist, the dramatist, and the poet that they seek their own kind of revelation. The present book is a sympathetic and reasonable survey in which scholars of varying beliefs and viewpoints have joined to explore this area in literature. Their studies show us that what we find in modern literature, when we find any religious wisdom at all, is not a coherent intellectual view of life but a creative effort to penetrate the meaning of man's suffering and aspirations in symbols that are imaginatively authentic. If God does appear in such symbols, we can expect to find Him expressed negatively and obscurely rather than with the positive and rewarding effulgence that we find in the poetry of other ages.

No sense can be made of modern literature if we are not willing to accept the fact that we live in an age of doubt. But even in the midst of this doubt we can find authentic assurances of hope and understanding, provided that we are willing to tolerate theological discomfort. Derek Stanford's quotation from Dylan Thomas sums up the casual but unimpeachable sincerity of modern sapiential literature:

"These poems, with all their crudities, doubts, and confusions, are written for the love of Man and in praise of God, and I'd be a damn' fool if they weren't."

And many of our writers can be called, as Dylan Thomas is called in Stanford's essay, writers "of religious temperament nourished in a literary culture of doubt"; they make no commitments and they contrive to affirm and to deny the spirit at the same time.

30

Ishi: A Meditation

On January 30, 1967, Merton writes in his journal of reading Theodora Kroeber's *Ishi in Two Worlds* (1964), a "heartrending book about the last of the Yahi Indians—victims of genocide a hundred years ago" (*Learning to Love*, 189). On February 4 he has finished the book (*Learning to Love*, 191), and five days later writes Dorothy Day about "doing a little piece" on it for *The Catholic Worker* (*Hidden Ground of Love*, 152). On February 22 he notes, "Monday or Tuesday—finished some notes on Ishi for the *Catholic Worker*" (*Learning to Love*, 201), and the essay was first published in *The Catholic Worker* 33 (March 1967), 5-6, and then in *Peace News* (June 30, 1967), 6-7. It appeared posthumously in *Ishi Means Man* (25-32), a collection of five of Merton's articles on Native Americans, and was reprinted in *The Nonviolent Alternative* (248-53) and *Passion for Peace* (263-69). The subtitle "A Meditation" is particularly apt, as Merton reflects not only on the circumstances of Ishi's biography, his early life as part of the dwindling remnant of the Yahi, or Mill Creek, tribe, and his final years among the anthropologists at Berkeley (including Kroeber's husband, Alfred), but also on the insights it provides on the American experience and the human condition generally. "It is a book to think deeply about and to take notes on, not only because of its extraordinary factual interest but because of its special quality as a kind of parable." He considers the ways in which dehumanizing "the other" allows one to marginalize and then eliminate those who are different; the fact that the last survivors of the tribe were able to live a totally undetected "hidden life" for twelve years because they were on their "home ground," completely integrated with their natural surroundings in a way no longer available to urban, "civilized" cultures; the psychic and spiritual integrity of Ishi and his kin, who were able to endure their sufferings and deprivations sustained by the realization that their cause was just; the sensitivity of Ishi's academic rescuers who treated him not as a specimen but as a friend; the haunting analogies between the brutality of the ethnic cleansing in nineteenth-century California and attempts to "wipe out" the enemy in Vietnam; and finally the remarkable revelation about Ishi's "name" that provided the collection of Indian essays its title.

GENOCIDE IS A NEW WORD. Perhaps the word is new because technology has now got into the game of destroying whole races at once. The destruction of races is not new—just easier. Nor is it a specialty of totalitarian regimes. We have forgotten that a century ago white America was engaged in the destruction of entire tribes and ethnic groups of Indians. The trauma of California gold. And the vigilantes who, in spite of every plea from Washington for restraint and understanding, repeatedly took matters into their own hands and went out slaughtering Indians. Indiscriminate destruction of the "good" along with the "bad"—just so long as they were Indians. Parties of riffraff from the mining camps and saloons suddenly constituted themselves defenders of civilization. They armed and went out to spill blood and gather scalps. They not only combed the woods and canyons—they even went into the barns and ranch houses, to find and destroy the Indian servants and hired people, in spite of the protests of the ranchers who employed them.

The Yana Indians (including the Yahi, or Mill Creeks) lived around the foothills of Mount Lassen, east of the Sacramento River. Their country came within a few miles of Vina, where the Trappist monastery in California stands today. These hill tribes were less easy to subdue than their valley neighbors. More courageous and more aloof, they tried to keep clear of the white man altogether. They were not necessarily more ferocious than other Indians, but because they kept to themselves and had a legendary reputation as "fighters," they were more feared. They were understood to be completely "savage." As they were driven farther and farther back into the hills, and as their traditional hunting grounds gradually narrowed and emptied of game, they had to raid the ranches in order to keep alive. White reprisals were to be expected, and they were ruthless. The Indians defended themselves by guerilla warfare. The whites decided that there could be no peaceful coexistence with such neighbors. The Yahi, or Mill Creek Indians, as they were called, were marked for complete destruction. Hence they were regarded as subhuman. Against them there were no restrictions and no rules. No treaties need be made for no Indian could be trusted. Where was the point in "negotiation"?

Ishi, the last survivor of the Mill Creek Indians, whose story was published by the University of California at Berkeley in 1964*, was born during the war of extermination against his people. The fact that the last Mill Creeks were able to go into hiding and to survive for another fifty years in their woods and canyons is extraordinary enough. But the courage, the resourcefulness, and the sheer

---

Ishi in Two Worlds: A Biography of the Last Wild Indian in North America, by Theodora Kroeber (Berkeley: University of California Press, 1964).

nobility of these few stone age men struggling to preserve their life, their autonomy, and their identity as a people rises to the level of tragic myth. Yet there is nothing mythical about it. The story is told with impeccable objectivity—though also with compassion—by the scholars who finally saved Ishi and learned from him his language, his culture, and his tribal history.

To read this story thoughtfully, to open one's heart to it, is to receive a most significant message: one that not only moves, but disturbs. You begin to feel the inner stirrings of that pity and dread which Aristotle said were the purifying effect of tragedy. "The history of Ishi and his people," says the author, Theodora Kroeber, "is inexorably part of our own history. We have absorbed their lands into our holdings. Just so must we be the responsible custodians of their tragedy, absorbing it into our tradition and morality." Unfortunately, we learned little or nothing about ourselves from the Indian wars.

"THEY HAVE SEPARATED MURDER into two parts and fastened the worse on me"—words which William Carlos Williams put on the lips of a Viking exile, Eric the Red. Men are always separating murder into two parts: one which is unholy and unclean: for "the enemy." Another which is a sacred duty: "for our side." He who first makes the separation, in order that he may kill, proves his bad faith. So too in the Indian wars. Why do we always assume the Indian was the aggressor? We were in *his* country, we were taking it over for ourselves, and we likewise refused even to share any with him. We were the people of God, always in the right, following a manifest destiny. The Indian could only be a devil. But once we allow ourselves to see all sides of the question, the familiar perspectives of American history undergo a change. The "savages" suddenly become human and the "whites," the "civilized," can seem barbarians. True, the Indians were often cruel and inhuman (some more than others). True also, the humanity, the intelligence, the compassion, and understanding which Ishi met with in his friends the scholars, when he came to join our civilization, restore the balance in our favor. But we are left with a deep sense of guilt and shame. The record is there. The Mill Creek Indians, who were once seen as bloodthirsty devils, were peaceful, innocent, and deeply wronged human beings. In their use of violence they were, so it seems, generally very fair. It is we who were the wanton murderers, and they who were the innocent victims. The loving kindness lavished on Ishi in the end did nothing to change that fact. His race had been barbarously, pointlessly destroyed.

The impact of the story is all the greater because the events are so deeply charged with a natural symbolism: the structure of these happenings is such that it leaves a haunting imprint on the mind. Out of that imprint come disturbing and potent reflections.

Take for example the scene in 1870 when the Mill Creeks were down to their last twenty or thirty survivors. A group had been captured. A delegation from the tiny remnant of the tribe appeared at a ranch to negotiate. In a symbolic gesture, they handed over five bows (five being a sacred number) and stood waiting for an answer. The gesture was not properly understood, though it was evident that the Indians were trying to recover their captives and promising to abandon all hostilities. In effect, the message was: "Leave us alone, in peace, in our hills, and we will not bother you any more. We are few, you are many, why destroy us? We are no longer any menace to you." No formal answer was given. While the Indians were waiting for some intelligible response, one of the whites slung a rope over the branch of a tree. The Indians quietly withdrew into the woods.

From then on, for the next twelve years, the Yahi disappeared into the hills without a trace. There were perhaps twenty of them left, one of whom was Ishi, together with his mother and sister. In order to preserve their identity as a tribe, they had decided that there was no alternative but to keep completely away from white men, and have nothing whatever to do with them. Since co-existence was impossible, they would try to be as if they did not exist for the white man at all. To be there as if they were not there.

In fact, not a Yahi was seen. No campfire smoke rose over the trees. Not a trace of fire was found. No village was discovered. No track of an Indian was observed. The Yahi remnant (and that phrase takes on haunting biblical resonances) systematically learned to live as invisible and as unknown.

To anyone who has ever felt in himself the stirrings of a monastic or solitary vocation, the notion is stirring. It has implications that are simply beyond speech. There is nothing one can say in the presence of such a happening and of its connotations for what our spiritual books so glibly call "the hidden life." The "hidden life" is surely not irrelevant to our modern world; nor is it a life of spiritual comfort and tranquility which a chosen minority can happily enjoy, at the price of a funny costume and a few prayers. The "hidden life" is the extremely difficult life that is forced upon a remnant that has to stay completely out of sight in order to escape destruction.

This so called "long concealment" of the Mill Creek Indians is not romanticized by any means. The account is sober, objective, though it cannot help being an admiring tribute to the extraordinary courage and ingenuity of these lost stone-age people. Let the book speak for itself.

The long concealment failed in its objective to save a people's life but it would seem to have been brilliantly successful in its psychology and techniques of living. . . . Ishi's group was a master of the difficult art of communal and peaceful coexistence in the presence of alarm and in a tragic and deteriorating prospect. . . .

It is a curious circumstance that some of the questions which arise about the concealment are those for which in a different context psychologists and neurologists are trying to find answers for the submarine and outer space services today. Some of these are: what makes for morale under confining and limiting life-conditions? What are the presumable limits of claustrophobic endurance? . . . It seems that the Yahi might have qualified for outer space had they lasted into this century.

There is something challenging and awe inspiring about this thoughtful passage by a scientifically trained mind. And that phrase about "qualifying for outer space" has an eerie ring about it. Does someone pick up the half-heard suggestion that the man who wants to live a normal life span during the next two hundred years of our history must be the kind of person who is "qualified for outer space"? Let us return to Ishi. The following sentences are significant:

In contrast to the Forty niners . . . . whose morality and morale had crumbled, Ishi and his band remained incorrupt, humane, compassionate, and with their faith intact even unto starvation, pain and death. The questions then are: what makes for stability? For psychic strength? For endurance, courage, faith?

The answers given by the author to these questions are mere suggestions. The Yahi were on their own home ground. This idea is not developed. The reader should reflect a little on the relation of the Indian to the land on which he lived. In this sense, most modern men never know what it means to have a "home ground." Then there is a casual reference to the "American Indian mystique" which could also be developed. William Faulkner's hunting stories, particularly "The Bear," give us some idea of what this "mystique" might involve. The word "mystique" has unfortunate connotations: it suggests an emotional icing on an ideological cake. Actually the Indian lived by a deeply religious wisdom which can be called in a broad sense mystical, and that is certainly much more than "a mystique." The book does not go into religious questions very deeply, but it shows us Ishi as a man sustained by a deep and unassailable spiritual strength which he never discussed.

Later, when he was living "in civilization" and was something of a celebrity as well as an object of charitable concern, Ishi was questioned about religion by a well-meaning lady. Ishi's English was liable to be unpredictable, and the language of his reply was not within its own ironic depths of absurdity:

"Do you believe in God?" the lady inquired.

"Sure, Mike!" he retorted briskly.

There is something dreadfully eloquent about this innocent short-circuit in communication.

One other very important remark is made by the author. The Yahi found strength in the incontrovertible fact that they were in the right. *"Of very great importance to their psychic health was the circumstance that their suffering and curtailments arose from wrongs done to them by others.* They were not guilt ridden."

Contrast this with the spectacle of our own country with its incomparable technological power, its unequalled material strength, and its psychic turmoil, its moral confusion and its profound heritage of guilt which neither the righteous declarations of Cardinals nor the moral indifference of "realists" can do anything to change! Every bomb we drop on a defenseless Asian village, every Asian child we disfigure or destroy with fire, only adds to the moral strength of those we wish to destroy for our own profit. It does not make the Viet Cong cause just; but by an accumulation of injustice done against innocent people we drive them into the arms of our enemies and make our own ideals look like the most pitiful sham.

Gradually the last members of the Yahi tribe died out. The situation of the survivors became more and more desperate. They could not continue to keep up their perfect invisibility: they had to steal food. Finally the hidden camp where Ishi lived with his sister and sick mother was discovered by surveyors who callously walked off with the few objects they found as souvenirs. The mother and sister died and finally on August 29, 1911, Ishi surrendered to the white race, expecting to be destroyed.

Actually, the news of this "last wild Indian" reached the anthropology department at Berkeley and a professor quickly took charge of things. He came and got the "wild man" out of jail. Ishi spent the rest of his life in San Francisco, patiently teaching his hitherto completely unknown (and quite sophisticated) language to experts like Sapir. Curiously enough, Ishi lived in an anthropological museum where he earned his living as a kind of caretaker and also functioned, on occasion, as a live exhibit. He was well treated, and in fact the affection and charm of his relations with his white friends are not the least moving part of his story. He adapted to life in the city without too much trouble and returned once, with his friends, to live several months in his old territory, under his natural conditions, showing them how the Yahi had carried out the fantastic operation of their invisible survival. But he finally succumbed to one of the diseases of civilization. He died of tuberculosis in 1916, after four and a half years among white men.

For the reflective reader who is—as everyone must be today—deeply concerned about man and his fate, this is a moving and significant book, one of those unusually suggestive works that *must* be read, and perhaps more than once. It is a book to think deeply about and to take notes on, not only because of its extraordinary factual interest but because of its special quality as a kind of parable.

One cannot help thinking today of the Vietnam War in terms of the Indian wars of a hundred years ago. Here again, one meets the same myths and misunderstandings, the same obsession with "completely wiping out" an enemy regarded as diabolical. The language of the Vigilantes had overtones of puritanism in it. The backwoods had to be "completely cleaned out," or "purified" of Indians—as if they were vermin. I have read accounts of American GI's taking the same attitude toward the Viet Cong. The jungles are thought to be "infested" with communists, and hence one goes after them as one would go after ants in the kitchen back home. And in this process of "cleaning up" (the language of "cleansing" appeases and pacifies the conscience) one becomes without realizing it a murderer of women and children. But this is an unfortunate accident, what the moralists call "double effect." Something that is just too bad, but which must be accepted in view of something more important that has to be done. And so there is more and more killing of civilians and less and less of the "something more important" which is what we are trying to achieve. In the end, it is the civilians that are killed in the ordinary course of events, and combatants only get killed by accident. No one worries any more about double effect. War is waged against the innocent to "break enemy morale."

What is most significant is that Vietnam seems to have become an extension of our old western frontier, complete with enemies of another "inferior" race. This is a real "new frontier" that enables us to continue the cowboys-and-indians game which seems to be part and parcel of our national identity. What a pity that so many innocent people have to pay with their lives for our obsessive fantasies.

One last thing. Ishi never told anyone his real name. The California Indians apparently never uttered their own names, and were very careful about how they spoke the names of others. Ishi would never refer to the dead by name either. "He never revealed his own private Yahi name," says the author. "It was as though it had been consumed in the funeral pyre of the last of his loved ones."

In the end, no one ever found out a single name of the vanished community. Not even Ishi's. For Ishi simply means MAN.

31

Learning to Live

On December 12, 1967, Merton grumbled in his journal, "I am sick of responding to requests for articles for this or that collection that someone is editing. Several times lately I have written such and heard nothing more about them. Wesley First and some Columbia Collection" (*Other Side of the Mountain*, 23). The reference is to the article "Learning to Live," dated July 1967 on its typescript, written for a projected collection of essays by Columbia University alumni. Evidently Merton was sufficiently pessimistic about publication in that venue that he revised the piece, now retitled "Monastery or University," by generalizing it somewhat, removing the explicit references to Columbia (apparently a rather hasty process, since in one instance he substituted "my own school" not for "Columbia" but for "Columbus"!) and cancelling some of the more personal material. In any event, the original version did appear the year after Merton's death in *University on the Heights*, edited by Wesley First (Garden City, NY: Doubleday, 1969), 187-99, and was later included as the opening essay in *Love and Living* (3-14); it also appears with a helpful headnote in *Thomas Merton, Spiritual Master* (357-67), and is the version reprinted here. The essay is both an expression of Merton's philosophy, or more properly his spirituality, of education, and an affectionate reminiscence of his own experience at Columbia. His focus on education as most fundamentally a process of self-discovery that makes possible a participation in the transformation of society, rather than as professional or vocational training, is rooted in the historical development of the medieval university from the cathedral school, devoted to a search for wisdom analogous to that of the monastery, a quest for the vision, and praxis, of a rightly ordered world that can be described as a recovery of paradise and as a sacred humanism, "the flash of the Absolute recognizing itself in me." In this essay Merton explicitly identifies himself as a "Christian existentialist," and relates the famous anecdote of his sardonic response to a request for a contribution to a book on how one becomes "a success." His concluding testimonial to Columbia, where he was allowed and encouraged to be himself and consequently was "turned on like a pinball machine" by encounters with great figures of the past and illuminated by the "small bursts of light" from interaction with friends and mentors like Mark Van Doren, eventually comes full circle with his return to campus in 1964 to drink tea with D. T. Suzuki, an extraordinary experience of the commonplace that functions as a final archetype of the potential of education to serve as a catalyst for authentic self-realization.

⌒

L IFE CONSISTS IN LEARNING to live on one's own, spontaneous, free-
 wheeling: to do this one must recognize what is one's own—be familiar
 and at home with oneself. This means basically learning who one is, and
learning what one has to offer to the contemporary world, and then learning
how to make that offering valid.

The purpose of education is to show a person how to define himself authentically and spontaneously in relation to his world—not to impose a prefabricated
definition of the world, still less an arbitrary definition of the individual himself.
The world is made up of the people who are fully alive in it: that is, of the people
who can be themselves in it and can enter into a living and fruitful relationship
with each other in it. The world is, therefore, more real in proportion as the
people in it are able to be more fully and more humanly alive: that is to say,
better able to make a lucid and conscious use of their freedom. Basically, this
freedom must consist first of all in the capacity to choose their own lives, to
find themselves on the deepest possible level. A superficial freedom to wander
aimlessly here or there, to taste this or that, to make a choice of distractions (in
Pascal's sense) is simply a sham. It claims to be a freedom of "choice" when it has
evaded the basic task of discovering who it is that chooses. It is not free because
it is unwilling to face the risk of self-discovery.

The function of a university is, then, first of all to help the student to discover
himself: to recognize himself, and to identify who it is that chooses.

This description will be recognized at once as unconventional and, in fact,
monastic. To put it in even more outrageous terms, the function of the university is to help men and women save their souls and, in so doing, to save their
society: from what? From the hell of meaninglessness, of obsession, of complex
artifice, of systematic lying, of criminal evasions and neglects, of self-destructive
futilities.

It will be evident from my context that the business of saving one's soul
means more than taking an imaginary object, "a soul," and entrusting it to some
institutional bank for deposit until it is recovered with interest in heaven.

Speaking as a Christian existentialist, I mean by "soul" not simply the Aris-
totelian essential form but the mature personal identity, the creative fruit of an
authentic and lucid search, the "self" that is found after other partial and exterior selves have been discarded as masks.

This metaphor must not mislead: this inner identity is not "found" as an
object, but is the very self that finds. It is lost when it forgets to find, when it

does not know how to seek, or when it seeks itself as an object. (Such a search is futile and self-contradictory.) Hence the paradox that it finds best when it stops seeking: and the graduate level of learning is when one learns to sit still and be what one has become, which is what one does not know and does not need to know. In the language of Sufism, the end of the ascetic life is *Rida*, satisfaction. Debts are paid (and they were largely imaginary). One no longer seeks something else. One no longer seeks to be told by another who one is. One no longer demands reassurance. But there is the whole infinite depth of *what is* remaining to be revealed. And it is not revealed to those who seek it from others.

Education in this sense means more than learning; and for such education, one is awarded no degree. One graduates by rising from the dead. Learning to be oneself means, therefore, learning to die in order to live. It means discovering in the ground of one's being a "self" which is ultimate and indestructible, which not only survives the destruction of all other more superficial selves but finds its identity affirmed and clarified by their destruction.

The inmost self is naked. Nakedness is not socially acceptable except in certain crude forms which can be commercialized without any effort of imagination (topless waitresses). Curiously, this cult of bodily nakedness is a veil and a distraction, a communion in futility, where all identities get lost in their nerve endings. Everybody claims to like it. Yet no one is really happy with it. It makes money.

Spiritual nakedness, on the other hand, is far too stark to be useful. It strips life down to the root where life and death are equal, and this is what nobody likes to look at. But it is where freedom really begins: the freedom that cannot be guaranteed by the death of somebody else. The point where you become free not to kill, not to exploit, not to destroy, not to compete, because you are no longer afraid of death or the devil or poverty or failure. If you discover this nakedness, you'd better keep it private. People don't like it. But can you keep it private? Once you are exposed . . . Society continues to do you the service of keeping you in disguises, not for your comfort, but for its own. It is quite willing to strip you of this or that outer skin (a stripping which is a normal ritual and which everybody enjoys). The final metaphysical stripping goes too far, unless you happen to be in Auschwitz.

If I say this description is "monastic," I do not necessarily mean "theological." The terms in which it has been stated here are open to interpretation on several levels: theologically, ascetically, liturgically, psychologically. Let's assume that this last is the more acceptable level for most readers. And let's assume that I am simply speaking from experience as one who, from a French lycée and an English public school, has traveled through various places of "learning" and has, in these, learned one thing above all: to keep on going. I have described the itinerary elsewhere, but perhaps a few new ideas may be added here. The journey went from Europe to America, from Cambridge to Columbia. At Columbia, having got the necessary degrees, I crossed the boundary that separates those who learn as students from those who learn as teachers. Then I went to teach English at a Catholic college (St. Bonaventure). After which I went to be a novice in a Trappist monastery, where I also "learned" just enough theology to renounce all desire to be a theologian. Here also (for I am still in Kentucky) I learned by teaching: not theology as such, but the more hazardous and less charted business of monastic education, which deals with the whole person in a situation of considerable ambiguity and hazard: the novice, the young monk who wants to become a contemplative and who is (you sooner or later discover) trapped both by the institution and by his own character in a situation where what he desperately wants beyond all else on earth will probably turn out to be impossible. Perhaps I would have been safer back at Columbia teaching elementary English composition. Fortunately, I am no longer teaching anybody anything.

On the basis of this experience, I can, anyhow, take up an ancient position that views monastery and university as having the same kind of function. After all, that is natural enough to one who could walk about Cambridge saying to himself, "Here were the Franciscans at one time, here the Dominicans, here—at my own college—Chaucer was perhaps a clerk."

A university, like a monastery (and here I have medievalists to back me up, but presume that footnotes are not needed), is at once a microcosm and a paradise. Both monastery and university came into being in a civilization open to the sacred, that is to say, in a civilization which paid a great deal of attention to what it considered to be its own primordial roots in a mythical and archetypal holy ground, a spiritual creation. Thus the *Logos* or *Ratio* of both monastery and university is pretty much the same. Both are "schools," and they teach not so much by imparting information as by bringing the clerk (in the university) or the monk (in the monastery) to direct contact with "the beginning," the archetypal paradise world. This was often stated symbolically by treating the various disciplines of university and monastic life, respectively, as the "four rivers of paradise." At the same time, university and monastery tended sometimes to be in very heated conflict, for though they both aimed at "participation" in an "experience" of the hidden and sacred values implanted in the "ground" and the "beginning," they arrived there by different means: the university by *scientia*, intellectual knowledge, and the monastery by *sapientia*, or mystical contemplation. (Of course, the monastery itself easily tended to concentrate on *scientia*— the science of the Scriptures—and in the university there could be mystics like

Aquinas, Scotus, and Eckhart. So that in the end, in spite of all the fulminations of the Cistercian St. Bernard, a deeper *sapientia* came sometimes from schools than from monasteries.)

The point I am making here is this: far from suggesting that Columbia ought to return to the ideal of Chartres and concentrate on the trivium and quadrivium, I am insinuating that this archetypal approach, this "microcosm-paradise" type of sacred humanism, is basically personalistic.

I admit that all through the Middle Ages men were actively curious about the exact location of the earthly paradise. This curiosity was not absent from the mind of Columbus. The Pilgrim Fathers purified it a little, spiritualized it a little, but New England to them was a kind of paradise: and to make sure of a paradisic institution they created, of all things, Harvard. But the monks of the Middle Ages, and the clerks too, believed that the inner paradise was the ultimate ground of freedom in man's heart. To find it one had to travel, as Augustine had said, not with steps, but with yearnings. The journey was from man's "fallen" condition, in which he was not free not to be untrue to himself, to that original freedom in which, made in the image and likeness of God, he was no longer able to be untrue to himself. Hence, he recovered that nakedness of Adam which needed no fig leaves of law, of explanation, of justification, and no social garments of skins (Gregory of Nyssa). Paradise is simply the person, the self, but the radical self in its uninhibited freedom. The self no longer clothed with an ego.

One must not forget the dimension of relatedness to others. True freedom is openness, availability, the capacity for gift. But we must also remember that the difficult dialectic of fidelity to others in fidelity to oneself requires one to break through the veils of infidelity which, as individual egoists or as a selfish community, we set up to prevent ourselves from living in the truth.

This sacred humanism was, of course, abused and perverted by the sacred institution, and in the end monasticism, by a curious reversal that is so usual in the evolution of societies, identified the fig leaf with the paradise condition and insisted on the monk having at least enough of a self to serve the organization—itself pressed into the service of more mundane interests. Freedom, then, consisted in blind obedience, and contemplation consisted in renouncing nakedness in favor of elaborate and ritual vestments. The "person" was only what he was in the eyes of the institution because the institution was, for all intents and purposes, Paradise, the domain of God, and indeed God himself. To be in Paradise, then, consisted in being defined by the paradisic community—or by Academe. Hence, the dogmatic absolutism for which the late Middle Ages are all too well known—and for which they are by no means uniquely responsible.

The original and authentic "paradise" idea, both in the monastery (*paradisus claustralis*) and in the university, implied not simply a celestial store of theoretic ideas to which the Magistri and Doctores held the key, but the inner self of the student who, in discovering the ground of his own personality as it opened out into the center of all created being, found in himself the light and the wisdom of his Creator, a light and wisdom in which everything comprehensible could be comprehended and what was not comprehensible could nevertheless be grasped in the darkness of contemplation by a direct and existential contact.

Thus, the fruit of education, whether in the university (as for Eckhart) or in the monastery (as for Ruysbroeck) was the activation of that inmost center, that *scintilla animae*, that "apex" or "spark" which is a freedom beyond freedom, an identity beyond essence, a self beyond all ego, a being beyond the created realm, and a consciousness that transcends all division, all separation. To activate this spark is not to be, like Plotinus, "alone with the Alone," but to recognize the Alone which is by itself in everything because there is nothing that can be apart from It and yet nothing that can be with It, and nothing that can realize It. It can only realize itself. The "spark" which is my true self is the flash of the Absolute recognizing itself in me.

This realization at the apex is a coincidence of all opposites (as Nicholas of Cusa might say), a fusion of freedom and unfreedom, being and unbeing, life and death, self and non-self, man and God. The "spark" is not so much a stable entity which one finds but an event, an explosion which happens as all opposites clash within oneself. Then it is seen that the ego is not. It vanishes in its non-seeing when the flash of the spark alone is. When all things are reduced to the spark, who sees it? Who knows it? If you say "God," you are destroyed; and if you say no one, you will plunge into hell; and if you say I, you prove you are not even in the ballgame.

The purpose of all learning is to dispose man for this kind of event.

The purpose of various disciplines is to provide ways or paths which lead to this capacity for ignition.

Obviously it would be a grave mistake to do, as some have done and still do, and declare that the only way is to be found in a cloister and the only discipline is asceticism or Zen sitting or, for that matter, turning on with a new drug. The whole of life is learning to ignite without dependence on any specific external means, whether cloistered, Zenist, Tantric, psychedelic, or what have you. It is learning that the spark, being a flash at the apex and explosion of all freedoms, can never be subject to control or to enlightenment, can never be got by pressing buttons. A spark that goes off when you swallow something or stick yourself with something may be a fairly passable imitation of the real thing, but it is not the real thing. (I will not argue that it cannot teach you a great deal about the real thing.) In the same way a cloistered complacency—a "peace" that is guaranteed only by getting out of the traffic, turning off the radio, and forgetting the world—is not by itself the real thing either.

THE DANGER OF EDUCATION, I have found, is that it so easily confuses means with ends. Worse than that, it quite easily forgets both and devotes itself merely to the mass production of uneducated graduates—people literally unfit for anything except to take part in an elaborate and completely artificial charade which they and their contemporaries have conspired to call "life."

A few years ago a man who was compiling a book entitled *Success* wrote and asked me to contribute a statement on how I got to be a success. I replied indignantly that I was not able to consider myself a success in any terms that had a meaning to me. I swore I had spent my life strenuously avoiding success. If it so happened that I had once written a best seller, this was a pure accident, due to inattention and naïveté, and I would take very good care never to do the same again. If I had a message to my contemporaries, I said, it was surely this: Be anything you like, be madmen, drunks, and bastards of every shape and form, but at all costs avoid one thing: success. I heard no more from him and I am not aware that my reply was published with the other testimonials.

Thus, I have undercut all hope of claiming that Columbia made me a success. On the contrary, I believe I can thank Columbia, among so many other things, for having helped me learn the value of unsuccess. Columbia was for me a microcosm, a little world, where I exhausted myself in time. Had I waited until after graduation, it would have been too late. During the few years in which I was there, I managed to do so many wrong things that I was ready to blow my mind. But fortunately I learned, in so doing, that this was good. I might have ended up on Madison Avenue if I hadn't. Instead of preparing me for one of those splendid jobs, Columbia cured me forever of wanting one. Instead of adapting me to the world downtown, Columbia did me the favor of lobbing me half conscious into the Village, where I occasionally came to my senses and where I continued to learn. I think I have sufficiently explained, elsewhere, how much I owed, in this regard, to people like Mark Van Doren (who lived around the corner from me in the Village) and Joseph Wood Krutch (who became, as I have become, a hermit). Such people taught me to imitate not Rockefeller but Thoreau. Of course, I am not trying to say that one has to be Thoreau rather than Rockefeller, nor am I slyly intimating that I have discovered a superior form of resentment, an offbeat way of scoring on everybody by refusing to keep score.

What I am saying is this: the score is not what matters. Life does not have to be regarded as a game in which scores are kept and somebody wins. If you are too intent on winning, you will never enjoy playing. If you are too obsessed with success, you will forget to live. If you have learned only how to be a success, your life has probably been wasted. If a university concentrates on producing successful people, it is lamentably failing in its obligation to society and to the students themselves.

Now I know that even in the thirties, at Columbia, the business of wanting to be a success was very much in the air. There was, in fact, a scandal about the year-book senior poll. The man who was voted "most likely to succeed" was accused of having doctored the results in his own favor after a surreptitious deal with a yearbook staff member who was voted "best dressed." Incidentally, I was voted best writer. I was not accused of trickery, but everyone understood that the vote, which had been between me and Hank Liebermann, had been decided by my fraternity brothers. (Incidentally, whatever became of the man "most likely to succeed"?)

In any case, no one really cared. Since that time many of my classmates have attained to eminence with all its joys and all its sorrows, and the ones I have seen since then are marked by the signature of anguish. So am I. I do not claim exemption. Yet I never had the feeling that our alma mater just wanted us to become well-paid operators, or to break our necks to keep on the front pages of the *Times*. On the contrary—maybe this is a delusion, but if it is a delusion it is a salutary one—I always felt at Columbia that people around me, half amused and perhaps at times half incredulous, were happy to let me be myself. (I add that I seldom felt this way at Cambridge.) The thing I always liked best about Columbia was the sense that the university was on the whole glad to turn me loose in its library, its classrooms, and among its distinguished faculty, and let me make what I liked out of it all. I did. And I ended up by being turned on like a pinball machine by Blake, Thomas Aquinas, Augustine, Eckhart, Cooma-raswamy, Traherne, Hopkins, Maritain, and the sacraments of the Catholic Church. After which I came to the monastery in which (this is public knowl-edge) I have continued to be the same kind of maverick and have, in fact, ended as a hermit who is also fully identified with the peace movement, with Zen, with a group of Latin American hippie poets, etc., etc.

The least of the work of learning is done in classrooms. I can remember scores of incidents, remarks, happenings, encounters that took place all over the cam-pus and sometimes far from the campus: small bursts of light that pointed out my way in the dark of my own identity. For instance, Mark Van Doren saying to me as we crossed Amsterdam Avenue: "Well, if you have a vocation to the monastic life, it will not be possible for you to decide not to enter" (or words to that effect). I grasped at once the existential truth of this statement.

One other scene, much later on. A room in Butler Hall, overlooking some campus buildings. Daisetz Suzuki, with his great bushy eyebrows and the hearing aid that aids nothing. Mihoko, his beautiful secretary, has to repeat everything. She is making tea. Tea ceremony, but a most unconventional one, for there are no rites and no rules. I drink my tea as reverently and attentively as I can. She goes into the other room. Suzuki, as if waiting for her to go, hastily picks up his cup and drains it.

It was at once as if nothing at all had happened and as if the roof had flown off the building. But in reality nothing had happened. A very very old deaf Zen man with bushy eyebrows had drunk a cup of tea, as though with the complete wakefulness of a child and as though at the same time declaring with utter finality: "This is not important!"

The function of a university is to teach a man how to drink tea, not because anything is important, but because it is usual to drink tea, or, for that matter, anything else under the sun. And whatever you do, every act, however small, can teach you everything—provided you see who it is that is acting.

32

The Wild Places

On February 25, 1968, Merton wrote in his journal, "Yesterday I wrote a short piece on Wilderness (the Nash book) in the afternoon. Importance of the 'ecological conscience'" (*Other Side of the Mountain*, 58). On May 14 he noted, "My piece on the 'Wild Places' is to be printed in *Center Magazine*" (*Other Side of the Mountain*, 99). This review-essay of Roderick Nash's *Wilderness and the American Mind* actually appeared first in *The Catholic Worker* 34 (June 1968), 4, 6, and the following month in *Center Magazine* (the journal of the Center for the Study of American Institutions) 1 (1968), 40-44; it was reprinted in an appendix to Merton's 1968 dialogue at the Center in *Preview of the Asian Journey* (95-107). In fact, however, the text found in *Center Magazine* and *Preview of the Asian Journey*, the most easily accessible and therefore most widely read version, was significantly abridged, altering or excising more than nine hundred words, almost a quarter of the original text, with changes ranging from single words to omission of entire paragraphs. *The Catholic Worker* printed the entire text, though with a few mis-transcriptions, but also including some evidently authorial alterations not found in the extant typescript. The complete form of the text presented here is basically that found in *The Catholic Worker*, with corrections based on the original typescript carbon. This essay is the most extensive presentation of Merton's developing ecological awareness in the final years of his life, otherwise evident mainly in journal entries and in correspondence. (For overviews of the topic, see Kathleen Deignan, CND, "'Love for the Paradise Mystery': Thomas Merton, Contemplative Ecologist," *CrossCurrents* 58.4 [December 2008], 545-69; Patrick O'Connell, "The Traditional Sources of Thomas Merton's Environmental Spirituality," *Spiritual Life* 56.3 [Fall 2010], 154-71; Monica Weis, SSJ, "The Wilderness of Compassion: Nature's Influence in Thomas Merton's Writing," *The Merton Annual* 14 [2001], 56-80; and especially Monica Weis, *The Environmental Vision of Thomas Merton* [Lexington: University Press of Kentucky, 2010].) The essay follows Nash's book in its chronological survey of American attitudes toward wilderness, but considered from Merton's own spiritual and contemplative perspective. He focuses on three seminal figures of American environmental consciousness, Henry David Thoreau, John Muir, and Aldo Leopold, each of whom emphasized the crucial necessity for a holistic understanding that situates the human person not apart from but as an integral part of the natural world, in Leopold's words, "*as a dependent member of the biotic community*." For Merton, alienation from the created world is an intrinsic and inevitable result of "the profound dehumanization and alienation of modern Western man," who has lost touch with his own ontological roots and so with his rootedness in the material world, which no longer functions as a sacramental revelation of its divine source but is reduced to a commodity to be exploited for pleasure and profit. The war on creation is simply another form of the war on other people, graphically illustrated by the massive use of defoliants and other chemical agents in Vietnam. Merton prophetically concludes (in a line cut from the *Center Magazine* text): "Catholic theology ought to take note of the ecological conscience and do it fast," one further instance of his sensitivity to crucial moral and spiritual issues that would become generally recognized as significant only years or even decades later.

MAN IS A CREATURE of ambiguity. His salvation and his sanity depend on his ability to harmonize the deep conflicts in his thought, his emotions, his personal mythology. Honesty and authenticity do not depend on complete freedom from contradictions—such freedom is impossible—but on recognizing our self-contradictions and not masking them with bad faith. The conflicts in individuals are not entirely of their own making. On the contrary, many of them are imposed, ready made, by an ambivalent culture. This poses a very special problem, because he who accepts the ambiguities of his culture without protest and without criticism is rewarded with a sense of security and moral justification. A certain kind of unanimity satisfies our emotions, and easily substitutes for truth. We are content to think like the others, and in order to protect our common psychic security, we readily become blind to the contradictions—or even the lies—that we have all decided to accept as "plain truth."

One of the more familiar ambiguities in the American mind operates in our frontier mythology, which has grown in power in proportion as we have ceased to be a frontier or even a rural people. The pioneer, the frontier culture hero, is a product of the wilderness. But at the same time he is a destroyer of the wilderness. His success as pioneer depends on his ability to fight the wilderness and win. Victory consists in reducing the wilderness to something else, a farm, a village, a road, a canal, a railway, a mine, a factory, a city—and finally an urban nation. A recent study[1] of *Wilderness and the American Mind* by Roderick Nash is an important addition to an already significant body of literature about this subject. It traces the evolution of the wilderness idea from the first Puritan set-

---

1. Roderick Nash, *Wilderness and the American Mind* (New Haven: Yale University Press, 1967).

tlers via Thoreau and Muir to the modern ecologists and preservationists—and to their opponents in big business and politics. The really crucial issues of the present moment in ecology are barely touched. The author is concerned with the wilderness idea and with the "irony of pioneering [which was] that success necessarily involved the destruction of the primitive setting that made the pioneer possible."

Nash does not develop the tragic implications of this inner contradiction but he states them clearly enough for us to recognize their symptomatic importance. We all proclaim our love and respect for wild nature, and in the same breath we confess our firm attachment to values which inexorably demand the destruction of the last remnant of wildness. But when people like Rachel Carson try to suggest that our capacity to poison the nature around us is some indication of a sickness in ourselves, we dismiss them as fanatics.

Now one of the interesting things about this ambivalence toward nature is that it is rooted in our Biblical, Judeo-Christian tradition. We might remark at once that it is neither genuinely Biblical nor Jewish nor Christian. Nash is perhaps a little one-sided in his analysis here. But a certain kind of Christian culture has certainly resulted in a manichean hostility towards created nature. This, of course, we all know well enough. (The word "manichean" has become a cliché of reproof like "communist" or "racist.") But the very ones who use the cliché most may be the ones who are still unknowingly tainted, on a deep level, with what they condemn. I say on a deep level, an unconscious level. For there is a certain popular, superficial, and one-sided "Christian worldliness" that is, in its hidden implications, profoundly destructive of nature and of "God's good creation" even while it claims to love and extol them.

The Puritans inherited a half-conscious bias against the realm of nature, and the Bible gave them plenty of texts that justified what Nash calls "a tradition of repugnance" for nature in the wild. In fact, they were able to regard the "hideous and desolate wilderness" of America as though it were filled with conscious malevolence against them. They hated it as a *person*, an extension of the Evil One, the Enemy opposed to the spread of the Kingdom of God. And the wild Indian who dwelt in the wilderness was also associated with evil. The wilderness itself was the domain of moral wickedness. It favored spontaneity—therefore sin. The groves (like those condemned in the Bible) suggested wanton and licentious rites to imaginations haunted by repressed drives. To fight the wilderness was not only necessary for physical survival, it was above all a moral and Christian imperative. Victory over the wilderness was an ascetic triumph over the forces of impulse and of lawless appetite. How could one be content to leave any part of nature just as it was, since nature was "fallen" and "corrupt"? The elementary Christian duty of the Puritan settler was to attack the forest with an axe and to keep a gun handy in order to exterminate Indians and wild beasts, should they put in an appearance. The work of combating, reducing, destroying, and transforming the wilderness was purely and simply "God's work." The Puritan, and after him the pioneer, had an opportunity to prove his worth—or indeed his salvation and election—by the single-minded zeal with which he carried on this obsessive crusade against wildness. His reward was prosperity, real estate, money, and ultimately the peaceful "order" of civil and urban life. In a seventeenth-century Puritan book with an intriguing title—Johnson's *Wonder Working Providence* (The "Great Society"?)—we read that it was Jesus Himself, working through the Puritans, who "turned one of the most hideous, boundless and unknown wildernesses in the world ... to a well-ordered Commonwealth."

Max Weber and others have long since helped us recognize the influence of the Puritan ethos on the growth of capitalism. This is one more example. American capitalist culture is firmly rooted in a secularized Christian myth and mystique of struggle with nature. The basic article of faith in this mystique is that you prove your worth by overcoming and dominating the natural world. You justify your existence and you attain bliss (temporal, eternal, or both) by transforming nature into wealth. This is not only good, but self-evident. Until transformed, nature is useless and absurd. Anyone who refuses to see this or acquiesce in it is some kind of half-wit—or, worse, a rebel, an anarchist, a prophet of apocalyptic disorders.

Of course, let us immediately admit that there is also superimposed on this another mystique: a mystique of America the beautiful, America whose mountains are bigger and better than those of Switzerland, scenic America which is to be seen first, last, and always in preference to foreign parts, America which must be kept lovely for Lady Bird. (So don't throw that beer can in the river—even though it is polluted with all kinds of industrial waste. Business can mess up nature, but not *you*, Jack!) But here again nature is not valued for itself but as a business asset. Nevertheless a cult of nature appeared in the nineteenth century.

The romantic love of wild American nature began in the cities and was an import from Europe which benefitted, first of all, the rich. But at the same time it had a profound effect on American civilization. Not only did poets like William Cullen Bryant proclaim that the "groves were God's first temples," and not only did the nineteenth-century landscape painters make America realize that the woods and mountains were worth looking at; not only did Fenimore Cooper revive the ideal of the Noble Primitive who grew up in the "honesty of the woods," and was better than city people; but also it was now the villain in the story (perhaps a city slicker) who ravished the forest and callously misused the good things of nature.

The Transcendentalists above all reversed the Puritan prejudice against nature, and began to teach that in the forests and mountains God was nearer than in the cities. The silence of the woods whispered, to the man who listened, a message of sanity and healing. While the Puritans had assumed that man, being evil, would only revert to the most corrupt condition in the wilderness, the Transcendentalists held that since he was naturally good, and the cities corrupted his goodness, he needed contact with nature in order to recover his true self.

All this quickly turned into cliché. But nevertheless the prophetic work of Henry Thoreau went deeper than a mere surface enthusiasm for scenery and fresh air. It is true that Walden was not too far from Concord and was hardly a wilderness even in those days. But Thoreau did build himself a house in the woods and did live at peace with the wild things around the pond. He also proved what he set out to prove: that one could not only survive outside the perimeter of town or farm life but that one could live better and happier there. The fictions, rites, and conventions of New England society did not deserve the absolute allegiance that they claimed. There were other and better values.

On the other hand, Thoreau explored the Maine woods and had enough experience of the real wilds to recognize that life there could be savage and dehumanizing. Hence he produced a philosophy of *balance* which, he thought, was right and necessary for America. He already saw that American capitalism was set on a course that would ultimately ravage all wild nature on the continent—perhaps even in the world. And he warned that some wilderness must be preserved. If it were not, man would destroy himself in destroying nature.

Thoreau had enough sense to realize that civilization was necessary and right. But *an element of wildness was necessary as a component in civilized life itself.* The American still had a priceless advantage over the European, one that would enable him to develop a greater and better civilization if he did not miss his chance. He could, in Thoreau's words, "combine the hardiness of the Indian with the intellectualness of civilized man." For that reason, said Thoreau, "I would not have every part of a man cultivated." To try to subject everything in man to rational and conscious control would be to warp, diminish, and barbarize him. So too, the reduction of all nature to use for profit would end in the dehumanization of man. The passion and savagery that the Puritan had projected onto nature in order to justify his hatred of it and his fanatical combat against it, turned out to be within man himself. And when man turned the green forests into asphalt jungles the price he paid was that they were precisely that: jungles.

The savagery of urban man, untempered by wilderness discipline, can be arbitrary, ruthless, and pure. It is wanton savagery for its own sake.

Thoreau, basing himself on the Chinese cosmology of Yang and Yin, preached an inner integration and proportion between the conscious and unconscious that anticipated the discoveries of Freud and Jung; civilized man needed an element of irrationality, spontaneity, impulse, nature to balance his rationalism, his discipline, his controlled endeavor. These two should have the same "proportion that night bears to day, winter to summer, thought to experience." For this reason, Thoreau was one of the first to advocate wilderness preservation. He thought that every township ought to include an area of wild nature "for modesty and reverence's sake."

It has been consistently proved true that what early nature philosophers, like Thoreau, said in terms that seemed merely poetic or sentimental turned out to have realistic and practical implications. Soon a few people began to realize the bad effects of deforestation, and already in 1864 the crucial importance of the Adirondack woods for New York's water supply was recognized. About this time, too, the movement to set up National Parks was begun, though not always for the most fundamental reasons. The arguments for and against Yellowstone Park (1872) are instructive. First of all, the area was "no use for business anyway." And then the geysers, hot springs, and other "decorations" were helpful manifestations of scientific truth. Then of course the place would provide "a great breathing place for the national lungs." Against this, one representative advanced a typical argument: "I cannot understand the sentiment which favors the retention of a few buffaloes to the development of mining interests amounting to millions of dollars."

John Muir is the great name in the history of American wilderness preservation. Muir's Scotch Calvinist father was the kind of man who believed that only a sinner or a slacker would approach the wilderness without taking an axe to it. To leave wild nature unattacked or unexploited was, in his eyes, not only foolish but morally reprehensible. It is curious, incidentally, that this attitude has rather consistently been associated with the American myth of virility. To be in the wilderness without fighting it, or at least without killing the animals in it, is regarded as a feminine trait. When a dam was about to be built in a canyon in Yosemite Park (1913) to provide additional water for San Francisco, those who opposed it were treated as "short haired women and long haired men." Theodore Roosevelt, though a friend of John Muir, associated camping and hunting in the wilds with his virility cult, and this has remained a constant in the American mystique. Muir tried without success to persuade Roosevelt to stop hunting.

Muir seems to have worked out his wilderness philosophy on a very deep symbolic level in personal conflict and crisis through which he attained an unusual level of psychic integration. His decision to travel on foot through a thousand miles of wild country from Indiana to the Gulf of Mexico seems to have been an act of self-liberation from a father-dominated superego. And the reason he gave: "There is a love of wild nature in everybody, an ancient mother love, showing itself whether recognized or no, and however covered by cares and duties." This was not mere regression, but a recognition of the profoundly ambiguous imbalance in the American mind. Muir saw intuitively that the aggressive, compulsive, exploitative attitude of the American male toward nature reflected not strength but insecurity and fear. The American cult of success implied a morbid fear of failure and resulted in the overkill mentality so costly not only to nature but to every real or imaginary competitor to our "manifest destiny." A psychological study in depth of John Muir would probably reveal some very salutary information for modern America, and help us deliver ourselves from the demon of overkill.

Muir was of course completely committed to wilderness preservation. But at first he thought he could accept the compromise of those conservationists who were content with a policy of forest management. There is an important difference. Forest management implies exploitation of the woods by selective cutting which "helps" the woods by "weeding out unwanted trees." It also puts emphasis on the development of forest areas for recreation, opening up roads, campsites, hotels, and so on. Muir soon saw that this was only a milder form of exploitation. He felt it was essential to preserve areas of *actual wilderness*, completely undeveloped and even without roads, in which no cutting, no hunting, no exploitation whatever would be permitted. These areas would be open only to those who were willing to camp out in the most primitive conditions in direct contact with wild nature.

Muir's basic insight was not simply the romantically religious one that "God's good tidings" are heard in the mountains, but the realization that man needed to feel a part of wild nature. He needed to recognize his kinship with all other living beings and to participate in their unchanged natural existence. In other words, he had to look at other living beings, especially wild things, not in terms of whether or not they were good *for him*, but as *good for themselves*. Instead of self-righteously assuming that man is absolute Lord of all nature and can exterminate other forms of life according to his own real or imagined needs, Muir reminded us that man is *part of nature*. He must remember the rights of other beings to *exist on their own terms* and not purely and simply on his. In other words, as Nash remarks, Muir here anticipated the teachings of the recent ecologists who have shown us that *unless man learns this fundamental respect for all life, he himself will be destroyed.*

An investigation of the wilderness mystique and of the contrary mystique of exploitation and power reveals the tragic depth of the conflict that now exists in the American mind. The ideal of freedom and creativity which has been celebrated with such optimism and self-assurance runs the risk of being turned completely inside out if the natural ecological balance, on which it depends for its vitality, is destroyed. Take away the space, the freshness, the rich spontaneity of a wildly flourishing nature, and what will become of the creative pioneer mystique? A pioneer in a suburb is a sick man tormenting himself with projects of virile conquest. In a ghetto he is a policeman shooting every black man who gives him a dirty look. Obviously, the frontier is a thing of the past, the bison has vanished, and only by some miracle have a few Indians managed to survive. There are still some forests and wilderness areas, but we are firmly established as an urban culture. Nevertheless, the problem of ecology exists in a most acute form. The danger of fallout and atomic waste is only one of the more spectacular ones. There is an almost infinite number of others.

Much of the stupendous ecological damage that has been done in the last fifty years is completely irreversible. Industry and the military, especially in America, are firmly set on policies which make further damage inevitable. There are plenty of people who are aware of the need for "something to be done"; but just consider the enormous struggle that has to be waged, for instance in eastern Kentucky, to keep mining interests from completing the ruin of an area that is already a ghastly monument to callous human greed. Everyone will agree that "deforestation is bad," and when flash floods pull down the side of a mountain and drown a dozen wretched little towns in mud, everyone will agree that it's too bad the strip-miners peeled off the tops of the mountains with bulldozers. But when a choice has to be made, it is almost invariably made in the way that is good for a quick return on somebody's investment—and a permanent disaster for everybody else.

Aldo Leopold, a follower of Muir and one of the great preservationists, understood that the erosion of American land was only part of a more drastic erosion of American freedom—of which it was a symptom. If "freedom" means purely and simply an uncontrolled power to make money in every possible way, regardless of consequences, then freedom becomes synonymous with ruthless, mindless, and absolute exploitation. Such freedom is in fact nothing but the arbitrary tyranny of a wasteful and destructive process, glorified with big words that have lost their meaning. Aldo Leopold saw the connection and expressed it in the quiet language of ecology: "*Is it not a bit beside the point to be so solicitous about preserving American institutions without giving so much as a thought to preserving the environment which produced them and which may now be one of the effective means of keeping them alive?"*

Aldo Leopold brought into clear focus one of the most important moral discoveries of our time. This can be called the *ecological conscience*. The ecological conscience is centered in an awareness of *man's true place as a dependent member of the biotic community*. Man must become fully aware of his *dependence* on a balance which he is not only free to destroy but which he has already begun to destroy. He must recognize his obligations toward the other members of that vital community. And incidentally, since he tends to destroy nature in his frantic efforts to exterminate other members of his own species, it would not hurt if he had a little more respect for human life too. The respect for life, the affirmation of *all* life, is basic to the ecological conscience. In the words of Albert Schweitzer: *"A man is ethical only when life as such is sacred to him, that of plants and animals as well as that of his fellow man."*

The tragedy which has been revealed in the ecological shambles created by business and war is a tragedy of ambivalence, aggression, and fear cloaked in virtuous ideas and justified by pseudo-Christian clichés. Or rather a tragedy of pseudo-creativity deeply impregnated with hatred, megalomania, and the need for domination. This is evident in the drama of the Vietnam War, cloaked as it is in the specious language of freedom and democracy. The psychological root of it is doubtless in the profound dehumanization and alienation of modern Western man, who has gradually come to mistake the artificial value of inert objects and abstractions (goods, money, property) for the power of life itself, and who is willing to place immediate profit above everything else. Money is more important, more alive than life, including the life and happiness of his closest and most intimate companions. This he can always justify by a legalistic ethic or a casuistical formula of some sort; but his formulas themselves betray him and eventually lose even the meaning which has been arbitrarily forced upon them.

As against this ethic of money and legal verbalism, Aldo Leopold laid down this basic principle of the ecological conscience: "A THING IS RIGHT WHEN IT TENDS TO PRESERVE THE INTEGRITY, STABILITY AND BEAUTY OF THE BIOTIC COMMUNITY. IT IS WRONG WHEN IT TENDS OTHERWISE."

In the light of this principle, an examination of our social, economic, and political history in the last hundred years would be a moral nightmare, redeemed only by a few gestures of good will on the part of those—and they are many—who obscurely realize that there *is* a problem. Yet compared to the size of the problem, these efforts are at best pitiful; and what is more, the same gestures are made with great earnestness by the very people who continue to ravage, destroy, and pollute the country. They honor the wilderness myth while they proceed to destroy nature.

Aldo Leopold has defined the ecological conscience. Can such a conscience be formed and become really effective in America today? Is it likely to be? The ecological conscience is also essentially a peace-making conscience. A country that seems to be more and more oriented to permanent hot or cold war-making does not give much promise of developing either one. But perhaps the very character of the war in Vietnam—with crop poisoning, the defoliation of forest trees, the incineration of villages and their inhabitants with napalm—presents enough of a stark and critical example to remind us of this most urgent moral need. Catholic theology ought to take note of the ecological conscience and do it fast.

Meanwhile some of us are wearing the little yellow and red button with a flower on it and the words "Celebrate Life!" We bear witness as best we can to these tidings.

33

Final Integration:
Toward a "Monastic Therapy"

On January 22, 1968, Merton contacted the editor of *Monastic Studies*, Basil DePinto, offering to write a review of the Persian-American psychoanalyst A. Reza Arasteh's book *Final Integration in the Adult Personality* (Leiden: E. J. Brill, 1965), which he called "a most important book which most people will not run across easily" and which he thought "could be of decisive importance for some of us in monastic renewal" (*School of Charity*, 363). Merton had previously written a brief review, published in French translation in *Collectanea Cisterciensia* 29.1 (1967), 179-80, of Arasteh's 1965 article with the same title from the *American Journal of Psychoanalysis*. (For a very helpful article straightening out the confusion entailed by these two reviews of two works by Arasteh, see Patricia A. Burton, "Final Integration of a Bibliographical Puzzle," *The Merton Seasonal* 35.4 [Winter 2010], 30-36.) On March 21 Merton wrote in his journal, "I took advantage of the quiet to write my review of the Arasteh book, *Final Integration*, which I found excellent" (*Other Side of the Mountain*, 70), and on the following day he wrote to Arasteh himself, "I have finished your excellent book and have written a long review article, which I will send along in due course" (*Hidden Ground of Love*, 42). The article appeared in *Monastic Studies* 6 (1968), 87-99, and was included in *Contemplation in a World of Action* (205-17). As suggested by his comments to DePinto and by the article's subtitle, "Toward a 'Monastic Therapy,'" Merton found Arasteh's approach, strongly influenced by the Persian Sufi tradition as well as by such humanistic psychotherapists as Viktor Frankl and Merton's friend Erich Fromm, so attractive because it aimed not merely at adjustment to prevailing social norms but at an inner transformation of consciousness, a psychological and spiritual "rebirth" that is also the ultimate goal of authentic monasticism. This "final integration" transcending the limitations of any specific social or cultural milieu is a liberation that Merton associates with Zen enlightenment and particularly with the freedom of the Spirit announced by Christ in the Gospel of John. What Arasteh offers on the psychological level Merton reconceives on the spiritual level, a transformation that is ultimately eschatological, "a rebirth into the transformed and redeemed time, the time of the Kingdom, the time of the Spirit, the time of 'the end' . . . . a disintegration of the social and cultural self, the product of merely human history, and the reintegration of that self in Christ, in salvation history, in the mystery of redemption, in the Pentecostal 'new creation.'" This reflection on Arasteh's theory of final integration becomes Merton's own final sustained reflection on the central Christian mystery of paschal transformation, which of course is also the fundamental theme underlying and unifying his own spiritual teaching: the radical surrender of the false self, the illusory identity created by one's own fears and desires, so that the true self, the self known and loved by God from all eternity, might become fully present, fully alive, through and with and in the risen Christ.

CONSIDERABLE AMOUNT of uneasiness and ambivalence in the monastic life today is due perhaps to the fact that though we possess clear conceptual formulas to explain what our "contemplative life" is all about, and though those formulas may well accord with what we would like to do, it seems they do not help us much with what we are actually doing. Thus we find ourselves with several different sets of problems which, however, we do not manage to distinguish. We have defined our ends in certain terms (a life of prayer and penance, apart from the world but not alien to it; seeking God alone, but in community and fraternal love; purifying our hearts by renunciation in order to pray more intently and simply, eventually attaining to contemplative experience; thus our community is a living sign of God's presence, etc.). But meanwhile, before we can get around to doing these things, we have to wrestle with a multitude of other problems: how to make our own living efficiently and yet remain "monastic"; how to keep our atmosphere of silence and yet communicate more spontaneously with one another; how to arrange the office, time for work, study, etc.; above all, how to cope with the contradictions in a system which at the same moment—but from different quarters—urges us to go forward and forbids us to move.

Thus, though we may be fairly clear about what we want to do, we are so confused about the way to do it that our ends become almost entirely theoretical, and our energies become involved in a rather different form of life from the one we claim to be living. This naturally causes a lot of anxiety, ambivalence, tension, not to say discouragement and even despair. Then we summon psychiatry to the rescue—and create still further problems: for the kind of adjustment that ordinary psychotherapy calls for is a realistic acceptance of our social situation, an acquiescence in fulfilling a moderately useful role and in being more or less the sort of person our society would like us to be. And yet the monastic role defined by the ideal to which we hold is one thing, and the role as defined by the actual situation of our community and of ourselves in it, quite another. This difficulty becomes all the greater and more confusing when sociology gets into the act, for then we are summoned to live at the same time by an unworldly ideal and by a worldly one: or to be monks according to norms and standards based on statistics which have nothing to do with our kind of life.

To put it quite simply: many people come to the monastery with a strong, if inchoate, sense that they are called to make something out of their lives. But after a few years of struggle they find that this "thing" they are supposed to do is not clarified, and though they may have become acquainted with formulas which explain the monastic life and justify it, they still do not feel that they are able to do anything about them. In addition, they begin to question the relevance of such formulas to modern man. The most difficult kind of vocation crisis is that in which a monk with genuine monastic aspirations comes to feel that such aspirations cannot be fulfilled in a monastery. Which means that they probably cannot be fulfilled anywhere.

The idea of "rebirth" and of life as a "new man in Christ, in the Spirit," of a "risen life" in the Mystery of Christ or in the Kingdom of God, is fundamental to Christian theology and practice—it is, after all, the whole meaning of baptism. All the more so is this idea central to that peculiar refinement of the theology of baptism which is the monastic *conversatio*—the vocation to a life especially dedicated to self-renewal, liberation from all sin, and the transformation of one's entire mentality "in Christ."

The notion of "rebirth" is not peculiar to Christianity. In Sufism, Zen Buddhism, and in many other religious or spiritual traditions, emphasis is placed on the call to fulfill certain obscure yet urgent potentialities in the ground of one's being, to "become someone" that one already (potentially) is, the person one is truly meant to be. Zen calls this awakening a recognition of "your original face before you were born."

In Asian traditions as well as in Christian monasticism, there has been considerable stress on the need for a guide or spiritual father, an experienced elder who knows how to bring the less experienced to a decisive point of breakthrough where this "new being" is attained. Strictly speaking, Christian monasticism is less dependent on the aid of a guide than some of the other traditions. In Sufism and Zen the spiritual master is as essential as the analyst in psychoanalysis. In Christian monasticism, a fervent community, a living and "spiritual" (*pneumatikos*) celebration of the liturgical mysteries and of the office might compensate, to some extent, for the lack of an experienced and charismatic teacher. But if there is no sense at all of the urgency of inner development, no aspiration to growth and "rebirth," or if it is blandly assumed that all this is automatically taken care of by a correct and lively communal celebration, something essential is missing.

The monastic life is not justified simply by a sort of contractual fulfillment of a "work" on behalf of the Church—even if it be the spiritual work of the *opus Dei*, the official public celebration of divine praise, or, for that matter, the cultivation of meditative prayer in silence, strict enclosure, in an austere regime. The monastic community does not effectively act as a sign of God's presence and of His Kingdom merely by the fulfillment of certain symbolic functions. For instance, it is not enough to keep the monks strictly enclosed and remote from all external activity—this does not by itself constitute a sign of the eschatological kingdom. On the contrary, very often this limitation constitutes a serious impoverishment of the personalities of the monks and at the same time serves to prevent that impoverishment from becoming public! It is of course perfectly true that solitude and silence are essential to the monastic way of life, and discipline does contribute very much to the ends for which monastic communities exist. But the fact remains that people are called to the monastic life so that they may grow and be transformed, "reborn" to a new and more complete identity, and to a more profoundly fruitful existence in peace, in wisdom, in creativity, in love. When rigidity and limitation become ends in themselves they no longer favor growth, they stifle it.

Sometimes it may be very useful for us to discover new and unfamiliar ways in which the human task of maturation and self-discovery is defined. The book of a Persian psychoanalyst, Dr. Reza Arasteh, who practices and teaches in America, might prove very valuable in this respect.[1]

Dr. Arasteh has developed and deepened ideas suggested by the humanistic psychoanalysis of Erich Fromm, by existential psychotherapy, and by the logo-therapy of Viktor Frankl. But—and this is what is most interesting—he has also incorporated into his theories material from the mystical tradition of Persian Sufism. The *Final Integration* which is the object of his research is not just the "cure" of neurosis by adaptation to society. On the contrary, it presupposes that any psychoanalytic theory that is content merely with this is bound to be inadequate. Dr. Arasteh is interested not only in the partial and limited "health" which results from contented acceptance of a useful role in society, but in the final and complete maturing of the human psyche on a transcultural level. This requires a little clarification.

Contrary to the accepted theory and practice of most psychotherapy derived from Freud and popular in America today, Dr. Arasteh holds that adaptation to society at best helps a man "to live with his illness rather than cure it," particu-

---

1. Reza Arasteh, *Final Integration in the Adult Personality* (Leiden, E. J. Brill, 1965).

larly if the general atmosphere of the society is unhealthy because of its over-emphasis on cerebral, competitive, acquisitive forms of ego-affirmation. Such an atmosphere may favor an apparently very active and productive mode of life but in reality it stifles true growth, leaves people lost, alienated, frustrated, and bored without any way of knowing what is wrong with them. In fact, in many cases, psychoanalysis has become a technique for making people conform to a society that prevents them from growing and developing as they should. Quoting E. Knight's book *The Objective Society*, Arasteh says:

> The Western individual, while opposing the integration of the Russian and Chinese models, not only accepts the herd values of his society but he has invented psychoanalysis to prevent him from straying from them. ... The stresses that modern life often produce in sensitive and intelligent people are no longer considered to call for a change in society; it is the individual who is wrong and he consequently becomes a neurotic, not a revolutionary. No more remarkable device than psychoanalysis has ever been devised by a society for preventing its superior citizens from giving it pain.

This interesting passage, quoted out of context, might give undue comfort to those who assume that, because they enjoy their masochism, they are superior. Nevertheless it does show to what extent psychotherapy and other techniques have been frankly drafted into the service of a massive, affluent organization that is dedicated to "freedom" and yet tolerates less and less dissent. The masochism, the anxiety, the alienation which are almost universal in such a society are forms of organized evasion. The energies that might otherwise go into productive or even revolutionary change are driven into stagnant backwaters of frustration and self-pity. People are not only made ill, but they prefer to be ill rather than face the risk of real dissent. (Note the important distinction between real and pseudo-dissent, the latter being merely a token and a symbol expressing and justifying an underlying neurosis.) We know well enough that this pattern, so familiar in "the world," is even more familiar in "the cloister."

Nevertheless there is an important distinction between mere neurotic anxiety which comes from a commitment to defeat and existential anxiety which is the healthy pain caused by the blocking of vital energies that still remain available for radical change. This is one of the main points made by Dr. Arasteh's book: the importance of existential anxiety seen not as a symptom of something wrong, but as a summons to growth and to painful development.

Carefully distinguishing existential anxiety from the petulant self-defeating sorrows of the neurotic, Dr. Arasteh shows how this anxiety is a sign of health and generates the necessary strength for psychic rebirth into a new transcultural identity. This new being is entirely personal, original, creative, unique, and it transcends the limits imposed by social convention and prejudice. Birth on this higher level is an imperative necessity for man.

The infant who lives immersed in a symbiotic relationship with the rest of nature—immersed, that is, in his own narcissism—must be "born" out of this sensual self-centeredness and acquire an identity as a responsible member of society. Ordinary psychotherapy is fully aware of this. But once one has grown up, acquired an education, and assumed a useful role as a worker and provider, there is still another birth to be undergone. Dr. Arasteh studies this birth to final integration in three exceptional individuals: Rumi, the Persian mystic and poet; Goethe; and a young modern Turk who was one of Arasteh's patients.

In the past, final integration was generally a matter only for unusually gifted people. We shall return to this point later. Even today, though the need for final integration makes itself more and more widely felt, the majority not only do not try to attain it, but society, as we have seen, provides them with ways to evade the summons. Clearly, in many cases, that summons takes the form of a monastic, religious, or priestly vocation. Clearly, too, there are many who leave the monastery because they feel that the way the monastic life is structured, or the way they themselves are fitted into the structure, makes a genuine response to the summons impossible.

All of us who have had to work through vocation problems with professed monks can, on reflection, easily distinguish obvious neurotics from men whose monastic crisis has taken the form of existential anxiety: this is a crisis of authentic growth which cannot be resolved in the situation in which they find themselves, and the situation cannot be changed. (Very often, in similar situations, it is the mildly neurotic who manage to stay and make some sort of compromise adjustment, nestling fearfully in the protection of the monastery with the obscure sense that further painful growth will not be demanded!)

Since his investigation is purely psychological, not theological, the question of "sanctity" or holiness does not really arise from Dr. Arasteh. But let us make clear that ordinarily a full spiritual development and a supernatural, even charismatic, maturity, evidenced in the "saint," normally includes the idea of complete psychological integration. Doubtless many saints have been neurotics, but they have used their neurosis in the interests of growth instead of capitulating and succumbing to its dubious comforts.

Final integration is a state of transcultural maturity far beyond mere social adjustment, which always implies partiality and compromise. The man who is "fully born" has an entirely "inner experience of life." He apprehends his life fully and wholly from an inner ground that is at once more universal than the empirical ego and yet entirely his own. He is in a certain sense "cosmic" and "universal man." He has attained a deeper, fuller identity than that of his limited ego-self which is only a fragment of his being. He is in a certain sense identified with everybody: or in the familiar language of the New Testament (which Arasteh evidently has not studied) he is "all things to all men." He is able to experience their joys and sufferings as his own, without however becoming dominated by them. He has attained to a deep inner freedom—the Freedom of the Spirit we read of in the New Testament. He is guided not just by will and reason, but by "spontaneous behavior subject to dynamic insight." Now, this calls to mind the theology of St. Thomas on the Gifts of the Holy Spirit which move a man to act "in a superhuman mode." Though Dr. Arasteh takes no account of specifically supernatural agencies, it is clear that such considerations might become relevant here. But of course they cannot be investigated by experimental science.

Again, the state of insight which is final integration implies an openness, an "emptiness," a "poverty" similar to those described in such detail not only by the Rhenish mystics, by St. John of the Cross, by the early Franciscans, but also by the Sufis, the early Taoist masters, and Zen Buddhists. Final integration implies the void, poverty, and nonaction which leave one entirely docile to the "Spirit" and hence a potential instrument for unusual creativity.

The man who has attained final integration is no longer limited by the culture in which he has grown up. "He has embraced *all of life*. . . . He has experienced qualities of every type of life": ordinary human existence, intellectual life, artistic creation, human love, religious life. He passes beyond all these limiting forms, while retaining all that is best and most universal in them, "finally giving birth to a fully comprehensive self." He accepts not only his own community, his own society, his own friends, his own culture, but all mankind. He does not remain bound to one limited set of values in such a way that he opposes them aggressively or defensively to others. He is fully "Catholic" in the best sense of the word. He has a unified vision and experience of the one truth shining out in all its various manifestations, some clearer than others, some more definite and more certain than others. He does not set these partial views up in opposition to each other, but unifies them in a dialectic or an insight of complementarity. With this view of life he is able to bring perspective, liberty, and spontaneity into the lives of others. The finally integrated man is a peacemaker, and that is why there is such a desperate need for our leaders to become such men of insight.

It will be seen at once that this kind of maturity is exactly what the monastic life should produce. The monastic ideal is precisely this sort of freedom in the spirit, this liberation from the limits of all that is merely partial and fragmentary in a given culture. Monasticism calls for a breadth and universality of vision that sees everything in the light of the One Truth as St. Benedict beheld all creation embraced "in one ray of the sun." This too is suggested at the end of Chapter 7 of the Rule where St. Benedict speaks of the new identity, the new mode of being of the monk who no longer practices the various degrees of humility with concentrated and studied effort, but with dynamic spontaneity "in the Spirit." It is suggested also in the "Degrees of Truth" and the "Degrees of Love" in St. Bernard's tracts on humility and on the love of God.

Unfortunately, we can see at once that if too many people developed in this way, if entire communities were all at once to reach final integration, the effect on the community structure itself might be revolutionary. Hence, in fact, our community life is unconsciously organized to make sure that any such development will be subject to human control. We will not let the Holy Spirit get out of hand! And yet with all its shortcomings and deficiencies, the monastic life is charismatic and the Spirit does work in our midst. But in monastic communities as well as in the Church at large we are conscious of the obscure and difficult struggle between charism and institution, in which the overwhelming need to channel and control the energies of the Spirit (and of course to distinguish them clearly from other more destructive energies) has led to a kind of neutralization of Spirit by organization. This institutional strait-jacketing does not prevent individuals from breaking through in their own way and achieving an integration that is perhaps warped and singular but nevertheless authentic (sometimes in amusing ways). But the community itself cannot be truly charismatic, except in a very subdued and harmless way. The penalty paid for this is a prevalence of neurosis, of masochism, of obsessions and compulsions, of fanaticism, intolerance, narrow-mindedness, and various petty forms of destructive cruelty which have proved so ruinous in the past. The present changes and relaxations have been first-aid measures to relieve these tensions at any price: but merely opening the windows is not enough. We must still be ready to face anxieties, and realize the difference between those that are fruitless and those that offer a promise of fruitful development. Sometimes the latter are even more painful and seemingly more dangerous than the former. After all, the rebirth which precedes final integration involves a crisis which is extremely severe—something like the Dark Night described by St. John of the Cross. And it is evident that anyone who chanced to fall into the Dark Night of the Soul today would (if discovered) soon find himself getting shock treatments, which would effectively take care of any further disturbing developments!

Dr. Arasteh describes the breakthrough into final integration, in the language of Sufism. The consecrated term in Sufism is *Fana*, annihilation or disintegration, a loss of self, a real spiritual death. But mere annihilation and death are not enough: they must be followed by reintegration and new life on a totally different level. This reintegration is what the Sufis call *Baqa*. The process of disintegration and reintegration is one that involves a terrible interior solitude and an "existential moratorium," a crisis and an anguish which cannot be analyzed or intellectualized. It also requires a solitary fortitude far beyond the ordinary, "an act of courage related to the root of all existence." It would be utterly futile to try to "cure" this anguish by bringing the "patient" as quickly and as completely as possible into the warm bosom of togetherness. Jung, with whom Arasteh has much in common, says this:

> [The development of the person to full ripeness] is at once a charisma and a curse because its first fruit is the conscious and unavoidable segregation of the individual from the undifferentiated and unconscious herd. This means isolation, and there is no more comforting word for it. Neither family nor society nor position can save him from the fate, nor yet the most successful adaptation to his environment. . . . [quoted by Arasteh]

Seen from the viewpoint of monastic tradition, the pattern of disintegration, existential moratorium, and reintegration on a higher, universal level is precisely what the monastic life is meant to provide. In the strictly limited, authoritarian, caste societies of medieval Europe, of India, of China, of Japan, the individual lived within extreme restriction in a framework that denied him social mobility. But the unusual person, from any caste, could become a monk. If he were able to live as an authentic beggar and pilgrim, accept the sacrifices, the insecurities, the risks, the challenges of the solitary adventure, he was freed from social limitations. He was on his own, on the road, in the jungle or in the desert, and he was entitled to develop in his own way, indeed to devote himself with passionate dedication to a freedom even from the limits of his contingency as a creature: he could get lost in the light of eternity, provided he found the way!

In the modern world, things have somehow become reversed. We live in an extremely mobile society in which, though we may not be nearly as free as we think we are, limits are still very flexible and sometimes do not exist at all. To enter a monastery is to enter into the most restricted form of life there is. This restriction has a purpose: it is imposed in order to liberate us from attachments and from self-will. But the big question is: Does it? Yes and no.

The ascesis of communal service and obedience cannot be dismissed as totally irrelevant, antiquated, repressive, and sterile. It is necessary and salutary for people who have had little or no discipline at all. But on the other hand it does definitely operate in such a way that while it initiates a certain growth, it goes only so far. It frustrates and stifles growth beyond a median level. It makes no provision for anything but formal adaptation to a rather narrow and limited communal pattern. Within that pattern it tolerates "safe," moderate growth and blesses lack of growth. In fact, it is in practice more tolerant of those who do not grow.

The crisis, the challenge, and the demands that Arasteh describes in terms of final integration would seldom be really acceptable in a monastery. They would be too disturbing, too exceptional, too "irregular." They would open up possibilities that would be regarded as altogether too hazardous. The result is that for many authentic vocations today the monastery has become merely a way station. To stay in the cloister for life would be to renounce their full development. And yet there is no guarantee that by leaving it they will develop any better.

Dr. Arasteh has nothing direct to say about the monastic life, but obviously those who have sufficient background and understanding will be able to apply his principles very fruitfully to our general predicament today. He will help us recover some sense of the real aim of that monastic *conversatio* which we have not only mentally approved but actually vowed. We have dedicated ourselves to rebirth, to growth, to final maturity, and integration. Monastic renewal means a reshaping of structures so that they will not only permit such growth but favor and encourage it in everyone.

However, as Christian monks, we cannot properly understand the full meaning of "final integration" if we see it only in the terms of psychology. For a Christian, a transcultural integration is eschatological. The rebirth of man and of society on a transcultural level is a rebirth into the transformed and redeemed time, the time of the Kingdom, the time of the Spirit, the time of "the end." It means a disintegration of the social and cultural self, the product of merely human history, and the reintegration of that self in Christ, in salvation history, in the mystery of redemption, in the Pentecostal "new creation." But this means entering into the full mystery of the eschatological Church.

Now, as Dr. Arasteh points out, whereas final psychological integration was, in the past, the privilege of a few, it is now becoming a need and aspiration of mankind as a whole. The whole world is in an existential crisis to which there are various reactions, some of them negative, tragic, destructive, demonic, others proffering a human hope which is yet not fully clear.

The destructive and tragic solutions are not solutions at all: they simply marshal the immense resources of military, economic, and political power to block real development and to maintain established patterns—in the interests of those who know best how to profit from them, and at the expense of everybody else.

The humanly optimistic answers foresee radical changes of a purely secular sort which will initiate a kind of hippie kingdom of love in a cybernated and peace-loving mega-city (presumably with free LSD for everybody). Many Christians feel that the Spirit is really summoning us to renounce our sense of spiritual privilege and enter into a fully turned-on solidarity with these secular hopes. Others, of course, and perhaps the majority, have lined up on the side of the armies and the "powers" under the mistaken idea that Christ is fully identified with the capitalist Western establishment which still refers to itself (when convenient) as "Christian."

At this point, the best one can do is hazard a personal guess that neither of these solutions is truly Christian, and neither offers a hope of final, eschatological integration to the individual Christian, to the Church, or to the monastic community. Both of these are reducible to identification with one form or other of culture, one form or other of "given" society. They are historical decisions that are merely historical and not eschatological. (Though of course they may contribute in a disastrous way to the ironies of eschatological judgment upon the organizational Church.)

Where are we to look for the true solutions? Precisely from the Spirit who will speak clearly at the right time through a renewed ecclesiastical and monastic community. The path to final integration for the individual, and for the community, lies, in any case, beyond the dictates and programs of any culture ("Christian culture" included).

Appendix

Merton's Essays: A Chronology

The following list of all of Thomas Merton's essays (including review essays but not simple book reviews) is in chronological order of publication, with bibliographical information on initial journal appearance and subsequent inclusion (if any) in book form (abbreviations are identified in the bibliography that follows this list). If an essay has variant titles, the primary title is that used in the final book publication, and any others are given in brackets. For posthumously published material, dates of composition (if available) are provided. Essays included in this volume are printed in bold type. (Because the essays are printed in order of composition, in some cases this will differ from the order of publication as found in this list.)

1938

"Huxley and the Ethics of Peace"
  Columbia Review 19 (March 1938), 13-18; *LE* 457-61

1939

"The Art of Richard Hughes"
  Columbia Review 21 (Nov. 1939), 13-18; *LE* 483-87

1940

"Huxley's Pantheon"
  Catholic World 152 (Nov. 1940), 206-9; *LE* 490-94

1947

"Poetry and the Contemplative Life"
  Commonweal 46 (4 July 1947), 280-86; *FA* 93-111
"The Trappists Go to Utah"
  Commonweal 46 (29 Aug. 1947), 470-73
"Death of a Trappist"
  Integrity 2 (Nov. 1947), 3-8
"Active and Contemplative Orders"
  Commonweal 47 (5 Dec. 1947), 192-96; *SSM* 414-19

"A Christmas Devotion"
   Commonweal 47 (26 Dec. 1947), 270-72

1948

"The Transforming Union in St. Bernard and St. John of the Cross"
   Collectanea OCR 9.2 (1948), 107-17; 9.3 (1948),
   210-23; 10.1 (1949), 41-52; 10.3 (1949), 353-61;
   11.1 (1950), 25-38; *TMSB* 159-226
"A Trappist Speaks on People, Priests and Prayer"
   Messenger of the Sacred Heart 83 (April 1948), 51-61, 89-90
"Contemplation in a Rocking Chair"
   Integrity 2 (August 1948), 15-23

1949

"The Pope of the Virgin Mary"
   Marian Literary Studies 62 (April 1949), 1-15
"The Contemplative Life: Its Meaning and Necessity"
   Dublin Review 223 (Winter 1949), 26-35
"Is Mysticism Normal?"
   Commonweal 51 (4 Nov. 1949), 94-98

1950

"The Primacy of Contemplation"
   Cross and Crown 2.2 (March 1950), 3-16
"Christian Self-Denial" ["Self-Denial and the Christian"]
   Commonweal 51 (31 March 1950), 649-53; *SC* 125-43
"The White Pebble"
   Sign 29 (July 1950), 26-28, 69; *Where I Found Christ* (1950), 235-50

1952

"Christ Suffers Again"
   Action Now! 5 (March 1952), 13
"St. John of the Cross"
   Saints for Now, ed. Claire Booth Luce (1952), 250-60; *TMR* 306-14;
   rev. ed. 285-94

1953

"St. Bernard: Monk and Apostle"
"Saint Bernard, moine et apôtre"
Preface to *Bernard de Clairvaux* (1953), vii-xv [in French]
   The Tablet 201 (23 May 1953), 438-39, 466-67; *DQ* 274-90
"Light in Darkness: The Ascetic Doctrine of St. John of the Cross"
   Introduction to *Counsels of Light and Love* (1953), 9-20; *DQ* 208-17
"The Sacrament of Advent in the Spirituality of St. Bernard"
   Dieu Vivant 23 (1953), 23-43 [in French]; *SC* 61-87

"Action and Contemplation in St. Bernard"
Collectanea OCR 15.1 (Jan. 1953), 26-31; 15.2
(July 1953), 203-61; 16.2 (April 1954), 105-21; *TMSB* 23-104
"St. Bernard"
Jubilee 1.4 (Aug. 1953), 32-37; Foreword to
St. Bernard of Clairvaux, Selected Letters (1958), v-viii

1955

"A Renaissance Hermit: Blessed Paul Giustiniani"
Preface to Jean Leclercq, *Seul avec Dieu* (1955),
7-18; *Alone with God* (1961), xiii-xxvii; *DQ* 165-76
"In Silentio"
Silence dans le Ciel (1955), 12-18;
Silence in Heaven (1956), 17-30; *SC* 204-15
"Notes for a Philosophy of Solitude"
["Dans le Désert de Dieu"]
Témoignages 48 (March 1955), 132-36; *DQ* 177-207
"The Christmas Sermons of Blessed Guerric of Igny"
Collectanea OCR 17.4 (Oct.-Dec. 1955), 229-44; *CSBGI* 1-25

1956

"Two Meditations for Our Members: The Priest in Union with Mary Immaculate"
Convivium 1 (1956), 27-37
"Notes on Sacred and Profane Art"
Jubilee 4.7 (Nov. 1956), 25-32
"Time and the Liturgy"
Worship 31 (Dec. 1956), 2-10; *SC* 45-60

1957

"The Feast of Freedom: Monastic Formation according to Adam of Perseigne"
["Christian Freedom and Monastic Formation"]
"La Formation Monastique selon Adam de Perseigne," *Collectanea*
OCR 19 (1957), 1-17; *American Benedictine Review* 13 (Sept.
1962), 289-313; Introduction to *Letters of Adam of Perseigne* (1976), 3-48
"The Monk and Sacred Art"
Sponsa Regis 28 (May 1957), 231-34

1958

"Prometheus: A Meditation"
King Library Press (1958); *BT* 11-23; *RU* 79-88
"Letter to an Innocent Bystander"
Informations Catholiques Internationales 77
(Aug. 1958), 29-31 [in French]; *BT* 51-64; *RU* 53-62
"Poetry and Contemplation: A Reappraisal"
Commonweal 69 (24 Oct. 1958), 87-92; *SP* 107-35; *LE* 338-54

1959

"Ash Wednesday"
Worship 33 (Feb. 1959), 165-70; *SC* 113-24

"Easter: The New Life"
Worship 33 (April 1959), 276-84; *SC* 144-57

"The Meaning and Purpose of Spiritual Direction"
Sponsa Regis 30 (June 1959), 249-54; *SDM* 3-12

"Christianity and Totalitarianism" ["Christianity and Mass Movements"]
Cross Currents 30 (Summer 1959), 201-10; *DQ* 127-48

"Manifestation of Conscience and Spiritual Direction"
Sponsa Regis 30 (July 1959), 277-82; *SDM* 23-36

"The Pasternak Affair II: The People with Watch-Chains"
["Boris Pasternak and the People with Watch Chains"]
Jubilee 7.3 (July 1959), 17-31; *DQ* 7-24

"Mount Athos"
Jubilee 7.4 (Aug. 1959), 8-16; *DQ* 68-82

"The Pasternak Affair III: Its Spiritual Dimension"
["The Pasternak Affair in Perspective"]
Thought 34 (Winter 1959-60), 485-517; *DQ* 25-67

"Advent: Hope or Delusion" ["The Advent Mystery"]
Worship 33 (Dec. 1959), 17-25; *SC* 88-100

"My Visits to the Secular Bookhouse"
Staff Log [Louisville Public Library] 2 (Dec. 1959), 1-4

"The Nativity Kerygma"
Worship 34 (Dec. 1959), 2-9; *SC* 101-12

"Art and Worship"
Sponsa Regis 31 (Dec. 1959), 114-17

1960

"Sacred Art and the Spiritual Life"
Sponsa Regis 31 (Jan. 1960), 133-40; *DQ* 151-64

"The Spirituality of Sinai: St. John of the Ladder" ["The Ladder of Divine Ascent"]
Jubilee 7.10 (Feb. 1960), 37-40; *DQ* 83-93

"What Is Meditation?"
Sponsa Regis 31 (Feb. 1960), 80-87; *SDM* 43-48

"Meditation, Action and Union"
Sponsa Regis 31 (March 1960), 191-98; *SDM* 56-67

"How to Meditate" ["Presuppositions to Meditation"]
Sponsa Regis 31 (April 1960), 231-40; *SDM* 68-83

"Absurdity in Sacred Decoration"
Worship 34 (April 1960), 248-55; *DQ* 264-73

"The Study of Meditation"
Sponsa Regis 31 (May 1960), 268-74; *SDM* 84-89

"Temperament and Meditation"
Sponsa Regis 31 (June 1960), 296-99; *SDM* 94-97

"The Solitary Life"
  Louisville: Stamperia del Santuccio, 1960; *MJ* 151-62
"St. Peter Damian and the Medieval Monk"
  Jubilee 8.4 (Aug. 1960), 39-44
"The Power and Meaning of Love" ["Love and Person / Love and Maturity"]
  Sponsa Regis 32 (Sept. 1960), 6-11; (Oct. 1960), 44-53; *DQ* 97-126
"Theology of Creativity" ["The Catholic and Creativity:
Theology of Creativity"]
  American Benedictine Review 11 (Sept.-Dec. 1960), 197-213; *LE* 355-70
"Herakleitos the Obscure" ["Herakleitos: A Study"]
  Jubilee 8.5 (Sept. 1960), 24-31; *BT* 75-84; *TMR* 258-71
"A Signed Confession of Crimes Against the State"
  Carleton Miscellany 1 (Fall 1960), 21-23; *BT* 65-71
"Let the Poor Man Speak"
  Jubilee 8.6 (Oct. 1960), 18-21
"Liturgy and Spiritual Personalism"
  Worship 34 (Oct. 1960), 494-507; *SC* 1-27
"The Pasternak Affair I: In Memoriam"; *DQ* 3-7
"The Primitive Carmelite Ideal"; *DQ* 218-63

1961

"The Recovery of Paradise: Wisdom in Emptiness, A Dialogue:
D. T. Suzuki and Thomas Merton"
  New Directions in Prose and Poetry 17 (1961), 65-101; *ZBA* 99-138
"Classic Chinese Thought"
  Jubilee 8.9 (Jan. 1961), 26-32; *MZM* 65-91
"The English Mystics"
  Collectanea Cisterciensia 23 (1961), 362-67
  Jubilee 9.5 (Sept. 1961), 36-40; *MZM* 128-53
"The Shelter Ethic" ["The Machine Gun in the Fallout Shelter"]
  The Catholic Worker 28 (Nov. 1961), 1, 5; *NA* 103-6; *PP* 20-26
"Atlas and the Fatman"; *BT* 24-48; *RU* 91-107

1962

"Letter to Pablo Antonio Cuadra concerning Giants"
  Blackfriars 43 (Feb. 1962), 69-81; *ESF* 70-89; *CP* 372-81
"Itinerary to Christ: The Art of William Congdon"
  Liturgical Arts 30 (Feb. 1962), 70
"A Martyr for Peace and Unity" ["Testament to Peace"]
  Jubilee 9.11 (March 1962), 22-25; *NA* 139-43; *PP* 53-55
"Nuclear War and Christian Responsibility"
  Commonweal 75 (9 Feb. 1962), 509-13; *PP* 37-47
"Red or Dead: The Anatomy of a Cliché"
  Fellowship 28 (March 1962), 21-23; *PP* 48-52

"Christian Ethics and Nuclear War" ["Christian Morality and Nuclear War"]
  Catholic Worker 28 (March-April 1962), 2; *NA* 82-87; *PP* 56-64
"We Have to Make Ourselves Heard"
  Catholic Worker 28 (May 1962), 4-6; (June 1962), 4-5
"Religion and the Bomb"
  Jubilee 10.1 (May 1962), 7-13; *PP* 65-79
"Love and Tao" [**Christian Culture Needs Oriental Wisdom** /
Two Chinese Classics"]
  Catholic World 195 (May 1962), 72-79; *TMR* 295-303
  Chinese Culture Quarterly 4 (June 1962), 34-41; *MZM* 69-80
"Christian Action in World Crisis"
  Blackfriars 43 (June 1962), 256-68; *NA* 219-26; *PP* 80-91
"The Jesuits in China"
  Jubilee 10.5 (Sept. 1962), 35-38; *MZM* 81-90
"Breakthrough to Peace: Introduction"
  Breakthrough to Peace 7-14; *NA* 76-81; *PP* 92-98
"Peace: A Religious Responsibility"
  Breakthrough to Peace 88-116; *NA* 107-28; *PP* 99-123
J. F. Powers—*Morte D'Urban*: Two Celebrations"
  Worship 36 (Nov. 1962), 645-50; *LE* 147-51

1963

"A Note on the Psychological Causes of War by Erich Fromm"
  War Within Man (1963), 44-50; *FV* 111-18
"Church and Bishop in St. Ignatius of Antioch"
  Worship 37 (Jan. 1963), 110-20; *SC* 28-44
"The Christian Failure" ["Passivity and Abuse of Authority"]
  Catholic Worker 29 (Jan. 1963), 5-8; *NA* 129-33; *PP* 56-64
"Virginity and Humanism in the Western Fathers"
  Sponsa Regis 34 (Jan. 1963), 131-44; *MZM* 113-27
"The Prison Meditations of Fr. Delp" ["A Martyr to the Nazis /
The Church in a Disillusioned World"]
  Jubilee 10.11 (March 1963), 32-35; *FV* 47-68
"Mystics and Zen Masters" ["Monastic Christianity Encounters
the Spirit of Zen" / "The Zen Revival"]
  Pilot (13 April 1963), 10
  Continuum 1 (Winter 1964), 523-28
  Chinese Culture Quarterly 6 (1965), 1-18; *MZM* 3-44
"Zen: Sense and Sensibility"
  America 108 (25 May 1963), 752-54
"On Writing"
  Catholic Worker 30 (July-Aug. 1963), 6
"Danish Nonviolent Resistance to Hitler"
  Catholic Worker 30 (July-Aug. 1963), 1, 3; *NA* 165-67; *PP* 150-53
"The Legend of Tucker Caliban" ["The Negro Revolt"]
  Jubilee 11.5 (Sept. 1963), 39-43; *SD* 72-90

"Self-Knowledge in Gertrude More and Augustine Baker" ["Examination of Conscience and *Conversatio Morum*"]
   Collectanea Cisterciensia 25 (1963), 355-69; *MZM* 154-77
"A Homily on Light and the Virgin Mary"
   Worship 37 (Oct. 1963), 572-80; *SC* 158-70
"Letters to a White Liberal" ["The Black Revolution"]
   New Blackfriars 2 (Nov. 1963), 467-77; (Dec. 1963), 503-16; *SD* 3-71
"Advent: Hope or Delusion" ["The Advent Mystery"]
   Worship 37 (Dec. 1963), 17-25; *SC* 88-100

1964

"Martin's Predicament; or Atlas Watches Every Evening"
   New Directions in Prose and Poetry 18 (1964), 10-15; *RU* 111-21
"A Devout Meditation in Memory of Adolf Eichmann"
   New Directions in Prose and Poetry 18 (1964), 16-18; *RU* 45-49
"Pleasant Hill, A Shaker Village in Kentucky" ["The Shakers"]
   Jubilee 11.9 (Jan. 1964), 36-41; *MZM* 193-202
"The Name of the Lord"
   Worship 38 (Feb. 1964), 142-51; *SC* 182-203
"Protestant Monasticism"
   Critic 22 (June/July 1964), 54-56; *MZM* 188-92
"The Council and Sacred Art"
   Continuum 2 (Spring 1964), 136-38; (Summer 1964), 292-94
"The Christian in the Diaspora II" ["The Monk in the Diaspora"]
   Commonweal 79 (20 March 1964), 741-45; *SD* 199-213
"Message to Poets"
   Americas 16 (April 1964), 29; *RU* 155-61
"To Each His Darkness: Notes on a Novel of Julien Green"
   Charlatan 1 (Spring 1964), n.p.; *RU* 27-33
"Honest to God" ["The Honest to God Debate: Demythologizing Bishop Robinson"]
   Commonweal 80 (21 Aug. 1964), 573-78; *FV* 225-38
"Seven Qualities of the Sacred"
   Good Work 27 (Winter 1964), 15-20
"The Humanity of Christ in Monastic Prayer"
   Monastic Studies 2 (Oct. 1964), 1-37; *MJ* 87-106
"Flannery O'Connor—A Prose Elegy"
   Jubilee 12.7 (Nov. 1964), 49-53; *RU* 37-42
"From Pilgrimage to Crusade"
   Cithara 4 (Nov. 1964), 3-21; *MZM* 91-112
"Is Man a Gorilla with a Gun?" ["Man is a Gorilla with a Gun: Reflections on an American Best-Seller"]
   Quest (Dec. 1964), 67-70; *FV* 96-105
"A Tribute to Gandhi" ["Gandhi, the Gentle Revolutionary"]
   Ramparts 3 (Dec. 1964), 29-32; *SD* 221-34

"Liturgical Renewal: The Open Approach"
   Critic 33 (Dec. 1964), 10-15; *SC* 231-48

1965
"The Good Samaritan" [1961]; *SC* 171-82
"Community of Pardon" [1963]; *SC* 216-30
"Answers on Art and Freedom"
   Lugano Review 1 (1965), 43-45; *RU* 165-75
"Gandhi and the One-Eyed Giant"
   Jubilee 12.9 (Jan. 1965), 12-17; *GNV* 1-22
"The Case for a Renewal of Eremitism in the Monastic State"
   Collectanea Cisterciensia 27 (1965), 121-49; *CWA* 294-327
"Religion and Race in the United States"
   New Blackfriars 46 (Jan. 1965), 218-25; *FV* 130-44
"The Unbelief of Believers" ["Review of *Varieties of Unbelief*
by Martin Marty"]
   Commonweal 81 (8 Jan. 1965), 90-91; *FV* 199-204
"An Enemy of the State"
   Peace News 5 (29 Jan. 1965), 1; *FV* 69-75
"The Reply of *Pacem in Terris*" ["The Challenge of Responsibility"]
   Saturday Review 48 (13 Feb. 1965), 28-30; *SD* 163-83
"The Function of a Monastic Review"
   Collectanea Cisterciensia 27.1 (1965), 9-13
"A Priest and His Mission"
   Continuum 3 (Spring 1965), 126-30
"The Climate of Mercy"
   Cord 15 (April 1965), 89-96; *LL* 203-19
"Contemplation and Dialogue" ["Contemplation and Ecumenism"]
   Season 3 (Fall 1965), 133-42; *MZM* 203-14
"Pacifism and Resistance in Simone Weil" ["The Answer of Minerva"]
   Peace News (April 1965), 5, 8; *FV* 76-84
"Rain and the Rhinoceros"
   Holiday 37 (May 1965), 8, 10, 12, 15-16; *RU* 9-23
"Reflections on Some Recent Studies of St. Anselm"
   Monastic Studies 3 (1965), 221-34
"Schema XIII: An Open Letter to the American Hierarchy"
   Unity 2 (July-Aug. 1965), 3-4; *WF* 88-94
"The Brothers and Aggiornamento"
   Brothers Newsletter 7 (Summer 1965), 8-11
"The Place of Obedience [in Monastic Renewal]"
   American Benedictine Review 16 (Sept. 1965), 359-68; *CWA* 117-28
"The Poorer Means"
   Cord 15 (Sept. 1965), 243-47
"St. Maximus the Confessor on Non-Violence"
   Catholic Worker 32.1 (Sept. 1965), 1-2; *NA* 172-77; *PP* 241-47

"The Contemplative Life in the Modern World"
  Mountain Path 2 (Oct. 1965), 223-27; *FV* 215-24
"The Council and Religious Life" ["The Council and Monasticism"]
  New Blackfriars 47 (Oct. 1965), 5-17
  The Impact of Vatican II, ed. Jude P. Dougherty (1966), 44-60
"The Other Side of Despair"
  Critic 24 (Oct.-Nov. 1965), 12-23; *MZM* 255-80
"St. Francis and Peace"
  St. Anthony Messenger 73 (Oct. 1965), 39
"The Good News of the Nativity"
  Bible Today 21 (Dec. 1965), 1367-75; *LL* 220-32
"The Time of the End Is the Time of No Room"
  Motive 26 (Dec. 1965), 4-9; *RU* 65-75
"The Christian in World Crisis"; *SD* 93-183
"The Christian in the Diaspora"; *SD* 184-220

1966

"Rubén Dario"
  Continuum 4 (Autumn 1966), 469-70; *LE* 305-306
Nonviolence and the Christian Conscience"
  Preface to Regamey, *Nonviolence and the Christian Conscience*
  (1966), 7-14; *FV* 30-39
"The Zen Koan"
  Lugano Review 1 (1966), 126-39; *MZM* 235-54
"The Church and the 'Godless World'"
  Redeeming the Time, 7-92
"Conversion of Life" ["*Conversatio Morum*"]
  Cistercian Studies 1 (1966), 130-44; *MJ* 107-20
"Events and Pseudo-Events: Letter to a Southern Churchman"
  Katallagete (Summer 1966), 10-17; *FV* 145-64
"Is the World a Problem?"
  Commonweal 84 (3 June 1966), 305-309; *CWA* 143-56
"St. Anselm and His Argument"
  American Benedictine Review 17 (June 1966), 238-62
"Nhat Hanh Is My Brother"
  Jubilee 14.4 (Aug. 1966), 11; *FV* 106-108
"Buddhism and the Modern World"
  Cross Currents 16 (Fall 1966), 495-99; *MZM* 281-88
"[Who Is It That Has a] Transcendent Experience"
  R. M. Bucke Society Newsletter-Review (Sept. 1966), 5-8; *ZBA* 71-78
"Love and Solitude"
  Critic 25 (Oct.-Nov. 1966), 13-17; *LL* 15-24
"Vocation and Modern Thought" ["Monastic Vocation and Modern Thought"]
  Monastic Studies 4 (Advent 1966), 17-54; *CWA* 26-55

"Symbolism: Communication or Communion?"
   Mountain Path 3 (Oct. 1966), 339-48; *LL* 54-79
"Apologies to an Unbeliever" ["How It Is: Apologies to an Unbeliever"]
   Harper's 233 (Nov. 1966), 36-39; *FV* 205-14
"[Albert] Camus and the Church"
   Catholic Worker 33 (Dec. 1966), 4-5, 8; *LE* 261-74
"Peace and Protest: A Statement"
   Continuum 3 (Winter 1966), 509-12; *FV* 40-46
"Orthodoxy and the World"
   Monastic Studies 4 (Advent 1966), 105-15
"Franciscan Eremitism"
   Cord 16 (Dec. 1966), 356-64; *CWA* 260-68
"Love and Need: Is Love a Package or a Message?" ["A Buyer's
Market for Love?"]
   Ave Maria 104 (24 Dec. 1966), 7-10, 27; *LL* 25-37
"A Christian Looks at Zen"
   Introduction to John Wu, *The Golden Age of Zen* (1966), 1-27; *ZBA* 33-58

1967

"Taking Sides on Vietnam"
   Authors Take Sides on Vietnam (1967), 51; *FV* 109-10
"Nishida: A Zen Philosopher"
   Collectanea Cisterciensia 29.1 (1967), 185-88; *ZBA* 67-70
"Russian Mystics"; *MZM* 178-87
"Blessed Are the Meek"
   Fellowship 33 (May 1967), 18-22; *FV* 14-29
"Monastic Attitudes: A Matter of Choice"
   Cistercian Studies 2 (1967), 3-14; *MJ* 121-32
"Wilderness and Paradise"
   Cistercian Studies 2 (1967), 83-89; *MJ* 144-50
"Louis Zukovsky: The Paradise Ear [Paradise Bugged]"
   Critic 25 (Feb.-March 1967), 69-71; *LE* 128-33
"Christian Solitude[: Notes on an Experiment]"
   Current 7 (Feb. 1967), 14-28; *CWA* 237-51
"Ishi: A Meditation"
   Catholic Worker 33 (March 1967), 5-6; *IMM* 25-32
"The New Consciousness" ["The Self of Modern Man
in the New Christian Consciousness"]
   Theoria to Theory 3 (Jan. 1967), 5-8; *ZBA* 15-32
"Faulkner and his Critics" ["The Sounds Are Furious"]
   Critic 25 (April-May 1967), 76-80; *LE* 117-23
"The True Legendary Sound: The Poetry and Criticism of Edwin Muir"
   Sewanee Review 75 (Spring 1967), 307-24; *LE* 29-36

"Prophetic Ambiguities: Milton and Camus" ["Can We
Survive Nihilism? Satan, Milton and Camus"]
　　Saturday Review 50 (15 April 1967), 16-19; *LE* 252-60
"The Meaning of Malcolm X"
　　Continuum 5 (Summer 1967), 432-35; *FV* 182-88
"The Angel and the Machine"
　　Season 5 (Summer 1967), 5-11
"Christian Humanism in the Nuclear Era" ["The Church in World Crisis"]
　　Redeeming the Time 64-82; *LL* 151-70
　　Katallagete (Summer 1967), 30-36
"The Death of a Holy Terror: The Strange Story of Frère Pascal"
　　Jubilee 15.2 (June 1967), 35-38
"The Shoshoneans"
　　Catholic Worker 33 (June 1967), 5, 6; *IMM* 5-16
"Day of a Stranger"
　　Hudson Review 20 (Summer 1967), 211-18; *DS*
"Zen in Japanese Art"
　　Catholic Worker 33 (July-Aug. 1967), 8; *ZBA* 89-92
"Contemplatives and the Crisis of Faith"
　　L'Osservatore Romano (12 Oct. 1967) [French]; *MJ* 174-78
"The Cell" ["Solitude"]
　　Sobernost 5 (Summer 1967), 332-38; *CWA* 252-59
　　Spiritual Life 14 (Fall 1968), 171-78
"On Remembering Monsieur Delmas"
　　The Teacher, ed. Morris L. Ernst (1967), 45-53
"D. T. Suzuki: The Man and His Work"
　　Eastern Buddhist 2 (Aug. 1967), 3-9; *ZBA* 59-66
"The Hot Summer of Sixty-Seven"
　　Katallagete 1 (Winter 1967-68), 28-34; *FV* 165-81
"Rafael Alberti [and His Angels]"
　　Continuum (Spring 1967), 175-79; *LE* 313-17
"The Death of God and the End of History"
　　Theoria to Theory (Oct. 1967), 3-16; *FV* 239-58
"Isaac of Stella: An Introduction to Selections from his *Sermons*"
　　Cistercian Studies 2 (1967), 243-51
"Openness and Cloister"
　　Cistercian Studies 2 (1967), 312-22; *CWA* 129-42
"Camus: Journals of the Plague Years"
　　Sewanee Review 75 (Autumn 1967), 717-30; *LE* 218-31
"Teilhard's Gamble: Betting on the Whole Human Species"
　　Commonweal 87 (27 Oct. 1967), 185-91; *LL* 185-91
"Auschwitz: A Family Camp"
　　Catholic Worker 33 (Nov. 1967), 4-5, 8; *NA* 150-59; *PP* 276-86
"Christian Humanism"
　　Spiritual Life 13 (Winter 1967), 219-30; *LL* 135-50

"'Godless Christianity'?"
  Katallagete (Winter 1967-68); *Redeeming the Time* 21-39; *FV* 259-87
"War and Vision: The Autobiography of a Crow Indian"
  Catholic Worker 23 (Dec. 1967), 4, 6; *IMM* 17-24
"Zen Buddhist Monasticism" [July 1965]; *MZM* 215-34
"Baptism in the Forest: Wisdom and Initiation in William Faulkner"
  Mansions of the Spirit, ed. George Panichas (1967), 19-44; *LE* 92-116
**"Terror and the Absurd: Violence and Nonviolence
in Albert Camus"**
  Gandhi Marg 42 (April 1967), 85-101; *LE* 232-51
"Nirvana"
  Foreword to Sally Donnelly, *Marcel and Buddha:
  A Metaphysics of Enlightenment*
  Journal of Religious Thought 24 (1967/1968), 51-57; *ZBA* 79-88

1968

"The Significance of the *Bhagavad Gita*"
  The Bhagavad Gita as It Is (1968), 18-22; *AJ* 348-53
"William Styron: Who is Nat Turner?"
  Katallagete (Spring 1968), 20-23; *LE* 152-58
"Notes for a Statement on Aid to Civilian War Victims in Vietnam"
  Fellowship 34 (Jan. 1968), 15, 29; *NA* 265-67
"The Cross-Fighters"
  Unicorn Journal 1 (1968), 26-40; *IMM* 35-52
"The Sacred City"
  Catholic Worker 34 (Jan. 1968), 4, 5, 6; *IMM* 53-71
"Focus on Religious Life"
  Focus: A Bulletin of the Sisters of Loretto 1 (19 Feb. 1968), 2
"The Spiritual Father in the Desert Tradition"
  Cistercian Studies 3 (1968), 3-23; *CWA* 269-93
"Dialogue and Renewal [in the Contemplative Life]"
  Spiritual Life 14 (Spring 1968), 41-52; *CWA* 83-97
"Vietnam: An Overwhelming Atrocity"
  Catholic Worker 34 (March 1968), 1, 6, 7; *FV* 87-95
"The Monk Today"
  Latitudes 2 (Spring 1968), 10-14; *CWA* 225-34
"Contemplation in a World of Action"
  BloomiNewman 2 (April 1968), 1-5; *CWA* 157-65
"Ecumenism and Renewal"
  Journal of Ecumenical Studies 5 (Spring 1968), 268-83; *CWA* 181-97
"The Historical Experience"
  Contemplative Review 1 (May 1968), 2-3
"The Study of Zen"
  Cimarron Review 4 (June 1968), 38-49; *ZBA* 1-14

"The Wild Places"
  Catholic Worker 34 (June 1968), 4, 6
  Center Magazine 1 (July 1968), 40-44; *PAJ* 95-107
"The Need for a New Education" ["Renewal in Monastic Education"]
  Cistercian Studies 3 (1968), 247-52; *CWA* 198-204
"A Footnote from *Ulysses*: Peace and Revolution"
  Peace 3 (Fall-Winter 1968), 4-10; *LE* 23-28
"Note on the New Church at Gethsemani"
  Liturgical Arts 36 (Aug. 1968), 100-101
"Three Saviors in Camus: Lucidity and the Absurd"
  Thought (Spring 1968), 5-23; *LE* 275-91
"Nonviolence Does Not . . . Cannot Mean Passivity" ["Note for *Ave Maria*"]
  Ave Maria 108 (7 Sept. 1968), 9-10; *NA* 231-33; *PP* 322-25
"Blake and the New Theology"
  Sewanee Review 76 (Autumn 1968), 673-82; *LE* 3-11
"*The Stranger*: Poverty of an Antihero"
  Unicorn Journal 1 (Fall 1968), 10-19; *LE* 292-302
"Final Integration: Toward a 'Monastic Therapy'"
  Monastic Studies 6 (1968), 87-99; *CWA* 205-17
"Toward a Theology of Resistance"; *FV* 3-13
"From Non-Violence to Black Power"; *FV* 121-29
"Violence and the Death of God: or God as Unknown Soldier"; *FV* 191-98
"Is Buddhism Life-Denying?"; *ZBA* 93-95

1969

"War and the Crisis of Language"
  The Critique of War, ed. Robert Ginsberg (1969),
  99-119; *NA* 234-47; *PP* 300-14
"A Letter on the Contemplative Life" ["As Man to Man"]
  [21 Aug. 1967]
  Cistercian Studies 4 (1969), 90-94; *MJ* 169-73
"Learning to Live"
  University on the Heights, ed. Wesley First (1969), 187-99; *LL* 3-14
"Seven Words [1966]"
"'Purity' / 'Death'"
  Prophetic Voices, ed. Ned O'Gorman (1969), 164-72, 230-38; *LL* 95-132
"Creative Silence"
  Baptist Student 48 (Feb. 1969), 18-22; *LL* 38-45
"Notes on the Future of Monasticism"
  L'Osservatore Romano [English ed.] 4.43 (23 Jan. 1969), 5; *CWA* 218-25
"The Japanese Tea Ceremony"
  Good Work 32 (Spring 1969), 6-7
"News of the Joyce Industry" [July 1968]
  Sewanee Review 77 (Summer 1969), 543-54; *LE* 12-22

"Roland Barthes—Writing as Temperature" [Sept. 1968]
  Sewanee Review 77 (Summer 1969), 535-42; *LE* 140-46
"The Street Is for Celebration"
  Mediator 20 (Summer 1969), 2-4; *LL* 46-53

1970

"The Contemplative and the Atheist"
  Schema XIII 1 (1970), 11-18; *CWA* 166-80
"Renewal and Discipline [in the Monastic Life]"
  Cistercian Studies 5 (1970), 3-18; *CWA* 98-116

1971

"Concerning the Collection in the Bellarmine College Library" [10 Nov. 1963]
  Merton Studies Center (1971), 13-17
"Peace: Christian Duties and Perspectives" [Oct. 1961]
  NA 12-19
"Target Equals City" [1962]
  NA 94-102; *PP* 27-36
"Christianity and Defense in the Nuclear Age" [1963]
  NA 88-93
"A Note on Civil Disobedience and Nonviolent Revolution"
  NA 227-30
"**[The Monastic Renewal:] Problems and Prospects**" [1967]; *CWA* 3-25
"The Identity Crisis [and Monastic Vocation]" [Oct. 1964]; *CWA* 56-82

1977

"Project for a Hermitage"; *MJ* 135-43
"Monastic Renewal: A Memorandum" [1964]; *MJ* 165-68

1978

"Pasternak's *Letters to Georgian Friends*" ["The Ascesis of Sacrifice . . ."]
  New Lazarus Review 1 (Spring 1978), 55-62; *LE* 84-91

1979

"The Universe as Epiphany" [1967]; *LL* 171-84
"Rebirth and the New Man in Christianity" [Oct. 1967]; *LL* 192-202

1981

"The Trial of Pope Pius XII: Rolf Hochhuth's *The Deputy*" [1963]; *LE* 162-67
"Why Alienation Is for Everybody" [1968]; *LE* 381-84

1988

"The Zen Insight of Shen Hui" [1968]
  Merton Annual 1 (1988), 3-15

1992

"The Neurotic Personality in the Monastic Life" [c. 1955]
  Merton Annual 4 (1992), 3-19

1995

"Vocations to the Lay Apostolate" [1941];
  Merton Annual 7 (1995), 6-13

1996

"A Very Early Essay" ["Oakham School 24 July 1931"]
  Merton Seasonal 21.3 (Fall 1996), 3-9

2009

"Your Will and Your Vocation" [Nov. 1955]
  Merton Seasonal 34.2 (Summer 2009), 3-11
"Christian Worship and Social Reform" [c. 1963]
  Merton Seasonal 34.4 (Winter 2009), 3-11

2011

"Monastic Vows: A Memorandum"
  Merton Seasonal 36.2 (Summer 2011), 3-5

2012

"Solitary Life in the Shadow of a Cistercian Monastery"
  Merton Seasonal 37.4 (Winter 2012), 308

Bibliography

BOOKS INCLUDING ESSAYS BY THOMAS MERTON

The Asian Journal, ed. Naomi Burton Stone, Brother Patrick Hart, and James Laughlin. New York: New Directions, 1973 [*AJ*].

The Behavior of Titans. New York: New Directions, 1961 [*BT*].

Breakthrough to Peace: Twelve Views on the Threat of Thermonuclear Extermination, ed. Thomas Merton. New York: New Directions, 1962 [*BP*].

The Christmas Sermons of Blessed Guerria of Igny. Trappist, KY: Abbey of Gethsemani, 1959 [*CSBGI*].

The Collected Poems of Thomas Merton. New York: New Directions, 1977 [*CP*].

Contemplation in a World of Action. Garden City, NY: Doubleday, 1971 [*CWA*].

Day of a Stranger. Salt Lake City: Gibbs M. Smith, 1981 [*DS*].

Disputed Questions. New York: Farrar, Straus & Cudahy, 1960 [*DQ*].

Emblems of a Season of Fury. New York: New Directions, 1963 [*ESF*].

Faith and Violence: Christian Teaching and Christian Practice. Notre Dame, IN: University of Notre Dame Press, 1968 [*FV*].

Figures for an Apocalypse. New York: New Directions, 1947 [*FA*].

Gandhi on Non-Violence: Selected Texts from Non-Violence in Peace and War, ed. Thomas Merton. New York: New Directions, 1964 [*GNV*].

Ishi Means Man. Greensboro, NC: Unicorn Press, 1976 [*IMM*].

The Literary Essays of Thomas Merton, ed. Patrick Hart, OCSO. New York: New Directions, 1981 [*LE*].

Loretto and Gethsemani. Trappist, KY: Abbey of Gethsemani, 1962 [*LG*].

Love and Living, ed. Naomi Burton Stone and Brother Patrick Hart. New York: Farrar, Straus, Giroux, 1979 [*LL*].

The Monastic Journey, ed. Brother Patrick Hart. Kansas City: Sheed, Andrews & McMeel, 1977 [*MJ*].

Mystics and Zen Masters. New York: Farrar, Straus & Giroux, 1967 [*MZM*].

The Nonviolent Alternative, ed. Gordon C. Zahn. New York: Farrar, Straus & Giroux, 1980 [*NA*].

Passion for Peace: The Social Essays, ed. William H. Shannon. New York: Crossroad, 1995 [*PP*].

Preview of the Asian Journey, ed. Walter H. Capps. New York: Crossroad, 1989 [*PAJ*].

Raids on the Unspeakable. New York: New Directions, 1966 [*RU*].

Seasons of Celebration. New York: Farrar, Straus & Giroux, 1965 [*SC*].

Seeds of Destruction. New York: Farrar, Straus & Giroux, 1964 [*SD*].

Selected Poems. New York: New Directions, 1959; enlarged ed. 1967 [*SP*].

The Seven Storey Mountain. New York: Harcourt, Brace, 1948 [*SSM*].

Spiritual Direction and Meditation. Collegeville, MN: Liturgical Press, 1960 [*SDM*].

Thomas Merton on St. Bernard. Kalamazoo, MI: Cistercian Publications, 1980 [*TMSB*].

A Thomas Merton Reader, ed. Thomas P. McDonnell. New York: Harcourt, Brace, 1962; rev. ed. Garden City, NY: Doubleday Image, 1974 [*TMR*].

Thomas Merton: Spiritual Master, ed. Lawrence S. Cunningham. New York: Paulist, 1992.

Zen and the Birds of Appetite. New York: New Directions, 1968 [*ZBA*].

OTHER MERTON BOOKS CITED

The Ascent to Truth. New York: Harcourt, Brace, 1951.

Cassian and the Fathers: Initiation into the Monastic Tradition, ed. Patrick F. O'Connell. Kalamazoo, MI: Cistercian Publications, 2005.

The Climate of Monastic Prayer. Washington, DC: Cistercian Publications, 1969.

Conjectures of a Guilty Bystander. Garden City, NY: Doubleday, 1966.

The Courage for Truth: Letters to Writers, ed. Christine M. Bochen. New York: Farrar, Straus, Giroux, 1993.

Dancing in the Water of Life: Seeking Peace in the Hermitage. Journals, vol. 5: 1963-1965, ed. Robert E. Daggy. San Francisco: HarperCollins, 1997.

Entering the Silence: Becoming a Monk and Writer. Journals, vol. 2: 1941-1952, ed. Jonathan Montaldo. San Francisco: HarperCollins, 1996.

The Hidden Ground of Love: Letters on Religious Experience and Social Concerns, ed. William H. Shannon. New York: Farrar, Straus, Giroux, 1985.

"Honorable Reader": Reflections on My Work, ed. Robert E. Daggy. New York: Crossroad, 1989.

The Inner Experience: Notes on Contemplation, ed. William H. Shannon. San Francisco: HarperCollins, 2003.

In the Dark before Dawn: New Selected Poems, ed. Lynn R. Szabo. New York: New Directions, 2005.

The Intimate Merton: His Life from His Journals, ed. Patrick Hart and Jonathan Montaldo. San Francisco: HarperCollins, 1999.

An Introduction to Christian Mysticism: Initiation into the Monastic Tradition 3, ed. Patrick F. O'Connell. Kalamazoo, MI: Cistercian Publications, 2008.

Learning to Love: Exploring Solitude and Freedom. Journals, vol. 6: 1966-1967, ed. Christine M. Bochen. San Francisco: HarperCollins, 1997.

A Life in Letters: The Essential Collection, ed. William H. Shannon and Christine M. Bochen. San Francisco: Harper One, 2008.

Monastic Observances: Initiation into the Monastic Tradition 5, ed. Patrick F. O'Connell. Collegeville, MN: Cistercian Publications, 2010.

The New Man. New York: Farrar, Straus and Cudahy, 1961.

New Seeds of Contemplation. New York: New Directions, 1961.

The Other Side of the Mountain: The End of the Journey. Journals, vol. 7: 1967-1968, ed. Patrick Hart. San Francisco: HarperCollins, 1998.

Peace in the Post-Christian Era, ed. Patricia A. Burton. Maryknoll, NY: Orbis, 2004.

Pre-Benedictine Monasticism: Initiation into the Monastic Tradition 2, ed. Patrick F. O'Connell. Kalamazoo, MI: Cistercian Publications, 2006.

The Road to Joy: Letters to New and Old Friends, ed. Robert E. Daggy. New York: Farrar, Straus, Giroux, 1989.

The School of Charity: Letters on Religious Renewal and Spiritual Direction, ed. Patrick Hart. New York: Farrar, Straus, Giroux, 1990.

A Search for Solitude: Pursuing the Monk's True Life. Journals, vol. 3: 1952-1960, ed. Lawrence S. Cunningham. San Francisco: HarperCollins, 1996.

Seeds of Contemplation. New York: New Directions, 1949.

The Sign of Jonas. New York: Harcourt, Brace, 1953.

The Solitary Life. Lexington, KY: Stamperia del Santuccio, 1960.

Turning Toward the World: The Pivotal Years. Journals, vol. 4: 1960-1963, ed. Victor A. Kramer. San Francisco: HarperCollins, 1996.

The Way of Chuang Tzu. New York: New Directions, 1965.

What Is Contemplation? Holy Cross, IN: Saint Mary's College, 1948; rev. ed. Springfield, IL: Templegate, 1981.

The Wisdom of the Desert: Sayings from the Desert Fathers of the Fourth Century. New York: New Directions, 1960.

Witness to Freedom: Letters in Times of Crisis, ed. William H. Shannon. New York: Farrar, Straus, Giroux, 1994.

Woods, Shore, Desert: A Notebook, May 1968, ed. Joel Weishaus. Santa Fe, NM: Museum of New Mexico Press, 1982.

* * *

Thomas Merton, John Howard Griffin, and Monsignor [Alfred] Horrigan, *The Thomas Merton Studies Center*. Santa Barbara, CA: Unicorn Press, 1971.

Thomas Merton and James Laughlin, *Selected Letters*, ed. David D. Cooper. New York: Norton, 1997.

Thomas Merton and Jean Leclercq, *Survival or Prophecy? The Letters of Thomas Merton and Jean Leclercq*, ed. Brother Patrick Hart. New York: Farrar, Straus and Giroux, 2002.

* * *

Bernadette Dieker and Jonathan Montaldo, eds., *Merton and Hesychasm: The Prayer of the Heart*. Louisville, KY: Fons Vitae, 2003.

Index

the absurd, absurdity, 67, 87, 92, 216, 222, 332, 361–67, 370–79, 381, 423

action, and contemplation, 24–38

activism, demonic, 138, 139

Ad Petri Cathedram, 132

Adam, Karl, 269

Adhemar, Bishop, 197

Aetheria (Egeria), 186, 187, 188

African American. *See* Negro(es)

Alcuin, 194

alienation, 25, 59, 87, 93, 97, 124, 166, 187, 202, 247, 250, 258, 264, 268, 271, 273, 339, 341, 369, 372, 422, 442, 450, 456

Ambrose Autpert, 168–71

Ambrose, Saint, 58

anawim, 277, 280

Anselm, Saint, 336

Anthony, Saint, 58, 155, 317, 322, 330

anxiety, existential, 456, 457

Apophthegmata, 312, 313, 317, 322

Arasteh, A. Reza, 452, 455–61

Aristotle, 111, 406, 428

Arsenius, Saint, 314, 316, 317, 322

art
    and contemplation, 26, 27, 36, 37, 38
    modern, 88
    and spirituality, 32
    and symbol, 251, 252, 257

artist
    cult of, 91–93
    Zen, 94–96

asceticism, 10, 12, 37, 75, 154, 163, 314, 319, 320, 329, 360, 438
    Irish, and *peregrinatio*, 188–96

Auden, W. H., 31

Augustine, Saint, 32, 59, 60, 61, 62, 100, 440

Baez, Joan, 284

baptism, 4, 6, 7, 9, 26, 27, 132, 218, 312, 412, 416, 454

"baptism in the forest," 412, 416

Baqa, 460

Baudelaire, Charles, 31, 92

beatitude, of the Meek, and nonviolence, 284–95

Beauvoir, Simone de, 273

Bede, Saint, 163, 164, 165

Benedict, Saint, 21, 235, 459

Benedict Biscop, Saint, 191

Bennett, Gloria, 361

Berdyaev, Nicolai, 269

Bernard, Saint, 21, 31, 62, 99, 198, 199, 200, 201, 437, 459

Bessarion, Abba, 318

Birnbaum, Milton, 404

Black Power, 208, 209

blacks. *See* Negro(es)

Blake, William, 32, 440

Blehl, Vincent Ferrar, 404

Bonaventure, Saint, 28, 31, 32, 34, 100, 334, 336, 436

Bonhoeffer, Dietrich, 296, 297, 298, 299, 307, 309, 338, 386

Boniface, Saint, 194

Born, Bertrand de, 201

Brendan, Saint, 188, 189, 190, 423

Brendan legend, 201

Bryant, William Cullen, 445

Bu Ji, 108

Buber, Martin, 267, 269
Buddhism, 54, 58, 63, 183, 342, 343, 349, 351, 353, 355, 359,
    and personality, 94
    Pure Land, 347
    and Zen, 261, 323, 344, 345, 346, 347, 454
Budge, E. A. Wallis, 310
Bultmann, Rudolf, 269, 275, 276
Burchard of Worms, 195
Burton, Patricia, 126

Cadroe, Saint, 189
Campbell, Will, 296
Camus, Albert, 259, 260, 269, 273, 402, 403, 405, 406, 423
    between capitalism and communism, 364, 371, 377, 378
    and early Franciscans, 369, 370, 371
    and ethic of love, 370, 371
    and ethic of revolt, 364–68, 371–81
    and faith, 366, 367
    and problem of God, 367
    and the Rebel, 364–69, 371–81
    and values of Western civilization, 363, 365
    violence and nonviolence in, 362–81
Cardenal, Ernesto, 113, 401
Carson, Rachel, 444
Casanata, Cardinal, 152
Cassian, John, 62, 63, 150, 314, 320, 325, 326
    on monastic life and prayer, 153–58
censorship, Trappist, vii, viii, xiv
Chaigne, Père Hervé, 205
Ching, 104, 105
Christ
    birth of, 278–82
    divinity and humanity of, 152–71
    encountering, 119, 120, 121
    humanity of, and prayer, 151–71
    as inspiration of Christian poets, 31
    Mystical, 4, 5, 54, 63, 70
    as New Adam, 52, 54, 63, 100
    presence of, 12, 150, 165
    as Prince of Peace, 132, 133

    and pure prayer, 156, 157, 158
    union with, 10, 38, 54, 55, 69, 358
Christianity
    and Buddhism, 54, 349, 350, 351, 355
    dialogue with Marxism, 338, 339
    and explanation, 347, 348, 352, 355
    and Zen, 347, 348, 349, 350, 351, 352
Christians, American, and civil rights movement, 206, 207, 211–15
Chuang Tzu, 111, 245
Church Fathers, on creation in the image of God, 57, 58
Church
    and existentialism, 270, 271, 272, 273
    post–Vatican II view of the world, 336, 337, 338
    relation to the world, 299, 300, 307, 308
    and the solitary, 77, 78
    as world-denying and world affirming, 334, 335, 336, 337, 338
Cistercians, 154, 196, 388, 389, 390
Civil Rights Bill, 206, 207, 208
civil rights movement, 206–15
Claudel, Paul, 29
Clement of Alexandria, 120, 410
Coindreau, Maurice-Edgar, 403, 420
Cold War, 42, 113, 118, 128, 129, 130, 131, 137, 138, 179, 451
colonialism, American, 209
Columba, Saint, 188, 189
Columbia University, 8, 433, 436, 437, 439, 440
Columbus, Christopher, 201, 433, 437
communication, 247–57
    and communion, 249–57
    and the modern world, 309
    and symbol, 242, 243, 249–57
communion
    and communication, 249–57
    between contemplative and scientific disciplines, 256, 257
Communism, 8, 40, 45, 48, 133, 135, 136, 137, 148, 210, 212, 371, 373, 378

defense against, by Christianity, 134–37

community
and existentialism, 267
monastic, 385, 387, 392, 393, 394, 400, 455, 459
and the solitary, 84
compunction, 163, 168, 318, 324, 325
Confucian ideal, 110
connaturality, 32, 33
conquistador, 202, 203
consciousness, environmental, 446–51
contemplation, 151, 154–58, 161–63, 166–71, 313, 314
and action, 24–38
active, 27, 29, 31
as experience of God, 28
infused. *See* contemplation, mystical
levels of, 26
mystical, 27, 28, 29, 33–38, 436
natural, 32, 33, 34, 36, 37, 38, 46
and ordinary life, 26
passive. *See* contemplation, mystical
as perception of life at its Source, 26
and poetry, 24–38
and the solitary life, 75
in technological world, 225, 226, 227, 231
contemplative life, and modern world, 225–31
contemplatives, mission of, in modern world, 229, 230
conversatio, 160, 286, 325, 454, 461
conversion, of Merton, 4, 7, 8, 9, 10, 11, 12
Coomaraswamy, Ananda, 86, 440
on the artist and cult of the artist, 96, 97, 101
Cooper, James Fenimore, 445
Cornford, F. M., 405, 409
creativity
and Christ, 100, 101
and the cult of the artist, 91–93
delusions about, 90–93
and destructiveness, 86, 87, 88, 89
and God, 98, 99, 100, 101

and history, 90, 91
and productiveness, 91
and self-expression, 90
theology of, 98–101
Cross, of Christ, 231, 253, 334, 358, 359
Cruickshank, John, 404
Crusades, 196–201
and courtly love, 200
as pilgrimage, 198
and repentance, 197, 198, 199
Cuadra, Pablo Antonio, 113, 114
culture, Christian, and Oriental wisdom, 103–12
Cunningham, Lawrence, xvi, 232

da Todi, Jacopone, 29
Daggy, Robert E., 232
Dalrymple, John, 275
Daniélou, Jean, 339
Dante, 29, 98, 334
Dark Night of the Soul, 18, 20, 459
David (Old Testament king), 29
Dawson, Christopher, 111, 147, 148
Day, Dorothy, 426
de Sola Pinto, Vivian, 422
Desert Fathers, 52, 53, 55, 58, 59, 61, 62, 69, 75, 310, 312–30
and the devil, 58, 59
on paradise, 53
sayings of, 52, 58, 310, 318, 320, 323. *See also Apophthegmata*
destruction
of the environment, 444, 445, 446, 448, 449, 450, 451
by superpowers, 115, 118, 123, 124, 125
destructiveness, and creativity, 86, 87, 88, 89
Detweiler, Robert, 411
devil, 18, 58, 59, 61, 93, 202, 302, 303, 304, 323, 334, 428, 435
diacrisis, 325
Dickinson, Emily, 65, 66
discernment of spirits, 62, 325
discipleship, and nonviolence, 286, 287, 288

discretio, 62

disintegration and reintegration, 460, 461

diversion, and the solitary, 66–71

doctrine, priority of, in Christianity, 347, 348, 351, 352

Dostoevsky, Fyodor, 43, 44, 45, 52, 53, 403

Dr. Zhivago, 39–48

Dr. Zhivago, as mankind, 40

drama, and religious literature, 406, 407

drugs, hallucinogenic, and mysticism, 226, 227, 256

Du Bay, William, 212

Eckhart, Meister, 336, 341, 349, 357, 359, 438, 440

ecological conscience, 450, 451

ecology, mental, of Thomas Merton, 234

education, 434–41
    purpose of, 434, 438–41

Ehrenburg, Ilya, 43

El Greco, 15

Eliot, T. S., 31, 288, 409

Ellis, Msgr. John Tracy, 126

Emerson, Ralph Waldo, 103

emptiness, 54, 55, 56, 57, 58, 61, 62, 63, 64, 73, 74, 75, 78, 79, 94, 95, 220, 340
    and way of wisdom, 228, 229, 230, 231

the End, 277–83

end of the world, 131, 132

enemy, image of God in, 288, 289

enlightenment, 345, 346, 353

equality, of all men, 119–22

eremitism. *See* hermit(s)
    wandering, 195

eros, communal, 247

eschatology, realized, 286, 287, 288, 293

ethics
    atheistic, 362, 363, 366, 369, 370
    Confucian, 109, 110
    situation, 259

Eucherius, Saint, 79

Evagrius Ponticus, 63, 153, 154, 314

Evdokimov, Paul, 271

event
    and pseudo-events, 301, 305, 306, 307, 308, 309
    saving, 308, 309

exile, 192, 193, 194, 195

existentialism, 259–76
    Christian, 269–76
    and community, 267
    theistic and atheistic, 269

experience
    aesthetic, 32, 37, 38
    Christian, of mystery of Christ, 348, 352
    immediate: and Zen, 258, 342, 343, 345, 346, 347, 348, 350, 354, 355; in Christianity and Zen, 347, 348, 349, 350, 352, 356, 357, 358, 359, 360

faith, 269, 270

Fana, 460

Faulkner, William, 209, 386, 401–25
    and sapiential literature, 411–25

filial love, 104, 105, 109, 110, 111, 312

filial piety, 109, 110

final integration, 453, 457–62
    and monastic life, 457–62

Fox, Abbot James, vii

Francis de Sales, Saint, 311, 312

Francis of Assisi, Saint, 21, 29, 204, 370

Franciscans, Camus' view of, 369, 370, 371

Frankl, Viktor, 455

freedom, 57, 58, 99
    and Christian existentialism, 269–75
    and education, 435, 437, 438
    and exploitation of nature, 449, 450
    and final integration, 458, 459
    and Pasternak, 51
    and solitude, 219–23

Freud, Sigmund, 8, 110, 338, 447, 455

Fromm, Erich, 452, 455

Gandhi, Mahatma, 177–84, 211, 286, 378

and Christianity, 180, 181, 183, 184
in England, 178, 179
and politics and religion, 180, 181,
182, 183
as revolutionary, 42, 43
Garaudy, Roger, 338
García Lorca, Federico, 31
genocide, 146, 148, 179, 371, 372, 426,
427, 432
Gill, Eric, 96, 97
Gilson, Etienne, 9, 269
Go Down, Moses, as sapiential literature,
411, 412, 413, 415, 418, 424
God
contemplative experience of, 154, 155,
156, 157, 158
death of, 363, 366, 367, 371, 378,
408, 416, 417; and death of man,
241, 242
image of, 33, 54, 57, 60, 70, 86; and
creativity, 99, 100, 101
as source of all reality, 9
union with, 5, 6
Gog and Magog, 113–25
Goss-Mayr, Jean and Hildegard, 126, 284
Graham, Dom Aelred, 360
Great Joy, 278, 280, 282, 283
Greene, Graham, 404
Gregory of Nyssa, Saint, 46, 63, 99, 100,
187, 437
and humanity of Christ and prayer,
159, 160, 161, 162, 165, 166, 167,
168
Gregory the Great, Saint, 28, 150
Gregory VII, Pope, 196
Grinberg, Miguel, 172

Hanna, Thomas L., 404, 405
Harrison, Jane, 409
Hausherr, Irénée, SJ, 327
Hegel, Georg Wilhelm Friedrich, 366
Heidegger, Martin, 260, 269, 270, 272,
274, 275
Heinemann, F. H., 259
Heisenberg, Werner, 243, 244, 245
Heraclitus, 70, 120

hermit(s), 57, 58, 71, 74, 75, 79, 80, 81,
82, 109, 156, 186, 192, 196, 219,
221, 232, 234, 235, 236, 237, 310,
313, 314, 315, 317, 318, 322, 390,
393, 394, 439, 440
and life with Christ, 156
Hinduism, 180, 183, 252, 310
history, and creativity, 90, 91
Hitler, Adolf, 89, 337, 366
home ground, 430
Honorius of Autun, Saint, 201
Hopkins, Gerard Manley, 29, 440
Hsiao Ching, 104, 105, 109, 110
hubris, 225, 263, 273, 279, 406
Hui Neng, 353
human person, as part of natural world,
442, 448, 449, 450
humanism
without God, 124, 125
of superpowers, 116, 123, 123
humility, 8, 19, 22, 28, 44, 59, 62, 70, 73,
94, 104, 120, 163, 166, 170, 204,
228, 256, 275, 284, 286, 287, 319,
320, 325, 373, 384, 398, 415, 459
and nonviolence, 290, 291, 292, 293
Huxley, Aldous, 404

I, inner, and Christ, 85
I–Thou, 267
identity
authentic, 3–14
and solitude, 219, 220, 221, 222, 223
idolatry, 301, 302, 303, 308, 322
image of God, in man, 33, 54, 57, 60, 70,
86, 99
imperialism, Eastern and Western, 364,
365
Incarnation, 277–83, 299
Indians. *See* Native Americans
dehumanization of, 428
industria, 34
inequality, of rich and poor, 289, 290
innocence
lost, 99
original, 53, 55–58, 61–63, 99
and the poet, 173, 174, 175

Institute of Asian Studies (St. John's
    University), 103
interior life, human need for, 25
intuition, aesthetic, 32, 33, 34, 35, 36,
    37, 38
Ionesco, Eugène, 222, 223
Ishi, 426–32

Jaeger, Werner, 409
Jarrett-Kerr, Martin, 405, 406, 407
Jaspers, Karl, 266, 268, 269, 270
Jerome, Saint, 79, 332, 333
Jerusalem, as source and center, 186, 187
John, Abba, 328
John Chrysostom, Saint, 315
John of Salisbury, 336
John of the Cross, Saint, 15–22, 25, 26,
    29, 31, 34, 36, 38, 55, 268, 332,
    344, 458, 459
John the Baptist, Saint, 233
John the Dwarf, Abbot, 61
John the Solitary, 310, 328, 329, 330
John XXIII, Pope, viii, 132, 135, 144, 204
Joseph, Abba, 319, 320
journey
    as archetype, 185, 187, 191, 204, 423
    sacred, 186, 423
joy, natural, and John of the Cross, 19, 20
Joyce, James, 43
Jung, Carl, 8, 447, 460
just war, 128, 129, 133, 134, 144, 146,
    371
Justin Martyr, Saint, 120

kairos, and Negro Christian nonviolent
    movement, 205, 206, 213, 214
Karma Yoga, 180
Karuna (compassion), 347
Kelley, William Melvin, 205
kenosis, 284, 343, 358, 416
Kierkegaard, Søren, 259, 264, 265, 270,
    416
King, Martin Luther, Jr., 205, 206
Kingdom of God, 63, 132, 154, 365, 366,
    387, 444, 454
    and nonviolence, 286, 287, 288, 293

Knight, E., 456
Kroeber, Theodora and Alfred, 426, 428
Krutch, Joseph Wood, 409, 439

language
    and Pasternak, 48, 49
    poetic, 174, 175
    and silence, 77
Lao Tzu, 104, 105, 109, 234
Latin Americans, North American lack
    of understanding of, 123
Laughlin, James, 232, 240, 277
Lavelle, Louis, 269
Lawrence, D. H., 408, 409, 422
Leclercq, Dom Jean, 150, 161, 192, 196
leitourgia, 180
Lentfoehr, Sr. Thérèse, xii
Leo the Great, Saint, and humanity of
    Christ and prayer, 158, 159, 160,
    161, 163
Leonard, Fr. M., 32
Leopold, Aldo, 441, 449, 450
Léras, Ponce de, 195
leveling, 264, 265, 266, 267, 270, 271
liberty, absolute, 365, 366
life
    and Boris Pasternak, 40, 41, 43
    as revolutionary, 41, 42
Lin Yutang, 108, 109
literature
    and religion, 402–25
    See also religious literature; sapiential
        literature
liturgy, 26, 27, 29, 30, 31, 166, 180, 187,
    243, 306, 307, 389, 392
    cosmic, 39, 44, 46
Living Flame of Love (John of the Cross),
    21
Lord of the Flies, 222
Lost Island, 201, 202
love
    of Christ, 13, 14, 22, 38, 286, 309
    and contemplation, 26, 27
    Gandhi's devotion to, 181, 182, 183,
        184
    and hate, 116

Luce, Claire Boothe, 15
Luther, Martin, 300

Macquarrie, John, 274, 275
Magog, Christianity of, 120
man
  and God as creator, 99, 100, 101
  likeness of God in, 99, 100, 101
  See also human person
Mara (the tempter), 58
Marcel, Gabriel, 259, 266, 268, 269, 359
Maritain, Jacques, 9, 32, 269, 409, 440
  on creativity and the artist, 92, 97, 98
Marx, Harpo, 333
Marx, Karl, 124, 250, 289, 337, 338, 366, 379
Marxism, dialogue with Christianity, 338, 339
maturation, 455–62
Maximus, Saint, 63
McDonnell, Fr. Kilian, xiii
McDonnell, Thomas, xvi
media, and manipulation, 300, 301, 305, 308, 309
meditatio, and *contemplatio,* 162, 163
meekness, 287, 288, 289, 293
Melville, Herman, 409
Mennonites, 128
mercy, 108, 109
Merleau–Ponty, Maurice, 371
Merton, Thomas
  autobiographical reflections of, 7, 8, 9, 10, 11, 12, 233–39, 332, 333, 433–41
  as Christian existentialist, 434
  defense of Gandhi, 178, 179
  as essayist, ix–xviii
  hermit vocation of, 233–35
  life in the hermitage, 235–39
  as world–denying contemplative, 332, 333
metanoia, 185, 325
Mill Creek Indians, 426, 427, 428, 429
Miller, J. Hillis, 417
Milton, John, 409

monachos, 65, 78, 82, 84
monasteries, and universities, shared function of, 436–38
monastic community, and final integration, 459
monastic life, 233–39, 335, 455
  and community, 393, 394
  and engagement in the world, 297, 298, 300
  as institution, 391, 392, 394, 395, 396, 400
  philosophy of, 65–85
  purpose of, 62–64
  renewal of, 383–400
  as search for God, 11
monastic vocation, 454, 455, 457
  charism of, 391, 392, 393, 394, 395, 396, 397, 398
  as life of freedom and detachment, 385–93, 398–400
monasticism, 153–71
  early, 312–30
  medieval, 384, 385
monk, as critic of the world, 387
Moseley, Edwin M., 405
Muir, John, 442, 444, 447, 448
Murder in the Cathedral, 288, 289
Murray, John Courtney, 134
Muthues, Abba, 318
Mystical Body of Christ, 5, 6, 7, 9, 14, 38, 74, 132, 142, 170
mysticism, Christian and Zen, 349, 350, 351
myth, 411, 412, 416, 420, 421, 422
The Myth of Sisyphus (Camus), 374, 375, 376

nakedness, spiritual, 435
Nash, Roderick, 443, 444, 448
nationalism, 145, 147, 148
Native Americans, 427–32
nature
  biblical ambivalence toward, 444, 445
  destruction of, 444, 445, 446, 448, 449, 450, 451

Negro(es)
    and Christian nonviolence, 206–15
    and civil rights movement, 206–15
    in United States, 290
The New Tenant (Ionesco), 223
New World, conquering of, 202, 203
Nicholas of Cusa, 438
Nietzsche, Friedrich, 241, 366, 417
Night at the Opera, 333
Nirvana, 347
Nishida, Kitaro, 269
no room, for Jesus/God/man, 278–83
non–Christian world, and war and peace,
    134, 135
nonviolence, 179
    Christian, 285–95
    and civil rights movement, 206, 207,
        208, 209
    conditions for practice of, 290–92
    Hindu, 208
    religious, 378, 379
    and unity of man, 286
nothingness, 268
    and the mystic void, 268
nuclear war, 127, 128, 129, 130
    and just war theory, 128, 129, 133,
        134, 142, 143, 144
nuclear weapons, 118, 128, 129, 130,
        131, 143, 146, 248
    as deterrents, 131

O'Brien, John A., 3
O'Connor, Flannery, 261, 262, 263, 304,
    411
obedience
    and desert fathers, 327
    monastic, 391, 392, 395, 396, 399
openness, 267
ordination, and priesthood, 11–14
Origen, 46, 100, 120
ourselves, image of, and idolatry, 303,
    304, 309

Pacem in Terris, viii, 204, 292
Pachomius, Saint, 313, 315, 316, 317,
    318, 328

Pai Chang, 356, 357
Palemon, Abba, 317, 318
Pambo, Abba, 319
Panichas, George A., 401, 411
paradise, 53–64, 437, 438
    as both present and future, 53
    as lost innocence, 53, 56, 63
    of the West, 201–4
The Paradise of the Fathers, 310
Parousia, 4, 6
Pascal, Blaise, 66, 366, 417
passivity, moral, 138, 139
Pasternak, Boris, 31, 39–51, 409
    as Christian and mystic, 43, 44, 45,
        46, 50, 51
    and Communism, 45, 46, 47, 48, 50,
        51
    as contemplative, 25, 26
    and Gandhi, 42, 43, 46
    and liturgy of the universe, 44, 45, 46,
        50
    as revolutionary, 42
    and Soviet society, 47, 48
    as spiritual genius, 42
peace, religious responsibility for,
    127–49
peace Churches, 128
peace movements, 127
peacemakers, Christians as, 132–34, 142,
    143
peacemaking, 139
penance, 10
    public, and pilgrimage, 192, 193, 194,
        195
peregrinatio, and Irish asceticism, 188–96
Perfectae Caritatis, 383, 390
Perse, St.-John, 409
personality, in Christianity and
    Buddhism, 54
Peter Damian, Saint, 162
pharisaism, and nonviolence, 286
Philoxenos, 219, 220, 221, 222, 223, 224
Picard, Max, 268
pilgrimage, 185–204
    and penitential system, 192–96
Pius XI, Pope, 385

Pius XII, Pope, 129, 134, 139, 140, 143, 144, 148
The Plague (Camus), 273, 372, 375
Plato, 105, 175, 410
Pleroma, 4, 6, 14
Plotinus, 37, 365, 438
pneumatikos, and *psychicos,* 328, 329, 330
Poemen, Abba, 57, 318, 319, 328
poetry, and contemplation, 24–38
poets
    Christian, 29, 38; as mystics, 30
    as dervishes, 176
    Latin American, 171–76
    solidarity of, 173, 174
positivism, 263, 264, 265, 405
poverty, spiritual, 81–85
power
    and monastic life, 396
    and nonviolence, 289, 290
powers and elements, 300
pragmatism, 133, 177, 264, 392
Prajna, 353, 356, 357, 359
prayer, 12, 13, 14
    contemplative, and John of the Cross, 22
    and humanity of Christ, 151–71
    mental, 151. *See also* contemplation
    monastic, 151–71
    and the solitary, 81, 82
priesthood, and ordination, 11, 12, 13, 14
Primitive Benedictines, 389, 390
productiveness, and creativity, 91
prophecy, and poetry, 175
Proust, Marcel, 43
pura oratio, 154, 155, 156, 157, 158
Puritans, 444, 445, 446
purity of heart, 52, 53, 54, 55, 56, 57, 58, 62, 63, 79, 154, 306, 314, 320, 327, 330, 374

Quakers, 128
quies, 63, 313, 314, 315, 316, 318, 320, 321, 323, 324, 326, 327, 330
quietism, 152
Quiroga, Vasco de, 203

racism, American, 206–15
Rahner, Karl, as existentialist, 260
rain, as image of renewal, 216, 217, 218, 219, 224
rebel, 364, 365, 366, 367, 368, 371, 372
The Rebel (Camus), 361, 365, 367
rebirth, 452, 454, 456, 457, 459, 461
religion
    and existentialism, 271, 272, 273
    of Faulkner, 402, 403, 404, 405, 423, 424
    religionless, 298
religious literature, 403, 404, 405, 406, 407, 408
repentance, and Crusades, 197, 198, 199, 200
resignation, passive, to injustice, 361, 368, 369
revolt, ethic of, 364–68, 371–81
revolution
    Camus' view of, 365, 366
    totalist, 361, 365, 373
Rhinoceros (Ionesco), 222, 223
Rice, Ed, xii, 102, 382
Richard III, 197
Richards, I. A., 406
Rida, 435
Rilke, Rainer Maria, 31
Rimbaud, Arthur, 31, 92
Robbe-Grillet, Alain, 405
Robert II, 197
Rockefeller, John D., 439
Roosevelt, Theodore, 447
Rossi, Don Giovanni, ix, xv
Rudel, Jaufré, 200
Russell, Bertrand, 345, 346
Russian revolution, 40, 51
Rustin, Bayard, 206
Ruysbroek, John, 31, 438

sage, and the Tao, 107, 108, 109
Salinger, J. D., 411
Salt March, 178
salvation, 415
sanctity, and suffering, 18, 19
sapientia, 38, 60, 402, 408, 409, 436, 437

sapiential literature, 408–25
    writings of Faulkner as, 411–25
sapiential writers and critics, 409
Sartre, Jean-Paul, 259, 260, 265, 268,
    269, 273, 274, 364, 365, 366,
    371
satyagraha, 181, 182
Schweitzer, Albert, 450
scientia (realm of knowledge), 56, 58, 59,
    60, 61, 408, 436,
Scotus, John Duns, 334, 336
self
    discovery of, 434, 435, 438
    true, and solitude, 84, 85
self-expression, and creativity, 90
self-realization, in Zen, 94, 95
Sengai, 108, 234
Seraphim of Sarov, Saint, 315
Sermon on the Mount, 104, 177, 180,
    287, 293
Shakespeare, William, 409
Shannon, William, xv, 126
Sholokhov, Mikhail, 43
Sih, Paul K. T., 102
Silva, Ludovico, 232
simulacra, 301, 302, 303
slavery, 209, 412
Smith, Gibbs M., 232
snake-handling, mental, 304–7
social image, 72
society, and the solitary, 66, 69, 70, 71,
    72, 73, 76, 77
Socrates, 120
solitary
    every person as, 68, 69
    true and false, 69, 71–79, 82
solitary life, 65–85, 429, 430
solitary spirit, 65, 66
solitude, 65–85, 429, 430
    common human, 73
    of desert fathers, 313, 314, 317, 318,
        321, 322, 323, 324
    and John of the Cross, 19, 20
    and the Mass, 14
    monk as witness to value of, 386, 387,
        390, 391, 392, 393, 398, 399, 400

and Pasternak, 42
and solitary life, 219-23
and the true self, 84, 85
and vocation, 78, 79
Sortais, Abbot Gabriel, vii, viii, xii, xiv
soul, inferior and superior, 32, 33
Soviet Writers' Union, 41, 43
Spender, Stephen, 31
Spirit of Medieval Philosophy, 9
Spirit/spirit
    freedom of, 458, 459
    unity of, 54
Spiritual Canticle (John of the Cross),
    16, 17
spiritual director, 311
spiritual experience, as idol, 255, 256
spiritual Father, 312–30, 454
    as *pneumatikos,* 328, 329, 330
    choice of, 326, 327
spirituality
    and art, 32
    and John of the Cross, 22
Stanford, Derek, 424, 425
Stone, Naomi Burton, 277
stranger
    encountering, 121, 122, 123
    presence of God/Christ in, 121, 122,
        123, 132, 204
The Stranger (Camus), 363, 372
success, 107, 439, 440, 448
suffering
    in Christianity and Buddhism, 355
    and John of the Cross, 16, 18
Sufism, 435, 454, 455, 460
suicide, global, 145, 146
superpowers, 113, 114, 115, 116, 117
supranational authority, and abolition of
    war, 142
Suzuki, D. T., 52, 54–59, 61, 62, 86, 94,
    95, 234, 269, 310, 344, 346, 349,
    354, 356, 357, 359, 360, 409, 433,
    441
    on art and Zen experience, 94–96
svadharma, 177, 180, 181, 182
symbol(s)
    and allegory, 21

and communication, 242, 243, 249,
    250–57
and communion, 242, 243, 249, 250,
    251, 252, 253
and communion with one another in
    God, 253, 254, 255
desecration of, 250, 251, 255
and religious literature, 408, 410
and sign, 242, 243
symbolism, 241–57
    and communal eros, 247
    death of, 242
    and spiritual wisdom, 246, 247
Tao Te Ching, 103–6, 108, 109
Tao, 104–9, 112, 253, 343, 356, 423
Tao, and Christianity, 108, 109
technology
    and communication, 247
    and dehumanization, 339
    and symbolism, 241–45, 257
Teilhard de Chardin, Pierre, 338, 386
Theodore (desert father), 313, 316, 319,
    324
Theodore of Canterbury, 195
theologia, 63, 314
theology, existential, 269, 273, 274, 275
theoria, 32, 192, 313, 411
Theresa of Avila, Saint, 16, 21, 31, 151,
    152, 311
third world, outlook of, 118, 123
Thomas à Becket, Saint, 288
Thomas Aquinas, Saint, 9, 25, 28, 34, 107,
    269, 334, 335, 336, 349, 440, 458
Thomas, Dylan, 31, 424, 425
Thoreau, Henry David, 65, 66, 103, 218,
    233, 332, 439, 442, 444, 446, 447
Tillich, Paul, 269, 422
    and communal eros, 247
    on creativity and the artist, 93–94, 97,
    98
    on symbol, 252, 252
Toledo, El Greco's view of, 15, 16
Tolstoy, Leo, 43, 180
tragedy
    and Faulkner, 402–8
    Greek, 403, 405, 406, 407, 408, 428

Traherne, Thomas, 440
tranquility, and desert fathers, 313, 314–
    18, 320, 321, 327, 330
Truce of God, 197, 198
truth
    commitment to, 285–92
    Gandhi's devotion to, 181–84
Tzu (ideogram), 105

Umbratilem, 385
United Nations, and war, 130
United States and Soviet Union, as Gog
    and Magog, 113–25
university
    function of, 434
    as paridisic institution, 437, 438
unlimited light, and monastic
    contemplation, 165–68
Urban II, Pope, 197, 198, 199

Van Doren, Mark, xi, 216, 409, 433, 439,
    440
Vatican II
    and nonviolence, 295, 296
    and renewal of monastic life, 383
Vietnam War, 209, 238, 331, 333, 336,
    339, 379, 426, 432, 443, 450, 451
violence, Christian, 212, 215
virtue, way of, 107
Vital, Oderic, 199

Waggoner, Hyatt, 404
Walden, 218, 446
war
    abolition of, 127, 142, 144
    Christian choice against, 146, 147,
    148
    Christian obligation to protest, 139,
    140
    limited, 126, 128, 129, 134, 143, 144,
    145
    moral problem of, 140, 141, 142, 143,
    144, 145, 146
    opposition to, 127
    and peace, 116, 126–49
    preemptive, 127, 131, 134, 136

weapons, spiritual, 135, 136
Weber, Max, 445
Weil, Simone, 377
West
     arrogance of, 119, 121
     paradise of the, 201–4
Western civilization, 119
white pebble, as symbol of authentic
     identity, 3–14
Whitehead, Alfred North, on symbolism,
     245, 246, 247
wilderness, American attitudes toward,
     442–51
Wilkes, Paul, xiv
William of Conches, 201
Williams, William Carlos, 409, 428
Winandy, Dom Jacques, 390
wisdom
     contemplative, 225, 227–31
     and education, 111, 112
     spiritual, 246, 358
     See also sapientia, sapiential literature
Wittgenstein, Ludwig, 354
world
     Christian approach to, 341
     future of, 118

optimistic view of, 334, 335
problem of, 332–41
real, 340
worldview, Carolingian, 334, 335, 336
worship, and contemplation, 26, 27
Wu, John C. H., 102, 103, 105, 107, 108,
     109, 342, 343, 344
wu wei, 107, 108

Yahi Indians, 426, 427, 428, 429, 431
Yeats, William Butler, 409

Zahn, Gordon, xv, 126
Zen, 54, 56, 58, 61, 228, 235, 310, 454
     and apophatic Christian mysticism,
     345
     and Buddhism, 345, 346, 347
     Christian view of, 342–60
     and Christianity, 347, 348, 349, 350,
     351, 352
     and communication of consciousness,
     352, 353, 354, 356
     language of, 353, 354
Zurburan, Francisco de, 15